GLEIM®

2021 EDITION

CPA REVIEW

FINANCIAL ACCOUNTING & REPORTING

by

Irvin N. Gleim, Ph.D., CPA, CIA, CMA, CFM

and

Michael Kustanovich, CPA

with the assistance of
Grady M. Irwin, J.D.

Gleim Publications, Inc.
PO Box 12848
Gainesville, Florida 32604
(800) 87-GLEIM or (800) 874-5346
(352) 375-0772
www.gleim.com/cpa
CPA@gleim.com

For updates to this 2021 edition of
CPA Review: Financial Accounting and Reporting

Go To: www.gleim.com/CPAupdate

Or: Email update@gleim.com with **CPA FAR 2021-1** in the subject line. You will receive our current update as a reply.

Updates are available until the next edition is published.

ISSN: 1547-8025

ISBN: 978-1-61854-390-5 *CPA Review: Auditing and Attestation*
ISBN: 978-1-61854-391-2 *CPA Review: Business Environment and Concepts*
ISBN: 978-1-61854-392-9 *CPA Review: Financial Accounting and Reporting*
ISBN: 978-1-61854-393-6 *CPA Review: Regulation*
ISBN: 978-1-61854-394-3 *CPA Exam Guide: A System for Success*

First Printing: November 2020

ACKNOWLEDGMENTS

Material from *Uniform CPA Examination, Selected Questions and Unofficial Answers*, Copyright © 1974-2020 by the American Institute of Certified Public Accountants, Inc., is reprinted and/or adapted with permission. Visit the AICPA's website at www.aicpa.org for more information.

The authors are indebted to the Institute of Certified Management Accountants for permission to use problem materials from past CMA Examinations. Questions and unofficial answers from the Certified Management Accountant Examinations, copyright by the Institute of Certified Management Accountants, are reprinted and/or adapted with permission.

The authors are grateful for permission to reproduce Certified Internal Auditor Examination Questions, Copyright © 1991-2020 by The Institute of Internal Auditors, Inc.

Environmental Statement -- This book is printed on recyclable paper sourced from suppliers certified using sustainable forestry management processes and is produced either TCF (Totally Chlorine-Free) or ECF (Elementally Chlorine-Free).

ABOUT THE AUTHORS

Irvin N. Gleim is Professor Emeritus in the Fisher School of Accounting at the University of Florida and is a member of the American Accounting Association, Academy of Legal Studies in Business, American Institute of Certified Public Accountants, Association of Government Accountants, Florida Institute of Certified Public Accountants, The Institute of Internal Auditors, and the Institute of Management Accountants. He has had articles published in the *Journal of Accountancy*, *The Accounting Review*, and *The American Business Law Journal* and is author/coauthor of numerous accounting books, aviation books, and CPE courses. Other exam prep and textbook titles from Dr. Gleim include Gleim CMA Review, Gleim CIA Review, Gleim EA Review, and the Gleim Exam Questions and Explanations Series.

Michael Kustanovich, M.A., CPA, is a Clinical Assistant Professor in the Department of Accountancy at the University of Illinois at Urbana-Champaign. He teaches advanced financial accounting courses at both the undergraduate and graduate levels, and he is the instructor of the CPA Exam Review Course there. He is an editor of accounting books, the author of many CPE courses, and a member of the American Accounting Association. Previously, Mr. Kustanovich worked in the assurance departments of KPMG and PwC.

REVIEWERS AND CONTRIBUTORS

Garrett W. Gleim, CPA, CGMA, leads production of the Gleim CPA, CMA, CIA, and EA exam review systems. He is a member of the American Institute of Certified Public Accountants and the Florida Institute of Certified Public Accountants and holds a Bachelor of Science in Economics with a Concentration in Accounting from The Wharton School, University of Pennsylvania. Mr. Gleim is coauthor of numerous accounting and aviation books and the inventor of multiple patents with educational applications. He is also an avid pilot who holds a commercial pilot rating and is a certified flight instructor. In addition, as an active supporter of the local business community, Mr. Gleim serves as an advisor to several start-ups.

Grady M. Irwin, J.D., is a graduate of the University of Florida College of Law, and he has taught in the University of Florida College of Business. Mr. Irwin provided substantial editorial assistance throughout the project.

Joseph Mauriello, CPA, CIA, CISA, CFE, CMA, CFSA, CRMA, is a Senior Lecturer as well as the Director of the Center for Internal Auditing Excellence at the University of Texas at Dallas. Professor Mauriello is the lead CIA and CPA FAR Gleim Instruct lecturer.

Mark S. Modas, M.S.T., CPA, holds a Bachelor of Arts in Accounting from Florida Atlantic University and a Master of Science in Taxation from Nova Southeastern University. Prior to joining Gleim, he worked in internal auditing, accounting and financial reporting, and corporate tax compliance in the public and private sectors. Mr. Modas provided substantial editorial assistance throughout the project.

Lisa M. Sedor, Ph.D., CPA, is an Associate Professor in the School of Accountancy and Management Information Systems at DePaul University, where she teaches auditing. She is a member of the American Accounting Association and the American Institute of Certified Public Accountants. Her articles have been published in *The Accounting Review*, *Contemporary Accounting Research*, and *Behavioral Research in Accounting*. Ms. Sedor worked in public accounting for 9 years and is one of the CPA Gleim Instruct lecturers.

Chun Nam Wo, M.S. Acc., received a Master of Science in Accountancy with a concentration in Data Analytics from the University of Illinois at Urbana-Champaign. Mr. Wo provided substantial editorial assistance throughout the project.

A PERSONAL THANKS

This manual would not have been possible without the extraordinary effort and dedication of Jacob Bennett, Julie Cutlip, Ethan Good, Doug Green, Fernanda Martinez, Bree Rodriguez, Veronica Rodriguez, Teresa Soard, Justin Stephenson, Joanne Strong, Elmer Tucker, Candace Van Doren, and Ryan Van Tress, who typed the entire manuscript and all revisions and drafted and laid out the diagrams, illustrations, and cover for this book.

The authors also appreciate the production and editorial assistance of Sirene Dagher, Michaela Giampaolo, Jessica Hatker, Sonora Hospital-Medina, Katie Larson, Michael Lupi, Bryce Owen, Shane Rapp, Alyssa Thomas, and Valerie Wendt.

The authors also appreciate the critical reading assistance of Ali Band, Corey Connell, Adrianna Cuevas, Allen Lin, Martin Salazar, Maris Silvestri, and Miranda Valcarcel.

The authors also appreciate the video production expertise of Gary Brook, Philip Brubaker, Matthew Church, Andrew Johnson, and Mackenzie O'Connell, who helped produce and edit our Gleim Instruct Video Series.

Finally, we appreciate the encouragement, support, and tolerance of our families throughout this project.

TABLE OF CONTENTS

DETAILED TABLE OF CONTENTS

A MESSAGE FROM OUR AUTHORS

Welcome to the 2021 Edition of Gleim CPA Review! The purpose of this book is to facilitate your preparation to pass the Financial Accounting and Reporting (FAR) section of the CPA Exam.

The CPA Exam is continuously changed in order to maintain its relevance and prestige in the world of accounting. As technology develops, accountants and auditors face new and increasingly complex challenges, which are reflected in the AICPA Blueprints. Our team of accounting experts ensures our materials are always up-to-date, so regardless of when you're preparing for the CPA Exam with Gleim, you have everything you need to succeed.

Our goal is to provide a comprehensive, effective, affordable, and easy-to-use study program. Our course

1. Explains how to maximize your score through learning strategies and exam-taking techniques.
2. Outlines all of the content topics described in the AICPA Blueprints and tested on the FAR section of the exam in 20 easy-to-use study units.
3. Presents multiple-choice questions taken or modeled from CPA Examinations to prepare you for the types of questions you will find on your CPA Exam.
    a. In our book, the answer explanations are presented to the immediate right of each multiple-choice question for your convenience. Use a piece of paper to cover our detailed explanations as you answer the question and then review all answer choices to learn why the correct one is correct and why the other choices are incorrect.
    b. You also should practice answering these questions through our online platform, which mimics Prometric's user interface, so you are comfortable answering questions online like you will do on test day. Our adaptive course will focus and target your weak areas.
4. Contains an appendix explaining the different types of Task-Based Simulations (TBSs) and how to get the most points possible on the TBS testlets.

The outline format, spacing, and question and answer formats in this book are designed to increase readability, learning, understanding, and success on the CPA Exam. Our most successful candidates use the Gleim Premium CPA Review System, which includes Gleim Instruct videos; our Access Until You Pass Guarantee; our innovative SmartAdapt technology; expertly authored books; the largest test bank of multiple-choice questions and simulations; audio lectures; flashcards; and the support of our team of accounting experts.

Since the release of our first CPA Review book in 1974, Gleim has helped candidates pass more than 1 million CPA Exams with our study materials and recommended learning techniques. With our cutting-edge adaptive technology creating personalized learning paths, we will help candidates pass millions more. Candidates' success is based on the Gleim system of teaching not only the topics tested, but also what you can expect on exam day. We want you to feel confident and in control when you sit for the exam.

We want your feedback immediately after you take the exam and receive your exam score. Please go to www.gleim.com/feedbackFAR to share suggestions on how we can improve this edition. The CPA Exam is a **nondisclosed** exam, which means you must maintain the confidentiality of the exam by not divulging the nature or content of any CPA question or answer under any circumstances. We ask only for information about our materials and any improvements that can be made regarding topics that need to be added or expanded or need more emphasis. Our approach has AICPA approval.

Good Luck on the Exam,

– Dr. Irvin N. Gleim *– Michael Kustanovich*

November 2020

OPTIMIZING YOUR FINANCIAL ACCOUNTING AND REPORTING SCORE

UNIFORM CPA EXAMINATION

CPA Exam Section	Auditing & Attestation	Business Environment & Concepts	**Financial Accounting & Reporting**	Regulation
Acronym	AUD	BEC	**FAR**	REG
Exam Length	4 hours	4 hours	**4 hours**	4 hours
Testlet 1: Multiple-Choice	36 questions	31 questions	**33 questions**	38 questions
Testlet 2: Multiple-Choice	36 questions	31 questions	**33 questions**	38 questions
Testlet 3: Task-Based Simulations	2 tasks	2 tasks	**2 tasks**	2 tasks
Standardized Break	Clock stops for 15 minutes			
Testlet 4: Task-Based Simulations	3 tasks	2 tasks	**3 tasks**	3 tasks
Testlet 5: Task-Based Simulations or Written Communications	3 tasks	3 written communications	**3 tasks**	3 tasks

Passing the CPA Exam is a serious undertaking. Begin by becoming an expert in the content, formatting, and functionality of the FAR exam before you take it. The objective is no surprises on exam day. Also, you will save time and money, decrease frustration, and increase your probability of success by learning all you can about how to prepare for and take FAR.

Review *CPA Exam Guide: A System for Success* at www.gleim.com/PassCPA for a complete explanation of how to prepare for and take each section of the CPA Exam. This free guide includes 40 pages of test-taking techniques, time management strategies, and more.

More exam tactics and information, as well as breaking news and updates from the AICPA and NASBA, are available in our Resource Center at www.gleim.com/CPAresources and on our blog at www.gleim.com/CPAblog. Follow us on all your favorite social media networks for blog updates and other critical information.

CPA Exam Pass Rates

	Percentage of Candidates		
	2017	2018	2019
AUD	49	52	51
BEC	52	58	60
FAR	45	45	46
REG	48	53	56

The implication of these pass rates for you as a CPA candidate is that you have to be, on average, in the top 50% of all candidates to pass. The major difference between CPA candidates who pass and those who do not is their preparation program. You have access to the best CPA review material; it is up to you to use it. Even if you are enrolled in a review course that uses other materials, you will benefit with the Gleim Premium CPA Review System.

GLEIM PREMIUM CPA REVIEW WITH SMARTADAPT

Gleim Premium CPA Review features the most comprehensive coverage of exam content and employs the most efficient learning techniques to help you study smarter and more effectively. The Gleim Premium CPA Review System is powered by SmartAdapt technology, an innovative platform that continually zeros in on areas you should focus on when you move through the following steps for optimized CPA review:

Step 1:

Complete a Diagnostic Quiz. Your quiz results set a baseline that our SmartAdapt technology will use to create a custom learning track.

Step 2:

Solidify your knowledge by studying the suggested Knowledge Transfer Outline(s) or watching the suggested Gleim Instruct video(s).

Step 3:

Focus on weak areas and perfect your question-answering techniques by taking the adaptive quizzes and simulations that SmartAdapt directs you to.

Final Review:

After completing all study units, take the first Exam Rehearsal. Then, SmartAdapt will walk you through a Final Review based on your results. Finally, a few days before your exam date, take the second Exam Rehearsal so you feel confident that you are ready to pass.

To facilitate your studies, the Gleim Premium CPA Review System uses the most comprehensive test bank of exam-quality CPA questions on the market. Our system's content and presentation are the most realistic representation of the whole exam environment so you feel completely at ease on test day.

Learning from Your Mistakes

One of the main building blocks of the Gleim studying system is that learning from questions you answer incorrectly is very important. Each question you answer incorrectly is an **opportunity** to avoid missing actual test questions on your CPA Exam. Thus, you should carefully study the answer explanations provided so you understand why the original answer you chose is wrong as well as why the correct answer indicated is correct. This learning technique is the difference between passing and failing for many CPA candidates.

The Gleim Premium CPA Review System has built-in functionality for this step. After each quiz and simulation you complete, the Gleim system directs you to study why you answered questions incorrectly so you can learn how to avoid making the same errors in the future. Reasons for answering questions incorrectly include

1. Misreading the requirement (stem)
2. Not understanding what is required
3. Making a math error
4. Applying the wrong rule or concept
5. Being distracted by one or more of the answers
6. Incorrectly eliminating answers from consideration
7. Not having any knowledge of the topic tested
8. Using a poor educated-guessing strategy

SUBJECT MATTER FOR FINANCIAL ACCOUNTING AND REPORTING

Below, we have provided the AICPA's major content areas from the Blueprint for Financial Accounting and Reporting (FAR). The averaged percentage of coverage for each topic is indicated.

I. (30%) Conceptual Framework, Standard-Setting, and Financial Reporting
II. (35%) Select Financial Statement Accounts
III. (25%) Select Transactions
IV. (10%) State and Local Governments

Appendix B contains the AICPA's Blueprint for FAR with cross-references to the subunits in our materials where topics are covered. Remember that we have studied and restudied the Blueprint and explain the subject matter thoroughly in our CPA Review. Accordingly, you do not need to spend time with Appendix B. Rather, it should give you confidence that Gleim CPA Review is the best review available to help you PASS the CPA Exam.

Candidates are expected to demonstrate knowledge and skills related to the financial accounting and reporting frameworks used by business entities (public and nonpublic), not-for-profit entities, and state and local government entities. The FAR section will test standards and regulations issued by the Financial Accounting Standards Board (FASB), the U.S. Securities and Exchange Commission (U.S. SEC), the American Institute of Certified Public Accountants (AICPA), the Governmental Accounting Standards Board (GASB), and the International Accounting Standards Board (IASB).

To demonstrate the knowledge and skills associated with financial accounting and reporting, the following general topics will be tested:

- FASB
  - Conceptual framework
  - Standards-setting process
  - Accounting Standards Codification
    - ☐ General-purpose financial statements applicable to for-profit entities, not-for-profit entities, and employee benefit plans
    - ☐ Disclosures specific to public companies
    - ☐ Select financial statement accounts: for-profit and not-for-profit
    - ☐ Select transactions: for-profit and not-for-profit
- IASB standards
  - Select transactions: differences between IFRS and U.S. GAAP
- U.S. SEC
  - Interim, annual, and periodic filing requirements for U.S. registrants
- AICPA Codification of Statements on Auditing Standards
  - Financial statements prepared under special purpose frameworks
- GASB
  - Conceptual framework
  - Requirements for state and local governments

WHICH LAWS, RULES, AND PRONOUNCEMENTS ARE TESTED?

The following is the AICPA's pronouncement policy:

Changes in accounting and auditing pronouncements are eligible to be tested on the Uniform CPA Examination in the later of: (1) the first calendar quarter beginning after the pronouncement's earliest mandatory effective date, regardless of entity type or (2) the first calendar quarter beginning six (6) months after the pronouncement's issuance date.*

Changes in the Internal Revenue Code, and federal taxation regulations are eligible to be tested in the calendar quarter beginning six (6) months after the change's effective date or enactment date, whichever is later.

Changes in federal laws outside the area of federal taxation are eligible to be tested in the calendar quarter beginning six (6) months after their effective date.

Changes in uniform acts are eligible to be tested in the calendar quarter beginning one (1) year after their adoption by a simple majority of the jurisdictions.

For all other subjects covered in the Uniform CPA Examination, changes are eligible to be tested in the later of: (1) the first calendar quarter beginning after the earliest mandatory effective date, regardless of entity type or (2) six (6) months after the issuance date.*

Once a change becomes eligible for testing in the Uniform CPA Examination, previous content impacted by the change is removed. [This simply means that once a new pronouncement is testable, you will no longer be tested on the old pronouncement.]

** Note the following example: A pronouncement issued on February 1, 2019, is effective for public business entities for fiscal years beginning after December 15, 2019, and is effective for all other entities for fiscal years beginning after December 15, 2020. For purposes of the Uniform CPA Examination: (1) the pronouncement is eligible for testing on January 1, 2020 for all entity types and (2) the prior pronouncement is deemed superseded and no longer eligible for testing as of January 1, 2020.*

AICPA's NONDISCLOSURE AGREEMENT

As part of the AICPA's nondisclosure policy and to prove each candidate's willingness to adhere to this policy, a confidentiality and break policy statement must be accepted by each candidate during the introductory screens at the beginning of each exam. Nonacceptance of this policy means the exam will be terminated and the test fees will be forfeited. This statement from the AICPA's Sample Test is reproduced here to remind all CPA candidates about the AICPA's strict policy of nondisclosure, which Gleim consistently supports and upholds.

"**Policy Statement and Confidentiality Agreement**

I hereby agree that I will maintain the confidentiality of the Uniform CPA Exam.
In addition, I agree that I will not:

- Divulge the nature or content of any Uniform CPA Exam question or answer under any circumstances
- Engage in any unauthorized communication during testing
- Refer to unauthorized materials or use unauthorized equipment during testing
- Remove or attempt to remove any Uniform CPA Exam materials, notes, or any other items from the exam room

I understand and agree that liability for test administration activities, including but not limited to the adequacy or accuracy of test materials and equipment, and the accuracy of scoring and score reporting, will be limited to score correction or test retake at no additional fee. I waive any and all right to all other claims. I further agree to report to the AICPA any exam question disclosures, or solicitations for disclosure, of which I become aware.

I affirm that I have had the opportunity to read the Candidate Bulletin and I agree to all of its terms and conditions.

I understand that breaks are only allowed between testlets. I understand that I will be asked to complete any open testlet before leaving the testing room for a break. In addition, I understand that failure to comply with this Policy statement and Confidentiality Agreement could result in the invalidation of my scores, disqualification from future exams, expulsion from the testing facility, and possibly civil or criminal penalties."

GLEIM CPA REVIEW ESSENTIALS

Gleim CPA Review has the following features to make studying easier:

1. **Backgrounds:** In certain instances, we have provided historical background or supplemental information. This information is intended to illuminate the topic under discussion and is set off in bordered boxes with shaded headings. This material does not need to be memorized for the exam.

BACKGROUND 4-1 Fair Value Measurement of Financial Instruments
Historical cost is an appropriate measurement attribute for property, plant, and equipment. An entity often holds these assets for years. Historical cost is not appropriate for financial instruments, which often are current assets. The FASB therefore requires all entities either to report on the face of the balance sheet or disclose in the notes the fair values of all financial instruments. Current GAAP are found in FASB ASC 825.

2. **Examples:** Illustrative examples, both hypothetical and those drawn from actual events, are set off in shaded, bordered boxes.

EXAMPLE 1-1 Representation Based on an Unobservable Price
The accuracy of an unobservable price cannot be determined. But the entity can disclose that the estimate is in fact an estimate. It also can explain the estimation process and its limits. Given this disclosure and explanation, if no errors have been made in choosing and performing the process, the representation is faithful.

3. **Gleim Success Tips:** These tips supplement the core exam material by suggesting how certain topics might be presented on the exam or how you should prepare for an issue.

SUCCESS TIP

The AICPA has previously tested candidates on their knowledge of what the classification of current liabilities entails. Potentially, candidates could see a list of fixed accounts with a question on the amount of current liabilities of the firm.

4. **Memory Aids:** These mnemonic devices are designed to assist you in memorizing important concepts.

The following memory aid is helpful for learning the enhancing qualitative characteristics:

E = Enhancing	Enhancing
C = Comparability	Comparability
V = Verifiability	Verifies
T = Timeliness	Timely
U = Understandability	Understanding

5. **Detailed Table of Contents:** This information at the beginning of the book is a complete listing of all study units and subunits in the Gleim CPA Financial Review program. Use this list as a study aid to mark off your progress and to provide jumping-off points for review.
6. **IFRS Differences:** The CPA Exam began testing international standards for the first time in 2011. When international standards diverge significantly from U.S. GAAP, the differences are highlighted. Questions that apply to IFRS include phrases such as "under IFRS" or "according to IFRS."

NOTE: All CPA Exam questions that mention IFRS test the differences between IFRS and U.S. GAAP. No question that mentions IFRS tests the convergence of IFRS and U.S. GAAP. For an example of the kind of IFRS question you might see on the CPA Exam, please see page 661 in Appendix A, "IFRS Differences."

IFRS DIFFERENCE

Each part of an item with a cost significant to the total cost must be depreciated separately. But an entity may separately depreciate parts that are not significant.

7. **Blueprint with Gleim Cross-References:** Appendix B contains a reprint of the AICPA Blueprint for FAR along with cross-references to the corresponding Gleim study units.
8. **Optimizing Your Score on the Task-Based Simulations (TBSs):** Appendix C explains how to approach and allocate your time for the TBS testlets. It also presents several example TBSs for your review.
9. **Core Concepts:** We have also provided additional study materials to supplement the Knowledge Transfer Outlines in the digital Gleim CPA Review Course. The Core Concepts, for example, are consolidated documents providing an overview of the key points of each subunit that serve as the foundation for learning. As part of your review, you should make sure that you understand each of them.

TIME BUDGETING AND QUESTION-ANSWERING TECHNIQUES FOR FAR

To begin the exam, you will enter your Launch Code on the Welcome screen. If you do not enter the correct code within 5 minutes of the screen appearing, the exam session will end.

Next, you will have an additional 5 minutes to view a brief exam introduction containing two screens: the nondisclosure policy and a section information screen. Accept the policy and then review the information screen, but be sure to click the Begin Exam button on the bottom right of the screen within the allotted 5 minutes. If you fail to do so, the exam will be terminated and you will not have the option to restart your exam.

These 10 minutes, along with the 5 minutes you may spend on a post-exam survey, are not included in the 240 minutes of exam time.

Once you complete the introductory screens and begin your exam, expect two testlets of 33 multiple-choice questions (MCQs) each and three testlets of Task-Based Simulations (TBSs) (one with 2 TBSs and two with 3 TBSs each). You will have 240 minutes to complete the five testlets.

1. **Budget your time so you can finish before time expires.**
   a. Here is our suggested time allocation for Financial Accounting and Reporting:

	Minutes	Start Time	
Testlet 1 (MCQ)	41*	4 hours	00 minutes
Testlet 2 (MCQ)	41*	3 hours	19 minutes
Testlet 3 (TBS)	36	2 hours	38 minutes
Break	15	Clock stops	
Testlet 4 (TBS)	54	2 hours	02 minutes
Testlet 5 (TBS)	54	1 hour	08 minutes
**Extra time	14	0 hours	14 minutes

   *Rounded down

   b. Before beginning your first MCQ testlet, prepare a Gleim Time Management plan as recommended in *CPA Exam Guide: A System for Success*.
   c. As you work through the individual questions, monitor your time. In Financial, we suggest 41 minutes (1.25 minutes per question) for each testlet of 33 MCQs. If you answer five items in 6 minutes, you are fine, but if you spend 8 minutes on five items, you need to speed up. In the TBS testlets, spend no more than 18 minutes on each TBS. For more information on TBS time budgets, refer to Appendix C, "Optimizing Your Score on the Task-Based Simulations (TBSs)."

   **Remember to allocate your budgeted extra time, as needed, to each testlet. Your goal is to answer all of the items and achieve the maximum score possible. As you practice answering TBSs in the Gleim Premium CPA Review System, you will be practicing your time management.

2. **Answer the questions in consecutive order.**
   a. Do not agonize over any one question. **Stay within your time budget.**
   b. Never leave an MCQ unanswered. Your score is based on the number of correct responses. You will not be penalized for answering incorrectly. If you are unsure about a question,
      1) Make an educated guess.
      2) Flag it for review by clicking on the flag icon at the bottom of the screen.
      3) Return to it before you submit the testlet as time allows. Remember, once you have selected the Submit Testlet option, you will no longer be able to review or change any answers in the completed testlet.

3. **Read the question carefully to discover exactly what is being asked.**
   a. Ignore the answer choices so they do not affect your precise reading of the question.
   b. Focusing on what is required allows you to
      1) Reject extraneous information
      2) Concentrate on relevant facts
      3) Proceed directly to determining the best answer
   c. **Careful!** The requirement may be an exception that features negative words.
   d. Decide the correct answer before looking at the answer choices.
4. **Read the answer choices, paying attention to small details.**
   a. Even if an answer choice appears to be correct, do not skip the remaining choices. Each choice requires consideration because you are looking for the best answer provided.
   b. **Only one answer option is the best.** In the MCQs, four answer choices are presented, and you know one of them is correct. The remaining choices are distractors and are meant to appear correct at first glance. Eliminate them as quickly as you can.
   c. Treat each answer choice like a true/false question as you analyze it.
   d. In computational MCQs, the distractor answers are carefully calculated to be the result of common mistakes. Be careful, and double-check your computations if time permits.
      1) There will be a mix of conceptual and calculation questions. When you take the exam, it may appear that more of the questions are calculation-type because they take longer and are more difficult.
5. **Click on the best answer.**
   a. You have a 25% chance of answering correctly by guessing blindly, but you can improve your odds with an educated guess.
   b. For many MCQs, you can **eliminate two answer choices with minimal effort** and increase your educated guess to a 50/50 proposition.
      1) Rule out answers that you think are incorrect.
      2) Speculate what the AICPA is looking for and/or why the question is being asked.
      3) Select the best answer or guess between equally appealing answers. Your first guess is usually the most intuitive.
6. **Do not click the Submit Testlet button until you have consulted the question status list at the bottom of each MCQ screen.**
   a. Return to flagged questions to finalize your answer choices if you have time.
   b. Verify that you have answered every question.
   c. Stay on schedule because time management is critical to exam success.

Doing well on the **task-based simulations** requires you to be an expert on how to approach them both from a question-answering and a time-allocation perspective. Refer to Appendix C, "Optimizing Your Score on the Task-Based Simulations (TBSs)," for a complete explanation of task-based simulations and how to optimize your score on each one.

HOW TO BE IN CONTROL

Remember, you must be in control to be successful during exam preparation and execution. Perhaps more importantly, control can also contribute greatly to your personal and other professional goals. Control is the process whereby you

1. Develop expectations, standards, budgets, and plans
2. Undertake activity, production, study, and learning
3. Measure the activity, production, output, and knowledge
4. Compare actual activity with expected and budgeted activity
5. Modify the activity, behavior, or study to better achieve the expected or desired outcome
6. Revise expectations and standards in light of actual experience
7. Continue the process or restart the process in the future

Exercising control will ultimately develop the confidence you need to outperform most other CPA candidates and PASS the CPA Exam!

QUESTIONS ABOUT GLEIM MATERIALS

Gleim has an efficient and effective way for candidates who have purchased the Gleim Premium CPA Review System to submit an inquiry and receive a response regarding Gleim materials **directly through their course**. This system also allows you to view your Q&A session online in your Gleim Personal Classroom.

Questions regarding the information in this **introduction and/or the Gleim *CPA Exam Guide*** (study suggestions, study plans, exam specifics) may be emailed to personalcounselor@gleim.com.

Questions concerning **orders, prices, shipments, or payments** should be sent via email to customerservice@gleim.com and will be promptly handled by our competent and courteous customer service staff.

For **technical support**, you may use our automated technical support service at www.gleim.com/support, email us at support@gleim.com, or call us at (800) 874-5346.

CITATIONS TO AUTHORITATIVE PRONOUNCEMENTS

Throughout the book, we refer to certain authoritative accounting pronouncements by the following abbreviations:

GAAP – The sources of authoritative U.S. generally accepted accounting principles (GAAP) recognized by the FASB as applicable by nongovernmental entities are (1) the FASB's Accounting Standards Codification (ASC) and (2) (for SEC registrants only) pronouncements of the SEC. All guidance in the Codification is equally authoritative. SEC pronouncements must be followed by registrants regardless of whether they are reflected in the codification.

IFRS and IASs – International Financial Reporting Standards (IFRS) are issued by the current standard-setter, the International Accounting Standards Board (IASB). International Accounting Standards (IASs), related Interpretations, and the framework for the preparation and presentation of financial statements were issued by the predecessor entity. IFRS also is the collective term for IASs.

GASB Statements – The Governmental Accounting Standards Board issues statements that apply to state and local governments.

SFAC – FASB Statements of Financial Accounting Concepts establish financial accounting and reporting objectives and concepts. SFACs are other accounting literature. They are considered only in the absence of applicable authoritative guidance (the FASB Accounting Standards Codification or SEC pronouncements). They were designed for use by the FASB in developing their other authoritative pronouncements.

ASC – The FASB's Accounting Standards Codification is "the single source of authoritative nongovernmental U.S. generally accepted accounting principles" for entities that are not SEC registrants. The Codification organizes the many pronouncements that constitute U.S. GAAP into a consistent, searchable format accessible through the Internet.

FEEDBACK

Please fill out our online feedback form (www.gleim.com/feedbackFAR) IMMEDIATELY after you take the CPA Financial section so we can adapt our material based on where candidates say we need to increase or decrease coverage. Our approach has been approved by the AICPA.

STUDY UNIT ONE

THE FINANCIAL REPORTING ENVIRONMENT

(20 pages of outline)

This study unit addresses

1) The domestic and international bodies that set accounting and reporting standards;
2) The financial reporting objectives for business entities, nongovernmental not-for-profit entities, and state and local governments;
3) The guidance in the FASB's conceptual framework for accounting and reporting; and
4) The reporting requirements of the U.S. Securities and Exchange Commission (SEC).

1.1 STANDARDS SETTING FOR FINANCIAL ACCOUNTING

1. **Nature of Financial Accounting**
   a. Financial accounting produces information about an entity's assets, liabilities, revenues, expenses, and other elements of financial statements.
      1) **Financial statements** are the primary method of communicating to external parties information about the results of operations, financial position, and cash flows.
   b. For general-purpose financial statements to be useful to external parties, they must be prepared in accordance with generally accepted accounting principles **(GAAP)** in the U.S.
      1) GAAP include pronouncements issued by the bodies designated by the AICPA Council to establish accounting and reporting principles. The following bodies have been designated:
         a) Financial Accounting Standards Board (FASB)
         b) International Accounting Standards Board (IASB)
         c) Governmental Accounting Standards Board (GASB)
         d) Federal Accounting Standards Advisory Board (FASAB)
   c. **Financial** accounting differs from **management** accounting.
      1) Management accounting information assists management decision making, planning, and control. It is primarily for internal use. It need not follow GAAP but is often derived from financial accounting records.

2. **SEC**
   a. The SEC has the legal authority to establish financial reporting requirements for publicly traded companies (referred to as issuers) in the United States. Issuers are firms that issue stocks and bonds.
      1) The SEC delegated this authority to the FASB.
      2) The SEC enforces those principles by ensuring that issuers meet certain periodic reporting requirements for the disclosure of financial and other information.
         a) This approach allows investors to evaluate investments for themselves using standardized reports filed with the SEC.
3. **Financial Accounting Foundation (FAF)**
   a. The FAF is an independent body established by the accounting profession in 1972. It oversees the following bodies involved in the establishment of U.S. GAAP for nongovernmental entities:
      1) The **Financial Accounting Standards Board (FASB)** establishes financial accounting and reporting standards (i.e., **U.S. GAAP**) for public and private companies and not-for-profit organizations.
         a) The FASB's Accounting Standards Codification (ASC) is the single source of U.S. GAAP.
         b) The FASB updates U.S. GAAP by issuing Accounting Standards Updates (ASUs).
      2) The Financial Accounting Standards Advisory Council (FASAC) advises the FASB on priorities and proposed standards and evaluates its performance.
      3) The Private Company Council (PCC)
         a) Proposes exceptions to and modifications of U.S. GAAP for private companies and
         b) Advises the FASB on private company issues before new pronouncements are issued.
      4) The Emerging Issues Task Force (EITF) addresses new and unusual accounting issues that require prompt action to avoid differences in accounting treatments.
         a) Many consensus positions of the EITF have been included in **Accounting Standards Updates (ASUs)**.
4. **Standard Setting by the FASB**
   a. The FASB follows a **due process** procedure before issuing final pronouncements. This procedure includes consideration of whether the benefits of change exceed its costs.
      1) Financial reporting issues are identified based on communications with stakeholders (e.g., investors, creditors, businesses, academics, and accountants), research, and other activities.
      2) The decision to add a project to the technical agenda is based on an analysis by the FASB's staff.

3) Deliberation of the issues occurs at a public meeting(s).
4) An Exposure Draft is published to solicit broad stakeholder responses before voting on the final draft proposal.
    a) In some projects, a Discussion Paper also may be issued at an early stage to seek input during the process of drafting the proposal.
5) A public meeting regarding the Exposure Draft may be held if needed.
6) The staff analyzes the information obtained in the preceding steps. The FASB then redeliberates the proposals with stakeholder input at a public meeting(s).
7) The FASB votes on a final draft proposal. If a majority of the seven board members approves, an ASU is issued to amend the Accounting Standards Codification (ASC).
    a) When an ASU has been incorporated into the FASB's ASC, it has the status of U.S. GAAP.

5. **IASB**

a. The International Accounting Standards Board (IASB) was founded in 2001. It is an independent group of experts that are responsible for
    1) The development and publication of International Financial Reporting Standards (IFRS), including the IFRS for Small and Medium-sized Enterprises (SMEs).
    2) Approving Interpretations of IFRS as developed by the IFRS Interpretations Committee.

6. **GASB**

a. The GASB is a private, not-for-profit, nongovernmental organization established by the FAF as the primary standard setter for state and local governmental entities. (The GASB does not establish GAAP for the federal government.)
    1) Governmental and nongovernmental environments have many similarities and many differences.
        a) The GASB and its predecessor were established because of the differences, especially the unique informational needs that must be met by governmental accounting systems and reports.
    2) GASB Statements have the status of GAAP for state and local governments. (Governmental accounting is covered in Study Units 18 and 19.)

7. **FASAB**

a. The FASAB establishes accounting principles for the federal government and issues Statements of Federal Financial Accounting Standards.

STOP & REVIEW

You have completed the outline for this subunit.
Study multiple-choice questions 1 and 2 beginning on page 32.

1.2 THE OBJECTIVE OF GENERAL-PURPOSE FINANCIAL REPORTING

1. The FASB's conceptual framework is a set of interrelated objectives, qualitative characteristics, elements, and other fundamental concepts. It is described in the **Statements of Financial Accounting Concepts (SFACs)**.
   a. But SFACs are not authoritative and are not included in the ASC. Instead, they are intended to guide the development and application of U.S. GAAP.
2. This subunit is based on SFAC 8, *Conceptual Framework for Financial Reporting*, Chapter 1, *The Objective of General Purpose Financial Reporting*.

SUCCESS TIP

The FASB's Conceptual Framework is frequently tested on the CPA Exam. It is covered in this subunit and in Subunits 1.5 through 1.7.

3. The **objective of general-purpose financial reporting** is to provide financial information about the reporting entity that is useful to existing and potential investors and creditors in making decisions about providing resources to the entity.
   a. **Primary users** of financial information are current or potential investors and creditors who cannot obtain it directly. Management and regulators are **not** primary users.
      1) Financial reporting may help the primary users to estimate the value of the reporting entity. But it does not directly show the value of the entity.
      2) Primary users' decisions depend on the expected return. Accordingly, primary users need information that helps them assess the amount, timing, and uncertainty of the entity's **future net cash inflows**.
4. The information reported is about the entity's economic resources, claims against the entity, and changes in those resources and claims. It helps primary users make decisions about (a) providing resources to the entity and (b) assessing the entity's ability to generate future net cash inflows.
   a. Financial reporting (statement of financial position) provides information about the nature and amount of the entity's economic resources (assets) and claims (liabilities and equity). This information may be used to assess the entity's liquidity and solvency.
   b. The changes in economic resources and claims may result from the entity's financial performance and other transactions, such as issuing debt or equity instruments.
      1) Financial performance reflected by accrual accounting (statement of comprehensive income) is a means of assessing the entity's ability to generate net cash inflows through its operations rather than by obtaining additional resources from investors and creditors. (The accrual basis is explained in Subunit 1.7.)
      2) Financial performance reflected by cash flows (statement of cash flows) helps to understand the entity's operations, evaluate its financing and investing activities, and assess its liquidity and solvency.
         a) Information about financial performance helps to (1) understand the return that the entity produced on its economic resources and (2) evaluate management performance.
      3) The entity's economic resources and claims may change when equity instruments are issued (statement of changes in equity).

STOP & REVIEW

You have completed the outline for this subunit.
Study multiple-choice questions 3 and 4 on page 33.

1.3 OBJECTIVES OF FINANCIAL REPORTING BY NONGOVERNMENTAL NOT-FOR-PROFIT ENTITIES

1. This subunit is based on SFAC 4, *Objectives of Financial Reporting by Nonbusiness Organizations.*
2. This outline uses the acronym **NFP** to denote a nongovernmental not-for-profit entity.
   a. The financial reporting model used by an NFP is outlined in Study Unit 20.
3. **Distinguishing Characteristics**
   a. NFPs receive significant resources from providers who do not expect to receive repayment or proportionate economic benefits (nonreciprocal transactions).
      1) They have transactions that are infrequent in businesses, such as grants and contributions.
   b. NFPs have operating purposes other than to provide goods or services at a profit.
   c. NFPs have no single indicator of performance, e.g., net income. Thus, other performance indicators are needed.
   d. NFPs lack defined ownership interests that (1) can be sold, transferred, or redeemed or (2) entitle an owner to distributions upon liquidation of the entity.
      1) They report net assets rather than equity (Assets – Liabilities).
      2) Investor-owned entities that provide economic benefits directly to owners, members, or participants (e.g., credit unions or employee benefit plans) are **not** considered not-for-profit entities.
      3) An entity may have some characteristics of an NFP but not others.
         a) Examples include private not-for-profit hospitals and schools that receive small amounts of contributions but are essentially dependent on debt issues and user fees. For such entities, the reporting objectives of businesses may be more appropriate.
   e. However, the operating environments of NFPs and business entities are similar. For example, both
      1) Produce and distribute goods and services using scarce resources
      2) Obtain resources from contributors and are accountable to them
      3) Must be financially sound in the long run
      4) Are subject to laws and regulations
   f. Stakeholders of for-profit entities primarily need information about financial return.
      1) But stakeholders of NFPs (managers, constituents, oversight bodies, and resource providers) primarily need information about the services provided and the continuing ability to provide those services.

4. **Objectives**
   a. Financial reporting should provide information
      1) Useful to providers in making resource allocation decisions
      2) Useful in assessing services and the ability to provide services
      3) Useful in assessing management stewardship and performance
      4) About economic resources, obligations, net resources, and changes in them, including
         a) Performance of an organization during a period
         b) Nature of, and relationship between, resource inflows and outflows
         c) Service efforts and accomplishments
         d) Factors that may affect an organization's liquidity, such as
            i) Sources and uses of cash and other liquid assets and
            ii) Borrowing and repayment activities
      5) About managers' explanations and interpretations to help users understand financial information

STOP & REVIEW

You have completed the outline for this subunit.
Study multiple-choice questions 5 and 6 on page 34.

1.4 OBJECTIVES OF FINANCIAL REPORTING BY STATE AND LOCAL GOVERNMENTS

1. The Governmental Accounting Standards Board's (GASB) conceptual framework provides a basis for the development and application of accounting standards for state and local governments. This subunit is based on GASB Concepts Statement 1, *Objectives of Financial Reporting*.
2. **Governmental-Type Activities**
   a. The following are **characteristics** of the governmental environment:
      1) The representative form of government and the separation of powers
      2) National, state, county, and city governments and the interflow of revenues
      3) The expectations of taxpayers about the services they receive
      4) A budget as a policy decision and a legally binding control
      5) Use of fund accounting
      6) Governments at the same level with dissimilar functions
      7) Assets, e.g., highways and bridges that do not earn revenue
      8) Citizens who want the maximum services for the minimum taxes
   b. The following are **users** of financial reporting for governmental-type activities:
      1) Citizens (those to whom the government is directly accountable)
      2) Legislative and oversight bodies (representatives of the citizenry)
      3) Investors and creditors (providers of financing)
   c. The following are **uses** of governmental reporting:
      1) Comparing actual results with budgeted amounts
      2) Assessing financial condition and operating results
      3) Determining compliance with laws, rules, and regulations
      4) Evaluating efficiency and effectiveness

3. **Business-Type Activities**
   a. Business-type activities
      1) Involve exchange (reciprocal) transactions.
      2) Have large investments in revenue-producing capital assets (e.g., toll roads).
      3) Often have one function. Thus,
         a) Comparisons among governments are simpler and
         b) Fund accounting is less likely to be used.
      4) May still be influenced by the political process (e.g., rate setting).
      5) May have budgets that lack legal force.

4. **Accountability and Interperiod Equity**
   a. Accountability is the primary objective of all governmental financial reporting. It is based on the public's right to know.
      1) **Fiscal accountability** is the responsibility of a government to justify that its actions comply with public decisions about obtaining and expending public resources in the short term.
      2) **Operational accountability** is the responsibility to report the extent to which accounting objectives have been met efficiently and effectively using available resources. It is also the responsibility to report whether those objectives can be met for the foreseeable future.
      3) **Interperiod equity** is part of accountability. Financial resources received during a period should suffice to pay for the services provided during that period. Moreover, debt should be repaid during the period of usefulness of the assets acquired.
         a) Thus, governmental reporting should help users assess whether future taxpayers must pay for services already provided.
         b) Governmental reporting also should help users (e.g., citizens, lawmakers, and oversight bodies) to make economic, political, and social decisions.

5. **Objectives**
   a. **Public accountability.** The government should provide information about
      1) Whether current revenues suffice to pay for current services
      2) Compliance with the budget and other requirements
      3) Service efforts, costs, and accomplishments
   b. **Evaluating operating results.** The government should provide information about
      1) Sources and uses of financial resources
      2) How its activities were financed and its cash needs were met
      3) Whether its financial condition improved or declined
   c. **Assessing services provided.** The government should provide information about
      1) Financial position and condition
      2) Noncurrent nonfinancial resources
      3) Legal or contractual restrictions and potential risks

NOTE: Study Units 18 and 19 address accounting and reporting by state and local governments.

STOP & REVIEW

You have completed the outline for this subunit.
Study multiple-choice question 7 on page 35.

1.5 QUALITATIVE CHARACTERISTICS OF USEFUL FINANCIAL INFORMATION

1. This subunit is based on
   a. SFAC 8, *Conceptual Framework for Financial Reporting*, Chapter 3, *Qualitative Characteristics of Useful Financial Information* (as amended), and
   b. GASB Concepts Statement 6, *Measurement of Elements of Financial Statements*.
2. **Fundamental Qualitative Characteristics**
   a. For financial information to be useful, it must include the fundamental qualitative characteristics of relevance and faithful representation.
   b. **Relevance.** Information is relevant if it can make a difference in user decisions. To do so, it must be material and have predictive value and/or confirmatory value.
      1) Information has **predictive value** if it can be used to generate predictions as an input in a predictive process.
      2) Information has **confirmatory value** for prior evaluations if it provides feedback that confirms or changes (corrects) them.
         a) Predictive value and confirmatory value are interrelated. For example, current revenue may confirm a prior prediction and also be used to predict the next period's revenue.
      3) Information is **material** if it is probable that an omission or misstatement of an item in a financial report will affect the judgment of a reasonable person who relies on this information.
         a) **Materiality is entity-specific**, whereas relevance is a general idea about what information is useful to investors.
         b) Materiality has no specific quantitative threshold. The dollar amount of an item, without regard to the nature of the item, generally is not a sufficient basis for a materiality judgment.
   c. **Faithful representation.** Useful information faithfully represents economic events. A perfectly faithful representation has the following characteristics:
      1) **Completeness** (containing what is needed for user understanding)
      2) **Neutrality** (unbiased in its selection and presentation)
      3) **Freedom from error**
         a) Information that is faithfully represented is not necessarily accurate in all respects. Free from error means no errors or omissions exist in the
            i) Descriptions of the phenomena and
            ii) Selection and application of the reporting process.

EXAMPLE 1-1	Representation Based on an Unobservable Price
The accuracy of an unobservable price cannot be determined. But the entity can disclose that the estimate is in fact an estimate. It also can explain the estimation process and its limits. Given this disclosure and explanation, if no errors have been made in choosing and performing the process, the representation is faithful.	

   d. The process for applying the fundamental qualitative characteristics is to
      1) Identify what may be useful to users of the financial reports,
      2) Identify the relevant information, and
      3) Determine whether the information is available and can be faithfully represented.

e. The memory aids below are helpful for learning the fundamental qualitative characteristics:

R = Relevance	Relevance
P = Predictive value	Predicts or
C = Confirmatory value	Confirms
M = Materiality	Materiality

F = Faithful representation	a Faithful representation is
C = Completeness	Complete
N = Neutrality	Neutral and
F = Freedom from error	error Free

3. **Enhancing Qualitative Characteristics**

a. The following enhance the usefulness of relevant and faithfully represented information:

1) **Comparability.** Information should be comparable with similar information for (a) other entities and (b) the same entity for another period or date. Thus, comparability allows users to understand similarities and differences.

a) Consistency is a means of achieving comparability over time and between periods. It is the use of the same methods (e.g., accounting principles) for the same items.

2) **Verifiability.** Information is verifiable (directly or indirectly) if knowledgeable and independent observers can reach a consensus (not necessarily unanimity) that it is faithfully represented.

a) For example, consensus-based fair value (e.g., transaction price) is verifiable.

b) Besides a point estimate, a range of possible amounts and their related possibilities can also be verified. An example is the expected cash flow approach outlined in Subunit 1.7.

3) **Timeliness.** Information is timely when it is available in time to influence decisions.

4) **Understandability.** Understandable information is clearly and concisely classified, characterized, and presented.

a) Information should be readily understandable by diligent users who have a reasonable knowledge of business and economic activities but should not be excluded because of its complexity.

b) The general public is thus not the target audience of financial reporting.

b. The memory aid below is helpful for learning the enhancing qualitative characteristics:

E = Enhancing	Enhancing
C = Comparability	Comparability
V = Verifiability	Verifies
T = Timeliness	Timely
U = Understandability	Understanding

SUCCESS TIP

Do not confuse the fundamental qualitative characteristics and the enhancing characteristics. Also, be aware of the aspects of each fundamental characteristic.

4. **Cost Constraint**

   a. Cost is a pervasive constraint on the information provided by financial reporting. The benefits of reporting specific information must justify the costs incurred to provide and use that information.

      1) Provider costs (collection, processing, verification, and distribution) ultimately are incurred by users as reduced returns.

      2) Other user costs include those to analyze and interpret the information provided.

      3) When the FASB develops financial reporting standards, it considers costs and benefits in relation to financial reporting generally and not in relation to individual reporting entities.

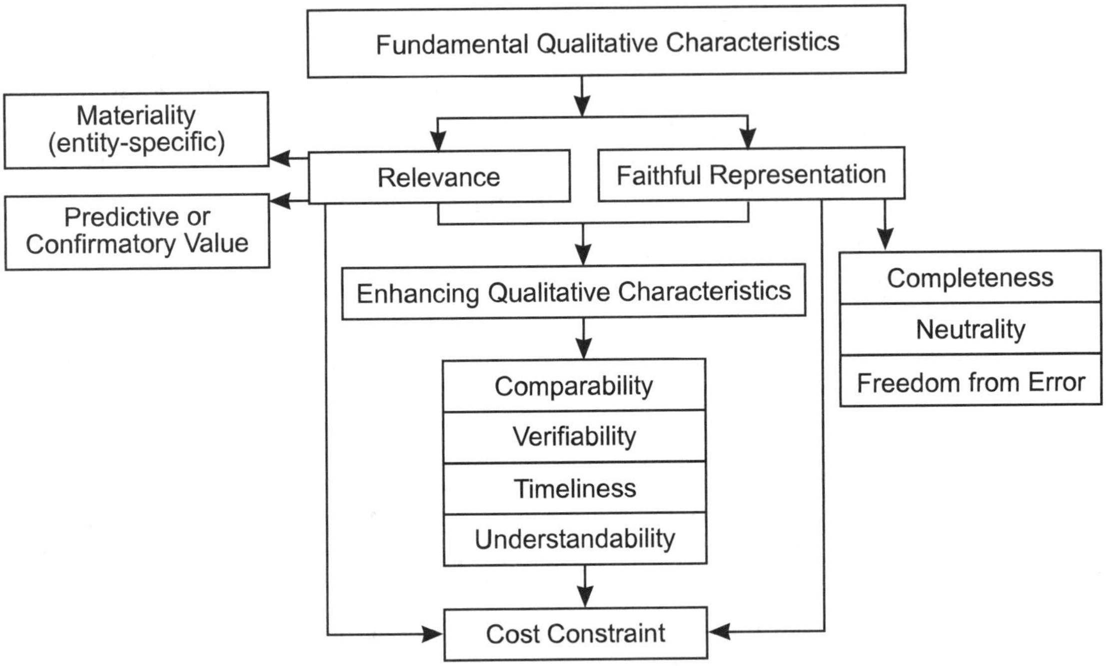

Figure 1-1

5. GASB Concepts Statement 6, *Measurement of Elements of Financial Statements*, defines the following qualitative characteristics of state and local governmental reporting:

   a. Understandability
   b. Reliability
   c. Relevance
   d. Timeliness
   e. Comparability
   f. Cost-benefit limitations

NOTE: Study Units 18 and 19 address accounting and reporting by state and local governments.

STOP & REVIEW

You have completed the outline for this subunit.
Study multiple-choice questions 8 through 11 beginning on page 35.

1.6 ELEMENTS OF FINANCIAL STATEMENTS

1. This subunit is based on
   a. SFAC 6, *Elements of Financial Statements*;
   b. GASB Concepts Statement 4, *Elements of Financial Statements*; and
   c. GASB Concepts Statement 6, *Measurement of Elements of Financial Statements*.
2. **Financial Statements**
   a. Financial statements are the primary, but not the only, means of communicating financial information to external parties.
      1) **Notes** supplement or further explain financial information on the face of the statements.
         a) Examples of such information are descriptions of the accounting policies used and other disclosures required by GAAP.
         b) Notes may **not** be used (1) to correct an improper presentation in the statements or (2) as a substitute for recognition in the statements.
         c) The notes should contain information about
            i) Financial statement line items.
            ii) The reporting entity.
            iii) Unrecognized past events and current circumstances that can affect cash flows.
      2) **Supplementary information**, such as management's discussion and analysis (MD&A) (described in Subunit 1.8), provides information additional to that in the statements and notes.
   b. A **full set of financial statements** should report the following:
      1) Financial position at the end of the period
      2) Earnings for the period
      3) Comprehensive income for the period
      4) Cash flows during the period
      5) Investments by and distributions to owners (changes in owners' equity) during the period
3. **Elements** are the classes of items in the financial statements. They are distributed as follows among the financial statements other than the statement of cash flows:
   a. **Statement of Financial Position (Balance Sheet)**
      1) **Assets** are probable future economic benefits obtained or controlled by an entity as a result of past transactions or events.
         a) **Valuation** allowances, such as (1) accumulated depreciation, (2) credit losses, or (3) premium on bonds receivable, are part of the carrying amount of the related assets, not assets or liabilities.

2) **Liabilities** are probable future sacrifices of economic benefits. They are existing obligations of a specific entity to transfer assets or provide services to other entities as a result of previous transactions or events.

   a) Valuation allowances, such as discounts on bonds payable, are part of the carrying amount of the related liability, not liabilities or assets.

3) **Equity** is the residual interest in the assets of an entity after subtracting liabilities. In a business entity, equity is the ownership interest.

4) **Investments by owners** are increases in equity of a business entity during a period. They result from transfers by other entities of something of value to increase ownership interests. Assets (e.g., cash or property) are the most commonly transferred items, but services also can be exchanged for equity interests.

5) **Distributions to owners** are decreases in equity during a period. They result from transferring assets, providing services, or incurring liabilities to owners.

b. **Statement of Earnings and Comprehensive Income**

1) **Revenues** are inflows or other enhancements of assets or settlements of liabilities (or both) from

   a) Delivering or producing goods,
   b) Providing services, or
   c) Other activities that qualify as ongoing major or central operations.

2) **Gains** are increases in equity from peripheral or incidental transactions or other events and circumstances except revenues or investments by owners.

3) **Expenses** are outflows or other uses of assets or incurrences of liabilities (or both) from

   a) Delivering or producing goods,
   b) Providing services, or
   c) Other activities that qualify as ongoing major or central operations.

4) **Losses** are decreases in equity from peripheral or incidental transactions or other events and circumstances except expenses or distributions to owners.

5) **Comprehensive income** includes all the changes in equity of a business entity during a period except those resulting from investments by owners and distributions to owners (owner sources).

4. **Elements of Financial Statements of State and Local Governments**
   a. **Statement of Net Position**
      1) **Assets** are resources with current service capacity that are currently controlled.
      2) **Liabilities** are present obligations to sacrifice resources that the government has little or no discretion to avoid.
      3) A **deferred outflow of resources** is a consumption of net assets that applies to a future reporting period.
      4) A **deferred inflow of resources** is an acquisition of net assets that applies to a future reporting period.
      5) **Net position** is the residual of all other elements in a statement of net financial position (net assets).
   b. **Resource Flows Statements**
      1) An **outflow of resources** is a consumption of net assets that applies to the reporting period.
      2) An **inflow of resources** is an acquisition of net assets that applies to the reporting period.
5. **Measurement Approaches**
   a. An **initial amount** reflects a transaction date. It is a price or amount assigned when an asset was acquired or a liability was incurred, including later modifications derived from the initial amount (e.g., depreciation or impairment).
   b. A **remeasured amount** reflects conditions on the financial statement date. It is a new carrying value not based on prior amounts reported.
      1) Remeasured amounts are appropriate for
         a) Financial assets (assets to be converted to cash) and
         b) Liabilities for which the timing and amount of payments is uncertain.
6. **Measurement Attributes**
   a. **Historical cost** is (a) the price paid to acquire an asset or (b) the amount received for the incurrence of a liability in an actual exchange transaction.
   b. **Fair value** is the price that would be (a) received to sell an asset or (b) paid to transfer a liability in an orderly transaction between market participants at the measurement date.
   c. **Replacement cost** is the price that would be paid to acquire an asset with equivalent service potential in an orderly market transaction at the measurement date.
   d. **Settlement amount** is the amount at which (a) an asset could be realized or (b) a liability could be liquidated with the counterparty, other than in an active market.

NOTE: Study Units 18 and 19 address accounting and reporting by state and local governments.

STOP & REVIEW

You have completed the outline for this subunit.
Study multiple-choice questions 12 through 14 on page 37.

1.7 ASSUMPTIONS, RECOGNITION, AND MEASUREMENT CONCEPTS

1. **Assumptions**

   a. **Economic-entity assumption.** The reporting (accounting) entity is separately identified for the purpose of economic and financial accountability.

      1) The legal entity and the economic entity are not necessarily the same.

         a) For example, a parent and its subsidiary are a single economic entity but are distinct legal entities.

   b. **Going-concern assumption.** Unless evidence indicates otherwise, every business is assumed to be a going concern that operates for the foreseeable future.

      1) As a result, the **liquidation** basis of accounting is **not** used. It is assumed that the entity will not be liquidated in the near future.

         a) For example, fixed assets are depreciated at their useful life based on the assumption that the reporting entity has a long-enough life to fulfill its objectives and commitments.

   c. **Monetary-unit assumption.** Accounting records are stated in units of money. The changing purchasing power of the monetary unit (inflation) is assumed not to be material.

   d. **Periodicity assumption.** Economic activity can be divided into distinct time periods.

      1) This assumption requires reporting estimates in the financial statements. It sacrifices some degree of faithful representation of information (e.g., completeness) for increased relevance.

2. **Fundamental Recognition Criteria**

   a. **Recognition** is the formal recording or incorporation of an item in the financial statements as an asset, liability, revenue, expense, gain, loss, etc.

   b. Recognition criteria determine whether and when items are incorporated into the financial statements, either initially or as changes in existing items.

   c. Four fundamental recognition criteria apply:

      1) The item must meet the **definition** of an element of financial statements.

      2) It must have a relevant attribute **measurable** with sufficient reliability.

      3) The information must be **relevant**. It must be capable of making a difference in user decisions.

      4) The information must be **reliable**. It must be representationally faithful, verifiable, and neutral.

   d. Incorporation of any item is subject to the pervasive **cost** constraint and the **materiality** threshold.

   e. The following memory aid is helpful for learning the recognition criteria:

R = Recognition criteria	Recognition
D = Definition	Defines
M = Measurable	Measurable
R = Relevant	Relevance and
R = Reliable	Reliability

3. **Accrual Accounting**
   a. Elements of financial statements that meet the recognition and measurement criteria are accounted for in the financial statements using accrual accounting.
   b. Accrual accounting records the financial effects of transactions and other events and circumstances on an entity's economic resources and claims to them when they occur. Thus, recording is not necessarily when the direct cash flows occur. Accrual accounting is based on the following concepts:
      1) **Accruals** anticipate future cash flows. They recognize related assets, liabilities, revenues, expenses, gains, or losses. Sales or purchases on account, interest, and taxes are common accruals.
      2) **Deferrals** reflect past cash flows. They recognize liabilities (for receipts) and assets (for payments), with deferral of the related revenues, expenses, gains, and losses. The deferral ends when the obligation is satisfied or the future economic benefit is used up. Prepaid insurance is an example.
   c. Accrual accounting is the financial reporting framework used in GAAP. **Special purpose frameworks** are comprehensive bases of accounting other than GAAP. They are described in Study Unit 2, Subunit 5.
4. **Revenue Recognition Principle**
   a. Generally, revenue is recognized when an entity satisfies a performance obligation by transferring a promised good or service (an asset) to a customer.
      1) An asset is transferred when the customer obtains control of that asset.
   b. Control of an asset is transferred when the customer
      1) Has the ability to direct the use of the asset and
      2) Obtains substantially all of the remaining benefits (potential cash flows) from the asset.
   c. The accounting for revenue from contracts with customers is described in Study Unit 3, Subunits 4 and 5.
5. **Expenses and Losses Recognition Principle**
   a. Generally, expenses are recognized when an entity consumes economic benefits in its revenue-generating activities.
      1) Some expenses (e.g., cost of goods sold) are **matched** with revenue. They are simultaneously recognized with the revenue that directly result from the same transactions.
      2) Certain other expenses (e.g., utilities and administrative employees' salaries) are recognized during the period in which cash is spent or liabilities incurred.
      3) Still other expenses (e.g., straight-line depreciation and amortization) are **systematically and rationally** allocated to the periods during which the related assets provide benefits.
   b. Losses are recognized when
      1) Future economic benefits of an asset have been reduced or eliminated (e.g., impairment of an asset).
      2) Liabilities have been incurred or increased without receipt of an associated economic benefit (e.g., a contingent liability incurred due to a lawsuit against the entity).

6. **Measurement Attributes**
   a. Assets and liabilities may be measured using different attributes.
   b. **Historical cost** is the amount of cash paid to acquire an asset. It ordinarily is adjusted subsequently for amortization (which includes depreciation) or other allocations. It is the relevant measurement attribute for property, plant, and equipment.
   c. **Current (replacement) cost** is the amount of cash that would have to be paid for a current acquisition of the same or an equivalent asset. It may be used to measure LIFO and retail method inventories.
   d. **Current market value** is the amount of cash that could be obtained by selling an asset in an orderly liquidation.
   e. **Net realizable value** is the amount of cash expected to be received for an asset in the due course of business, minus the costs of completion and sale. It is used to measure some inventories.
      1) **Net settlement value** is the relevant attribute for trade payables. It is the sum of the undiscounted amount of cash expected to be paid to liquidate an obligation in the ordinary course of business.
   f. **Present value** of future cash flows incorporates time value of money concepts.
      1) Calculating the present value of future cash flows requires (a) identifying an appropriate interest rate (or discount rate) and (b) identifying the timing and amount of future cash flows. It may be used to measure noncurrent receivables and payables.
7. **Cash Flow Information and Present Value Measurement**
   a. Accounting measurements ordinarily use an observable amount determined by the market. Otherwise, estimated cash flows often are used to measure an asset or a liability.
   b. The objective is to estimate **fair value** by distinguishing the economic differences between sets of future cash flows that may vary in amount, timing, and uncertainty.
   c. The following are elements of a present value measurement:
      1) Estimates of future cash flows
      2) Expected variability of their amount and timing
      3) The time value of money based on the risk-free interest rate
      4) The price of uncertainty inherent in an asset or liability
      5) Other factors, such as lack of liquidity or market imperfections
         a) For example, the discount rate is increased to account for a lack of liquidity (a liquidity premium).
   d. Based on SFAC 7, *Using Cash Flow Information and Present Value in Accounting Measurements*, the following are two approaches to calculating present value:
      1) The **traditional approach** uses one set of estimated cash flows and one interest rate.
         a) Uncertainty is reflected solely in the choice of an interest rate.
         b) This approach is expected to continue to be used in many cases, for example, when cash flows are required by a contract.

2) The **expected cash flow (ECF)** approach applies in more complex circumstances, such as when no market or no comparable item exists for an asset or liability.

a) The ECF results from multiplying each possible estimated amount by its probability and adding the products. The emphasis is on explicit assumptions about the possible estimated cash flows and their probabilities.

b) By allowing for a range of possibilities, the ECF approach permits the use of expected present value when the timing of cash flows is uncertain.

c) **Expected present value** is the sum of the present values of estimated cash discounted using the same interest rate and weighted according to their probabilities.

e. The purpose of a present value measurement of the fair value of a liability is to estimate the value of assets required currently to

1) Settle the liability or
2) Transfer the liability to an entity of comparable credit standing.

a) The effect of an entity's credit standing on the measurement of its liabilities is captured in an adjustment to the interest (discount) rate.

STOP & REVIEW

You have completed the outline for this subunit.
Study multiple-choice questions 15 through 17 on page 38.

1.8 SEC REPORTING

1. The Securities and Exchange Commission (SEC) was created by the Securities Exchange Act of 1934 to regulate the trading of securities and otherwise to enforce securities legislation.

   a. The basic purposes of the securities laws are to prevent fraud and misrepresentation and to require full and fair disclosure so investors can evaluate investments.

2. Under the Securities Exchange Act of 1934, all regulated, publicly held companies must register with the SEC. Registration is required of all securities listed on a national exchange.

   a. Under the 1934 act, disclosures about subsequent trading of securities are made by filing periodic reports using the Electronic Data Gathering, Analysis, and Retrieval (EDGAR) system that are available to the public for review.

3. **Regulation S-X** describes the form and content of, and requirements for, financial statements filed with SEC. It applies to the reporting of **interim** and **annual financial statements**, including notes and schedules.
    a. The following are examples of information that must be provided in addition to the financial statements:
        1) **Management's discussion and analysis (MD&A)** of financial condition and results of operations
            a) This information includes the entity's outlook and significant effects of known trends, events, and uncertainties. It addresses such matters as (1) liquidity, (2) capital resources, (3) results of operations, and (4) the effect of changing prices.
        2) Management and general data for each director and officer
        3) Compensation of the five highest-paid directors and officers
        4) Security holdings of directors, officers, and those owning 5% or more of the security
        5) Matters submitted to shareholders for approval
        6) Pending litigation, e.g., principal parties, allegations, and relief sought
4. **Periodic Reporting**
    a. After registration with the SEC and the initial issuance of the securities under the Securities Act of 1933, the SEC requires the issuer to file many different forms (reports).
    b. The following forms filed with the SEC may be tested on the CPA Exam:
        1) **Form 10-K** is the **annual report** to the SEC. It must be **audited** by an independent public accountant.
            a) Annual financial statements include
                i) Balance sheets for the two most recent fiscal year ends
                ii) Statements of income, cash flows, and changes in equity for the three most recent fiscal years.
            b) The annual report must be filed within
                i) 60 days of the last day of the fiscal year by **large accelerated filers** [companies with a public float (the market value of shares held by the public) of $700 million or more]
                ii) 75 days by **accelerated filers** (public float of $75 million to $700 million and annual revenues of $100 million or more)
                iii) 90 days by **nonaccelerated filers** [(a) public float of less than $75 million or (b) public float of $75 to $700 million and annual revenues of less than $700 million]

2) **Form 10-Q** is the **quarterly report** of operations and financial condition filed with the SEC. It must be **reviewed** by an independent public accountant. A review offers a lower level of assurance than an audit regarding financial condition and the results of operations.

   a) An entity required to file Form 10-K also must file Form 10-Q for each of the first three quarters. No filing for the fourth quarter is required; Form 10-K is filed instead.

   b) The quarterly report must be filed within

      i) 40 days of the last day of the fiscal quarter by large accelerated filers and accelerated filers

      ii) 45 days by nonaccelerated filers

<table>
<tr><th>Status</th><th>Public Float</th><th>Annual Revenues</th><th>10-K is Filed within</th><th>10-Q is Filed within</th></tr>
<tr><td>Large accelerated filer</td><td>$700 million or more</td><td>Any</td><td>60 days</td><td>40 days</td></tr>
<tr><td>Accelerated filer</td><td>$75 million to $700 million</td><td>$100 million or more</td><td>75 days</td><td>40 days</td></tr>
<tr><td rowspan="2">Nonaccelerated filer</td><td>$75 million to $700 million</td><td>Less than $100 million</td><td rowspan="2">90 days</td><td rowspan="2">45 days</td></tr>
<tr><td>Less than $75 million</td><td>Any</td></tr>
</table>

3) **Form 8-K** is a **current report** to disclose material events.

   a) It must be filed within 4 business days after the material event occurs.

   b) The following are some examples of material events:

      i) A change in control of the registrant

      ii) Acquisition or disposition of a significant amount of assets not in the ordinary course of business

      iii) Bankruptcy or receivership

      iv) Resignation of a director

      v) A change in the registrant's certifying accountant

4) **Form 20-F** is the annual report to the SEC filed by **foreign** private issuers. It is similar to Form 10-K. The financial statements in Form 20-F may be prepared in accordance with U.S. GAAP or IFRS.

Periodic Issuer Reporting to SEC under the 1934 Act

Report	Form	Content	Timing
Annual (certified by CEO and CFO)	10-K	Audited financial statements and many other matters	60, 75, or 90 days after fiscal year end
Quarterly (certified by CEO and CFO)	10-Q	Reviewed quarterly financial information and changes during quarter	40 or 45 days after fiscal quarter end
Current	8-K	Material events	Within 4 business days of event

5. The SEC Rule, "Interactive Data to Improve Financial Reporting," requires domestic and foreign companies using U.S. GAAP and foreign private issuers using IFRS to provide their financial statements in the XBRL format as an exhibit in their periodic and current reports.

   a. **XBRL** (eXtensible Business Reporting Language) is derived from XML (eXtensible Markup Language), a programming language used to organize and define data online.

      1) XBRL, which is the standard for transmitting business information, uses a uniform format to tag each piece of business and financial data being transmitted.

   b. The tags allow computers to automatically search for and assemble data so those data can be readily accessed and analyzed by investors, analysts, SEC staff, etc.

   c. One application of XBRL is in the field of publishing financial statements, for example, in Form 10-K filed with the SEC.

      1) Instead of retrieving the financial statements in plain text, which may require the retriever to manually type or copy and paste the statements, XBRL allows those statements to be directly transmitted to spreadsheets for analysis.

STOP & REVIEW

You have completed the outline for this subunit.
Study multiple-choice questions 18 through 20 on page 39.

QUESTIONS

1.1 Standards Setting for Financial Accounting

1. The FASB makes changes to the Accounting Standards Codification by issuing

A. Accounting Standards Updates.

B. Emerging Issues Task Force Releases.

C. Statements of Financial Accounting Standards.

D. Staff Technical Bulletins.

Answer (A) is correct.

REQUIRED: The means used by the FASB to change the ASC.

DISCUSSION: An Accounting Standards Update (ASU) is issued when the FASB approves an amendment to the Accounting Standards Codification (ASC). However, an ASU is not authoritative until it has been incorporated into the ASC. The ASC is the single source of U.S. GAAP.

Answer (B) is incorrect. The Emerging Issues Task Force (EITF) addresses new and unusual accounting issues that require prompt action to avoid differences in accounting treatments. The FASB has included many consensus positions of the EITF in ASUs. **Answer (C) is incorrect.** The FASB no longer issues Statements of Financial Accounting Standards. **Answer (D) is incorrect.** FASB Technical Bulletins, Staff Positions, and Implementation Guides were included in the initial ASC as of July 1, 2009. But amendments to the accounting guidance in the ASC are made only by the FASB's issuance of ASUs.

2. Arpco, Inc., a for-profit provider of healthcare services, recently purchased two smaller companies and is researching accounting issues arising from the two business combinations. Which of the following accounting pronouncements are the most authoritative?

A. FASB Accounting Standards Updates.

B. FASB Statements of Financial Accounting Concepts.

C. FASB Statements of Financial Accounting Standards.

D. The Accounting Standards Codification.

Answer (D) is correct.

REQUIRED: The most authoritative pronouncements.

DISCUSSION: The FASB's Accounting Standards Codification is the single source of U.S. GAAP. All other sources of guidance are nonauthoritative.

Answer (A) is incorrect. Accounting Standards Updates are authoritative only to the extent they have been incorporated in the Accounting Standards Codification. **Answer (B) is incorrect.** Statements of Financial Accounting Concepts are nonauthoritative. **Answer (C) is incorrect.** Statements of Financial Accounting Standards are no longer issued. Their guidance is authoritative only to the extent it has been incorporated in the Accounting Standards Codification.

1.2 The Objective of General-Purpose Financial Reporting

3. General purpose external financial reporting of a corporation focuses primarily on the needs of which of the following users?

A. Regulatory and taxing authorities.

B. Investors and creditors and their advisors.

C. The board of directors of the corporation.

D. The management of the corporation.

Answer (B) is correct.

REQUIRED: The primary users of general purpose external financial reporting.

DISCUSSION: The objective is to report financial information that is useful in making decisions about providing resources to the reporting entity. Primary users of financial information are current and potential investors and creditors who cannot obtain it directly.

Answer (A) is incorrect. Regulatory and taxing authorities have an indirect stake in a corporation and are able to demand access to its financial information. Accordingly, they are not primary users. **Answer (C) is incorrect.** Directors are internal users of the entity's financial information and can obtain it directly. **Answer (D) is incorrect.** External financial reporting focuses primarily on the needs of external users such as investors and creditors. Management is an internal user with direct access to accounting information.

4. What is the primary objective of financial reporting?

A. To provide economic information that is comprehensible to all users.

B. To provide management with an accurate evaluation of their financial performance.

C. To provide forecasts for future cash flows and financial performance.

D. To provide information that is useful for economic decision making.

Answer (D) is correct.

REQUIRED: The primary purpose of financial reporting.

DISCUSSION: The overall objective is to report financial information that is useful to current and potential investors and creditors in making decisions about providing resources to an individual reporting entity.

Answer (A) is incorrect. "Financial reports are prepared for users who have a reasonable knowledge of business and economic activities and who review and analyze the information diligently" (SFAC No. 8 Ch. 3). **Answer (B) is incorrect.** Information about financial performance of an entity helps to evaluate management performance, but it is not the primary objective of financial reporting. **Answer (C) is incorrect.** Although financial reporting is helpful in creating forecasts of future cash flows, this is not its primary purpose.

1.3 Objectives of Financial Reporting by Nongovernmental Not-for-Profit Entities

5. The reporting model described in the guidance on not-for-profit financial statements applies to

A. Business entities and governmental not-for-profit entities.

B. Business entities and nongovernmental not-for-profit entities.

C. Nongovernmental not-for-profit entities.

D. Governmental not-for-profit entities that also use proprietary fund accounting.

Answer (C) is correct.

REQUIRED: The application of the reporting model for not-for-profit financial statements.

DISCUSSION: The reporting model for not-for-profit financial statements applies to nongovernmental not-for-profit entities (NFPs). The information needs of resource providers of NFPs differ from those of resource providers of business entities. Resource providers of business entities primarily need information about financial return. Resource providers of NFPs primarily need information about the services provided by the NFP and its continuing ability to provide those services.

6. All of the following are objectives of financial reporting by nongovernmental not-for-profit entities **except**

A. To provide information that is useful to current and potential resource providers in making resource allocation decisions.

B. To provide information about the sources and uses of liquid assets, borrowing and repayment activities, and other factors affecting liquidity.

C. To provide information about performance, including a single indicator comparable to a business enterprise's net income, that permits resource providers to assess how effectively the entity is competing with others.

D. To provide information about economic resources, liabilities, net resources, and the effects of changes in resources and interests.

Answer (C) is correct.

REQUIRED: The objectives of financial reporting by NFPs.

DISCUSSION: NFPs often have no single indicator of performance comparable to a business enterprise's net income. Accordingly, other performance indicators are needed. The most useful is information measuring the changes in the amount and nature of net resources that is combined with information about service efforts and accomplishments.

Answer (A) is incorrect. Among the objectives of financial reporting by NFPs is to provide information that is useful to current and potential resource providers in making resource allocation decisions. **Answer (B) is incorrect.** Among the objectives of financial reporting by NFPs is to provide information about (1) the sources and uses of cash and other liquid assets, (2) borrowing and repayment activities, and (3) other factors affecting liquidity. **Answer (D) is incorrect.** Among the objectives of financial reporting by NFPs is to provide information about (1) economic resources, (2) liabilities, (3) net resources, and (4) the effects of changes in resources and interests.

1.4 Objectives of Financial Reporting by State and Local Governments

7. Which of the following is **not** a characteristic of the governmental reporting environment?

A. Interperiod equity.

B. Balance sheet equity.

C. Legally binding budget.

D. Accountability.

Answer (B) is correct.

REQUIRED: The item not a characteristic of the governmental reporting environment.

DISCUSSION: State and local governments report net position or fund balances, not equity.

Answer (A) is incorrect. Interperiod equity implies that current citizens should treat future citizens fairly. Later generations should not have to pay for services received by prior generations. This principle implies that current-year revenues should be sufficient to cover current-year services. **Answer (C) is incorrect.** A legally binding budget is one of the control characteristics inherent in the structure of government. **Answer (D) is incorrect.** Accountability is the essence of governmental reporting. Accountability requires that a governmental body justify how it spends the resources it collects in pursuit of the goals the citizens have set for it.

1.5 Qualitative Characteristics of Useful Financial Information

8. According to the FASB's conceptual framework, what does the concept of faithful representation in financial reporting include?

A. Predictive value.

B. Certainty.

C. Perfect accuracy.

D. Neutrality.

Answer (D) is correct.

REQUIRED: The item included in the concept of faithful representation.

DISCUSSION: Faithful representation and relevance are the fundamental qualitative characteristics of accounting information. A perfectly faithful representation is complete, neutral, and free from error. Faithfully represented information is neutral if it is unbiased in its selection or presentation of information.

Answer (A) is incorrect. Relevant information has predictive value and/or confirmatory value. **Answer (B) is incorrect.** Certainty and perfect accuracy are not implied by faithful representation. **Answer (C) is incorrect.** Faithful representation does not mean accurate in all respects. Free from error means there are no errors or omissions in (1) the descriptions of the phenomena and (2) the selection and application of the reporting process.

9. According to *Statements of Financial Accounting Concepts*, predictive value relates to

	Relevance	Faithful Representation
A.	No	No
B.	Yes	Yes
C.	No	Yes
D.	Yes	No

Answer (D) is correct.

REQUIRED: The qualitative characteristic to which predictive value relates.

DISCUSSION: Relevance is a general idea that is a fundamental qualitative characteristic of useful financial information. It is the capacity of information to make a difference in a decision. It must have (1) predictive value and/or (2) confirmatory value. Moreover, materiality is a related concept that is entity-specific.

10. According to the FASB's conceptual framework, which of the following enhances information that is relevant and faithfully represented?

A. Comparability.

B. Confirmatory value.

C. Neutrality.

D. Materiality.

Answer (A) is correct.

REQUIRED: The item that enhances information that is relevant and faithfully represented.

DISCUSSION: Comparability is a qualitative characteristic that enhances the usefulness of relevant and faithfully represented information. It enables users to identify similarities in and differences among items.

Answer (B) is incorrect. Relevance is a fundamental qualitative characteristic. Relevant information is able to make a difference in user decisions. To do so, it must have predictive value and/or confirmatory value. Something has confirmatory value with respect to prior evaluations if it provides feedback that confirms or changes (corrects) them. **Answer (C) is incorrect.** Faithful representation is a fundamental qualitative characteristic. A perfectly faithful representation is complete, neutral, and free from error. Faithfully represented information is neutral if it is unbiased in its selection or presentation of information. **Answer (D) is incorrect.** Information is material if it is probable that an omission or misstatement of an item in a financial report will affect the judgment of a reasonable person who relies on the information. Materiality is entity-specific, whereas relevance is a general idea about what is useful to investors. Materiality has no specific quantitative threshold. The dollar amount of an item, without regard to the nature of the item, generally does not suffice for a materiality judgment.

11. Under SFAC 8, the ability, through consensus among measurers, to ensure that information represents what it purports to represent is an example of the concept of

A. Relevance.

B. Verifiability.

C. Comparability.

D. Predictive value.

Answer (B) is correct.

REQUIRED: The ability to ensure that information represents what it purports to represent.

DISCUSSION: Verifiability is a qualitative characteristic that enhances relevance and faithful representation. Information is verifiable (directly or indirectly) if knowledgeable and independent observers can reach a consensus (not necessarily unanimity) that it is faithfully represented.

Answer (A) is incorrect. Relevance (a fundamental qualitative characteristic) is the capacity of information to make a difference in a decision. **Answer (C) is incorrect.** Comparability (an enhancing qualitative characteristic) is the quality of information that enables users to identify similarities and differences among items. **Answer (D) is incorrect.** Relevant information is able to make a difference in user decisions. To do so, it must have predictive value and/or confirmatory value. Something has predictive value if it can be used as an input in a predictive process.

1.6 Elements of Financial Statements

12. According to the FASB's conceptual framework, asset valuation accounts are

A. Assets.

B. Neither assets nor liabilities.

C. Part of equity.

D. Liabilities.

Answer (B) is correct.

REQUIRED: The conceptual framework's definition of asset valuation accounts.

DISCUSSION: Asset valuation accounts are separate items sometimes found in financial statements that reduce or increase the carrying amount of an asset. The conceptual framework considers asset valuation accounts to be part of the related asset account. They are not considered to be assets or liabilities in their own right.

Answer (A) is incorrect. Asset valuation accounts are not assets. **Answer (C) is incorrect.** An asset valuation account is part of the related asset account. **Answer (D) is incorrect.** Asset valuation accounts are not liabilities.

13. According to the FASB's conceptual framework, which of the following is an essential characteristic of an asset?

A. The claims to an asset's benefits are legally enforceable.

B. An asset is tangible.

C. An asset is obtained at a cost.

D. An asset provides future benefits.

Answer (D) is correct.

REQUIRED: The essential characteristic of an asset.

DISCUSSION: Assets are probable future economic benefits obtained or controlled by an entity as a result of a past transaction or event. One of the three essential characteristics of an asset is that the transaction or event giving rise to the entity's right to or control of its assets has already occurred. It is not expected to occur in the future. A second essential characteristic of an asset is that an entity can obtain the benefits of and control others' access to the asset. The third essential characteristic is that an asset must embody a probable future benefit that involves a capacity to contribute to future net cash inflows.

Answer (A) is incorrect. Claims to an asset's benefits may not be legally enforceable. Goodwill is an example. **Answer (B) is incorrect.** Some assets are intangible. **Answer (C) is incorrect.** Assets may be obtained through donations or investments by owners.

14. According to the FASB's conceptual framework, which of the following decreases shareholder equity?

A. Investments by owners.

B. Distributions to owners.

C. Issuance of stock.

D. Acquisition of assets in a cash transaction.

Answer (B) is correct.

REQUIRED: The item that decreases equity.

DISCUSSION: Equity equals assets minus liabilities. Accordingly, transactions that decrease assets without affecting liabilities also decrease equity. Distributions to owners, such as payments of dividends (debit retained earnings and credit dividends payable, then debit dividends payable and credit cash), are such transactions.

Answer (A) is incorrect. Investments by owners increase assets and equity. **Answer (C) is incorrect.** An issuance of stock results either in no change in equity (e.g., a stock split or stock dividend) or an increase. **Answer (D) is incorrect.** Acquisition of assets in a cash transaction has no effect on equity.

1.7 Assumptions, Recognition, and Measurement Concepts

15. According to the FASB's conceptual framework, which of the following attributes should **not** be used to measure inventory?

A. Historical cost.

B. Replacement cost.

C. Net realizable value.

D. Present value of future cash flows.

Answer (D) is correct.

REQUIRED: The attribute not used to measure inventory.

DISCUSSION: The present value of future cash flows is not an acceptable measure of inventory. Present value is typically used for long-term receivables and payables.

16. Some costs cannot be directly related to particular revenues but are incurred to obtain benefits that are exhausted in the period in which the costs are incurred. An example of such a cost is

A. Salespersons' monthly salaries.

B. Salespersons' commissions.

C. Transportation to customers' places of business.

D. Prepaid insurance.

Answer (A) is correct.

REQUIRED: The costs not directly related to particular revenues but incurred to obtain benefits exhausted in the same period in which they are incurred.

DISCUSSION: Expenses should be recognized when a benefit has been consumed. The consumption of benefit may occur when (1) the expenses are matched with the revenues, (2) they are allocated on a systematic and rational basis to the periods in which the related assets are expected to provide benefits, or (3) the cash is spent or liabilities are incurred for goods and services that are used up either simultaneously with the acquisition or soon after. An example of a cost that (1) cannot be directly related to particular revenues but (2) is incurred to obtain benefits that are exhausted in the same period in which the cost is incurred is salespersons' monthly salaries.

Answer (B) is incorrect. Salespersons' commissions (not salaries) are recognized upon recognition of revenues that result directly and jointly from the same transactions or other events as the cost. **Answer (C) is incorrect.** Transportation to customers' places of business is recognized upon recognition of revenues that result directly and jointly from the same transactions or other events as the cost. **Answer (D) is incorrect.** Prepaid insurance benefits more than one accounting period. Its cost should be allocated on a systematic and rational basis to the accounting periods benefited.

17. According to the FASB's conceptual framework, certain assets are reported in financial statements at the amount of cash or its equivalent that would have to be paid if the same or equivalent assets were acquired currently. What is the name of the reporting concept?

A. Current replacement cost.

B. Current market value.

C. Historical cost.

D. Net realizable value.

Answer (A) is correct.

REQUIRED: The measurement attribute that results in reporting assets at the cash amount (or equivalent) that would have to be paid currently for them.

DISCUSSION: Replacement (current) cost is the amount of cash that would have to be paid for a current acquisition of the same or an equivalent asset.

Answer (B) is incorrect. Current market value is the amount of cash that could be obtained by selling an asset in orderly liquidation. **Answer (C) is incorrect.** Historical cost is the price paid for an asset adjusted for amortization and other allocations. **Answer (D) is incorrect.** Net realizable value is the cash or cash equivalent expected to be received for the asset in the due course of business, minus costs of completion and sale.

1.8 SEC Reporting

18. The management's discussion and analysis (MD&A) section of an annual report

A. Includes the company president's letter.

B. Covers three financial aspects of a firm's business: liquidity, capital resources, and results of operations.

C. Is a technical analysis of past results and a defense of those results by management.

D. Covers marketing and product line issues.

Answer (B) is correct.

REQUIRED: The item that is an aspect of MD&A.

DISCUSSION: The MD&A section is included in SEC filings. It addresses in a nonquantified manner the prospects of a filer. The SEC examines it to determine that management has disclosed material information affecting future results. Disclosures about commitments and events that may affect operations or liquidity are mandatory. Thus, the MD&A section pertains to liquidity, capital resources, and results of operations.

Answer (A) is incorrect. The MD&A section may be separate from the president's letter. **Answer (C) is incorrect.** A technical analysis and a defense are not required in the MD&A section because it is primarily forward-looking. **Answer (D) is incorrect.** The MD&A section need not address marketing and product line issues.

19. Each of the following events is required to be reported to the United States Securities and Exchange Commission on Form 8-K, **except**

A. The creation of an obligation under an off-balance sheet arrangement of a registrant.

B. The unregistered sale of equity securities.

C. A change in a registrant's certifying accountant.

D. The quarterly results of operations and financial condition of a registrant.

Answer (D) is correct.

REQUIRED: The event not reported on Form 8-K.

DISCUSSION: Form 8-K is a current report to disclose material events within 4 business days after such an event occurs. However, the quarterly results of operations and financial condition of a registrant (interim financial information) must be reported not on Form 8-K but on Form 10-Q, the quarterly report to the SEC.

Answer (A) is incorrect. Disclosure on Form 8-K is required when the registrant becomes (1) obligated on a material direct financial obligation or (2) liable for a material obligation arising from an off-balance sheet arrangement. **Answer (B) is incorrect.** The unregistered sale of equity securities must be disclosed on Form 8-K. **Answer (C) is incorrect.** The registrant's principal auditor (or an auditor of a significant subsidiary whose report was relied upon) may (1) decline to be reappointed after completion of the audit or (2) resign or be dismissed. These events must be disclosed on Form 8-K.

20. U.S. Securities and Exchange Commission (SEC) regulations for the financial statement presentation and disclosure requirements of SEC filings can be found in

A. Regulation S-B.

B. Regulation S-K.

C. Regulation S-T.

D. Regulation S-X.

Answer (D) is correct.

REQUIRED: The source of SEC regulations for financial statement presentation and disclosure.

DISCUSSION: Regulation S-X applies to the reporting of financial statements, including notes and schedules.

Answer (A) is incorrect. Regulation S-B applies to smaller reporting companies (small business issuers and nonaccelerated filers). **Answer (B) is incorrect.** Regulation S-K provides integrated disclosure standards, many of which are nonfinancial. It does not state requirements for financial statements. **Answer (C) is incorrect.** Regulation S-T governs the types of documents the SEC requires to be filed electronically.

STUDY UNIT TWO

FINANCIAL STATEMENTS

(14 pages of outline)

This study unit covers the **basic financial statements** other than the statement of cash flows. Detailed explanations of line items in these financial statements are discussed in later study units. However, specific names and formats for these statements are **not** specified under GAAP. Instead, the formats of these statements have evolved to fulfill the requirements of GAAP.

The accompanying **notes** are an integral part of the financial statements. The notes and statements together are a means of achieving the objectives of financial reporting. Supplementary information (e.g., on changing prices) and various other methods of financial reporting (such as management's discussion and analysis) also are useful.

Financial statements **complement** each other. They describe different aspects of the same transactions, and more than one statement is necessary to provide information for a specific economic decision. Moreover, the **elements** of one statement **articulate** (interrelate) with those of other statements.

2.1 BALANCE SHEET (STATEMENT OF FINANCIAL POSITION)

1. **Overview**
   a. The balance sheet (statement of financial position) reports assets, liabilities, equity, and their relationships at a moment in time. It helps users to assess liquidity, financial flexibility, and risk.
   b. The balance sheet is a detailed presentation of the basic accounting equation:

      Assets = Liabilities + Equity

      1) The left side of this equation depicts the entity's resource structure. The right side depicts the financing structure.

c. Assets are generally reported in order of liquidity.

1) Some variation of the following classifications is used by most entities:

EXAMPLE 2-1 Comparative Statement of Financial Position

CURRENT ASSETS:	Current Year End	Prior Year End	CURRENT LIABILITIES:	Current Year End	Prior Year End
Cash and equivalents	$ 325,000	$ 275,000	Accounts payable	$ 200,000	$ 125,000
Available-for-sale debt securities	165,000	145,000	Accrued interest on note	5,000	5,000
Accounts receivable	120,000	115,000	Current maturities of L.T. debt	100,000	100,000
Notes receivable	55,000	40,000	Accrued salaries and wages	15,000	10,000
Inventories	85,000	55,000	Income taxes payable	70,000	35,000
Prepaid expenses	10,000	5,000			
Total current assets	**$ 760,000**	**$ 635,000**	**Total current liabilities**	**$ 390,000**	**$ 275,000**
NONCURRENT ASSETS:			**NONCURRENT LIABILITIES:**		
Equity-method investments	$ 120,000	$ 115,000	Bonds payable	$ 500,000	$ 600,000
Property, plant, and equipment	1,000,000	900,000	Long-term notes payable	90,000	60,000
Minus: Accum. depreciation	(85,000)	(55,000)	Employee-related obligations	15,000	10,000
Goodwill	5,000	5,000	Deferred income taxes	5,000	5,000
Total noncurrent assets	**$1,040,000**	**$ 965,000**	**Total noncurrent liabilities**	**$ 610,000**	**$ 675,000**
			Total liabilities	**$1,000,000**	**$ 950,000**
			EQUITY:		
			Common stock $1 par	$ 500,000	$ 500,000
			Additional paid-in capital	200,000	80,000
			Accumulated OCI	30,000	20,000
			Retained earnings	70,000	50,000
			Total equity	**$ 800,000**	**$ 650,000**
Total assets	**$1,800,000**	**$1,600,000**	**Total liabilities and equity**	**$1,800,000**	**$1,600,000**

2. **Current Assets**

a. Current assets consist of "cash and other assets or resources commonly identified as reasonably expected to be realized in cash or sold or consumed **during the normal operating cycle** of the business."

b. The operating cycle is the average time between the acquisition of resources and the final receipt of cash from their sale as the culmination of revenue generating activities. If the cycle is less than a year, **1 year** is the period used for segregating current from noncurrent assets.

1) Thus, an asset is classified as current on the statement of financial position if it is expected to be realized within the entity's **operating cycle or 1 year**, whichever is **longer**.

c. Current assets include

1) Cash and cash equivalents;
2) Certain individual trading, available-for-sale, and held-to-maturity debt securities;
3) Receivables;
4) Inventories;
5) Prepaid expenses; and
6) Certain individual investments in equity securities.

3. **Noncurrent Assets**
   a. Noncurrent assets are those not qualifying as current.
   b. **Investments and funds** include nonoperating items intended to be held beyond the longer of 1 year or the operating cycle. The following assets are typically included:
      1) Investments in equity securities made to control or influence another entity
      2) Other noncurrent equity securities
         a) Certain individual available-for-sale and held-to-maturity debt securities may be noncurrent.
      3) Funds restricted as to withdrawal or use for other than current operations, for example, to
         a) Retire long-term debt,
         b) Satisfy pension obligations, or
         c) Pay for the acquisition or construction of noncurrent assets
      4) Capital assets not used in current operations, such as
         a) Idle facilities or
         b) Land held for a future plant site
   c. **Property, plant, and equipment (PPE)** are tangible operating items recorded at cost and reported net of any accumulated depreciation. They include
      1) Land and natural resources subject to depletion, e.g., oil and gas
      2) Buildings, equipment, furniture, fixtures, leasehold improvements, land improvements, noncurrent assets under construction, and other depreciable assets
   d. **Intangible assets** are nonfinancial assets without physical substance. Examples are patents and goodwill.
   e. **Other noncurrent assets** include noncurrent assets not readily classifiable elsewhere. Examples are deferred tax assets and long-term receivables.
   f. The category **deferred charges** (long-term prepayments) appears on some balance sheets.

SUCCESS TIP

The AICPA has previously tested candidates on their knowledge of what the classification of current liabilities entails. Potentially, candidates could see a list of fixed accounts with a question on the amount of current liabilities of the firm.

4. **Current Liabilities**
    a. Current liabilities are "obligations whose liquidation is reasonably expected to require the use of existing resources properly classifiable as current assets, or the creation of other current liabilities."
        1) Current liabilities generally are expected to be settled or liquidated in the ordinary course of business during the longer of 1 year or the operating cycle.
    b. Current liabilities include
        1) **Trade payables** for items entering into the operating cycle, e.g., for materials and supplies used in producing goods or services for sale.
        2) **Other payables** arising from operations, such as accrued wages, salaries, rentals, royalties, and taxes.
        3) **Unearned revenues** arising from collections in advance of delivering goods or performing services, e.g., ticket sales revenue.
    c. Other current liabilities include
        1) Short-term notes given to acquire capital assets
        2) Payments on the current portion of serial bonds or other noncurrent debt
    d. **Noncurrent obligations callable** by the creditor because of the debtor's violation of the debt agreement at the balance sheet date are classified as current.
    e. Current liabilities **do not include**
        1) Current obligations if an entity (a) intends to refinance them on a noncurrent basis and (b) demonstrates an ability to do so.
            a) The ability to refinance may be demonstrated by
                i) Entering into a financing agreement meeting all conditions before the balance sheet is issued.
                ii) Issuing a noncurrent obligation or equity securities after the end of the reporting period but before issuance of the balance sheet.
            b) The amount excluded from current liabilities must not exceed the proceeds from the new obligation or equity securities issued.
        2) Debts to be paid from funds accumulated in noncurrent asset accounts. Thus, a liability for bonds payable in the next period will not be classified as current if payment is to be from a noncurrent fund.
    f. The difference between current assets and current liabilities is working capital.
5. **Noncurrent Liabilities**
    a. Noncurrent liabilities are those not qualifying as current. The noncurrent portions of the following items are reported in this section of the balance sheet:
        1) Noncurrent notes and bonds
        2) Lease liability
        3) Most postretirement benefit obligations
        4) Obligations under product or service warranty agreements
        5) Advances for noncurrent commitments to provide goods or services
        6) Deferred revenue
    b. Deferred tax liabilities arising from interperiod tax allocation are classified as noncurrent.

6. **Equity**
   a. Equity is the residual after total liabilities are subtracted from total assets.
      1) Equity consists of the following:
         a) Capital contributed by owners (par value of common and preferred stock issued and additional paid-in capital)
         b) Retained earnings (income reinvested)
         c) Accumulated other comprehensive income (all comprehensive income items not included in net income)
         d) The noncontrolling interest in a consolidated entity (covered in Study Unit 15)
      2) Treasury stock is the entity's own common stock that it has repurchased. Treasury stock is presented as a reduction of total equity (discussed in Study Unit 14).

STOP & REVIEW

You have completed the outline for this subunit.
Study multiple-choice questions 1 through 5 beginning on page 55.

2.2 STATEMENT OF INCOME

BACKGROUND 2-1 Temporary vs. Permanent Accounts

The accounts presented on the balance sheet are temporary or permanent accounts. They report an entity's resources and financing elements that exist from period to period. The accounts presented on the income statement are nominal or temporary accounts. They are reported for a period of time, closed at the end of the period, and reopened at the beginning of the next period with zero balances.

1. **Nature of the Income Statement**
   a. The results of operations are reported in the income statement (statement of earnings) on the **accrual basis** using an approach oriented to historical transactions.
      1) The traditional income statement reports **revenues** from, and **expenses** of, the entity's major activities and **gains** and **losses** from other activities.
      2) The sum of these income statement elements is net income (loss) for an interval of time.

         Revenues – Expenses + Gains – Losses = Net income or loss
   b. Income statement elements are reported in temporary **(nominal)** accounts that are periodically closed to permanent **(real)** accounts. The accountant need not close each transaction directly to equity.
      1) Income or loss is **closed to retained earnings** at the end of the period.
   c. Any recognized amounts not included in continuing operations are reported in a separate section for **discontinued operations**.
      1) The term "continuing operations" is used only when a discontinued operation is reported.

d. The **transactions not included** in net income are

1) Transactions with owners,
2) Error corrections,
3) Items reported initially in other comprehensive income,
4) Transfers to and from appropriated retained earnings, and
5) Effects on prior periods of accounting changes.

2. **Income Statement Format**

a. **Three formats** are commonly used for presentation of recurring items:

1) The **single-step income statement** provides one grouping for revenues and gains and one for expenses and losses. The single step is the one subtraction necessary to arrive at net income.

EXAMPLE 2-2 Single-Step Income Statement

Bouffie Company
Income Statement
For Year Ended December 31, Year 1

Revenues and gains:		
Net sales	$1,050,000	
Other revenues	580,000	
Gains	495,000	
Total revenues and gains		$ 2,125,000
Expenses and losses:		
Costs of goods sold	$ 820,000	
Selling and administrative expenses	148,000	
Interest expense	124,000	
Losses	198,000	
Income tax expense	85,000	
Total expenses and losses		(1,375,000)
Net income		$ 750,000
Earnings per common share (simple capital structure) -- assuming 20,000 shares issued and outstanding		$37.50

2) The **multiple-step income statement** matches operating revenues and expenses in a section separate from nonoperating items. It enhances disclosure by presenting subtotals.

EXAMPLE 2-3 Multiple-Step Income Statement

Bouffie Company
Income Statement
For Year Ended December 31, Year 1

Revenues:			
Gross sales			$1,600,000
Minus: Sales discounts		$ (350,000)	
Sales returns and allowances		(200,000)	(550,000)
Net sales			$1,050,000
Cost of goods sold:			
Beginning inventory		$1,200,000	
Purchases	$ 500,000		
Minus: Purchase returns and discounts	(100,000)		
Net purchases	$ 400,000		
Transportation-in	50,000	450,000	
Goods available for sale		$1,650,000	
Minus: Ending inventory		(830,000)	
Cost of goods sold			(820,000)
Gross profit			$ 230,000
Operating expenses:			
Selling expenses:			
Sales salaries and commissions	$18,000		
Freight-out	5,000		
Travel	25,000		
Advertising	10,000		
Office supplies	12,000	$ 70,000	
Administrative expenses:			
Executive salaries	$40,000		
Professional salaries	7,000		
Wages of office staff	19,000		
Depreciation	7,000		
Office supplies	5,000	78,000	
Total operating expenses			(148,000)
Income from operations			$ 82,000
Other revenues and gains:			
Gain on investments		$495,000	
Dividend revenue		580,000	1,075,000
Other expenses and losses:			
Interest expense		$124,000	
Loss on disposal of equipment		198,000	(322,000)
Income before taxes*			$ 835,000
Income taxes			(85,000)
Net income*			$ 750,000
Earnings per common share (simple capital structure) -- assuming 20,000 shares issued and outstanding			$37.50

* If a discontinued operation is reported, these line items are "Income from continuing operations before taxes" and "Income from continuing operations," respectively.

3) The **condensed income statement** is the most common method of presentation. It includes only the section totals of the multiple-step format. The enhanced disclosure of each line item is presented in the notes to the financial statements.

EXAMPLE 2-4 Condensed Income Statement

Bouffie Company
Income Statement
For Year Ended December 31, Year 1

Net sales	$1,050,000
Cost of goods sold	(820,000)
Gross profit	$ 230,000
Selling and administrative expenses	(148,000)
Income from operations	$ 82,000
Other revenues and gains	1,075,000
Interest expense	(124,000)
Other expenses and losses	(198,000)
Income before taxes*	$ 835,000
Income taxes	(85,000)
Net income*	$ 750,000
Earnings per common share (simple capital structure) -- assuming 20,000 shares issued and outstanding	$37.50

* If a discontinued operation is reported, these line items are "Income from continuing operations before taxes" and "Income from continuing operations," respectively.

3. Income Statement Sections

SUCCESS TIP

Previous CPA Exams have included questions with cost and inventory information that require candidates to calculate cost of goods sold or cost of goods manufactured.

a. **Cost of goods sold** equals purchases for a retailer or cost of goods manufactured (COGM) for a manufacturer, adjusted for the change in finished goods (FG) in inventory.

	Beginning FG inventory
+	Purchases or COGM
	Goods available for sale
–	Ending FG inventory
	Cost of goods sold

b. **Cost of goods manufactured** equals the period's manufacturing costs adjusted for the change in work-in-process. It also may be stated as cost of goods sold adjusted for the change in finished goods inventory.

	Beginning work in process		Ending FG inventory
+	Sum of periodic manufacturing costs	+	Cost of goods sold
–	Ending work-in-process	–	Beginning FG inventory
	Cost of goods manufactured		Cost of goods manufactured

NOTE: Study Unit 7, Subunit 1, contains a more detailed explanation of this topic.

c. **Selling expenses** are incurred in selling or marketing.
   1) Examples include
      a) Sales representatives' salaries, commissions, and traveling expenses;
      b) Sales department rent, salaries, and depreciation; and
      c) Communications (e.g., Internet) costs.
   2) Shipping costs also may be classified as selling costs.
   3) Advertising costs should be expensed either as incurred or when advertising first occurs.
      a) Sellers may agree to reimburse customers for the customers' advertising costs (cooperative advertising). The revenues related to the transactions that created such obligations generally are recognized before reimbursement. Accordingly, the obligations must be accrued and the advertising costs expensed when the related revenues are recognized.
d. **Administrative (general) expenses** are incurred for the direction of the entity as a whole and are not related entirely to a specific function, e.g., selling or manufacturing. They include
   1) Accounting, legal, and other fees for professional services;
   2) Officers' salaries;
   3) Insurance;
   4) Wages of office staff;
   5) Miscellaneous supplies; and
   6) Office occupancy costs.
e. **Interest expense** is recognized based on the passage of time. In the case of bonds, notes, and finance leases, the effective interest method is used.
f. Material items that are **unusual in nature, infrequent in occurrence, or both** are reported as a separate component of income from **continuing operations**.
   1) These items must **not** be reported net of taxes.
   2) Gains or losses of a similar nature that are not individually material must be aggregated.
   3) The nature and financial effect of each item is disclosed in the notes to the financial statements or reported in the income statement.
   4) The effects of such items on earnings per share must **not** be presented on the income statement.

g. When an entity reports a **discontinued operation**, it must be presented in a separate section **after** income from continuing operations.

1) **Intraperiod tax allocation** is required. Thus, income tax expense or benefit is allocated to

a) Continuing operations,
b) Discontinued operations,
c) Other comprehensive income, and
d) Items debited or credited directly to other components of equity.

2) The following items are reported separately in the **discontinued operations** section:

a) Income or loss from operations of the component unit (including any gain or loss on disposal)

b) Income tax expense or benefit

3) Appropriate earnings per share amounts must be disclosed, either on the face of the statement or in the accompanying notes.

EXAMPLE 2-5 Presentation of Income from Discontinued Operations

Income from continuing operations		$ 90,000
Discontinued operations:		
Income from discontinued component unit (net of loss on disposal of $5,000)	$45,000	
Income tax expense	(6,750)	
Income from discontinued operations		38,250
Net income		**$128,250**
Basic and diluted EPS:	Basic	Diluted
Income from continuing operations	$4.50	$2.50
Income from discontinued component unit, net of tax	1.91	1.06
Net income -- assuming 20,000 shares outstanding	**$6.41**	**$3.56**

STOP & REVIEW

You have completed the outline for this subunit.
Study multiple-choice questions 6 through 10 beginning on page 58.

2.3 COMPREHENSIVE INCOME

1. **Overview**

   a. **Comprehensive income** includes all changes in equity of a business during a period except those from investments by and distributions to owners. It includes all components of

      1) **Net income** and
      2) **Other comprehensive income (OCI)**.

   b. OCI includes all items of comprehensive income not included in net income. Under existing accounting standards, items of OCI include, among others,

      1) Unrealized holding gains and losses on **available-for-sale debt securities** (Study Unit 5).
      2) Gains and losses on **derivatives** designated and qualifying as **cash flow hedges** (Study Unit 16).
      3) Certain amounts associated with recognition of the **funded status of postretirement defined benefit plans** (Study Unit 11).
      4) **Certain foreign currency items** (Study Unit 16).
      5) Changes in fair value attributable to instrument-specific credit risk of financial liabilities for which the fair value option is elected (Study Unit 5).

   c. Each component of OCI must be presented **net of tax**, or one amount must be presented for the aggregate tax effect on the total of OCI. In either case, the tax effect on each component must be disclosed.

2. **Reporting**

   a. An entity that presents a full set of financial statements but has no items of OCI need not report OCI or comprehensive income. Otherwise, an entity must present all items of comprehensive income recognized for the period either

      1) In one continuous financial statement or
      2) In two separate but consecutive statements.

   b. **One continuous statement** must have two sections: net income and OCI. It must include

      1) A total of net income with its components,
      2) A total of OCI with its components, and
      3) A total of comprehensive income.

   c. **Separate but consecutive statements** must be presented as follows:

      1) The first statement (the income statement) presents the components of net income and total net income.
      2) The second statement (the statement of OCI) is presented immediately after the first. It presents

         a) The components of OCI,
         b) The total of OCI, and
         c) A total for comprehensive income.

      3) The entity must begin the second statement with net income.

d. The following is an example of the **single-statement** presentation for reporting comprehensive income:

EXAMPLE 2-6 Single-Statement Presentation

CI Company
Statement of
Comprehensive Income (in millions)
Year Ended December 31, Year 1

Statement of Income	Revenues and gains:		
	Net revenues	$250	
	Gain on sale of available-for-sale debt securities	10	
	Gains reclassified from OCI	14	$274
	Expenses and losses:		
	Expenses	$122	
	Amortized prior service cost reclassified from OCI	12	(134)
	Income from continuing operations		$140
	Income tax expense		(30)
	Net income		**$110**
Statement of OCI	OCI, net of tax:		
	Foreign currency translation adjustments		20
	Unrealized holding gains	40	
	Minus: Reclassification of gains included in net income	(14)	26
	Defined benefit pension plan:		
	Prior service cost	(33)	
	Minus: Amortization of prior service cost	12	(21)
	OCI		**$ 25**
	Comprehensive income		**$135**

1) A **two-statement** presentation is easily derived from the example above.

a) The final component of the **statement of net income** is net income.

b) The first component of the **statement of OCI** is net income, and the final component is comprehensive income.

IFRS DIFFERENCE

An entity must group items of OCI as follows: (1) those that will not be reclassified to profit or loss (e.g., actuarial gains and losses on defined benefit pension plans) and (2) those that may be (e.g., exchange differences arising from foreign operations).

e. The **components of OCI** are recorded initially in a temporary (nominal) account. At the end of each reporting period, the total OCI for a period is **closed to accumulated OCI**, a permanent account that is reported in the equity section of the balance sheet.

1) Other comprehensive income for the period increases accumulated OCI.
2) Other comprehensive loss for the period decreases accumulated OCI.

STOP & REVIEW

You have completed the outline for this subunit.
Study multiple-choice questions 11 through 15 beginning on page 60.

2.4 STATEMENT OF CHANGES IN EQUITY

1. **Overview**

   a. A statement of changes in equity is presented as part of a full set of financial statements. This statement provides disclosure of changes during the accounting period in the separate equity accounts. These are retained earnings, common stock, preferred stock, additional paid-in capital, accumulated OCI, and noncontrolling interest.

EXAMPLE 2-7 Statement of Changes in Equity

CI Company
For the Year Ended December 31, Year 1

	Total Equity	Retained Earnings	Accumulated Other Comprehensive Income	Common Stock	Additional Paid-in Capital	Treasury Stock
Beginning balance	$500	$350	$100	$40	$ 30	$(20)
Net income for the period	110	110				
OCI for the period	25		25			
Common stock issued	90			10	80	
Dividends declared	(60)	(60)				
Repurchase of common stock	(15)					(15)
Ending balance	$650	$400	$125	$50	$110	$(35)

2. **Statement of Retained Earnings**

   a. A statement of retained earnings reconciles the beginning and ending balances of the account. This statement is not separately reported. Instead, it is reported as part of the statement of changes in equity in a separate column.

   b. The changes in retained earnings can result from the following adjustments:

      1) Net income (loss) for the period;

      2) Any prior-period adjustments, net of tax (discussed in Study Unit 3);

      3) Dividends declared; and

      4) Certain other rare items, e.g., reissuance of treasury stock under the cost method (discussed in Study Unit 14).

   c. Retained earnings are sometimes appropriated (restricted) to a special account to disclose that earnings retained in the business (not paid out in dividends) are being used for special purposes (discussed in Study Unit 14).

STOP & REVIEW

You have completed the outline for this subunit.
Study multiple-choice questions 16 and 17 on page 62.

2.5 SPECIAL PURPOSE FRAMEWORKS

1. **Other Bases of Accounting**
   a. Financial statements may be prepared using a comprehensive basis of accounting that is not in accordance with GAAP.
   b. Common examples are the following:
      1) The cash basis or modified cash basis
      2) A basis used for tax purposes
      3) A basis used to comply with the requirements of a regulator
   c. Statements using a basis other than GAAP should include a summary of significant accounting policies that discusses the basis used and how it differs from GAAP.
2. **Cash Basis**
   a. Under the strict cash basis of accounting, revenues and expenses are recognized when cash is received or paid, respectively, regardless of when goods are delivered or received or when services are rendered.
      1) The cash basis ignores the revenue and expense recognition principles that are fundamental to the accrual basis.
      2) This method may be appropriate for small businesses operated as sole proprietorships.
3. **Modified Cash Basis**
   a. The modified cash basis uses the cash basis for typical operating activities with modifications having substantial support, for example, reporting inventory, accruing income taxes, and capitalizing and depreciating fixed assets.
      1) This method often is used by professional services firms, such as physicians, realtors, and architects.
4. **Income Tax Basis**
   a. This basis must be applied to calculate income tax liability.
   b. Certain doctrines underlying the federal tax code differ significantly from those in the conceptual framework. For example, the code requires use of the modified accelerated cost recovery system (MACRS), a depreciation method not recognized under GAAP.

STOP & REVIEW

You have completed the outline for this subunit.
Study multiple-choice questions 18 through 20 beginning on page 63.

QUESTIONS

2.1 Balance Sheet (Statement of Financial Position)

1. Brite Corp. had the following liabilities at December 31, Year 6:

Accounts payable	$ 55,000
Unsecured notes, 8%, due 7/1/Year 7	400,000
Accrued expenses	35,000
Contingent liability	450,000
Deferred income tax liability	25,000
Senior bonds, 7%, due 3/31/Year 7	1,000,000

The contingent liability is an accrual for possible losses on a $1 million lawsuit filed against Brite. Brite's legal counsel expects the suit to be settled in Year 8 and has estimated that Brite will be liable for damages in the range of $450,000 to $750,000. The deferred income tax liability is not related to an asset for financial reporting and is expected to reverse in Year 8. What amount should Brite report in its December 31, Year 6, balance sheet for current liabilities?

A. $515,000

B. $940,000

C. $1,490,000

D. $1,515,000

Answer (C) is correct.

REQUIRED: The amount reported for current liabilities.

DISCUSSION: The following are current liabilities: (1) Obligations that, by their terms, are or will be due on demand within 1 year (or the operating cycle if longer) and (2) obligations that are or will be callable by the creditor within 1 year because of a violation of a debt covenant. Deferred tax assets and liabilities are classified as noncurrent. Thus, current liabilities are calculated as

Accounts payable	$ 55,000
Unsecured notes, 8%, due 7/1/Year 7	400,000
Accrued expenses	35,000
Senior bonds, 7%, due 3/31/Year 7	1,000,000
Current liabilities	$1,490,000

Answer (A) is incorrect. The amount of $515,000 excludes the senior bonds due within 1 year and includes the deferred income tax liability that will not reverse within 1 year. Deferred tax assets and liabilities are classified as noncurrent amounts. **Answer (B) is incorrect.** The amount of $940,000 includes the contingent liability not expected to be settled until Year 8 and excludes the senior bonds. **Answer (D) is incorrect.** The amount of $1,515,000 includes the deferred income tax liability that should be classified as noncurrent.

Questions 2 and 3 are based on the following information.

The following trial balance of Trey Co. at December 31, Year 6, has been adjusted except for income tax expense.

	Dr.	Cr.
Cash	$ 550,000	
Accounts receivable	1,650,000	
Prepaid taxes	300,000	
Accounts payable		$ 120,000
Common stock		500,000
Additional paid-in capital		680,000
Retained earnings		630,000
Foreign currency translation adjustment	430,000	
Revenues		3,600,000
Expenses	2,600,000	
	$5,530,000	$5,530,000

Additional Information

- During Year 6, estimated tax payments of $300,000 were charged to prepaid taxes. Trey has not yet recorded income tax expense. There were no differences between financial statement and income tax income, and Trey's tax rate is 30%.
- Included in accounts receivable is $500,000 due from a customer. Special terms granted to this customer require payment in equal semiannual installments of $125,000 every April 1 and October 1.

2. In Trey's December 31, Year 6, balance sheet, what amount should be reported as total current assets?

A. $1,950,000

B. $2,200,000

C. $2,250,000

D. $2,500,000

Answer (A) is correct.

REQUIRED: The total current assets.

DISCUSSION: Trey's current assets include cash, accounts receivable, and prepaid taxes. However, income tax expense is $300,000 [($3,600,000 revenues – $2,600,000 expenses) × 30%]. After recording income tax expense, prepaid taxes equal $0. Moreover, $250,000 of the receivables is due in Year 8 and is therefore noncurrent. Thus, total current assets equal $1,950,000 [$550,000 cash + ($1,650,000 – $250,000 noncurrent A/R)].

Answer (B) is incorrect. The amount of $2,200,000 includes the noncurrent accounts receivable. **Answer (C) is incorrect.** The amount of $2,250,000 includes $300,000 of prepaid taxes. **Answer (D) is incorrect.** The amount of $2,500,000 includes $300,000 of prepaid taxes and the noncurrent accounts receivable.

3. In Trey's December 31, Year 6, balance sheet, what amount should be reported as total retained earnings?

A. $1,029,000

B. $1,200,000

C. $1,330,000

D. $1,630,000

Answer (C) is correct.

REQUIRED: The total retained earnings.

DISCUSSION: Retained earnings equal $1,330,000 {$630,000 beginning retained earnings + [($3,600,000 revenues – $2,600,000 expenses) × (1.0 – .30 tax rate)]}.

Answer (A) is incorrect. The amount of $1,029,000 results from subtracting the $430,000 foreign currency translation adjustment from retained earnings and subtracting $171,000 of taxes [($1,000,000 – $430,000) × 30%]. **Answer (B) is incorrect.** The amount of $1,200,000 results from subtracting the $430,000 foreign currency translation adjustment and from not subtracting the $300,000 in taxes. **Answer (D) is incorrect.** The amount of $1,630,000 results from not subtracting the $300,000 in taxes.

4. In analyzing a company's financial statements, which financial statement will a potential investor primarily use to assess the company's liquidity and financial flexibility?

A. Balance sheet.

B. Income statement.

C. Statement of retained earnings.

D. Statement of cash flows.

Answer (A) is correct.

REQUIRED: The statement used to assess liquidity and financial flexibility.

DISCUSSION: The balance sheet includes information that is often used in assessing liquidity and financial flexibility but should be used at minimum with a cash flow statement. Liquidity reflects nearness to cash. Financial flexibility is the ability to take action to alter cash flows so that the entity can respond to unexpected events.

Answer (B) is incorrect. The income statement is primarily concerned with profitability. **Answer (C) is incorrect.** The statement of retained earnings shows changes in the balance of retained earnings for the period. **Answer (D) is incorrect.** The statement of cash flows provides an incomplete basis for assessing future cash flows. It cannot show interperiod relationships.

5. A company has outstanding accounts payable of $30,000 and a short-term construction loan in the amount of $100,000 at year end. The loan was refinanced through issuance of long-term bonds after year end but before issuance of financial statements. How should these liabilities be recorded in the balance sheet?

A. Noncurrent liabilities of $130,000.

B. Current liabilities of $130,000.

C. Current liabilities of $30,000, noncurrent liabilities of $100,000.

D. Current liabilities of $130,000, with required footnote disclosure of the refinancing of the loan.

Answer (C) is correct.

REQUIRED: The classification of liabilities.

DISCUSSION: Accounts payable are properly classified as current liabilities because they are for items entering into the operating cycle. Short-term debt that is refinanced by a post-balance-sheet-date issuance of long-term debt should be classified as noncurrent. (The ability to refinance on a long-term basis has been demonstrated.) Thus, the short-term construction loan is classified as noncurrent. Accordingly, the entity records current liabilities of $30,000 and noncurrent liabilities of $100,000.

Answer (A) is incorrect. Outstanding accounts payable are normally classified as current liabilities. **Answer (B) is incorrect.** The $100,000 that is to be refinanced on a long-term basis should be reclassified as noncurrent. **Answer (D) is incorrect.** The $100,000 that is to be refinanced on a long-term basis should be reclassified as noncurrent.

2.2 Statement of Income

6. The effect of a material transaction that is infrequent in occurrence and unusual in nature should be presented separately as a component of income from continuing operations when the transaction results in a

	Gain	Loss
A.	Yes	Yes
B.	Yes	No
C.	No	No
D.	No	Yes

Answer (A) is correct.

REQUIRED: The circumstances in which an infrequent and unusual transaction is presented in a separate component of income from continuing operations.

DISCUSSION: A material event or transaction that is unusual in nature, infrequent in occurrence, or both must be reported as a separate component of income from continuing operations. Whether the item is a gain or loss is irrelevant to the presentation.

7. The following items were among those that were reported on Lee Co.'s income statement for the year ended December 31, Year 1:

Legal and audit fees	$170,000
Rent for office space	240,000
Interest on inventory floor plan	210,000
Loss on abandoned data processing equipment used in operations	35,000

The office space is used equally by Lee's sales and accounting departments. What amount of the above-listed items should be classified as general and administrative expenses in Lee's multiple-step income statement?

A. $290,000
B. $325,000
C. $410,000
D. $500,000

Answer (A) is correct.

REQUIRED: The general and administrative expenses for the year.

DISCUSSION: The interest expense and the loss on the abandoned data processing equipment should be classified as other expenses. The legal and audit fees and one-half of the rent for the office space should be classified as general and administrative expenses. The total is $290,000 [$170,000 + ($240,000 × 50%)].

Answer (B) is incorrect. The amount of $325,000 includes the loss. **Answer (C) is incorrect.** The amount of $410,000 includes the legal and audit fees as well as the total rent for the office space. **Answer (D) is incorrect.** The amount of $500,000 includes the interest.

8. The following data were available from Mith Co.'s records on December 31:

Finished goods inventory, 1/1	$120,000
Finished goods inventory, 12/31	110,000
Cost of goods manufactured	520,000
Loss on sale of plant equipment	50,000

The cost of goods sold for the year was

A. $510,000
B. $520,000
C. $530,000
D. $580,000

Answer (C) is correct.

REQUIRED: The cost of goods sold.

DISCUSSION: Cost of goods sold equals cost of goods manufactured (or purchases for a retailer) adjusted for the change in finished goods inventory. The loss on sale of equipment is not an inventoriable cost. Thus, cost of goods sold is $530,000 ($520,000 COGM + $120,000 BI – $110,000 EI).

Answer (A) is incorrect. The amount of $510,000 results from subtracting, rather than adding, the inventory decrease. **Answer (B) is incorrect.** The amount of $520,000 equals the cost of goods manufactured. **Answer (D) is incorrect.** The amount of $580,000 includes the loss.

9. The changes in account balances of the Vel Corporation during Year 6 are presented below:

	Increase
Assets	$356,000
Liabilities	108,000
Capital stock	240,000
Additional paid-in capital	24,000

Vel has no items of other comprehensive income (OCI), and the only charge to retained earnings was for a dividend payment of $52,000. Thus, the net income for Year 6 is

A. $16,000

B. $36,000

C. $52,000

D. $68,000

Answer (B) is correct.

REQUIRED: The net income for the year given the increase in assets, liabilities, and paid-in capital.

DISCUSSION: Assets equal the sum of liabilities and equity (contributed capital, retained earnings, and accumulated OCI). To calculate net income, the dividend payment ($52,000) should be added to the increase in assets ($356,000). The excess of this sum ($408,000) over the increase in liabilities ($108,000) gives the total increase in equity ($300,000). Given no items of OCI, the excess of this amount over the combined increases in the capital accounts ($264,000) equals the increase in retained earnings ($36,000) arising from net income.

Answer (A) is incorrect. The amount of $16,000 is the excess of the sum of the increases in the capital accounts other than retained earnings over the increase in net assets. **Answer (C) is incorrect.** The amount of $52,000 is the dividend. **Answer (D) is incorrect.** The amount of $68,000 equals the sum of the dividend and the excess of the sum of the increases in the capital accounts other than retained earnings over the increase in net assets.

10. Pak Co.'s professional fees expense account had a balance of $82,000 at December 31, Year 1, before considering year-end adjustments relating to the following:

- Consultants were hired for a special project at a total fee not to exceed $65,000. Pak has recorded $55,000 of this fee based on billings for work performed in Year 1.
- The attorney's letter requested by the auditors dated January 28, Year 2, indicated that legal fees of $6,000 were billed on January 15, Year 2, for work performed in November Year 1, and unbilled fees for December Year 1 were $7,000.

What amount should Pak report for professional fees expense for the year ended December 31, Year 1?

A. $105,000

B. $95,000

C. $88,000

D. $82,000

Answer (B) is correct.

REQUIRED: The professional fees expense for the year.

DISCUSSION: Pak should recognize an expense only for the work done by the attorneys in Year 1. Thus, no adjustment is necessary for the consulting fees, but the legal fees, billed and unbilled, for November and December Year 1 should be debited to the account. The professional fees expense for the year is therefore $95,000 ($82,000 + $6,000 + $7,000).

Answer (A) is incorrect. The amount of $105,000 includes the maximum fee that may be payable to the consultants. **Answer (C) is incorrect.** The amount of $88,000 excludes the attorneys' fees for December. **Answer (D) is incorrect.** The amount of $82,000 excludes the attorneys' fees for November and December.

2.3 Comprehensive Income

11. When a full set of general-purpose financial statements is presented, comprehensive income and its components

A. Appear as a part of discontinued operations.

B. Must be reported net of related income tax effects in total and individually.

C. Appear only in a supplemental schedule in the notes to the financial statements.

D. Must be reported in a presentation that includes the components of other comprehensive income and their total.

Answer (D) is correct.

REQUIRED: The presentation of comprehensive income and its components.

DISCUSSION: If an entity that reports a full set of financial statements has items of other comprehensive income (OCI), it must report comprehensive income in one continuous statement or in two separate but consecutive statements. One continuous statement has two sections: net income and OCI. It must include (1) a total of net income with its components, (2) a total of OCI with its components, and (3) a total of comprehensive income. In separate but consecutive statements, the first statement (the income statement) must present the components of net income and total net income. The second statement (the statement of OCI) must be presented immediately after the first. It presents (1) the components of OCI, (2) the total of OCI, and (3) a total for comprehensive income. The entity must begin the second statement with net income.

Answer (A) is incorrect. Discontinued operations is a component of net income, a component of comprehensive income. **Answer (B) is incorrect.** The components of OCI must be presented either (1) net of related tax effects or (2) pretax, with one amount shown for the aggregate tax effect related to the total of OCI. No amount is displayed for the tax effect related to total comprehensive income. **Answer (C) is incorrect.** Comprehensive income must be reported in one continuous statement or in two separate but consecutive statements.

12. Rock Co.'s financial statements had the following balances at December 31:

Infrequently occurring gain	$ 50,000
Foreign currency translation gain	100,000
Net income	400,000
Unrealized holding gain on available-for-sale debt securities	20,000

What amount should Rock report as comprehensive income for the year ended December 31?

A. $400,000

B. $420,000

C. $520,000

D. $570,000

Answer (C) is correct.

REQUIRED: The amount to report as comprehensive income.

DISCUSSION: Comprehensive income includes all changes in equity of a business entity except those changes resulting from investments by owners and distributions to owners. Comprehensive income includes two major categories: net income and other comprehensive income (OCI). Net income includes the results of continuing and discontinued operations. Components of comprehensive income not included in the determination of net income are included in OCI. These include unrealized holding gains and losses on available-for-sale debt securities and certain foreign currency items, such as a translation adjustment. The infrequently occurring gain of $50,000 has already been included in the determination of net income. Thus, comprehensive income equals $520,000 ($400,000 net income + $100,000 translation gain + $20,000 unrealized holding gain on available-for-sale securities).

Answer (A) is incorrect. Certain foreign currency items and unrealized holding gains on available-for-sale debt securities are components of OCI. **Answer (B) is incorrect.** A foreign currency translation gain is a component of OCI. **Answer (D) is incorrect.** The infrequently occurring gain already is included in the net income amount of $400,000.

13. Which of the following describes how comprehensive income is reported under U.S. GAAP?

A. No specific format is required.

B. It should be disclosed in the notes but not reported in the financial statements.

C. It may be reported in a statement of equity.

D. It must be reported in two separate but consecutive statements or in one continuous statement.

Answer (D) is correct.

REQUIRED: The reporting of comprehensive income.

DISCUSSION: Two reporting formats for comprehensive income are allowed: (1) two separate but consecutive statements and (2) one continuous statement. One continuous statement must have two sections: net income and other comprehensive income (OCI). It must include (1) a total of net income with its components, (2) a total of OCI with its components, and (3) a total of comprehensive income. If separate but consecutive statements are presented, the first statement (the income statement) presents the components of net income and total net income. The second statement (the statement of OCI) is presented immediately after the first. It presents (1) the components of OCI, (2) the total of OCI, and (3) a total for comprehensive income. The entity must begin the second statement with net income.

Answer (A) is incorrect. Comprehensive income must be reported in (1) one continuous financial statement or (2) two separate but consecutive financial statements. **Answer (B) is incorrect.** Comprehensive income and its components must be presented in a financial statement. **Answer (C) is incorrect.** Reporting in a statement of equity is prohibited under U.S. GAAP.

14. A company reports the following information as of December 31:

Sales revenue	$800,000
Cost of goods sold	600,000
Operating expenses	90,000
Unrealized holding gain on available-for-sale debt securities, net of tax	30,000

What amount should the company report as comprehensive income as of December 31?

A. $30,000

B. $110,000

C. $140,000

D. $200,000

Answer (C) is correct.

REQUIRED: The amount to report as comprehensive income.

DISCUSSION: Comprehensive income includes net income and other comprehensive income. Net income equals $110,000 ($800,000 sales revenue – $600,000 COGS – $90,000 operating expenses). Unrealized holding gains on available-for-sale debt securities ($30,000) are included in other comprehensive income. Thus, comprehensive income is $140,000 ($110,000 + $30,000).

Answer (A) is incorrect. The amount of other comprehensive income is $30,000. Comprehensive income includes net income and other comprehensive income. **Answer (B) is incorrect.** The amount of net income is $110,000. Comprehensive income includes net income and other comprehensive income. **Answer (D) is incorrect.** The excess of sales revenue over cost of goods sold is $200,000.

15. Comprehensive income includes

	Net Income	Unrealized Holding Gains and Losses on Available-for-Sale Debt Securities
A.	Yes	No
B.	Yes	Yes
C.	No	Yes
D.	No	No

Answer (B) is correct.

REQUIRED: The item(s), if any, included in comprehensive income.

DISCUSSION: The components of comprehensive income are net income and other comprehensive income (OCI). Under existing accounting standards, items of OCI include, among others, (1) unrealized holding gains and losses on available-for-sale debt securities; (2) foreign currency translation adjustments; (3) gains or losses on a derivative designated and qualifying as a cash flow hedge; and (4) certain amounts associated with recognition of the funded status of postretirement benefit plans.

2.4 Statement of Changes in Equity

16. Zinc Co.'s adjusted trial balance at December 31, Year 6, includes the following account balances:

Common stock, $3 par	$600,000
Additional paid-in capital	800,000
Treasury stock, at cost	50,000
Net unrealized holding loss on available-for-sale securities	20,000
Retained earnings: Appropriated for uninsured earthquake losses	150,000
Retained earnings: Unappropriated	200,000

What amount should Zinc report as total equity in its December 31, Year 6, balance sheet?

A. $1,680,000

B. $1,720,000

C. $1,780,000

D. $1,820,000

Answer (A) is correct.

REQUIRED: The total equity.

DISCUSSION: Total credits to equity equal $1,750,000 ($600,000 common stock at par + $800,000 additional paid-in capital + $350,000 retained earnings). The treasury stock recorded at cost is subtracted from (debited to) total equity, and the unrealized holding loss on available-for-sale securities is debited to other comprehensive income, a component of equity. Because total debits equal $70,000 ($50,000 cost of treasury stock + $20,000 unrealized loss on available-for-sale securities), total equity equals $1,680,000 ($1,750,000 – $70,000).

Answer (B) is incorrect. The amount of $1,720,000 treats the unrealized loss as a credit. **Answer (C) is incorrect.** The amount of $1,780,000 treats the treasury stock as a credit. **Answer (D) is incorrect.** The amount of $1,820,000 treats the treasury stock and the unrealized loss as credits.

17. Data regarding Ball Corp.'s investment in available-for-sale debt securities follow:

	Cost	Fair Value
December 31, Year 3	$150,000	$130,000
December 31, Year 4	150,000	160,000

Differences between cost and fair values are not due to credit losses. The decline in fair value was properly accounted for at December 31, Year 3. Ball's Year 4 statement of changes in equity should report an increase of

A. $30,000

B. $20,000

C. $10,000

D. $0

Answer (A) is correct.

REQUIRED: The increase reported in the statement of changes in equity because of a change in the fair value of available-for-sale securities.

DISCUSSION: Available-for-sale debt securities are measured at fair value in the financial statements. Unrealized holding gains or losses on their remeasurement to fair value, that are not related to credit losses, are reported in OCI. On 12/31/Year 3, the amount reported was $130,000. The increase in the fair value in Year 4 of $30,000 ($160,000 – $130,000) is recognized as an unrealized holding gain in Year 4 OCI. The OCI for the period (a temporary account) is closed to accumulated OCI (a permanent account) that is reported in the equity section of the balance sheet. Thus, the unrealized holding gain of $30,000 increases the accumulated OCI in Year 4. The statement of changes in equity reports the changes in all the equity accounts, including accumulated OCI.

Answer (B) is incorrect. The amount of $20,000 is the excess of cost over fair value on 12/31/Year 3. **Answer (C) is incorrect.** The amount of $10,000 is the excess of fair value over cost on 12/31/Year 4. **Answer (D) is incorrect.** Equity increases when the unrealized holding gain is reported in other comprehensive income.

2.5 Special Purpose Frameworks

18. Which of the following is **not** a comprehensive basis of accounting other than generally accepted accounting principles?

A. Cash receipts and disbursements basis of accounting.

B. Basis of accounting used by an entity to file its income tax returns.

C. Basis of accounting used by an entity to comply with the financial reporting requirements of a government regulatory agency.

D. Basis of accounting used by an entity to comply with the financial reporting requirements of a lending institution.

Answer (D) is correct.

REQUIRED: The item not a comprehensive basis of accounting other than GAAP.

DISCUSSION: A comprehensive basis of accounting other than GAAP may be (1) a basis that the reporting entity uses to comply with the requirements or financial reporting provisions of a regulatory agency; (2) a basis used for tax purposes; (3) the cash basis, and modifications of the cash basis having substantial support, such as recording depreciation on fixed assets or accruing income taxes; or (4) a definite set of criteria having substantial support that is applied to all material items, for example, the price-level basis. However, a basis of accounting used by an entity to comply with the financial reporting requirements of a lending institution does not qualify as governmentally mandated or as having substantial support.

19. On April 1, Julie began operating a service proprietorship with an initial cash investment of $1,000. The proprietorship provided $3,200 of services in April and received a payment of $2,500 in May. The proprietorship incurred expenses of $1,500 in April that were paid in June. During May, Julie drew $500 from her capital account. What was the proprietorship's income for the 2 months ended May 31 under the following methods of accounting?

	Cash-Basis	Accrual-Basis
A.	$500	$1,200
B.	$1,000	$1,700
C.	$2,000	$1,200
D.	$2,500	$1,700

Answer (D) is correct.

REQUIRED: The income for a proprietorship under the cash basis and accrual basis.

DISCUSSION: Under the cash basis, $2,500 of income is recognized for the payments received in May for the services rendered in April. The $1,500 of expenses is not recognized until June. Under the accrual basis, the $3,200 of income and the $1,500 of expenses incurred in April but not paid until June are recognized. The net income is $1,700 under the accrual basis. The cash investment and capital withdrawal are ignored because they do not affect net income.

Answer (A) is incorrect. The $500 withdrawal should not be recognized in the computation of net income under either method, and the $1,500 of expenses should not be recognized under the cash basis.
Answer (B) is incorrect. The cash basis does not recognize the $1,500 in expenses until June. **Answer (C) is incorrect.** The $500 withdrawal should not be recognized in the computation of net income under either method.

20. Hahn Co. prepared financial statements on the cash basis of accounting. The cash basis was modified so that an accrual of income taxes was reported. Are these financial statements in accordance with the modified cash basis of accounting?

A. Yes.

B. No, because the modifications are illogical.

C. No, because there is no substantial support for recording income taxes.

D. No, because the modifications result in financial statements equivalent to those prepared under the accrual basis of accounting.

Answer (A) is correct.

REQUIRED: The true statement about whether cash-basis statements may be modified for accrual of income taxes.

DISCUSSION: A comprehensive basis of accounting other than GAAP includes the cash basis. Modifications of the cash basis having substantial support, such as accruing income taxes or recording depreciation on fixed assets, may be made when preparing financial statements on the cash basis (AU-C 800).

Answer (B) is incorrect. Accrual of quarterly income taxes is a logical modification of the cash basis of accounting. **Answer (C) is incorrect.** Substantial support exists for accrual of a reasonably estimable expense such as income taxes. **Answer (D) is incorrect.** A modification of the cash basis that accrues income taxes but incorporates no other accruals or deferrals will not result in financial statements equivalent to those prepared under the accrual basis.

STUDY UNIT THREE

INCOME STATEMENT ITEMS

(28 pages of outline)

The first three subunits of this study unit apply to the presentation of certain items on the income statement. The next two subunits address various revenue recognition issues.

3.1 DISCONTINUED OPERATIONS

1. **Overview**
   a. A **discontinued operation** includes a component of an entity (or a group of components) that meets the following criteria:
      1) It (a) has been **disposed of** or (b) is classified as **held for sale**.
         a) Held-for-sale classification criteria are discussed in Study Unit 8, Subunit 9.
      2) Its disposal is a **strategic shift** that has (or will have) a major effect on an entity's operations and financial results.
         a) Examples are disposal of
            i) A major geographical area,
            ii) A major line of business,
            iii) A major equity method investment, or
            iv) Other major parts of an entity.
   b. A **component** of an entity has operations and cash flows that are clearly distinguishable for operating and financial reporting purposes. A component may be
      1) A reportable segment,
      2) An operating segment,
      3) A reporting unit,
      4) A subsidiary, or
      5) An asset group.

2. Income Statement Presentation

a. The operating results of a discontinued operation are reported **separately net of tax** in the income statement. This section is presented **after the results of continuing operations**.

b. If a component (discontinued operation) is disposed of during the period, any **gain or loss on disposal** must be disclosed on the face of the income statement or in the notes.

c. When a component (discontinued operation) is classified as **held for sale**, it is measured at the **lower** of its **carrying amount** or **fair value minus cost to sell**.

1) Operating results reported in discontinued operations include any **income** earned or loss incurred during the **entire** reporting period (i.e., before and after the component was classified as held for sale).

2) Operating results also include any loss for a writedown to fair value minus cost to sell recognized on the initial classification as held for sale and subsequently.

3) From the moment the component is classified as held for sale, operating results do **not** include **depreciation or amortization** of assets.

d. The results of discontinued operations are reported **minus (plus) income tax expense (benefit)**.

EXAMPLE 3-1 Discontinued Operations

On July 1, Year 1, Emkay Co. approved a plan to dispose of Segment X on October 1, Year 1. As a result, Segment X (a component of the entity) was properly classified as a discontinued operation. It was sold on October 1, Year 1, for $480,000. Emkay's income tax rate is 40%. The following data pertain to Segment X:

- Operating losses were $110,000 for the period January 1 to June 30, Year 1.
- Operating losses were $100,000 for the period July 1 to October 1, Year 1.
- The operating losses presented above do not include a loss on disposal or a write-down to fair value minus cost to sell.
- The carrying amount on July 1, Year 1, was $600,000.
- Fair value minus cost to sell on July 1, Year 1, was $450,000.

The following are Emkay's Year 1 income statement items excluding Segment X's operating results:

Revenues	$950,000
Cost of goods sold	380,000
General and administrative expenses	90,000
Interest expense	50,000

Year 1 operating results of Segment X are reported in discontinued operations. The loss from discontinued operations for the year ended December 31, Year 1, includes all of the following:

- Operating losses incurred during the entire reporting period were $210,000 ($110,000 + $100,000).
- The loss on write-down to fair value minus cost to sell on July 1 was $150,000 ($600,000 carrying amount – $450,000 fair value minus cost to sell).
- The gain on disposal of the segment on October 1 was $30,000 ($480,000 – $450,000).

The total Year 1 loss from discontinued operations before tax is $330,000 ($210,000 + $150,000 – $30,000). The loss on discontinued operations (net of tax) reported in the income statement is $198,000 [$330,000 × (1 – 40%)].

-- Continued on next page --

EXAMPLE 3-1 -- Continued

The following format may be used by Emkay to present its Year 1 income statement:

Emkay Co.
Income Statement
For the Year Ended 12/31/Yr 1

Revenues		$950,000
Cost of goods sold		(380,000)
Gross profit		$570,000
General and administrative expenses	$ 90,000	
Interest expense	50,000	(140,000)
Income from continuing operations before income taxes		$430,000
Income taxes		(172,000)
Income from continuing operations		**$258,000**
Discontinued operations		
Loss from operations of component unit – Segment X (including gain on disposal of $30,000)	$(330,000)	
Income tax benefit	132,000	
Loss from discontinued operations		**(198,000)**
Net income		**$ 60,000**

1) The operating results of a discontinued operation also must be reported in the comparative financial statements.

e. If a disposal of an individually significant component does **not** qualify for discontinued operation reporting, a gain or loss on its sale is included in income from continuing operations.

1) A pretax profit or loss of such a component must be disclosed in the notes.

3. **Statement of Financial Position Presentation**

a. The assets and liabilities of a discontinued operation classified as held for sale must be presented separately in the relevant sections of the statement of financial position for (1) the current period and (2) all comparative periods reported.

1) These items must **not** be offset and presented as one amount.

2) A discontinued operation may be classified **initially** as held for sale in the current period. The carrying amount(s) of its major classes of assets and liabilities then must be

a) Presented on the face of the statement of financial position or
b) Disclosed in the notes for all periods reported.

STOP & REVIEW

You have completed the outline for this subunit.
Study multiple-choice questions 1 through 3 beginning on page 93.

3.2 ACCOUNTING CHANGES AND ERROR CORRECTIONS

SUCCESS TIP

The AICPA tests candidates' knowledge of how to account for the effects of (1) a change in accounting principle, (2) a change in accounting estimate, and (3) the correction of errors. Be prepared for questions that ask for (1) a description of the accounting, (2) calculation of amounts, or (3) the journal entries.

1. **Accounting Changes -- Overview**
   a. If financial information is to be comparable and consistent, entities must not make voluntary changes in accounting principles unless they can be justified as **preferable**.
      1) Thus, the assumption is that an adopted **principle must be applied consistently** in preparing financial statements.
   b. The three types of accounting changes are
      1) A change in accounting principle,
      2) A change in accounting estimate, and
      3) A change in the reporting entity.
2. **Change in Accounting Principle (Retrospective Application)**
   a. A change in accounting principle occurs when an entity (1) adopts a generally accepted principle different from the one previously used, (2) changes the **method** of applying a generally accepted principle, or (3) changes to a generally accepted principle when the principle previously used is no longer generally accepted.
      1) A change in principle does **not** include the initial adoption of a principle because of an event or transaction occurring for the first time.
   b. **Retrospective application** is required for all direct effects and the related income tax effects of a change in principle.
      1) An example of a direct effect is an adjustment of an inventory balance to implement a change in the method of measurement.
      2) Retrospective application must **not include indirect effects**. These are changes in current or future cash flows from a change in principle applied retrospectively.
         a) An example of an indirect effect is a required profit-sharing payment based on a reported amount that was directly affected (e.g., revenue).
         b) Indirect effects are recognized and reported in the period of change.
   c. Retrospective application requires the carrying amounts of (1) assets, (2) liabilities, and (3) retained earnings (or other components of equity or net assets) at the beginning of the first period reported to be adjusted for the **cumulative effect (CE)** of the new principle on the prior periods.
      1) All periods presented must be individually adjusted for the **period-specific effects (PSE)** of the new principle.
   d. It may be **impracticable** to determine the CE of a new principle on any prior period.
      1) The new principle then must be applied as if the change had been made prospectively at the earliest date practicable.
   e. It may be **practicable** to determine the CE of applying the new principle to all prior periods but **not** the PSE.
      1) In these circumstances, CE adjustments must be made to the beginning balances for the first period to which the new principle can be applied.

IMPRACTICABILITY EXCEPTIONS

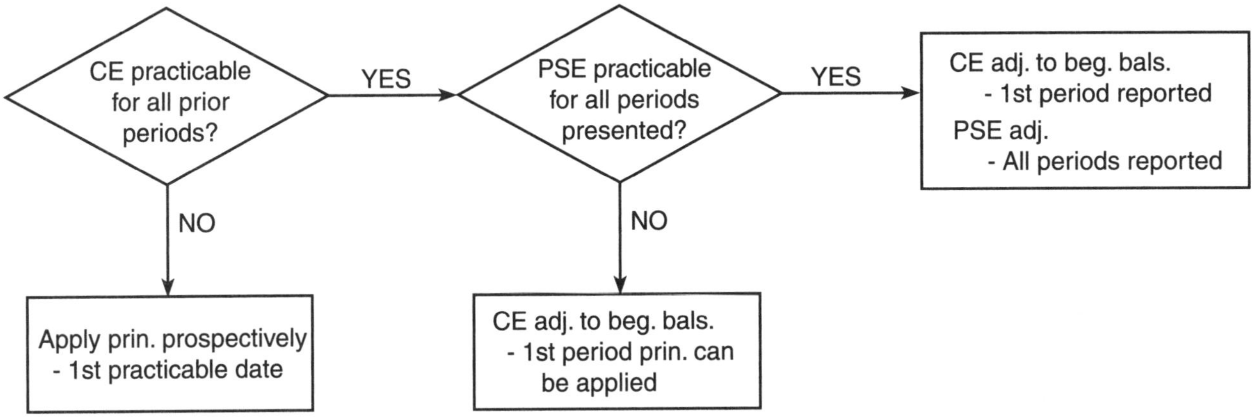

Figure 3-1

3. **Change in Accounting Estimate (Prospective Application)**

   a. A change in accounting estimate results from new information. It is a reassessment of the future status, benefits, and obligations of assets and liabilities. Its effects must be accounted for only in (1) the period of change and (2) any future periods affected **(prospectively)**.

      1) The prospective application must be applied from the beginning of the accounting period in which the accounting estimate was changed.

      2) For a change in estimate, the entity **must not**

         a) Restate or retrospectively adjust prior-period statements or
         b) Report pro forma amounts for prior periods.

EXAMPLE 3-2 Change in Accounting Estimate

On January 1, Year 1, Entity D purchased a machine for $98,000. Depreciation is based on the straight-line method using an estimated useful life of 10 years with a salvage value of $8,000. During Year 3, Entity D determined that the machine has a useful life of 8 years from the date of acquisition and that its salvage value is $2,000. Entity D reports only annual financial statements.

Annual depreciation on the machine in Years 1 and 2 is $9,000 [($98,000 historical cost – $8,000 salvage value) ÷ 10 years]. On December 31, Year 2, the carrying amount of the machine is $80,000 [$98,000 historical cost – ($9,000 annual depreciation × 2 years elapsed)].

The annual depreciation of the machine from the beginning of Year 3 is based on revised estimates of the machine's useful life (8 years) and salvage value ($2,000). The carrying amount of the machine ($80,000) at the beginning of the accounting period in which the change in estimates occurred is used in the new calculation.

- The new depreciable base of the machine is **$78,000** ($80,000 – $2,000).
- The remaining useful life of the machine from the beginning of the accounting period in which the change in estimates occurred (January 1, Year 3) is **6** years (8 – 2).
- Annual depreciation on the machine in Years 3 through 8 is **$13,000** ($78,000 ÷ 6).
- The carrying amount of the machine on December 31, Year 3, is **$67,000** ($80,000 January 1, Year 3, carrying amount – $13,000 depreciation expense in Year 3).

   b. A **change in estimate inseparable from a change in principle** is accounted for as a **change in estimate**, i.e., prospective application.

      1) An example is a change in a method of depreciation, amortization, or depletion of long-lived, nonfinancial assets.

4. **Change in the Reporting Entity**
   a. A change in the reporting entity results in statements that are effectively those of a different entity.
      1) Most such changes occur when
         a) Consolidated or combined statements replace those of individual entities,
         b) Consolidated statements include different subsidiaries, or
         c) Combined statements include different entities.
      2) A business combination or consolidation of a variable interest entity is not a change in the reporting entity.
   b. A change in the reporting entity is retrospectively applied to interim and annual statements.
5. **Error Correction**
   a. An error in prior statements results from
      1) A mathematical mistake,
      2) A mistake in the application of GAAP, or
      3) An oversight or misuse of facts existing when the statements were prepared.
   b. A change to a generally accepted accounting principle from one that is not generally accepted is an error correction, **not an accounting change**.
      1) Any error related to a prior period discovered after the statements are, or are available to be, used must be reported as an error correction by restating the prior-period statements. In addition to the revision of the previously issued financial statements, **restatement** requires the same adjustments as **retrospective application** of a new principle.
         a) The carrying amounts of (1) assets, (2) liabilities, and (3) retained earnings **at the beginning of the first period reported** are adjusted for the cumulative effect of the error on the prior periods.
         b) Corrections of prior-period errors **must not** be included in net income.

EXAMPLE 3-3 Error Correction

On January 1, Year 1, Entity E acquired a machine at a cost of $240,000. The freight-in and site preparation costs for the machine of $30,000 were mistakenly expensed as incurred by the bookkeeper. The machine was depreciated on the straight-line basis over a 6-year period with no residual value. During Year 3, Entity E's controller discovered the error made by the bookkeeper in Year 1.

All the costs necessarily incurred to bring the machine to the condition and location necessary for its intended use ($30,000) must be capitalized as part of the historical cost of the machine and depreciated in future periods. Ignoring the tax effect, the following error correction should be made by Entity E in Year 3:

- The incorrect carrying amount of the machine on January 1, Year 3, is **$160,000** [$240,000 historical cost – ($40,000 annual depreciation × 2 years)].
- The correct carrying amount of the machine on January 1, Year 3, is **$180,000** [$270,000 historical cost – ($45,000 annual depreciation × 2 years)].
- The cumulative effect of the error for the two prior periods on the carrying amount of retained earnings is **$20,000**. This amount is the difference between (1) cumulative expenses actually recognized for Years 1 and 2 of $110,000 ($30,000 freight-in and site preparation costs + $80,000 depreciation expense in the first 2 years) and (2) cumulative expenses that should have been recognized of $90,000 (depreciation expense in Years 1 and 2). The carrying amount of retained earnings should be credited (i.e., increased) for the cumulative effect. The correct expense in Years 1 and 2 is $20,000 lower. Thus, the correct net income (ignoring tax effect) for these years is $20,000 greater, and the beginning balance of retained earnings on 1/1/Year 3 also should be $20,000 greater.
- The error correction journal entry in Year 3 is

Machine -- cost ($270,000 – $240,000)	$30,000	
Retained earnings January 1, Year 3		$20,000
Accumulated depreciation ($90,000 – $80,000)		10,000

- The annual depreciation expense recognized in Years 3 to 6 is **$45,000** ($270,000 historical cost ÷ 6 years of useful life).

2) Error corrections must be reported in **single-period** statements as adjustments of the opening balance of retained earnings.

   a) If comparative statements are presented, corresponding adjustments must be made to net income (and its components) and retained earnings (and other affected balances) for all periods reported.

6. **Error Analysis**

   a. A correcting journal entry combines the reversal of the error with the correct entry. Thus, it requires a determination of the

      1) Journal entry originally recorded,
      2) Event or transaction that occurred, and
      3) Correct journal entry.

EXAMPLE 3-4 Correcting Journal Entry

If the purchase of a fixed asset on account had been debited to purchases:

Incorrect Entry	Correct Entry	Correcting Entry
Purchases	Fixed asset	Fixed asset
Payables	Payables	Purchases

If cash had been incorrectly credited:

Incorrect Entry	Correct Entry	Correcting Entry
Purchases	Fixed asset	Fixed Asset
Cash	Payables	Cash
		Purchases
		Payables

   b. Error analysis addresses

      1) Whether an error affects prior-period statements,
      2) The timing of error detection,
      3) Whether comparative statements are presented, and
      4) Whether the error is counterbalancing.

   c. An error affecting **prior-period statements** may or may not affect prior-period net income. For example, misclassifying an item as a gain rather than a revenue does not affect income and is readily correctable. No prior-period adjustment to retained earnings is required.

   d. An error that affects prior-period net income is **counterbalancing** if it self-corrects over two periods. However, despite the self-correction, the financial statements remain misstated. They should be restated if presented comparatively in later periods. The flowchart on inventory errors in Study Unit 7, Subunit 7, illustrates this concept.

   e. An example of a **noncounterbalancing** error is a misstatement of depreciation. Such an error does not self-correct over two periods. Thus, a prior-period adjustment will be necessary.

STOP & REVIEW

You have completed the outline for this subunit.
Study multiple-choice questions 4 through 7 beginning on page 94.

3.3 EARNINGS PER SHARE (EPS)

1. **Overview**

   a. **Earnings per share (EPS)** is the amount of current-period earnings that can be associated with a single share of a corporation's common stock.

      1) The guidance regarding calculation and presentation of EPS must be followed by **public entities** and by other entities that choose to report EPS.

      2) EPS is calculated only for common stock.

SUCCESS TIP

The topic of earnings per share has been tested continually on CPA Exams, often through calculations. Several questions testing earnings per share will likely appear on the exam.

2. **Basic Earnings per Share (BEPS)**

   a. All corporations must report two BEPS amounts on the face of the income statement. Their numerators are **income from continuing operations** and **net income**, respectively.

$$\text{BEPS} = \frac{\text{Income available to common shareholders}}{\text{Weighted-average number of common shares outstanding}}$$

EXAMPLE 3-5 Basic Earnings per Share (BEPS)

At year end, an entity's capital structure consisted of 10,000,000 shares of $1 par-value common stock. The entity issued no new shares during the year. Its income from continuing operations and net income for the year were $1,278,000 and $1,141,000, respectively.

<u>BEPS calculations:</u>

Income from continuing operations:	$1,278,000 ÷ 10,000,000 = $0.128
Net income:	$1,141,000 ÷ 10,000,000 = $0.114

   b. If an entity has no discontinued operations, the income from continuing operations equals net income. Thus, one amount of BEPS for net income available to common shareholders is presented on the face of the income statement.

   c. If a discontinued operation is reported, basic and diluted EPS amounts for the discontinued operation are presented on the face of the income statement or in the notes.

3. **Calculation of the BEPS Numerator**

   a. **Income available to common shareholders** is the BEPS numerator.

      1) Thus, neither BEPS amount (income from continuing operations or net income) is calculated directly from the amount reported for that line item on the income statement.

         a) Income in the BEPS numerator is reduced by dividends

            i) **Declared in the current period on preferred stock (whether or not paid)** and

            ii) **Accumulated for the current period on cumulative preferred stock (whether or not declared).**

         b) Dividends paid in the current period for undistributed accumulated preferred dividends for prior years do not affect the calculation. They were included in BEPS of prior years.

      2) The following calculation is performed for net income and income from continuing operations (or other number):

Income statement amount
– Dividends on preferred stock for the current period (cumulative or declared noncumulative)
Income available to common shareholders

EXAMPLE 3-6 BEPS Numerator

An entity has two classes of preferred stock. It declared a 4% dividend on its $100,000 of noncumulative preferred stock. The entity did not declare a dividend on its $200,000 of 6% cumulative preferred stock. Undistributed dividends for the past 4 years have accumulated on this stock. The following is an excerpt from the entity's condensed income statement for the year:

Income from continuing operations before income taxes		$1,666,667
Income taxes		(666,667)
Income from continuing operations		**$1,000,000**
Discontinued operations:		
Loss from operations of component unit -- Pipeline Division (including gain on disposal of $30,000)	$(216,667)	
Income tax benefit	86,667	
Loss on discontinued operations		(130,000)
Net income		**$ 870,000**

The numerators for income from continuing operations and for net income are calculated as follows:

	Income from Continuing Operations	**Net Income**
Income statement amounts	**$1,000,000**	**$870,000**
Declared or accumulated preferred dividends:		
Dividends declared on noncumulative preferred stock in the current period	(4,000)	(4,000)
Dividends accumulated on cumulative preferred stock in the current period	(12,000)	(12,000)
Income available to common shareholders	**$ 984,000**	**$854,000**

4. **Calculation of the BEPS Denominator**

   a. The **weighted-average number of common shares outstanding** is determined by relating the portion of the period that the shares were outstanding to the total time in the period.

      1) Weighting is necessary because some shares may have been issued or reacquired during the period.

EXAMPLE 3-7 BEPS Denominator

Using the data from Example 3-6, assume the following common stock transactions during the year just ended:

Date	Stock Transactions	Common Shares Outstanding		Portion of Year		Weighted Average
Jan 1	Beginning balance	240,000	×	2 ÷ 12	=	40,000
Mar 1	Issued 60,000 shares	300,000	×	5 ÷ 12	=	125,000
Aug 1	Repurchased 20,000 shares	280,000	×	3 ÷ 12	=	70,000
Nov 1	Issued 80,000 shares	360,000	×	2 ÷ 12	=	60,000
	Total					**295,000**

The **BEPS** amounts for income from continuing operations and net income are **$3.335** ($984,000 ÷ 295,000) and **$2.895** ($854,000 ÷ 295,000), respectively. Basic loss per share (negative BEPS) from discontinued operations of $0.44 ($130,000 ÷ 295,000) is reported on the face of the income statement or in the notes.

   b. **Stock dividends** and **stock splits** require an adjustment to the weighted-average of common shares outstanding.

      1) EPS amounts for all periods presented are adjusted **retroactively** to reflect the change in capital structure as if it had occurred at the **beginning** of the **first period** presented.

      2) Adjustments are made for such changes even if they occur after the end of the current reporting period but before issuance (or the availability for issuance) of the financial statements.

EXAMPLE 3-8 Effect of Stock Dividend and Stock Split on BEPS Denominator

Using the data from Example 3-6, assume declaration of a 50% common stock dividend on June 1 and a 2-for-1 common stock split on October 1:

Date	Stock Transactions	Common Shares Outstanding		Restate for Stock Div.		Restate for Stock Split		Portion of Year		Weighted Average
Jan 1	Beginning balance	240,000	×	1.5	×	2	×	2 ÷ 12	=	120,000
Mar 1	Issued 60,000 shares	300,000	×	1.5	×	2	×	5 ÷ 12	=	375,000
Jun 1	Distributed 50% stock dividend	450,000								
Aug 1	Repurchased 20,000 shares	430,000			×	2	×	3 ÷ 12	=	215,000
Oct 1	Distributed 2-for-1 stock split	860,000								
Nov 1	Issued 80,000 shares	940,000					×	2 ÷ 12	=	156,667
	Total									**866,667**

The **BEPS** amounts for income from continuing operations and net income are **$1.135** ($984,000 ÷ 866,667) and **$0.985** ($854,000 ÷ 866,667), respectively. Basic loss per share (negative BEPS) from discontinued operations of $0.15 ($130,000 ÷ 866,667) is reported in the income statement or in the notes.

   c. **Contingently issuable shares** are shares issuable for little or no cash consideration upon satisfaction of certain conditions.

      1) Contingently issuable common shares are treated as outstanding and included in the calculation of the BEPS denominator from the date when the conditions for contingent issuance have been met.

5. **Diluted Earnings per Share (DEPS)**

   a. An entity with **only common stock** outstanding (a simple capital structure) must report only BEPS amounts but not DEPS.

      1) An entity that does not have a simple capital structure must report DEPS as well as BEPS. Thus, the DEPS calculation includes the effects of **dilutive potential common shares (PCS)**.

         a) PCS are securities or other contracts that may entitle the holder to obtain common stock.

         b) PCS are included in the DEPS calculation only if they are dilutive.

   b. **Dilution** is a reduction in BEPS (or an increase in loss per share) resulting from the assumption that

      1) **Convertible** securities (preferred stock or debt) were converted;
      2) **Options, warrants**, and their equivalents were exercised; or
      3) **Contingently** issuable common shares were issued.

         a) The conditions for contingent issuance may be satisfied by year end. The shares are then deemed to have been issued at the beginning of the period or date of the contingent stock agreement, if later.

         b) However, the conditions may not have been met at year end. In this case, the shares included in the DEPS denominator equal those that would have been issued if the end of the year were the end of the contingency interval.

EXAMPLE 3-9 **Contingently Issuable Shares**

The contingency may involve earnings. The contingently issuable shares equal those issuable (if any) based on the current period's earnings if the result is dilutive.

6. **Calculation of DEPS**

   a. DEPS measures performance after considering the effect on the numerator and denominator of dilutive PCS. DEPS is calculated as follows:

      1) **The BEPS denominator is increased** to include the weighted-average number of additional shares of common stock that would have been outstanding if dilutive PCS had been issued.

      2) **The BEPS numerator** is adjusted to **add back** any dividends on convertible preferred stock and the after-tax interest expense (an amount that includes amortization of discount or premium) related to any convertible debt.

$$\text{DEPS} = \frac{\text{BEPS numerator + Effect of dilutive PCS}}{\text{BEPS denominator + Effect of dilutive PCS}}$$

EXAMPLE 3-10 Calculation of DEPS

Green Company's current year BEPS is $40 ($400,000 income available to common shareholders ÷ 10,000 weighted-average number of common shares outstanding). No dividend was declared this year, and the company's effective tax rate is 30%. The following PCS were outstanding during the year:

- $500,000 face amount, 10-year, 6%, convertible bonds. The bonds were originally issued at par, and each $5,000 bond is convertible into 10 of Green's common shares.
- 10,000 shares of $20 par, 10%, cumulative, convertible preferred stock. The conversion ratio is 5 shares of preferred stock to 2 shares of common stock.

Assuming that the bonds and the preferred stock are dilutive securities, the DEPS for the period is calculated as follows:

Adjustment of BEPS Numerator

Convertible bonds: The BEPS numerator is adjusted to add back the after-tax amount of interest expense recognized in the current period associated with the convertible bonds. Because the bonds were issued at par, interest expense is calculated using the bonds' stated rate. Thus, the amount added back is calculated as follows:

$500,000 face amount × 6% × (1.0 – .30) = $21,000

Cumulative convertible preferred stock: The BEPS numerator is adjusted to add back any convertible preferred dividends that were declared or accumulated. No dividends were declared. However, the income available to common shareholders of $400,000 reflected the dividends accumulated for the current period on cumulative convertible preferred stock. Thus, the amount added back is calculated as follows:

10,000 preferred shares × $20 par × 10% = $20,000

Adjustment of BEPS Denominator

Convertible bonds: The BEPS denominator is increased to include the weighted-average number of additional shares of common stock that would have been outstanding if the dilutive convertible bonds (PCS) had been converted. Thus, the increase is calculated as follows:

($500,000 face amount ÷ $5,000 par) × 10 = 1,000 common shares

Cumulative convertible preferred stock: The BEPS denominator is increased to include the weighted-average number of additional shares of common stock that would have been outstanding if the dilutive convertible preferred stock (PCS) had been converted. Thus, the increase is calculated as follows:

10,000 preferred shares ÷ (5 ÷ 2) conversion ratio = 4,000 common shares

$$\text{The DEPS for the year is \$29.40} = \frac{\$400{,}000 + \$21{,}000 + \$20{,}000}{10{,}000 + 1{,}000 + 4{,}000}$$

3) The calculation of DEPS does not assume the conversion, exercise, or contingent issuance of antidilutive securities, i.e., securities that increase EPS or decrease loss per share.

4) Dilutive PCS issued during a period are included in the DEPS denominator for the period they were outstanding.

   a) Moreover, dilutive convertible securities that were actually converted are included for the period **before** conversion. Common shares actually issued are included for the period **after** conversion.

5) Previously reported DEPS is not retroactively adjusted for subsequent conversions or changes in the market price of the common stock.

b. Three methods are used to determine the **dilutive effect** of PCS: (1) the if-converted method for convertible securities, (2) the treasury stock method for call options and warrants, and (3) the reverse treasury stock method for put options.

7. **The If-Converted Method**

   a. The if-converted method calculates DEPS assuming the conversion of all dilutive convertible securities at the **beginning** of the period or at the **time of issue, if later**.

      1) The conversion of **antidilutive** securities (those whose conversion increase EPS or decrease loss per share) is **not assumed**. Thus, convertible PCS are antidilutive if the current dividend or after-tax interest per common share issuable exceeds BEPS.

   b. In determining whether PCS are dilutive, each issue or series of issues of PCS are considered separately (rather than in the aggregate) and in sequence from the most dilutive to the least dilutive. The goal of this process is to maximize the dilution of BEPS (lowest possible DEPS).

      1) The **control number** to establish whether PCS are dilutive or antidilutive is the BEPS for the period.

         a) If a discontinued operation is reported, the control number is BEPS from continuing operations.

      2) The issue with the lowest earnings per incremental share is included in DEPS before issues with higher earnings per incremental share. If the issue with the lowest earnings per incremental share is found to be dilutive with respect to BEPS, it is included in a trial calculation of DEPS.

      3) If the issue with the next lowest earnings per incremental share is dilutive with respect to the first trial calculation of DEPS, it is included in a new DEPS calculation that adjusts the numerator and denominator from the prior calculation.

      4) This process continues until all issues of PCS have been tested.

EXAMPLE 3-11 The If-Converted Method for DEPS

Using the data from Example 3-10 on the previous page, assume that Green's current-year BEPS is $23.20 ($232,000 income available to common shareholders ÷ 10,000 weighted-average number of common shares outstanding). The DEPS for the period is calculated as follows:

The earnings per incremental share of the convertible bonds is $21 ($21,000 ÷ 1,000). The earnings per incremental share of the cumulative convertible preferred stock is $5 ($20,000 ÷ 4,000).

Because the preferred stock's earnings per incremental share ($5) is lower than bond's earnings per incremental share ($21), it is more dilutive. Thus, it is compared first with the BEPS for the period (the control number). Because $5 is lower than $23.20, the cumulative convertible preferred stock is dilutive. Accordingly, it is included in the trial calculation of DEPS.

The result is $\$18 = \dfrac{\$232{,}000 + \$20{,}000}{10{,}000 + 4{,}000}$

The next step is to compare the earnings per incremental share of the convertible bonds ($21) with the new control number ($18). Because it is higher than the control number, the convertible bonds are antidilutive and must not be included in the calculation of DEPS. Thus, the DEPS for the period is **$18**.

NOTE: The inclusion of convertible bonds and preferred stock in the calculation of DEPS results in DEPS of $18.20 [($232,000 + $20,000 + $21,000) ÷ (10,000 + 4,000 + 1,000)]. This amount ($18.20) is not the lowest possible DEPS ($18).

NOTE: The inclusion of only convertible bonds in the calculation of DEPS results in DEPS of $23 [($232,000 + $21,000) ÷ (10,000 + 1,000)]. This amount also is not the lowest DEPS possible ($18).

c. If a discontinued operation is reported, the same number of shares used to adjust the denominator for income from continuing operations is used to adjust the DEPS denominator for income from discontinued operations. This rule applies even if the effect on the other amounts is antidilutive.

8. **Treasury Stock Method**

a. The second method used to determine the dilutive effect of PCS is the treasury stock method. It is used to determine the dilutive effect of outstanding **call options, warrants**, and their equivalents.

1) Call options and warrants are **dilutive** only if the **average market price** for the period of the common shares is **greater** than the **exercise price** of the options or warrants (they are in the money).

2) Equivalents include nonvested stock granted to employees, stock purchase contracts, and partially paid stock subscriptions.

b. The treasury stock method assumes that

1) The options and warrants are exercised at the beginning of the period (or time of issuance, if later),

2) Common shares are issued, and

3) The proceeds of exercise are used to purchase common stock at the average market price for the period.

c. If the options or warrants are dilutive, their exercise affects only the denominator in the computation of DEPS. Any additional number of common shares outstanding (incremental shares) is added as an adjustment of the BEPS denominator.

1) Because the numerator in the computation of DEPS is not affected, the earnings per incremental share is $0. Thus, options and warrants are generally the most dilutive PCS. They should be included first (before other series of PCS) in the trial calculation of DEPS.

d. The number of incremental shares from dilutive call options or warrants that must be included in the denominator of the DEPS computation is determined by calculating the following:

1) Proceeds from exercising the options or warrants (Number outstanding × Exercise price).

2) Number of shares assumed purchased (Proceeds from exercise ÷ Average market price for the period of common shares).

3) Number of incremental shares (Number of common shares assumed issued – Number of common shares assumed purchased).

a) The number of common shares assumed issued is the amount of common shares that would have been issued assuming all the options or warrants were exercised.

EXAMPLE 3-12 The Effect of Call Options on DEPS

Troupe Company's current-year BEPS is $11 ($440,000 net income ÷ 40,000 weighted-average number of common shares outstanding). Unexercised call options to purchase 20,000 shares of Troupe's common stock at $20 per share were outstanding at the beginning and end of the year. For the year, the average market price per share of Troupe's common stock was $25. The DEPS for the current year is calculated as follows:

- The call options are dilutive because the exercise price ($20) is less than the average market price ($25).
- The proceeds from exercising the options are $400,000 (20,000 number of call options outstanding × $20 exercise price of the options).
- The number of shares assumed purchased is 16,000 ($400,000 proceeds from exercising the options ÷ $25 average market price).
- The number of incremental shares is **4,000** (20,000 number of common shares assumed issued – 16,000 number of common shares assumed purchased).
- The number of incremental shares is added to the BEPS denominator in the computation of DEPS.

Thus, DEPS for the current year is $10 = $\frac{\$440{,}000}{40{,}000 + 4{,}000}$

9. **Reverse Treasury Stock Method**

   a. The third method used to determine the dilutive effect of PCS is the reverse treasury stock method. It is used when the entity has entered into contracts to repurchase its own stock, for example, when it has **written put options** held by other parties.

      1) When the contracts are **in the money** (the exercise price exceeds the average market price), the potential dilutive effect on EPS is calculated by

         a) Assuming the issuance at the beginning of the period of sufficient shares to raise the proceeds needed to satisfy the contracts,

         b) Assuming those proceeds are used to repurchase shares, and

         c) Including the excess of shares assumed to be issued over those assumed to be repurchased in the calculation of the DEPS denominator.

   b. Options held by the entity on its own stock, whether they are puts or calls, are not included in the DEPS denominator because their effect is antidilutive.

10. **Income Statement Disclosure**

   a. EPS disclosures are made for **all periods** for which an income statement or earnings summary is presented. For each period for which an income statement is presented, the following are disclosed:

      1) A reconciliation by individual security of the numerators and denominators of BEPS and DEPS for income from continuing operations, including income and share effects

      2) The effect of preferred dividends on the BEPS numerator

      3) PCS not included in DEPS because it would have had an antidilutive effect in the periods reported

   b. If DEPS data are reported for at least one period, they are reported for all periods shown, even if they are equal to BEPS amounts.

STOP & REVIEW

You have completed the outline for this subunit.
Study multiple-choice questions 8 through 11 beginning on page 96.

3.4 REVENUE FROM CONTRACTS WITH CUSTOMERS

1. **Overview**

   a. The guidance for recognition of revenue from contracts with customers (ASC 606) provides a **single, principles-based** model for all contracts with customers regardless of the industry-specific or transaction-specific fact pattern.

   b. The **core principle** is that an entity recognizes revenue for the transfer of promised goods or services to customers in an amount that reflects the consideration to which the entity expects to be entitled in the exchange.

   c. This guidance applies to all contracts with customers **except** the following:

      1) Leases
      2) Financial instruments
      3) Contractual rights and obligations within the scope of specific topics, such as receivables, derivatives and hedging, insurance, and guarantees (other than product or service warranties)
      4) Nonmonetary exchanges between entities in the same line of business to facilitate sales to customers or potential customers

   d. Below is the **five-step model** for recognizing revenue from contracts with customers.

      Step 1: Identify the contract(s) with a customer.
      Step 2: Identify the performance obligations in the contract.
      Step 3: Determine the transaction price.
      Step 4: Allocate the transaction price to the performance obligations in the contract.
      Step 5: Recognize revenue when (or as) a performance obligation is satisfied.

2. **Step 1: Identify the Contract with a Customer**

   a. A contract is an agreement between two or more parties that creates enforceable rights and obligations.

   b. A contract is accounted for under ASC 606 if **all** of the following criteria are met:

      1) The contract was approved by the parties.
      2) The contract has commercial substance.
      3) Each party's rights can be identified regarding
         a) Goods or services to be transferred and
         b) The payment terms.
      4) It is probable that the entity will collect substantially all of the consideration to which it is entitled according to the contract.
         a) **Probable** means the future event is likely to occur.

c. If the criteria described on the previous page are not met (e.g., if collectibility cannot be reliably estimated), the consideration received is recognized as a liability, and **no revenue is recognized** until the criteria are met.

1) However, even when the criteria described on the previous page are not met, revenue in the amount of **nonrefundable consideration** received from the customer is recognized if at least one of the following has occurred:

a) The contract has been terminated.

b) Control over the goods or services was transferred to the customer and the entity has stopped transferring (and has no obligation to transfer) additional goods or services to the customer.

c) The entity (1) has no obligation to transfer goods or services and (2) has received substantially all consideration from the customer.

d. A **contract modification** exists when the parties approve a change in the scope or price of a contract.

1) It is accounted for as a **separate contract** if the following conditions are met:

a) The scope of the contract increases because of the addition of promised goods or services that are distinct, and

b) The price of the contract increases by an amount of consideration that reflects the entity's standalone selling prices of the additional promised goods or services.

3. **Step 2: Identify the Performance Obligations in the Contract**

a. A **performance obligation** is a promise in a contract with a customer to transfer to the customer

1) A good or service that is distinct or

2) A series of distinct goods or services that are substantially the same and have the same pattern of transfer to the customer.

b. Promised goods or services are **distinct** if

1) The customer can benefit from them either on their own or together with other resources that are readily available **(capable of being distinct)** and

2) The entity's promise to transfer them to the customer is separately identifiable from other promises in the contract **(distinct within the context of the contract)**. A **separately identifiable good or service**

a) Does not significantly modify or customize another good or service promised in the contract and

b) Is not highly dependent on, or highly interrelated with, other goods or services promised in the contract.

c. Customer options to acquire **additional goods or services for free or at a discount** have many forms, such as sales incentives, coupons, customer award points, or other discounts on future goods or services.

   1) When the option to acquire additional goods or services (e.g., a coupon or discount voucher) provides a material right to the customer, it results in a separate performance obligation in the contract.

      a) A material right is an option that the customer would not receive without entering into that contract. An example is a discount in addition to the range of discounts typically given for those goods or services.

      b) But an option to acquire an additional good or service at a price that reflects its standalone selling price does **not** provide a material right.

4. **Step 3: Determine the Transaction Price**

   a. The **transaction price** is the amount of consideration to which an entity expects to be entitled in exchange for transferring promised goods or services to a customer.

      1) It excludes amounts collected on behalf of third parties (e.g., sales taxes).

      2) Any consideration payable to the customer, such as coupons, credits, or vouchers, reduces the transaction price.

      3) To determine the transaction price, an entity should consider the effects of the **time value of money** and **variable consideration**.

   b. The revenue recognized must reflect the price that a customer would have paid for the promised goods or services if the cash payment had been made when they were transferred to the customer (i.e., the cash selling price).

      1) Thus, the transaction price is adjusted for the effect of the time value of money when the contract includes a **significant financing component**.

      2) The following factors should be considered in assessing whether a contract includes a significant financing component:

         a) The difference between

            i) The cash selling price of the promised goods or services and
            ii) The amount of consideration to be received

         b) The combined effect of

            i) The expected time between the payment and the delivery of the promised goods or services and

            ii) Market interest rates

   c. The transaction price should **not** be adjusted for the effect of the time value of money if

      1) The time between the payment and the delivery of the promised goods or services to the customer is **1 year or less**

      2) The customer paid in advance and the transfer of goods or services is at the discretion of the customer

         a) An example is a bill-and-hold contract in which the seller provides storage services for goods it sold to the buyer.

      3) A substantial amount of the consideration promised is **variable** and its amount or timing varies with future circumstances that are **not** within the control of the entity or the customer

         a) An example is consideration in the form of a sales-based royalty.

d. Interest income or expense is recognized using the **effective interest method**.

   1) It must be presented in the income statement **separately** from revenue from contracts with customers.

EXAMPLE 3-13 Significant Financing Component

On January 1, Year 1, BIF Co. sold and transferred a machine to a customer for $583,200 that is payable on December 31, Year 2. Other customers pay $500,000 upon delivery of the same machine at contract inception. The cost of the machine to BIF is $400,000. BIF determined that the contract includes a significant financing component because of the difference between the consideration ($583,200) and the cash selling price ($500,000). The contract includes an implicit interest rate of 8%. The following entries are recorded by BIF:

<u>January 1, Year 1</u>					
Accounts receivable	$500,000		Cost of goods sold	$400,000	
Revenue		$500,000	Machine inventory		$400,000
<u>December 31, Year 1</u>					
Accounts receivable ($500,000 × 8%)	$40,000				
Interest income		$40,000			
<u>December 31, Year 2</u>					
Accounts receivable ($540,000 × 8%)	$43,200		Cash	$583,200	
Interest income		$43,200	Accounts receivable		$583,200

EXAMPLE 3-14 Significant Financing Component -- Advance Payment

On January 1, Year 1, Eva Co. received a payment of $100,000 for delivering a machine to a customer at the end of Year 2. The cost of the machine to Eva is $70,000. Eva determined that (1) the contract includes a significant financing component and (2) a financing rate of 10% is an appropriate discount rate. The following entries are recorded by Eva:

<u>January 1, Year 1</u>			<u>December 31, Year 1</u>		
Cash	$100,000		Interest expense ($100,000 × 10%)	$10,000	
Contract liability		$100,000	Contract liability		$10,000
<u>December 31, Year 2</u>					
Interest expense ($110,000 × 10%)	$11,000		Contract liability	$121,000	
Contract liability		$11,000	Revenue		$121,000
Cost of goods sold	70,000				
Machine inventory		70,000			

e. **Variable Consideration**

   1) If a contract includes a variable amount, an entity must estimate the consideration to which it will be entitled in exchange for transferring the promised goods or services to a **customer**. For example, the contract price may vary because of the following:

      a) Refunds due to a right of return provided to customers (Study Unit 7, Subunit 1)
      b) Prompt payment discounts (Study Unit 6, Subunit 1)
      c) Volume discounts
      d) Other uncertainties in contract price based on the occurrence or nonoccurrence of some future event

   2) Variable consideration is **estimated** using one of the following methods:

      a) The **expected value** is the sum of probability-weighted amounts in the range of possible consideration amounts. This method may provide an appropriate estimate if an entity has many contracts with similar characteristics.
      b) The **most likely amount** is the single most likely amount in a range of possible consideration amounts. This method may provide an appropriate estimate if the contract has only two possible outcomes. For example, a construction entity either will receive a performance bonus for finishing construction on time or will not.

3) The estimated transaction price must be updated at the **end** of each reporting period.

4) **Constraint**

   a) Revenue from variable consideration is recognized only to the extent that it is **probable** that a **significant reversal** will **not** occur when the uncertainty associated with the variable consideration is subsequently resolved.

5) A **volume discount** offered as an incentive to increase future sales requires the customer to purchase a specified quantity of goods or services to receive a discount. The discount may be applied (a) **prospectively** on additional goods purchased in the future or (b) **retrospectively** on all goods purchased to date.

   a) A **prospective volume discount** that provides a **material right** to the customer is accounted for as a separate performance obligation in the contract (Study Unit 10, Subunit 4).

   b) **Retrospective volume discounts** are accounted for as **variable consideration**. The uncertainty of the contract price for current goods sold is based on the occurrence or nonoccurence of some future event (i.e., whether the customer completes the specified volume of purchase).

EXAMPLE 3-15 Retrospective Volume Discount

Barashka Co. manufactures wool coats. On October 1, Year 1, Barashka entered into a 2-year contract with a customer to sell coats for $200 per unit. Based on the contract, if the customer purchased more than 3,000 coats over the contract period, the contract price per coat would be retroactively reduced to $150. The cost per coat to Barashka is $80. Barashka determined that the contract has no significant financing component.

The retrospective volume discount is variable consideration. In Year 1, the customer purchased with cash 100 coats, and Barashka estimated that the customer's purchases would not exceed 3,000 during the contract period. Thus, based on the most likely amount method, the contract price per coat was $200.

The following entries were recorded by Barashka in Year 1:

Cash (100 × $200)	$20,000		Cost of goods sold (100 × $80)	$8,000	
Sales revenue		$20,000	Inventory of coats		$8,000

The winter in Year 2 was colder than expected. The customer purchased an additional 2,200 coats. Accordingly, Barashka estimated that the customer would purchase more than 3,000 coats over the contract period. The price per coat therefore was retrospectively reduced to $150, and Year 2 revenue is calculated as a cumulative catch up adjustment. Year 2 revenue of $325,000 was the difference between total revenue that should be recognized for Year 1 and Year 2 of $345,000 [(2,200 + 100) × $150)] minus revenue recognized in Year 1 of $20,000. A contract liability is recognized for the excess of consideration received over the amount of revenue recognized. It equals the future amount of goods to be transferred to the customer for which the consideration was already received.

The following entries were recorded by Barashka in Year 2:

Cash (2,200 × $200)	$440,000		Cost of goods sold (2,200 × $80)	$176,000	
Sales revenue		$325,000	Inventory of coats		$176,000
Contract liability		115,000			

As expected, the customer purchased an additional 1,100 coats in Year 3. Accordingly, 3,400 (100 + 2,200 + 1,100) coats were purchased during the contract period. In Year 3, the customer retroactively received the discount on all the coats previously purchased, paying cash of $50,000 [(3,400 × $150) – ($440,000 + $20,000)].

The following entries were recorded by Barashka in Year 3

Cash	$ 50,000		Cost of goods sold (1,100 × $80)	$88,000	
Contract liability	115,000		Inventory of coats		$88,000
Sales revenue (1,100 × $150)		$165,000			

f. **Consideration payable to a customer** includes cash amounts that an entity pays, or expects to pay, to the customer (or to other parties that purchase the entity's goods or services from the customer).

   1) Consideration payable to a customer is recognized as a **reduction** of the **transaction price** and therefore of revenue.

EXAMPLE 3-16	**Consideration Paid to a Customer**

Haf Company is a manufacturer of printing machines, and Gary Company is a large electronics retail store. On January 1, Year 1, Haf entered into a 1-year contract with Gary to sell 5,000 printing machines for $400 each. The contract also required Haf to make a nonrefundable payment of $150,000 to Gary at the inception of the contract. The $150,000 payment compensates Gary for needed changes in shelving to accommodate the new printing machines.

The consideration payable to Gary of $150,000 is accounted for as a reduction of the transaction price. Accordingly, (1) the total transaction price is $1,850,000 [(5,000 × $400) – $150,000], and (2) the revenue recognized on the sale of each printing machine is $370 ($1,850,000 ÷ 5,000).

   2) Revenue is reduced for consideration payable to a customer at the **later** of when the entity

      a) Recognizes revenue for the transfer of the related goods or services to the customer or

      b) Promises to pay the consideration to the customer.

5. **Step 4: Allocate the Transaction Price to the Performance Obligations in the Contract**

   a. After separate performance obligations are identified and the total transaction price is determined, the transaction price is allocated to performance obligations on the basis of relative standalone selling prices.

   b. A **standalone selling price** is the price at which an entity would sell a promised good or service separately to a customer.

      1) The best evidence of a standalone selling price is the **observable price** of a good or service when it is (a) sold separately (b) in similar circumstances and (c) to similar customers (e.g., the list price of a good or service).

c. If the standalone price is **not directly observable**, it must be estimated. The following are suitable approaches:

1) **Adjusted market assessment.** An entity evaluates the market in which it sells goods or services and estimates the price that a customer in that market would be willing to pay for them.

a) For example, the prices of competitors for similar goods or services adjusted for the entity's costs and margins are estimates of standalone selling prices.

2) **Expected cost plus an appropriate margin.** An entity forecasts its expected costs of satisfying a performance obligation and adds an appropriate margin for that cost.

3) **Residual.** An entity estimates the standalone selling price by reference to the total transaction price minus the sum of the observable standalone selling prices of other goods or services promised in the contract. The residual approach may be used only in limited circumstances.

EXAMPLE 3-17 Allocation of Contract Price

A company entered into a contract with a customer to sell a machine and provide 3 years of maintenance services for the machine. The total consideration is $200,000. The company determined that the machine and the maintenance services are distinct performance obligations. The company regularly sells machines separately at a directly observable standalone selling price of $160,000. But it does not sell maintenance services on a standalone basis. Based on the expected cost plus an appropriate margin approach, the estimated standalone selling price for 3 years of maintenance services was $90,000. The transaction price is allocated to each performance obligation in the contract using relative standalone selling prices.

Performance Obligation	Standalone Selling Price	Allocation of the Contract Price
Machine	$160,000	**$128,000** = ($160,000 ÷ $250,000) × $200,000
Maintenance Services	90,000	**72,000** = ($90,000 ÷ $250,000) × $200,000
Total	**$250,000**	**$200,000**

6. **Step 5: Recognize Revenue when (or as) a Performance Obligation Is Satisfied**

a. An entity recognizes revenue when (or as) it satisfies a performance obligation by transferring a promised good or service (an asset) to a **customer**.

1) An **asset** is transferred when (or as) the customer obtains control of that asset.

b. **Control** of an asset is transferred when the customer

1) Has the ability to direct the use of the asset and

2) Obtains substantially all of the remaining benefits (potential cash flows) from the asset.

c. A performance obligation can be satisfied either over time or at a point in time.

1) Recognizing revenue **over time** requires transfer of the control of goods or services to a customer over time and therefore satisfaction of a performance obligation over time. **One** of the following criteria must be met:

a) The customer **simultaneously** receives and consumes the benefits provided by the entity's performance as the entity performs. For example, cleaning services are provided to a customer's offices every day throughout the accounting period.

b) The entity's performance **creates or enhances an asset** that the customer controls as the asset is created or enhanced. For example, a construction company erects a building on the customer's land.

c) The asset created has **no alternative use** to the entity, and the entity has an enforceable **right** to payment for the performance completed to date. For example, an aerospace company contracts to build a satellite designed for the unique needs of a specific customer.

i) An entity does not have an alternative use for an asset if the entity is restricted contractually or limited practically from directing the asset for another use.

2) The accounting for contracts in which revenue is recognized over time is described in Subunit 3.5.

3) If a performance obligation is **not satisfied over time**, an entity satisfies the performance obligation **at a point in time**.

a) Revenue is recognized at a point in time when the customer obtains **control** over the promised asset. The following indicators of the transfer of control should be considered:

i) The entity has a present right to payment for the asset.

ii) The customer has legal title to the asset.

iii) The entity has transferred physical possession of the asset.

iv) The customer has the significant risks and rewards of ownership of the asset.

v) The customer has accepted the asset.

7. **Balance Sheet Presentation**

a. A **contract liability** is recognized for an entity's obligation to transfer goods or services to a customer for which the entity has received consideration from the customer.

1) Deposits and other advance payments by the customer, such as sales of gift certificates, are recognized as contract liabilities (Study Unit 10, Subunit 4).

b. A **contract asset** is recognized for an entity's right to consideration in exchange for goods or services that the entity has transferred to a customer.

1) However, the entity must have an **unconditional** right to the consideration to recognize a **receivable**.

2) A right to consideration is unconditional if only the passage of time is required before payment of that consideration is due.

c. Contract assets and contract liabilities resulting from different contracts must not be presented net in the statement of financial position.

8. **Costs to Obtain or Fulfill a Contract**

   a. **Incremental Costs of Obtaining a Contract**

      1) The incremental costs of obtaining a contract with a customer must be capitalized **(recognized as an asset)** if the entity expects to recover them.

         a) The asset recognized must be **amortized** on a systematic basis consistent with the transfer to the customer of the goods or services to which the asset relates.

      2) The cost of obtaining a contract may be **expensed as incurred** if its amortization period is **1 year or less**.

      3) Costs to obtain a contract that would have been incurred **regardless** of whether the contract was obtained must be **expensed as incurred**.

         a) But costs explicitly chargeable to the customer regardless of whether the contract is obtained are capitalized.

EXAMPLE 3-18 Costs of Obtaining a Contract

A company wins a bid to provide consulting services for 5 years to a new customer. The following costs were incurred to obtain the contract:

External legal fees for due diligence	$30,000
Commissions to sales employees	20,000
Total costs incurred to obtain the contract	$50,000

The commissions to sales employees of $20,000 are incremental costs of obtaining the contract. Because the company expects to recover those costs through future fees for consulting services, they must be capitalized. The costs capitalized are amortized over 5 years as the services are delivered to the customer. The external legal fees for due diligence of $30,000 must be expensed as incurred. Such costs are not incremental costs of obtaining the contract. They would have been incurred regardless of whether the contract was obtained.

   b. **Costs Incurred to Fulfill a Contract**

      1) Costs incurred to fulfill a contract must be capitalized (recognized as an asset) only if they meet all of the following criteria:

         a) The costs relate directly to a current or anticipated contract.

         b) The costs generate or enhance resources of the entity that will be used in satisfying performance obligations **in the future**.

         c) The costs are expected to be recovered.

      2) The asset recognized must be **amortized** on a systematic basis consistent with the transfer to the customer of the goods or services to which the asset relates.

STOP & REVIEW

You have completed the outline for this subunit.
Study multiple-choice questions 12 through 16 beginning on page 98.

3.5 RECOGNITION OF REVENUE OVER TIME

1. For each performance obligation satisfied over time, an entity must recognize revenue over time. For this purpose, the entity measures the **progress toward complete satisfaction** using the **output method** or the **input method**.
   a. To determine the appropriate method, an entity must consider the nature of the good or service that it promised to transfer to the customer.
   b. The chosen method should describe the entity's performance in transferring control of the promised asset to the customer.
2. At the end of each reporting period, the progress toward complete satisfaction of the performance obligation must be **remeasured** and updated for any changes in the outcome of the performance obligation.
   a. Such changes must be accounted for prospectively as a **change in accounting estimate**.
3. The **input method** recognizes revenue on the basis of (a) the entity's inputs to the satisfaction of the performance obligation relative to (b) the total expected inputs to the satisfaction of that performance obligation.
   a. Examples of input include
      1) Costs incurred,
      2) Labor hours expended,
      3) Resources consumed,
      4) Time elapsed, or
      5) Machine hours used.
   b. In long-term construction contracts, **costs incurred relative to total estimated costs** often are used to measure the progress toward completion. This method is the **cost-to-cost** method.
      1) Only costs that contribute to progress in satisfying the performance obligation are used in the cost-to-cost method. Thus, the following costs must not be included in measuring the progress:
         a) Costs incurred that relate to significant inefficiencies in the entity's performance (e.g., abnormal amounts of wasted materials or labor) that were not chargeable to the customer under the contract
         b) General and administrative costs not directly related to the contract
         c) Selling and marketing costs

c. When an entity's inputs are incurred evenly over time, recognition of revenue on a straight-line basis may be appropriate.

EXAMPLE 3-19 Cost-to-Cost Method

On January 1, Year 1, a contractor agrees to build on the customer's land a bridge that is expected to be completed at the end of Year 3. The promised bridge is a single performance obligation to be satisfied over time. The contractor determines that the progress toward completion of the bridge is reasonably measurable using the input method based on costs incurred. The contract price is $2,000,000, and expected total costs of the project are $1,200,000.

	Year 1	Year 2	Year 3
Costs incurred during each year	$300,000	$600,000	$550,000
Costs expected in the future	900,000	600,000	

Year 1

By the end of Year 1, 25% [$300,000 ÷ ($300,000 + $900,000)] of the total expected costs have been incurred. Using the input method based on costs incurred, the contractor recognizes 25% of the total expected revenue ($2,000,000 contract price × 25% = $500,000) and cost of goods sold ($1,200,000 × 25% = $300,000). The difference between these amounts is the gross profit for Year 1.

Revenue	$500,000
Cost of goods sold	(300,000)
Gross profit -- Year 1	$200,000*

* The gross profit in Year 1 of $200,000 also may be calculated as total expected gross profit from the project of $800,000 ($2,000,000 – $1,200,000) times the progress toward completion of the contract of 25%.

Year 2

By the end of Year 2, total costs incurred are $900,000 ($300,000 + $600,000). Given that $600,000 is expected to be incurred in the future, the total expected cost is $1,500,000 ($900,000 + $600,000). The change in the total cost of the contract must be accounted for prospectively. By the end of Year 2, 60% ($900,000 ÷ $1,500,000) of expected costs have been incurred. Thus, $1,200,000 ($2,000,000 × 60%) of cumulative revenue and $900,000 ($1,500,000 × 60%) of cumulative cost of goods sold should be recognized for Years 1 and 2. Because $500,000 of revenue and $300,000 of cost of goods sold were recognized in Year 1, revenue of $700,000 ($1,200,000 cumulative revenue – $500,000) and cost of goods sold of $600,000 ($900,000 cumulative cost of goods sold – $300,000) are recognized in Year 2.

Revenue	$700,000
Cost of goods sold	(600,000)
Gross profit -- Year 2	$100,000*

* The gross profit in Year 2 of $100,000 also may be calculated as the cumulative gross profit for Years 1 and 2 of $300,000 [($2,000,000 – $1,500,000) × 60%] minus the gross profit recognized in Year 1 of $200,000.

Year 3

At the end of Year 3, the project is completed, and the total costs incurred for the contract are $1,450,000 ($300,000 + $600,000 + $550,000). Given $1,200,000 of cumulative revenue and $900,000 of cumulative cost of goods sold for Years 1 and 2, $800,000 ($2,000,000 contract price – $1,200,000) of revenue and $550,000 ($1,450,000 total costs – $900,000) of cost of goods sold are recognized in Year 3.

Revenue	$800,000
Cost of goods sold	(550,000)
Gross profit -- Year 3	$250,000

NOTE: (1) The total gross profit from the project of $550,000 ($200,000 + $100,000 + $250,000) equals the contract price of $2,000,000 minus the total costs incurred of $1,450,000. (2) When progress toward completion is measured using the cost-to-cost method, as in the example above, the cost of goods sold recognized for the period equals the costs incurred during that period.

4. The **output method** recognizes revenue based on direct measurement of (a) the value of goods or services transferred to the customer to date relative to (b) the remaining goods or services promised under the contract.

   a. Examples of output methods include

      1) Appraisals of results achieved,
      2) Milestones reached,
      3) Units produced, and
      4) Units delivered.

   b. An entity may have a right to consideration from a customer in an amount corresponding directly with the value to the customer of performance to date. Using a practical expedient, revenue may be recognized at the amounts to which the entity has a **right to invoice the customer**.

EXAMPLE 3-20 Output Method -- Practical Expedient

A law firm enters into a contract to provide consulting services to a customer for a 1-year period for a fixed amount per hour of service provided. Because the customer simultaneously receives and consumes the benefits provided by the law firm's performance as it performs, revenue is recognized over time. Under the practical expedient, the law firm may recognize revenue that it has a right to bill to the customer.

5. An entity recognizes revenue for a performance obligation satisfied over time only if progress toward complete satisfaction of the performance obligation can be reasonably measured.

   a. However, revenue can be recognized to the **extent of the cost incurred** (zero profit margin) when

      1) An entity is not able to reasonably measure the outcome of a performance obligation or its progress toward satisfaction of that obligation, but
      2) An entity expects to recover the costs incurred in satisfying the performance obligation.

EXAMPLE 3-21 Revenue Recognition to the Extent of the Costs Incurred

On January 1, Year 1, Sadik Co. agrees to build on the customer's land a bridge that is expected to be completed at the end of Year 3. The contract price is $2 million. The promised bridge is a single performance obligation to be satisfied over time. Because Sadik has no experience with this type of contract, it cannot reasonably determine the total expected costs of the project. Accordingly, by the end of Year 1, progress toward completion of the bridge is not reasonably determinable. In Year 1, $300,000 of costs were incurred and paid by Sadik. However, the contract specified that Sadik has an enforceable right to payment of the costs incurred. Sadik therefore expects to recover these costs.

In Year 1, revenue and cost of goods sold are recognized at the amount of costs incurred of $300,000, and no gross profit is recognized. The following entries are recorded by Sadik in Year 1:

Accounts receivable	$300,000		Cost of goods sold	$300,000	
Revenue		$300,000	Cash		$300,000

6. As soon as an **estimated loss** on any project becomes apparent, it must be recognized in full, regardless of the methods used.

STOP & REVIEW

You have completed the outline for this subunit.
Study multiple-choice questions 17 through 20 beginning on page 101.

QUESTIONS

3.1 Discontinued Operations

1. During January of Year 6, Doe Corp. agreed to sell the assets and product line of its Hart division. The sale was completed on January 15, Year 7, and resulted in a gain on disposal of $900,000. Hart's operating losses were $600,000 for Year 6 and $50,000 for the period January 1 through January 15, Year 7. Disregarding income taxes and assuming that the criteria for reporting a discontinued operation are met, what amount of net gain (loss) should be reported in Doe's comparative Year 7 and Year 6 income statements?

	Year 7	Year 6
A.	$0	$250,000
B.	$250,000	$0
C.	$850,000	$(600,000)
D.	$900,000	$(650,000)

Answer (C) is correct.

REQUIRED: The amounts reported in comparative statements for discontinued operations.

DISCUSSION: The results of operations of a component that meets the definition of a discontinued operation are reported separately in the income statement under discontinued operations in the periods when they occur. Thus, in its Year 6 income statement, Doe should recognize a $600,000 loss. For Year 7, a gain of $850,000 should be recognized ($900,000 – $50,000).

Answer (A) is incorrect. The amount of $250,000 is the net gain for Year 6 and Year 7. However, the results for Year 7 may not be anticipated. **Answer (B) is incorrect.** The results for Year 6 should not be deferred. **Answer (D) is incorrect.** The operating loss for January Year 7 should be recognized in Year 7.

2. On September 30, Year 1, a component that represents a major line of an entity's business was properly classified as held for sale. This transaction is probable and is expected to qualify for recognition as a completed sale within 1 year. The component's operating loss for the period October 1 through December 31, Year 1, should be included in the Year 1 income statement as part of

A. Gain or loss on disposal of the discontinued component.

B. Operating gain or loss of the discontinued component.

C. Income or loss from continuing operations.

D. Other comprehensive income.

Answer (B) is correct.

REQUIRED: The treatment of the segment operating loss for the period from the measurement date to the balance sheet date.

DISCUSSION: A component of an entity, e.g., an operating segment, reporting unit, subsidiary, or asset group, may be disposed of or classified as held for sale. In these circumstances, the component's results of operations are reported in discontinued operations if the component has a major effect on an entity's operations and financial results (e.g., major line of business, major geographical area, major equity method investment, or other major part of an entity). The income statement reports the component's results of operations, including (1) any gain or loss from measuring the component at fair value minus cost to sell or (2) any gain or loss on disposal in discontinued operations in the period(s) when they occur. Accordingly, the operating loss of the component for the last quarter of Year 1 should be included in the operating gain or loss of the discontinued component reported in the discontinued operations section of the income statement.

3. On January 1, Year 4, Dart, Inc., entered into an agreement to sell the assets and product line of its Jay Division, which met the criteria for classification as an operating segment. The sale was consummated on December 31, Year 4, and resulted in a gain on disposal of $400,000. The division's operations resulted in losses before income tax of $225,000 in Year 4 and $125,000 in Year 3. For both years, Dart's income tax rate is 30%, and the criteria for reporting a discontinued operation have been met. In a comparative statement of income for Year 4 and Year 3, under the caption discontinued operations, Dart should report a gain (loss) of

	Year 4	Year 3
A.	$122,500	$(87,500)
B.	$122,500	$0
C.	$(157,500)	$(87,500)
D.	$(157,500)	$0

Answer (A) is correct.

REQUIRED: The amounts reported for discontinued operations in comparative statements.

DISCUSSION: When a component (e.g., an operating segment) has been disposed of or is classified as held for sale, and the criteria for reporting a discontinued operation have been met, the income statements for current and prior periods (in this case, Year 3 and Year 4) must report its operating results in discontinued operations. The gain from operations of the component for Year 4 is the net of the $225,000 operating loss for Year 4 and the $400,000 gain on disposal. The pretax gain is therefore $175,000 ($400,000 – $225,000), and the after-tax amount is $122,500 [$175,000 × (1.0 – .30)]. The $125,000 pretax loss for Year 3 should be reported in the comparative statements for Years 3 and 4 as an $87,500 [$125,000 × (1.0 – .30)] loss from discontinued operations.

Answer (B) is incorrect. The comparative statement of income for Year 4 and Year 3 should report a loss on discontinued operations for Year 3. **Answer (C) is incorrect.** An after-tax loss of $157,500 for Year 4 does not consider the gain on disposal. **Answer (D) is incorrect.** The comparative statement of income for Year 4 and Year 3 should report a loss on discontinued operations for Year 3, and an after-tax loss of $157,500 for Year 4 does not consider the gain on disposal.

3.2 Accounting Changes and Error Corrections

4. On January 2, Year 1, Air, Inc., agreed to pay its former president $300,000 under a deferred compensation arrangement. Air should have recorded this expense in Year 1 but did not do so. Air's reported income tax expense would have been $70,000 lower in Year 1 had it properly accrued this deferred compensation. In its December 31, Year 2, financial statements, Air should adjust the beginning balance of its retained earnings by a

A. $230,000 credit.

B. $230,000 debit.

C. $300,000 credit.

D. $370,000 debit.

Answer (B) is correct.

REQUIRED: The adjustment to the beginning balance of retained earnings.

DISCUSSION: Error corrections in single-period statements are reflected net of applicable income taxes as changes in the opening balance in the statement of retained earnings of the current period. The net effect of the error on Year 1 after-tax income was to understate expenses and overstate income by $230,000 ($300,000 expense – $70,000 tax savings). Consequently, beginning retained earnings should be debited (decreased) by $230,000.

5. Volga Co. included a foreign subsidiary in its Year 6 consolidated financial statements. The subsidiary was acquired in Year 4 and was excluded from previous consolidations. The change was caused by the elimination of foreign currency controls. Including the subsidiary in the Year 6 consolidated financial statements results in an accounting change that should be reported

A. By note disclosure only.

B. Currently and prospectively.

C. Currently with note disclosure of pro forma effects of retrospective application.

D. By retrospective application to the financial statements of all prior periods presented.

Answer (D) is correct.

REQUIRED: The reporting of the change in the subsidiaries included in consolidated financial statements.

DISCUSSION: A change in the reporting entity requires retrospective application to all prior periods presented to report information for the new entity. The following are changes in the reporting entity: (1) presenting consolidated or combined statements in place of statements of individual entities, (2) changing the specific subsidiaries included in the group for which consolidated statements are presented, and (3) changing the entities included in combined statements.

Answer (A) is incorrect. The change requires recognition in the financial statements. **Answer (B) is incorrect.** A change in reporting entity requires retrospective application. **Answer (C) is incorrect.** The change must apply to the financial statements for all periods presented.

6. How should the effect of a change in accounting estimate be accounted for?

A. By retrospectively applying the change to amounts reported in financial statements of prior periods.

B. By reporting pro forma amounts for prior periods.

C. As a prior-period adjustment to beginning retained earnings.

D. By prospectively applying the change to current and future periods.

Answer (D) is correct.

REQUIRED: The accounting for the effect of a change in accounting estimate.

DISCUSSION: The effect of a change in accounting estimate is accounted for in the period of change, if the change affects that period only, or in the period of change and future periods, if the change affects both. For a change in accounting estimate, the entity may not (1) restate or retrospectively adjust prior-period statements or (2) report pro forma amounts for prior periods.

7. On January 2, Year 4, Raft Corp. discovered that it had incorrectly expensed a $210,000 machine purchased on January 2, Year 1. Raft estimated the machine's original useful life to be 10 years and its salvage value at $10,000. Raft uses the straight-line method of depreciation and is subject to a 30% tax rate. In its December 31, Year 4, financial statements, what amount should Raft report as a prior period adjustment?

A. $102,900

B. $105,000

C. $165,900

D. $168,000

Answer (B) is correct.

REQUIRED: The prior period adjustment to correct the expensing of an asset purchase.

DISCUSSION: Expensing the machine in Year 1 resulted in an after-tax understatement of net income equal to $147,000 [$210,000 × (1.0 – .30 tax rate)]. Not recognizing annual depreciation of $20,000 [($210,000 – $10,000 salvage value) ÷ 10 years] in Years 1-3 resulted in an after-tax overstatement of net income equal to $42,000 [($20,000 × 3 years) × (1.0 – .30 tax rate)]. Thus, the prior period adjustment is for a net understatement of $105,000 ($147,000 – $42,000).

Answer (A) is incorrect. The amount of $102,900 assumes no salvage value. **Answer (C) is incorrect.** The amount of $165,900 equals $102,900 plus $63,000 (total pre-tax effect of omitting depreciation for three years and assuming no salvage value). **Answer (D) is incorrect.** The amount of $168,000 equals $105,000 plus $63,000 (total pre-tax effect of omitting depreciation for three years and assuming no salvage value).

3.3 Earnings per Share (EPS)

8. Deck Co. had 120,000 shares of common stock outstanding at January 1. On July 1, it issued 40,000 additional shares of common stock. Outstanding all year were 10,000 shares of nonconvertible cumulative preferred stock. What is the number of shares that Deck should use to calculate basic earnings per share?

A. 140,000

B. 150,000

C. 160,000

D. 170,000

Answer (A) is correct.

REQUIRED: The weighted-average number of shares used to calculate BEPS.

DISCUSSION: Basic earnings per share (BEPS) is used to measure earnings performance based on common stock outstanding during the period. BEPS equals income available to common shareholders divided by the weighted-average number of common shares outstanding. The weighted-average number of common shares outstanding relates the portion of the period that the shares were outstanding to the total time in the period. Consequently, the number of shares used to calculate BEPS is 140,000 {120,000 shares outstanding throughout the period + [40,000 shares × (6 months ÷ 12 months)]}.

Answer (B) is incorrect. The figure of 150,000 includes the preferred shares. **Answer (C) is incorrect.** The figure of 160,000 includes the unweighted number of additional shares. **Answer (D) is incorrect.** The figure of 170,000 includes the preferred shares and does not weight the additional common shares.

9. A firm has basic earnings per share of $1.29. If the tax rate is 30%, which of the following securities would be dilutive?

A. Cumulative 8%, $50 par preferred stock.

B. Ten percent convertible bonds, issued at par, with each $1,000 bond convertible into 20 shares of common stock.

C. Seven percent convertible bonds, issued at par, with each $1,000 bond convertible into 40 shares of common stock.

D. Six percent, $100 par cumulative convertible preferred stock, issued at par, with each preferred share convertible into four shares of common stock.

Answer (C) is correct.

REQUIRED: The dilutive securities given BEPS and the tax rate.

DISCUSSION: The calculation of dilutive EPS (DEPS) gives effect to dilutive potential common shares (e.g., options and convertible securities). Dilution is a reduction in basic EPS (BEPS) resulting from the assumption that (1) convertible securities were converted, (2) options or warrants were exercised, or (3) contingently issuable shares were issued. The conversion of the bonds would eliminate after-tax interest expense per bond of $49 [($1,000 par × 7%) × (1.0 – 30% tax rate)]. (The bonds were issued at par, so amortization of premium or discount does not affect the calculation.) The per-share effect is $1.225 ($49 ÷ 40 shares per bond). Thus, the convertible debt is dilutive ($1.225 < $1.29 BEPS).

Answer (A) is incorrect. Unless the preferred stock is convertible, it is not dilutive. Nonconvertible preferred shares are not potential common stock and therefore are not considered in the calculation of DEPS. **Answer (B) is incorrect.** The conversion of the bonds would eliminate after-tax interest expense per bond of $70 [($1,000 par × 10%) × (1.0 – 30% tax rate)]. (The bonds were issued at par, so amortization of premium or discount does not affect the calculation.) The per-share effect is $3.50 ($70 ÷ 20 shares per bond). Thus, the convertible debt is antidilutive ($3.50 > $1.29 BEPS). **Answer (D) is incorrect.** If the preferred stock is converted, the EPS numerator increases by the dividend savings of $6 ($100 par × 6%) per share of preferred stock (the additional income available to common shareholders). The per-share effect is $1.50 ($6 ÷ 4 common shares per share of preferred stock). Thus, the preferred stock is antidilutive ($1.50 > $1.29 BEPS).

10. During the current year, Comma Co. had outstanding: 25,000 shares of common stock; 8,000 shares of $20 par, 10% cumulative preferred stock; and 3,000 bonds that are $1,000 par and 9% convertible. The bonds were originally issued at par, and each bond was convertible into 10 shares of common stock. During the year, net income was $200,000, no dividends were declared, and the tax rate was 30%. What amount was Comma's basic earnings per share for the current year?

A. $6.78

B. $7.36

C. $7.07

D. $8.00

Answer (B) is correct.

REQUIRED: The basic earnings per share.

DISCUSSION: The numerator of the basic earnings per share (BEPS) ratio is income available to common shareholders. Declared dividends and accumulated dividends on preferred stock are removed from net income for the period to arrive at this amount. The undeclared but cumulative dividends on preferred stock equal $16,000 (8,000 shares × $20 par × 10%). Thus, given no dividends declared, the income available to common shareholders is $184,000 ($200,000 – $16,000). This amount is divided by the weighted-average common shares outstanding. All 25,000 of the common shares were outstanding during the entire period. Accordingly, BEPS equals $7.36 ($184,000 ÷ 25,000 shares).

Answer (A) is incorrect. The amount of $6.78 is diluted EPS [(BEPS numerator + $189,000 after-tax bond interest saved by a hypothetical bond conversion) ÷ (BEPS denominator + 30,000 common shares assumed to have been issued at the beginning of the period after the conversion of the bonds)]. **Answer (C) is incorrect.** The amount of $7.07 is the diluted EPS amount if the preferred stock were not cumulative. **Answer (D) is incorrect.** The amount of $8.00 ignores the undeclared cumulative preferred dividends.

11. The following information pertains to Ceil Co., a company whose common stock trades in a public market:

Shares outstanding at 1/1	100,000
Stock dividend at 3/31	24,000
Stock issuance at 6/30	5,000

What is the weighted-average number of shares Ceil should use to calculate its basic earnings per share (BEPS) for the year ended December 31?

A. 120,500

B. 123,000

C. 126,500

D. 129,000

Answer (C) is correct.

REQUIRED: The weighted-average number of shares used to calculate BEPS.

DISCUSSION: BEPS measures earnings performance based on common stock outstanding during all or part of the period. BEPS equals income available to common shareholders divided by the weighted-average number of shares of common stock outstanding. The weighted-average number of common shares outstanding is determined by relating the portion of the reporting period that the shares were outstanding to the total time in the period. Weighting is necessary because some shares may have been issued or reacquired during the period. The stock dividend is assumed to have occurred at the beginning of the period. The BEPS denominator is 126,500, based on 124,000 shares outstanding for the entire year (100,000 beginning balance + 24,000 stock dividend) and 5,000 additional shares issued on June 30.

124,000 × (6 ÷ 12)	=	62,000
129,000 × (6 ÷ 12)	=	64,500
		126,500

Answer (A) is incorrect. This figure is based on the assumption that the stock dividend was outstanding for 9 months. **Answer (B) is incorrect.** This figure is based on the assumption that (1) the stock dividend was outstanding for 9 months, and (2) the 6/30 issuance was outstanding for 12 months. **Answer (D) is incorrect.** This figure is the number outstanding at year-end.

3.4 Revenue from Contracts with Customers

12. On January 1, Year 1, an entity receives a payment of $20,000 for delivering a product to a customer at the end of Year 3. Based on the contract's terms, the performance obligation will be satisfied at a point in time (upon delivery of the product). The entity determined that (1) the contract includes a significant financing component and (2) a financing rate of 6% is an appropriate discount rate. What amount of interest expense and contract liability will be recognized in the entity's December 31, Year 2, financial statements?

	Year 2 Interest Expense	Contract Liability on December 31, Year 2
A.	$1,200	$21,200
B.	$2,400	$22,400
C.	$1,272	$22,472
D.	$1,348	$0

Answer (C) is correct.
REQUIRED: The interest expense and contract liability recognized for a performance obligation satisfied at a point in time.
DISCUSSION: Until the product is delivered to the customer, all payments received are recognized as a contract liability. Because the contract includes a significant financing component, interest expense is recognized using the effective interest method. The contract liability at the beginning of Year 2 equals $21,200 ($20,000 × 1.06). Thus, Year 2 interest expense equals $1,272 ($21,200 × 6%), and the contract liability at the end of Year 2 equals $22,472 ($21,200 × 1.06).
Answer (A) is incorrect. The amounts of $1,200 and $21,200 are the Year 1 interest expense and the December 31, Year 1, contract liability, respectively. **Answer (B) is incorrect.** The contract includes a significant financing component, so interest expense is recognized using the effective interest method, not a simple interest method. **Answer (D) is incorrect.** The amounts of $1,348 and $0 are the Year 3 interest expense and December 31, Year 3, contract liability, respectively.

13. The transaction price from contracts with customers generally should **not** be adjusted for the effect of the time value of money when

A. The transfer of goods is at the discretion of the seller.

B. A substantial amount of the consideration is contingent on a future event that is not within the control of the seller.

C. The time between the payment and the delivery of the promised goods in the contract to the customer is 18 months.

D. The selling price of the product and the consideration promised in the contract differ significantly.

Answer (B) is correct.
REQUIRED: The reason not to adjust the transaction price for the time value of money.
DISCUSSION: The transaction price should not be adjusted for the effect of the time value of money if

- The time between the payment and the delivery of the promised good or service to the customer is 1 year or less.
- The transfer of goods or services is at the discretion of the customer (e.g., a bill-and-hold contract in which the seller provides storage services for goods it sold to the buyer).
- A substantial amount of the consideration promised is variable, and its amount or timing varies on the basis of future circumstances that are not within the control of the entity or the customer. An example is a sales-based royalty contract in which the amount of consideration depends on sales by the customer to third parties.

Answer (A) is incorrect. The transaction price should not be adjusted when the transfer of goods or services is at the discretion of the customer. **Answer (C) is incorrect.** The transaction price should not be adjusted for the effect of the time value of money if the time between the payment and the delivery of the promised good or service to the customer is 1 year or less. **Answer (D) is incorrect.** The transaction price should be adjusted for the effect of the time value of money when the contract includes a significant financing component. A significant difference between (1) the selling price of the product and (2) the consideration promised in the contract may indicate that the financing component is significant.

14. Which of the following can be used to estimate the standalone selling price of a performance obligation in a contract with customers when that price is **not** directly observable?

	Adjusted Market Assessment	Expected Cost Plus an Appropriate Margin
A.	Yes	No
B.	Yes	Yes
C.	No	No
D.	No	Yes

Answer (B) is correct.

REQUIRED: The method(s), if any, of estimating the standalone selling price when the price is not directly observable.

DISCUSSION: The transaction price is allocated to performance obligations in the contract based on their standalone selling prices. The best evidence of a standalone selling price is the observable price of a good or service when it is sold separately in similar circumstances and to similar customers. The adjusted market assessment and the expected cost plus an appropriate margin are acceptable estimates of the standalone selling price of a performance obligation when that price is not directly observable. Using the adjusted market assessment approach, an entity evaluates the market in which it sells goods or services and estimates the price that a customer in that market would be willing to pay for them. Using the expected cost plus an appropriate margin approach, an entity forecasts its expected costs of satisfying a performance obligation and adds an appropriate margin for that cost.

Answer (A) is incorrect. The expected cost plus an appropriate margin approach also is an acceptable estimate of the standalone selling price of a performance obligation when that price is not directly observable. **Answer (C) is incorrect.** If the standalone price of a performance obligation is not directly observable, it can be estimated by the following approaches: (1) adjusted market assessment, (2) expected cost plus an appropriate margin, and (3) residual. **Answer (D) is incorrect.** The adjusted market assessment also is an acceptable estimate of the standalone selling price of a performance obligation when that price is not directly observable.

15. A promised asset is transferred in full satisfaction of a performance obligation in a contract when the customer

A. Obtains control of the asset.

B. Can direct use of the product.

C. Has physical possession of the asset.

D. Pays for the asset in full.

Answer (A) is correct.

REQUIRED: The time when an asset transfer fully satisfies a performance obligation.

DISCUSSION: Revenue is recognized when a performance obligation is satisfied by transferring a promised good or service to a customer. It happens when the customer obtains control of the good or service (i.e., an asset). Control of an asset is transferred to the customer when the customer (1) has the ability to direct the use of the asset and (2) obtains substantially all of the remaining benefits (potential cash flows) from the asset.

Answer (B) is incorrect. Control of the asset is not transferred to the customer unless the customer also obtains substantially all of the remaining benefits from the asset. **Answer (C) is incorrect.** Transfer of a physical possession is only one of the indicators for transfer of control. However, according to the terms of some contracts, the control of an asset may be transferred to a customer even when the product is still physically in the seller's warehouse. An example is a bill-and-hold contract in which the transfer of goods or services is at the discretion of the customer. **Answer (D) is incorrect.** Control of an asset is transferred to the customer when the customer (1) has the ability to direct the use of the asset and (2) obtains substantially all of the remaining benefits (potential cash flows) from the asset. Control can be transferred to a customer before (installment sale contract) or after (prepaid contract) the full payment is made.

16. According to ASC 606, the incremental costs of obtaining a contract with a customer that are expected to be recovered must be

A. Reported as an item of other comprehensive income.

B. Recognized as an item of equity.

C. Recognized as an asset and amortized in subsequent periods.

D. Recognized directly in the income statement.

Answer (C) is correct.

REQUIRED: The accounting for incremental costs of obtaining a contract with a customer.

DISCUSSION: The incremental costs of obtaining a contract with a customer must be capitalized (recognized as an asset) if the entity expects to recover them. These costs would not have been incurred if the contract had not been obtained. The cost capitalized (asset recognized) must be amortized on a systematic basis that is consistent with the transfer to the customer of the goods or services to which the asset relates.

Answer (A) is incorrect. The incremental costs of obtaining a contract with a customer must be capitalized if the entity expects to recover them. **Answer (B) is incorrect.** The incremental costs of obtaining a contract with a customer are not an item of equity. These costs must be capitalized if they are expected to be recovered. **Answer (D) is incorrect.** The incremental costs of obtaining a contract with a customer must be capitalized (recognized as an asset) if those costs are expected to be recovered.

3.5 Recognition of Revenue over Time

17. An entity is calculating the income recognized in the third year of a 5-year construction contract. It uses the input method based on costs incurred to measure the progress toward completion. The ratio used in calculating income is

A. Costs incurred in Year 3 to total billings.

B. Costs incurred in Year 3 to total estimated costs.

C. Total costs incurred to date to total billings.

D. Total costs incurred to date to total estimated costs.

Answer (D) is correct.

REQUIRED: The ratio used in calculating income under the input method based on costs incurred to measure the progress toward completion.

DISCUSSION: The entity is using a cost-to-cost accounting method. The input method based on costs incurred to measure the progress toward completion recognizes gross profit or revenue based on the ratio of costs to date to estimated total costs.

Answer (A) is incorrect. The estimate of progress may be based on various methods, e.g., units delivered, units of work performed, efforts expended, or cost incurred. However, billings do not necessarily measure progress. Also, the elements of the ratio should be measured on the same basis, but billings are not measured in terms of costs. Moreover, the gross profit or revenue recognized to date should be based on a cumulative calculation that reflects changes in estimates. **Answer (B) is incorrect.** The ratio of costs in one year to total costs does not estimate progress. **Answer (C) is incorrect.** Billings do not necessarily measure progress, and the elements of the ratio should be measured on the same basis.

18. Haft Construction Co. has consistently used the input method based on costs incurred to measure progress toward completion of the project. On January 10, Year 3, Haft began work on a $3 million construction contract. At the inception date, the estimated cost of construction was $2,250,000. The following data relate to the progress of the contract:

Gross profit recognized at 12/31/Yr 3	$ 300,000
Costs incurred 1/10/Yr 3 through 12/31/Yr 4	1,800,000
Estimated cost to complete at 12/31/Yr 4	600,000

In its income statement for the year ended December 31, Year 4, what amount of gross profit should Haft report?

A. $450,000

B. $300,000

C. $262,500

D. $150,000

Answer (D) is correct.

REQUIRED: The amount of gross profit reported using the input method based on costs incurred to measure progress toward completion of the project.

DISCUSSION: The input method based on costs incurred provides for the recognition of gross profit based on the relationship between the costs incurred to date and estimated total costs for the completion of the contract. The total anticipated gross profit is multiplied by the ratio of the costs incurred to date to the total estimated costs, and the product is reduced by previously recognized gross profit. The percentage-of-completion at 12/31/Yr 4 is 75% [$1,800,000 ÷ ($1,800,000 + $600,000)]. The total anticipated gross profit is $600,000 ($3,000,000 contract price – $2,400,000 expected total costs). Consequently, a gross profit of $150,000 [($600,000 total gross profit × 75%) – $300,000 previously recognized gross profit] is recognized for Year 4.

Answer (A) is incorrect. The current year's profit equals the cumulative income minus the previously recognized gross profit. **Answer (B) is incorrect.** The amount of $300,000 is the previously recognized gross profit. **Answer (C) is incorrect.** The amount of $262,500 assumes the total estimated gross profit is $750,000 ($3,000,000 price – $2,250,000 originally estimated total cost).

19. Frame Construction Company's contract requires the construction of a bridge in 3 years. The expected total cost of the bridge is $2,000,000, and Frame will receive $2,500,000 for the project. The actual costs incurred to complete the project were $500,000, $900,000, and $600,000, respectively, during each of the 3 years. Progress payments received were $600,000, $1,200,000, and $700,000, respectively. Frame uses the input method based on costs incurred to recognize revenue from a performance obligation satisfied over time. What amount of gross profit should Frame report during the last year of the project?

A. $120,000

B. $125,000

C. $140,000

D. $150,000

Answer (D) is correct.

REQUIRED: The recognized gross profit during the last year of the project.

DISCUSSION: The expected gross profit is $500,000 ($2,500,000 price – $2,000,000 expected cost). Cumulative recognized gross profit in Year 2 is $350,000 {$500,000 × [($500,000 + $900,000) ÷ $2,000,000]}. Recognized gross profit in Year 3 is $150,000 [($2,500,000 price – $500,000 – $900,000 – $600,000) actual gross profit – $350,000 previously recognized].

Answer (A) is incorrect. The amount of $120,000 is the recognized gross profit in the first year based on the percentage of the price paid ($600,000 ÷ $2,500,000). **Answer (B) is incorrect.** The amount of $125,000 is the amount recognized in the first year. **Answer (C) is incorrect.** The amount of $140,000 is the recognized gross profit in the third year based on the percentage of the price paid ($700,000 ÷ $2,500,000).

20. An entity recognizes revenue from a long-term contract over time. However, early in the performance of the contract, it cannot reasonably measure the outcome, but it expects to recover the costs incurred. Revenue should be recognized based on

A. The output method.

B. A straight-line calculation.

C. A zero profit margin.

D. The completed-contract method.

Answer (C) is correct.

REQUIRED: The basis for recognizing revenue for a performance obligation satisfied over time if the outcome cannot be reasonably measured but cost recovery is expected.

DISCUSSION: When the outcome of the contract is not reasonably measurable but the costs incurred in satisfying the performance obligation are expected to be recovered, revenue must be recognized only to the extent of the costs incurred. Revenue recognized is based on a zero profit margin until the entity can reasonably measure the outcome of the performance obligation.

Answer (A) is incorrect. When the outcome of the contract is not reasonably measurable but the costs incurred in satisfying the performance obligation are expected to be recovered, revenue must be recognized only to the extent of the costs incurred. Thus, neither the input nor the output method is used until the entity can reasonably measure the outcome of the performance obligation. **Answer (B) is incorrect.** When the outcome of the contract is not reasonably measurable but the costs incurred in satisfying the performance obligation are expected to be recovered, revenue must be recognized only to the extent of the costs incurred. **Answer (D) is incorrect.** When the outcome of the contract is not reasonably measurable but the costs incurred in satisfying the performance obligation are expected to be recovered, revenue is recognized to the extent of the costs incurred.

STUDY UNIT FOUR

FINANCIAL STATEMENT DISCLOSURE

(19 pages of outline)

According to the **full disclosure principle**, understandable information capable of affecting user decisions should be reported. The financial statements are the primary means of disclosure. However, almost all accounting pronouncements require additional disclosures in the notes. Because memorizing them is virtually impossible, candidates should anticipate the disclosure requirements before reading the summary, outline, or actual pronouncement. The appropriate perspective is that of an informed creditor or investor.

The study unit begins with significant accounting policies to set the tone for the types of disclosures required by GAAP.

4.1 SIGNIFICANT ACCOUNTING POLICIES

1. **Overview**
   a. Accounting policies are the specific principles and the methods of applying them used by the reporting entity. Management selects these policies as the most appropriate for fair presentation of financial statements.
   b. Business and not-for-profit entities **must disclose** all significant accounting policies as an **integral part** of the financial statements.
      1) Disclosure of accounting policies in unaudited interim financial statements is not required when the reporting entity has not changed its policies since the end of the preceding fiscal year.
2. **Presentation and Disclosure**
   a. The preferred presentation is a **summary of accounting policies** in a separate section preceding the notes or in the initial note.
   b. The disclosure should include accounting principles adopted and the methods of applying them that materially affect the financial statements. Disclosure extends to accounting policies that involve
      1) A selection from existing acceptable alternatives,
      2) Policies unique to the industry in which the entity operates, even if they are predominantly followed in that industry, and
      3) GAAP applied in an unusual or innovative way.
   c. Certain disclosures about policies of business entities are commonly required. These items include the following:
      1) Basis of consolidation
      2) Depreciation methods
      3) Amortization of intangibles
      4) Inventory pricing
      5) Recognition of revenue from contracts with customers
      6) Recognition of revenue from leasing operations
   d. Disclosure of accounting policies should **not duplicate details** presented elsewhere.
      1) For example, the summary of significant policies should not contain the composition of plant assets or inventories or the maturity dates of noncurrent debt.

STOP & REVIEW

You have completed the outline for this subunit.
Study multiple-choice questions 1 and 2 on page 122.

4.2 SEGMENT REPORTING

1. **Overview**

   a. Segment reporting includes interim financial reports and annual financial statements of **public** business entities. The objective is to provide information about the different business activities of the entity and the economic environments in which it operates.

      1) Ordinarily, information is to be reported on the basis that is used internally for evaluating performance and making resource allocation decisions. This approach aligns external and internal reporting.

      2) Disclosure of information is **not** required if it is not prepared for internal use, and reporting it would not be feasible.

   b. An **operating segment** has three characteristics:

      1) It is a business component of the entity that may recognize revenues and incur expenses.

      2) Its operating results are regularly reviewed by the entity's **chief operating decision maker (CODM)** for the purpose of resource allocation and performance assessment.

      3) Its discrete financial information is available.

   c. Operating segments may be **aggregated** if

      1) Doing so is consistent with the objective;

      2) They have similar economic characteristics; and

      3) They have similar products and services, production processes, classes of customers, distribution methods, and regulatory environments.

2. **Quantitative Thresholds**

   a. **Reportable segments** are operating segments that must be separately disclosed if one of the following quantitative thresholds is met:

      1) **Revenue test.** Reported revenue, including sales to external customers and intersegment sales or transfers, is at least 10% of the combined revenue (external and internal) of all operating segments.

      2) **Asset test.** Assets are at least 10% of the combined assets of all operating segments.

      3) **Profit (loss) test.** The absolute amount of reported profit or loss is at least 10% of the greater, in absolute amount, of either the combined reported **profit** of all operating segments that did **not** report a loss or the combined reported **loss** of all operating segments that **did** report a loss.

b. If an operating segment does not meet any threshold, management still may report it if such information would be useful.

Test Amount	Percent of Relevant Amount
Revenue	≥ 10% of all operating segments
Assets	≥ 10% of all operating segments
Absolute Profit or Loss	≥ 10% of greater of absolute sum of (1) all profitable OSs or (2) all loss-reporting OSs

EXAMPLE 4-1 Identification of Reportable Segments

Greque Co. operates in four industries. Which of the following operating segments should be identified as a reportable segment under the operating profit or loss test?

Operating Segment	Operating Profit (Loss)
Rho	$ 90,000
Sigma	(100,000)
Tau	910,000
Upsilon	(420,000)

An operating segment is identified as a reportable segment if it meets the profit or loss test (among others). The segment is reportable if the absolute amount of the operating profit or loss equals at least 10% of the greater, in absolute amount, of (1) the combined operating profit of all operating segments not reporting an operating loss or (2) the combined operating loss of all operating segments reporting an operating loss.

The first step in applying the operating profit (loss) test is to classify the segments into those reporting profits and those reporting losses and summing the amounts.

Segment	Operating Profit	Operating Loss
Rho	$ 90,000	$ 0
Sigma	0	100,000
Tau	910,000	0
Upsilon	0	420,000
	$1,000,000	$520,000

The greater sum, in absolute dollars, is that of the operating profit segments. The reporting threshold is therefore $100,000 ($1,000,000 × 10%). Segments Sigma, Tau, and Upsilon report absolute amounts greater than this threshold, and they are the reportable segments.

c. If the **total external revenue** of the operating segments meeting the quantitative thresholds is **less than 75%** of consolidated revenue, additional operating segments are identified as reportable until the 75% level is reached.

d. Information about nonreportable activities and segments is combined and disclosed in an **all other** category as a reconciling item.

e. As the number of reportable segments increases above 10, the entity may decide that it has reached a practical limit.

Reportable Segments

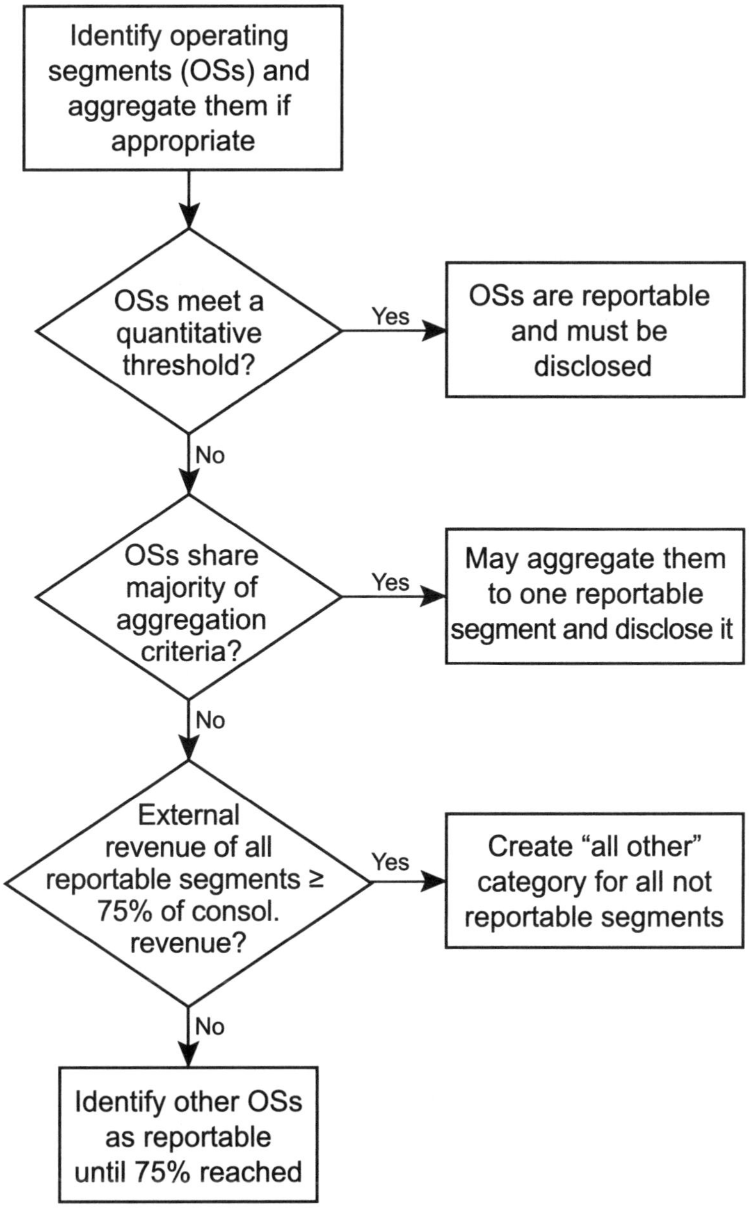

Figure 4-1

3. **Disclosures for Each Reportable Segment**

   a. **General information** disclosed includes

      1) The factors used to identify reportable segments, such as the basis of organization, and

      2) Revenue-generating products and services.

   b. A **measure of profit or loss and total assets** should be reported. Moreover, the following amounts should be disclosed if they are included in the measure of profit or loss reviewed by the CODM:

      1) Revenues from external customers and other operating segments,
      2) Interest revenue and expense,
      3) Depreciation,
      4) Depletion and amortization,
      5) Unusual items,
      6) Equity in the net income of equity-based investees,
      7) Income tax expense or benefit, and
      8) Other significant noncash items.

EXAMPLE 4-2 Segment Reporting Disclosures

Lucas Co., a public company, has three reportable segments: software, hardware, and inspection. The following is an example of its disclosures about these segments in the notes to the financial statements:

(Dollars in Millions)	Software	Hardware	Inspection	All Other	Totals
Revenues from external customers	$150	$110	$ 90	$ 60	$ 410
Intersegment revenues	30	--	20	--	50
Interest expense	15	20	22	14	71
Interest revenue	8	27	--	18	53
Depreciation and amortization expense	10	15	9	13	47
Segment net profit (loss)	33	40	(10)	28	91
Segment total assets	320	400	280	210	1,210
Expenditures for segment long-lived assets	10	14	13	--	37

4. **Measurement**

   a. The external information reported is measured in the same way as the internal information used for resource allocation and performance evaluation. The amount of a reported segment item, such as assets, is the measure reported to the CODM.

5. **Reconciliations**

   a. Reconciliations to the consolidated amounts must be provided for the total reportable segments' amounts for significant items of information disclosed. These significant items include (1) revenues, (2) profit or loss, (3) total assets, etc.

EXAMPLE 4-3 Reconciliation Disclosure in Segment Reporting

The following is an example of the reconciliation of Lucas Co.'s total revenues for reportable segments to the total revenues presented in the consolidated income statement:

Revenues (In Millions of Dollars)	
Total revenues for reportable segments	$400
Other revenues	60
Elimination of intersegment revenues	(50)
Total consolidated revenue	$410

6. **Restatements**

   a. Restatement of previously reported information is required if changes in internal organization cause the composition of reportable segments to change.

   b. The entity may choose not to restate segment information for earlier periods, including interim periods. Segment information for the year of the change then must be disclosed under the old basis and the new basis of segmentation if feasible.

7. **Entity-Wide Disclosures**

   a. Such disclosures must be provided only if they are not given in the reportable operating segment information.

   b. Revenues from external customers for each product and service (or each group of similar products and services) are reported if feasible based on the financial information used to produce the general-purpose financial statements.

   c. The following information about **geographic areas** is also reported if feasible:

      1) External revenues attributed to the home country and to all foreign countries,
      2) Material external revenues attributed to an individual foreign country,
      3) The basis for attributing revenues from external customers, and
      4) Certain information about assets.

   d. If 10% or more of revenue is derived from sales to any single customer, (1) that fact, (2) the amount from each such customer, and (3) the segment(s) reporting the revenues must be disclosed. Single customers include entities under common control and each federal, state, local, or foreign government.

STOP & REVIEW

You have completed the outline for this subunit.
Study multiple-choice questions 3 through 8 beginning on page 123.

4.3 INTERIM FINANCIAL REPORTING

1. Overview

a. GAAP do not require reporting of interim financial information. But GAAP must be applied when entities report such information, including when **publicly traded companies** issue summarized interim information. Moreover, federal securities law requires certain entities that meet the definition of an **issuer** to report interim quarterly information on Form 10-Q.

   1) For many reasons, the usefulness of interim financial information is limited. Thus, their best qualitative characteristic is **timeliness**.

b. Each interim period is treated primarily as an **integral part** of an annual period. Ordinarily, the results for an interim period should be based on the **same accounting principles** the entity uses in preparing annual statements, but certain principles may require modification at interim dates.

IFRS DIFFERENCE

Each interim period is a discrete reporting period.

2. Revenue and Associated Costs

a. **Revenue** should be recognized as earned during an interim period on the same basis as followed for the full year.

b. **Costs associated with revenue** are treated similarly for annual and interim reporting. However, some exceptions are appropriate for inventory accounting at interim dates.

   1) The gross profit method may be used for estimating cost of goods sold and inventory because a physical count at the interim date may not be feasible (described in Study Unit 7, Subunit 7).

   2) An inventory loss from a write-down below cost may be deferred if no loss is reasonably anticipated for the year.

      a) But inventory losses from nontemporary declines below cost must be recognized at the interim date. If the loss is recovered during the year (in another quarter), it is treated as a change in estimate. The amount recovered is limited to the losses previously recognized. (Study Unit 7, Subunit 6, contains the relevant outlines.)

IFRS DIFFERENCE

For an interim period, an inventory loss from a market decline must be recognized even if no loss is reasonably expected for the year.

3. **All Other Costs and Expenses**
   a. Costs and expenses other than product costs are either charged to income in interim periods as incurred or allocated among interim periods.
   b. The **allocation** is based on the (1) benefits received, (2) estimates of time expired, or (3) activities associated with the period. If an item expensed for annual reporting benefits more than one interim period, it should be allocated.
      1) **Gains and losses** that are similar to gains and losses that would not be deferred at year end are not deferred to later interim periods.
         a) For example, an unusual or infrequently occurring item and a gain or loss on the disposal of an asset are **recognized in full** in the quarter in which they occur. They **must not** be prorated over the fiscal year.
      2) Some items expensed in annual statements should be allocated to the interim periods that are clearly benefited.
      3) **Quantity discounts** based on annual sales volume should be charged to interim periods based on periodic sales.
      4) **Interest, rent, and property taxes** may be accrued or deferred at interim dates to assign an appropriate cost to each period.

EXAMPLE 4-4 Interim Reporting -- Costs and Expenses

On March 15 of the current year, Chen Company paid property taxes of $120,000 on its factory building for the current calendar year. On April 1, Chen made $240,000 in unanticipated repairs to its equipment. The repairs will benefit operations for the remainder of the calendar year.

The benefit from the payment of the property taxes relates to all four quarters of the current year and should be prorated at $30,000 ($120,000 ÷ 4) per quarter. The benefit from the unanticipated repairs to plant equipment relates to the second, third, and fourth quarters. It should be spread evenly over these quarters at $80,000 ($240,000 ÷ 3) per quarter.

      5) **Advertising costs** may be deferred within a fiscal year if the benefits clearly extend beyond the interim period of the expenditure.
      6) Certain costs and expenses, such as (a) inventory shrinkage, (b) allowance for credit losses, and (c) discretionary bonuses, are subject to **year-end adjustment**. To the extent possible, these adjustments should be estimated and assigned to interim periods.

4. **Seasonality**
   a. If interim information is issued, certain disclosures are mandatory for businesses that have material seasonal fluctuations. These fluctuations cannot be smoothed in interim information.
   b. Accordingly, reporting entities must disclose the seasonal nature of their activities. They also should consider supplementing interim reports with information for the 12-month period that ended at the interim date for the current and preceding years.

5. **Interim Period Tax Expense (Benefit)**

   a. At the end of each interim period, the entity should estimate the annual effective tax rate.

   b. **Interim period tax expense (benefit)** equals the **estimated annual effective tax rate**, times year-to-date ordinary income (loss) before income taxes, minus the tax expense (benefit) recognized in previous interim periods.

      1) Ordinary in this context means excluding unusual or infrequently occurring items and results of discontinued operations.

   c. The **estimated annual effective tax rate** is based on the statutory rate adjusted for the current year's expected conditions. These include (1) anticipated tax credits, (2) foreign tax rates, (3) capital gains rates, and (4) other tax planning alternatives.

      1) The rate also includes the effect of any expected valuation allowance at year end for deferred tax assets related to deductible temporary differences and carryforwards arising during the year.

      2) The rate is determined without regard to (a) significant unusual or infrequently occurring items to be reported separately or (b) items reported net of tax effect. However, such items are recognized in the interim period when they occur. The method of intraperiod tax allocation described in Study Unit 10 is used.

   d. A **tax benefit** is recognized for a loss early in the year if the benefits are expected to be realized during the year or recognizable as a deferred tax asset at year end.

      1) A valuation allowance must be recognized if it is more likely than not that a deferred tax asset will not be fully realized. Accordingly, the tax benefit of an ordinary loss early in the year is not recognized to the extent that this criterion is met.

         a) However, no income tax expense is recognized for subsequent ordinary income until the earlier unrecognized tax benefit is used.

      2) The foregoing principles are applied in determining the estimated tax benefit of an ordinary loss for the fiscal year used to calculate (a) the annual effective tax rate and (b) the year-to-date tax benefit of a loss.

EXAMPLE 4-5 Interim Reporting – Income Tax Expense

The information below was used in preparing quarterly income statements during the first half of the current year.

Quarter	Income before Income Taxes	Estimated Effective Annual Income Tax Rate
1	$80,000	45%
2	70,000	45%
3	50,000	40%

The tax expense for the third quarter equals the estimated annual effective tax rate determined at the end of the third quarter, times the cumulative year-to-date ordinary income (loss), minus the cumulative tax expense for the first two quarters. At the end of the third quarter, the year-to-date ordinary income is $200,000 ($80,000 + $70,000 + $50,000), and the cumulative tax expense is $80,000 ($200,000 × 40%). Because the cumulative tax expense at the end of the second quarter was $67,500 [($80,000 + $70,000) × 45%], $12,500 ($80,000 – $67,500) should be reported as income tax expense in the income statement for the third quarter.

   e. Taxes on all items other than continuing operations are determined at incremental rates. Thus, their marginal effect on taxes is calculated.

6. **Interim Period Accounting Changes**

   a. In interim as well as annual periods, a change in accounting principle is **retrospectively** applied unless it is impracticable to determine the cumulative or period-specific effects of the change.

   b. The **cumulative effect** of the change on periods prior to those presented is reflected in the carrying amounts of assets, liabilities, and retained earnings (or other appropriate components of equity or net assets) at the beginning of the first period presented.

      1) All periods presented must be adjusted for **period-specific effects**.

   c. A **change in an accounting estimate**, including a change in the estimated effective annual tax rate, is accounted for **prospectively** in the interim period in which the change is made and in future periods. Prior-period information is not retrospectively adjusted.

7. **Prior Interim Period Adjustments**

   a. The following items apply to adjustment or settlement of (1) litigation, (2) income taxes (except for the effects of retroactive tax legislation), or (3) renegotiation proceedings.

      1) All or part of the adjustment or settlement must relate specifically to a prior interim period of the current year.

         a) Moreover, its effect must be material, and the amount must have become reasonably estimable only in the current interim period.

      2) If an **item of profit or loss** occurs in other than the first interim period and meets the criteria for an adjustment, the portion of the item allocable to the current interim period is included in net income for that period.

         a) The financial statements for the **prior interim periods are restated** to include their allocable portions of the adjustment.

         b) The portion of the adjustment directly related to prior fiscal years is included in net income of the first interim period of the current fiscal year.

EXAMPLE 4-6 Prior Interim Period Adjustments

On June 1, Year 5, a calendar-year entity settled a patent infringement lawsuit. The court awarded it $3,000,000 in damages. Of this amount, $1,000,000 related to Year 3, $1,000,000 to Year 4, and $500,000 to each of the first two quarters in Year 5. The applicable tax rate is 40%. Prior interim periods should be restated to include their allocable portions of the adjustment. Accordingly, $2,500,000 of the settlement is included in earnings for the first quarter and $500,000 of the settlement should be included in earnings for the second quarter. Given a tax rate of 40%, the settlement increases net income of the first and second quarter by $1,500,000 and $300,000, respectively.

SUCCESS TIP

Expect to possibly be tested on interim financial reporting, as the AICPA has traditionally tested candidates' knowledge of this topic. Candidates could see either a conceptual question or a calculation question.

STOP & REVIEW

You have completed the outline for this subunit.
Study multiple-choice questions 9 through 14 beginning on page 126.

4.4 SIGNIFICANT RISKS, UNCERTAINTIES, AND GOING CONCERN

1. **Overview**
   a. Disclosures should be made at the balance sheet date about certain items that could significantly affect reported amounts in the near term, that is, within 1 year of the balance sheet date.
   b. Disclosures should be made in the notes of annual and interim financial statements when substantial doubt
      1) Exists about an entity's ability to continue as a going concern or
      2) Was alleviated as a result of management's plans.
2. **Nature of Operations**
   a. One set of disclosures applies to risks and uncertainties relating to the nature of operations. Thus, entities must disclose their
      1) Major products or services,
      2) Principal markets, and
      3) The locations of those markets.
   b. They also should disclose (1) all industries in which they operate; (2) the relative importance of each; and (3) the basis for determining the relative importance, e.g., assets, revenue, or earnings. However, this set of disclosures need not be quantified.
3. **Use of Estimates**
   a. A second type of disclosures concerns the use of estimates in the preparation of financial statements. Financial statements should explain that conformity with GAAP requires management to use numerous estimates.
   b. Disclosure about certain **significant estimates** used to value assets, liabilities, or contingencies is required when the estimated effects of a condition, situation, or set of circumstances at the balance sheet date are subject to a **reasonable possibility** of change in the near term and the effects will be material.
4. **Concentrations**
   a. A third set of disclosures relates to current vulnerability due to concentrations, for example, when entities fail to diversify.
   b. Disclosure is necessary if management knows prior to issuance of the statements that
      1) The concentration **exists** at the balance sheet date,
      2) It makes the entity vulnerable to a near-term **severe impact**, and
      3) Such impact is at least **reasonably possible** in the near term.

c. Disclosable concentrations include those in

   1) The volume of business with a given customer, supplier, lender, grantor, or contributor;
   2) Revenue from given products, services, or fund-raising events;
   3) The available suppliers of materials, labor, services, or rights (e.g., licenses) used in operations; and
   4) The market or geographic area where the entity operates.
      a) For concentrations of operations in another country, disclosure should include the carrying amounts of net assets and the areas where they are located.

5. **Going Concern**

   a. When preparing annual or interim financial statements, management must evaluate whether conditions and events raise substantial doubt about the entity's ability to continue as a going concern.
      1) Substantial doubt exists when it is probable that the entity cannot meet its obligations as they come due within 1 year after the date that the financial statements are issued (or available to be issued).
   b. When a **substantial doubt** exists about an entity's ability to continue as a going concern, an entity must disclose the following:
      1) A statement in the notes that substantial doubt exists
      2) Principal conditions or events that raise substantial doubt
      3) Management's evaluation of the significance of those conditions or events
      4) Management's plans to mitigate those conditions or events
   c. When substantial doubt about an entity's ability to continue as going **was alleviated** as a result of management's plans, the entity must disclose the following:
      1) Principal conditions or events that raised the substantial doubt
      2) Management's evaluation of the significance of those conditions or events
      3) Management's plans that alleviated the substantial doubt

STOP & REVIEW

You have completed the outline for this subunit.
Study multiple-choice question 15 on page 128.

4.5 SUBSEQUENT EVENTS

1. **Overview**
   a. Subsequent events are events or transactions that occur **after the balance sheet date** and **prior to the issuance or availability for issuance of the financial statements**.
      1) An SEC filer evaluates subsequent events through the date the statements are issued (become widely available for general use).
      2) Other entities evaluate subsequent events through the date statements are available for issuance (are complete in accordance with GAAP and approved).
         a) The entity must disclose the date through which subsequent events have been evaluated.
2. **Recognized Subsequent Events**
   a. One type of subsequent event provides additional evidence about **conditions that existed at the date of the balance sheet**, including the estimates inherent in statement preparation.
      1) This type of event **must be recognized** in the financial statements.
      2) Subsequent events affecting the realization of assets (such as receivables and inventories) or the settlement of estimated liabilities ordinarily require recognition.
         a) They usually reflect the resolution of conditions that existed over a relatively long period. Examples are
            i) The settlement of litigation for an amount differing from the liability recorded in the statements and
            ii) A loss on a receivable resulting from a customer's bankruptcy.
      3) Adjustments to earnings per share (EPS) are made as a result of stock dividends and stock splits that occurred after the balance sheet date but prior to the issuance (or availability for issuance) of the financial statements (discussed in Study Unit 3, Subunit 3).
3. **Unrecognized Subsequent Events**
   a. The second type of subsequent event provides evidence about **conditions that did not exist at the date of the balance sheet**. These events **do not require recognition**, but some of them do require disclosure.
      1) Examples of nonrecognized subsequent events requiring **disclosure only** include
         a) Sale of a bond or capital stock issue
         b) A business combination
         c) Settlement of litigation when the event resulting in the claim occurred after the balance sheet date
         d) Loss of plant or inventories as a result of a fire or natural disaster
         e) Losses on receivables resulting from conditions (e.g., a customer's major casualty) occurring after the balance sheet date
      2) Some events of the second type may be so significant that the most appropriate disclosure is to supplement the historical statements with pro forma financial data.

STOP & REVIEW

You have completed the outline for this subunit.
Study multiple-choice questions 16 and 17 on page 128.

4.6 FINANCIAL INSTRUMENTS

BACKGROUND 4-1 Fair Value Measurement of Financial Instruments

Historical cost is an appropriate measurement attribute for property, plant, and equipment. An entity often holds these assets for years. Historical cost is not appropriate for financial instruments, which often are current assets. The FASB therefore requires all entities either to report on the face of the balance sheet or disclose in the notes the fair values of all financial instruments. Current GAAP are found in FASB ASC 825.

1. **Definition**
   a. A financial instrument is cash, evidence of an ownership interest in an entity, or a contract that both
      1) Imposes on one entity a **contractual obligation** to
         a) Deliver cash or another financial instrument to a second entity or
         b) Exchange other financial instruments on potentially unfavorable terms with the second entity **and**
      2) Conveys to that second entity a **contractual right** to
         a) Receive cash or another financial instrument from the first entity or
         b) Exchange other financial instruments on potentially favorable terms with the first entity.
2. **Financial Statements Presentation**
   a. On the balance sheet or in the notes to the financial statements, financial assets and financial liabilities are separately presented by
      1) **Measurement category** (i.e., amortized cost, fair value through net income, and fair value through OCI) and
      2) **Form of financial asset** (i.e., loans, securities, and receivables).
3. **Disclosures**
   a. Public business entities must disclose, either in the body of the financial statements or in the notes, the
      1) **Fair value** of financial instruments, regardless of whether they are recognized (e.g., financial instruments measured at amortized cost) or not recognized in the balance sheet (e.g., unrecognized firm commitments), and
      2) **Level of the fair value hierarchy** (Level 1, 2, or 3) in which the fair value measurements of the financial instruments are categorized.
   b. Fair value disclosure is not required for certain financial instruments, such as trade receivables and payables due in 1 year or less and investments accounted for under the equity method.
   c. Ordinarily, disclosures should **not** net the fair values of instruments even if they are of the same class or are related, e.g., by a risk management strategy.

4. **Concentration of Credit Risk**

   a. **Credit risk** is the risk of accounting loss from a financial instrument because of the possible failure of another party to perform.

      1) With certain exceptions, for example, (a) instruments of pension plans, (b) certain insurance contracts, (c) warranty obligations and rights, and (d) unconditional purchase obligations, an entity must disclose significant **concentrations of credit risk** arising from financial instruments, whether from one counterparty or groups.

         a) Group concentrations arise when multiple counterparties have similar activities and economic characteristics that cause their ability to meet obligations to be similarly affected by changes in conditions.

      2) **Disclosures** (in the body of the statements or the notes) should include

         a) Information about the shared activity, region, or economic characteristic that identifies the concentration.

         b) The **maximum loss** due to credit risk if parties failed completely to perform and the security, if any, proved to be of no value.

         c) The **policy of requiring collateral** or other security, information about access to that security, and the nature and a brief description of the security.

         d) The policy of entering into **master netting arrangements** to mitigate the credit risk; information about them; and a description of the terms, including the extent to which they reduce the maximum amount of loss.

5. **Market Risk**

   a. An entity is encouraged, but not required, to disclose quantitative information about the **market risks** of instruments that is consistent with the way the entity manages those risks.

STOP & REVIEW

You have completed the outline for this subunit.
Study multiple-choice questions 18 and 19 on page 129.

4.7 FAIR VALUE MEASUREMENTS

1. **Overview**

   a. GAAP establish a framework for fair value measurements (FVMs) required by other pronouncements. But they do not determine when FVMs are required. Accordingly, they

      1) Define **fair value**,
      2) Discuss **valuation** techniques,
      3) Establish a **fair value hierarchy** of inputs to valuation techniques, and
      4) Require expanded **disclosures** about FVMs.

2. **Definitions**

   a. **Fair value** is the **price** that would be **received** to sell an asset or paid to transfer a liability in an **orderly transaction between market participants** at the measurement date.

   b. The FVM is for a particular asset or liability that may stand alone (e.g., a financial instrument) or constitute a group (e.g., a business). The definition also applies to instruments measured at fair value that are classified as equity.

   c. The price is an **exit price** paid or received in a hypothetical transaction considered from the perspective of a market participant.

   d. **Market participants** are not related parties. They are independent of the reporting entity.

      1) They are knowledgeable (i.e., they have a reasonable understanding based on all available information).

      2) They are willing and able (but not compelled) to engage in transactions involving the asset or liability.

      3) The FVM is market-based, not entity-specific.

   e. An **orderly transaction** is not forced, and time is assumed to be sufficient to allow for customary marketing activities.

      1) The transaction is assumed to occur in the reporting entity's **principal market** for the asset or liability.

      2) In the absence of such a market, it is assumed to occur in the most advantageous market. This market is the one in which the specific reporting entity can

         a) Maximize the amount received for selling the asset or

         b) Minimize the amount paid for transferring the liability, after considering transaction costs.

      3) Given a principal (or most advantageous) market, the FVM is the price in that market **without adjustment for transaction costs**.

EXAMPLE 4-7 Fair Value Measurement

On January 1, Year 1, Brooke Co. acquired 50 shares of common stock of John Co. In its December 31, Year 1, balance sheet, Brooke must report the investment in shares of John at fair value. (The accounting for an investment in equity securities is discussed in detail in Study Unit 5, Subunit 3.) John's shares are actively traded on two different stock exchanges (London and Madrid). Below is the information for the stock price and transaction costs of John's stock on the two stock exchanges on December 31, Year 1:

12/31/Year 1	Quoted Stock Price	Transaction Costs	Net Proceeds
London	$100	$4	$96
Madrid	102	7	95

- If one of the two stock exchanges is a principal market, the **quoted stock price** on this stock exchange is the fair value.
- If neither of the two stock exchanges is a principal market, the most advantageous market is the market in which Brooke can receive the maximum proceeds from selling the shares (quoted stock price – transaction costs). Consequently, London is the most advantageous market, and the **quoted stock price** of $100 on the London stock exchange is the fair value measurement of John's shares.

On December 31, Year 1, Brooke reports the investment in shares of John Co. at $5,000 (50 shares × $100 fair value per share).

f. **Assets.** The FVM is based on the **highest and best use (HBU)** by market participants.

1) The HBU is in-use if the value-maximizing use is in combination with other assets in a group. An example is machinery in a factory.

2) The HBU is in-exchange if the value-maximizing use is as a stand-alone asset. An example is a financial asset.

g. **Liabilities.** The FVM assumes transfer, not settlement.

3. **Valuation Techniques**

a. The following valuation techniques (approaches) are used to measure fair value:

1) The **market approach** is based on information, such as multiples of prices, from market transactions involving identical or comparable items.

2) The **income approach** uses valuation methods based on current market expectations about future amounts, e.g., earnings or cash flows.

a) It converts future amounts to one present discounted amount.
b) Examples are present value methods and option-pricing models.

3) The **cost approach** is based on current replacement cost. It is the cost to buy or build a comparable asset.

b. Inputs to valuation techniques are the pricing assumptions of market participants.

1) **Observable inputs** are based on market data obtained from independent sources.

2) **Unobservable inputs** are based on the entity's own assumptions about the assumptions of market participants that reflect the best available information.

a) An entity should maximize the use of relevant observable inputs and minimize the use of unobservable inputs.

4. **The Fair Value Hierarchy**

   a. **Level 1 inputs** are the **most reliable**. They are unadjusted quoted prices in active markets for identical assets or liabilities that the entity can access at the measurement date.

      1) EXAMPLE: If the entity has an investment in securities that are traded in an active market, the investment is measured within Level 1. The FVM equals the quantity of securities held times the securities' quoted price.

   b. **Level 2 inputs** are **observable**. But they exclude quoted prices included within Level 1. The following are examples:

      1) Quoted prices for similar items in active markets,
      2) Quoted prices in markets that are not active, and
      3) Observable inputs that are not quoted prices.

   c. **Level 3 inputs** are the **least reliable**. They are **unobservable** inputs that are used given no observable inputs. They should be based on the best available information in the circumstances. An example of a Level 3 input is the reporting entity's own data.

5. **Disclosures**

   a. **Quantitative disclosures** in a tabular format are made for **each class** of assets and liabilities measured at fair value in the balance sheet after initial recognition. The following are examples:

      1) Fair value measurement at the end of the reporting period
      2) The level of the fair value hierarchy within which the fair value measurements are categorized (Level 1, 2, or 3)
      3) A description of the valuation technique(s) and the inputs used in the fair value measurements categorized within Level 2 and Level 3
      4) Quantitative information about the significant unobservable inputs used in the fair value measurements categorized within Level 3
      5) A reconciliation from the opening balances to the closing balances for fair value measurements categorized within Level 3

   b. The appropriate classes of assets and liabilities are determined on the basis of the following:

      1) The nature, characteristics, and risks of the asset or liability
      2) The level of the fair value hierarchy within which the fair value measurement is categorized

STOP & REVIEW

You have completed the outline for this subunit.
Study multiple-choice questions 20 through 22 on page 130.

QUESTIONS

4.1 Significant Accounting Policies

1. Which of the following must be included in a summary of significant accounting policies in the notes to the financial statements?

A. Description of current year equity transactions.

B. Summary of long-term debt outstanding.

C. Schedule of fixed assets.

D. Revenue recognition policies.

Answer (D) is correct.

REQUIRED: The item in the summary of significant accounting policies.

DISCUSSION: Disclosure should include "important judgments as to appropriateness of principles related to recognition of revenue and allocation of asset costs to current and future periods."

2. Which of the following information should be included in Melay, Inc.'s current-year summary of significant accounting policies?

A. Property, plant, and equipment is recorded at cost with depreciation computed principally by the straight-line method.

B. During the current year, the consulting services operating segment was sold.

C. Operating segment current-year sales are $2 million for the software segment, $4 million for the book production segment, and $6 million for the technical services segment.

D. Future common share dividends are expected to approximate 60% of earnings.

Answer (A) is correct.

REQUIRED: The item properly disclosed in the summary of significant accounting policies.

DISCUSSION: The commonly required disclosures in a summary of significant accounting policies include (1) the basis of consolidation, (2) depreciation methods, (3) amortization of intangible assets, (4) inventory pricing, (5) recognition of profit on long-term construction-type contracts, (6) recognition of revenue from franchising and leasing operations, and (7) the policy for defining cash equivalents. Hence, the summary of significant accounting policies should include information about property, plant, and equipment depreciated by the straight-line method.

Answer (B) is incorrect. The sale of an operating segment is a transaction, not an accounting principle. It is reflected in the discontinued operations section of the income statement. **Answer (C) is incorrect.** Specific operating segment information does not constitute an accounting policy. An accounting policy is a specific principle or a method of applying it. **Answer (D) is incorrect.** Future dividend policy is not an accounting policy.

4.2 Segment Reporting

3. Which of the following qualifies as a reportable operating segment?

A. Corporate headquarters, which oversees $1 billion in sales for the entire company.

B. North American segment, whose assets are 12% of the company's assets of all segments, and management reports to the chief operating officer.

C. South American segment, whose results of operations are reported directly to the chief operating officer, and has 5% of the company's assets, 9% of revenues, and 8% of the profits.

D. Eastern Europe segment, which reports its results directly to the manager of the European division, and has 20% of the company's assets, 12% of revenues, and 11% of profits.

Answer (B) is correct.

REQUIRED: The reportable operating segment.

DISCUSSION: An operating segment engages in business activities, is reviewed by the company's chief operating decision maker, and has discrete financial information available. For an operating segment to be reportable, it must meet one or more of the following quantitative thresholds: (1) Reported revenue is at least 10% of the combined revenue of all operating segments; (2) reported profit or loss is at least 10% of the greater (in absolute amount) of the combined reported profit of all operating segments that did not incur a loss, or the combined reported loss of all operating segments that did report a loss; or (3) its assets are at least 10% of the combined assets of all operating segments. The North American segment holds 12% of the company's assets and reports to the chief operating officer, so it meets the requirements of an operating segment.

Answer (A) is incorrect. A corporate headquarters is not an operating segment. Any revenues it earns are incidental to the entity's activities. **Answer (C) is incorrect.** This segment does not meet the asset, revenue, or profit or loss quantitative threshold to qualify as an operating segment. **Answer (D) is incorrect.** This segment does not report to the chief operating decision maker.

4. Terra Co.'s total revenues from its three operating segments were as follows:

Segment	Sales to External Customers	Inter-segment Sales	Total Revenues
Lion	$ 70,000	$ 30,000	$100,000
Monk	22,000	4,000	26,000
Nevi	8,000	16,000	24,000
Combined	$100,000	$ 50,000	$150,000
Elimination	--	(50,000)	(50,000)
Consolidated	$100,000	$ --	$100,000

Which operating segment(s) can be deemed reportable?

A. None.

B. Lion only.

C. Lion and Monk only.

D. Lion, Monk, and Nevi.

Answer (D) is correct.

REQUIRED: The reportable operating segments in conformity with the revenue test.

DISCUSSION: For the purpose of identifying reportable operating segments, revenue is defined to include sales to external customers and intersegment sales or transfers. In accordance with the revenue test, a reportable operating segment has revenue equal to 10% or more of the total combined revenue, internal and external, of all of the entity's operating segments. Given combined revenues of $150,000, Lion, Monk, and Nevi all qualify because their revenues are at least $15,000 ($150,000 × 10%).

5. Opto Co. is a publicly traded, consolidated entity reporting segment information. Which of the following items is a required entity-wide disclosure regarding external customers?

A. The fact that transactions with a particular external customer constitute more than 10% of the total entity revenues.

B. The identity of any external customer providing 10% or more of a particular operating segment's revenue.

C. The identity of any external customer considered to be "major" by management.

D. Information on major customers is not required in segment reporting.

Answer (A) is correct.

REQUIRED: The entity-wide disclosure about external customers.

DISCUSSION: Information about products and services and geographical areas is reported if it is feasible to do so. If 10% or more of revenues is derived from one external customer, (1) that fact, (2) the amount from each such customer, and (3) the segment(s) reporting the revenues must be disclosed.

Answer (B) is incorrect. The identity of the segment(s) reporting the revenues must be disclosed, not that of the customer. **Answer (C) is incorrect.** The identity of any external customer, regardless of whether it meets the revenue criterion or is considered to be "major" by management, does not have to be disclosed. **Answer (D) is incorrect.** The entity must disclose information about sales to each major customer, that is, one providing at least 10% of revenues.

6. Hyde Corp. has three manufacturing divisions, each of which has been determined to be a reportable operating segment. In Year 4, Clay division had sales of $3 million, which was 25% of Hyde's total sales, and had traceable operating costs of $1.9 million. In Year 4, Hyde incurred operating costs of $500,000 that were not directly traceable to any of the divisions. In addition, Hyde incurred interest expense of $300,000 in Year 4. The calculation of the measure of segment profit or loss reviewed by Hyde's chief operating decision maker does not include an allocation of interest expense incurred by Hyde. However, it does include traceable costs. It also includes nontraceable operating costs allocated based on the ratio of divisional sales to aggregate sales. In reporting segment information, what amount should be shown as Clay's operating profit for Year 4?

A. $875,000

B. $900,000

C. $975,000

D. $1,100,000

Answer (C) is correct.

REQUIRED: The amount to be shown as profit for a reportable operating segment.

DISCUSSION: The amount of a segment item reported, such as profit or loss, is the measure reported to the chief operating decision maker for purposes of making resource allocation and performance evaluation decisions regarding the segment. However, the FASB does not stipulate the specific items included in the calculation of that measure. Consequently, allocation of revenues, expenses, gains, and losses are included in the determination of reported segment profit or loss only if they are included in the measure of segment profit or loss reviewed by the chief operating decision maker. Given that this measure for Clay reflects traceable costs and an allocation of nontraceable operating costs, the profit is calculated by subtracting the $1,900,000 traceable costs and the $125,000 ($500,000 × 25%) of the allocated costs from the division's sales of $3,000,000. The profit for the division is $975,000.

Sales	$ 3,000,000
Traceable costs	(1,900,000)
Allocated costs (25%)	(125,000)
Profit	$ 975,000

Answer (A) is incorrect. No amount of interest expense should be included in the calculation. **Answer (B) is incorrect.** Clay's share of interest expense ($300,000 × 25% = $75,000) is excluded from the calculation of profit. **Answer (D) is incorrect.** The allocated nontraceable operating costs must also be subtracted.

7. Correey Corp. and its divisions are engaged solely in manufacturing operations. The following data (consistent with prior years' data) pertain to the industries in which operations were conducted for the year ended December 31, Year 2:

Operating Segment	Total Revenue	Profit	Assets at 12/31/Yr 2
A	$10,000,000	$1,750,000	$20,000,000
B	8,000,000	1,400,000	17,500,000
C	6,000,000	1,200,000	12,500,000
D	3,000,000	550,000	7,500,000
E	4,250,000	675,000	7,000,000
F	1,500,000	225,000	3,000,000
	$32,750,000	$5,800,000	$67,500,000

In its segment information for Year 2, how many reportable segments does Correy have?

A. Three.

B. Four.

C. Five.

D. Six.

Answer (C) is correct.

REQUIRED: The number of reportable operating segments.

DISCUSSION: Four operating segments (A, B, C, and E) have revenue equal to or greater than 10% of the $32,750,000 total revenue of all operating segments. These four segments also have profit equal to or greater than 10% of the $5,800,000 total profit. Five segments (A, B, C, D, and E) have assets greater than 10% of the $67,500,000 total assets. Because an operating segment is reportable if it meets one or more of the three tests, Correy Corp. has five reportable segments for Year 2.

8. Bean Co. included interest expense and depreciation expense in its determination of segment profit, which Bean's chief financial officer considered in determining the segment's operating budget. Bean is required to report the segment's financial data in accordance with GAAP. Which of the following items should Bean disclose in reporting segment data?

	Interest expense	Depreciation expense
A.	No	No
B.	No	Yes
C.	Yes	No
D.	Yes	Yes

Answer (D) is correct.

REQUIRED: The items disclosed in segment data.

DISCUSSION: The objective is to provide information about the different types of business activities of the entity and the economic environments in which it operates. Disclosures include a measure of profit or loss and total assets for each reportable segment. Other items typically disclosed include revenues from external customers and other operating segments, interest revenue and expense, depreciation, depletion, amortization, unusual items, equity in the net income of equity-based investees, income tax expense or benefit, and other significant noncash items.

Answer (A) is incorrect. Items that contribute to the profit and loss of a segment and are reviewed by the chief operating decision maker should be disclosed in the segment's data. **Answer (B) is incorrect.** Interest expense affects the profit and loss of a reportable segment and is reviewed by the chief operating decision maker. It should be reported. **Answer (C) is incorrect.** Depreciation expense affects the profit and loss of a reportable segment and is reviewed by the chief operating decision maker. It should be reported.

4.3 Interim Financial Reporting

9. On January 16, Tree Co. paid $60,000 in property taxes on its factory for the current calendar year. On April 2, Tree paid $240,000 for unanticipated major repairs to its factory equipment. The repairs will benefit operations for the remainder of the calendar year. What amount of these expenses should Tree include in its third quarter interim financial statements for the 3 months ended September 30?

A. $0

B. $15,000

C. $75,000

D. $95,000

Answer (D) is correct.

REQUIRED: The expenses included in the interim statements.

DISCUSSION: Property taxes are accrued or deferred at interim dates to assign an appropriate cost to each period. Moreover, annual major repairs are allocated to the periods benefited. Thus, the benefit from the payment of the property taxes relates to all four quarters of the current year. It should be prorated at $15,000 ($60,000 ÷ 4) per quarter. The benefit from the unanticipated repairs relates to the second, third, and fourth quarters. It should be allocated to these quarters at $80,000 ($240,000 ÷ 3) per quarter. Thus, the amount of these expenses recognized in the third quarter is $95,000 ($15,000 + $80,000).

Answer (A) is incorrect. The property tax payments and repairs benefited the third quarter. **Answer (B) is incorrect.** An allocation of repairs expense should be made to the third quarter. **Answer (C) is incorrect.** The amount of $75,000 includes an allocation of repairs expense of only $60,000, implying an assignment to all four quarters instead of the three benefited.

10. Because of a decline in market price in the second quarter, Petal Co. incurred an inventory loss, but the market price was expected to return to previous levels by the end of the year. At the end of the year, the decline had not reversed. Petal accounts for its inventory using the LIFO method. When should the loss be reported in Petal's interim income statements?

A. Ratably over the second, third, and fourth quarters.

B. Ratably over the third and fourth quarters.

C. In the second quarter only.

D. In the fourth quarter only.

Answer (D) is correct.

REQUIRED: The true statement about reporting inventory at interim dates when a market decline is expected to reverse by year end but does not.

DISCUSSION: A decline below cost reasonably expected to be restored within the fiscal year may be deferred at an interim reporting date because no loss is anticipated for the year. (Inventory losses from nontemporary market declines must be recognized at the interim reporting date.) Consequently, Petal would not have reported the market decline until it determined at the end of the fourth quarter that the expected reversal would not occur.

11. During the first quarter of Year 4, Tech Co. had income before taxes of $200,000, and its effective income tax rate was 15%. Tech's Year 3 effective annual income tax rate was 30%, but Tech expects its Year 4 effective annual income tax rate to be 25%. In its first quarter interim income statement, what amount of income tax expense should Tech report?

A. $0

B. $30,000

C. $50,000

D. $60,000

Answer (C) is correct.

REQUIRED: The provision for income taxes for the first interim period.

DISCUSSION: At the end of each interim period, the entity should estimate the annual effective tax rate. This rate is used in providing for income taxes on a current year-to-date basis. Tech's income before taxes for the first quarter is $200,000, and the estimated annual effective tax rate for Year 4 is 25%. The provision for income taxes for the first interim period is therefore $50,000 ($200,000 × 25%).

Answer (A) is incorrect. Zero excludes any income tax expense. **Answer (B) is incorrect.** The amount of $30,000 uses Tech's quarterly effective income tax rate. **Answer (D) is incorrect.** The amount of $60,000 uses Tech's Year 3 effective annual income tax rate.

12. Conceptually, interim financial statements can be described as emphasizing

A. Timeliness over reliability.
B. Reliability over relevance.
C. Relevance over comparability.
D. Comparability over neutrality.

Answer (A) is correct.
REQUIRED: The emphasis of interim statements.
DISCUSSION: Interim financial statements cover periods of less than 1 year. Because of (1) the seasonality of some businesses, (2) the need for increased use of estimates, (3) the need for allocations of costs and expenses among interim periods, and (4) other factors, the usefulness of the information provided by interim financial statements may be limited. Hence, they emphasize timeliness over reliability.

13. In general, an enterprise preparing interim financial statements should

A. Defer recognition of seasonal revenue.
B. Disregard permanent decreases in the market value of its inventory.
C. Allocate revenues and expenses evenly over the quarters, regardless of when they actually occurred.
D. Use the same accounting principles followed in preparing its latest annual financial statements.

Answer (D) is correct.
REQUIRED: The method of preparing interim financial statements.
DISCUSSION: Each interim period is an integral part of an annual period. Ordinarily, interim results are based on the same principles applied in annual statements. Certain principles and practices used for annual reporting, however, may require modification so that interim reports may relate more closely to the results of operations for the annual period.
Answer (A) is incorrect. Seasonal revenue is not deferred. However, an entity with material seasonal fluctuations must disclose the seasonal nature of its activities and should consider making additional disclosures. **Answer (B) is incorrect.** Inventory losses from nontemporary market declines must be recognized at the interim date. Recovery during the fiscal year is treated as a change in estimate. **Answer (C) is incorrect.** Revenue is recognized as earned during an interim period on the same basis followed for the annual period.

14. A loss from a market price decline on inventory accounted for under the LIFO method occurred in the first quarter. The loss was not expected to be restored in the fiscal year. However, in the third quarter the inventory had a market price recovery that exceeded the market decline that occurred in the first quarter. For interim financial reporting, the dollar amount of net inventory should

A. Decrease in the first quarter by the amount of the market price decline and increase in the third quarter by the amount of the market price recovery.
B. Decrease in the first quarter by the amount of the market price decline and increase in the third quarter by the amount of decrease in the first quarter.
C. Decrease in the first quarter by the amount of the market price decline and not be affected in the third quarter.
D. Not be affected in either the first quarter or the third quarter.

Answer (B) is correct.
REQUIRED: The proper interim financial reporting of a market decline and a market price recovery.
DISCUSSION: A market price decline in inventory must be recognized in the interim period in which it occurs unless it is expected to be temporary, i.e., unless the decline is expected to be restored by the end of the fiscal year. This loss was not expected to be restored in the fiscal year, and the company should report the dollar amount of the market price decline as a loss in the first quarter. Inventory may never be written up to an amount above its original cost. Accordingly, the market price recovery recognized in the third quarter is limited to the extent of losses previously recognized in a prior interim period.
Answer (A) is incorrect. The recovery recognized in the third quarter is limited to the amount of the losses previously recognized. **Answer (C) is incorrect.** Assuming no market price decline had been recognized prior to the current year, the first quarter loss and the third quarter recovery would be offsetting. The recognized third quarter gain is limited to the amount of the first quarter loss, and the year-end results would not be affected. **Answer (D) is incorrect.** The inventory amount is affected in both the first and third quarters.

4.4 Significant Risks, Uncertainties, and Going Concern

15. Financial statements must disclose significant risks and uncertainties. The required disclosures include

A. Quantified comparisons of the relative importance of the different businesses in which the entity operates.

B. Information about a significant estimate used to value an asset only if it is probable that the financial statement effect of a condition existing at the balance sheet date will change materially in the near term.

C. Risk-reduction techniques that have successfully mitigated losses.

D. Vulnerability due to a concentration if a near-term severe impact is at least reasonably possible.

Answer (D) is correct.

REQUIRED: The required disclosure.

DISCUSSION: The current vulnerability due to concentrations must be disclosed if certain conditions are met. Disclosure is necessary if management knows prior to issuance of the statements that the concentration exists at the balance sheet date; it makes the entity vulnerable to a near-term severe impact; and such impact is at least reasonably possible in the near term. A severe impact may result from loss of all or a part of a business relationship, price or demand changes, loss of a patent, changes in the availability of a resource or right, or the disruption of operations in a market or geographic area.

Answer (A) is incorrect. Disclosures about the nature of operations need not be quantified. **Answer (B) is incorrect.** A material financial statement effect need only be reasonably possible in the near term. **Answer (C) is incorrect.** The criteria for required disclosures about significant estimates may not be met if the entity has successfully employed risk-reduction techniques. In these circumstances, disclosure of those techniques is encouraged but not required.

4.5 Subsequent Events

16. On January 15, Year 2, before the Mapleview Co. released its financial statements for the year ended December 31, Year 1, it settled a long-standing lawsuit. A material loss resulted and no prior liability had been recorded. How should this loss be disclosed or recognized in the Year 1 financial statements?

A. The loss should be disclosed, but the financial statements themselves need not be adjusted.

B. The loss should be disclosed in an explanatory paragraph in the auditor's report.

C. No disclosure or recognition is required.

D. The loss must be recognized in the financial statements.

Answer (D) is correct.

REQUIRED: The proper treatment of a material loss on an existing lawsuit after year end.

DISCUSSION: Subsequent events that provide additional evidence with the respect to conditions that existed at the balance sheet date, including the estimates inherent in preparing the financial statements, must be recognized in the financial statements of the year affected by the subsequent event. Settlement of a lawsuit is indicative of conditions existing at year end and calls for recognition in the statements.

Answer (A) is incorrect. The loss must be recognized in the financial statements. **Answer (B) is incorrect.** The audit report need not be modified. **Answer (C) is incorrect.** Failure to recognize a material loss on an asset that existed at year end is a departure from GAAP.

17. Zero Corp. suffered a loss that would have a material effect on its financial statements on an uncollectible trade account receivable due to a customer's bankruptcy. This occurred suddenly due to a natural disaster 10 days after Zero's balance sheet date but 1 month before the issuance of the financial statements. Under these circumstances,

	The Loss Must Be Recognized in the Financial Statements	The Event Requires Financial Statement Disclosure Only
A.	Yes	Yes
B.	Yes	No
C.	No	No
D.	No	Yes

Answer (D) is correct.

REQUIRED: The effect on the financial statements of a customer's bankruptcy after the balance sheet date but before the issuance of the statements.

DISCUSSION: Certain subsequent events may provide additional evidence about conditions at the date of the balance sheet, including estimates inherent in the preparation of statements. These events require recognition in the statements at year end. Other subsequent events provide evidence about conditions not existing at the date of the balance sheet but arising subsequent to that date and before the issuance of the statements or their availability for issuance. These events may require disclosure but not recognition in the statements. Thus, the loss must not be recognized in Zero's statements, but disclosure must be made.

4.6 Financial Instruments

18. Disclosure of information about significant concentrations of credit risk is required for

A. Most financial instruments.

B. Financial instruments with off-balance-sheet credit risk only.

C. Financial instruments with off-balance-sheet market risk only.

D. Financial instruments with off-balance-sheet risk of accounting loss only.

Answer (A) is correct.

REQUIRED: The financial instruments for which disclosure of significant concentrations of credit risk is required.

DISCUSSION: GAAP require the disclosure of information about the fair value of financial instruments, whether recognized or not (certain nonpublic entities and certain instruments, such as leases and insurance contracts, are exempt from the disclosure requirements). GAAP also require disclosure of all significant concentrations of credit risk for most financial instruments (except for obligations for deferred compensation, certain instruments of a pension plan, insurance contracts, warranty obligations and rights, and unconditional purchase obligations).

19. Where in its financial statements should a company disclose information about its concentration of credit risks?

A. No disclosure is required.

B. The notes to the financial statements.

C. Supplementary information to the financial statements.

D. Management's report to shareholders.

Answer (B) is correct.

REQUIRED: The method of disclosure about concentration of credit risk.

DISCUSSION: An entity must disclose significant concentrations of risk arising from most instruments. These disclosures should be made in the basic financial statements, either in the body of the statements or in the notes.

Answer (A) is incorrect. Disclosure in the basic statements is required. **Answer (C) is incorrect.** Disclosure in supplementary information is normally done when certain entities are excluded from the scope of the requirements. However, the required disclosures are to be made by all entities. **Answer (D) is incorrect.** Management's report to shareholders is not part of the basic statements.

4.7 Fair Value Measurements

20. Fair value measurement (FVM) of an asset or liability is based on a fair value hierarchy that establishes priorities among inputs to valuation techniques. According to the hierarchy,

A. Observable inputs are on Level 1.

B. Unobservable inputs are on Level 2.

C. Quoted prices for items similar to the asset or liability are on Level 3.

D. Unadjusted quoted prices for an identical asset or liability are on Level 1.

Answer (D) is correct.

REQUIRED: The appropriate level of the fair value hierarchy for inputs to valuation techniques.

DISCUSSION: The level of the FVM depends on the lowest level input significant to the entire FVM. Level 1 inputs are unadjusted quoted prices in active markets for identical assets (liabilities) that the entity can access at the measurement date. An adjustment for new information results in a lower level FVM.

Answer (A) is incorrect. Observable inputs that are not Level 1 quoted prices are on Level 2. Examples are quoted prices for similar items in active markets and quoted prices in markets that are not active. **Answer (B) is incorrect.** Level 3 inputs are unobservable. They are used in the absence of observable inputs and should be based on the best available information in the circumstances. **Answer (C) is incorrect.** Quoted prices for items similar (not identical) to the asset or liability are on Level 2.

21. For the purpose of a fair value measurement (FVM) of an asset or liability, a transaction is assumed to occur in the

A. Principal market if one exists.

B. Most advantageous market.

C. Market in which the result is optimized.

D. Principal market or most advantageous market at the election of the reporting entity.

Answer (A) is correct.

REQUIRED: The market in which a transaction is assumed to occur.

DISCUSSION: For FVM purposes, a transaction is assumed to occur in the principal market for an asset or liability if one exists. The principal market has the greatest volume or level of activity. If no such market exists, the transaction is assumed to occur in the most advantageous market.

22. Each of the following would be considered a Level 2 observable input that could be used to determine an asset or liability's fair value **except**

A. Quoted prices for identical assets and liabilities in markets that are not active.

B. Quoted prices for similar assets and liabilities in markets that are active.

C. Internally generated cash flow projections for a related asset or liability.

D. Interest rates that are observable at commonly quoted intervals.

Answer (C) is correct.

REQUIRED: The Level 2 observable inputs.

DISCUSSION: Internally generated cash flow projections are not observable and would be considered a Level 3 input. Level 3 inputs are unobservable inputs that are used in the absence of observable inputs. They should be based on the best available information in the circumstances.

Answer (A) is incorrect. Quoted prices for identical assets and liabilities in markets that are not active is an example of a Level 2 input. Level 2 inputs are observable. **Answer (B) is incorrect.** Quoted prices for similar assets and liabilities in markets that are active is an example of a Level 2 input. Level 2 inputs are observable. **Answer (D) is incorrect.** Interest rates that are observable at commonly quoted intervals are an example of a Level 2 input. Level 2 inputs are observable.

STUDY UNIT FIVE

CASH AND INVESTMENTS

(27 pages of outline)

The first subunit applies to **cash**, the most liquid of assets. It includes **cash equivalents**, a special category of assets so close to conversion to cash that they are classified with cash on the balance sheet. **Securities held as investments** are reported in different classifications on the balance sheet. Other matters, such as the **equity method** of accounting for investments in common stock and investments in **bonds**, also are covered.

5.1 CASH

1. **Nature of Cash**
   a. Cash is the **most liquid of assets**. Because of that liquidity and the ability to transfer it electronically, internal control of cash must be strong.
   b. As the customary **medium of exchange**, it also provides the **standard of value** (the unit of measurement) of the transactions that are reported in the financial statements.
   c. Cash is classified as a **current asset** unless its use is restricted to such purposes as payments to sinking funds.
      1) In this case, cash is reported as a noncurrent asset with an account title such as bond sinking fund.
2. **Readily Available**
   a. To be classified as current, cash must be readily available for use. The cash account on the balance sheet should consist of
      1) Coin and currency on hand, including petty cash and change funds
      2) Demand deposits (checking accounts)
      3) Time deposits (savings accounts)
      4) Near-cash assets
         a) They include many negotiable instruments, such as money orders, bank drafts, certified checks, cashiers' checks, and personal checks.
         b) They are usually in the process of being deposited (deposits in transit).
         c) They must be depositable. They exclude unsigned and postdated checks.
         d) Checks written to creditors but not mailed or delivered at the balance sheet date should be included in the payor's cash account (not considered cash payments at year end).

3. **Restricted Cash**
   a. Restricted cash is not actually set aside in special accounts. However, it is designated for special uses and should be separately presented and disclosed in the notes.
      1) Examples are bond sinking funds, new building funds, and restricted compensating balances.
      2) The nature of the use determines whether cash is current or noncurrent.
         a) A bond sinking fund used to redeem noncurrent bond debt is noncurrent, but a fund to be used to redeem bonds currently redeemable is a current asset.
4. **Compensating Balances**
   a. As part of an agreement regarding either an existing loan or the provision of future credit, a borrower may keep an average or minimum amount on deposit with the lender. This compensating balance increases the effective rate of interest paid by the borrower.
   b. It also creates a disclosure issue because the full amount reported as cash might not be available to meet general obligations.
5. **Cash Equivalents**
   a. Cash equivalents are short-term, highly liquid investments. Common examples are Treasury bills, money market funds, and commercial paper.
   b. Cash equivalents are
      1) Readily convertible to known amounts of cash and
      2) So near maturity that interest rate risk is insignificant.
         a) Only investments with an **original maturity to the holder of 3 months or less** qualify.

EXAMPLE 5-1 Cash Equivalents

Debtor issues a note with a 2-year maturity to Creditor. After 1 year and 10 months, Creditor sells the note to Holder. The original maturity to Holder is 2 months. If the note is highly liquid, it may be a cash equivalent. The note would not have been a cash equivalent to Creditor at the date of sale.

6. **Noncash Items**
   a. **Nonsufficient funds (NSF) checks** and postdated checks should be treated as receivables. Advances for expenses to employees may be classified as receivables (if expected to be paid by employees) or as prepaid expenses.
   b. An **overdraft** is a current liability unless the entity has sufficient funds in another account at the same bank to cover it.
   c. **Noncash short-term investments** are usually substantially restricted and thus not readily available for use by the entity. They should be classified as current or temporary investments, not cash. However, they may qualify as cash equivalents.
      1) Money market funds are essentially mutual funds that have portfolios of commercial paper and Treasury bills. However, a money market fund with a usable checking feature might be better classified as cash.
      2) Commercial paper (also known as negotiable instruments) consists of short-term (no more than 270 days) corporate obligations.
      3) Treasury bills are short-term, guaranteed U.S. government obligations.
      4) Certificates of deposit are formal debt instruments issued by a bank or other financial institution and are subject to penalties for withdrawal before maturity.

7. **Recording Cash**

   a. Cash may be recorded in a general ledger control account, with a subsidiary ledger for each bank account. An alternative is a series of general ledger accounts.

      1) On the balance sheet, one account is presented. It reflects all unrestricted cash.

      2) Each transfer of cash from one account to another requires an entry.

      3) At the end of each period, a schedule of transfers should be prepared and reviewed to make certain all cash transfers are counted only once.

8. **Bank Reconciliation**

SUCCESS TIP

The AICPA has released bank reconciliation problems that test cash reporting on the exam. CPA candidates may see a bank reconciliation problem on the CPA Exam.

   a. A bank reconciliation is a schedule comparing the cash balance per books with the balance per bank statement (usually received monthly). The common approach is to reconcile the bank balance to the book balance to reach the true balance.

      1) The bank and book balances usually vary. Thus, the reconciliation permits the entity to determine whether the difference is attributable to normal conditions, error, or fraud. It is also a basis for entries to adjust the books to reflect unrecorded items.

      2) The bank and the entity inevitably record many transactions at different times. Both also may make errors.

   b. **Items Known to Entity but Not Known to Bank**

      1) **Outstanding checks.** The books may reflect checks written by the entity that have not yet cleared the bank. These amounts are subtracted from the bank balance to arrive at the true balance.

      2) **Deposits in transit.** A time lag may occur between deposit of receipts and the bank's recording of the transaction. Thus, receipts placed in a night depository on the last day of the month are reflected only in the next month's bank statement. These receipts are added to the bank balance to arrive at the true balance.

      3) **Errors.** If the bank has wrongly charged or credited the entity's account (or failed to record a transaction at all), the error will be detected in the process of preparing the reconciliation.

   c. **Items Known to Bank but Not Known to Entity**

      1) **Amounts added by the bank.** Interest income added to an account may not be included in the book balance. Banks may act as collection agents, for example, for notes on which the depositor is the payee. If the depositor has not learned of a collection, it will not be reflected in its records.

         a) These amounts are added to the book balance to arrive at the true balance.

         b) They should be recorded on the entity's books, after which they are no longer reconciling items.

2) **Amounts subtracted (or not added) by the bank.** These amounts generally include service charges and customer checks returned for insufficient funds (NSF checks). Service charges cannot be recorded in the books until the bank statement is received. Customer checks returned for insufficient funds are not added to the bank balance but are still included in the book balance.

   a) These amounts are subtracted from the book balance to get the true balance.

   b) They should be recorded on the entity's books, after which they are no longer reconciling items.

3) **Errors.** Bookkeeping errors made by the entity will likewise be discovered.

d. **Common Reconciliation Items**

	To Book Balance	To Bank Balance
Additions	Interest earned Deposits collected Errors	Deposits in transit Errors
Subtractions	Service charges NSF checks Errors	Outstanding checks Errors

EXAMPLE 5-2 Bank Reconciliation

Raughley Company's bank statement on March 31 indicated a balance of $6,420. The book balance on that date was $7,812. The bank balance did not include $3,229 of receipts for March 31 that were deposited on that day but were not recorded until April 1 by the bank. It also did not include $450 of checks written in March that did not clear until April. The March bank statement revealed that (1) the bank had collected $1,500 in March on a note owed to Raughley, (2) a $160 customer check had been returned for insufficient funds, and (3) service charges totaled $7. Finally, a check for $60 written by Raughley cleared the bank for $6.

Book balance – March 31		$7,812
Add items on bank statement not on books:		
Note proceeds	$1,500	1,500
Subtract items on bank statement not on books:		
Service charges	$ (7)	
Deposited check returned NSF	(160)	(167)
True cash balance – March 31		**$9,145**
Bank balance – March 31		$6,420
Add items on books not on bank statement:		
Deposits in transit	$3,229	3,229
Subtract items on books not on bank statement:		
Bank error: $60 check cleared for $6	$ (54)	
Outstanding checks	(450)	(504)
True cash balance – March 31		**$9,145**

STOP & REVIEW

You have completed the outline for this subunit.
Study multiple-choice questions 1 through 3 beginning on page 158.

5.2 FAIR VALUE OPTION (FVO)

1. **Scope**
   a. The FVO allows entities to measure most recognized financial assets and liabilities at **fair value**.
   b. An entity **may elect** the **FVO** for most recognized financial assets and liabilities.
   c. The FVO **may not be elected** for the following:
      1) An investment that must be consolidated
         a) The FVO is not an alternative to consolidation.
         b) Consolidation is required for subsidiaries and variable interest entities. Study Unit 15 addresses these topics.
      2) Postretirement employee benefit obligations, employee stock option and purchase plans, and deferred compensation obligations
      3) Most financial assets and liabilities under leases
      4) Demand deposit liabilities
      5) Financial instruments at least partly classified in equity
2. **Election of the FVO**
   a. The decision whether to elect the FVO is **made irrevocably at an election date** (unless a new election date occurs).
      1) With certain exceptions, the decision is made **instrument by instrument** and only for an **entire instrument**.
      2) Thus, the FVO generally need **not** be applied to all instruments in a single transaction.
         a) For example, it might be applied only to some of the shares or bonds issued or acquired in a transaction.
   b. The election may be made only on the date of one of the following:
      1) Initial recognition of an eligible item
      2) Making an eligible firm commitment
      3) A change in accounting for an investment in another entity because it becomes subject to the **equity method**
      4) Deconsolidation of a subsidiary

3. FVO – Presentation of Financial Assets and Liabilities

a. Balance Sheet

1) Under the FVO, financial assets and liabilities are measured at **fair value** each balance sheet date.
2) Assets and liabilities measured using the FVO are reported by separating their reported fair values from the carrying amounts of similar items measured using another attribute, such as amortized cost or present value.

b. Income Statement

1) Transaction costs related to the acquisition of an item for which the FVO was elected must be expensed as incurred. They must not be capitalized at the initial cost of the item.
2) Dividends received from an investment that is accounted for using the FVO are recognized as dividend income.

c. Changes in the Fair Value of Financial Assets

1) Under the FVO, **unrealized holding gains and losses** on the remeasurement to fair value of financial assets are recognized in the **income statement** (net income) at each subsequent reporting date.

EXAMPLE 5-3 FVO for Financial Asset

On October 1, Year 1, Mill Co. purchased 5,000 shares of Floss Co.'s common stock, out of a total of 20,000 outstanding, for their fair value. Mill elected the fair value option for its investment in the common stock of Floss. The following are the fair values per share of Floss common stock:

Date	Fair Value
October 1, Year 1	$15
December 31, Year 1	13
December 31, Year 2	20

October 1, Year 1

Investment – FVO (5,000 × $15)	$75,000	
Cash		$75,000

December 31, Year 1

At each balance sheet date, an investment accounted for using the FVO is remeasured at fair value. Unrealized holding gains and losses are reported in earnings.

Unrealized holding loss on FVO investment [5,000 × ($15 – $13)]	$10,000	
Investment – FVO		$10,000

In Mill's December 31, Year 1, balance sheet, the investment in Floss is measured at year-end fair value of $65,000 (5,000 × $13).

December 31, Year 2

Investment – FVO [5,000 × ($20 – $13)]	$35,000	
Unrealized holding gain on FVO investment		$35,000

In Mill's December 31, Year 2, balance sheet, the investment in Floss is measured at year-end fair value of $100,000 (5,000 × $20).

d. **Changes in the Fair Value of Financial Liabilities**

1) Under the FVO, unrealized gains and losses on the remeasurement to fair value of **financial liabilities** are recognized in the statement of comprehensive income.

a) The portion of the total change in the fair value attributable to the **change in instrument-specific credit risk** is recognized as an item of **other comprehensive income** (OCI).

i) This amount is the difference between

- The total change in the fair value of the financial liability and
- The amount that results from a change in a base market risk, such as a risk-free interest rate.

b) The **remaining change in fair value** (total change in fair value – change attributable to instrument-specific credit risk) is recognized directly in the **income statement**.

c) When the financial liability is derecognized, the accumulated gains or losses due to changes in instrument-specific credit risk are reclassified from OCI to the income statement.

EXAMPLE 5-4 FVO for Financial Liability

The following amounts are for a financial liability accounted for using the fair value option:

Fair value on January 1, Year 1	$ 9,000
Fair value on December 31, Year 1	15,000
Change in fair value attributable to instrument-specific credit risk	2,000

Year 1 total unrealized loss on the financial liability is $6,000 ($15,000 – $9,000). The $2,000 change in fair value attributable to instrument-specific credit risk is recognized in OCI. The remaining $4,000 change in fair value ($6,000 – $2,000) is recognized in the income statement.

Unrealized loss – OCI	$2,000	
Unrealized loss – Income statement	4,000	
Financial liability – FVO		$6,000

STOP & REVIEW

You have completed the outline for this subunit.
Study multiple-choice questions 4 and 5 on page 160.

5.3 INVESTMENTS IN EQUITY SECURITIES

1. **Overview**
   a. An **equity security** is an **ownership** interest in an entity (e.g., common stock or preferred stock) or a right to acquire or dispose of such an interest (e.g., warrants or call options).
      1) Convertible debt securities are not equity interests in the issuer.
   b. This subunit applies to all investments in equity securities **except** for investments
      1) Accounted for under the equity method
      2) In consolidated subsidiaries
      3) For which the entity has elected the FVO
   c. The accounting method for an investment in voting stock depends on the presumed influence the investor has over the investee.
      1) The presumed influence usually is determined based on the ownership interest held.
      2) The following table depicts the three possibilities:

Percentage Ownership	Presumed Influence	Accounting Method
100% – 50%	Control	Consolidation
50% – 20%	Significant	Equity Method or FVO
20% – 0%	Little or none	Fair Value Measurement

Figure 5-1

2. **Measurement of an Investment in Equity Securities**
   a. The investment is measured at **fair value** at each balance sheet date.
   b. **Unrealized holding gains and losses** on the remeasurement of the investment to fair value are reported in the **income statement** (net income) at each subsequent reporting date.
   c. Dividends received from investments in equity securities are reported as dividend income in the income statement.
   d. Cash flows from purchases and sales of equity securities are classified in the statement of cash flows based on the nature and purpose for which the securities were acquired.

EXAMPLE 5-5 Fair Value through Net Income Approach

On November 1, Year 1, Abi Co. purchased 200 shares of Gail Co.'s common stock at fair value. This investment is less than 1% of the ownership interests in Gail Co. The following are the fair values per share of Gail common stock at the relevant dates:

Date	Fair Value
November 1, Year 1	$100
December 31, Year 1	90
December 31, Year 2	115

November 1, Year 1

Investment in equity securities (200 × $100)	$20,000	
Cash		$20,000

This investment in equity securities of Gail Co. is reported at fair value through net income on each balance sheet date.

December 31, Year 1

Unrealized holding loss [200 × ($90 – $100)]	$2,000	
Investment in equity securities		$2,000

In Abi's December 31, Year 1, balance sheet, the investment in equity securities of Gail Co. is reported at its fair value of $18,000 (200 × $90). In the Year 1 income statement, a loss of $2,000 is recognized.

December 31, Year 2

Investment in equity securities [200 × ($115 – $90)]	$5,000	
Unrealized holding gain		$5,000

In Abi's December 31, Year 2, balance sheet, the investment in equity securities of Gail Co. is reported at its fair value of $23,000 (200 × $115). In the Year 2 income statement, a gain of $5,000 is recognized.

3. **Measurement Alternative for Investment in Equity Securities without a Readily Determinable Fair Value**

   a. **Measurement Alternative**

      1) An entity may elect a measurement alternative for an investment in equity securities without a readily determinable fair value.

         a) This alternative is **cost minus impairment** (if any), **plus or minus** changes resulting from observable price changes for the identical or a similar investment of the same issuer.

      2) If the measurement alternative is selected, it must be applied until the investment has a readily determinable fair value.

         a) The entity must reassess at each reporting period whether the fair value of an equity investment is readily determinable.

         b) When the fair value of an equity investment is readily determinable, the investment is measured at fair value through net income.

b. **Impairment Test**

1) A qualitative assessment of whether an investment is impaired must be performed at each reporting date. An investment is impaired if the fair value of the investment is lower than its carrying amount.

a) A **qualitative** assessment may consider many impairment indicators, such as significant deterioration in earnings performance, credit rating, or asset quality.

2) If the qualitative assessment indicates potential impairment, the entity must estimate the fair value of the investment and perform a **quantitative** impairment test.

a) The carrying amount of the investment is compared with its fair value. An impairment loss is recognized in the income statement (net income) for the excess of the carrying amount over the fair value.

Impairment loss = Carrying amount – Fair value

c. **Observable Price Changes**

1) To identify observable price changes, a reasonable effort should be made to identify relevant transactions by the same issuer that occurred on or before the balance sheet date. Accordingly, an entity does not need to make an exhaustive search for all observable price changes.

d. **Similar Investment of the Same Issuer**

1) Different rights and obligations of the securities should be considered when identifying whether a security issued by the same issuer is similar to the equity investment.

4. **Decision Tree: Classification and Measurement of an Investment in Equity Securities**

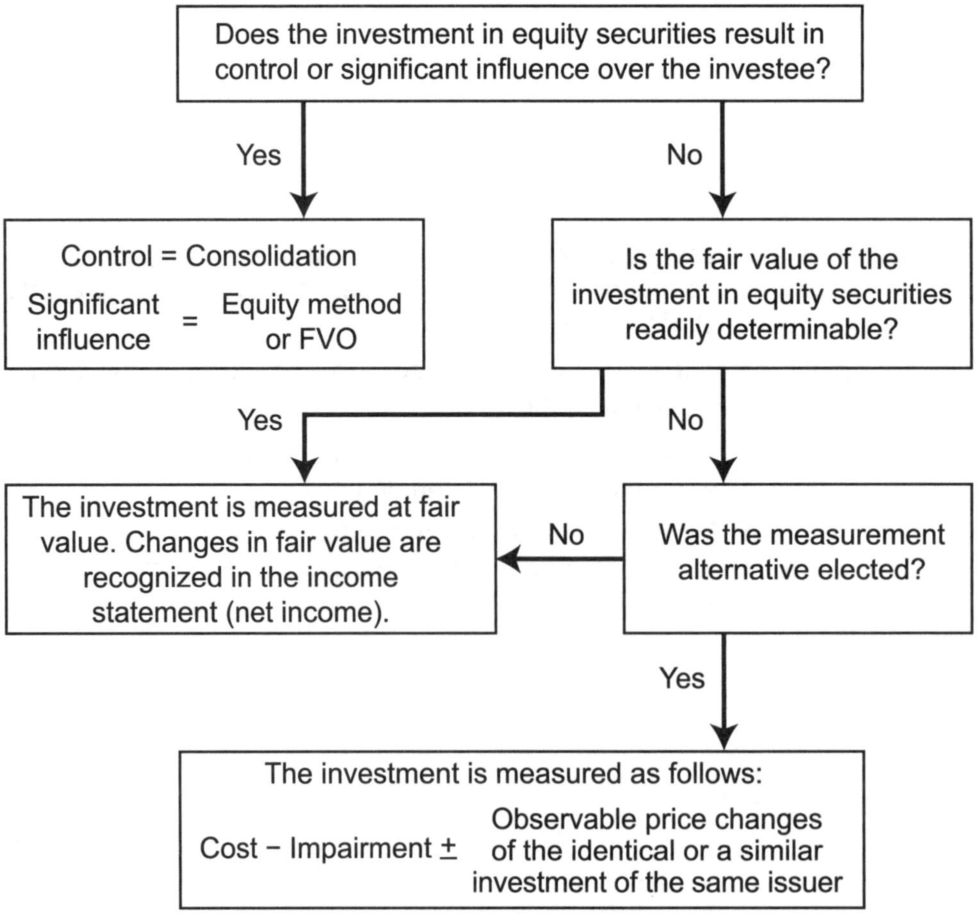

Figure 5-2

IFRS DIFFERENCE

1. An investment in equity securities that does not result in significant influence or in control over the investee is measured at **fair value through profit or loss** (as under U.S. GAAP). However, the investor also **may** irrevocably elect at initial recognition to measure the investment in equity securities that is not held for trading at **fair value through OCI**. The holding gains and losses accumulated in OCI are never reclassified to profit or loss even when the investment is sold.
2. The measurement alternative is not an option under IFRS. Under IFRS, an investment in equity securities that does not result in significant influence or in control over the investee is measured at fair value.
3. Decision Tree for Classification and Measurement of an Investment in Equity Securities

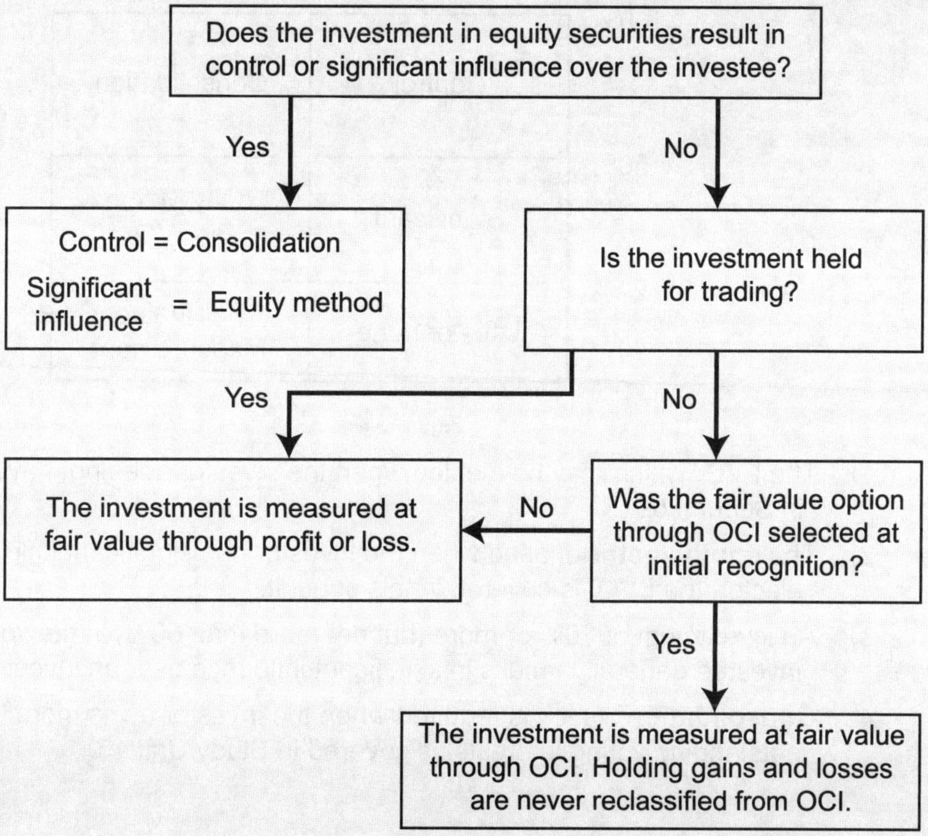

Figure 5-3

STOP & REVIEW

You have completed the outline for this subunit.
Study multiple-choice questions 6 through 8 beginning on page 161.

5.4 EQUITY METHOD

1. **Significant Influence**

   a. An investment in voting stock that enables the investor to exercise significant influence over the investee should be accounted for by the equity method (assuming no FVO election).

   b. The accounting method used by the investor depends on its presumed influence based on the ownership interest held. The following table depicts the three possibilities:

Percentage Ownership	Presumed Influence	Accounting Method
100% – 50%	Control	Consolidation
50% – 20%	Significant	Equity Method or FVO
20% – 0%	Little or none	Fair Value Measurement

Figure 5-4

      1) The **FVO**, which may be elected when the investor does not have control, is covered in Subunit 5.2.
      2) The **equity method**, used when the investor has significant influence and has not elected the FVO, is covered in this subunit.
      3) An investment of 20% or more (but not more than 50%) in the voting stock of the investee generally results in significant influence over an investee.
      4) **Consolidation**, which is required when the investor owns more than 50% of the outstanding voting interests, is covered in Study Unit 15.

IFRS DIFFERENCE

When the investor has significant influence, the equity method must be applied unless

1) The investment is classified as held for sale or
2) Conditions exist similar to those that would exempt a parent from preparing consolidated statements.

SUCCESS TIP

CPA candidates should expect to see questions on applying the equity method to investments. Past exam questions most often have required calculations to test candidates' understanding of this topic.

2. **Applying the Equity Method at the Acquisition Date**

   a. An equity method investment is initially recognized at cost. The difference between the cost of the investment and the underlying equity in the investee's net assets may consist of the following:

      1) **Equity method goodwill.** Goodwill resulting from the acquisition is the difference between the consideration transferred (cost of the investment) and the investor's equity in the fair value of the investee's net assets.

         a) Equity method goodwill is **not** a separately identifiable asset. Accordingly, it is **not recognized and presented separately** in the investor's financial statements. Instead, it is included in the carrying amount of the equity method investment.

         b) Equity method goodwill is not amortized. The equity method investment (but not the equity method goodwill itself, which is inseparable from the investment) is tested for impairment.

EXAMPLE 5-6 Equity Method Investment and Goodwill

On March 1, GRV Co. purchased 25% of Minion Co.'s outstanding common stock for $130,000. On that date, the carrying amount and fair value of Minion's net assets was $400,000.

Goodwill resulting from the acquisition is calculated as follows:

Cost of the investment	$130,000
Equity in the fair value of investee's net assets ($400,000 × 25%)	(100,000)
Equity method goodwill	$ 30,000

Investment in Minion Co.	$130,000	
Cash		$130,000

      2) The investor's equity is the difference between the acquisition date fair value and the carrying amount of each identifiable asset or liability of the investee.

EXAMPLE 5-7 Equity Method Investment and Goodwill -- Plant Asset

Using the data from Example 5-6, assume that on March 1, the fair values and the carrying amounts of Minion's net assets were the same for all items except for a plant asset. The fair value of this asset exceeded the carrying amount by $40,000.

Cost of the investment	$130,000	
Equity in the carrying amount of investee's net assets ($400,000 × 25%)	(100,000)	Equity in fair value
Equity in the excess of plant's fair value over its carrying amt. ($40,000 × 25%)	(10,000)	of net assets
Equity method goodwill	$ 20,000	

Investment in Minion Co.	$130,000	
Cash		$130,000

Private Companies Accounting

A **private company** is any entity that is not (1) a public business entity, (2) a not-for-profit entity, or (3) an employee benefit plan.

In accounting for subsequent measurement of **equity method goodwill**, a private company may

1. Use the general FASB codification guidance that applies to all entities or
2. May elect to apply the **goodwill accounting alternative**.

Under the goodwill accounting alternative, goodwill recognized must be **amortized on a straight-line basis over 10 years**. The amortization expense is recognized in the income statement.

1. A private company may amortize goodwill over a period shorter than 10 years if it can demonstrate that this useful life is more appropriate.

NOTE: Unless specifically stated otherwise, all questions and simulations are based on the FASB codification guidance applied to all entities. The guidance for private companies should be used only when the facts of a question or simulation state that (1) a company has elected the accounting alternative and (2) the company is private.

3. **Applying the Equity Method after the Acquisition Date**

   a. Under the equity method, the investor recognizes in income its **share of the investee's earnings or losses** in the periods for which they are reported by the investee. The journal entry is as follows:

Investee reported net income for the period		
Investment in X Co.	$XXX	
Equity method income --		
Share of X Co. earnings		$XXX

Investee reported net loss for the period		
Equity method loss --		
Share of X Co. losses	$XXX	
Investment in X Co.		$XXX

      1) The investor's share of the investee's earnings or losses is recognized only for the portion of the year that the investment was held under the equity method.
      2) The investor's share of the investee's earnings or losses is adjusted to eliminate intraentity profits and losses not realized in third-party transactions.

   b. Dividends from the investee are treated as a return of an investment. They **decrease the investment balance** but have no effect on the investor's income. The journal entry is

Cash or dividend receivable	$XXX	
Investment in X Co.		$XXX

EXAMPLE 5-8	**Equity Method Subsequent to Initial Recognition**	
On March 1, H.E. Bird Company purchased, at the market price, 40% of the outstanding common stock of Dowland Corporation. On March 1, Dowland had 50,000 shares of $1 par value common stock outstanding, and the market price was $12 per share.		
Investment in Dowland Corp. (50,000 × $12 × 40%)	$240,000	
Cash		$240,000
On September 13, Dowland declared and paid a $15,000 cash dividend.		
Cash ($15,000 × 40%)	$6,000	
Investment in Dowland Corp.		$6,000
For the year ending December 31, Dowland reported net income of $60,000, earned at a constant rate throughout the year. Bird held its equity-method investment in Dowland for 10 months of the year.		
Investment in Dowland Corp. [$60,000 × 40% × (10 ÷ 12)]	$20,000	
Income -- Equity-method investee		$20,000
Presentation in Bird's year-end financial statements:		
Balance sheet: Investment in Dowland Corp. ($240,000 + $20,000 – $6,000)		$254,000
Income statement: Equity method income from Dowland Corp.		20,000

c. The equity method requires the investor's share of the investee's earnings or losses to be adjusted for the difference at the acquisition date between the fair value and the carrying amount of the investee's net assets. This adjustment is made as the assets are sold or consumed in operations (e.g., depreciated).

1) For example, the investee's depreciable assets may be understated at the acquisition date. Thus, subsequent amortization of the excess of the fair value over the carrying amount decreases equity method income. It is recognized by the following entry:

Equity method loss	$XXX	
Investment in X Co.		$XXX

d. Use of the equity method is discontinued when the investment is reduced to zero by investee losses unless the investor has committed to providing additional financial support to the investee.

e. Disclosures about equity method investees should include

1) The entity's accounting policies for the investments;
2) The name of each investee and the entity's percentage of ownership;
3) The difference, if any, between the carrying amount of the investment and the underlying equity in the net assets of the investee; and
4) The accounting method applied to the difference.

4. **Change to the Equity Method -- Increase in Level of Ownership**
   a. When ownership of the voting stock of an investee **rises to the level of significant influence**, the investor must adopt the equity method or the FVO. A 20% or greater ownership interest is presumed to permit such influence absent strong contrary evidence.
   b. When significant influence is achieved in stages (step-by-step), the investor applies the equity method prospectively from the moment significant influence is achieved.
   c. On the date the investment becomes qualified for the equity method, the equity method investment equals (1) the cost of acquiring the additional equity interest in the investee plus (2) the current basis of the previously held equity interest in the investee.

5. **Change from the Equity Method**
   a. If an investor can **no longer be presumed** to exercise significant influence (for example, due to a decrease in the level of ownership), it ceases to account for the investment using the equity method.
      1) Any retained investment is measured based on the carrying amount of the investment on the date significant influence is lost.
      2) The shares retained ordinarily are measured at fair value through net income, unless the measurement alternative was selected because the fair value of shares was not readily determinable.

STOP & REVIEW

You have completed the outline for this subunit.
Study multiple-choice questions 9 through 11 beginning on page 162.

5.5 INVESTMENTS IN DEBT SECURITIES

1. **Overview**
   a. A **debt security** represents a **creditor** relationship with the issuer.
      1) In addition to the common forms of debt, this category includes (a) mandatorily redeemable preferred stock (stock that must be redeemed by the issuer), (b) preferred stock redeemable at the investor's option, and (c) collateralized mortgage obligations.
      2) Leases, options, financial futures contracts, and forward contracts are not debt securities.
   b. This subunit applies to all investments in debt securities.

c. Debt securities are classified at acquisition into one of **three categories**. The classification is reassessed at each reporting date.

Category	Criteria
Held-to-maturity	Debt securities that the reporting entity has the positive intent and ability to hold to maturity
Trading	Debt securities intended to be sold in the near term
Available-for-sale	Debt securities not classified as held-to-maturity or trading

2. **Held-to-Maturity Securities -- Amortized Cost**

a. An investment in a debt security is classified as held-to-maturity when the holder has both the **positive intent** and the **ability** to hold the security until its maturity date.

1) The investor may intend to hold the security for an indefinite period. Also, the possibility may exist that it will be sold before maturity to supply needed cash, avoid interest rate risk, etc. In these cases, the security cannot be classified as held-to-maturity.

2) If a sale before maturity takes place, the security still can be deemed to have been held-to-maturity if

a) Sale is near enough to the maturity or call date (e.g., within 3 months) so that interest rate risk (change in the market rate) does not have a significant effect on fair value, or

b) Sale is after collection of 85% or more of the principal.

b. Held-to-maturity securities are measured at **amortized cost**.

1) Amortized cost is the amount at which an investment in debt securities was recognized, adjusted for accrued interest, collection of cash, and amortization of premium or discount.

2) The purchase of held-to-maturity securities is recorded as follows:

Held-to-maturity securities	$XXX	
Cash		$XXX

c. An allowance for credit losses is a valuation account that is deducted from the amortized cost basis of held-to-maturity debt securities to present the net amount expected to be collected.

1) Initial recognition of the allowance for credit losses and subsequent changes in the allowance balance are recognized immediately in the income statement in the credit loss expense account.

d. **Presentation -- balance sheet.** On the face of the balance sheet, held-to-maturity securities are presented net of any unamortized premium or discount. (This topic is addressed in Subunit 5.6.)

1) Amortization of any discount (premium) is reported by a debit (credit) to held-to-maturity securities and a credit (debit) to interest income.
2) Individual securities are presented as current or noncurrent.
3) The allowance for credit losses must be separately presented as a deduction from the held-to-maturity securities' balance.

Balance sheet:	
Debt securities held-to-maturity	$X,XXX
(Allowance for credit losses)	(X,XXX)
Debt securities held-to-maturity, net of allowance for credit losses	$X,XXX

SUCCESS TIP

Unless the question indicates that a portion of the investment in debt securities is not expected to be collected, you can ignore the recognition of the allowance for credit losses.

e. **Presentation -- income statement.** Realized gains and losses and interest income (including amortization of premium or discount) are included in earnings.

f. **Presentation -- cash flow statement.** Cash flows are from investing activities.

3. **Trading Securities -- Fair Value through Net Income**

a. Trading securities are bought and held primarily for sale in the near term. They are purchased and sold frequently.

1) Each trading security is initially recorded at **cost** (including brokerage commissions and taxes).

Trading securities	$XXX	
Cash		$XXX

2) At each balance sheet date, trading securities are **remeasured at fair value**. (The fair value measurement framework is covered in Study Unit 4, Subunit 7.)

b. **Unrealized holding gains and losses** on trading securities are reported in the **income statement** (net income). A holding gain or loss is the net change in fair value during the period, not including recognized dividends or interest not received.

1) To retain historical cost in the accounts while reporting changes in the carrying amount from changes in fair value, a valuation allowance may be established.

a) For example, the entry below debits an allowance for an increase in the fair value of trading securities.

Securities fair value adjustment (trading)	$XXX	
Unrealized holding gain		$XXX

c. **Presentation -- balance sheet.** The balances of the securities and valuation allowances are netted. One amount is displayed for fair value.

   1) Trading securities are current assets.

d. **Presentation -- income statement.** Unrealized and realized holding gains and losses, dividends, and interest income (including premium or discount amortization) are included in earnings (income statement).

e. **Presentation -- cash flow statement.** Classification of cash flows depends on the nature of the securities and the purpose of their acquisition. They are typically considered to be from operating activities.

f. The accounting for (1) trading securities and (2) financial assets under the fair value option is similar. Under both methods, the investment is measured in the balance sheet at fair value. Unrealized holding gains or losses on the remeasurement to fair value then are recognized in earnings (income statement).

EXAMPLE 5-9 Trading Debt Securities

On October 1, Year 1, Maverick Co. purchased 1,000 shares of Larson Co. mandatorily redeemable preferred stock (i.e., debt securities) at fair value. Maverick classified this investment as trading securities. On March 1, Year 2, Maverick sold all of its investment at fair value. The following are the fair values per share of Larson mandatorily redeemable preferred stock at the relevant dates:

Date	Fair Value
October 1, Year 1	$15
December 31, Year 1	14
March 1, Year 2	21

<u>October 1, Year 1</u>

Trading securities (1,000 × $15)	$15,000	
Cash		$15,000

<u>December 31, Year 1</u>

At each balance sheet date, trading securities are remeasured at fair value. Unrealized holding gains and losses are reported in earnings.

Unrealized holding loss [1,000 × ($15 – $14)]	$1,000	
Securities fair value adjustment (trading)		$1,000

In Maverick's December 31, Year 1, balance sheet, the investment in Larson is reported in the current assets section as trading securities. It is measured at year-end fair value of $14,000 (1,000 × $14).

<u>March 1, Year 2</u>

Cash (1,000 × $21)	$21,000	
Trading securities		$14,000
Gain on disposal of trading securities		7,000

4. **Available-for-Sale Securities -- Fair Value through OCI**

   a. An investment in debt securities that are not classified as held-to-maturity or trading is considered available-for-sale. The initial acquisition is recorded at **cost** by a debit to available-for-sale securities and a credit to cash.

Available-for-sale securities	$XXX	
Cash		$XXX

   b. At each balance sheet date, available-for-sale securities are **remeasured at fair value**.

   c. **Unrealized holding gains and losses** resulting from the remeasurement to fair value are reported in **other comprehensive income** (OCI).

Unrealized holding loss -- OCI	$XXX	
Securities fair value adjustment (available-for-sale)		$XXX

      1) Tax effects are debited or credited directly to OCI.
      2) Amortization of any discount (premium) is reported by a debit (credit) to available-for-sale securities and a credit (debit) to interest income.
      3) All or part of unrealized gains and losses for an available-for-sale security designated and qualifying as the hedged item in a fair value hedge are recognized in earnings.

   d. **Presentation -- balance sheet.** On the face of the balance sheet, available-for-sale securities are reported at **fair value**. The amounts of the allowance for credit losses and amortized cost basis should be indicated within the text (presented parenthetically).

      1) Individual securities are presented as current or noncurrent.
      2) In the equity section, unrealized holding gains and losses are reported in accumulated OCI (the real account to which OCI is closed).

   e. **Presentation -- income statement.** Realized gains and losses, dividends, and interest income (including premium or discount amortization) are included in earnings.

   f. **Presentation -- statement of comprehensive income.** Unrealized holding gains and losses for the period are included in comprehensive income.

      1) Reclassification adjustments also must be made for each component of OCI. Their purpose is to avoid double counting when an item included in net income also was included in OCI for the same or a prior period. For example, if a gain on available-for-sale securities is realized in the current period, the prior-period recognition of an unrealized holding gain must be eliminated by debiting OCI and crediting a gain.

   g. **Presentation -- cash flow statement.** Cash flows are from investing activities.

EXAMPLE 5-10 Available-for-Sale Debt Securities

On April 1, Year 1, Maverick Co. purchased 1,000 shares of White Co. mandatorily redeemable preferred stock at fair value. Maverick classified this investment as available-for-sale securities. On May 1, Year 3, Maverick sold all of its investment at fair value. The following are the fair values per share of White mandatorily redeemable preferred stock at the relevant dates:

Date	Fair Value
April 1, Year 1	$25
December 31, Year 1	32
December 31, Year 2	27
May 1, Year 3	31

The changes in the fair value of White preferred shares are not due to credit losses.

April 1, Year 1, Journal Entry

Available-for-sale securities (1,000 × $25)	$25,000	
Cash		$25,000

December 31, Year 1, Journal Entry

At each balance sheet date, available-for-sale securities are remeasured at fair value. Unrealized holding gains and losses are included in OCI.

Available-for-sale securities fair value adjustment [1,000 × ($32 – $25)]	$7,000	
Unrealized holding gain (OCI item)		$7,000

Presentation in Maverick's December 31, Year 1, financial statements:

Balance sheet: Assets section -- Available-for-sale securities (1,000 × $32)	$32,000 ($25,000 + $7,000)
Equity section -- Accumulated OCI	7,000
Statement of comprehensive income -- Unrealized holding gain (OCI)	7,000

December 31, Year 2, Journal Entry

Unrealized holding loss [1,000 × ($27 – $32)]	$5,000	
Available-for-sale securities fair value adjustment		$5,000

Presentation in Maverick's December 31, Year 2, financial statements:

Balance sheet: Assets section -- Available-for-sale securities (1,000 × $27)	$27,000 ($25,000 + $2,000)
Equity section -- Accumulated OCI ($7,000 – $5,000)	2,000
Statement of comprehensive income -- Unrealized holding loss (OCI)	5,000

May 1, Year 3, Journal Entry

Cash (1,000 × $31)	$31,000	
Reclassification of holding gains from AOCI (OCI item)	2,000	
Available-for-sale securities		$25,000
Available-for-sale securities fair value adjustment		2,000
Realized gain on disposal of available-for-sale securities		6,000

Presentation in Maverick's December 31, Year 3, financial statements:

Income statement: Realized gain on disposal on AFS securities	$6,000
Statement of OCI: Reclassification of holding gains from accumulated OCI	(2,000)
Total comprehensive income for Year 3 ($31,000 – $27,000)	$4,000

5. **Impairment of Available-for-Sale (AFS) Securities**
   a. An available-for-sale debt security is impaired only if its fair value is less than its amortized cost basis.
   b. The accounting question is to determine the portion of the impairment that relates to credit losses (recognized in net income) and the noncredit losses portion (unrealized holding loss recognized in OCI).
   c. The debt security's fair value often may be lower than its amortized cost due to factors that are not related to credit losses (the issuer's ability to pay). For example, the fair value of the security may decline solely due to an increase in market interest rates.
      1) In these cases, the entire decline in the fair value of the security is recognized as an unrealized holding loss in OCI.
   d. A credit loss exists if the present value of cash flows expected to be collected from the security is less than its amortized cost basis.

      Amortized cost basis > Present value of cash flows = Credit loss exists

      1) The impairment for credit losses recognized is limited by the amount that the fair value of the security is less than the security's amortized cost basis.

   Amortized cost basis – Fair value = Maximum amount of impairment for credit losses

   e. The impairment for credit losses is recognized in the **income statement** and recorded through an allowance for credit losses. The following is the journal entry:

Credit loss expense	$XXX	
Allowance for credit losses		$XXX

   f. The following is the decision tree:

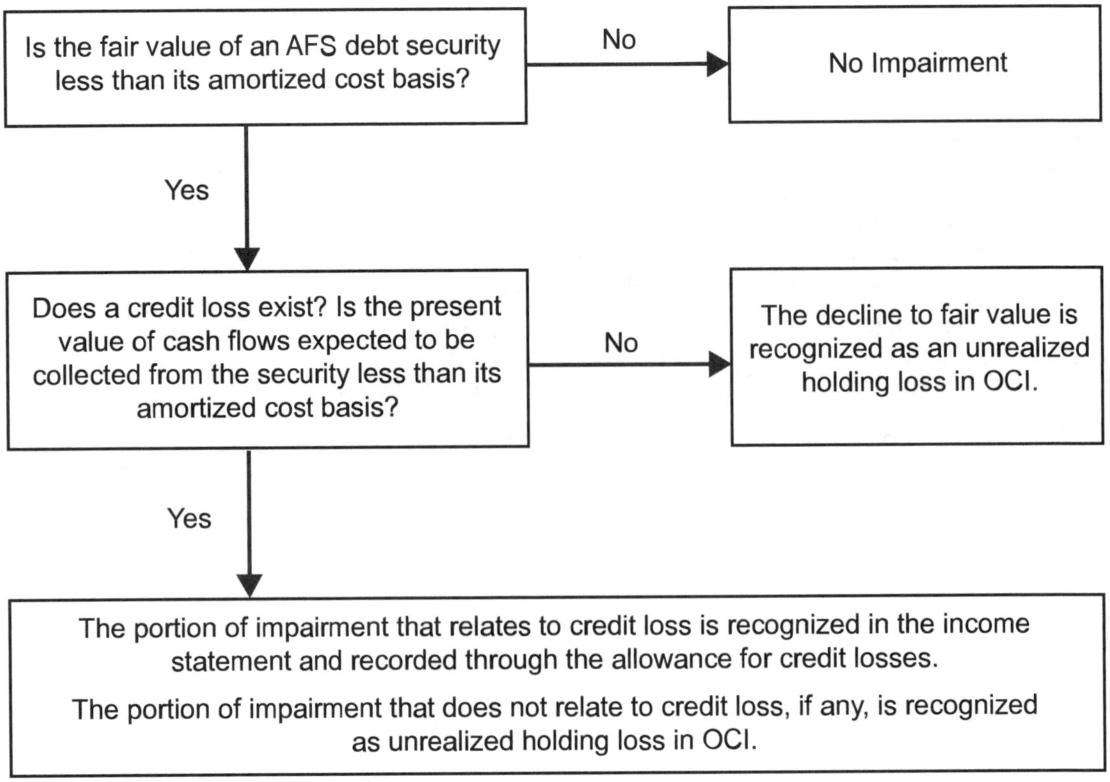

Figure 5-5

EXAMPLE 5-11 Impairment of AFS Debt Securities

The following year-end information pertains to Ariel Co's investment in available-for-sale debt securities:

Amortized cost basis	$100,000
Fair value	90,000
Discounted cash flows expected to be collected from the securities	88,000

The fair value is lower than amortized cost. Thus, the securities are impaired by $10,000 ($100,000 – $90,000). This entire amount is an impairment for credit losses that is recognized in the income statement. The journal entry is

Credit loss expense	$10,000	
Allowance for credit losses		$10,000

Balance sheet presentation:
Available-for-sale debt securities (amortized cost $100,000; allowance for credit losses $10,000) $90,000

EXAMPLE 5-12 Impairment of AFS Debt Securities

Using the data from Example 5-11, assume that the fair value of the securities is $85,000. The securities are impaired by $15,000 ($100,000 amortized cost basis – $85,000 fair value). The impairment for credit losses of $12,000 ($100,000 amortized cost – $88,000 discounted cash flows expected from the securities) is recognized in the income statement. The remaining decline in the securities' fair value of $3,000 ($15,000 – $12,000) is recognized in OCI. The following are the journal entries:

Credit loss expense	$12,000	
Allowance for credit losses		$12,000
Unrealized holding loss – OCI	$3,000	
AFS securities fair value adjustment		$3,000

Balance sheet presentation:
Available-for-sale debt securities (amortized cost $100,000; allowance for credit losses $12,000) $85,000

EXAMPLE 5-13 Impairment of AFS Debt Securities

Using the data from Example 5-11, assume that the discounted cash flows expected to be collected from the securities are $100,000. The securities are impaired by $10,000 ($100,000 – $90,000). Given that the discounted cash flows expected to be collected from the securities are not less than the amortized cost, no impairment for credit losses is recognized. The entire decline in the fair value of $10,000 is recognized in OCI. The journal entry is

Unrealized holding loss – OCI	$10,000	
AFS securities fair value adjustment		$10,000

g. The allowance for credit losses is reassessed each reporting period. Subsequent changes in the allowance for credit losses on available-for-sale debt securities are recognized in the income statement. The previously recorded allowance cannot be reversed below zero.

SUCCESS TIP

If the change in the fair value of the security is **not due to credit losses**, you can (1) ignore the recognition of the allowance for credit losses and (2) recognize the entire change in the fair value of the AFS security in OCI.

6. **Transfers between Categories**

   a. Transfers between categories are accounted for at **transfer-date fair value**. The following describes the treatment of **unrealized holding gains and losses** at that date:

      1) **From trading to any category.** Amounts already recognized in earnings are not reversed.
      2) **To trading from any category.** Amounts not already recognized in earnings are recognized in earnings.
      3) **To available-for-sale from held-to-maturity.** Amounts are recognized in OCI.
      4) **To held-to-maturity from available-for-sale.** Amounts recognized in OCI are not reversed but are amortized in the same way as a premium or discount.
      5) Transfers **from held-to-maturity** or **into or from trading** should be rare.

   b. **Summary of Transfers**

From	To	Earnings Recognition
Trading	Any category	Already recognized, not reversed
Any category	Trading	If not already recognized
Held-to-maturity	Available-for-sale	Unrealized gain (loss) recognized in OCI
Available-for-sale	Held-to-maturity	Amounts in OCI not reversed but are amortized in same way as premium (discount)

IFRS DIFFERENCE

The classification and measurement of investments in debt securities depends on (1) the investor's business model for managing them and (2) the nature of cash flows from them. The following is the decision tree:

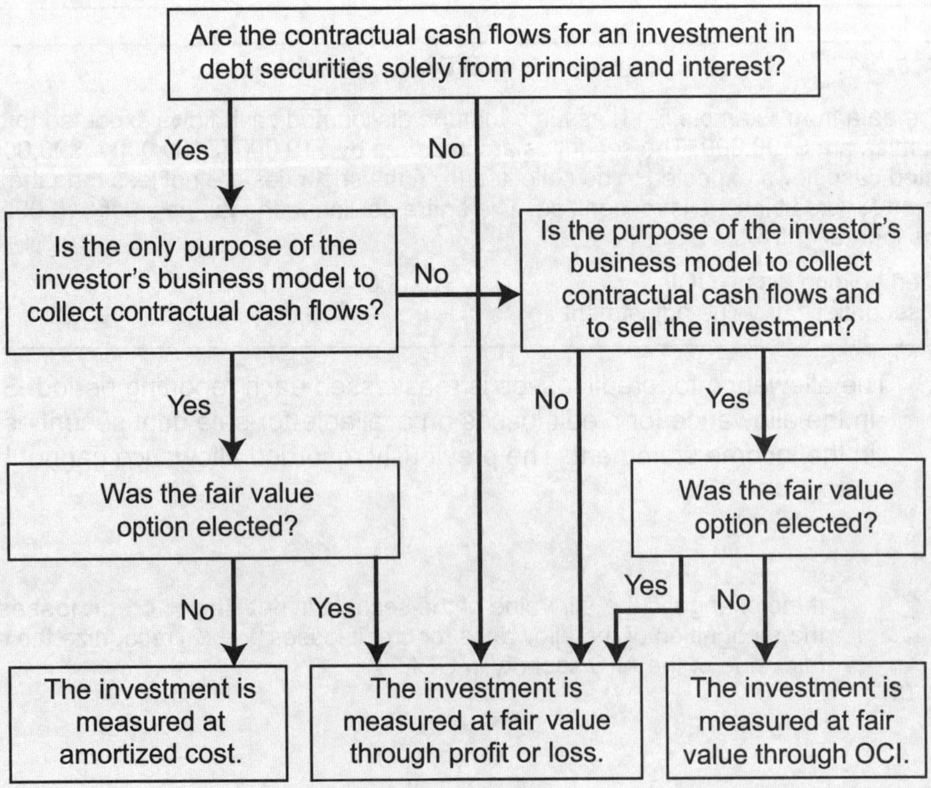

Figure 5-6

STOP & REVIEW

You have completed the outline for this subunit.
Study multiple-choice questions 12 through 15 beginning on page 164.

5.6 INVESTMENTS IN BONDS

1. Definition and Classification

a. A bond is a formal contractual agreement by an issuer to pay an amount of money (face amount) at the maturity date plus interest at the stated rate at specific intervals. All terms are stated in a document called an indenture.

1) An investment in a bond is a financial asset. Thus, the investor may elect the FVO.

2) Absent this election (or proper classification as a trading security), a bond is classified as held-to-maturity or available-for-sale.

3) Study Unit 12, Subunit 1, contains a description of the various types of bonds.

2. Purchase Price

a. An investment in a bond is recorded on the purchaser's books at the present value of the bond's two cash flows, discounted at the interest rate prevailing in the market at the time of the purchase. (Study Unit 12, Subunit 2, has a thorough outline of the time value of money.)

1) The **face amount** (also called the maturity amount) is received on the bond's maturity date, e.g., 20 years after the initial purchase.

2) The annual **cash interest** equals the bond's face amount times the stated (or coupon) rate, e.g., $1,000 face amount × 4% stated rate = $40 annual cash interest.

b. If the bond's stated (coupon) rate differs from the market rate at the time of the purchase, the price paid will not equal the face amount.

1) If the bond's stated rate is greater than the current market rate, the purchase price is higher than the face amount and the bond is purchased at a premium.

a) An investor in bonds rarely uses a separate premium or discount account, instead recording the investment at historical cost.

EXAMPLE 5-14 Bond Purchased at Premium

An investor purchases an 8%, 5-year, $5,000 bond when the prevailing interest rate in the market is 6%. The present value of $1 at 6% for 5 periods is 0.747, and the present value of an ordinary annuity of $1 at 6% for 5 periods is 4.213. The present value of the face amount is $3,735 ($5,000 × 0.747), and the present value of the annual cash interest is $1,686 ($5,000 face amount × 8% stated rate × 4.213 PV of ordinary annuity). Thus, the amount paid for the bond is $5,421 ($3,735 + $1,686). The premium on the bond is $421 ($5,421 cost – $5,000 face amount). The investor records the following entry:

Investment in bond	$5,421	
Cash		$5,421

2) If the bond's stated rate is less than the current market rate, the purchase price is lower than the face amount and the bond is purchased at a discount.

EXAMPLE 5-15 Bond Purchased at Discount

An investor purchases a 6%, 5-year, $5,000 bond at 92 (meaning 92% of par). The cost of the bond (the present value of the face amount and annual cash interest) is $4,600 ($5,000 × .92). The cost reflects a market rate of 8%. The discount at the date of purchase is $400 ($5,000 face amount – $4,600 present value). The investor records the following entry:

Investment in bond	$4,600	
Cash		$4,600

c. When a bond is purchased between interest dates, the investor generally pays to the issuer the amount of interest that has accrued since the last interest payment. On the next payment date, the investor receives a full interest payment.

1) The purchaser of the bond, in effect, "buys" the amount of interest that has accrued since the last payment.

3. **Amortizing a Premium or Discount**

a. Any premium or discount is amortized over the life of the bond using the effective-interest method.

1) The effective rate is the interest rate prevailing in the market at the time of the initial purchase (also called the yield).

2) The essence of the effective rate method is application of a constant interest rate. The total amount of interest revenue recognized changes every period.

3) Amortization results in the carrying amount of the asset (liability) being adjusted over time, reaching the face amount at maturity.

4) The straight-line method is used only if its results are not materially different from those of the effective-interest method.

EXAMPLE 5-16 Amortization of Premium and Discount on Bonds

The following are bond premium and discount amortization schedules:

Year	Beginning Carrying Amount	Times: Effective Rate	Equals: Interest Revenue	Minus: Interest Received	Equals: Premium Amortized	Ending Carrying Amount
1	$5,421	6%	$325	$400	$ (75)	$5,346
2	5,346	6%	321	400	(79)	5,267
3	5,267	6%	316	400	(84)	5,183
4	5,183	6%	311	400	(89)	5,094
5	5,094	6%	306	400	(94)	5,000
					$(421)	

Year	Beginning Carrying Amount	Times: Effective Rate	Equals: Interest Revenue	Minus: Interest Received	Equals: Discount Amortized	Ending Carrying Amount
1	$4,600	8%	$368	$300	$ 68	$4,668
2	4,668	8%	374	300	74	4,742
3	4,742	8%	379	300	79	4,821
4	4,821	8%	386	300	86	4,907
5	4,907	8%	393	300	93	5,000
					$400	

-- Continued on next page --

EXAMPLE 5-16 -- Continued

The entries recorded by the two investors in Examples 5-14 and 5-15 are shown here:

Amortization of Premium			Amortization of Discount		
End of Year 1:					
Cash	$400		Cash	$300	
Investment in bond		$ 75	Investment in bond	68	
Interest revenue		325	Interest revenue		$368
End of Year 2:					
Cash	$400		Cash	$300	
Investment in bond		$ 79	Investment in bond	74	
Interest revenue		321	Interest revenue		$374
End of Year 3:					
Cash	$400		Cash	$300	
Investment in bond		$ 84	Investment in bond	79	
Interest revenue		316	Interest revenue		$379
End of Year 4:					
Cash	$400		Cash	$300	
Investment in bond		$ 89	Investment in bond	86	
Interest revenue		311	Interest revenue		$386
End of Year 5:					
Cash	$400		Cash	$300	
Investment in bond		$ 94	Investment in bond	93	
Interest revenue		306	Interest revenue		$393

The bond's carrying amount at the maturity date equals its face amount.

End of Year 5:					
Cash	$5,000		Cash	$5,000	
Investment in bond		$5,000	Investment in bond		$5,000

STOP & REVIEW

You have completed the outline for this subunit.
Study multiple-choice questions 16 through 19 beginning on page 165.

QUESTIONS

5.1 Cash

1. Burr Company had the following account balances at December 31, Year 1:

Cash in banks	$2,250,000
Cash on hand	125,000
Cash legally restricted for additions to plant (expected to be disbursed in Year 2)	1,600,000

Cash in banks includes $600,000 of compensating balances related to short-term borrowing arrangements. The compensating balances are not legally restricted as to withdrawal by Burr. In the current assets section of Burr's December 31, Year 1, balance sheet, total cash should be reported at

A. $1,775,000

B. $2,250,000

C. $2,375,000

D. $3,975,000

Answer (C) is correct.

REQUIRED: The total cash reported in current assets given legal restrictions and compensating balance requirements.

DISCUSSION: Legally restricted amounts related to long-term arrangements should be classified separately as noncurrent. Thus, the amount restricted for additions should be classified as noncurrent because it relates to a plant asset. Compensating balances against short-term borrowing arrangements that are legally restricted should be reported separately among the cash and cash equivalents in the current assets section. Total cash reported as current assets therefore equals $2,375,000 ($2,250,000 + $125,000).

Answer (A) is incorrect. The amount of $1,775,000 results from subtracting the $600,000 of compensating balances from cash in banks. **Answer (B) is incorrect.** Cash on hand should be included in total cash. **Answer (D) is incorrect.** The legally restricted cash related to a long-term arrangement should be classified as noncurrent.

2. The following information pertains to Grey Co. at December 31, Year 4:

Checkbook balance	$12,000
Bank statement balance	16,000
Check drawn on Grey's account, payable to a vendor, dated and recorded 12/31/Yr 4 but not mailed until 1/10/Yr 5	1,800

On Grey's December 31, Year 4, balance sheet, what amount should be reported as cash?

A. $12,000

B. $13,800

C. $14,200

D. $16,000

Answer (B) is correct.

REQUIRED: The amount of cash that should be reported on the balance sheet.

DISCUSSION: The cash account on the balance sheet should consist of (1) coin and currency on hand, (2) demand deposits (checking accounts), (3) time deposits (savings accounts), and (4) near-cash assets (e.g., deposits in transit or checks written to creditors but not yet mailed). Thus, the cash balance should be $13,800 ($12,000 checkbook balance + $1,800 check drawn but not mailed). The checkbook balance is used instead of the bank balance in the calculation. It more closely reflects the amount of cash that is unrestricted at the balance sheet date.

Answer (A) is incorrect. The amount of $12,000 excludes the check that was recorded but not mailed. **Answer (C) is incorrect.** The amount of $14,200 equals the bank statement balance minus the check not mailed. **Answer (D) is incorrect.** The amount of $16,000 is the bank statement balance.

3. Ral Corp.'s checkbook balance on December 31, Year 7, was $5,000. In addition, Ral held the following items in its safe on that date:

Check payable to Ral Corp., dated January 2, Year 8, in payment of a sale made in December Year 7, not included in December 31 checkbook balance	$2,000
Check payable to Ral Corp., deposited December 15 and included in December 31 checkbook balance but returned by Bank on December 30 stamped "NSF." The check was redeposited on January 2, Year 8, and cleared on January 9	500
Check drawn on Ral Corp.'s account, payable to a vendor, dated and recorded in Ral's books on December 31, but not mailed until January 10, Year 8	300

The proper amount to be shown as cash on Ral's balance sheet at December 31, Year 7, is

A. $4,800

B. $5,300

C. $6,500

D. $6,800

Answer (A) is correct.

REQUIRED: The amount to be recorded as cash on the year-end balance sheet.

DISCUSSION: The December 31 checkbook balance is $5,000. The $2,000 check dated January 2, Year 8, is properly not included in this balance because it is not negotiable at year end. The $500 NSF check should not be included in cash because it is a receivable. The $300 check that was not mailed until January 10 should be added to the balance. This predated check is still within the control of the company and should not decrease the cash account. Consequently, the cash balance to be reported on the December 31, Year 7, balance sheet is $4,800.

Balance per checkbook	$5,000
Add: Predated check	300
Deduct: NSF check	(500)
Cash balance 12/31/Year 7	$4,800

Answer (B) is incorrect. The amount of $5,300 does not include the NSF check. **Answer (C) is incorrect.** The amount of $6,500 includes the postdated check but not the predated check. **Answer (D) is incorrect.** The amount of $6,800 includes the postdated check.

5.2 Fair Value Option (FVO)

4. During Year 3, Gilman Co. purchased 5,000 shares of the 500,000 outstanding shares of Meteor Corp.'s common stock for $35,000. During Year 3, Gilman received $1,800 of dividends from its investment in Meteor's stock. The fair value of Gilman's investment on December 31, Year 3, is $32,000. Gilman has elected the fair value option for this investment. What amount of income or loss that is attributable to the Meteor stock investment should be reflected in Gilman's earnings for Year 3?

A. Income of $4,800.

B. Income of $1,800.

C. Loss of $1,200.

D. Loss of $3,000.

Answer (C) is correct.

REQUIRED: The income or loss reflected in current-year earnings when the FVO for measuring investments is used.

DISCUSSION: Under the fair value option, dividends received and unrealized gains and losses on remeasurement of financial assets to fair value are reported in earnings. Thus, the $1,800 of dividend income received and the $3,000 ($35,000 – $32,000) of unrealized loss are reflected in Gilman's earnings for Year 3. This results in a total loss of $1,200 ($1,800 – $3,000) attributable to the Meteor stock investment.

Answer (A) is incorrect. Income of $4,800 is calculated by treating the change in fair value of the Meteor stock investment as a gain. However, the fair value has declined from $35,000 to $32,000, resulting in an unrealized loss of $3,000, not a gain. **Answer (B) is incorrect.** Income of $1,800 is calculated by excluding the unrealized loss from the Meteor stock investment from earnings. However, under the fair value option, unrealized gains and losses are reported in earnings. **Answer (D) is incorrect.** A loss of $3,000 is calculated by excluding the $1,800 of dividend income from Gilman's earnings for Year 3. However, under the fair value option, dividends received are treated as income and included in earnings for the year.

5. The reporting entity may elect the fair value option (FVO) for

A. An investment consisting of more than 50% of the outstanding voting interests of another entity.

B. An interest in a variable interest entity (VIE) if the reporting entity is the primary beneficiary.

C. Its obligation for pension and other postretirement employee benefits.

D. Most financial assets and liabilities.

Answer (D) is correct.

REQUIRED: The item eligible for the FVO election.

DISCUSSION: An entity may elect the FVO for most recognized financial assets and liabilities.

Answer (A) is incorrect. An investment in a subsidiary required to be consolidated is not an eligible item. **Answer (B) is incorrect.** The primary beneficiary must consolidate the VIE. Thus, the interest in the VIE is not an eligible item. **Answer (C) is incorrect.** Items eligible for the FVO election do not include employers' and plans' obligations for (1) employee pension benefits, (2) other postretirement employee benefits, (3) postemployment benefits, (4) employee stock option and stock purchase plans, or (5) other deferred compensation.

5.3 Investments in Equity Securities

6. On December 31, Ott Co. had investments in equity securities as follows:

	Cost	Fair Value
Man Co.	$10,000	$ 8,000
Kemo, Inc.	9,000	11,000
Fenn Corp.	11,000	9,000
	$30,000	$28,000

Ott's December 31 balance sheet should report the equity securities as

A. $26,000

B. $28,000

C. $29,000

D. $30,000

Answer (B) is correct.

REQUIRED: The amount at which the trading securities should be reported.

DISCUSSION: An investment in equity securities that does not result in significant influence or control over the investee is reported at fair value, and unrealized holding gains and losses are included in earnings. Consequently, the securities should be reported as $28,000.

Answer (A) is incorrect. The amount of $26,000 is the lower of cost or fair value determined on an individual security basis. **Answer (C) is incorrect.** The amount of $29,000 is the average of the aggregate cost and aggregate fair value. **Answer (D) is incorrect.** The aggregate cost is $30,000.

7. Plack Co. purchased 10,000 shares (2% ownership) of Ty Corp. on February 14 and did not elect the fair value option. Plack received a stock dividend of 2,000 shares on April 30, when the market value per share was $35. Ty paid a cash dividend of $2 per share on December 15. In its income statement for the year, what amount should Plack report as dividend income?

A. $20,000

B. $24,000

C. $90,000

D. $94,000

Answer (B) is correct.

REQUIRED: The amount of dividend income to be reported.

DISCUSSION: Plack Co. owns 2% of the stock of Ty Corp. Accordingly, this investment should be accounted for using the fair value method. If the fair value of the stock is not readily determinable, the measurement alternative may be selected. This alternative is cost minus any impairment, plus or minus changes resulting from observable price changes for the identical or a similar investment of the same issuer. Under either method, dividends from an investee are accounted for by the investor as dividend income unless a liquidating dividend is received. The recipient of a stock dividend does not recognize income. Thus, Plack should report dividend income of $24,000 [(10,000 shares + 2,000 shares received as a stock dividend on April 30) × $2 per share dividend].

Answer (A) is incorrect. The amount of $20,000 does not include the dividends received on the 2,000 shares from the April 30 stock dividend. **Answer (C) is incorrect.** The amount of $90,000 equals the sum of the $2 per share cash dividend on 10,000 shares and the April 30 market value of the 2,000-share stock dividend. However, the recipient of a stock dividend does not recognize income. **Answer (D) is incorrect.** The amount of $94,000 equals the sum of the $2 per share cash dividend on 12,000 shares and the April 30 market value of the 2,000-share stock dividend. However, the recipient of a stock dividend does not recognize income.

8. During Year 6, Wall Co. purchased 2,000 shares of Hemp Corp. common stock for $31,500. They represent 2% of ownership in Hemp Corp. The fair value of this investment was $29,500 at December 31, Year 6. Wall sold all of the Hemp common stock for $14 per share on December 15, Year 7, incurring $1,400 in brokerage commissions and taxes. In its income statement for the year ended December 31, Year 7, Wall should report a recognized loss of

A. $4,900

B. $3,500

C. $2,900

D. $1,500

Answer (C) is correct.

REQUIRED: The realized loss on the sale of equity securities.

DISCUSSION: A realized loss or gain is recognized when an individual equity security is sold or otherwise disposed of. Wall would have included the $2,000 ($31,500 – $29,500) decline in the fair value of the equity securities (an unrealized holding loss) in earnings at 12/31/Yr 6. Consequently, the realized loss on disposal at 12/15/Yr 7 is $2,900 [(2,000 shares × $14) – $29,500 carrying amount – $1,400].

Answer (A) is incorrect. The sum of the recognized losses for Year 6 and Year 7 is $4,900. **Answer (B) is incorrect.** The sum of the recognized losses for Year 6 and Year 7 without regard to the commissions and taxes is $3,500. **Answer (D) is incorrect.** Ignoring the commissions and taxes results in $1,500.

5.4 Equity Method

9. Birk Co. purchased 30% of Sled Co.'s outstanding common stock on December 31 for $200,000. On that date, Sled's equity was $500,000, and the fair value of its net assets was $600,000. On December 31, what amount of equity method goodwill results from this acquisition?

A. $0

B. $20,000

C. $30,000

D. $50,000

Answer (B) is correct.

REQUIRED: The amount of goodwill attributable to a purchase of 30% of the investee's common stock.

DISCUSSION: The equity method of accounting is used when the investor has significant influence over the investee (investment is at least 20% but not more than 50% of the voting interests) and the FVO was not elected. Equity method goodwill is the difference between the cost of the $200,000 investment and the investor's equity in the fair value of the investee's net assets of $180,000 (30% × $600,000). Accordingly, equity method goodwill equals $20,000 ($200,000 – $180,000).

Answer (A) is incorrect. Equity method goodwill exists if the cost of the investment exceeds the fair value of the underlying equity in net assets acquired. **Answer (C) is incorrect.** The amount of $30,000 equals 30% of the difference between the carrying amount of the investee's equity and the fair value of the underlying equity in net assets. **Answer (D) is incorrect.** The amount of $50,000 is the difference between 30% of the equity and the investment cost.

Questions 10 and 11 are based on the following information. Grant, Inc., acquired 30% of South Co.'s voting stock for $200,000 on January 2, Year 1, and did not elect the fair value option. The price equaled the carrying amount and the fair value of the interest purchased in South's net assets. Grant's 30% interest in South gave Grant the ability to exercise significant influence over South's operating and financial policies. During Year 1, South earned $80,000 and paid dividends of $50,000. South reported earnings of $100,000 for the 6 months ended June 30, Year 2, and $200,000 for the year ended December 31, Year 2. On July 1, Year 2, Grant sold half of its stock in South for $150,000 cash. South paid dividends of $60,000 on October 1, Year 2.

10. Before income taxes, what amount should Grant include in its Year 1 income statement as a result of the investment?

A. $15,000

B. $24,000

C. $50,000

D. $80,000

Answer (B) is correct.

REQUIRED: The income statement amount derived from an equity-based investment.

DISCUSSION: Under the equity method, Grant's share of South's revenue reported in the income statement is $24,000 ($80,000 × 30%). The cash dividends received are recorded as a decrease in the investment's carrying amount.

Answer (A) is incorrect. Grant's share of the cash dividends equals $15,000. **Answer (C) is incorrect.** The amount of cash dividends South paid is $50,000. **Answer (D) is incorrect.** The amount of South's Year 1 earnings is $80,000.

11. In its Year 2 income statement, what amount should Grant report as gain from the sale of half of its investment?

A. $24,500

B. $30,500

C. $35,000

D. $45,500

Answer (B) is correct.

REQUIRED: The gain reported from the sale of half of the investment.

DISCUSSION: At December 31, Year 1, the carrying amount of the investment is $209,000 ($200,000 original investment + $24,000 share of Year 1 earnings – $15,000 share of Year 1 dividends). At June 30, Year 2, the investment is increased to $239,000 by the $30,000 share of South's earnings. Half of the new carrying amount is $119,500. Grant received $150,000, so the gain is $30,500 ($150,000 – $119,500).

Answer (A) is incorrect. The amount of $24,500 is based on a carrying amount of $251,000. **Answer (C) is incorrect.** The amount of $35,000 is based on a carrying amount of $230,000. **Answer (D) is incorrect.** The amount of $45,500 is based on a carrying amount of $209,000, which does not include the $30,000 of Year 2 income.

5.5 Investments in Debt Securities

12. Kale Co. purchased bonds at a discount on the open market as an investment and has the intent and ability to hold these bonds to maturity. Absent an election of the fair value option, Kale should account for these bonds at

A. Cost.

B. Amortized cost.

C. Fair value.

D. Lower of cost or market.

Answer (B) is correct.

REQUIRED: The recording of held-to-maturity securities.

DISCUSSION: Without an election of the fair value option, investments in debt securities that the investor has the ability and positive intent to hold until maturity must be classified as held-to-maturity and measured at amortized cost.

Answer (A) is incorrect. The discount is amortized over the term of the bonds. **Answer (C) is incorrect.** Trading and available-for-sale debt securities are accounted for at fair value. **Answer (D) is incorrect.** LIFO or retail inventory is measured at lower of cost or market.

13. The following information pertains to Lark Corp.'s available-for-sale debt securities:

	December 31	
	Year 2	Year 3
Cost	$100,000	$100,000
Fair value	90,000	120,000

Differences between cost and fair values are not due to credit losses. The decline in fair value was properly accounted for at December 31, Year 2. Ignoring tax effects, by what amount should other comprehensive income (OCI) be credited at December 31, Year 3?

A. $0

B. $10,000

C. $20,000

D. $30,000

Answer (D) is correct.

REQUIRED: The credit to OCI if fair value exceeds cost.

DISCUSSION: Unrealized holding gains and losses on available-for-sale debt securities not related to credit losses are not included in earnings but ordinarily are reported in OCI, net of tax effects (ignored in this question). At December 31, Year 2, OCI should have been debited for $10,000 for the excess of cost over fair value to reflect an unrealized holding loss. At December 31, Year 3, OCI should be credited to reflect a $30,000 unrealized holding gain ($120,000 fair value at 12/31/Year 3 – $90,000 fair value at 12/31/Year 2).

Answer (A) is incorrect. Unrealized holding gains on available-for-sale securities are recognized. **Answer (B) is incorrect.** The amount of $10,000 is the recovery of the previously recognized unrealized holding loss. The recognition of gain is not limited to that amount. **Answer (C) is incorrect.** The excess of fair value over cost is $20,000.

14. When the fair value of an investment in debt securities exceeds its amortized cost, how should each of the following debt securities be measured at the end of the year, given no election of the fair value option?

	Debt Securities Classified As	
	Held-to-Maturity	Available-for-Sale
A.	Amortized cost	Amortized cost
B.	Amortized cost	Fair value
C.	Fair value	Fair value
D.	Fair value	Amortized cost

Answer (B) is correct.

REQUIRED: The measurement of debt securities classified as held-to-maturity and available-for-sale.

DISCUSSION: Investments in debt securities must be classified as held-to-maturity and measured at amortized cost in the balance sheet if the reporting entity has the positive intent and ability to hold them to maturity. Debt securities that are not expected to be sold in the near term and that are not held-to-maturity should be classified as available-for-sale. Available-for-sale debt securities should be reported at fair value, with unrealized holding gains and losses (excess of fair value over amortized cost).

15. The following information was extracted from Gil Co.'s December 31 balance sheet:

Noncurrent assets:	
Available-for-sale debt securities (carried at fair value)	$96,450
Equity:	
Accumulated other comprehensive income (OCI)	
Unrealized holding gains and losses on available-for-sale debt securities	(19,800)

Historical cost of the available-for-sale debt securities was

A. $63,595

B. $76,650

C. $96,450

D. $116,250

Answer (D) is correct.

REQUIRED: The historical cost of the available-for-sale debt securities.

DISCUSSION: The existence of an equity account with a debit balance signifies that the available-for-sale debt securities are reported at fair value that is less than historical cost. The difference is the net unrealized holding loss balance. Thus, historical cost must have been $116,250 ($96,450 available-for-sale securities at fair value + $19,800 net unrealized loss).

Answer (A) is incorrect. The amount of $63,595 is a nonsense figure. **Answer (B) is incorrect.** The amount of $76,650 results from subtracting the unrealized loss instead of adding. **Answer (C) is incorrect.** The amount of $96,450 ignores the unrealized loss balance.

5.6 Investments in Bonds

16. An investor purchased a bond as a long-term investment between interest dates at a premium. At the purchase date, the cash paid to the seller is

A. The same as the face amount of the bond.

B. The same as the face amount of the bond plus accrued interest.

C. More than the face amount of the bond.

D. Less than the face amount of the bond.

Answer (C) is correct.

REQUIRED: The cash paid for a bond issued at a premium.

DISCUSSION: At the date of purchase, the cash paid to the seller is equal to interest accrued since the last interest date, plus the face amount of the bonds, plus the premium. The carrying amount of the bonds (face amount plus the premium) is equal to the present value of the cash flows associated with the bond discounted at the market rate of interest (yield).

17. An investor purchased a bond classified as a long-term investment between interest dates at a discount. At the purchase date, the carrying amount of the bond is more than the

	Cash Paid to Seller	Face Amount of Bond
A.	No	Yes
B.	No	No
C.	Yes	No
D.	Yes	Yes

Answer (B) is correct.

REQUIRED: The carrying amount of a bond purchased at a discount between interest dates.

DISCUSSION: At the date of purchase, the carrying amount of the bond equals its face amount minus the discount. The cash paid equals the initial carrying amount plus accrued interest. Hence, the initial carrying amount is less than the cash paid by the amount of the accrued interest.

18. Jent Corp. purchased bonds at a discount of $10,000. Subsequently, Jent sold these bonds at a premium of $14,000. During the period that Jent held this investment, amortization of the discount amounted to $2,000. What amount should Jent report as gain on the sale of bonds?

A. $12,000

B. $22,000

C. $24,000

D. $26,000

Answer (B) is correct.

REQUIRED: The amount reported as gain on the sale of bonds.

DISCUSSION: The gain equals the sale price (Face amount + $14,000 premium) minus the carrying amount [Face amount – ($10,000 original discount – $2,000 amortization)]. Consequently, the gain is $22,000 [(Face amount + $14,000) – (Face amount – $8,000)].

Answer (A) is incorrect. The amount of $12,000 assumes a carrying amount equal to face amount plus the amortization. **Answer (C) is incorrect.** The amount of $24,000 ignores the amortization. **Answer (D) is incorrect.** The amount of $26,000 results from increasing the discount by the amortization.

19. On July 1, Year 4, Pell Co. purchased Green Corp. 10-year, 8% bonds with a face amount of $500,000 for $420,000. The bonds are classified as held-to-maturity, mature on June 30, Year 14, and pay interest semiannually on June 30 and December 31. Using the interest method, Pell recorded bond discount amortization of $1,800 for the 6 months ended December 31, Year 4. From this long-term investment, Pell should report Year 4 revenue of

A. $16,800

B. $18,200

C. $20,000

D. $21,800

Answer (D) is correct.

REQUIRED: The interest revenue when amortization of bond discount is known.

DISCUSSION: Interest income for a bond issued at a discount is equal to the sum of the periodic cash flows and the amount of bond discount amortized during the interest period. The periodic cash flows are equal to $20,000 ($500,000 face amount × 8% coupon rate × 1/2 year). The discount amortization is given as $1,800. Thus, revenue for the 6-month period from July 1 to December 31, Year 4, is $21,800 ($20,000 + $1,800).

Answer (A) is incorrect. The amount of $16,800 is 50% of 8% of $420,000. **Answer (B) is incorrect.** The amount of $18,200 equals the cash flow minus discount amortization. **Answer (C) is incorrect.** The amount of $20,000 equals the cash flow.

STUDY UNIT SIX

RECEIVABLES

(12 pages of outline)

This study unit primarily covers **accounts and notes receivable**, assets less liquid than available-for-sale securities but more liquid than inventories. **Accounts receivable** often are short-term, unsecured, and informal credit arrangements (open accounts). **Notes receivable** are evidenced by a formal instrument, such as a promissory note. A formal document provides its holder with a stronger legal status than does an account receivable.

6.1 ACCOUNTS RECEIVABLE -- FUNDAMENTALS

1. **Definition**
   a. A receivable is an asset recognized to reflect a claim against another party for the receipt of money, goods, or services. For most accounting purposes, the claim is expected to be settled in cash.
   b. The recording of a receivable, which often coincides with revenue recognition, is consistent with accrual accounting.
2. **Current vs. Noncurrent Receivables**
   a. A receivable is a **current** asset if it is reasonably expected to be collected within the longer of 1 year or the entity's normal operating cycle.
      1) Otherwise, it should be classified as **noncurrent**. Noncurrent receivables are measured at the present value of expected cash flows.
3. **Trade vs. Nontrade Receivables**
   a. **Trade receivables**, the majority of receivables, are current assets resulting from credit sales to customers in the normal course of business and due in customary trade terms.
      1) They are normally unsecured and noninterest-bearing.
      2) They represent unconditional rights to consideration from contracts with customers.
   b. **Nontrade receivables** are all other receivables. They include among others
      1) Lease receivables
      2) Interest, dividends, rent, or royalties accrued

4. **Trade Discounts**

   a. Trade discounts adjust the **gross (list) price** for different buyers, quantities, and costs. **Net price after the trade discount** is the basis for recognition.

EXAMPLE 6-1 Trade Discount
An item with a list price of $1,000 may be subject to a 40% trade discount in sales to wholesalers. Thus, $400 is subtracted from the list price in arriving at the actual selling price of $600. Only the $600 is recorded. The accounts do not reflect trade discounts.

   b. Some sellers offer **chain-trade discounts** such as 40%, 10%, which means certain buyers receive both a 40% discount and a 10% discount.

EXAMPLE 6-2 Chain-Trade Discount
In Example 6-1, an additional discount of $60 reduces the actual selling price to $540. All journal entries by the buyer and seller are for $540, with no recognition of the list price or the discount. The two discounts are not added but are calculated sequentially.

   c. Trade discounts are solely a means of calculating the sales price. They are not recorded.

5. **Cash Discounts**

   a. Cash discounts (prompt payment discounts) accelerate cash collection by rewarding customers for early payment.

      1) A common example of prompt payment discount is 2/10, n/30. It means a 2% discount if the invoice is paid within 10 days, or the entire balance is due in 30 days.

   b. Because of the uncertainty as to whether customers will pay during the discount period and receive the discount, the consideration in this type of contract is variable.

      1) At contract inception, an entity should estimate the number of customers that are expected to receive the discount and recognize revenue based on the expected amount of consideration to which it will be entitled.

6. **Measurement**

   a. Accounts receivable are presented at the net amount expected to be collected. They are measured using the amortized cost basis and reported minus the allowance for credit losses (previously called the allowance for uncollectible accounts).

   b. The amortized cost basis is the amount at which an account receivable is originated or acquired, adjusted for applicable accrued interest and amortization of premium or discount (in the case of noncurrent receivables), cash and trade discounts, collection of cash, and write-offs.

   c. The **allowance for credit losses** on accounts receivable must be recorded at the reporting date. It represents the portion of accounts receivable that the entity does not expect to collect.

      1) The allowance for credit losses is a valuation account that is deducted from the accounts receivable balance.

d. Initial recognition of the allowance for credit losses and subsequent changes in the allowance balance are recognized immediately in the income statement in the **credit loss expense** (previously called bad debt expense) account.

1) An increase in the balance of the allowance for credit losses is recognized as a credit loss expense.

Credit loss expense	$XXX	
Allowance for credit losses		$XXX

2) A decrease in the balance of the allowance for credit losses is recognized as a reversal of credit loss expense.

Allowance for credit losses	$XXX	
Credit loss expense		$XXX

e. The allowance for credit losses should be estimated based on entity's past experience taking into account current and forecasted economic conditions.

7. **Balance Sheet Presentation**

a. On the face of the balance sheet, the carrying amount of accounts receivable is presented net of any allowance for credit losses.

b. The allowance for credit losses must be separately presented as a deduction from the balance of accounts receivable.

Balance sheet:	
Accounts receivable	$X,XXX
(Allowance for credit losses)	(X,XXX)
Accounts receivable, net	$X,XXX

c. **Material receivables** should be segregated. Among the usual categories are

1) Notes receivable (with disclosure of the effective interest rates)
2) Trade receivables
3) Nontrade receivables

d. Receivables should be separated into **current and noncurrent** portions.

e. Discount or premium resulting from a present value measurement directly decreases or increases the face amount of a note.

f. **Disclosure** should be made of

1) Related party receivables, e.g., those arising from loans to employees or affiliates
2) Pledged or assigned receivables
3) Concentrations of credit risk (described in Study Unit 4, Subunit 6)

STOP & REVIEW

You have completed the outline for this subunit.
Study multiple-choice question 1 on page 179.

6.2 TRADE RECEIVABLES

1. **Overview**
   a. Trade receivables are current, noninterest-bearing accounts receivable that are reported at the net amount expected to be collected, i.e., net of an allowance for credit losses.
      1) Interest recognition (except for late payment) and present value calculations are not relevant.
   b. The principal measurement issue for accounts receivable is the estimation of the **allowance for credit losses** and calculation of **credit loss expenses** for the period.
      1) The two approaches to accounting for credit losses are the direct write-off method and the allowance method. However, only the allowance method is acceptable under GAAP.
2. **Direct Write-Off Method (not allowed under GAAP)**
   a. The direct write-off method expenses bad debts when they are determined to be uncollectible. It is **not acceptable under GAAP** because
      1) It does not match revenue and expense when the receivable and the write-off are recorded in different periods.
      2) It does not state receivables at the net amount expected to be collected.
   b. This method is acceptable for tax purposes.
3. **Allowance Method (required under GAAP)**
   a. The allowance method attempts to match credit loss expense with the related revenue. This method is **required under GAAP**.
      1) The periodic journal entry to record credit loss expense is

Credit loss expense	$XXX	
Allowance for credit losses		$XXX

      2) As specific accounts receivable are written off, they are charged to the allowance account.

Allowance for credit losses	$XXX	
Accounts receivable		$XXX

      3) Thus, the **write-off** of a particular account has no effect on expenses.
         a) Write-offs do not affect the carrying amount of the net accounts receivable balance because the reductions of gross accounts receivable and the allowance are the same.
      4) In the balance sheet, the carrying amount of accounts receivable is reported at the net amount expected to be collected.

Gross accounts receivable − **Allowance for credit losses** = **Carrying amount of accounts receivable**

4. **Measurement of the Allowance for Credit Losses**

   a. The ending balance of the allowance for credit losses is a percentage of the ending balance of accounts receivable.

      1) Credit loss expense reflects the adjustment of the allowance to its correct ending balance.

EXAMPLE 6-3 Allowance for Credit Losses

Midburg Co. has the following unadjusted account balances at year end:

Cash	$ 85,000 Dr.
Accounts receivable	100,000 Dr.
Allowance for credit losses	2,000 Cr.
Sales on credit	500,000 Cr.

Based on Midburg's experience, 6% of accounts receivable are determined to be uncollectible. Thus, the ending balance of the allowance for credit losses is $6,000 ($100,000 × 6%). Because the allowance currently has a balance of $2,000, the following journal entry is required:

Credit loss expense ($6,000 – $2,000)	$4,000	
Allowance for credit losses		$4,000

Balance sheet presentation	
Accounts receivable	$100,000
Minus: Allowance for credit losses	(6,000)
Accounts receivable, net	$ 94,000

   b. An entity rarely experiences a single rate of uncollectibility on all its accounts. For this reason, entities generally prepare an **aging schedule** for accounts receivable.

EXAMPLE 6-4 Aging Schedule for Accounts Receivable

Midburg prepares the following aging schedule for its accounts receivable:

Balance Range	Less than 30 Days	31-60 Days	61-90 Days	Over 90 Days	Total Balances
$0 - $100	$ 5,000	$ 200	$ 100	$ 100	$ 5,400
$100 - $1,000	8,000	3,800			11,800
$1,000 - $5,000	20,000	2,000	1,900		23,900
$5,000 - $10,000	38,000		8,000	900	46,900
Over $10,000		12,000			12,000
Totals	$71,000	$18,000	$10,000	$1,000	$100,000

Midburg then applies an appropriate percentage to each stratum based on experience.

Aging Intervals	Balance	Estimated Uncollectible	Ending Allowance
Less than 30 days	$ 71,000	2%	$1,420
30-60 days	18,000	12%	2,160
61-90 days	10,000	15%	1,500
Over 90 days	1,000	20%	200
Total	$100,000		$5,280

Because the allowance currently has a balance of $2,000, the following journal entry is required to establish the proper measurement:

Credit loss expense ($5,280 – $2,000)	$3,280	
Allowance for credit losses		$3,280

Balance sheet presentation	
Accounts receivable	$100,000
Minus: Allowance for credit losses	(5,280)
Accounts receivable, net	$ 94,720

5. Collection of Accounts Previously Written Off

a. Occasionally, a customer pays an account that was previously written off and was not expected to be recovered. The journal entry is

Cash	$XXX	
Allowance for credit losses		$XXX

SUCCESS TIP

The following equation illustrates the reconciliation of the beginning and ending balances of the allowance for credit losses:

Beginning allowance for credit losses	$XXX
Credit loss expense recognized for the period	XXX
Minus: Accounts receivable written off	(XXX)
Collection of accounts receivable previously written off	XXX
Ending allowance for credit losses	$XXX

The ending balance of the allowance is a percentage of the ending balance of accounts receivable, and credit loss expense is calculated using the equation above.

EXAMPLE 6-5 Collection of Written-Off Accounts

A retailer had the following account balances on January 1, Year 1:

- Accounts receivable 145,000 Dr.
- Allowance for credit losses 8,000 Cr.

The following information pertains to the retailer's accounts receivable in Year 1:

- Credit sales for the year $400,000
- Collections of current-year credit sales 240,000
- Accounts written off on 7/1/Year 1 5,000
- Collection of accounts that were written off last year that the retailer did not expect to collect 6,000

Based on past experience and considering current and forecasted economic conditions, the retailer estimates that 4% of year-end accounts receivable are expected to be uncollectible. The retailer recorded the following journal entries in Year 1:

	Sales on credit:		
(A)	Accounts receivable	$400,000	
	Sales		$400,000
	Collections on credit sales:		
(B)	Cash	$240,000	
	Accounts receivable		$240,000
	Accounts considered uncollectible written off:		
(C)	Allowance for credit losses	$5,000	
	Accounts receivable		$5,000
	Account previously written off collected:		
(D)	Cash	$6,000	
	Allowance for credit losses		$6,000

-- Continued on next page --

EXAMPLE 6-5 -- Continued

After the Year 1 activity is recorded, the year-end balance of accounts receivable is calculated as follows:

Accounts Receivable

1/1/Year 1	$145,000	
(A)	400,000	$240,000 (B)
		5,000 (C)
12/31/Year 1	$300,000	

The year-end balance of the allowance for credit losses is **$12,000** ($300,000 × 4%). The credit loss expense for Year 1 is calculated below as an adjustment of the allowance to its ending balance.

Allowance for Credit Losses

(C) $5,000	$ 8,000	1/1/Year 1
	6,000	(D)
	3,000	**Credit loss expense** (E)
	$12,000	12/31/Year 1

	Year-end adjustment of the allowance and credit loss expense recognition:		
(E)	Credit loss expense	$3,000	
	Allowance for credit losses		$3,000

On the balance sheet, the carrying amount of accounts receivable is reported as follows:

12/31/Year 1 balance sheet:	
Accounts receivable	$300,000
Minus: Allowance for credit losses	(12,000)
Accounts receivable, net	$288,000

In practice, the collection of accounts previously written off also may be recorded directly as a reduction of credit loss expense. However, both methods result in the same amounts of allowance for credit losses and credit loss expense for the period.

	Account previously written off collected and recorded in the credit loss expense account:		
(D)	Cash	$6,000	
	Credit loss expense		$6,000

The year-end allowance is still $12,000 ($300,000 × 4%), and the adjustment to its ending balance is $9,000.

Allowance for Credit Losses

(C) $5,000	$ 8,000	1/1/Year 1
	9,000	**Credit loss expense** (E)
	$12,000	12/31/Year 1

	Year-end adjustment of the allowance and credit loss expense recognition:		
(E)	Credit loss expense	$9,000	
	Allowance for credit losses		$9,000

Thus, the credit loss expense for Year 1 is $3,000 ($9,000 E – $6,000 D).

STOP & REVIEW

You have completed the outline for this subunit.
Study multiple-choice questions 2 through 6 beginning on page 179.

6.3 TRANSFERS OF RECEIVABLES AND OTHER FINANCIAL ASSETS

1. **Factoring**
   a. Factoring is a transfer of receivables to a third party (a factor) who assumes the responsibility of collection.
   b. Factoring discounts receivables on a **nonrecourse, notification basis**. Thus, payments by the debtors on the transferred assets are made to the factor. If the transferor (seller) surrenders control, the transaction is a sale of accounts receivable.
      1) If a sale is **with recourse**, the transferor (seller) may be required to make payments to the transferee or to buy back receivables in specified circumstances. For example, the seller may become liable for defaults up to a given percentage of the transferred receivables.
         a) The sale proceeds are reduced by the fair value of the recourse obligation.
         b) If the transfer with recourse does not qualify as a sale, the parties account for the transaction as a secured borrowing with a pledge of noncash collateral.
      2) If a sale is **without recourse**, the transferee (credit agency) assumes the risks and receives the rewards of collection. This sale is final, and the seller has no further liabilities to the transferee.
   c. A factor usually receives a high financing fee plus a fee for collection. Furthermore, the factor often operates more efficiently than its clients because of the specialized nature of its services.

EXAMPLE 6-6 Transfer of Accounts Receivable

A factor charges a 2% fee plus an interest rate of 18% on all cash advanced to a transferor of accounts receivable. Monthly sales are $100,000, and the factor advances 90% of the receivables submitted after deducting the 2% fee and the interest. Credit terms are net 60 days. What is the cost to the transferor of this arrangement?

Amount of receivables submitted	$100,000	
Minus: 10% reserve	(10,000)	
Minus: 2% factor's fee	(2,000)	
Amount accruing to the transferor	$ 88,000	
Minus: 18% interest for 60 days	(2,640)	[$88,000 × 18% × (60 ÷ 360)]
Amount to be received immediately	$ 85,360	

The transferor also will receive the $10,000 reserve at the end of the 60-day period if it has not been absorbed by sales returns and allowances. Thus, the total cost to the transferor to factor the receivables for the month is $4,640 ($2,000 factor fee + interest of $2,640). Assuming that the factor has approved the customers' credit in advance (the sale is without recourse), the transferor will not absorb any bad debts.

The journal entry to record the preceding transaction is

Cash	$85,360	
Due from factor	10,000	
Loss on sale of receivables	2,000	
Prepaid interest/interest expense	2,640	
Accounts receivable		$100,000

d. **Credit card sales** are a common form of factoring. The retailer benefits by prompt receipt of cash and avoidance of credit losses and other costs. In return, the credit card company charges a fee.

1) Two methods of accounting for credit card sales may be necessary depending upon the reimbursement method used.

a) If payment is after submission of credit card receipts, the retailer initially records a sale and a receivable. After payment, the entry is

Cash	$XXX	
Service charge expense	XXX	
Receivable		$XXX

b) If the retailer's checking account is increased by the direct deposit of credit card receipts, no receivable is recognized. The entry is to credit sales instead of a receivable.

Cash	$XXX	
Service charge expense	XXX	
Sales		$XXX

2. **Pledging**

a. A pledge (a general assignment) is the use of receivables as collateral (security) for a loan. The borrower agrees to use collections of receivables to repay the loan.

1) Upon default, the lender can sell the receivables to recover the loan proceeds.

b. Because a pledge is a relatively informal arrangement, it is not reflected in the accounts. A transfer of financial assets is a sale only when the transferor relinquishes control.

1) If the transfer (e.g., a pledge) of accounts receivable is not a sale, the transaction is a secured borrowing. The transferor becomes a debtor, and the transferee becomes a creditor in possession of collateral.

a) However, absent default, the collateral remains an asset of the transferor.

3. **Transfers of Financial Assets -- Objectives and Control**

a. The accounting for transfers of financial assets is based on a **financial-components approach** focused on control.

b. The objective is for each party to

1) Recognize the assets it controls and the liabilities it has incurred,
2) Derecognize assets when control has been given up, and
3) Derecognize liabilities when they have been extinguished.

c. Whether **control** exists depends, among other things, on the transferor's continuing involvement. **Continuing involvement** is the right to receive benefits from the assets or an obligation to provide additional assets to a party related to the transfer.

4. **Transfers of Financial Assets -- Sales**

   a. Transfers of financial assets include transfers of (1) an entire financial asset, (2) a group of entire financial assets, and (3) a participating interest in an entire financial asset.

      1) The holder of a **participating interest** receives cash in proportion to the share of ownership, and all holders have the same priority.

   b. A transfer of financial assets is a **sale** when the transferor **relinquishes control**. The transferor relinquishes control only if certain conditions are met:

      1) The transferred assets are beyond the reach of the transferor and its creditors;
      2) Transferees may pledge or exchange the assets or interests received; and
      3) The transferor does not maintain effective control through, for example,

         a) An agreement to reacquire the assets before maturity or
         b) An agreement making it probable that the transferee will require repurchase.

   c. If the transfer of an **entire financial asset** (or a group) qualifies as a sale, the financial components approach is applied. The transferor

      1) Derecognizes the financial assets transferred
      2) Recognizes and initially measures at fair value the assets obtained and liabilities incurred
      3) Recognizes any gain or loss in earnings

EXAMPLE 6-7 Transfer of a Financial Asset

A company transfers its entire financial interest in its notes receivable for $60,000. The receivable has a carrying amount of $62,500. The journal entry to record this transfer is

Cash	$60,000	
Loss on transfer	2,500	
Notes receivable		$62,500

5. **Transfers of Financial Assets -- Secured Borrowings**

   a. If the transfer is not a sale, the transaction is a secured borrowing. The transferor becomes a debtor, and the transferee becomes a creditor in possession of collateral.

   b. A secured borrowing is a formal borrowing arrangement. The borrower signs a promissory note and financing agreement, and specific receivables are pledged as **collateral**.

      1) The loan is at a specified percentage of the face amount of the collateral, and interest and service fees are charged to the borrower.

   c. The collateral may be segregated from other receivables on the balance sheet.

Accounts receivable assigned	$XXX	
Accounts receivable		$XXX

      1) The note payable is reported as a **liability**.

Cash	$XXX	
Notes payable		$XXX

STOP & REVIEW

You have completed the outline for this subunit.
Study multiple-choice questions 7 through 9 on page 182.

6.4 NOTES RECEIVABLE

1. **Definition**
   a. A note receivable is a debt evidenced by a two-party writing (a **promissory note**). Notes are more formal promises to pay than accounts receivable.
   b. Most notes bear interest (explicitly or implicitly) because they represent longer-term borrowings than accounts receivable.
   c. Notes with original maturities to the holder of **3 months or less** are treated as cash equivalents and accounted for at **net realizable value**.
      1) Because the interest implicit in the maturity amount is immaterial, no interest revenue is recognized.
   d. Notes classified as **current assets** are usually recorded at face amount and reported minus an allowance for credit losses.
   e. Notes classified as **noncurrent assets** are recorded at the **present value of the expected future cash flows** and reported minus an allowance for credit losses.
      1) Any difference between the proceeds and the face amount must be recognized as a premium or discount and amortized.
   f. When the note's stated interest rate is a reasonable rate (e.g., the market rate), the note is issued at its face amount, and no discount or premium is recognized.
2. **Noninterest-Bearing Notes**
   a. Sometimes notes are issued with no stated rate and an **unknown effective rate**. In these cases, the rate must be **imputed** from other facts surrounding the transaction. Such facts include the marketability of the note and the debtor's creditworthiness.
      1) Thus, the interest is **implicit**.
   b. A note may bear no explicit interest because interest is included in the amount to be paid at maturity. The accounting treatment is to debit notes receivable for its face (maturity) amount, credit cash (or other appropriate account), and credit discount. The discount is amortized to interest revenue.
      1) The entry for initial recognition is

Notes receivable	$XXX	
Cash		$XXX
Discount on note		XXX

         a) Notes receivable are reported in the financial statements at their face amount minus any unamortized discount.
      2) At the end of the period, the discount is amortized to interest revenue using the effective-interest method explained in Study Unit 5, Subunit 6.
         a) The entry for recognition of interest is

Discount on note	$XXX	
Interest revenue		$XXX

      3) When the note arises in the ordinary course of business and is "due in customary trade terms not exceeding approximately 1 year," the interest element need not be recognized.

3. **Unreasonable Interest**

   a. The term "noninterest-bearing" is confusing. It is used not only (1) when a note bears implicit interest but also (2) when no actual interest is charged (the cash proceeds equal the face amount).

      1) When a note is noninterest-bearing in the second scenario above or bears interest at a rate that is unreasonable in the circumstances, interest must be **imputed (estimated)**. A note with imputed interest also results in amortization of discount or premium.

   b. When a **note is exchanged solely for cash**, and no other right or privilege is exchanged, the proceeds are assumed to reflect the present value of the note. The effective interest rate is therefore the interest rate implicit in that present value.

   c. When a **note is exchanged for property, goods, or services**, the interest rate determined by the parties in an arm's-length transaction is presumed to be fair.

      1) That presumption is overcome when (a) no interest is stated, (b) the stated rate is unreasonable, or (c) the nominal amount of the note materially differs from the cash sales price of the item or the market value of the note.

         a) In these circumstances, the transaction should be recorded at the more clearly determinable of

            i) The fair value of the property, goods, or services or
            ii) The market value of the note.

         b) Absent established exchange prices or evidence of the note's market value, the present value of a note with no stated rate or an unreasonable rate should be determined by discounting future payments using an imputed rate. The prevailing rate for similar instruments of issuers with similar credit ratings normally helps determine the appropriate rate.

   d. The stated interest rate may be less than the effective rate applicable in the circumstances because the lender has received **other stated (or unstated) rights and privileges** as part of the bargain.

      1) The difference between the respective present values of the note computed at the stated rate and at the effective rate should be accounted for as the cost of the rights or privileges obtained.

4. **Discounting of Notes Receivable**

   a. When a note receivable is discounted (sold, usually at a bank), the gain or loss on disposition of the note must be calculated.

   b. The holder of the note receives the maturity amount (Principal + Interest at maturity) of the note minus the bank's discount. The bank usually collects the maturity amount from the maker of the note.

STOP & REVIEW

You have completed the outline for this subunit.
Study multiple-choice questions 10 through 18 beginning on page 183.

QUESTIONS

6.1 Accounts Receivable -- Fundamentals

1. The following information relates to Jay Co.'s accounts receivable for the year just ended:

Accounts receivable, 1/1	$ 650,000
Credit sales for the year	2,700,000
Sales returns for the year	75,000
Accounts written off during the year	40,000
Collections from customers during the year	2,150,000
Estimated uncollectible accounts at 12/31	110,000

What amount should Jay report for accounts receivable, before allowance for credit losses, at December 31?

A. $1,200,000

B. $1,125,000

C. $1,085,000

D. $1,165,000

Answer (C) is correct.

REQUIRED: The year-end balance in accounts receivable.

DISCUSSION: The ending balance in accounts receivable consists of the $650,000 beginning debit balance, plus debits for $2,700,000 of credit sales, minus credits for $2,150,000 of collections, $40,000 of accounts written off, and $75,000 of sales returns.

Accounts Receivable (in 000s)

1/1	$ 650	$ 75	Sales returns
Credit sales	2,700	2,150	Collections
		40	Write-offs
12/31	$1,085		

The $110,000 of estimated uncollectible receivables is not relevant because it affects the allowance account but not gross accounts receivable.

Answer (A) is incorrect. The amount of $1,200,000 does not subtract write-offs and sales returns from accounts receivable. **Answer (B) is incorrect.** The amount of $1,125,000 does not subtract sales returns from accounts receivable. **Answer (D) is incorrect.** The accounts written off during the year decrease, not increase, the gross balance of accounts receivable.

6.2 Trade Receivables

2. Rue Co.'s allowance for credit losses had a credit balance of $12,000 at December 31, Year 1. During Year 2, Rue wrote off uncollectible accounts of $48,000. The aging of accounts receivable indicated that a $50,000 allowance for credit losses was required at December 31, Year 2. What amount of credit loss expense should Rue report for Year 2?

A. $48,000

B. $50,000

C. $60,000

D. $86,000

Answer (D) is correct.

REQUIRED: The amount of credit loss expense for Year 2.

DISCUSSION: The beginning balance of the allowance for credit losses was a credit of $12,000. The account was debited for $48,000 when the uncollectible accounts were written off. Thus, the credit for credit loss expense must be $86,000 if the ending balance is $50,000.

Allowance for Credit Losses

		$12,000	1/1/Year 2
Write-offs	$48,000	86,000	Expense
		$50,000	12/3/Year 2

Answer (A) is incorrect. The amount of uncollectible accounts written off in Year 2 is $48,000. **Answer (B) is incorrect.** The ending balance is $50,000. **Answer (C) is incorrect.** The sum of the beginning balance and the amount written off is $60,000.

3. In its December 31, Year 3, balance sheet, Fleet Co. reported accounts receivable of $100,000 before allowance for credit losses of $10,000. Credit sales during Year 4 were $611,000, and collections from customers, excluding recoveries, totaled $591,000. During Year 4, accounts receivable of $45,000 were written off and $17,000 were recovered. Fleet estimated that $15,000 of the accounts receivable at December 31, Year 4, were uncollectible. In its December 31, Year 4, balance sheet, what amount should Fleet report as accounts receivable before allowance for credit losses?

A. $58,000

B. $67,000

C. $75,000

D. $82,000

Answer (C) is correct.

REQUIRED: The balance of accounts receivable.

DISCUSSION: The ending balance in accounts receivable consists of the beginning balance, plus credit sales, minus collections, and minus write-offs. The recovery of accounts that were previously written off does not affect the accounts receivable balance.

Accounts Receivable (in 000s)

1/1/Yr 4	$100	$591	Collections
Sales	611	45	Write-offs
12/31/Yr 4	$ 75		

Answer (A) is incorrect. Subtracting the recovered accounts results in $58,000. The collection of written-off accounts has no effect on the ending balance of accounts receivable. **Answer (B) is incorrect.** The amount of $67,000 equals the ending accounts receivable balance, plus the amount recovered, minus the beginning balance of the allowance for credit losses, minus the estimated uncollectible accounts at year end. **Answer (D) is incorrect.** The amount of $82,000 is calculated by adding the recovered accounts and subtracting the allowance for credit losses from Year 3.

4. For the year ended December 31, Beal Co. estimated its allowance for credit losses using the year-end aging of accounts receivable. The following data are available:

Allowance for credit losses, 1/1	$42,000
Uncollectible accounts written off, 11/30	46,000
Estimated uncollectible accounts per aging, 12/31	52,000

After year-end adjustment, the credit loss expense should be

A. $46,000

B. $48,000

C. $52,000

D. $56,000

Answer (D) is correct.

REQUIRED: The adjusted credit loss expense for the year.

DISCUSSION: As indicated in the T-account analysis presented below, the credit loss expense is calculated as follows:

Allowance

		$42,000	1/1
Write-offs	$46,000	56,000	Credit loss expense
		$52,000	12/31

Answer (A) is incorrect. The amount written off is $46,000. **Answer (B) is incorrect.** The amount of $48,000 would result if the beginning balance in the allowance account had been $46,000 and the write-offs had equaled $42,000. **Answer (C) is incorrect.** The estimate of uncollectible accounts at year end is $52,000.

5. An internal auditor is deriving cash flow data based on an incomplete set of facts. Credit loss expense was $2,000. Additional data for this period follows:

Credit sales	$100,000
Gross accounts receivable -- beginning balance	5,000
Allowance for credit losses -- beginning balance	(500)
Accounts receivable written off	1,000
Increase in net accounts receivable (after subtraction of allowance for credit losses)	30,000

How much cash was collected this period on credit sales?

A. $64,000

B. $68,000

C. $68,500

D. $70,000

Answer (B) is correct.

REQUIRED: The cash collected on credit sales.

DISCUSSION: The beginning balance of gross accounts receivable (A/R) was $5,000 (debit). Thus, net beginning A/R was $4,500 ($5,000 – $500 credit in the allowance for credit losses). The allowance was credited for the $2,000 credit loss expense. Accordingly, the ending allowance (credit) was $1,500 ($500 – $1,000 write-off + $2,000). Given a $30,000 increase in net A/R, ending net A/R must have been $34,500 ($4,500 beginning net A/R + $30,000), with ending gross A/R of $36,000 ($34,500 + $1,500). Collections were therefore $68,000 ($5,000 beginning gross A/R – $1,000 write-off + $100,000 credit sales – $36,000 ending gross A/R).

Gross A/R

$ 5,000	Beg. Bal.	$ 1,000	Write-off
100,000	Cr. Sales	68,000	Collections
$ 36,000	End. Bal.		

Answer (A) is incorrect. Credit sales minus the ending gross accounts receivable equals $64,000. **Answer (C) is incorrect.** The amount of $68,500 equals credit sales, minus the increase in net accounts receivable, minus the ending allowance. **Answer (D) is incorrect.** Credit sales minus the increase in net accounts receivable equals $70,000.

6. Foster Co. adjusted its allowance for credit losses at year end. The general ledger balances for the accounts receivable and the related allowance account were $1,000,000 and $40,000, respectively. Foster uses the percentage-of-receivables method to estimate its allowance for credit losses. Accounts receivable were estimated to be 5% uncollectible. What amount should Foster record as an adjustment to its allowance for credit losses at year end?

A. $10,000 decrease.

B. $10,000 increase.

C. $50,000 decrease.

D. $50,000 increase.

Answer (B) is correct.

REQUIRED: The adjustment of the allowance for credit losses.

DISCUSSION: Because the percentage of accounts receivable method is used to estimate the allowance, the accounts receivable balance must be multiplied by 5%. Thus, the allowance for credit losses should be $50,000 ($1,000,000 × 5%). Given that the pre-adjustment allowance for credit losses is $40,000, the year-end adjustment must increase the allowance by $10,000 (debit credit loss expense, credit the allowance).

Answer (A) is incorrect. The adjustment should be a $10,000 increase, not a decrease. **Answer (C) is incorrect.** The year-end allowance for credit losses is $50,000. **Answer (D) is incorrect.** The year-end allowance for credit losses is $50,000.

6.3 Transfers of Receivables and Other Financial Assets

7. Which of the following is a method to generate cash from accounts receivable?

	Assignment	Factoring
A.	Yes	No
B.	Yes	Yes
C.	No	Yes
D.	No	No

Answer (B) is correct.

REQUIRED: The method(s) of generating cash from accounts receivable.

DISCUSSION: Methods of generating cash from accounts receivable include both assignment and factoring. Assignment occurs when specifically named accounts receivable are pledged as collateral for a loan. The accounts receivable remain those of the assignor. However, when cash is collected from these accounts receivable, the cash must be remitted to the assignee. Accounts receivable are factored when they are sold outright to a third party. This sale may be with or without recourse.

Answer (A) is incorrect. Factoring is a way to generate cash from accounts receivable. **Answer (C) is incorrect.** Assignment is a way to generate cash from accounts receivable. **Answer (D) is incorrect.** Both assignment and factoring are ways to generate cash from accounts receivable.

8. Red Co. had $3 million in accounts receivable recorded on its books. Red wanted to convert the $3 million in receivables to cash in a more timely manner than waiting the 45 days for payment as indicated on its invoices. Which of the following would alter the timing of Red's cash flows for the $3 million in receivables already recorded on its books?

A. Change the due date of the invoice.

B. Factor the receivables outstanding.

C. Discount the receivables outstanding.

D. Demand payment from customers before the due date.

Answer (B) is correct.

REQUIRED: The action that alters the timing of cash flows from receivables.

DISCUSSION: Factoring transfers accounts receivable to a finance company or bank (the factor) on a nonrecourse, notification (to debtors) basis. The arrangement is an outright sale. If it meets certain criteria, it is accounted for as a sale of financial assets. The seller therefore accelerates cash inflows in exchange for the factor's fee.

Answer (A) is incorrect. Red and its customers have entered into contracts that establish the due date. It cannot be changed without a new agreement. **Answer (C) is incorrect.** Calculating the present value of the future amounts to be received does not result in cash flows. **Answer (D) is incorrect.** Customers are not contractually obligated to pay before the due date.

9. Gar Co. factored its receivables without recourse with Ross Bank. Gar received cash as a result of this transaction, which is best described as a

A. Loan from Ross collateralized by Gar's accounts receivable.

B. Loan from Ross to be repaid by the proceeds from Gar's accounts receivable.

C. Sale of Gar's accounts receivable to Ross, with the risk of uncollectible accounts retained by Gar.

D. Sale of Gar's accounts receivable to Ross, with the risk of uncollectible accounts transferred to Ross.

Answer (D) is correct.

REQUIRED: The effect of factoring receivables without recourse.

DISCUSSION: When receivables are factored without recourse, the transaction is treated as a sale and the buyer accepts the risk of collectibility. The seller bears no responsibility for credit losses. A sale without recourse is not a loan. In a sale without recourse, the buyer assumes the risk of uncollectible accounts.

6.4 Notes Receivable

10. On January 1, Year 3, Mill Co. exchanged equipment for a $200,000, noninterest-bearing note due on January 1, Year 6. The prevailing rate of interest for a note of this type at January 1, Year 3, was 10%. The present value of $1 at 10% for three periods is 0.75. What amount of interest revenue should be included in Mill's Year 4 income statement?

A. $0

B. $15,000

C. $16,500

D. $20,000

Answer (C) is correct.

REQUIRED: The interest income from a noninterest-bearing note received for property.

DISCUSSION: When a noninterest-bearing note is exchanged for property, and neither the note nor the property has a clearly determinable exchange price, the present value of the note should be determined by discounting all future payments using an appropriately imputed interest rate. Mill Company will receive $200,000 cash in 3 years. Assuming that 10% is the appropriate imputed rate of interest, the present value (initial carrying amount) of the note at January 1, Year 3, was $150,000 ($200,000 × 0.75). Interest revenue for Year 3 was $15,000 ($150,000 × 10%), and the entry was to debit the discount and credit interest revenue for that amount. Thus, the carrying amount of the note at January 1, Year 4, was $165,000 ($200,000 face amount – $35,000 unamortized discount). Interest revenue for Year 4 is therefore $16,500 ($165,000 carrying amount × 10% interest rate).

Answer (A) is incorrect. Interest should be recognized equal to the imputed rate times the carrying amount of the note. **Answer (B) is incorrect.** Interest income for Year 3 was $15,000. **Answer (D) is incorrect.** The amount of $20,000 is 10% of the face amount of the note.

11. A note payable was issued in payment for services received. The services had a fair value less than the face amount of the note payable. The note payable has no stated interest rate. How should the note payable be presented in the statement of financial position?

A. At the face amount.

B. At the face amount with a separate deferred asset for the discount calculated at the imputed interest rate.

C. At the face amount with a separate deferred credit for the discount calculated at the imputed interest rate.

D. At the face amount minus a discount calculated at the imputed interest rate.

Answer (D) is correct.

REQUIRED: The presentation of a noninterest bearing note on the statement of financial position.

DISCUSSION: When a note is exchanged for property, goods, or services, the interest rate determined by the parties in an arm's-length transaction is presumed to be fair. But when the note is issued with no stated rate, the transaction should be recorded at the more clearly determinable of (1) the fair value of goods or services received or (2) the market value of the note. Assuming that the market value of the note cannot be reliably determined, the transaction is recorded at the fair value of services received, if known. Because the fair value of services received is lower than the note's face amount, a discount on the note is recognized. The imputed interest rate on this note is the one that equates the present value of future payments on the note with the fair value of services received.

Answer (A) is incorrect. When a note exchanged for services has no stated rate, the transaction should be recorded at the more clearly determinable of (1) the fair value of services received or (2) the market value of the note. Thus, the note cannot be presented at its face amount. **Answer (B) is incorrect.** Issuance of a note for services received does not result in recognition of a deferred asset. **Answer (C) is incorrect.** Issuance of a note for services received does not result in recognition of a deferred credit.

12. On August 15, Benet Co. sold goods for which it received a note bearing the market rate of interest on that date. The 4-month note was dated July 15. Note principal, together with all interest, is due November 15. When the note was recorded on August 15, which of the following accounts increased?

A. Unearned discount.

B. Interest receivable.

C. Prepaid interest.

D. Interest revenue.

Answer (B) is correct.

REQUIRED: The account that increased when the note was recorded.

DISCUSSION: Because the note bears interest at a reasonable rate (in this case, the market rate), its present value at the date of issuance is the face amount. Accordingly, the note should be recorded at this amount. Interest receivable also may be debited, and unearned interest revenue may be credited. The simple alternative is to debit cash and credit interest revenue when payment is received. If the reporting period ends prior to November 15, the period-end entry is to debit interest receivable and credit accrued interest revenue.

Answer (A) is incorrect. The note bears interest at the market rate. Thus, no discount from its face amount is recorded. **Answer (C) is incorrect.** No prepayment of interest has been made. **Answer (D) is incorrect.** Interest revenue has not yet been earned.

13. On December 1, Year 4, Tigg Mortgage Co. gave Pod Corp. a $200,000, 12% loan. Pod received proceeds of $194,000 after the deduction of a $6,000 nonrefundable loan origination fee. Principal and interest are due in 60 monthly installments of $4,450, beginning January 1, Year 5. The repayments yield an effective interest rate of 12% at a present value of $200,000 and 13.4% at a present value of $194,000. What amount of accrued interest receivable should Tigg include in its December 31, Year 4, balance sheet?

A. $4,450

B. $2,166

C. $2,000

D. $0

Answer (C) is correct.

REQUIRED: The accrued interest receivable at year end.

DISCUSSION: Accrued interest receivable is always equal to the face amount times the nominal rate for the period of the accrual. Thus, the accrued interest receivable is $2,000 [$200,000 × 12% × (1 ÷ 12)].

Answer (A) is incorrect. The monthly installment is $4,450. It includes principal as well as interest. **Answer (B) is incorrect.** The amount of $2,166 is based on a present value of $194,000 and an effective rate of 13.4%. It is the interest revenue from the loan. **Answer (D) is incorrect.** One month's interest should be accrued.

14. On Merf's April 30, Year 4, balance sheet, a note receivable was reported as a noncurrent asset, and its accrued interest for 8 months was reported as a current asset. Which of the following terms would fit Merf's note receivable?

A. Both principal and interest amounts are payable on August 31, Year 4, and August 31, Year 5.

B. Principal and interest are due December 31, Year 4.

C. Both principal and interest amounts are payable on December 31, Year 4, and December 31, Year 5.

D. Principal is due August 31, Year 5. Interest is due August 31, Year 4, and August 31, Year 5.

Answer (D) is correct.

REQUIRED: The terms explaining classification of a note receivable as a noncurrent asset and its accrued interest as a current asset.

DISCUSSION: A noncurrent note receivable is one that is not expected to be converted into cash within 1 year or one operating cycle, whichever is longer. Because the principal is due more than 1 year from the balance sheet date, it must be regarded as noncurrent. However, the accrued interest is a current asset because it is due in 4 months.

Questions 15 and 16 are based on the following information. On January 2, Year 3, Emme Co. sold equipment with a carrying amount of $480,000 in exchange for a $600,000 noninterest-bearing note due January 2, Year 6. There was no established exchange price for the equipment, and the market value of the note cannot be reasonably approximated. The prevailing rate of interest for a note of this type at January 2, Year 3, was 10%. The present value of 1 at 10% for three periods is 0.75.

15. In Emme's Year 3 income statement, what amount should be reported as interest income?

A. $15,000

B. $45,000

C. $48,000

D. $60,000

Answer (B) is correct.

REQUIRED: The interest income from a noninterest-bearing note received for property.

DISCUSSION: When a noninterest-bearing note is exchanged for property, and neither the note nor the property has a clearly determinable exchange price, the present value of the note should be the basis for recording the transaction. The present value is determined by discounting all future payments using an appropriately imputed interest rate. Emme Co. will receive $600,000 cash in 3 years. Assuming that 10% is the appropriate imputed rate of interest, the present value (initial carrying amount) of the note at January 2, Year 3, was $450,000 ($600,000 × 0.75). Under the interest method, interest income for Year 3 was $45,000 ($450,000 × 10%), and the entry is to debit the discount and credit interest income for that amount.

Answer (A) is incorrect. The amount of $15,000 is the difference between 10% of the face amount and 10% of the carrying amount. **Answer (C) is incorrect.** Interest income is based on the present value of the note, not the carrying amount of the equipment. **Answer (D) is incorrect.** Interest income is based on the carrying amount of the note, not the face amount.

16. In Emme's Year 3 income statement, what amount should be reported as gain (loss) on sale of equipment?

A. $(30,000)

B. $30,000

C. $120,000

D. $150,000

Answer (A) is correct.

REQUIRED: The amount reported as gain (loss) on the sale of machinery.

DISCUSSION: Emme Co. sold equipment with a carrying amount of $480,000 and received a note with a present value of $450,000 ($600,000 × .75). Thus, Emme should report a $30,000 loss ($480,000 – $450,000).

Answer (B) is incorrect. The present value of the note is $30,000 less than the carrying amount surrendered. **Answer (C) is incorrect.** The amount of $120,000 is the difference between the face amount of the note and the carrying amount of the equipment. **Answer (D) is incorrect.** The amount of $150,000 is the discount (Face amount – Present value).

17. On December 1, Year 4, Money Co. gave Home Co. a $200,000, 11% loan. Money paid proceeds of $194,000 after the deduction of a $6,000 nonrefundable loan origination fee. Principal and interest are due in 60 monthly installments of $4,310, beginning January 1, Year 5. The repayments yield an effective interest rate of 11% at a present value of $200,000 and 12.4% at a present value of $194,000. What amount of income from this loan should Money report in its Year 4 income statement?

A. $0

B. $1,833

C. $2,005

D. $7,833

Answer (C) is correct.

REQUIRED: The amount of income from the loan at year end.

DISCUSSION: Under the effective-interest method, the effective rate of interest is applied to the net carrying amount of the receivable to determine periodic interest revenue. Thus, interest revenue from the loan for the month of December equals $2,005 [$194,000 × 12.4% × (1 ÷ 12)].

Answer (A) is incorrect. One month's interest should be accrued. **Answer (B) is incorrect.** The amount of $1,833 is the accrued interest receivable, which equals the face amount times the nominal rate for the period [$200,000 × 11% × (1 ÷ 12)]. **Answer (D) is incorrect.** The amount of $7,833 equals the $6,000 origination fee plus the accrued interest receivable of $1,833.

18. Leaf Co. purchased from Oak Co. a $20,000, 8%, 5-year note that required five equal, annual year-end payments of $5,009. The note was discounted to yield a 9% rate to Leaf. At the date of purchase, Leaf recorded the note at its present value of $19,485. What should be the total interest revenue earned by Leaf over the life of this note?

A. $5,045

B. $5,560

C. $8,000

D. $9,000

Answer (B) is correct.

REQUIRED: The total interest revenue earned on a discounted note receivable.

DISCUSSION: Leaf Co. will receive cash of $25,045 ($5,009 × 5). Thus, interest revenue is $5,560 ($25,045 – $19,485 present value).

Answer (A) is incorrect. The amount of $5,045 does not include the discount amortization. **Answer (C) is incorrect.** The amount of $8,000 equals $20,000 times 8% nominal interest for 5 years. **Answer (D) is incorrect.** The amount of $9,000 equals $20,000 times the 9% yield rate for 5 years.

STUDY UNIT SEVEN

INVENTORIES

(24 pages of outline)

Inventory consists of the tangible goods intended to be sold to produce revenue. The cost of inventory is a deferral. It is not included in earnings until the reporting period in which the inventory is sold (produces revenue). Many methods of costing inventory are acceptable. Inventory and related concepts always are tested on the CPA Exam.

7.1 INVENTORY FUNDAMENTALS

1. **Definition**

   a. Inventory is the total of tangible personal property

      1) Held for sale in the ordinary course of business,

      2) In the form of work-in-process to be completed and sold in the ordinary course of business, or

      3) To be used up currently in producing goods or services for sale.

   b. Inventory does not include long-term assets subject to depreciation.

2. **Sources of Inventories**

   a. **Retailing**

      1) A trading (retailing) entity purchases merchandise to be resold without substantial modification. Such entities may also have supplies inventories.

      2) For a retailer, **cost of goods sold** essentially equals beginning merchandise inventory, plus purchases for the period, minus ending merchandise inventory (purchases adjusted for the change in inventory).

Cost of Goods Sold for a Retailer

Beginning inventory		$ XXX,XXX
Purchases	$X,XXX,XXX	
Purchase returns and discounts	(XX,XXX)	
Freight-in	XX,XXX	
Net purchases		X,XXX,XXX
Goods available for sale		$X,XXX,XXX
Ending inventory		**(XXX,XXX)**
Cost of goods sold		$X,XXX,XXX

   b. **Manufacturing**

      1) An entity that acquires goods for conversion into substantially different products has inventories of goods consumed directly or indirectly in production (direct materials and supplies), goods in the course of production (work-in-process), and goods awaiting sale (finished goods).

      2) For a manufacturer, **cost of goods sold** essentially equals beginning finished goods inventory, plus the cost of goods manufactured, minus ending finished goods inventory.

3) **Cost of goods manufactured** equals beginning work-in-process, plus current manufacturing costs (Direct materials + Direct labor + Production overhead), minus ending work-in-process (current manufacturing costs adjusted for the change in work-in-process).

Cost of Goods Sold for a Manufacturer

Beginning materials inventory		$ XXX,XXX	
Purchases	$X,XXX,XXX		
Purchase returns and discounts	(XX,XXX)		
Freight-in	XX,XXX		
Net purchases		X,XXX,XXX	
Materials available for use		$X,XXX,XXX	
Ending materials inventory		**(XXX,XXX)**	
Direct materials used in production			$X,XXX,XXX
Direct labor costs			X,XXX,XXX
Manufacturing overhead costs			XXX,XXX
Total manufacturing costs for the period			$X,XXX,XXX
Beginning work-in-process inventory			XXX,XXX
Ending work-in-process inventory			**(XXX,XXX)**
Cost of goods manufactured			$X,XXX,XXX
Beginning finished goods inventory			XXX,XXX
Goods available for sale			$X,XXX,XXX
Ending finished goods inventory			**(XXX,XXX)**
Cost of goods sold			$X,XXX,XXX

3. **Inventory Accounting Systems**

   a. Entities that require continuous monitoring of inventory use a perpetual system. Entities that have no need to monitor continuously use a periodic system.

   b. **Perpetual System**

      1) In a perpetual system, purchases, purchase returns and allowances, purchase discounts, and freight-in (transportation in) are charged directly to inventory.

         a) Inventory and cost of goods sold are adjusted as sales occur.

         b) A physical count is needed to detect material misstatements in the records.

         c) The amount of inventory on hand and the cost of goods sold can be determined at any moment in time.

         d) Inventory over-and-short is debited (credited) when the physical count is less (greater) than the balance in the perpetual records.

            i) This account is either closed to cost of goods sold or reported separately under (a) other revenues and gains or (b) other expenses and losses.

Journal Entries in a Perpetual Inventory System

<u>Acquisition and Returns</u>		
Inventory	$XXX	
Accounts payable		$XXX
<u>Sale</u>		
Accounts receivable	$XXX	
Sales		$XXX
Cost of goods sold	XXX	
Inventory		XXX

c. **Periodic System**

1) In a periodic system, the inventory and cost of goods sold accounts are updated at specific intervals, such as quarterly or annually, based on the results of a **physical count**.

   a) The beginning inventory balance remains unchanged during the accounting period.

   b) Goods bought from suppliers, freight-in, and adjustments usually are tracked in a separate temporary account (i.e., **purchases**).

   c) Changes in inventory and cost of goods sold are recorded only at the end of the period, based on the physical count.

   d) After the physical count,

      i) The inventory balance is adjusted to match the physical count and
      ii) Cost of goods sold is calculated.

Journal Entries in a Periodic Inventory System

Acquisition and Returns		
Purchases	$XXX	
Accounts payable		$XXX
Accounts payable	XXX	
Purchase returns		XXX
Sale		
Accounts receivable	$XXX	
Sales		$XXX
Closing		
Inventory (physical count)	$XXX	
Cost of goods sold (difference)	XXX	
Purchases (total amount for period)		$XXX
Inventory (beginning balance)		XXX

EXAMPLE 7-1 Perpetual vs. Periodic Inventory System

Entity A's January 1, Year 1, inventory consists of 1,000 units with a cost of $5 per unit. The following are Entity A's Year 2 transactions:

April 1: Sold 600 inventory units for $4,800 in cash.

May 1: Purchased 250 inventory units for $5 in cash per unit.

-- Continued on next page --

EXAMPLE 7-1 -- Continued

The year-end result of the physical count was 650 inventory units. The following are Entity A's journal entries under the perpetual and periodic systems:

Perpetual System			Periodic System		
Inventory sale April 1:					
Cash	$4,800		Cash	$4,800	
Sales		$4,800	Sales		$4,800
Cost of goods sold (600 × $5)	$3,000				
Inventory		$3,000			
Inventory purchase May 1:					
Inventory (250 × $5)	$1,250		Purchases	$1,250	
Cash		$1,250	Cash		$1,250
After the physical count on December 31:					
No journal entry is needed because the physical count equals the amount of inventory on the books (1,000 – 600 + 250 = 650).			Inventory (year-end) (650 × $5)	$3,250	
			Cost of goods sold (difference)	3,000	
			Inventory (beginning)		$5,000
			Purchases		1,250

Beginning inventory	$5,000
Purchases of inventory during the period	1,250
Ending inventory	(3,250)
Cost of goods sold	**$3,000**

The perpetual and periodic systems have the same result. However, under the periodic system, the amounts of inventory and cost of goods sold are updated only at the end of the period after the physical count.

4. **Items Counted in Inventory**

   a. **Items in Transit**

      1) Not all inventory is on hand. Most sales are recorded by the seller at the time of shipment and by the buyer at the time of receipt.

         a) However, this procedure may misstate inventory, receivables, payables, and earnings at the end of the period.

      2) Proper cut-off is observed by determining when control has passed under the FOB (free on board) terms of the contract.

         a) **FOB shipping point** means control over goods passes to the buyer when the seller makes a proper tender of delivery of the goods to the carrier. The buyer then includes the goods in inventory.

         b) **FOB destination** means control over goods passes to the buyer when the seller makes a proper tender of delivery of the goods at the destination. The seller should include the goods in inventory until that time.

      3) **Shipping services** performed before control over the goods is transferred to the customer are activities to fulfill the contract. Thus, revenue from shipping activities is recognized when control over the goods transfers to the customer.

         a) Shipping services performed after control over the goods is transferred to the customers may be accounted for as either of the following:

            i) An additional promised service. In this case, revenue from shipping activities is recognized when shipping services occur.

            ii) A contract fulfillment activity. In this case, revenue from shipping activities is recognized when control over the goods transfers to the customer.

b. **Right of Return**

1) When sales are made with the understanding that unsatisfactory goods may be returned, the consideration in the contract is **variable**. Sales revenue then is recognized only to the extent that it is **probable** that a significant reversal will not occur when the uncertainty is resolved. To account for the transfer of products with a right of return at the time of the sale, an entity should recognize all of the following:

   a) **Sales** revenue is recognized only for the amount of consideration to which an entity expects to be entitled. Thus, no sales are recognized for the products expected to be returned.

   b) **A refund liability** is recognized for the amount of consideration expected to be returned to customers. The refund liability is estimated at each reporting period to reflect the changes in the expectations about the refund amount. The adjustments to the refund liability are recognized as revenue (or reductions of revenue).

   c) **A return asset** is recognized for the entity's right to recover products from customers. The return asset is measured initially at the former carrying amount of the products expected to be returned minus any expected costs to recover those products. The return asset is presented separately from (1) the refund liability and (2) inventory.

   d) **Cost of goods sold** is measured at the carrying amount of the products sold minus the return asset recognized.

2) Some entities differentiate between the gross sales amount and the sales amount that probably will be returned. In this situation, sales are recorded at their gross amount and **sales returns**, a contra sales revenue account, is recognized.

EXAMPLE 7-2 Sales with Right of Return

Zaya Company is a producer of printing machines. On January 1, Year 1, Zaya sold 20 machines for $500 in cash each. The cost of each machine is $400. Zaya allows customers to return any unused machine within 2 months and receive a full refund. Because the contract allows customers a **right of return**, the consideration received is variable. Zaya uses the expected value method to estimate the variable consideration. Based on its past experience, Zaya estimates that four machines will be returned. Only three machines were returned by the customers during the return period.

Because revenue is recognized for the products not expected to be returned, sales of $8,000 [(20 – 4) × $500] are recognized on the transaction date. The following journal entries were recorded by Zaya:

<u>January 1, Year 1</u>					
Cash (20 × $500)	$10,000		Cost of goods sold (16 × $400)	$6,400	
Sales (16 × $500)		$8,000	Return asset (4 × $400)	1,600	
Refund liability (4 × $500)		2,000	Inventory (20 × $400)		$8,000
<u>Return of three machines</u>					
Refund liability (3 × $500)	$1,500		Inventory (3 × $400)	$1,200	
Cash		$1,500	Return asset		$1,200
<u>March 1, Year 1 – End of the return period</u>					
Refund liability	$500		Cost of goods sold	$400	
Sales		$500	Return asset		$400

NOTE: If sales were recorded at their gross amount and sales returns were recognized, the following entries would be made on 1/1/Year 1:

Cash (20 × $500)	$10,000		Cost of goods sold (16 × $400)	$6,400	
Sales returns (contra revenue)	2,000		Return asset (4 × $400)	1,600	
Sales		$10,000	Inventory (20 × $400)		$8,000
Refund liability (4 × $500)		2,000			

3) The entity may not be able to make a reasonable estimate of the probability and the amount of a refund. If the entity also cannot conclude that a significant reversal of revenue recognized is not probable, no revenue or cost of goods sold is recognized until the right of return expires.

   a) The entire consideration received is recognized as a contract liability.

   b) The decrease in inventory is recognized as a contract asset to reflect the right to recover products from customers on settling the refund liability.

c. **Goods Out on Consignment** (discussed in detail in the next subunit)

EXAMPLE 7-3 Items Counted in Inventory

Entity A's December 31, Year 1, physical count of inventory results in a measurement of $50,000. The following is additional information about year-end inventory:

- During the year, Entity A (the consignor) consigned goods with a total cost of $60,000 to Entity B (the consignee). The annual statement sent by Entity B to Entity A indicates that 60% of the goods were sold for $42,000.
- Goods costing $40,000 were shipped FOB shipping point by a vendor on December 29, Year 1. They were received by Entity A on January 4, Year 2.
- Goods costing $70,000 were shipped FOB destination by a vendor on December 30, Year 1. They were received by Entity A on January 5, Year 2.
- Goods costing $25,000 were billed to a customer FOB destination on December 27, Year 1. They were shipped by Entity A on December 28, Year 1, and received by the customer on January 3, Year 2.

In Entity A's December 31, Year 1, financial statements, the inventory balance is $139,000. This amount consists of

Physical inventory count	$ 50,000
Goods out on consignment ($60,000 × 40%)	24,000
Goods shipped FOB shipping point (title and risk of loss passed to Entity A on December 29, Year 1, at the time of shipment)	40,000
Goods shipped FOB destination to customer (title and the risk of loss will pass to the customer only on January 3, Year 2)	25,000
December 31, Year 1, inventory balance	**$139,000**

SUCCESS TIP

CPA candidates have been asked to calculate amounts for inventory and cost of goods sold using information given in the question, such as shipping terms and consignment sales.

5. **Cost Basis of Inventory – Initial Measurement**
    a. The **cost of inventories** includes all costs incurred in bringing them to their existing condition and location.
    b. The **cost of purchased inventories** includes
        1) The price paid or consideration given to acquire the inventory, net of trade discounts, rebates, and other similar items;
        2) Import duties and other unrecoverable taxes; and
        3) Handling, insurance, freight-in, and other costs directly attributable to (a) acquiring finished goods and materials and (b) bringing them to their present location and condition (salable or usable condition).
    c. The **cost of manufactured inventories** (work-in-process and finished goods inventories) includes the cost of direct materials used, direct labor costs, and production overhead.
        1) Abnormal production costs are not inventoriable costs. They are expensed as incurred.
    d. **Period** costs, such as (1) general and administrative expenses or (2) selling expenses, should be expensed as incurred. They are not inventoriable costs.
6. **Purchases, Freight Costs, and Discounts**
    a. Purchased inventory is measured at invoice cost net of any discounts taken.
        1) **Trade discounts** are usually subtracted prior to invoicing.
            a) A chain discount applies more than one trade discount. The first discount is applied to the list price, the second is applied to the resulting amount, etc.
        2) Cash discounts are offered to induce early payment and improve cash flow.
    b. The buyer's **transportation (freight) costs** for purchased goods are inventoried.
        1) In a perpetual system, these costs can be assigned to specified purchases.
        2) In a periodic system, transportation costs are usually debited to purchases.

STOP & REVIEW

You have completed the outline for this subunit.
Study multiple-choice questions 1 and 2 on page 211.

7.2 CONSIGNMENT ACCOUNTING

1. **Overview**
   a. A consignment sale is an arrangement between the owner of goods and a sales agent. Consigned goods are not sold but rather transferred to an agent for possible sale.
      1) The consignor (owner) records sales only when the goods are sold to third parties by the consignee (agent).
      2) Goods out on consignment are **included in inventory** at cost. Costs of transporting the goods to the consignee are inventoriable costs, not selling expenses.
   b. The following are examples of indicators that the contract with an agent is a consignment arrangement:
      1) The product is controlled by the entity until a specified event occurs, such as the sale of the product to a third party, or until a specified period expires.
      2) The entity is able to require the return of the product or transfer the product to a third party.
      3) The dealer does not have an unconditional obligation to pay for the product.
2. **Consignor's Accounting**
   a. The **consignor** records the initial shipment by a debit to **consigned goods out** (a separate inventory account) and a credit to inventory at cost.
   b. Consigned goods out is used in a perpetual or periodic inventory system when consignments are recorded in separate accounts.
      1) If the consignor uses a perpetual system, the credit on shipment is to inventory.
      2) If a periodic system is used, the credit is to consignment shipments, a contra cost of goods sold account. Its balance is then closed at the end of the period when the inventory adjustments are made.
3. **Consignee's Accounting**
   a. The **consignee** never records the consigned goods as an asset.
      1) The basic account used in consignee accounting is **consignment-in**, a receivable (payable). Its balance is the amount payable to the consignor (a credit) or the amount receivable from the consignor (a debit).
         a) Before consigned goods are sold, expenses chargeable to the consignor (e.g., freight-in or service costs) are recorded in the consignment-in account as a receivable. After the consigned goods are sold, the credit balance reflects the consignee's net liability to the consignor.
         b) Sales are recorded with a debit to cash (or accounts receivable) and credits to consignment-in (a payable) and commission income.
         c) Payments to the consignor result in a debit to consignment-in and a credit to cash.

4. **Comparative Journal Entries**

EXAMPLE 7-4 Consignment Accounting

The consignor ships 100 units, costing $50 each, to the consignee.

Consignor			**Consignee**		
Consigned goods out	$5,000		Only a memorandum entry		
Inventory		$5,000			

The consignee pays $120 for freight-in.

Consignor			**Consignee**		
No entry at this time			Consignment-in	$120	
			Cash		$120

The consignee sells 80 units at $80 each. The consignee is to receive a 15% commission on all sales.

Consignor			**Consignee**		
No entry at this time			Cash (80 × $80)	$6,400	
			Consignment-in		$5,440
			Commission income ($6,400 × 15%)		960

The consignee sends a monthly statement to the consignor with the balance owed. The cost of shipping goods to the consignee, including the $120 payment by the consignee, is debited as a cost of consigned inventory.

Consignor			**Consignee**		
Cash	$5,320		Consignment-in	$5,320 ($5,440 – $120)	
Commission expense	960		Cash		$5,320
Consigned goods out	120				
Cost of goods sold	4,096 [($5,000 + $120) × 80%]				
Sales		$6,400			
Consigned goods out		4,096			

STOP & REVIEW

You have completed the outline for this subunit.
Study multiple-choice questions 3 and 4 on page 212.

7.3 COST FLOW METHODS -- APPLICATION

SUCCESS TIP

The AICPA has asked candidates to solve calculation questions concerning average-cost, FIFO, and LIFO inventory. Candidates may also see questions that ask for adjusting year-end entries.

1. **Specific Identification**
   a. Specific identification requires determining which specific items are sold and therefore reflects the actual physical flow of goods. It can be used for special inventory items, such as automobiles or heavy equipment.
   b. A practical weakness of specific identification is the need for detailed records.
2. **Average Cost**
   a. The assumption in an average cost system is that goods are indistinguishable and are therefore measured at an average of the costs incurred.
   b. The **moving-average** method requires determination of a new weighted-average cost after each purchase and thus is used only in a **perpetual system**.

EXAMPLE 7-5 Moving-Average Method

The following data relate to Entity A's Year 1 activities:

Date	Transaction	Number of units	Purchase price per unit ($)	Sale price per unit ($)
January 1	Beginning balance	100	20	
March 1	Purchase	20	32	
April 1	Sale	70		40
June 1	Purchase	30	14	
October 1	Sale	40		24

Under the **moving-average method**, the year-end inventory and Year 1 cost of goods sold are calculated as follows:

Date	Activity	Units	Price	Cost of inventory purchased (sold)	Inventory total balance	On-hand units	Cost per unit
Jan. 1	Beg. bal.	100	$20		$2,000 (100 × 20)	100	**$20**
Mar. 1	Purchase	20	$32	$640 = 20 × $32	$2,640 (2,000 + 640)	120	**$22** ($2,640 ÷ 120)
Apr. 1	Sale	70	**$22**	($1,540) = 70 × $22	$1,100 (2,640 – 1,540)	50	**$22** ($1,100 ÷ 50)
Jun. 1	Purchase	30	$14	$420 = 30 × $14	$1,520 (1,100 + 420)	80	**$19** ($1,520 ÷ 80)
Oct. 1	Sale	40	**$19**	($760) = 40 × $19	**$760** (1,520 – 760)	40	**$19** ($760 ÷ 40)

The cost of **inventory** on December 31, Year 1, is **$760**. The Year 1 **cost of goods sold** is **$2,300**.

Beginning inventory	$2,000
Purchases ($640 + $420)	1,060
Ending inventory	(760)
Cost of goods sold ($1,540 + $760)	**$2,300**

c. The **weighted-average method** is used under the **periodic** inventory accounting system. The average cost is determined only at the end of the period. The weighted-average cost per unit is used to determine the ending inventory and the cost of goods sold for the period. It is calculated as follows:

$$\frac{\text{Cost of beginning inventory (\$) + Cost of purchases during the period (\$)}}{\text{Units in beginning inventory + Number of units purchased during the period}}$$

EXAMPLE 7-6 Weighted-Average Method

Under the **weighted-average method**, Entity A's ending inventory and Year 1 cost of goods sold are determined as follows:

First, the weighted-average cost per unit is calculated.

$$\frac{\text{Cost of beginning inventory + Cost of purchases during the period}}{\text{Units in beginning inventory + Number of units purchased}} = \frac{\$2{,}000 + \$1{,}060}{100 + 20 + 30} = \mathbf{\$20.40}$$

Second, the ending inventory and Year 1 cost of goods sold are calculated using the weighted-average cost per unit (WACPU):

Beginning inventory	$2,000	
Purchases	1,060	
Ending inventory	**(816)**	(40 × $20.40) = (WACPU × Units in ending inventory)
Cost of goods sold	**$2,244**	(110 × $20.40) = (WACPU × Units sold during the period)

3. **First-in, First-out (FIFO)**

a. This method assumes that the first goods purchased are the first sold. Thus, ending inventory consists of the latest purchases.

b. Cost of goods sold includes the earliest goods purchased.

c. Under the FIFO method, year-end inventory and cost of goods sold for the period are **the same** regardless of whether the perpetual or the periodic inventory accounting system is used.

EXAMPLE 7-7 FIFO Method

The number of units in Entity A's ending inventory is 40. Under the FIFO method, the cost of these units is the cost of the **latest purchases ($740)**.

Date of purchase	Units	Price per unit	Total cost
June 1, Year 1	30	$14	$420
March 1, Year 1	10	32	320
Ending inventory	**40**		**$740**

The Year 1 cost of goods sold is $2,320.

Beginning inventory	$2,000
Purchases ($640 + $420)	1,060
Ending inventory	(740)
Cost of goods sold	**$2,320**

NOTE: The results are the same under the periodic and perpetual systems.

4. **Last-in, First-out (LIFO)**
   a. This method assumes that the newest items of inventory are sold first. Thus, the items remaining in inventory are recognized as if they were the oldest.
      1) Under the LIFO method, the perpetual and the periodic inventory accounting systems may result in different amounts for the cost of year-end inventory and cost of goods sold.
      2) Increasing inventory results in the creation of **LIFO layers**.
   b. **LIFO Periodic**
      1) In a periodic system, a purchases account is used. Cost of goods sold and ending inventory are determined only at the end of the period.

EXAMPLE 7-8 LIFO Method in a Periodic Inventory System

The number of units in Entity A's ending inventory is 40. Under the LIFO method, the cost of those units is the cost of the **earliest purchases** (beginning inventory) of **$800** (40 units × $20). The Year 1 cost of goods sold is **$2,260**.

Beginning inventory	$2,000
Purchases ($640 + $420)	1,060
Ending inventory	(800)
Cost of goods sold	**$2,260**

   c. **LIFO Perpetual**
      1) In a perpetual system, purchases are directly recorded in inventory. Cost of goods sold is calculated when a sale occurs and consists of the latest purchases.

EXAMPLE 7-9 LIFO Method in a Perpetual Inventory System

Date	Activity	Units	Cost per unit	Cost of inventory purchased/sold	Inventory total balance	Number of units
Jan. 1	Beg. bal.	100	$20		100 × $20 = $2,000	100
Mar. 1	Purchase	20	$32	20 × $32 = $640	January 1 layer 100 × $20 = $2,000 March 1 layer 20 × $32 = 640 $2,640	120
Apr. 1	Sale	70		20 × $32 = $ 640 50 × $20 = 1,000 $(1,640)	January 1 layer 50 × $20 = $1,000	50
Jun. 1	Purchase	30	$14	30 × $14 = $420	January 1 layer 50 × $20 = $1,000 June 1 layer 30 × $14 = 420 $1,420	80
Oct. 1	Sale	40		30 × $14 = $ 420 10 × $20 = 200 $(620)	January 1 layer 40 × $20 = **$800**	40

Entity A's cost of ending **inventory** is **$800** and the Year 1 **cost of goods sold** is **$2,260** ($1,640 + $620).

NOTE: The results of the LIFO method under the perpetual and periodic systems are the same in this example but may differ in other situations.

   d. **LIFO Conformity Rule**
      1) An IRS regulation requires LIFO to be used for financial reporting if it is used in the tax return.

e. **LIFO Valuation Allowance**

1) Entities that use a different inventory costing method for internal purposes must convert to LIFO for reporting purposes if they use LIFO for tax purposes.

2) To adjust the inventory to LIFO, an allowance, sometimes called the **LIFO reserve**, is created. This account is reported as a contra to inventory account.

3) At period end, this allowance is adjusted to reflect the difference between LIFO and the internal costing method.

Cost of goods sold	$XXX	
Allowance to reduce inventory to LIFO		$XXX

IFRS DIFFERENCE

LIFO is not permitted.

STOP & REVIEW

You have completed the outline for this subunit.
Study multiple-choice questions 5 through 7 beginning on page 213.

7.4 COST FLOW METHODS -- COMPARISON

1. **Varying Results under the Five Methods**

EXAMPLE 7-10 Comparison of Cost Flow Methods

The following are Entity A's varying results under each of the five cost flow methods:

	Ending Inventory	Cost of Goods Sold
Moving average	$760	$2,300
Weighted average	816	2,244
FIFO	740	2,320
LIFO periodic	800	2,260
LIFO perpetual	800	2,260

a. The cost flow model selected should be the one that most clearly reflects periodic income.

2. **FIFO vs. LIFO**

a. An advantage of FIFO is that ending inventory approximates the market value.

1) A disadvantage is that current revenues are matched with older costs.

b. Under LIFO, management can affect net income with an end-of-period purchase that immediately alters cost of goods sold.

1) An end-of-period FIFO purchase has no such effect.

c. In a time of **rising prices** (inflation), use of the **LIFO** method results in the lowest year-end inventory, the highest cost of goods sold, and the lowest gross profit.

   1) LIFO assumes that

      a) The earliest (and therefore the lowest-priced) goods purchased are in ending inventory and

      b) Cost of goods sold consists of the latest (and therefore the highest-priced) goods purchased.

   2) The results for the **FIFO** method are opposite of those for the LIFO method.

SUCCESS TIP

During a period of inflation	Ending Inventory	Cost of Goods Sold	Gross Profit (Net Income)
FIFO	Highest	Lowest	Highest
LIFO	Lowest	Highest	Lowest

STOP & REVIEW

You have completed the outline for this subunit.
Study multiple-choice questions 8 and 9 on page 215.

7.5 DOLLAR-VALUE LIFO

SUCCESS TIP

In recent years, dollar-value LIFO has been less tested on the CPA Exam.

1. **Pools of Specific Goods**

   a. The previous discussion of LIFO has assumed that the method is applied to specific units of inventory with specific unit costs. Dollar-value LIFO is applied to groups (pools) of inventory items that are substantially identical.

   b. Recordkeeping is simplified because all goods in a beginning inventory pool are presumed to have been acquired on the same date and at the same cost.

      1) Using the pooling method, beginning inventory is costed at a weighted-average unit price (Total cost ÷ Unit quantity).

      2) Usually, purchases of goods in a pool also are recorded at a weighted-average cost (Total cost ÷ Unit quantity). If the quantity of units in the pool increases during the year, a new LIFO layer will be formed at the new weighted-average cost.

   c. Each period's inventory layer equals the total change in inventory during that period. The example below illustrates this concept.

EXAMPLE 7-11 Dollar-Value LIFO -- Inventory Layers

Beginning inventory has a base-year cost and an end-of-year cost of $100,000. Ending inventory has a base-year cost and an end-of-year cost of $120,000 and $150,000, respectively. The year's inventory layer at base-year cost is $20,000 ($120,000 – $100,000). This layer at current-year cost is $50,000 ($150,000 – $100,000).

2. **Deriving a Price Index**

   a. Under dollar-value LIFO, changes in inventory are measured in terms of dollars of **constant purchasing power** rather than units of physical inventory. This calculation uses a specific price index for each year.

   b. Selecting an appropriate price index is crucial to dollar-value LIFO accounting.

      1) An entity may choose to use published indexes. Examples are the Consumer Price Index for All Urban Consumers (CPI-U) and indexes published by trade associations.

      2) Most often, an index is generated internally for each year.

   c. The **double-extension method** is the most common technique for internally generating a price index.

      1) Extending inventory is the process of multiplying the quantity of each good on hand by the unit cost to arrive at a total amount for inventory.

      2) To enable the calculation of price indexes, this operation must be performed twice: once using current-year cost and once using base-year cost.

EXAMPLE 7-12 Dollar-Value LIFO -- Data

Retailer B has the following extended inventory cost data. Note that LIFO liquidation occurred in Year 3.

	At Base-Year Cost	At Current-Year Cost
1/1/Year 1	$250,000	$250,000
Year 1 layer	50,000	50,000
Year 2 layer	40,000	74,000
Year 3 layer	(20,000)	10,000
Year 4 layer	30,000	71,000

   d. A price index can be computed for each year with the following ratio:

$$\text{Price index} = \frac{\text{Ending inventory at current-year cost}}{\text{Ending inventory at base-year cost}}$$

EXAMPLE 7-13 Dollar-Value LIFO -- Calculation of Price Indexes

Using the values provided in Example 7-12, the price indexes for computing Retailer B's dollar-value LIFO inventory are calculated as follows:

Year 1 price index = ($250,000 + $50,000) ÷ ($250,000 + $50,000)
= $300,000 ÷ $300,000
= 1.00

Year 2 price index = ($250,000 + $50,000 + $74,000) ÷ ($250,000 + $50,000 + $40,000)
= $374,000 ÷ $340,000
= 1.10

Year 3 price index = ($250,000 + $50,000 + $74,000 + $10,000) ÷ ($250,000 + $50,000 + $40,000 – $20,000)
= $384,000 ÷ $320,000
= 1.20

Year 4 price index = ($250,000 + $50,000 + $74,000 + $10,000 + $71,000) ÷
($250,000 + $50,000 + $40,000 – $20,000 + $30,000)
= $455,000 ÷ $350,000
= 1.30

3. **Dollar-Value LIFO Calculations**

   a. To arrive at dollar-value LIFO ending inventory, **each layer** must be inflated by the relevant price index.

EXAMPLE 7-14 Dollar-Value LIFO -- Year 1 and Year 2 Ending Inventory

The following example uses Retailer B's information from Examples 7-12 and 7-13:

Year 1 Calculation:	At Base-Year Cost		Price Index		At Dollar-Value LIFO Cost
1/1/Year 1	$250,000	×	1.00	=	$250,000
Year 1 layer	50,000	×	1.00	=	50,000
12/31/Year 1	$300,000				$300,000

Year 2 Calculation:	At Base-Year Cost		Price Index		At Dollar-Value LIFO Cost
1/1/Year 1	$250,000	×	1.00	=	$250,000
Year 1 layer	50,000	×	1.00	=	50,000
Year 2 layer	40,000	×	1.10	=	44,000
12/31/Year 2	$340,000				$344,000

   b. In any year when the balance declines, a portion of the most recent year's layer must be removed.

EXAMPLE 7-15 Dollar-Value LIFO -- Year 3 Ending Inventory

The following example uses Retailer B's information from Examples 7-12 and 7-13:

Year 3 Calculation:	At Base-Year Cost		Price Index		At Dollar-Value LIFO Cost
1/1/Year 1	$250,000	×	1.00	=	$250,000
Year 1 layer	50,000	×	1.00	=	50,000
Year 2 layer	40,000	×	1.10	=	44,000
Year 2 liquidation	(20,000)	×	1.10	=	(22,000)
12/31/Year 3	$320,000				$322,000

   c. Once liquidated, layers cannot be replaced.

EXAMPLE 7-16 Dollar-Value LIFO -- Year 4 Ending Inventory

The following example uses Retailer B's information from Examples 7-12 and 7-13:

Year 4 Calculation:	At Base-Year Cost		Price Index		At Dollar-Value LIFO Cost
1/1/Year 1	$250,000	×	1.00	=	$250,000
Year 1 layer	50,000	×	1.00	=	50,000
Year 2 layer	40,000	×	1.10	=	44,000
Year 2 liquidation	(20,000)	×	1.10	=	(22,000)
Year 4 layer	30,000	×	1.30	=	39,000
12/31/Year 4	$350,000				$361,000

STOP & REVIEW

You have completed the outline for this subunit.
Study multiple-choice questions 10 and 11 on page 216.

7.6 MEASUREMENT OF INVENTORY SUBSEQUENT TO INITIAL RECOGNITION

1. **Statement of Rule**
   a. The subsequent measurement of inventory depends on the cost method used.
      1) Inventory accounted for using LIFO or the retail inventory method is measured at the **lower of cost or market (LCM)**.
      2) Inventory accounted for using any other cost method (e.g., **FIFO or average cost**) is measured at the **lower of cost or net realizable value.**
   b. The **loss on write-down** of inventory to market or net realizable value (NRV) generally is presented as a component of cost of goods sold. However, if the amount of loss is material, it should be presented as a separate line item in the current-period income statement.
      1) A write-down of inventory below its cost may result from damage, deterioration, obsolescence, changes in price levels, changes in demand, etc.
   c. A reversal of a write-down of inventory recognized in the annual financial statements is **prohibited** in subsequent periods.
      1) Once inventory is written down below cost, the reduced amount is the new cost basis.
   d. Depending on the nature of the inventory, the rules for write-down below cost may be applied either directly to each item or to the total of the inventory (or in some cases, to the total of each major category). The method should be the one that most clearly reflects periodic income.
2. **Measurement of Inventory at the Lower of Cost or Market (LCM)**
   a. Inventory accounted for using the **LIFO or retail inventory method** must be written down to **market** if its utility is no longer as great as its cost.
      1) The excess of cost over market is recognized as a loss on write-down in the income statement.
   b. **Market** is the current cost to replace inventory, subject to certain limitations. Market should not (1) exceed a **ceiling** equal to **net realizable value (NRV)** or (2) be less than a **floor** equal to NRV reduced by an allowance for an approximately **normal profit margin**.
      1) NRV is the estimated selling price in the ordinary course of business minus reasonably predictable costs of completion, disposal, and transportation.
      2) Thus, **current replacement cost** (CRC) is not to be greater than NRV or less than NRV minus a normal profit (NRV – P).

MARKET (M)

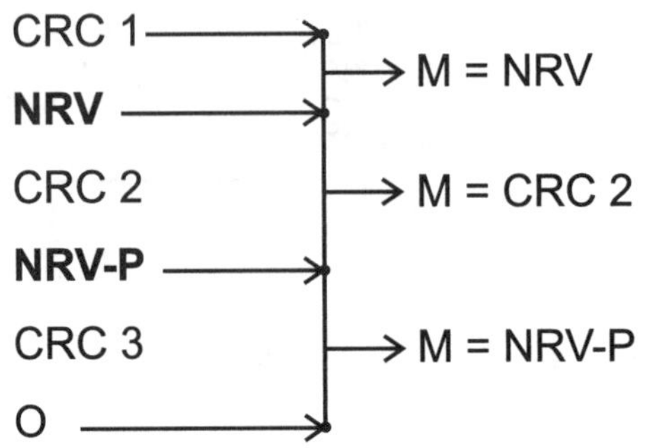

Figure 7-1

EXAMPLE 7-17 Measurement of Inventory at LCM

The following information is related to a company's year-end inventories:

Cost per inventory unit	Item A	Item B	Item C
Estimated selling price	$80	$70	$44
Minus: Cost of completion	(20)	--	(3)
Minus: Cost of disposal	(6)	(5)	(2)
NRV **(ceiling)**	**$54**	**$65**	**$39**
Minus: Normal profit margin	(3)	(7)	(4)
NRV – NPM **(floor)**	**$51**	**$58**	**$35**
Current replacement cost **(CRC)**	**53**	**55**	**40**
(a) Market	53 Ceiling > CRC > Floor	58 Floor > CRC	39 CRC > Ceiling
(b) Historical cost per unit	50	60	45
Lower of cost (b) or market (a)	50 Cost < Market	**58** Market < Cost	**39** Market < Cost

c. LCM by item always will be equal to or less than the other LCM measurements, and LCM in total always will be equal to or greater than the other LCM measurements.

1) Most entities use LCM by item. This method is required for **tax purposes**.

a) If **dollar-value LIFO** is used, LCM should be applied to pools of items.
b) An entity may not use LCM with LIFO for tax purposes.

EXAMPLE 7-18 Lower of Cost or Market

Lala Co. accounts for its inventory using the **LIFO** cost method. The following is its inventory information at the end of the fiscal year:

Historical cost	$100,000
Current replacement cost	82,000
Net realizable value (NRV)	90,000
Normal profit margin	5,000

Under the LIFO method, inventory is measured at the lower of cost or market (current replacement cost subject to certain limitations). Market cannot be higher than NRV ($90,000) or lower than NRV reduced by a normal profit margin ($90,000 – $5,000 = $85,000). Thus, market is $85,000. (The current replacement cost of $82,000 is below the floor.) Because market is lower than cost, the inventory is reported in the balance sheet at market of $85,000. The write-down of inventory of $15,000 ($100,000 – $85,000) is recognized as a loss in the income statement. The journal entry is as follows:

Loss from inventory write-down	$15,000	
Inventory		$15,000

IFRS DIFFERENCE

Inventories are measured at the lower of cost or net realizable value (NRV) regardless of the cost method used. NRV is the estimated selling price less the estimated costs of completion and disposal. NRV is assessed each period. Accordingly, a write-down **may be reversed** but not above original cost. The write-down and reversal are recognized in profit or loss.

Using the data from Example 7-18 above, NRV ($90,000) is lower than cost ($100,000). Thus, the inventory is reported in the statement of financial position at its NRV ($90,000). The write-down of inventory of $10,000 ($100,000 – $90,000) is recognized in profit or loss. The journal entry is as follows:

Loss from inventory write-down	$10,000	
Inventory		$10,000

3. **Measurement of Inventory at the Lower of Cost or NRV**

   a. Inventory measured using any method other than LIFO or retail (e.g., **FIFO or average cost**) must be measured at the **lower of cost or net realizable value**.

      1) **Net realizable value (NRV)** is the estimated selling price in the ordinary course of business minus reasonably predictable costs of completion, disposal, and transportation.

      2) The excess of cost over NRV is recognized as a loss on write-down in the income statement.

EXAMPLE 7-19 Measurement of Inventory at Lower of Cost or NRV

Using the data from Example 7-18, assume that Lala Co. accounts for its inventory using the **FIFO** cost method.

Under the FIFO method (or any other method except for LIFO or retail), inventory is measured at the **lower of cost or net realizable value**. NRV of $90,000 is lower than cost of $100,000. Thus, a loss on write-down to NRV of $10,000 is recognized. The journal entry is as follows:

Loss from inventory write-down	$10,000	
Inventory		$10,000

NOTE: The same loss on write-down is recognized under IFRS.

4. **Inventory Measurement at Interim Dates**

   a. A write-down of inventory below cost (to market for LIFO and retail and to NRV for all other methods) may be **deferred in the interim financial statements** if no loss is reasonably anticipated for the year.

      1) But inventory losses from a **nontemporary** decline below cost must be recognized at the interim date.

      2) If the loss is recovered in another quarter, it is recognized as a gain and treated as a change in estimate. The amount recovered is limited to the losses previously recognized.

EXAMPLE 7-20 Interim LCM Measurement -- Loss Expected

A company accounts for its inventory using the LIFO cost method. The following is its inventory information for the interim period ending March 31, Year 1:

Historical cost	$93,000
Current replacement cost	87,000
Net realizable value (NRV)	90,000
Normal profit margin	5,000

Under LIFO, inventory is measured at LCM. Additional information: (1) This inventory was sold on January 5, Year 2. (2) On March 31, Year 1, the company expects no changes during the year regarding inventory information determined. (3) On June 30, Year 1, as a result of an increase in the demand for the company's products, the company determines the following data:

Current replacement cost	$95,000
Net realizable value (NRV)	99,000
Normal profit margin	5,000

-- Continued on next page --

EXAMPLE 7-20 -- Continued

March 31, Year 1

The current replacement cost ($87,000) is below the ceiling of NRV ($90,000) and above the floor of NRV minus normal profit margin ($85,000). Thus, **market** is equal to the current replacement cost of **$87,000**. Because market is lower than cost, the inventory is reported in the balance sheet at market of $87,000. The loss is not expected to be restored in the fiscal year, and the write-down of inventory of $6,000 ($93,000 – $87,000) is recognized as a loss in the income statement. The journal entry is as follows:

Loss from inventory write-down	$6,000	
Inventory		$6,000

June 30, Year 1

The current replacement cost ($95,000) is below the ceiling of NRV ($99,000) and above the floor of NRV minus normal profit margin ($94,000). Thus, **market** is equal to current replacement cost of **$95,000**. The loss is recovered in the second quarter ($95,000 > $87,000). The amount of reversal of the write-down recognized in the first quarter is limited to the losses previously recognized. The inventory must not be reported above its cost. The journal entry is as follows:

Inventory	$6,000	
Loss from inventory write-down		$6,000

EXAMPLE 7-21 Interim LCM Measurement -- No Loss Expected

Tal Co. accounts for its inventory using the LIFO cost method. The following is its inventory information at the end of the interim period on March 31, Year 1:

Historical cost	$100,000
Current replacement cost	82,000
Net realizable value (NRV)	90,000
Normal profit margin	5,000

Tal expects that on December 31, Year 1, the inventory's NRV reduced by a normal profit margin will be at least $100,000.

No write-down of inventory is recognized in the interim financial statements on March 31, Year 1, because no loss is reasonably anticipated for the year.

IFRS DIFFERENCE

Under IFRS, each interim period is viewed as a discrete (individually separate) reporting period. Accordingly, the accounting treatment for inventory measurement in the interim statements is the same as in the annual statements. For an interim period, an inventory loss from a write-down to NRV must be recognized even if no loss is reasonably expected for the year.

Using the data from Example 7-21, in its interim financial statements on March 31, Year 1, Tal will recognize a loss of $10,000 ($100,000 historical cost – $90,000 NRV). Under IFRS, inventory is measured at the lower of cost or NRV regardless of its expected NRV at year end.

STOP & REVIEW

You have completed the outline for this subunit.
Study multiple-choice questions 12 through 15 beginning on page 217.

7.7 SPECIAL TOPICS IN INVENTORY ACCOUNTING

1. **Estimating Inventory**
   a. The estimated **gross profit method** is used to determine inventory for **interim statements**.
   b. Because of its imprecision, GAAP and federal tax law **do not permit** use of the gross profit method **at year end**. But other applications are possible.
      1) If inventory is destroyed, the method may be used to estimate the loss.
      2) External auditors apply the gross profit method as an analytical procedure to determine the fairness of the ending inventory balance.
      3) The method may be used internally to generate estimates of inventory throughout the year, e.g., as a verification of perpetual records.
   c. The gross profit method calculates ending inventory at a given time by subtracting an estimated cost of goods sold from the sum of beginning inventory and purchases (or cost of goods manufactured).
      1) The estimated cost of goods sold equals sales minus the gross profit.
      2) The gross profit equals sales multiplied by the gross profit percentage, an amount ordinarily computed on a historical basis.

$$\text{Gross profit percentage} = \frac{\text{Gross profit}}{\text{Sales}}$$

EXAMPLE 7-22 **Gross Profit Method**

Beginning inventory		$60,000
Purchases		20,000
Goods available for sale		$80,000
Sales (at selling price)	$50,000	
Gross profit (20% of sales)	(10,000)	
Cost of goods sold		(40,000)
Estimated ending inventory		**$40,000**

2. **Purchase Commitments**
   a. A commitment to acquire goods in the future is **not** recorded at the time of the agreement, e.g., by debiting an asset and crediting a liability.
      1) But a **loss** is recognized on a firm, noncancelable purchase commitment (unconditional purchase obligation) if the market price of the goods is less than the commitment price.
      2) The reason for current loss recognition is the same as that for inventory. A decrease (not an increase) in future benefits should be recognized when it occurs even if the contract is unperformed on both sides.
      3) Material losses expected on purchase commitments are measured in the same way as inventory losses, recognized, and separately disclosed.

b. The entry is

Unrealized holding loss -- earnings	$XXX	
Liability -- purchase commitment		$XXX

EXAMPLE 7-23 Purchase Commitment

During the year, the Lisbon Company signed a noncancelable contract to purchase 2,000 pounds of materials at $64 per pound during the forthcoming year. On December 31, the market price of the materials is $52 per pound, and the selling price of the finished product is expected to decline accordingly. A loss of $24,000 [2,000 × ($64 – $52)] should be reported in the annual income statement.

GAAP require recognition in the income statement of a material loss on a purchase commitment as if the inventory were already owned. Losses on firm purchase commitments are measured in the same way as inventory losses. If the cost is $128,000 and the market price is $104,000, a $24,000 loss should be recognized.

c. **Disclosure** of commitments to transfer funds for fixed or minimum amounts of goods or services at fixed or minimum prices is required.

1) A **take-or-pay contract** requires one party to purchase a certain number of goods from the other party or else pay a penalty.

2) **Sinking-fund requirements** for the retirement of noncurrent debt also are affected by the provisions of this pronouncement.

3) Disclosure of the aggregate amount of **payments** for unconditional purchase obligations is required for recorded obligations for each of the 5 years following the date of the latest balance sheet presented.

3. **Retail Method**

a. Some entities, such as major retailers, have a high volume of transactions in relatively low-cost merchandise. They often use the retail method because it is applied to the dollar amounts of goods, not quantities. The result is **easier and less expensive estimates** of ending inventory and cost of goods sold.

b. Records of the beginning inventory and net purchases are maintained at both cost and retail. Sales at retail and any other appropriate items are subtracted from goods available for sale at retail (the sum of beginning inventory and net purchases at retail) to provide ending inventory at retail.

NOTE: The retail method is rarely tested on the CPA Exam.

4. **Inventory Errors**

a. These errors may have a material effect on current assets, working capital (Current assets – Current liabilities), cost of goods sold, net income, and equity. A common error is inappropriate timing of the recognition of transactions.

b. If a purchase on account is not recorded and the goods are not included in ending inventory, cost of goods sold (BI + Purchases – EI) and net income are unaffected. But current assets and current liabilities are understated.

c. If purchases and beginning inventory are properly recorded but items are excluded from ending inventory, cost of goods sold is overstated. Net income, inventory, retained earnings, working capital, and the current ratio are understated.

d. If the goods are properly included in ending inventory but the purchase is not recorded, net income is overstated because cost of goods sold is understated. Also, current liabilities are understated and working capital overstated.

e. Errors arising from recording transactions in the wrong period may reverse in the subsequent period.

   1) If ending inventory is overstated, the overstatement of net income will be offset by the understatement in the following year that results from the overstatement of beginning inventory.

f. An **overstatement error in year-end inventory** of the current year affects the financial statements of 2 different years.

   1) The **first year's** effects may be depicted as follows:

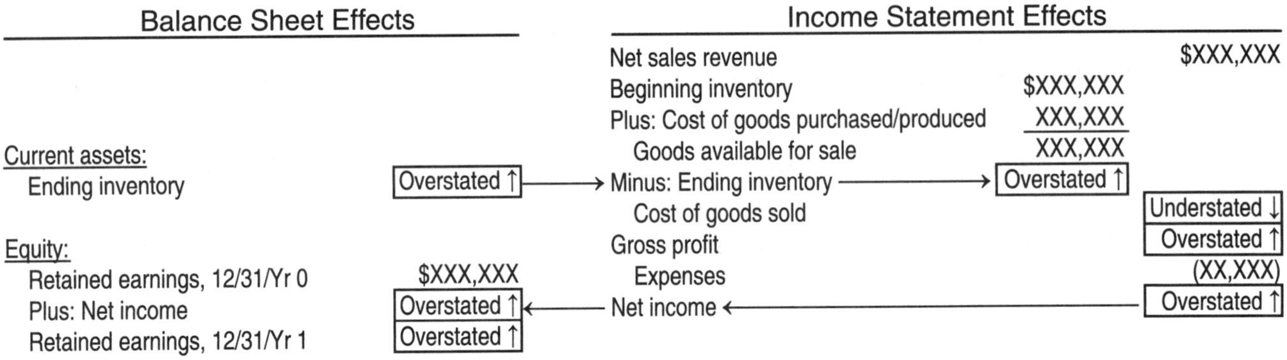

Figure 7-2

   2) At the end of the **second year**, retained earnings is correctly stated:

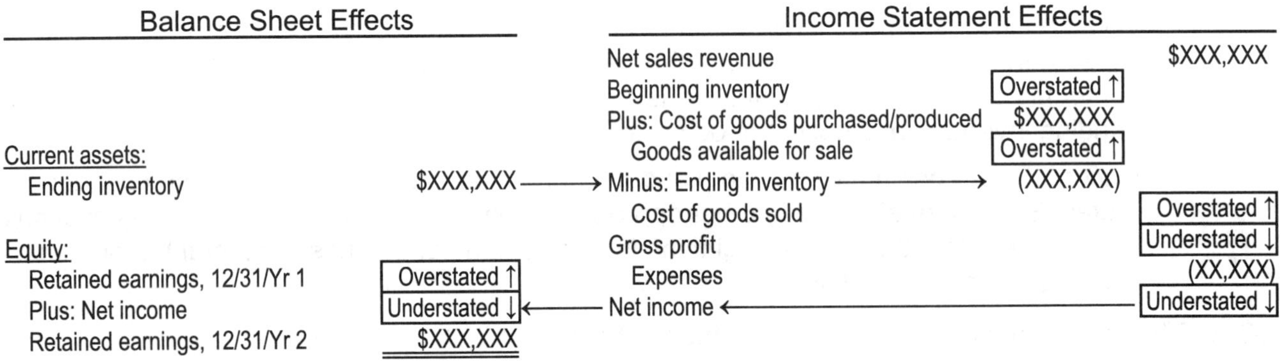

Figure 7-3

STOP & REVIEW

You have completed the outline for this subunit.
Study multiple-choice questions 16 through 20 beginning on page 219.

QUESTIONS

7.1 Inventory Fundamentals

1. How should the following costs affect a retailer's inventory?

	Freight-in	Interest on Inventory Loan
A.	Increase	No Effect
B.	Increase	Increase
C.	No effect	Increase
D.	No effect	No effect

Answer (A) is correct.

REQUIRED: The effect of certain costs on inventory.

DISCUSSION: Cost is "the sum of the applicable expenditures and charges directly or indirectly incurred in bringing an article to its existing condition and location." Freight costs are therefore an inventoriable cost to the extent they are not abnormal. However, interest cost for inventories is not capitalized. Interest cost is capitalized only for assets produced for an enterprise's own use or for sale or lease as discrete projects.

2. Herc Co.'s inventory at December 31, Year 1, was $1.5 million based on a physical count priced at cost, and before any necessary adjustment for the following:

- Merchandise costing $90,000 was shipped FOB shipping point from a vendor on December 30, Year 1, and was received and recorded on January 5, Year 2.
- Goods in the shipping area were excluded from inventory although shipment was not made until January 4, Year 2. The goods, billed to the customer FOB shipping point on December 30, Year 1, had a cost of $120,000.

What amount should Herc report as inventory in its December 31, Year 1, balance sheet?

A. $1,500,000

B. $1,590,000

C. $1,620,000

D. $1,710,000

Answer (D) is correct.

REQUIRED: The year-end inventory.

DISCUSSION: The inventory balance prior to adjustments was $1.5 million. The merchandise shipped FOB shipping point to Herc should be included because title passed when the goods were shipped. The goods in the shipping area should be included because title did not pass until the goods were shipped in Year 2. Thus, inventory reported at December 31, Year 1, should be $1,710,000 ($1,500,000 + $90,000 + $120,000).

Answer (A) is incorrect. The amount of $1,500,000 excludes the $90,000 of goods shipped by a vendor and the $120,000 of goods not shipped until January 4. **Answer (B) is incorrect.** The amount of $1,590,000 results from failing to include the $120,000 of goods not shipped until January 4. **Answer (C) is incorrect.** The amount of $1,620,000 does not include the $90,000 of goods shipped by a vendor FOB shipping point.

7.2 Consignment Accounting

3. The following items were included in Opal Co.'s inventory account at December 31:

Merchandise out on consignment, at sales price, including 40% markup on selling price	$40,000
Goods purchased, in transit, shipped FOB shipping point	36,000
Goods held on consignment by Opal	27,000

By what amount should Opal's inventory balance at December 31 be reduced?

A. $103,000

B. $67,000

C. $51,000

D. $43,000

Answer (D) is correct.

REQUIRED: The recognition of inventory for consignment sales and goods in transit.

DISCUSSION: Consigned goods are in the possession of the consignee but remain the property of the consignor and are included in the consignor's inventory count at cost, not selling price. Thus, Opal should reduce inventory by $16,000 ($40,000 selling price × 40%). Opal should also reduce inventory by $27,000 for the goods held on consignment. The goods in transit are properly included in inventory because title and risk of loss pass to the buyer at the shipping point when the shipping term is FOB shipping point. Consequently, inventory should be reduced by a total of $43,000 ($16,000 + $27,000).

Answer (A) is incorrect. The cost of goods on consignment and the cost of the goods in transit are included in inventory. **Answer (B) is incorrect.** The cost of goods on consignment is included in inventory. **Answer (C) is incorrect.** The amount of $51,000 is the result of deducting the cost, not the markup, of the goods on consignment.

4. On October 20, Grimm Co. consigned 40 freezers to Holden Co. for sale at $1,000 each and paid $800 in transportation costs. On December 30, Holden reported the sale of 10 freezers and remitted $8,500. The remittance was net of the agreed 15% commission. What amount should Grimm recognize as consignment sales revenue for the year?

A. $7,700

B. $8,500

C. $9,800

D. $10,000

Answer (D) is correct.

REQUIRED: The amount of consignment sales revenue to be recognized.

DISCUSSION: Under a consignment sales agreement, the consignor ships merchandise to the consignee, who acts as agent for the consignor in selling the goods. The goods are in the physical possession of the consignee but remain the property of the consignor and are included in the consignor's inventory account. Accordingly, sales revenue from these consigned goods should be recognized by the consignor when the merchandise is sold (delivered to the ultimate customer). Grimm should recognize sales revenue of $10,000 ($1,000 sales price × 10 units). Transportation costs and commissions are consignor inventory costs and selling expenses, respectively, and are not used to compute sales revenue.

Answer (A) is incorrect. The amount of $7,700 is the amount received from the consignee minus $800 of transportation costs. **Answer (B) is incorrect.** The amount of $8,500 is the amount received from the consignee. **Answer (C) is incorrect.** The amount of $9,800 equals the sales price of 10 freezers minus 25% (10 ÷ 40) of the transportation costs.

7.3 Cost Flow Methods -- Application

5. Flex Co. uses a periodic inventory system. The following are inventory transactions for the month of January:

1/1	Beginning inventory	10,000 units at $3
1/5	Purchase	5,000 units at $4
1/15	Purchase	5,000 units at $5
1/20	Sales at $10 per unit	10,000 units

Flex uses the average pricing method to determine the value of its inventory. What amount should Flex report as cost of goods sold on its income statement for the month of January?

A. $30,000

B. $37,500

C. $40,000

D. $100,000

Answer (B) is correct.

REQUIRED: The cost of goods sold using the average pricing method.

DISCUSSION: The total cost of beginning inventory and purchases is $75,000 ($30,000 + $20,000 + $25,000), and the total number units of beginning inventory and purchases is 20,000. The average price of the beginning inventory and purchases is $3.75 ($75,000 cost ÷ 20,000 units). The total cost of goods sold equals $37,500 (10,000 units sold × $3.75).

Answer (A) is incorrect. The amount of $30,000 is based on FIFO (10,000 units in beginning inventory × $3). **Answer (C) is incorrect.** The amount of $40,000 is based on the January 5 price. **Answer (D) is incorrect.** The amount of $100,000 is based on the selling price of the 10,000 units.

Questions 6 and 7 are based on the following information. During January, Metro Co., which maintains a perpetual inventory system, recorded the following information pertaining to its inventory:

	Units	Unit Cost	Total Cost	Units On Hand
Balance on 1/1	1,000	$1	$1,000	1,000
Purchased on 1/7	600	3	1,800	1,600
Sold on 1/20	900			700
Purchased on 1/25	400	5	2,000	1,100

6. Under the moving-average method, what amount should Metro report as inventory at January 31?

A. $2,640

B. $3,225

C. $3,300

D. $3,900

Answer (B) is correct.

REQUIRED: The ending inventory using the moving-average method.

DISCUSSION: The moving-average system is only applicable to perpetual inventories. It requires that a new weighted average be computed after every purchase. This moving average is based on remaining inventory held and the new inventory purchased. Based on the calculations below, the moving-average cost per unit for the 1/20 sale is $1.75, and the cost of goods sold (COGS) for January is $1,575 (900 units sold × $1.75). Thus, ending inventory is $3,225 ($1,000 beginning balance + $1,800 purchase on 1/7 – $1,575 COGS on 1/20 + $2,000 purchase on 1/25).

	Units	Moving-Average Cost/Unit	Total Cost
Balance 1/1	1,000	$1.00	$1,000
Purchase 1/7	600	3.00	1,800
	1,600	$1.75	$2,800

Answer (A) is incorrect. The amount of $2,640 is based on the weighted-average method. **Answer (C) is incorrect.** The amount of $3,300 is based on a cost of $3 being assigned to each unit in ending inventory. **Answer (D) is incorrect.** The amount of $3,900 is based on the FIFO method.

7. Under the LIFO method, what amount should Metro report as inventory at January 31?

A. $1,300

B. $2,700

C. $3,900

D. $4,100

Answer (B) is correct.

REQUIRED: The ending inventory using a perpetual LIFO system.

DISCUSSION: In a perpetual inventory system, purchases are directly recorded in the inventory account, and cost of goods sold (COGS) is determined as the goods are sold. Under LIFO, the latest goods purchased are assumed to be the first to be sold. Using LIFO perpetual, 600 of the 900 units sold on 1/20 are assumed to have come from the last purchase. Their cost was $1,800 (600 × $3). The remaining 300 came from the beginning balance at a cost of $300 (300 × $1). Hence, the total COGS for January was $2,100, and ending inventory must equal $2,700 ($1,000 beginning inventory + $1,800 purchase on 1/7 + $2,000 purchase on 1/25 – $2,100 COGS).

Answer (A) is incorrect. The amount of $1,300 is based on the periodic LIFO method. **Answer (C) is incorrect.** The amount of $3,900 is based on the periodic FIFO method. **Answer (D) is incorrect.** The amount of $4,100 is based on an ending inventory of 400 units at $5 per unit and 700 units at $3 per unit.

7.4 Cost Flow Methods -- Comparison

8. The UNO Company was formed on January 2, Year 1, to sell a single product. Over a 2-year period, UNO's costs increased steadily. Inventory quantities equaled 3 months' sales at December 31, Year 1, and zero at December 31, Year 2. Assuming the periodic system and no accounting changes, the inventory cost method that reports the highest amount for each of the following is

	Inventory 12/31/Year 1	Cost of Sales Year 2
A.	LIFO	FIFO
B.	LIFO	LIFO
C.	FIFO	FIFO
D.	FIFO	LIFO

Answer (C) is correct.

REQUIRED: The method resulting in the highest beginning inventory and cost of sales given zero ending inventory.

DISCUSSION: In a period of rising prices, FIFO inventory is higher than LIFO inventory. FIFO assumes that the latest and therefore the highest priced goods purchased are in inventory. But LIFO assumes that these goods were the first to be sold. Accordingly, the inventory at December 31, Year 1 (beginning inventory for Year 2), is higher for FIFO than LIFO. Given zero inventory at December 31, Year 2, the units sold in Year 2 must have equaled the sum of Year 2 purchases and beginning inventory. Because beginning inventory for Year 2 is reported at a higher amount under FIFO than LIFO, the result is a higher cost of goods sold under FIFO.

9. The Hastings Company began operations on January 1, Year 1, and uses the FIFO method in costing its raw material inventory. Management is contemplating a change to the LIFO method and is interested in determining what effect such a change will have on net income. Accordingly, the following information has been developed:

Final Inventory	Year 1	Year 2
FIFO	$240,000	$270,000
LIFO	200,000	210,000
Net income per FIFO	$120,000	$170,000

Based upon the above information, a change to the LIFO method in Year 2 results in net income for Year 2 of

A. $110,000

B. $150,000

C. $170,000

D. $230,000

Answer (B) is correct.

REQUIRED: The second-year net income after a change from FIFO to LIFO in the second year of operations.

DISCUSSION: A change in accounting principle requires retrospective application. All periods reported must be individually adjusted for the period-specific effects of applying the new principle. The difference in income in the second year is equal to the $20,000 difference between the FIFO inventory change and the LIFO inventory change (FIFO: $270,000 – $240,000 = $30,000 change; LIFO: $210,000 – $200,000 = $10,000 change; $30,000 – $10,000 = $20,000 difference). The $170,000 FIFO net income will decrease by $20,000. Net LIFO income will therefore be $150,000 ($170,000 – $20,000).

Answer (A) is incorrect. The amount of $110,000 incorrectly subtracts the difference from Year 1 from the net income under LIFO for Year 2. **Answer (C) is incorrect.** The amount of $170,000 is the income for Year 2 under FIFO. **Answer (D) is incorrect.** The amount of $230,000 incorrectly adds the cumulative difference between LIFO and FIFO to FIFO net income instead of subtracting the difference from FIFO net income.

7.5 Dollar-Value LIFO

10. Bach Co. adopted the dollar-value LIFO inventory method as of January 1, Year 4. A single inventory pool and an internally computed price index are used to compute Bach's LIFO inventory layers. Information about Bach's dollar-value inventory follows:

	Inventory:	
Date	At Base-Year Cost	At Current-Year Cost
1/1/Year 4	$90,000	$90,000
Year 4 layer	20,000	30,000
Year 5 layer	40,000	80,000

What was the price index used to compute Bach's Year 5 dollar-value LIFO inventory layer?

A. 1.09

B. 1.25

C. 1.33

D. 2.00

Answer (C) is correct.

REQUIRED: The price index used to compute the current year dollar-value LIFO inventory layer.

DISCUSSION: To compute the ending inventory under dollar-value LIFO, the ending inventory stated in year-end or current-year cost must be restated at base-year cost. The layers at base-year cost are computed using a LIFO flow assumption and then weighted (multiplied) by the relevant indexes to price the ending inventory. A price index for the current year may be calculated by dividing the ending inventory at current-year cost by the ending inventory at base-year cost. This index is then applied to the current-year inventory layer stated at base-year cost. Thus, the Year 5 index (rounded) is 1.33 {[($90,000 + $30,000 + $80,000) EI at current-year cost] ÷ [($90,000 + $20,000 + $40,000) EI at base-year cost]}.

Answer (A) is incorrect. The figure of 1.09 is the price index for Year 4. **Answer (B) is incorrect.** The figure of 1.25 is calculated by dividing the difference in the current-year cost of inventory layers for Year 4 and Year 5 by the Year 5 base-year cost. **Answer (D) is incorrect.** The figure of 2.00 equals the current year cost of the Year 5 layer divided by its base-year.

11. Walt Co. adopted the dollar-value LIFO inventory method as of January 1, when its inventory was valued at $500,000. Walt's entire inventory constitutes a single pool. Using a relevant price index of 1.10, Walt determined that its December 31 inventory was $577,500 at current-year cost and $525,000 at base-year cost. What was Walt's dollar-value LIFO inventory at December 31?

A. $525,000

B. $527,500

C. $552,500

D. $577,500

Answer (B) is correct.

REQUIRED: The dollar-value LIFO inventory cost reported in the balance sheet.

DISCUSSION: A price index for the current year may be calculated by dividing the ending inventory at current-year cost by the ending inventory at base-year cost. This index is then applied to the current-year inventory layer stated at base-year cost. Consequently, the index is 1.10 ($577,500 ÷ $525,000), and the dollar-value LIFO cost at December 31 is $527,500 {$500,000 base layer + [($525,000 – $500,000) × 1.10]}.

Answer (A) is incorrect. The base-year cost is $525,000. **Answer (C) is incorrect.** The amount of $552,500 results from using $525,000 as the base layer. **Answer (D) is incorrect.** The amount of $577,500 is the year-end inventory at current cost.

7.6 Measurement of Inventory Subsequent to Initial Recognition

12. Lialia Co. has determined the cost of its fiscal year-end unfinished FIFO inventory to be $300,000. Information pertaining to that inventory at year-end is as follows:

Estimated selling price	$330,000
Estimated cost of disposal	20,000
Normal profit margin	15%
Current replacement cost	280,000
Estimated completion costs	15,000

What amount should Lialia report as inventory on its year-end balance sheet?

A. $295,000

B. $280,000

C. $300,000

D. $330,000

Answer (A) is correct.

REQUIRED: The ending balance of inventory measured using FIFO.

DISCUSSION: Inventory accounted for using the FIFO method (or any cost method other than LIFO or retail) is measured at the lower of cost or net realizable value (NRV). NRV is the estimated selling price in the ordinary course of business, minus reasonably predictable costs of completion, disposal, and transportation. At year-end, the NRV of the inventory of $295,000 ($330,000 estimated selling price – $15,000 estimated completion costs – $20,000 estimated costs of disposal) is lower than its cost of $300,000. Thus, the inventory is reported at its NRV of $295,000.

Answer (B) is incorrect. If the inventory were accounted for under the LIFO or the retail inventory method, it would have been reported at its current replacement cost of $280,000. **Answer (C) is incorrect.** Inventory accounted for using the FIFO method is measured at the lower of cost or net realizable value (NRV). The NRV is lower than cost, so the inventory must be reported at its NRV. **Answer (D) is incorrect.** Inventory should not be reported at an amount greater than its historical cost.

13. Rose Co. sells one product and uses the last-in, first-out method to determine inventory cost. Information for the month of January follows:

	Total Units	Unit Cost
Beginning inventory, 1/1	8,000	$8.20
Purchases, 1/5	12,000	7.90
Sales	10,000	

Rose has determined that at January 31, the replacement cost of its inventory was $8 per unit, and the net realizable value was $8.80 per unit. Rose's normal profit margin is $1 per unit. Rose applies the lower-of-cost-or-market rule to total inventory and records any resulting loss. At January 31, what should be the net carrying amount of Rose's inventory?

A. $79,000

B. $78,000

C. $80,000

D. $81,400

Answer (C) is correct.

REQUIRED: The net carrying amount of LIFO-based inventory.

DISCUSSION: Subject to certain restrictions, inventory is valued at the lower of cost or market. Because Rose uses the LIFO method to determine inventory cost, the 10,000 units sold are treated as coming from the purchases made on 1/5. Thus, 2,000 units remain from the purchase, and 8,000 units remain from beginning inventory. The average cost of the remaining 10,000 units is $8.14 {[(8,000 × $8.20) + (2,000 × $7.90)] ÷ 10,000}. The replacement cost of $8, which exceeds NRV minus a normal profit ($8.80 – $1.00 = $7.80) but is lower than NRV ($8.80), is lower than the average cost of $8.14. Consequently, ending inventory on a LIFO-LCM basis is $80,000 (10,000 units × $8 replacement cost).

Answer (A) is incorrect. The amount of $79,000 assumes that LCM was applied using the FIFO method. **Answer (B) is incorrect.** The amount of $78,000 equals 10,000 units times $7.80 (NRV – a normal profit). **Answer (D) is incorrect.** The amount of $81,400 is based on the assumption that average unit cost is below the unit replacement cost.

14. Based on a physical inventory taken on December 31, Chewy Co. determined its chocolate inventory on a LIFO basis at $26,000 with a replacement cost of $20,000. Chewy estimated that, after further processing costs of $12,000, the chocolate could be sold as finished candy bars for $40,000. Chewy's normal profit margin is 10% of sales. Under the lower-of-cost-or-market rule, what amount should Chewy report as chocolate inventory in its December 31 balance sheet?

A. $28,000

B. $26,000

C. $24,000

D. $20,000

Answer (C) is correct.

REQUIRED: The LCM value of inventory.

DISCUSSION: Under LIFO, inventory is measured at the lower of cost or market (LCM). Market equals current replacement cost subject to maximum and minimum values. The maximum is NRV, and the minimum is NRV minus normal profit. When replacement cost is within this range, it is used as market. Cost is given as $26,000. NRV is $28,000 ($40,000 selling price – $12,000 additional processing costs), and NRV minus a normal profit equals $24,000 [$28,000 – ($40,000 × 10%)]. Because the lowest amount in the range ($24,000) exceeds replacement cost ($20,000), it is used as market. Because market value ($24,000) is less than cost ($26,000), it is also the inventory amount.

Answer (A) is incorrect. The NRV is $28,000. **Answer (B) is incorrect.** The cost is $26,000. **Answer (D) is incorrect.** The replacement cost is $20,000.

15. The original cost of an inventory item is above the replacement cost. The inventory item's replacement cost is above the net realizable value. Under the lower-of-cost-or-market method, the inventory item accounted for using the retail inventory method should be valued at

A. Original cost.

B. Replacement cost.

C. Net realizable value.

D. Net realizable value less normal profit margin.

Answer (C) is correct.

REQUIRED: The measurement of an inventory item under the LCM method given that cost exceeds replacement cost and replacement cost exceeds NRV.

DISCUSSION: Inventory accounted for using LIFO or the retail inventory method is measured at the lower of cost or market. Market is the current cost to replace inventory, subject to certain limitations. Market should not exceed a ceiling equal to net realizable value (NRV) or be less than a floor equal to NRV minus a normal profit margin. Because replacement cost exceeds NRV, the ceiling is NRV.

Answer (A) is incorrect. The inventory item should be written down to market if its utility is no longer as great as its cost. **Answer (B) is incorrect.** Market should not exceed a ceiling equal to NRV. **Answer (D) is incorrect.** Net realizable value minus a normal profit margin is the minimum amount (the floor) for market.

7.7 Special Topics in Inventory Accounting

16. On December 30, Year 1, Astor Corp. sold merchandise for $75,000 to Day Co. The terms of the sale were net 30, FOB shipping point. The merchandise was shipped on December 31, Year 1, and arrived at Day on January 5, Year 2. Due to a clerical error, the sale was not recorded until January Year 2, and the merchandise, sold at a 25% markup, was included in Astor's inventory at December 31, Year 1. As a result, Astor's cost of goods sold for the year ended December 31, Year 1, was

A. Understated by $75,000.

B. Understated by $60,000.

C. Understated by $15,000.

D. Correctly stated.

Answer (B) is correct.

REQUIRED: The cost of goods sold given delayed recording of a sale.

DISCUSSION: Astor should have debited a receivable and credited sales for $75,000, the net amount, on the date of shipment. Astor also should have debited cost of sales and credited inventory at cost on the same date. Under the shipping terms, the sale should have been recognized on December 31, Year 1, because title and risk of loss passed to the buyer on that date; that is, an earning process was complete. The error therefore understated cost sales by $60,000 ($75,000 sales price ÷ 125% of cost).

Answer (A) is incorrect. The selling price is $75,000. **Answer (C) is incorrect.** The amount of the markup is $15,000. **Answer (D) is incorrect.** Cost of goods was understated by $60,000.

17. Bren Co.'s beginning inventory at January 1 was understated by $26,000, and its ending inventory was overstated by $52,000. As a result, Bren's cost of goods sold for the year was

A. Understated by $26,000.

B. Overstated by $26,000.

C. Understated by $78,000.

D. Overstated by $78,000.

Answer (C) is correct.

REQUIRED: The misstatement of cost of goods sold.

DISCUSSION: When beginning inventory is understated, cost of goods sold will be understated. When ending inventory is overstated, cost of goods sold will be understated. Thus, Bren Co.'s cost of goods sold is understated by $78,000 ($26,000 + $52,000).

Answer (A) is incorrect. The overstatement of ending inventory also understates cost of goods sold. **Answer (B) is incorrect.** COGS was understated in the current year by the amounts of both the beginning inventory error and the ending inventory error. **Answer (D) is incorrect.** Both errors understate cost of goods sold.

18. On January 1, Year 4, Card Corp. signed a 3-year, noncancelable purchase contract that allows Card to purchase up to 500,000 units of a computer part annually from Hart Supply Co. The price is $.10 per unit, and the contract guarantees a minimum annual purchase of 100,000 units. During Year 4, the part unexpectedly became obsolete. Card had 250,000 units of this inventory at December 31, Year 4, and believes these parts can be sold as scrap for $.02 per unit. What amount of probable loss from the purchase commitment should Card report in its Year 4 income statement?

A. $24,000

B. $20,000

C. $16,000

D. $8,000

Answer (C) is correct.

REQUIRED: The amount of probable loss from the purchase commitment.

DISCUSSION: The entity must accrue a loss in the current year on goods subject to a firm purchase commitment if their market price declines below the commitment price. This loss should be measured in the same manner as inventory losses. Disclosure of the loss also is required. Consequently, given that 200,000 units must be purchased over the next 2 years for $20,000 (200,000 × $.10), and the parts can be sold as scrap for $4,000 (200,000 × $.02), the amount of probable loss for Year 4 is $16,000 ($20,000 – $4,000).

Answer (A) is incorrect. The amount of $24,000 includes the purchase commitment for the current year. **Answer (B) is incorrect.** The amount of $20,000 excludes the net realizable value of the parts from the calculation. **Answer (D) is incorrect.** The amount of $8,000 excludes the probable loss expected in the last year of the purchase commitment.

19. The following information was obtained from Smith Co.:

Sales	$275,000
Beginning inventory	30,000
Ending inventory	18,000

Smith's gross margin is 20%. What amount represents Smith purchases?

A. $202,000

B. $208,000

C. $220,000

D. $232,000

Answer (B) is correct.

REQUIRED: The amount of purchases given the gross margin.

DISCUSSION: Gross margin equals sales minus cost of goods sold. If it is 20% of sales, cost of goods sold equals $220,000 [$275,000 × (1.0 – .20)]. Cost of goods sold equals beginning inventory, plus purchases, minus ending inventory. Thus, purchases equals $208,000 ($220,000 COGS – $30,000 BI + $18,000 EI).

Answer (A) is incorrect. Cost of goods sold minus ending inventory equals $202,000. **Answer (C) is incorrect.** Cost of goods sold equals $220,000. **Answer (D) is incorrect.** The amount of $232,000 equals cost of goods sold plus beginning inventory, minus ending inventory.

20. Fireworks, Inc., had an explosion in its plant that destroyed most of its inventory. Its records show that beginning inventory was $40,000. Fireworks made purchases of $480,000 and sales of $620,000 during the year. Its normal gross profit percentage is 25%. It can sell some of its damaged inventory for $5,000. The insurance company will reimburse Fireworks for 70% of its loss. What amount should Fireworks report as loss from the explosion?

A. $50,000

B. $35,000

C. $18,000

D. $15,000

Answer (D) is correct.

REQUIRED: The loss from destruction of inventory.

DISCUSSION: The loss from the destruction of inventory equals the cost of the damaged inventory minus any sales of the damaged inventory and insurance proceeds.

Beginning inventory	$ 40,000
Purchases	480,000
Cost of goods sold [$620,000 × (1.0 – .25)]	(465,000)
Estimated inventory	$ 55,000
NRV	(5,000)
Loss before insurance proceeds	$ 50,000
Insurance ($50,000 × 70%)	(35,000)
Reported loss	$ 15,000

Answer (A) is incorrect. The loss without regard to the insurance proceeds equals $50,000. **Answer (B) is incorrect.** The insurance proceeds equal $35,000. **Answer (C) is incorrect.** The estimated selling price of damaged inventory should be included in the calculation of a loss.

STUDY UNIT EIGHT

PROPERTY, PLANT, EQUIPMENT, AND DEPLETABLE RESOURCES

(28 pages of outline)

This study unit covers tangible fixed assets. The next study unit addresses intangible assets. Depreciation and depletion are included in this study unit because income statement accounts traditionally are presented with the related balance sheet accounts.

8.1 INITIAL MEASUREMENT OF PROPERTY, PLANT, AND EQUIPMENT (PPE)

1. **Definition**

   a. These assets are called property, plant, and equipment; fixed assets; or plant assets. They provide benefits from their use in the production of goods and services, not from their consumption.

      1) PPE are tangible. They have physical existence.

      2) PPE may be either **personal property** (something movable, e.g., equipment) or **real property** (such as land or a building).

      3) PPE are used in the **ordinary operations** of an entity and are not held primarily for investment, resale, or inclusion in another product. But they are often sold.

      4) PPE are **noncurrent**. They are not expected to be used up within 1 year or the normal operating cycle of the business, whichever is longer.

2. **Carrying Amount**

   a. The carrying amount of an item of PPE is the amount at which it is presented in the financial statements. This amount is equal to the historical cost minus accumulated depreciation and impairment losses.

Historical or initial cost	$XXX
Accumulated depreciation	(XXX)
Impairment losses	(XXX)
Asset's carrying amount	$XXX

3. **Types of PPE**

   a. **Land**

   b. **Buildings**

   c. **Land improvements**, such as landscaping, drainage, streets, street lighting, sewers, sidewalks, parking lots, driveways, and fences

   d. **Machinery and equipment**, such as furniture, fixtures (personal property permanently attached to real property, such as a central heating system), and vehicles

   e. **Leasehold improvements**, such as buildings constructed on, and other modifications made to, the leased property by a lessee

   f. **Internally constructed assets**

   g. **Miscellaneous items**, such as tools, patterns and dies, and returnable containers

4. **Relevant Accounting Principles**

   a. PPE are initially measured at **historical cost**, which consists of

      1) The amount paid to acquire the asset and

      2) The costs needed to bring the asset to the condition and location necessary for its intended use.

         a) The initial measurement embraces all other costs to acquire PPE, transport them to the sites of their intended use, and prepare them for operations.

         b) Freight-in (transportation-in), installation costs, renovation or reconditioning costs, expenses of tests or trial runs, and insurance and taxes during the preoperations period are capitalized to the initial cost of the asset.

b. Historical cost is adjusted for changes in utility over the life of the asset, e.g., depreciation and impairment.

   1) In general, expenses should be recognized at the time related revenues are earned.

   2) However, no direct relationship ordinarily exists between the consumption of service potential and specific revenues. Thus, the **depreciation expense** must be **systematically and rationally allocated** to periods expected to be benefited.

c. Depreciation does not start until PPE are placed in operation and begin to contribute economic benefits.

d. Under GAAP, PPE are not revalued upward to reflect appraisal, market, current, or fair values that are above historical cost (or carrying amount) of PPE.

SUCCESS TIP

The AICPA often tests candidates' knowledge of the initial measurement of PPE with both conceptual and calculation questions. A common format for calculation questions gives information about the noncurrent asset and asks for the amount at which the asset should be initially recorded.

5. **Initial Costs -- Land**

   a. The costs of acquiring and preparing land for its expected use are capitalized.

   b. The price should include not only the cash price but also any **encumbrances assumed** (such as mortgages or tax liens).

   c. The cost of land also includes **transaction costs**, e.g., surveying costs, legal fees, brokers' commissions, title insurance, and escrow fees.

   d. **Site preparation costs** [clearing, draining, filling, leveling the property, and razing existing buildings, minus any proceeds (such as timber sales)] are costs of the land, not of the building to be constructed on the land.

   e. Certain **permanent improvements** of the land made by the entity that have **indefinite lives** are debited to the land account.

   f. Land has an indefinite useful life and therefore is **not depreciated**.

6. **Initial Costs -- Land Improvements**

   a. Land improvements with **finite useful lives** that are maintained and replaced by the reporting entity are capitalized separately from land and depreciated.

7. **Initial Costs -- Buildings**

   a. The costs that are necessary to the purchase or construction of a building and that will result in future economic benefits should be capitalized. These include

      1) The **purchase price**, including any liens assumed by the purchaser, etc.
      2) Costs of **renovating and preparing the structure** for its expected use.
      3) The expenses of **excavating the site** to build the foundation (but not site preparation costs).

         a) The **costs of razing an old building** are either debited to the land account or treated as an adjustment of a gain or loss on disposal. The accounting depends on whether the land was purchased as a site for the new structure or the old building was previously used in the entity's operations.
         b) The **carrying amount of an existing building** previously used in the entity's operations is not included in the cost of the new structure. It will not produce future benefits.

      4) The materials, labor, and overhead **costs of construction**
      5) Interest costs incurred during construction of a building for an entity's own use should be capitalized. (The outline for capitalization of interest is in Subunit 8.2.)

8. **Initial Costs -- Machinery and Equipment**

   a. **Costs** include

      1) Purchase price (including sales taxes)
      2) Freight-in, handling, insurance, and storage until use begins
      3) Preparation, installation, and start-up costs, such as testing and trial runs

EXAMPLE 8-1 Initial Cost of Equipment

On January 1, Year 1, an entity purchased a machine to be used in production. The machine was installed and ready for its intended use on July 1, Year 1. The following costs were incurred during Year 1:

Purchase price	$100,000
Year 1 insurance costs incurred evenly throughout year	10,000
Shipping costs	3,000
Installation costs	4,000
Testing costs	2,500

The historical (initial) cost of the machine is **$114,500** [$100,000 + ($10,000 × 0.5) + $3,000 + $4,000 + $2,500]. The $5,000 of insurance costs for the 6 months after the machine is ready for its intended use (after July 1, Year 1) should be expensed, not capitalized, as part of the machine's initial cost.

9. **Initial Costs -- Leasehold Improvements**

   a. Leasehold improvements, such as buildings constructed on leased land, are accounted for by the lessee in the same way as property to which title is held. However, the term of the lease may limit the depreciation period.

   b. If the useful life of the asset extends beyond the lease term and lease renewal is reasonably certain, the amortization period may include all or part of the renewal period. If renewal is uncertain, the useful life is the remaining term of the lease.

10. **Other Factors Affecting Initial Measurement**

    a. **Acquisition in exchange for a noncurrent obligation.** If an item of PPE is acquired in exchange for a noncurrent note, its cost is the present value of the consideration paid (the note). But the note's interest rate may be unstated or unreasonable, or the face amount may differ materially from the cash price of the PPE or the market value of the note. In these cases, the cost of the PPE should be the more clearly determinable of the cash price of the PPE or the market value of the note.

    b. **Donated assets.** In general, contributions received should be recognized as (1) revenues or gains in the period of receipt and (2) assets, or decreases in liabilities or expenses. They are measured at fair value.

PPE	$XXX	
Contribution revenue		$XXX

11. **Acquisition of a Group of Assets (Lump-Sum Purchase)**

    a. When two or more assets are acquired for a single price, the cost must be allocated to the individual assets in the group.

       1) Allocation is based on the **relative fair values** of the assets acquired.

EXAMPLE 8-2 Acquisition of a Group of Assets

Mike Co. paid a lump-sum purchase price of $100,000 to acquire the following assets:

Assets Acquired	Fair Value
Building	$ 72,000
Machine	36,000
Inventory	12,000
	$120,000

The lump-sum cost of the assets of $100,000 is allocated to the individual assets acquired based on their relative fair values.

Assets Acquired	Fair Value	Relative % of the Total Fair Value	Allocated Cost
Building	$ 72,000	60%	**$ 60,000** = $100,000 × 60%
Machine	36,000	30%	**30,000** = $100,000 × 30%
Inventory	12,000	10%	**10,000** = $100,000 × 10%
	$120,000	100%	$100,000

An entity may choose either the **cost model** (as under U.S. GAAP) or the **revaluation model** as its accounting policy. It must apply that policy to an entire class of PPE. A class is a grouping of assets of similar nature and use in an entity's operations, for example, land, office equipment, or motor vehicles.

Under the revaluation model, an item of PPE whose fair value can be reliably measured may be carried at a **revalued amount** equal to fair value at the revaluation date (minus subsequent accumulated depreciation and impairment losses).

Revaluation is needed whenever fair value and the asset's carrying amount differ materially. Accumulated depreciation is restated proportionately or eliminated.

A revaluation increase must be recognized in other comprehensive income and accumulated in equity as **revaluation surplus**. But the increase must be recognized in profit or loss to the extent it reverses a decrease of the same asset that was recognized in profit or loss.

A revaluation decrease must be recognized in profit or loss. But the decrease must be recognized in other comprehensive income to the extent of any credit in revaluation surplus for the same asset.

IFRS DIFFERENCE

IFRS EXAMPLE 8-1 IFRS Revaluation Model

On January 1, Year 1, a company purchased a machine with a 10-year estimated useful life and no residual value for $100,000. The company accounts for its machines using the revaluation model and revalues them at the end of each year. The company applies the straight-line depreciation method, and the fair value of the machine at the end of Year 1 is $94,000.

The carrying amount of the machine at the end of Year 1 just prior to revaluation is $90,000 [$100,000 historical cost – ($100,000 ÷ 10) accumulated depreciation]. According to the revaluation model, the machine must be carried at a revalued amount that equals its fair value of $94,000. A revaluation increase of $4,000 ($94,000 fair value – $90,000 carrying amount prior to the revaluation) is recognized as a revaluation surplus in other comprehensive income. The following are the balances in relation to this machine that will be recognized in the December 31, Year 1, financial statements:

Machine's carrying amount	$94,000
Revaluation surplus (item of OCI)	4,000
Depreciation expense	10,000

Under **IAS 40**, *Investment Property*, **investment property** is property (land, building, part of a building, or both) held by the owner or by the lessee as a right-of-use asset to earn rental income or for capital appreciation or both. Investment property may be accounted for according to (1) the **cost model** and carried at historical cost minus accumulated depreciation and impairment losses (as under U.S. GAAP) or (2) the **fair value model**. If the fair value model is chosen as the accounting policy, all of the entity's investment property must be measured at **fair value** at the end of the reporting period. A **gain or loss** arising from a change in the fair value of investment property must be recognized in profit or loss for the period in which it arises. Investment property that is accounted for according to the fair value model is **not depreciated**.

IFRS DIFFERENCE

IFRS EXAMPLE 8-2 Investment Property – IFRS Fair Value Model

Using the data from IFRS Example 8-1, assume that the company purchased a rental building (instead of a machine) for $100,000. The company accounts for its investment properties using the fair value model.

According to the fair value model, investment property must not be depreciated. Thus, the carrying amount of the building at the end of Year 1 just prior to the fair value measurement is $100,000. A loss of $6,000 ($94,000 fair value – $100,000 carrying amount prior to fair value measurement) arising from the change in the fair value of investment property is recognized in the income statement. The following are the balances in relation to this rental building that will be recognized in the December 31, Year 1, financial statements:

Rental building's carrying amount	$94,000
Impairment loss	6,000

If at the end of Year 1 the fair value of the building was $106,000, an appreciation gain of $6,000 ($106,000 fair value – $100,000 carrying amount prior to fair value measurement) would have been recognized in profit or loss.

STOP & REVIEW

You have completed the outline for this subunit.
Study multiple-choice questions 1 through 3 beginning on page 248.

8.2 INTERNALLY CONSTRUCTED ASSETS (ICAs) -- CAPITALIZATION OF INTEREST

1. **Capitalization of Interest**

   a. The costs necessary to bring an asset to the condition and location of its intended use are part of the historical cost. **Interest incurred during construction** is such a cost and must be capitalized as part of an asset's initial cost. An imputed cost of equity capital is not recognized.

2. **Qualifying Assets**

   a. Qualifying assets are assets for which interest must be capitalized. The following are qualifying assets:

      1) Assets that are constructed or produced by the entity for its own use
      2) Assets that are constructed or produced for the entity by others for which deposits or progress payments have been made
      3) Assets that are constructed or produced for sale or lease as separate projects, such as real estate developments or ships

3. **Nonqualifying Assets**
    a. The following are assets for which interest must not be capitalized (nonqualifying assets):
        1) Inventories routinely produced in large quantities on a repetitive basis
        2) Assets in use or ready for their intended use in earning activities
        3) Assets not being used in earning activities that are not undergoing the activities necessary to ready them for use
4. **Capitalization Period for Interest Costs**
    a. This period is the time required to carry out the activities necessary to bring a qualifying asset to the condition and location necessary for its intended use.
    b. **The period begins and continues** as long as
        1) Expenditures for a qualifying asset are being made,
        2) Activities necessary to make the asset ready for its intended use (i.e., construction) are in progress, and
        3) Interest cost is being incurred.
    c. **Capitalization ends** when the asset is substantially complete and ready for its intended use. Also, interest capitalization must cease if substantially all asset-related activities are suspended.
5. **Limitation on Capitalized Interest**
    a. Interest cost includes interest (1) on obligations with explicit interest rates (including amortization of issue costs and discount or premium), (2) imputed on certain payables, and (3) on a finance lease.
    b. Capitalizable interest is limited to the **amount theoretically avoidable** if expenditures for ICAs had not been made. For example, if the entity had not incurred costs for ICAs, it might have used the funds to repay debt or to avoid issuing new debts.
    c. Interest capitalized may not exceed the actual total interest cost incurred during the period.
    d. Interest earned on borrowed funds is ordinarily not offset against interest cost to determine either capitalization rates or limitations on interest costs to be capitalized.
6. **Amount of Interest to be Capitalized**
    a. Capitalized interest equals the weighted **average accumulated expenditures (AAE)** for the qualifying asset during the capitalization period times the interest rate(s). The weighting is based on the time expenditures incurred interest.
    b. If a specific new borrowing outstanding during the period can be identified with the asset, the rate on that obligation may be applied to the extent that the AAE do not exceed the amount borrowed.
    c. To the extent that AAE exceed the amount of specific new borrowings, a weighted-average rate must be applied that is based on other (not the specific) borrowings outstanding during the period.

EXAMPLE 8-3 Capitalization of Interest

Lyssa Co. constructed a building for its own use. The capitalization period began on 1/1/Year 1 and ended on 12/31/Year 1. The AAE are based on the following construction-related expenditures and the amounts of time they incurred interest:

Quarter Beginning					AAE
1/1/Year 1:	$500,000	×	(12 ÷ 12)	=	$ 500,000
4/1/Year 1:	$400,000	×	(9 ÷ 12)	=	300,000
7/1/Year 1:	$600,000	×	(6 ÷ 12)	=	300,000
10/1/Year 1:	$400,000	×	(3 ÷ 12)	=	100,000
12/31/Year 1:	$900,000	×	(0 ÷ 12)	=	0
					$1,200,000

On 1/1/Year 1, Lyssa specifically borrowed $1,000,000 at a rate of 10% to finance the construction. Its other borrowings outstanding during the entire construction period consisted of a $2,000,000 bond issue bearing 8% interest and a $6,000,000 bond issue bearing 9%. All interest is paid at fiscal year end. Accordingly, the weighted-average rate on other borrowings is 8.75%.

		Interest		Principal		Rate
$2,000,000 × 8%	=	$160,000		$2,000,000		
$6,000,000 × 9%	=	540,000		6,000,000		
		$700,000	÷	$8,000,000	=	8.75%

Total actual interest cost for the fiscal year is $800,000.

$1,000,000 × 10%	=	$100,000
$2,000,000 × 8%	=	160,000
$6,000,000 × 9%	=	540,000
		$800,000

The AAE for the qualifying asset ($1,200,000) exceed the amount of specific borrowing associated with that asset ($1,000,000). The capitalization rate to be applied to this excess ($1,200,000 – $1,000,000 = $200,000) must be the weighted average of rates applicable to other borrowings of Lyssa (8.75%). Thus, the amount of avoidable interest is $117,500.

$1,000,000 × 10%	=	$100,000
($1,200,000 – $1,000,000) × 8.75%	=	17,500
		$117,500

The amount of $117,500 is capitalized as part of the initial cost of the building because it is less than actual interest.

Interest expense recognized in Year 1 is $682,500 ($800,000 – $117,500).

7. **Disclosures**

   a. If no interest cost is capitalized, the amount incurred and expensed during the period should be reported. If some interest cost is capitalized, the total incurred and the amount capitalized should be disclosed.

STOP & REVIEW

You have completed the outline for this subunit.
Study multiple-choice questions 4 and 5 on page 250.

8.3 SUBSEQUENT EXPENDITURES FOR PPE

1. **Accounting Issues**
   a. The issues are to determine whether subsequent expenditures should be capitalized or expensed and to determine the accounting methods to be used.
   b. **Capital expenditures** are capitalized. They provide additional benefits by improving the quality of services rendered by the asset, extending its useful life, or increasing its output.
   c. **Revenue expenditures** (expenses) maintain an asset's normal service capacity.
      1) These costs are recurring, are not expected to benefit future periods, and are expensed when incurred.
      2) An entity usually specifies a materiality threshold below which all costs are expensed, thereby avoiding the burden of depreciating immaterial amounts.
2. **Additions**
   a. Substantial expenditures for extensions or expansions of existing assets are **capitalized**. An example is an additional floor for a building.
   b. If the addition is essentially a separate asset, it is recorded in a separate account and depreciated over its own useful life. Otherwise, the addition should be debited to the original asset account and depreciated over the life of that asset.
   c. The basic entry is

Asset (new or old)	$XXX	
Cash, etc.		$XXX

3. **Replacements and Improvements (Betterments)**
   a. A **replacement** substitutes a new component of an asset for a similar one, for example, a tile roof for a tile roof. But an **improvement** substitutes a better component, such as a more efficient heating system.
   b. **Substitution method.** If the old component was recorded separately, e.g., recording a central air conditioning system separately from the building, the procedure is to remove it from the ledger, along with accumulated depreciation, and to **substitute the cost of the new component**. A loss may be recognized.
      1) The new component will be depreciated over the shorter of its useful life or that of the entire asset.
      2) The basic entry is

New asset	$XXX	
Accumulated depreciation of old asset	XXX	
Loss	XXX	
Old asset		$XXX
Cash, etc.		XXX

   c. If (1) the component replaced or improved has not been separately accounted for or (2) the old component has been modified, the substitution method is not used.
      1) If the replacement or improvement increases the asset's service potential but does not extend its estimated useful life, the asset is debited. The carrying amount of the old component is not removed.

2) If the replacement or improvement primarily extends the useful life without enhancing service potential, the entry is to debit accumulated depreciation. The expenditure is a recovery of depreciation, not an increase in the quality of service.

Accumulated depreciation	$XXX	
Cash, etc.		$XXX

4. **Rearrangements, Reinstallations, Relocations**
   a. Rearranging the configuration of plant assets, reinstalling such assets, or relocating operations may require material outlays that are separable from recurring expenses and provide probable future benefits.
   b. The **substitution method** of accounting for these costs may be used if the original installation costs and accumulated depreciation **are known**.
   c. Otherwise, if these costs are material, they should be debited to a new account and amortized over the period benefited.
   d. Relocation (moving) costs often are expensed as incurred.
5. **Repairs and Maintenance**
   a. Routine, **minor expenditures** made to maintain the operating efficiency of PPE are **ordinarily expensed as incurred**. However, as the amounts involved become more significant and the benefits to future periods increase, treatment of a **major repair as an addition, etc.**, may be more appropriate.
   b. Although a repair or maintenance cost ordinarily should be allocated to a single annual period only, its full recognition at the interim date when incurred may distort the interim statements.
      1) Accordingly, may be allocated to the interim periods that will benefit.
6. **Summary**

Action	Accounting Treatment	
Additions	Debit separate asset or debit old asset	
Replacements/Improvements – Carrying Amount Known	Substitution method	
Replacements/Improvements – Carrying Amount Not Known	Increase service potential only: debit asset	Extend useful life only: debit accumulated depreciation
Rearrangements/Reinstallations	Cost known: substitution method	Otherwise, material costs debited to new asset
Repairs	Minor: expense	Major: treatment as addition, etc.

STOP & REVIEW

You have completed the outline for this subunit.
Study multiple-choice questions 6 and 7 on page 251.

8.4 DEPRECIATION METHODS -- CALCULATIONS

SUCCESS TIP

CPA candidates can expect to answer questions that test depreciation concepts. CPA Exam questions often ask for depreciation calculations but not in the manner of simply calculating the depreciation amount using a depreciation method. The question may state that the useful life of the asset has increased/decreased and ask for the amount of accumulated depreciation.

1. **Definition**
   a. Depreciation is the process of systematically and rationally **allocating the depreciable base** of a tangible capital asset over its expected useful life.
      1) It is not a process of valuation.
   b. The periodic depreciation expense is recognized in the income statement. Accumulated depreciation is a contra-asset account. The journal entry is

Depreciation expense	$XXX	
Accumulated depreciation		$XXX

   c. An asset's **depreciable base** is the total amount that is to be systematically and rationally allocated.

Depreciable base = Historical cost – Salvage value – Recognized impairment loss

      1) **The estimated useful life** is an estimated period over which services (economic benefits) are expected to be obtained from the use of the asset.
      2) **Salvage value** is the amount that an entity expects to obtain from disposal of the asset at the end of the asset's useful life.

EXAMPLE 8-4 Depreciable Base of an Asset

Jayhawk Co. recently acquired a robot to be used in its fully automated factory for a purchase price of $850,000. Jayhawk spent another $150,000 installing and testing the robot. The company estimates that the robot will have a 5-year useful life and can be sold at the end of that time for $100,000.

The depreciable base for this asset is calculated as follows:

Purchase price	$ 850,000
Installation and testing	150,000
Historical cost	$1,000,000
Estimated salvage value	(100,000)
Depreciable base	$ 900,000

   d. The depreciation method chosen should reflect the pattern in which economic benefits (services) from the assets are expected to be received. The chosen method allocates the cost of the asset as equitably as possible to the periods during which services (economic benefits) are obtained from the use of the asset.

2. **Depreciation Methods -- Straight-Line**
   a. Straight-line depreciation is the simplest method because an equal amount of depreciation is charged to each period of the asset's useful life.
      1) The easiest way to calculate straight-line depreciation is to divide the depreciable base by the estimated useful life.

Periodic expense = Depreciable base ÷ Estimated useful life

2) The straight-line percentage is 100% divided by the number of years in the asset's estimated useful life.

EXAMPLE 8-5 Straight-Line Depreciation Method

If Jayhawk applies the straight-line method, depreciation expense over the life of the asset will be calculated as follows:

	Depreciable Base	Divided by: Estimated Useful Life	Equals: Depreciation Expense	Accumulated Depreciation	Carrying Amount, End of Year
Year 1:	$900,000	5	$180,000	$180,000	$820,000
Year 2:	900,000	5	180,000	360,000	640,000
Year 3:	900,000	5	180,000	540,000	460,000
Year 4:	900,000	5	180,000	720,000	280,000
Year 5:	900,000	5	180,000	900,000	100,000
Total			$900,000		

The straight-line percentage for Jayhawk's new robot is 20% (100% ÷ 5-year estimated useful life).

3. **Depreciation Methods -- Declining Balance**

a. **Accelerated methods** were popularized when they became allowable on tax returns. But the same method need not be used for tax and financial statement purposes.

1) Accelerated methods are time-based. They result in decreasing depreciation charges over the life of the asset. The two major time-based methods are declining balance and sum-of-the-years'-digits.

b. Declining balance determines depreciation expense by multiplying the carrying amount (not the depreciable base equal to cost minus salvage value) at the beginning of each period by some percentage (e.g., 200% or 150%) of the straight-line rate of depreciation.

Periodic expense = Carrying amount × Declining-balance percentage

1) The carrying amount decreases by the depreciation recognized. The result is the use of a constant rate against a declining balance.

2) Salvage value is ignored in determining the carrying amount, but the asset is not depreciated below salvage value.

EXAMPLE 8-6 Declining-Balance Depreciation Method

If Jayhawk applies double-declining-balance (DDB) depreciation to the robot, the declining-balance percentage will be 40% (20% straight-line rate × 2). Depreciation expense over the life of the asset will be calculated as follows:

	Carrying Amount, First of Year	Times: DDB Rate	Equals: Depreciation Expense	Accumulated Depreciation	Carrying Amount, End of Year
Year 1:	$1,000,000	40%	$400,000	$400,000	$600,000
Year 2:	600,000	40%	240,000	640,000	360,000
Year 3:	360,000	40%	144,000	784,000	216,000
Year 4:	216,000	40%	86,400	870,400	129,600
Year 5:	129,600	40%	29,600*	900,000	100,000
			$900,000		

*Year 5 depreciation expense is $29,600 because the carrying amount cannot be less than salvage value.

4. **Depreciation Methods -- Sum-of-the-Years'-Digits**

   a. Sum-of-the-years'-digits (SYD) multiplies not the carrying amount but the constant depreciable base (cost minus salvage value) by a declining fraction. It is a declining-rate, declining-charge method.

$$\text{Periodic expense} = \text{Depreciable base} \times \frac{\text{Remaining years in useful life}}{\text{Sum of all years in useful life}}$$

EXAMPLE 8-7 Sum-of-the-Years'-Digits Depreciation Method

If Jayhawk applies sum-of-the-years'-digits depreciation, the denominator of the SYD fraction is 15 (1 + 2 + 3 + 4 + 5). Depreciation expense over the life of the asset will be calculated as follows:

	Depreciable Base	SYD Fraction	Depreciation Expense	Accumulated Depreciation	Carrying Amount, Year End
Year 1:	$900,000	(5 ÷ 15)	$300,000	$300,000	$700,000
Year 2:	900,000	(4 ÷ 15)	240,000	540,000	460,000
Year 3:	900,000	(3 ÷ 15)	180,000	720,000	280,000
Year 4:	900,000	(2 ÷ 15)	120,000	840,000	160,000
Year 5:	900,000	(1 ÷ 15)	60,000	900,000	100,000
			$900,000		

5. **Depreciation Methods -- Usage-Centered**

   a. Usage-centered activity methods calculate depreciation as a function of an asset's use rather than the time it has been held.

   b. The **units-of-output method** allocates cost based on production. As production varies, so will the depreciation expense.

$$\text{Periodic depreciation expense} = \text{Depreciable base} \times \frac{\text{Units produced during current period}}{\text{Estimated total lifetime units}}$$

EXAMPLE 8-8 Units-of-Production Depreciation Method

On the date of purchase, Jayhawk anticipated that the robot would produce 8,000 units of product over its 5-year life. In actuality, the robot produced the following:

Year 1	Year 2	Year 3	Year 4	Year 5	Total
2,300 units	2,000 units	1,800 units	1,200 units	700 units	8,000 units

Depreciation expense over the life of the asset will be calculated as follows:

	Depreciable Base	Times: Units-of-Production Fraction	Equals: Depreciation Expense	Accumulated Depreciation	Carrying Amount, Year End
Year 1:	$900,000	(2,300 ÷ 8,000)	$258,750	$258,750	$741,250
Year 2:	900,000	(2,000 ÷ 8,000)	225,000	483,750	516,250
Year 3:	900,000	(1,800 ÷ 8,000)	202,500	686,250	313,750
Year 4:	900,000	(1,200 ÷ 8,000)	135,000	821,250	178,750
Year 5:	900,000	(700 ÷ 8,000)	78,750	900,000	100,000
Total			$900,000		

6. **Group and Composite Depreciation**

   a. These methods apply **straight-line** accounting to a collection of assets depreciated as if they were a single asset. The composite method applies to groups of **dissimilar assets** with varying useful lives, and the group method applies to **similar assets**. They provide an efficient way to account for large numbers of depreciable assets. They also result in the offsetting of under- and overstated depreciation estimates.

   b. Each method calculates (1) the total depreciable cost (Total acquisition cost – Salvage value) for all the assets debited to a control account, (2) the weighted-average estimated useful life (Total depreciable cost ÷ Total annual straight-line depreciation), and (3) the weighted-average depreciation rate based on cost (Total annual straight-line depreciation ÷ Total acquisition cost). One accumulated depreciation account also is maintained.

   c. **Early and late retirements** are expected to offset each other. Thus, gains and losses on retirements of single assets are not recognized but are treated as adjustments of accumulated depreciation. The entry is

Cash (proceeds)	$XXX	
Asset (cost)		$XXX
Accumulated depreciation (dr. or cr.)		XXX

   d. **Periodic depreciation** equals the weighted-average rate times the beginning balance of the asset account for the period. Thus, depreciation is calculated based on the cost of assets in use during the period. Prior-period retirements are reflected in this balance.

EXAMPLE 8-9 Composite Depreciation Method

For its first year of operations, Argent Co. used the composite method of depreciation and prepared the following schedule of machinery owned:

	Total Cost	Estimated Salvage Value	Estimated Life in Years
Machine X	$320,000	$40,000	20
Machine Y	180,000	20,000	10
Machine Z	80,000	--	8

Argent computes depreciation using the straight-line method. The composite or average useful life of the assets is essentially a weighted average. As illustrated below, the annual straight-line depreciation for each asset should be calculated. The total cost, estimated salvage value, and depreciable base of the assets should then be computed. Dividing the composite depreciable base ($520,000) by the total annual straight-line depreciation ($40,000) gives the composite life (13 years) of these assets.

	Total Cost	Estimated Salvage Value	Depreciable Base	Est. Life	Annual S-L Dep.
Machine X	$320,000	$40,000	$280,000	20	$14,000
Machine Y	180,000	20,000	160,000	10	16,000
Machine Z	80,000	0	80,000	8	10,000
	$580,000	$60,000	$520,000		$40,000

The average composite rate is 6.9% ($40,000 total annual straight-line depreciation ÷ $580,000 total cost).

7. Depreciation for a Fractional Period

a. An asset is most likely to be acquired or disposed of at a time other than the beginning or end of a fiscal year. Thus, depreciation may need to be calculated for a fraction of a period. Time-based methods most often compute depreciation to the nearest month of a partial year, but other conventions also are permitted.

EXAMPLE 8-10 Depreciation for a Fractional Period

Using the data from Example 8-4, assume that Jayhawk purchased the robot on October 1, Year 1. Using the straight-line depreciation method, the annual depreciation expense is $180,000 ($900,000 ÷ 5 years). Thus, the depreciation expense recognized in Year 1 is $45,000 [$180,000 × (3 months ÷ 12 months)]. Annual depreciation expense recognized in Years 2 through 5 is $180,000. Depreciation expense recognized in Year 6 is $135,000 [$180,000 × (9 months ÷ 12 months)].

b. Each entity might have different policies for depreciation of a fractional period. For example,

1) A full year's depreciation may be recognized in the year of acquisition and none in the year of disposal or vice versa.
2) Depreciation may be recognized to the nearest full year or the nearest half-year.
3) A half-year's depreciation may be recognized in both the year of acquisition and the year of disposal.

8. Disclosure

a. Full disclosure should be made of depreciation methods and practices, including

1) Depreciation expense for the period
2) Balances of major classes of depreciable assets by nature or function
3) Accumulated depreciation either by major class or in total
4) Description of depreciation methods for each major class of assets

IFRS DIFFERENCE

Each part of an item with a cost significant to the total cost must be depreciated separately. But an entity may separately depreciate parts that are not significant.

STOP & REVIEW

You have completed the outline for this subunit.
Study multiple-choice questions 8 and 9 on page 252.

8.5 DEPRECIATION METHODS -- CHANGES AND COMPARISON

1. **Effects on Net Income**
    a. Because the accelerated methods charge higher amounts to depreciation expense in the earlier years of an asset's economic life, those methods result in lower net income than the straight-line method in those years.
2. **Effects of Accounting Changes**
    a. A change in the estimates for depreciation is accounted for prospectively (from the beginning of the period in which the change in estimate was made). The new estimates are used in the year of the change, and no "catch-up" amounts are recorded.

EXAMPLE 8-11 Change in Estimates for Depreciation

On January 2, Year 1, a company purchased a machine for $500,000 and depreciated it by the straight-line method using an estimated useful life of 10 years with no salvage value. On January 2, Year 4, the company determined that the machine had a useful life of 6 years from the date of acquisition and will have a salvage value of $20,000. An accounting change was made in Year 4 to reflect the additional data.

For Years 1 through 3, the amount of depreciation was $50,000 per year ($500,000 depreciable base ÷ 10 years estimated useful life), resulting in a balance of accumulated depreciation at December 31, Year 3, of $150,000 ($50,000 × 3 years). The company calculates the new depreciable base as follows:

Historical cost	$500,000
Revised salvage value	(20,000)
Revised depreciable base	$480,000
Balance of accumulated depreciation, 1/1/Year 4	(150,000)
Remaining depreciable base, 1/1/Year 4	$330,000

Annual depreciation for the remaining years of the machine's estimated life is $110,000 ($330,000 depreciable base ÷ 3 years estimated remaining useful life).

STOP & REVIEW

You have completed the outline for this subunit.
Study multiple-choice questions 10 and 11 on page 253.

8.6 EXCHANGES OF ASSETS

1. Exchanges Measured at Fair Value

a. Accounting for exchanges of monetary assets (receivables, financial instruments, etc.) is straightforward because they are stated in terms of units of money.

1) **Monetary exchanges** are measured at the fair value of the assets involved, with gain or loss recognized immediately.

2) The **fair value of the assets given up** generally is used to measure the cost of the assets acquired unless the fair value of the assets received is more clearly evident.

b. **Nonmonetary exchange** of assets is treated as a monetary exchange when the fair value of both assets is determinable.

1) The asset received is measured at the fair value of the asset given up, and any gain or loss is recognized immediately.

2) This gain or loss is the difference between the fair value of the asset given up and its carrying amount.

a) If the fair value of the asset given up is greater (lower) than its carrying amount, a gain (loss) for the difference is recognized.

EXAMPLE 8-12 Nonmonetary Exchange of Assets

Jayhawk Co. and Wildcat Corp. agree to exchange pieces of machinery. No exception to fair-value accounting applies. The following information is gathered from the two companies' books:

	Jayhawk Co.	Wildcat Corp.
Historical cost	$ 280,000	$ 300,000
Accumulated depreciation	(150,000)	(160,000)
Carrying amount	130,000	140,000
Fair value	250,000	275,000

The journal entries to record the exchange are as follows:

Jayhawk's entry

Machinery and equipment (total fair value given up)	$250,000	
Accumulated depreciation (balance in account)	150,000	
Machinery and equipment (historical cost of old machine)		$280,000
Gain on exchange of machinery ($250,000 fair value – $130,000 carrying amount)		120,000

Wildcat's entry

Machinery and equipment (total fair value given up)	$275,000	
Accumulated depreciation (balance in account)	160,000	
Machinery and equipment (historical cost of old machine)		$300,000
Gain on exchange of machinery ($275,000 fair value – $140,000 carrying amount)		135,000

c. One of the parties to a nonmonetary exchange also may transfer cash **(boot)**. The party paying boot includes this amount in the total fair value of assets given up in the exchange.

1) The party receiving the boot measures the asset received at the fair value of the asset given up minus the boot (i.e., the net fair value of the asset given up).

EXAMPLE 8-13 Nonmonetary Exchange with Boot

The same facts apply from Example 8-12, but Jayhawk also pays Wildcat $25,000. The journal entries to record the exchange are as follows:

Jayhawk's entry		
Machinery and equipment (total fair value given up)	$275,000	
Accumulated depreciation (balance in account)	150,000	
Machinery and equipment (historical cost of old machine)		$280,000
Gain on exchange of machinery ($250,000 fair value – $130,000 carrying amount)		120,000
Cash (boot given)		25,000

Wildcat's entry		
Machinery and equipment ($275,000 fair value given up – $25,000 boot received)	$250,000	
Accumulated depreciation (balance in account)	160,000	
Cash (boot received)	25,000	
Machinery and equipment (historical cost of old machine)		$300,000
Gain on exchange of machinery ($275,000 fair value – $140,000 carrying amount)		135,000

d. The fair value of the asset received may be more clearly evident. For example, the fair value of the asset given up is not known, but the fair value of the asset received can be determined. Accordingly, the asset received is measured at its fair value.

1) The gain or loss on the exchange is the difference between the fair value of all the assets received (Fair value of assets received + Any cash received) and the carrying amount of all the assets given up (Carrying amount of assets given up + Any cash paid).

2. **Exchanges Measured at Carrying Amount**

a. When certain exceptions apply, the accounting for a nonmonetary exchange is based on the **carrying amount** of the assets given up. Unless boot is received, no gain is recognized. The following are the exceptions:

1) Neither the fair value of the assets given up nor the fair value of the assets received is reasonably determinable,

2) The exchange involves inventory sold in the same line of business that facilitates sales to customers not parties to the exchange, or

3) The exchange **lacks commercial substance** because it is not expected to change the entity's cash flows significantly.

b. If (1) an exchange is based on the carrying amount of the assets given up and (2) the fair value of the asset to be exchanged is lower than its carrying amount, the total loss must be recognized for the difference.

1) First, the asset to be exchanged is written down to its fair value and an impairment loss is recognized.

2) Second, the exchange is measured at the new carrying amount of the asset given up (fair value of the asset on the exchange date).

c. If boot is given as part of an exchange measured at carrying amount, the recipient of the boot must recognize a proportionate amount of any potential gain. The amount of gain is calculated in the following steps:

   1) Calculate the total potential gain on the exchange.

	Fair value of other assets received
+	Boot received
–	Carrying amount of assets given up
	Total potential gain

   2) Calculate the proportion of assets received represented by boot.

$$\frac{\text{Boot received}}{\text{Fair value of other assets received + Boot received}}$$

   3) Determine the amount of gain to be recognized.

Total potential gain × Proportion represented by boot

d. If boot constitutes 25% or more of the fair value of the exchange, the exchange is treated as a monetary exchange. Both parties record the transaction at fair value and recognize any gain or loss in full.

EXAMPLE 8-14 Nonmonetary Exchange Lacks Commercial Substance

The same facts apply from Example 8-13, but the transaction lacks commercial substance.

Jayhawk's entry

Machinery and equipment (total carrying amount given up)	$155,000	
Accumulated depreciation (balance in account)	150,000	
Machinery and equipment (historical cost of old machine)		$280,000
Cash (boot given)		25,000

Wildcat's proportional gain

Fair value of other assets received	$250,000
Boot received	25,000
Carrying amount of assets given up ($300,000 – $160,000)	(140,000)
Total potential gain	$135,000

Proportion represented by boot = $25,000 ÷ ($250,000 + $25,000)
= 9.091% (< 25% of total)

Gain recognized = $135,000 × 9.091%
= $12,272

Wildcat's entry

Machinery and equipment	$127,272	
Accumulated depreciation (balance in account)	160,000	
Cash (boot received)	25,000	
Machinery and equipment (historical cost of old machine)		$300,000
Gain (calculated above)		12,272

3. **Summary**

Measure of Exchange	Gain	Loss
Fair value	Total	Total
Carrying amount -- no boot received	None	Total
Carrying amount -- boot received	Partial	Total

STOP & REVIEW

You have completed the outline for this subunit.
Study multiple-choice questions 12 through 14 beginning on page 254.

8.7 DISPOSALS OTHER THAN BY EXCHANGE

1. **Procedures**
   a. Depreciation is recorded up to the time of disposal so that periodic depreciation expense is not understated and the carrying amount of the asset is not overstated.
   b. The asset's carrying amount is removed from the accounts by eliminating the asset, its accumulated depreciation, and any other valuation account.
   c. Any consideration (proceeds) received is debited appropriately.
   d. Gain or loss is recognized for the difference between the proceeds received and the carrying amount of an asset.
2. **Sale**
   a. Accounting for a cash sale of PPE (including a scrap sale) is straightforward.
      1) Depreciation, if any, is recognized to the date of sale, the carrying amount is removed from the books, the proceeds are recorded, and any gain or loss is recognized.

EXAMPLE 8-15 Disposal of an Item of PPE

A company sold a machine with a carrying amount of $100,000 ($180,000 historical cost – $80,000 accumulated depreciation) for $135,000 in cash. The gain on disposal recognized is $35,000 ($135,000 – $100,000). The journal entry is

Cash	$135,000	
Accumulated depreciation	80,000	
Machine		$180,000
Gain on disposal		35,000

If the machine were sold for $90,000 in cash, the loss on disposal recognized would be $10,000 ($90,000 – $100,000). The journal entry would be

Cash	$90,000	
Accumulated depreciation	80,000	
Loss on disposal	10,000	
Machine		$180,000

3. **Abandonment**
   a. An asset to be abandoned is disposed of when it is no longer used.
   b. If the asset to be abandoned is still in use, it is normally not immediately written down to zero. Continued use indicates that the asset has service potential. However, depreciation estimates should be revised to account for the reduced service period.
      1) A noncurrent asset that is temporarily idled is not treated as abandoned.
4. **Involuntary Conversion**
   a. An item of PPE is involuntarily converted when it is (1) lost through a casualty (flood, earthquake, fire, etc.), (2) expropriated (seized by a foreign government), or (3) condemned (through the governmental power of eminent domain).
      1) The accounting is the same as for other nonexchange dispositions.
      2) The **gain or loss** on an involuntary conversion is reported in income from continuing operations.
      3) A nonmonetary asset may be involuntarily converted to monetary assets (e.g., insurance proceeds).
      4) Gain or loss recognition is required even though the entity reinvests or is required to reinvest the proceeds in replacement nonmonetary assets.
         a) Hence, the replacement property should be recorded at its cost. The involuntary conversion and replacement are not equivalent to a single exchange transaction between entities.

EXAMPLE 8-16 Involuntary Conversion

A state government condemned Owner Co.'s parcel of real estate. Owner will receive $1,500,000 for this property, which has a carrying amount of $1,150,000. Owner incurred the following costs as a result of the condemnation:

Appraisal fees to support a $1,500,000 fair value	$5,000
Attorney fees for the closing with the state	7,000
Attorney fees to review contract to acquire replacement property	6,000
Title insurance on replacement property	8,000

Gain or loss must be recognized even if the entity reinvests or is required to reinvest the monetary assets in replacement nonmonetary assets. The gain equals the consideration received ($1,500,000) minus the sum of the carrying amount ($1,150,000) and the direct costs of condemnation ($7,000 attorney fees + $5,000 appraisal fees = $12,000). The gain is therefore $338,000 ($1,500,000 – $1,162,000). The costs of acquiring the replacement property (attorney fees and title insurance) are included in its carrying amount.

STOP & REVIEW

You have completed the outline for this subunit.
Study multiple-choice questions 15 and 16 on page 256.

8.8 IMPAIRMENT OF LONG-LIVED ASSETS

1. **Two-Step Impairment Test**
   a. Testing for impairment occurs when events or changes in circumstances indicate that the carrying amount of the asset may not be recoverable, for example, when
      1) The market price has decreased significantly, or
      2) The use or physical condition of the asset has changed significantly and adversely.
   b. The test for impairment has **two steps**.
      1) **Recoverability test.** The carrying amount of a long-lived asset to be held and used is not recoverable if it exceeds the sum of the **undiscounted** future cash flows expected from the use and disposition of the asset.
      2) If the carrying amount is not recoverable, an impairment loss may be recognized. It equals the excess of the carrying amount of the asset over its fair value.
         a) An impairment loss is recognized in income from continuing operations.
   c. The entry for an impairment of a depreciable asset is

Impairment loss	$XXX	
Accumulated depreciation		$XXX

Determination of an Impairment Loss
1. Events or changes in circumstances indicate a possible loss
2. Carrying amount > Sum of undiscounted cash flows
3. Loss = Carrying amount – Fair value

d. The carrying amount of a long-lived asset adjusted for an impairment loss is its new cost basis. A previously recognized impairment loss **must not be reversed**.

EXAMPLE 8-17 Impairment Test for an Item of PPE

Lisa Co. purchased a machine with a 10-year estimated useful life for $200,000 on January 1, Year 1. On December 31, Year 2, as a result of low demand for Lisa's products, management concludes that the carrying amount of the machine may not be recoverable. Management estimates that the undiscounted future cash flows over the remaining useful life of the machine will be $150,000. On that date, the machine's estimated fair value is $136,000.

Annual straight-line depreciation expense is $20,000 ($200,000 depreciable base ÷ 10 years), and the machine's carrying amount on December 31, Year 2, is $160,000 ($200,000 historical cost – $20,000 Year 1 depreciation – $20,000 Year 2 depreciation). On December 31, Year 2, the carrying amount of the machine exceeds the undiscounted future cash flows expected from the machine ($160,000 > $150,000). Thus, the carrying amount is not recoverable. Accordingly, the amount of impairment loss recognized is the excess of the machine's carrying amount over its fair value ($160,000 – $136,000 = **$24,000**). The December 31, Year 2, journal entries are

Depreciation expense ($200,000 ÷ 10)	$20,000	
Accumulated depreciation		$20,000
Impairment loss	$24,000	
Accumulated depreciation		$24,000

The carrying amount of the machine reported in the financial statements on December 31, Year 2, is

Historical (initial) cost	$200,000
Accumulated depreciation	(40,000)
Impairment losses	(24,000)
Asset's carrying amount	$136,000

The carrying amount of an asset adjusted for an impairment loss is its new depreciation base.

Year 3 depreciation expense is $17,000 ($136,000 carrying amount ÷ 8 years remaining useful life). The carrying amount of the machine in Lisa's December 31, Year 3, financial statements is $119,000 ($136,000 – $17,000).

The entity assesses at each reporting date whether an indication of impairment exists. Given such an indication, IFRS require a **one-step impairment test**.

- The carrying amount of an asset is compared with its recoverable amount. An impairment loss is recognized equal to the excess of the carrying amount over the recoverable amount.

Determination of an Impairment Loss
1. Reporting-date assessment indicates a possible loss
2. Impairment loss = Carrying amount – Recoverable amount

The **recoverable amount** is the greater of an asset's (1) fair value minus cost to sell or (2) value in use. Value in use of the asset is the present value of its expected cash flows.

IFRS DIFFERENCE

An impairment loss on an asset (besides goodwill) **may be reversed** in a subsequent period if a change in the estimates used to measure the recoverable amount has occurred. The reversal of an impairment loss is recognized immediately in profit or loss as income from continued operations.

An impairment loss on a revalued asset is treated as a revaluation decrease.

IFRS EXAMPLE 8-3 IFRS Impairment Test

Using the data from Example 8-17, assume that on December 31, Year 2, the estimated cost to sell of the machine is $6,000, and the present value of future cash flows over the remaining useful life of the machine is $133,000.

IFRS require a one-step impairment test. Impairment loss is recognized for the excess of the carrying amount of the machine ($160,000) over its recoverable amount. The recoverable amount is the greater of the machine's fair value minus the cost to sell of $130,000 ($136,000 fair value – $6,000 cost to sell) or value in use of $133,000 (present value of the machine's expected cash flows). The value in use is greater than the fair value minus the cost to sell. Thus, the recoverable amount equals the machine's value in use of $133,000. The impairment loss recognized in Year 2 income statement is **$27,000** ($160,000 carrying amount – $133,000 recoverable amount).

STOP & REVIEW

You have completed the outline for this subunit.
Study multiple-choice questions 17 and 18 on page 257.

8.9 ASSETS CLASSIFIED AS HELD FOR SALE

1. **Classification Criteria**
   a. An asset (disposal group) is classified as **held for sale** when six conditions are met:
      1) Management has committed to a **plan to sell**.
      2) The asset is **available for immediate sale** in its current condition on usual and customary terms.
      3) Actions (such as actively seeking a buyer) have begun to complete the plan.
      4) Completion of sale **within 1 year is probable**.
      5) The asset is **actively marketed** at a price reasonably related to current fair value.
      6) The likelihood is low of significant change in, or withdrawal of, the plan.
   b. The **disposal group** consists of assets to be disposed of together in one transaction and directly associated liabilities to be transferred in the same transaction (for example, warranties associated with an acquired customer base).
   c. Whenever the conditions are not met, the asset or disposal group must be reclassified as held and used.
   d. If disposition is to be **other than by sale**, for example, by abandonment or exchange, the asset is classified as **held and used** until disposal. It will continue to be depreciated or amortized.
2. **Measurement**
   a. Assets held for sale are measured at the **lower of carrying amount or fair value minus cost to sell**.
      1) An asset classified as held for sale is **not depreciated or amortized**, but expenses related to the liabilities of a disposal group are accrued.
      2) Costs to sell are the incremental direct costs. Examples are brokers' commissions, legal and title transfer fees, and closing costs (but not future operating losses expected to be incurred).
      3) A **loss** is recognized for a write-down to fair value minus cost to sell. A **gain** is recognized for any subsequent increase but only to the extent of previously recognized losses for write-downs.
      4) A gain or loss from the sale is recognized at the date of sale.
   b. **A plan of sale may change** because of circumstances (previously unlikely) that result in a decision not to sell. The asset (disposal group) then must be reclassified as held and used.
      1) A reclassified long-lived asset is measured individually at the lower of
         a) Carrying amount before the asset (disposal group) was classified as held for sale, minus any depreciation (amortization) that would have been recognized if it had always been classified as held and used, or
         b) Fair value at the date of the decision not to sell.

3. **Reporting**
   a. If a long-lived asset is held for sale, it is reported **separately**.
      1) If a disposal group is held for sale, its assets and liabilities are reported separately in the balance sheet and are not presented as one amount.
   b. When a component of an entity is **reclassified** as held and used, its results of operations previously reported in discontinued operations are reclassified and included in income from continuing operations for all periods presented.

STOP & REVIEW

You have completed the outline for this subunit.
Study multiple-choice question 19 on page 258.

8.10 DEPLETION

1. **Overview**
   a. **Natural resources** (wasting assets) are held for direct resale or consumption in other products. Examples are petroleum, gold, silver, timber, iron ore, gravel, and coal.
   b. Natural resources differ from depreciable assets because they
      1) Lose their separate character during extraction and consumption
      2) Are produced only by natural processes
      3) Are recorded as inventory after extraction
         a) The entry to record the inventory and the depletion of the natural resource is

Inventory	$XXX	
Accumulated depletion (a contra account)		$XXX

         b) But some entities credit the natural resource account directly.
   c. Depletion is similar to depreciation. It is an accounting process of allocating the historical cost of a tangible asset to the periods benefited by its uses.
2. **Components of the Depletion Base**
   a. **Acquisition costs** of land (but not the costs of extractive machinery, which are depreciated and recognized as separate items of PPE)
   b. **Development costs** to prepare the site for extraction (added)
   c. **Restoration costs** required by law to return the land to its original condition (added)
   d. The **residual value** of the property (subtracted)

3. **Calculating Periodic Depletion**

   a. Depletion is similar to usage-centered depreciation because it is most often determined by applying the units-of-output (production) method.

   b. The per-unit depletion rate is determined by dividing the depletion base by the total number of units estimated to be economically recoverable during the property's useful life.

$$\text{Per-unit depletion rate} = \frac{\text{Depletion base}}{\text{Total estimated recoverable units}}$$

   c. Units extracted times the depletion rate equals periodic depletion.

      1) To the extent that extracted units are sold, cost of goods sold is debited.
      2) Unsold units remain in inventory.

EXAMPLE 8-18 Depletion

Mullinax Mining acquired a mine in Idaho for $3.2 million. The company estimates that the mine contains 1,125 recoverable grams of a particular rare earth. Mullinax further estimates that it will eventually be able to sell the mine for $600,000 after spending $200,000 on restoration. The company must spend $800,000 to prepare the site for mining. The depletion base for this mine is calculated as follows:

Purchase price	$3,200,000
Add: Preparation costs	800,000
Add: Restoration costs	200,000
Minus: Residual value	(600,000)
Depletion base	$3,600,000

The depletion charge for this mine will therefore be $3,200 per gram ($3,600,000 depletion base ÷ 1,125 total recoverable grams). During the first year of operations, the mine produced 200 grams of ore. The depletion charge for the first year was thus $640,000 (200 grams × $3,200 per gram).

STOP & REVIEW

You have completed the outline for this subunit.
Study multiple-choice question 20 on page 258.

QUESTIONS

8.1 Initial Measurement of Property, Plant, and Equipment (PPE)

1. Merry Co. purchased a machine costing $125,000 for its manufacturing operations and paid shipping costs of $20,000. Merry spent an additional $10,000 testing and preparing the machine for use. What amount should Merry record as the cost of the machine?

A. $155,000

B. $145,000

C. $135,000

D. $125,000

Answer (A) is correct.

REQUIRED: The amount to be recorded as the acquisition cost.

DISCUSSION: The amount to be recorded as the acquisition cost of a machine includes all costs necessary to prepare it for its intended use. Thus, the cost of a machine used in the manufacturing operations of a company includes the cost of testing and preparing the machine for use and the shipping costs. The acquisition cost is $155,000 ($125,000 + $20,000 + $10,000).

Answer (B) is incorrect. The amount of $145,000 does not include the $10,000 cost of testing and preparation. **Answer (C) is incorrect.** The amount of $135,000 does not include the shipping costs. **Answer (D) is incorrect.** The amount of $125,000 does not include the shipping, testing, and preparation costs.

2. During January, Yana Co. incurred landscaping costs of $120,000 to improve leased property. The estimated useful life of the landscaping is 15 years. The remaining term of the lease is 8 years, with an option to renew for an additional 4 years. However, Yana has not reached a decision with regard to the renewal option. In Yana's December 31 balance sheet, what should be the net carrying amount of landscaping costs?

A. $0

B. $105,000

C. $110,000

D. $112,000

Answer (B) is correct.

REQUIRED: The net amount of leasehold improvements reported in the balance sheet.

DISCUSSION: General improvements to leased property should be capitalized as leasehold improvements and amortized in accordance with the straight-line method over the shorter of their expected useful life or the lease term. However, if the useful life of the asset extends beyond the lease term and renewal of the lease is reasonably certain, the amortization period may include all or part of the renewal period. If renewal is uncertain, the useful life is the remaining term, and the salvage value is the amount, if any, to be paid by the lessor to the lessee at the expiration of the lease. Consequently, the amortization period is the 8-year lease term, and the net carrying amount at December 31 of the landscaping costs incurred in January is $105,000 [$120,000 × (7 years ÷ 8 years)].

Answer (A) is incorrect. Land improvements with limited lives should be capitalized. **Answer (C) is incorrect.** The amount of $110,000 assumes that renewal for 4 years is likely. **Answer (D) is incorrect.** The amount of $112,000 assumes amortization over 15 years.

3. Star Co. leases a building for its product showroom. The 10-year nonrenewable lease will expire on December 31, Year 6. In January Year 1, Star redecorated its showroom and made leasehold improvements of $48,000. The estimated useful life of the improvements is 8 years. Star uses the straight-line method of amortization. What amount of leasehold improvements, net of amortization, should Star report in its June 30, Year 1, balance sheet?

A. $45,600

B. $45,000

C. $44,000

D. $43,200

Answer (C) is correct.

REQUIRED: The net amount of leasehold improvements reported in the balance sheet.

DISCUSSION: General improvements to leased property should be capitalized as leasehold improvements and amortized in accordance with the straight-line method over the shorter of their expected useful life or the lease term. Because the remaining lease term is less than the estimated life of the improvements, the cost should be amortized equally over 6 years. On 6/30/Year 1, $44,000 {$48,000 – [($48,000 ÷ 6 years) × 1/2 year]} should be reported for net leasehold improvements.

Answer (A) is incorrect. The amount of $45,600 assumes the amortization period is 10 years. **Answer (B) is incorrect.** The amount of $45,000 assumes the amortization period is 8 years. **Answer (D) is incorrect.** The amount of $43,200 assumes that 1 year's amortization has been recorded and that the amortization period is 10 years.

8.2 Internally Constructed Assets (ICAs) -- Capitalization of Interest

4. A company is constructing an asset for its own use. Construction began in Year 3. The asset is being financed entirely with a specific new borrowing. Construction expenditures were made in Year 3 and Year 4 at the end of each quarter. The total amount of interest cost capitalized in Year 4 should be determined by applying the interest rate on the specific new borrowing to the

A. Total accumulated expenditures for the asset in Year 3 and Year 4.

B. Average accumulated expenditures for the asset in Year 3 and Year 4.

C. Average expenditures for the asset in Year 4.

D. Total expenditures for the asset in Year 4.

Answer (B) is correct.

REQUIRED: The expenditures used in determining the capitalizable interest.

DISCUSSION: An asset constructed for an entity's own use qualifies for capitalization of interest if (1) relevant expenditures have been made, (2) activities necessary to prepare the asset for its intended use are in progress, and (3) interest is being incurred. The capitalized amount is determined by applying an interest rate to the average qualifying expenditures accumulated during the period. These expenditures in any given period include those incurred in that period plus those incurred in the construction of the asset in all previous periods. Thus, the total interest cost capitalized in Year 4 equals the interest rate on the specific new borrowing times the average accumulated expenditures for the asset in Year 3 and Year 4.

Answer (A) is incorrect. The basis is an average for Year 3 and Year 4, not the total. **Answer (C) is incorrect.** The basis includes expenditures during the entire construction period. **Answer (D) is incorrect.** The basis is an average for Year 3 and Year 4.

5. Clay Company started construction of a new office building on January 1, Year 8, and moved into the finished building on July 1, Year 9. Of the building's $2.5 million total cost, $2 million was incurred in Year 8 evenly throughout the year. Clay's incremental borrowing rate was 12% throughout Year 8, and the total amount of interest incurred by Clay during Year 8 was $102,000. What amount should Clay report as capitalized interest at December 31, Year 8?

A. $102,000

B. $120,000

C. $150,000

D. $240,000

Answer (A) is correct.

REQUIRED: The amount of interest to be capitalized as a cost of an asset.

DISCUSSION: The new office building qualifies for capitalization of interest cost because (1) the asset is being constructed for the entity's own use, (2) expenditures relative to the qualifying asset have been made, (3) activities necessary to prepare the asset for its intended use are in progress, and (4) interest cost is being incurred. The amount capitalized is determined by applying an interest rate to the average accumulated expenditures (AAE) for the period. The AAE equal the simple average of any cost that is incurred evenly throughout the year. Here, the AAE are $1,000,000 ($2,000,000 × .5). The amount of interest to be capitalized is the $1,000,000 AAE times the rate of interest paid during Year 8, which is given as 12%. Because the $120,000 result ($1,000,000 × 12%) exceeds the $102,000 total amount of interest incurred, $102,000 is the maximum amount of interest that can be capitalized during the period ending 12/31/Year 8.

8.3 Subsequent Expenditures for PPE

6. On June 18, Dell Printing Co. incurred the following costs for one of its printing presses:

Purchase of collating and stapling attachment	$84,000
Installation of attachment	36,000
Replacement parts for overhaul of press	26,000
Labor and overhead in connection with overhaul	14,000

The overhaul resulted in a significant increase in production. Neither the attachment nor the overhaul increased the estimated useful life of the press. What amount of the above costs should be capitalized?

A. $0

B. $84,000

C. $120,000

D. $160,000

Answer (D) is correct.

REQUIRED: The amount of costs to be capitalized.

DISCUSSION: Expenditures that increase the quality or quantity of a machine's output should be capitalized whether or not its useful life is extended. Thus, the amount of the cost to be capitalized equals $160,000 ($84,000 + $36,000 + $26,000 + $14,000).

Answer (A) is incorrect. Zero omits all of the listed capital expenditures. **Answer (B) is incorrect.** The installation and overhaul costs are capitalized. **Answer (C) is incorrect.** The amount of $120,000 excludes the overhaul costs.

7. Tomson Co. installed new assembly line production equipment at a cost of $175,000. Tomson had to rearrange the assembly line and remove a wall to install the equipment. The rearrangement cost $12,000, and the wall removal cost $3,000. The rearrangement did not increase the life of the assembly line, but it did make it more efficient. What amount of these costs should be capitalized by Tomson?

A. $175,000

B. $178,000

C. $187,000

D. $190,000

Answer (D) is correct.

REQUIRED: The capitalized cost of a new assembly line.

DISCUSSION: The initial measurement equals the sum of the cost to acquire the equipment and the costs necessarily incurred to bring it to the condition and location necessary for its intended use. A rearrangement is the movement of existing assets to provide greater efficiency or to reduce production costs. If the rearrangement expenditure benefits future periods, it should be capitalized. If the wall removal costs likewise improve future service potential, they too should be capitalized. Thus, the capitalized cost is $190,000 ($175,000 + $12,000 + $3,000).

Answer (A) is incorrect. The amount capitalized must include all costs incurred to bring the equipment to use. **Answer (B) is incorrect.** The rearrangement cost must be included in the amount capitalized. If this cost was incurred for the benefit of existing equipment, different rules apply. **Answer (C) is incorrect.** Cost of removal of the wall is capitalized.

8.4 Depreciation Methods -- Calculations

8. Ichor Co. reported equipment with an original cost of $379,000 and $344,000 and accumulated depreciation of $153,000 and $128,000, respectively, in its comparative financial statements for the years ended December 31, Year 2 and Year 1. During Year 2, Ichor purchased equipment costing $50,000 and sold equipment with a carrying amount of $9,000. What amount should Ichor report as depreciation expense for Year 2?

A. $19,000

B. $25,000

C. $31,000

D. $34,000

Answer (C) is correct.

REQUIRED: The depreciation given comparative information and a purchase and a sale of equipment.

DISCUSSION: The reported equipment cost increased by $35,000 ($379,000 – $344,000), and the reported accumulated depreciation increased by $25,000 ($153,000 – $128,000) from December 31, Year 1, to December 31, Year 2. Given that the equipment purchased had a cost of $50,000, the cost of the equipment sold must have been $15,000 ($50,000 – $35,000 increase in the equipment cost balance). Given also that the equipment sold had a carrying amount of $9,000, the accumulated depreciation removed from the books must have been $6,000 ($15,000 cost – $9,000). Accordingly, the depreciation expense for Year 2 must have been $31,000 ($25,000 net increase in accumulated depreciation + $6,000).

Answer (A) is incorrect. The amount of $19,000 equals the $10,000 increase in the net equipment balance ($35,000 increase in cost – $25,000 increase in accumulated depreciation) plus $9,000. **Answer (B) is incorrect.** The amount of $25,000 is the increase in accumulated depreciation. **Answer (D) is incorrect.** The amount of $34,000 equals the increase in accumulated depreciation plus $9,000.

9. Rye Co. purchased a machine with a 4-year estimated useful life and an estimated 10% salvage value for $80,000 on January 1, Year 6. In its income statement, what should Rye report as the depreciation expense for Year 8 using the double-declining-balance (DDB) method?

A. $9,000

B. $10,000

C. $18,000

D. $20,000

Answer (B) is correct.

REQUIRED: The DDB depreciation expense.

DISCUSSION: Under the DDB method, a constant rate is applied to a declining carrying amount of an asset. Salvage value is ignored except that the asset is not depreciated below salvage value. Because the straight-line rate for this machine is 25% (100% ÷ 4 years), the DDB rate is 50% (25% × 2).

	Carrying Amount		DDB %		Depreciation Expense
Year 6:	$80,000	×	.50	=	$40,000
Year 7:	$40,000	×	.50	=	$20,000
Year 8:	$20,000	×	.50	=	$10,000

Answer (A) is incorrect. The amount of $9,000 includes the $8,000 residual value in the calculation. **Answer (C) is incorrect.** The amount of $18,000 is the Year 7 depreciation expense if the residual value is included in the calculation. **Answer (D) is incorrect.** The amount of $20,000 is the depreciation expense for Year 7.

8.5 Depreciation Methods -- Changes and Comparison

10. On January 1, Year 5, Crater, Inc., purchased equipment having an estimated salvage value equal to 20% of its original cost at the end of a 10-year life. The equipment was sold December 31, Year 9, for 50% of its original cost. If the equipment's disposition resulted in a reported loss, which of the following depreciation methods did Crater use?

A. Double-declining balance.

B. Sum-of-the-years'-digits.

C. Straight-line.

D. Composite.

Answer (C) is correct.

REQUIRED: The method that results in a reported loss upon disposition.

DISCUSSION: The straight-line method of depreciation is the only one of the generally accepted methods that is not an accelerated method. It thus yields the lowest amount of depreciation for the early part of the depreciable life of the asset. Because only 50% of the original cost was received and straight-line accumulated depreciation equaled 40% of cost {[(100% – 20%) ÷ 10 years] × 5 years} at the time of sale, a 10% loss [50% – (100% – 40%)] results.

Answer (A) is incorrect. The DDB method results in 5-year accumulated depreciation that is greater than 50% of cost. **Answer (B) is incorrect.** The SYD method results in 5-year accumulated depreciation that is greater than 50% of cost. **Answer (D) is incorrect.** The composite method of depreciation applies to the weighted average of multiple useful lives of assets, whereas only one asset is mentioned in this question. Moreover, it recognizes no gain or loss on disposition.

11. On January 2, Year 1, Union Co. purchased a machine for $264,000 and depreciated it by the straight-line method using an estimated useful life of 8 years with no salvage value. On January 2, Year 4, Union determined that the machine had a useful life of 6 years from the date of acquisition and will have a salvage value of $24,000. An accounting change was made in Year 4 to reflect the additional data. The accumulated depreciation for this machine should have a balance at December 31, Year 4, of

A. $179,000

B. $160,000

C. $154,000

D. $146,000

Answer (D) is correct.

REQUIRED: The accumulated depreciation for a machine given changes in estimates.

DISCUSSION: A change in the estimates for depreciation is accounted for prospectively. The new estimates are used in the year of the change, and no cumulative-effect adjustments are recorded. For Years 1 through 3, the amount of depreciation was $33,000 per year ($264,000 old depreciable base ÷ 8 years old estimate of useful life), resulting in a balance of accumulated depreciation at December 31, Year 3, of $99,000 ($33,000 × 3 years). On January 2, Year 4, Union estimates the machine's original depreciable base to be $240,000 ($264,000 historical cost – $24,000 revised salvage value). The remaining depreciable base at January 2, Year 4, is thus $141,000 ($240,000 revised depreciable base – $99,000 accumulated depreciation), resulting in a new annual depreciation expense of $47,000 ($141,000 ÷ 3 years revised estimated life remaining). Thus, accumulated depreciation at December 31, Year 4, is $146,000 ($99,000 + $47,000).

Answer (A) is incorrect. The amount of $179,000 does not reflect subtraction of prior depreciation in calculating depreciation for Year 4. **Answer (B) is incorrect.** The amount of $160,000 would be the accumulated depreciation if the revised estimates had been used from the beginning. **Answer (C) is incorrect.** The amount of $154,000 does not reflect subtraction of the salvage value in calculating depreciation for Year 4.

8.6 Exchanges of Assets

12. Iona Co. and Siena Co. exchanged goods held for resale with equal fair values. Each will use the other's goods to promote its own products. The retail price of the wickets that Iona gave up is less than the retail price of the wombles received. What gain should Iona recognize on the nonmonetary exchange?

A. A gain is not recognized.

B. A gain equal to the difference between the retail prices of the wombles received and the wickets.

C. A gain equal to the difference between the retail price and the cost of the wickets.

D. A gain equal to the difference between the fair value and the cost of the wickets.

Answer (D) is correct.

REQUIRED: The gain to be recognized on a nonmonetary exchange of inventory.

DISCUSSION: The accounting for a nonmonetary transaction should be based on the carrying amount of the asset given up in an exchange of goods held for sale in the ordinary course of business for goods to be sold in the same line of business. The exchange also must be designed to facilitate sales to customers other than the parties to the exchange. Because Iona will use the wombles to promote its own product, the requirement that the product be used to facilitate sales to customers other than Iona or Siena is not met. Accordingly, this transaction is a nonmonetary exchange that should be measured at the fair value of the assets given up. Iona should record a gain equal to the difference between the fair value (the same for both assets) and the cost (carrying amount) of the asset surrendered.

Answer (A) is incorrect. A gain should be recognized. **Answer (B) is incorrect.** The appropriate basis at which the asset received should be recognized is fair value, not retail prices. **Answer (C) is incorrect.** The appropriate basis at which the asset received should be recognized is fair value, not retail prices.

13. Amble, Inc., exchanged a truck with a carrying amount of $12,000 and a fair value of $20,000 for another truck and $5,000 cash. The fair value of the truck received was $15,000. The exchange was not considered to have commercial substance. At what amount should Amble record the truck received in the exchange?

A. $7,000

B. $9,000

C. $12,000

D. $15,000

Answer (D) is correct.

REQUIRED: The amount at which a nonmonetary asset should be recorded in a transaction involving boot.

DISCUSSION: A transaction involving nonmonetary assets and boot is monetary if the boot equals or exceeds 25% of the fair value of the exchange. In this exchange, the $5,000 of boot equals 25% of the $20,000 ($5,000 + $15,000) fair value of the exchange. Thus, the exchange is monetary. Accounting for monetary transactions should be based on the fair value of the assets involved, with gain or loss recognized immediately. The party receiving boot measures the asset received at the fair value of the asset given up minus boot. Accordingly, Amble should record the truck received at $15,000 ($20,000 fair value of truck given up – $5,000 boot received).

Answer (A) is incorrect. The amount of $7,000 is the $12,000 carrying amount of the asset given up minus the $5,000 boot received. **Answer (B) is incorrect.** The amount of $9,000 is the $12,000 carrying amount of the truck given up, minus the $5,000 boot received, plus the $2,000 ($8,000 × 25%) proportionate gain that would have been recognized had the transaction been nonmonetary. **Answer (C) is incorrect.** The amount of $12,000 is the carrying amount of the truck given up.

14. On January 1, Feld traded a delivery truck and paid $10,000 cash for a tow truck owned by Baker. The delivery truck had an original cost of $140,000, accumulated depreciation of $80,000, and an estimated fair value of $90,000. Feld estimated the fair value of Baker's tow truck to be $100,000. The transaction had commercial substance. What amount of gain should be recognized by Feld?

A. $0

B. $3,000

C. $10,000

D. $30,000

Answer (D) is correct.

REQUIRED: The gain recognized in an exchange of nonmonetary assets.

DISCUSSION: The transaction had commercial substance. Thus, Feld should account for this exchange of nonmonetary assets at fair value. The asset received is measured at the total fair value of assets given up. The truck given up has a carrying amount of $60,000 ($140,000 cost – $80,000 acc. dep.). Thus, the recognized gain on the appreciation of the truck is $30,000 ($90,000 FV – $60,000 CA). Because the assets given up have a fair value of $100,000 ($90,000 FV of truck + $10,000 cash), the truck received is measured at $100,000. The entry is

Tow truck (fair value of assets given up)	$100,000	
Accumulated depreciation	80,000	
Delivery truck		$140,000
Cash		10,000
Gain		30,000

Answer (A) is incorrect. The full amount of the gain should be recognized because the transaction had commercial substance. **Answer (B) is incorrect.** The cash paid is 10% of the fair value of the consideration transferred ($90,000 + $10,000), and $3,000 is 10% of the $30,000 gain. **Answer (C) is incorrect.** The cash paid is $10,000.

8.7 Disposals Other than by Exchange

15. A state government condemned Cory Co.'s parcel of real estate. Cory will receive $750,000 for this property, which has a carrying amount of $575,000. Cory incurred the following costs as a result of the condemnation:

Appraisal fees to support a $750,000 value	$2,500
Attorney fees for the closing with the state	3,500
Attorney fees to review contract to acquire replacement property	3,000
Title insurance on replacement property	4,000

What amount of cost should Cory use to determine the gain on the condemnation?

A. $581,000

B. $582,000

C. $584,000

D. $588,000

Answer (A) is correct.

REQUIRED: The amount of cost used to determine the gain on the condemnation.

DISCUSSION: A gain or loss must be recognized on an involuntary conversion. The determination of the gain is based on the carrying amount ($575,000) and the costs incurred as a direct result of the condemnation ($2,500 appraisal fees and $3,500 attorney fees), a total of $581,000. Because the recipient is not obligated to reinvest the condemnation proceeds in other nonmonetary assets, the costs associated with the acquisition of the replacement property (attorney fees and title insurance) should be treated as part of the consideration paid for that property.

Answer (B) is incorrect. The amount of $582,000 includes the costs associated with the replacement property but not the costs incurred as a direct result of the condemnation. **Answer (C) is incorrect.** The amount of $584,000 includes the attorney fees associated with the replacement property. **Answer (D) is incorrect.** The amount of $588,000 includes the costs associated with the replacement property.

16. On July 1, one of Rudd Co.'s delivery vans was destroyed in an accident. On that date, the van's carrying value was $2,500. On July 15, Rudd received and recorded a $700 invoice for a new engine installed in the van in May and another $500 invoice for various repairs. In August, Rudd received $3,500 under its insurance policy on the van, which it plans to use to replace the van. What amount should Rudd report as gain (loss) on disposal of the van in its income statement for the year?

A. $1,000

B. $300

C. $0

D. $(200)

Answer (B) is correct.

REQUIRED: The gain (loss) on disposal of the van.

DISCUSSION: Gain (loss) is recognized on an involuntary conversion equal to the difference between the proceeds and the carrying amount. The carrying amount includes the carrying value at July 1 ($2,500) plus the capitalizable cost ($700) of the engine installed in May. This cost increased the carrying amount because it improved the future service potential of the asset. Ordinary repairs, however, are expensed. Consequently, the gain is $300 [$3,500 – ($2,500 + $700)].

Answer (A) is incorrect. The amount of $1,000 results from expensing the cost of the engine. **Answer (C) is incorrect.** Gain (loss) is recognized on an involuntary conversion. **Answer (D) is incorrect.** The amount of $(200) assumes the cost of repairs increased the carrying amount.

8.8 Impairment of Long-Lived Assets

17. Which of the following conditions must exist in order for an impairment loss to be recognized?

I. The carrying amount of the long-lived asset is less than its fair value.

II. The carrying amount of the long-lived asset is not recoverable.

A. I only.

B. II only.

C. Both I and II.

D. Neither I nor II.

Answer (B) is correct.

REQUIRED: The condition(s), if any, for recognition of an impairment loss.

DISCUSSION: A long-lived asset (or asset group) to which the guidance for impairment or disposal applies is tested for recoverability whenever events or changes in circumstances indicate that its carrying amount may not be recoverable. The carrying amount is not recoverable when it exceeds the sum of the undiscounted cash flows expected to result from the use and disposition of the asset (or asset group). If the carrying amount is not recoverable, an impairment loss is recognized equal to the excess of the carrying amount over the fair value.

18. A company has a long-lived asset with a carrying value of $120,000, expected future cash flows of $130,000, present value of expected future cash flows of $100,000, and a market value of $105,000. What amount of impairment loss should be reported?

A. $0

B. $5,000

C. $15,000

D. $20,000

Answer (A) is correct.

REQUIRED: The impairment loss.

DISCUSSION: An impairment loss is recognized when a long-lived asset's carrying amount exceeds the sum of its undiscounted cash flows. Because the sum of the undiscounted cash flows ($130,000) exceeds the carrying amount ($120,000), the carrying amount is recoverable. Thus, no impairment is recognized.

Answer (B) is incorrect. The difference between the fair value of the asset and the present value of the expected future cash flows is $5,000. **Answer (C) is incorrect.** The excess of the carrying amount over the fair value of the asset is $15,000. This unrealized holding loss is not recognized because the recoverability test has not been met. **Answer (D) is incorrect.** The difference between the carrying amount and the present value of the future cash flows is $20,000.

8.9 Assets Classified as Held for Sale

19. If a long-lived asset satisfies the criteria for classification as held for sale,

A. Its carrying amount is the cost at the acquisition date if the asset is newly acquired.

B. It is not depreciated.

C. Interest attributable to liabilities of a disposal group to which the asset belongs is not accrued.

D. It is classified as held for sale even if the criteria are not met until after the balance sheet date but before issuance of the financial statements.

Answer (B) is correct.

REQUIRED: The treatment of a long-lived asset that meets the criteria for classification as held for sale.

DISCUSSION: A long-lived asset is not depreciated (amortized) while it is classified as held for sale and measured at the lower of carrying amount or fair value minus cost to sell. The reason is that depreciation (amortization) would reduce the carrying amount below fair value minus cost to sell. Furthermore, fair value minus cost to sell must be evaluated each period, so any future decline will be recognized in the period of decline.

Answer (A) is incorrect. The carrying amount of a newly acquired long-lived asset classified as held for sale is its fair value minus cost to sell at the acquisition date. **Answer (C) is incorrect.** Interest and other expenses attributable to liabilities of a disposal group to which the asset belongs are accrued. **Answer (D) is incorrect.** If the criteria are not met until after the balance sheet date but before issuance of the financial statements, the long-lived asset continues to be classified as held and used in those statements.

8.10 Depletion

20. In January, Vorst Co. purchased a mineral mine with removable ore estimated at 1.2 million tons for $2,640,000. After it has extracted all the ore, Vorst will be required by law to restore the land to its original condition at an estimated cost of $180,000. Vorst believes it will be able to sell the property afterwards for $300,000. During the year, Vorst incurred $360,000 of development costs preparing the mine for production and removed and sold 60,000 tons of ore. In its income statement for the year, what amount should Vorst report as depletion?

A. $135,000

B. $144,000

C. $150,000

D. $159,000

Answer (B) is correct.

REQUIRED: The amount of depletion to be reported.

DISCUSSION: Vorst's per-ton depletion charge is calculated as follows:

Purchase price	$2,640,000
Add: Restoration costs	180,000
Minus: Residual value	(300,000)
Add: Preparation costs	360,000
Depletion base	$2,880,000
Divided by: Estimated removable tons	÷1,200,000
Depletion charge per ton	$ 2.40

Accordingly, Vorst should report $144,000 (60,000 tons sold × $2.40 per ton) as depletion in its income statement for the year.

Answer (A) is incorrect. The amount of $135,000 does not include the $180,000 restoration costs. **Answer (C) is incorrect.** The amount of $150,000 does not consider the restoration costs and the residual value of the land. **Answer (D) is incorrect.** The amount of $159,000 adds the $180,000 restoration cost instead of deducting the $120,000 net residual value of the land.

STUDY UNIT NINE

INTANGIBLE ASSETS AND OTHER CAPITALIZATION ISSUES

(18 pages of outline)

Intangible assets can take many forms. The following are the common categories:

1) Marketing-related (e.g., trademarks),
2) Customer-related (e.g., customer lists),
3) Artistic-related (e.g., copyrights),
4) Contract-related (e.g., franchise rights),
5) Technology-related (e.g., computer software), and
6) Goodwill (recognized only in business combinations).

9.1 INTANGIBLE ASSETS DISTINCT FROM GOODWILL -- INITIAL RECOGNITION

1. **Definition**
   a. They **lack physical substance**.
      1) In general, intangible assets convey to the holder a contractual or legal right to receive future economic benefits.
      2) Common examples are patents, trademarks, copyrights, and franchise arrangements.
   b. They **are not financial assets**.
      1) Intangible assets thus do not include such items as cash, equity investments, accounts and notes receivable, bonds receivable, or prepaid expenses.
   c. Because the accounting treatment of goodwill is different from that of other intangible assets, goodwill is discussed in Subunit 9.3.
2. **Initial Recognition**
   a. **Externally acquired** intangibles other than goodwill are initially recorded at acquisition cost plus any incidentals such as legal fees.
   b. **Internally developed** intangibles other than goodwill are most often initially recorded at the amount of the incidental costs (e.g., legal fees) only.
      1) Most of the costs of an internally generated intangible asset consist of research and development (R&D), which must be expensed as incurred.

EXAMPLE 9-1 Internally Developed Intangible Asset

A company invested $200,000 and $300,000 in the research phase and development phase, respectively, for the internal development of a patent. In addition, the company paid $10,000 and $15,000 for patent registration fees and legal fees, respectively.

The patent is recorded at the amount of the incidental costs, or $25,000 ($10,000 patent registration fees + $15,000 legal fees). The amounts paid for research and development must be expensed as incurred and are never capitalized as part of the cost of the asset.

3. **Organization and Start-up Costs**
   a. Organization costs are those incurred in the formation of a business entity. They include payments to promoters, legal and accounting fees, and costs of registering with the state of incorporation.
   b. For financial accounting purposes, nongovernmental entities **must expense** all start-up and organization costs as incurred.

STOP & REVIEW

You have completed the outline for this subunit.
Study multiple-choice questions 1 and 2 on page 277.

9.2 INTANGIBLE ASSETS DISTINCT FROM GOODWILL -- ACCOUNTING SUBSEQUENT TO ACQUISITION

1. **Useful Life and Amortization**
   a. The useful life of an asset is the period during which it is expected to contribute either directly or indirectly to the future cash flows of the reporting entity.
   b. An intangible asset with a **finite useful life** to the reporting entity is **amortized** over that useful life.
      1) The useful life should be reevaluated each reporting period. A change in the estimate results in a prospective change in amortization.
   c. Amortization is based on the pattern of consumption of economic benefits, if reliably determinable. Otherwise, the straight-line method must be used.
      1) The **amortizable amount** equals the amount initially assigned minus the residual value. The **residual value** is the estimated fair value to the entity at the end of the asset's useful life minus disposal costs. This amount is zero unless
         a) A third party has committed to purchase the asset, or
         b) It can be determined from an exchange transaction in an existing market for the asset that is expected to exist at the end of the useful life.

IFRS DIFFERENCE

Intangible assets may be accounted for under either the **cost model** (as under U.S. GAAP) or the **revaluation model** (described in the IFRS Difference box on page 226). The revaluation model can be applied only if the intangible asset is traded in an active market.

   d. An intangible asset with an **indefinite useful life** is **not amortized**.
   e. If an amortized intangible asset is later determined to have an **indefinite useful life**, it must (1) no longer be amortized and (2) be tested for impairment.
   f. The carrying amount of an intangible asset is the amount at which it is reported in the financial statements.
      1) The carrying amount of an intangible asset with a **finite useful** life equals its historical cost minus accumulated amortization and impairment losses.
      2) The carrying amount of an intangible asset with an **indefinite useful** life equals its historical cost minus impairment losses.

EXAMPLE 9-2 Amortization of Intangible Assets

An intangible asset was purchased on the first day of the fiscal year for $1,000,000. Its useful life is 5 years, and it has a residual value of $100,000. However, its pattern of consumption of economic benefits is not reliably determinable. The year-end amortization entry is

Amortization expense	$180,000	
Accumulated amortization/Intangible asset		$180,000

[($1,000,000 – $100,000) ÷ 5 years = $180,000 straight-line amortization]

The intangible asset is reported in the year-end financial statements at the amount of $820,000 ($1,000,000 historical cost – $180,000 accumulated amortization).

2. **Testing for Impairment**

   a. An **intangible asset with a finite useful life** (an **amortized** intangible asset) is reviewed for impairment when events or changes in circumstances indicate that its carrying amount may not be recoverable.

      1) The test for impairment is the same as the test for long-lived tangible assets described in Study Unit 8, Subunit 8. It is a **two-step test**:

         a) **Recoverability test.** The carrying amount is not recoverable if it exceeds the sum of the **undiscounted** future cash flows expected from the use and disposition of the asset.

         b) If the carrying amount is **not** recoverable, an impairment loss may be recognized. It equals the excess of the carrying amount of the asset over its fair value.

         c) An impairment loss is recognized in income from continuing operations.

Determination of an Impairment Loss
1. Events or changes in circumstances indicate a possible loss.
2. Carrying amount > Sum of undiscounted cash flows
3. Loss = Carrying amount – Fair value

      2) The carrying amount of an intangible asset adjusted for an impairment loss is its new cost basis. A previously recognized impairment loss **must not be reversed**.

EXAMPLE 9-3 Impairment Test for Finite Useful Life of Intangible Assets

A patent was purchased on the first day of the fiscal year for $900,000. Its useful life is 5 years with no residual value. At the end of Year 3, an event occurred indicating that the asset may be impaired. The patent's fair value is $350,000, and its undiscounted future net cash inflows are $355,000.

Step 1 -- The carrying amount of the patent at the end of Year 3 of $360,000 {$900,000 historical cost – [($900,000 ÷ 5 years) × 3 years] accumulated amortization} exceeds its undiscounted future net cash flows of $355,000. Thus, the carrying amount is not recoverable.

Step 2 -- The impairment loss is $10,000 ($360,000 carrying amount – $350,000 fair value). The journal entry to record the impairment is

Impairment loss	$10,000	
Patent		$10,000

The patent is reported in the year-end financial statements at the amount of **$350,000** ($900,000 historical cost – $540,000 accumulated amortization – $10,000 impairment loss recognized).

IFRS DIFFERENCE

An impairment loss for an asset (except goodwill) may be reversed if a change has occurred in the estimates used to measure the recoverable amount. The test for impairment of assets other than goodwill has one step: determine whether an asset's carrying amount is greater than its recoverable amount (greater of fair value minus costs to sell or value in use). The impairment test for long-lived assets under IFRS is described in Study Unit 8, Subunit 8.

Using the data from Example 9-3, assume that the present value of the patent's expected cash flows is $320,000 and the estimated cost to sell the patent is $5,000. Fair value minus cost to sell is thus $345,000 ($350,000 – $5,000). Under IFRS, the patent's recoverable amount is $345,000 [the greater of (1) fair value minus cost to sell of $345,000 or (2) value in use of $320,000]. The impairment loss recognized is $15,000 ($360,000 carrying amount – $345,000 recoverable amount).

b. An **intangible asset with an indefinite useful life** (a **nonamortized** intangible asset) must be reviewed for impairment at least annually. It is tested more often if events or changes in circumstances suggest that the asset may be impaired. An entity may perform a **qualitative assessment** prior to determining whether it is necessary to perform the **quantitative impairment test**. The performance of the qualitative assessment is at the discretion of the entity. The entity may decide to bypass the qualitative assessment and directly perform the quantitative test.

1) **Qualitative assessment.** After the assessment of qualitative factors, the entity may determine that it is more likely than not (probability > 50%) that an indefinite-lived intangible asset is not impaired. In this case, the quantitative impairment test is not required. If potential impairment is found, the quantitative impairment test must be performed.

2) **Quantitative assessment.** The carrying amount of an asset is compared with its fair value. If the carrying amount exceeds the fair value, the asset is impaired, and the excess is the recognized loss.

a) This loss also is **nonreversible**, so the adjusted carrying amount is the new accounting basis.

Determination of an Impairment Loss
1. Review for impairment
2. Loss = Carrying amount – Fair value

EXAMPLE 9-4 Impairment Test for Indefinite Useful Life of Intangible Assets

A company has a trademark with a carrying amount of $750,000 and an indefinite useful life. At the end of Year 4, an event occurred indicating that the asset may be impaired. The trademark's fair value is $700,000, and its undiscounted future net cash inflows are $790,000. The company decided to bypass the qualitative assessment and directly perform the quantitative test.

The impairment loss is $50,000 ($750,000 carrying amount – $700,000 fair value).

The journal entry to record the impairment is

Impairment loss	$50,000	
Trademark		$50,000

The trademark is reported in the year-end financial statements at the amount of $700,000 ($750,000 historical cost – $50,000 impairment loss recognized).

NOTE: The undiscounted future net cash inflows are not considered when testing an intangible asset with an indefinite life. The cash flows could continue for many years.

IFRS DIFFERENCE

A one-step quantitative impairment test is performed. No qualitative assessment exists.

3. **Patents**

a. Patents may be purchased or developed internally.

1) The initial capitalized cost of a **purchased patent** is normally the fair value of the consideration given, that is, its purchase price plus incidental costs, such as registration and attorneys' fees.

2) **Internally developed patents** are less likely to be capitalized because related R&D costs must be expensed when incurred.

a) Thus, only relatively minor costs can be capitalized, for example, patent registration fees and legal fees.

b. The **amortization period** for a patent is the **shorter** of (1) its useful life or (2) the legal life remaining after acquisition or the moment the application was filed.

1) The useful life may be substantially shorter than the legal life because of (a) changes in consumer tastes, (b) delays in marketing the product or service, and (c) development of substitutes or improvements.

c. The accounting treatment of the costs of the **legal defense of a patent** depends upon the outcome of the litigation.

1) The costs of **successful litigation** are **capitalized** because they will benefit future periods.

a) They are amortized over the shorter of the remaining legal life or the estimated useful life of the patent.

2) The costs of **unsuccessful litigation** (damages, attorneys' fees) are **expensed** as incurred.

a) An unsuccessful suit also indicates that the unamortized cost of the patent has no value and should be recognized as a loss.

EXAMPLE 9-5 Accounting for Patents

A company has two patents, patent A1 and patent B2, both with an estimated useful life of 10 years. Both patents have allegedly been infringed by competitors. On January 1, Year 1, the company incurred legal costs in its attempt to stop the infringement of $20,000 and $25,000 for patents A1 and B2, respectively. The rights to patent A1 were defended successfully for an additional 12 years. The rights to patent B2 were unsuccessfully defended.

The costs of successful litigation of $20,000 for patent A1 are capitalized and recognized as part of the intangible asset. These costs are amortized over its estimated useful life of 10 years because the estimated useful life (10 years) is shorter than the legal life (12 years). The costs of unsuccessful litigation must be expensed as incurred.

The company records the following journal entries:

1/1/Year 1		
Patent -- Capitalized legal costs	$20,000	
Cash		$20,000
Legal expense	$25,000	
Cash		$25,000

12/31/Year 1		
Amortization expense ($20,000 ÷ 10)	$2,000	
Patent -- Capitalized legal costs		$2,000

d. Patents may be sold or temporarily licensed. A **license of a patent** is considered a license of functional intellectual property (IP). Other common examples of functional IP are a software license, a drug formula, and completed media content (e.g., films or music).

1) **Revenue from a license of the right to use the functional IP is recognized at the point in time** at which the license is granted (but not before the customer can benefit from the license).

EXAMPLE 9-6 Revenue from a Licensed Patent

On 1/1/Year 1, GWG Co. licensed patent rights for an approved drug compound for a 5-year period. In exchange for the license, GWG received fixed consideration of $100,000 per year starting from 12/31/Year 1. Because the payments are over a 5-year period, GWG determines that the contract includes a significant financial component. The present value of the five annual payments of $100,000 at the interest rate implicit in the contract is $382,000.

Because the licensed patent is a license of functional IP, revenue is recognized at the point in time at which the license is granted. Thus, a revenue of $382,000 from patent license fee is recognized by GWG on 1/1/Year 1.

4. **Royalties from Licensed Intellectual Property**

a. Revenue for sales-based or usage-based royalties from licensed IP (both functional and symbolic IP) is recognized when (or as) the later of the following occurs:

1) The subsequent sale or usage occurs.

2) The entity satisfied the performance obligations to which the sales-based or usage-based royalty relates.

STOP & REVIEW

You have completed the outline for this subunit.
Study multiple-choice questions 3 through 7 beginning on page 278.

9.3 GOODWILL

1. **Definition**
   a. Goodwill is recognized only in a business combination. It is "an asset representing the future economic benefits arising from other assets acquired in a business combination that are not individually identified and separately recognized" (ASC 350-20-20).
      1) Internally generated goodwill must not be recognized in the financial statements. Study Unit 15 covers the accounting for the initial recognition of goodwill.
   b. Goodwill is **not amortized**. Instead, goodwill of a reporting unit is tested for impairment each year at the same time.
2. **Impairment Test for Goodwill**
   a. Goodwill is tested for impairment at the reporting unit level. All goodwill is assigned to the reporting units that will benefit from the business combination.
      1) Different reporting units may be tested at different times.
   b. A **reporting unit** is an operating segment or one of its components (one level of reporting below an operating segment).
   c. As with the impairment test of other intangible assets with indefinite useful lives, an entity may first perform a **qualitative assessment** to determine whether it is necessary to perform the **quantitative impairment test**.
   d. **Qualitative assessment.** The entity may choose to assess whether qualitative factors indicate that it is more likely than not (probability > 50%) that the **fair value of the reporting unit** is less than its **carrying amount**.
      1) The qualitative assessment considers relevant events and circumstances. Among many others, they may include (a) macroeconomic, industry, and market conditions; (b) cost increases; (c) overall financial performance; (d) other entity-specific events; and (e) events affecting the reporting unit.
      2) The quantitative test need not be performed if the qualitative assessment does not indicate impairment.
   e. If the qualitative assessment indicates that **potential impairment exists**, the quantitative impairment test below is performed to determine whether goodwill is impaired.
      1) The **fair value of the reporting unit is compared with its carrying amount, including goodwill**.
      2) A goodwill impairment loss is recognized for the amount that the carrying amount of a reporting unit, including goodwill, exceeds its fair value. The loss is limited to the total amount of goodwill allocated to that reporting unit. The journal entry is as follows:

Impairment loss	$XXX	
Goodwill		$XXX

      3) The goodwill impairment loss is recognized in the income statement and cannot be reversed in subsequent periods.

EXAMPLE 9-7 Goodwill Impairment Test

On January 1, Year 1, Thom Co. purchased all of the outstanding common stock of Preston Co. for $200,000 and recognized $50,000 of goodwill. It properly classifies Preston as a reporting unit. At the end of Year 2, the following information is available for Preston:

Carrying amount of assets (including goodwill of $50,000)	$290,000
Carrying amount of liabilities	100,000
Fair value	150,000

Thom decided to bypass the qualitative assessment and directly performed the quantitative impairment test.

The carrying amount of the reporting unit, including goodwill, of $190,000 ($290,000 – $100,000) exceeds the fair value of the reporting unit by $40,000 ($190,000 – $150,000). Because this amount is lower than the carrying amount of the reporting unit's goodwill, $40,000 is recognized as the goodwill impairment loss. Thom records the following journal entry on December 31, Year 2:

Impairment loss	$40,000	
Goodwill		$40,000

Goodwill is reported in Thom's Year 2 consolidated balance sheet at $10,000 ($50,000 – $40,000). The impairment loss of $40,000 is reported in the Year 2 consolidated income statement.

EXAMPLE 9-8 Goodwill Impairment Test

Using the data from Example 9-7, assume that the fair value of Preston at the end of Year 2 is $120,000.

The excess of the reporting unit's carrying amount, including goodwill, over its fair value is $70,000 ($190,000 – $120,000). Because this amount is greater than the carrying amount of the reporting unit's goodwill, the goodwill impairment loss is the carrying amount of the reporting unit's goodwill of $50,000. Thom records the following journal entry on December 31, Year 2:

Impairment loss	$50,000	
Goodwill		$50,000

Private Companies Accounting

A private company is any entity that is not (1) a public business entity, (2) a not-for-profit entity, or (3) an employee benefit plan.

In accounting for subsequent measurement of **goodwill**, a private company may

a) Use the FASB codification guidance that applies to all entities (the accounting treatment described on the previous page and above) or

b) Elect to apply the **goodwill accounting alternative**.

Under the accounting alternative, goodwill must be **amortized on a straight-line basis over a 10-year period**. The amortization expense is recognized in the income statement.

a) The amortization period for goodwill cannot exceed 10 years.

b) A private company may amortize goodwill over a period shorter than 10 years if it can demonstrate that this useful life is more appropriate.

The goodwill impairment test under the accounting alternative is the same as under the general FASB codification guidance except that goodwill

a) Can be tested for impairment on an entity level and

b) Is tested for impairment only when a triggering event occurs indicating that the fair value of the entity is below its carrying amount.

NOTE: Unless specifically stated otherwise, all questions and simulations are based on the FASB codification guidance applied to all entities. The guidance for private companies should be used only when the facts of a question or simulation state that a private company has elected the accounting alternative.

3. **Presentation in the Financial Statements**
   a. In the **balance sheet**, intangible assets are required to be presented, at a minimum, as a single aggregated line item. But individual intangible assets or classes of these assets may be separately presented.
      1) Goodwill is presented in the aggregate as a separate line item.
   b. In the **income statement**, amortization expense and impairment losses related to intangible assets are presented as line items under continuing operations.

IFRS DIFFERENCE

A qualitative assessment is not an option. The following quantitative impairment test must be performed.

For the purpose of impairment testing, goodwill is allocated to the entity's **cash-generating units (CGUs)** that will benefit from the business combination.

- A CGU is the lowest level at which goodwill is monitored and must not be larger than an operating segment.

The test for impairment of a CGU to which goodwill has been allocated is whether the **carrying amount of the CGU** (including allocated goodwill) exceeds its **recoverable amount** (greater of fair value minus costs to sell or value in use). An impairment loss for a CGU is allocated first to reduce allocated goodwill to zero and then pro rata to other assets of the CGU.

STOP & REVIEW

You have completed the outline for this subunit.
Study multiple-choice questions 8 and 9 on page 280.

9.4 FRANCHISE ACCOUNTING

1. **Franchises**
   a. A franchise is a contractual agreement by a **franchisor** (grantor of the franchise) to permit a **franchisee** (purchaser) to operate a certain business.
      1) Thus, an exclusive right may be granted to sell a specified product or service in a given geographical area and to use trademarks, patents, trade secrets, etc.
2. **Franchisee Accounting**
   a. The franchisee should capitalize the costs of acquiring the franchise. The **capitalizable amount** includes the initial fee and other expenditures (e.g., legal fees) necessary to acquire the franchise that will provide future benefits.
      1) If the initial fees are paid over a period longer than 1 year, the present value of the payments is capitalized as part of franchise costs and recognized as an intangible asset.
   b. Franchise costs (the amounts capitalized) are **amortized** over their **estimated useful life** if such life is **finite**.
   c. Future payments based on a percentage of revenues or for franchisor services are expensed as incurred. They benefit only the period of payment.
3. **Franchisor Accounting**
   a. A franchise right is considered symbolic intellectual property (IP). Other common examples of symbolic IP are trade names, brands, and logos. **Revenue from a license of the right to access symbolic IP is recognized over time.** Thus, franchise fee revenue is recognized over the franchise license period (or over its remaining economic life, if shorter).
      1) Revenue from initial fixed fees received generally is recognized evenly over the entire franchise license period.
      2) Revenue from sales-based royalties typically is recognized when the sales occur.

EXAMPLE 9-9 Revenue from Licensing a Franchise

Abik Corp. has a franchise for a restaurant business. On January 1, Year 1, Abik granted Mika a license for 10 years to operate as a franchisee of one of its restaurants for an initial fixed fee of $3 million and a royalty of 2% of Mika's restaurant sales. The sales-based royalty is paid at the end of each year. In Year 1, Mika's restaurant had $600,000 of sales.

The initial fixed fee of $3 million is initially recorded as contract liability (unearned revenue) and recognized evenly over the franchise license period of 10 years. Thus, in Year 1, Abik recognized franchise fee revenue of $312,000 [($3,000,000 ÷ 10 years) + ($600,000 × 2%)]. The following journal entries were recorded by Abik in Year 1:

1/1/Year 1			12/31/Year 1		
Cash	$3,000,000		Cash ($600,000 × 2%)	$ 12,000	
Contract liability		$3,000,000	Contract liability	300,000	
			Franchise fee revenue		$312,000

STOP & REVIEW

You have completed the outline for this subunit.
Study multiple-choice question 10 on page 281.

9.5 RESEARCH AND DEVELOPMENT

1. **Overview**

   a. Research and development (R&D) costs must be **expensed as incurred**.

      1) This rule does not apply to R&D activities conducted for others.

      2) This rule also does not apply to assets (tangible or intangible) acquired in a business combination that are used in R&D activities. Such assets are initially recognized and measured at fair value even if they have no alternative use.

IFRS DIFFERENCE

Research costs must be expensed as incurred.

Development costs may result in **recognition of an intangible asset** if the entity can demonstrate the

1) Technical feasibility of completion of the asset,
2) Intent to complete,
3) Ability to use or sell the asset,
4) Way in which it will generate probable future economic benefits,
5) Availability of resources to complete and use or sell the asset, and
6) Ability to measure reliably expenditures attributable to the asset.

IFRS EXAMPLE 9-1 R&D Costs under IFRS

A company invested $200,000 and $300,000 in the research phase and the development phase, respectively, of the internal development of a patent. The company also paid $10,000 and $15,000 for patent registration fees and legal fees, respectively. Assume that all the criteria above are met. Under IFRS, the patent is recorded at the amount of $325,000 ($300,000 development costs + $25,000 incidental costs). The research costs of $200,000 are expensed as incurred and are never capitalized as part of the cost of the asset.

   b. **Research** is planned search or critical investigation aimed at discovery of new knowledge with the hope that it will be useful in developing a new (or significantly improving an existing) product, service, process, or technique (product or process).

   c. **Development** is translation of research findings or other knowledge into a plan or design for a new or improved product or process.

      1) It includes conceptual formulation, design, and testing of product alternatives; prototype construction; and operation of pilot plants.

      2) Development does **not** include routine alterations to existing products, production lines, processes, and other ongoing operations.

         a) Market research or testing also is excluded.

2. **R&D Activities**
   a. The following are examples of activities typically included in R&D unless conducted for others under a contract (reimbursable costs are not expensed):
      1) Laboratory research aimed at discovery of new knowledge
      2) Searching for applications of new research findings or other knowledge
      3) Conceptual formulation and design of possible product or process alternatives
      4) Testing in search for, or evaluation of, product or process alternatives
      5) Modification of the formulation or design of a product or process
      6) Design, construction, and testing of preproduction prototypes and models
      7) Design of tools, jigs, molds, and dies involving new technology
      8) Design, construction, and operation of a pilot plant that is not of a scale economically feasible to the entity for commercial production
      9) Engineering activity required to advance the design of a product until it meets specific functional and economic requirements and is ready for manufacture
3. **Activities Not Classified as R&D**
   a. The following are examples of activities that typically are not classified as R&D:
      1) Engineering follow-through in an early phase of commercial production
      2) Quality control during commercial production, including routine testing of products
      3) Troubleshooting in connection with breakdowns during commercial production
      4) Routine, ongoing efforts to refine, enrich, or otherwise improve upon the qualities of an existing product
      5) Adaptation of an existing capability to a particular requirement or customer's need as part of a continuing commercial activity
      6) Seasonal or other periodic design changes to existing products
      7) Routine design of tools, jigs, molds, and dies
      8) Activity, including design and construction engineering, related to the construction, relocation, rearrangement, or start-up of facilities or equipment other than pilot plants and facilities or equipment whose sole use is for a particular R&D project
      9) Legal work in connection with patent applications or litigation and the sale or licensing of patents

4. **Elements of R&D Costs**

   a. **Materials, equipment, and facilities.** The costs of such items acquired or constructed for R&D and having alternative future uses (in R&D projects or otherwise) are capitalized as tangible assets and depreciated over their estimated useful lives.

      1) The costs of materials consumed in R&D and the depreciation of equipment or facilities used in R&D are R&D costs and are expensed when incurred.

      2) The costs of materials, equipment, or facilities acquired (but not in a business combination) or constructed for a particular project and having no alternative future uses (and no separate economic values) are R&D costs and are expensed when incurred.

   b. **Personnel.** Salaries, wages, and other related costs of personnel engaged in R&D are included in R&D costs and are expensed when incurred.

   c. **Intangible assets purchased from others.** These costs of R&D assets having alternative future uses are capitalized as intangible assets. They are amortized if their useful lives are finite.

      1) The amortization of those intangible assets is an R&D cost.

      2) The costs of intangible assets purchased from others (but not in a business combination) for a particular project and having no alternative future uses (and no separate economic values) are R&D costs and are expensed when incurred.

   d. **Contract services.** The costs of services performed by others in connection with the R&D activities of an entity, including R&D conducted by others on behalf of the entity, are R&D costs and are expensed when incurred.

   e. **Indirect costs.** R&D costs include a reasonable allocation of indirect costs, which also are expensed.

      1) General and administrative costs not clearly related to R&D are excluded.

   f. **Disclosure** is made in the financial statements of the total R&D costs charged to expense in each period for which an income statement is presented.

5. **R&D Funded by Others**

   a. Sometimes an entity's R&D is funded wholly or partly by others.

      1) If the entity is **obligated to repay** any of the funds provided by the other party regardless of the outcome of the project, it recognizes a **liability**.

      2) If repayment depends solely on the results of the R&D having future economic benefit, the entity accounts for its obligation as a contract to perform R&D for others.

SUCCESS TIP

CPA candidates should expect to be tested on research and development costs. Common questions have focused on what activities are classified as R&D activities, and both theoretical and calculation formats have been utilized.

STOP & REVIEW

You have completed the outline for this subunit.
Study multiple-choice questions 11 and 12 on page 282.

9.6 COMPUTER SOFTWARE

1. **Overview**

   a. Accounting for the costs of developing or obtaining computer software depends on whether the software is (1) sold to external customers or (2) used internally.

      1) Costs of software may be

         a) Expensed as incurred,
         b) Capitalized as computer software costs, or
         c) Included in inventory.

      2) Costs of software to be used **internally** are either expensed or capitalized.

2. **Software to Be Marketed**

   a. **Costs Expensed**

      1) Costs incurred before technological feasibility is established (coding, testing, etc.) are expensed as incurred. Thus, they are treated as R&D costs.

      2) Technological feasibility is established when either a detailed program design is complete or the entity has created a working model.

   b. **Costs Capitalized**

      1) Costs incurred after technological feasibility is established (coding, testing, producing product masters) are capitalized as computer software costs.

      2) Amortization begins and capitalization ends when the product is available for general release.

      3) If purchased software to be marketed has **no alternative future use**, the entity accounts for its cost as if it had been developed internally to be marketed. If purchased software to be marketed **has an alternative future use**, the entity **capitalizes** the costs when it purchases the software and accounts for it according to use.

   c. **Costs Included in Inventory**

      1) Costs incurred to prepare the product for sale (duplication of software, training materials, packaging) are capitalized as inventory.

Costs of Software to Be Marketed

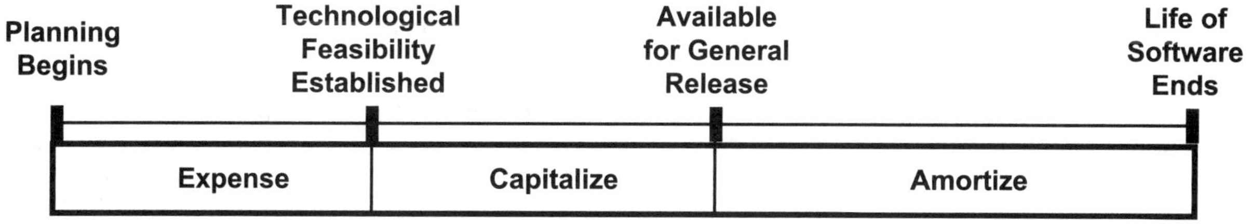

Figure 9-1

EXAMPLE 9-10 Costs Incurred for Software to Be Marketed

During Year 1, TriloByte, Inc., incurred and properly classified the following costs to prepare a software package for the market:

	Costs	Expensed	Capitalized	Inventory
Work on detail program design	$93,000	$ 93,000		
Coding to establish technological feasibility	58,000	58,000		
Testing to establish technological feasibility	64,000	64,000		
Coding after establishment of technological feasibility	60,000		$ 60,000	
Testing after establishment of technological feasibility	45,000		45,000	
Production of product masters	20,000		20,000	
Duplication of software	80,000			$ 80,000
Preparation of training materials	15,000			15,000
Packaging	27,000			27,000
Totals		$215,000	$125,000	$122,000

d. **Annual Amortization of Capitalized Software Costs**

1) Annual amortization is the **greater** of

a) Total capitalized cost times the revenue ratio (Annual gross software revenue ÷ Total projected gross revenue) **or**

b) Straight-line amortization (Total capitalized cost ÷ Estimated economic life of the software).

e. **Balance Sheet Measurement**

1) Capitalized software costs are reported at the lower of unamortized cost or net realizable value (NRV).

2) A loss on the write-down to NRV is recognized in the income statement. After the write-down, the carrying amount of computer software is the new cost basis.

a) The amount of the write-down to NRV must **not** be subsequently restored.

EXAMPLE 9-11 Measurement of Capitalized Software Costs

TriloByte, Inc., expected its software package to have an economic life of 6 years. Sales during Year 2 were 20% of the projected total revenues expected over the life of the software. The net realizable value of the software at December 31, Year 2, was $90,000. TriloByte calculates annual amortization of software costs as follows:

Revenue ratio: $125,000 × 20% = $25,000
Straight-line: $125,000 ÷ 6 = $20,833

Amortization based on the revenue ratio ($25,000) is greater than the straight-line amount ($20,833). Consequently, unamortized software costs at December 31, Year 2, are $100,000 ($125,000 – $25,000). But NRV ($90,000) is lower than unamortized software costs ($100,000), and the software must be written-down to NRV. In the Year 2 income statement, an amortization expense of $25,000 and a loss on write-down to NRV of $10,000 ($100,000 – $90,000) are recognized. The software is reported at its new carrying amount of $90,000 on the 12/31/Year 2 balance sheet.

3. **Software to Be Used Internally**

   a. **Costs Expensed**

      1) Costs incurred during the preliminary project stage (planning, evaluation) are expensed as incurred.

      2) Costs incurred for training and maintenance are also expensed.

   b. **Costs Capitalized**

      1) Costs incurred during the application development stage (coding, testing) are capitalized as computer software costs. They include

         a) External direct costs of materials and services,
         b) Payroll costs directly associated with the project, and
         c) Interest costs associated with the project.

      2) When software is replaced, unamortized costs of the old software are expensed.

   c. **Annual Amortization**

      1) Annual amortization of the capitalized costs of software to be used internally is on a straight-line basis over the estimated economic life of the software.

EXAMPLE 9-12 Software for Internal Use

Dancy Corp. spent $22,000,000 during the current year developing a new software package that will only be used internally. Of this amount, $6,000,000 was spent before the project reached the application development stage. The package was completed during the year and is expected to have a 4-year useful life. Dancy's policy is to take a full year's amortization in the first year. After the application development stage, Dancy spent $125,000 on training materials and sessions. Dancy will calculate expense associated with this software package for the current year as follows:

Costs incurred during preliminary project stage	$ 6,000,000
Amortization expense [($22,000,000 – $6,000,000) ÷ 4]	4,000,000
Costs incurred for training	125,000
Current-year expense	$10,125,000

   d. **Subsequent Sale**

      1) Occasionally, software developed for internal use is sold to outside parties.

         a) The net proceeds from these sales reduce the carrying amount of capitalized software costs.

         b) When the carrying amount is $0, net proceeds are recognized as revenue.

STOP & REVIEW

You have completed the outline for this subunit.
Study multiple-choice questions 13 through 16 beginning on page 283.

9.7 PREPAYMENTS AND OTHER ISSUES

1. **Prepayments**

   a. An asset provides future economic benefits. If a cash payment is made in one period and the recognition of the related expense (receipt of the benefit) is not appropriate until a later period, the **deferred cost** is recorded as an **asset**.

      1) Examples include prepaid insurance, rent, interest, and income taxes.

      2) The amount of the prepaid expense that will be used up within the longer of 1 year or the next operating cycle of the entity is classified as a current asset.

   b. Adjusting entries are made as of the balance sheet date to record the effects on periodic revenue and expense of deferrals (prepaid expenses) and accruals. The adjusting journal entry recorded depends on how the original transaction was initially recorded.

      1) If the payment is initially recorded as an asset (prepaid expenses), the year-end adjusting entry credits the asset and debits an expense for the expired portion.

      2) If the payment is initially recorded as an expense, the year-end adjusting entry debits an asset (prepaid expenses) and credits (decreases) expense for the unexpired portion.

EXAMPLE 9-13 Adjusting Entries for Prepayments

On January 1, Year 1, a calendar-year company made an advance payment of $120,000 for 3 years of insurance coverage. The company did not record any additional journal entries in Year 1 related to the payment.

Payment was initially recorded as insurance expense. The insurance expense account and prepaid insurance account are reported in the unadjusted trial balance at $120,000 and $0, respectively. Because only one-third of the amount paid is for current-year insurance, the balances that should be reported in the financial statements are $40,000 for insurance expense and $80,000 for prepaid insurance. Thus, the year-end adjusting entry is to decrease insurance expense by $80,000 and recognize prepaid insurance for $80,000.

Prepaid insurance	$80,000	
Insurance expense		$80,000

Payment was initially recorded as prepaid insurance. The insurance expense account and prepaid insurance account are reported in the unadjusted trial balance at $0 and $120,000, respectively. Thus, the year-end adjusting entry is to recognize insurance expense of $40,000 and decrease prepaid insurance by $40,000.

Insurance expense	$40,000	
Prepaid insurance		$40,000

2. **Deferred Charges**

   a. Deferred charges (other assets) is a catchall category. It includes long-term prepayments and any noncurrent assets not classified elsewhere.

   b. Such a classification has been criticized because many assets (e.g., PPE) are deferred charges. Thus, they are noncurrent prepayments that will be depreciated or amortized.

STOP & REVIEW

You have completed the outline for this subunit.
Study multiple-choice questions 17 and 18 on page 286.

QUESTIONS

9.1 Intangible Assets Distinct from Goodwill -- Initial Recognition

1. An entity purchases a trademark and incurs the following costs in connection with the trademark:

One-time trademark purchase price	$100,000
Nonrefundable VAT taxes	5,000
Training sales personnel on the use of the new trademark	7,000
Research expenditures associated with the purchase of the new trademark	24,000
Legal costs incurred to register the trademark	10,500
Salaries of the administrative personnel	12,000

Assuming that the trademark meets all of the applicable initial asset recognition criteria, the entity should recognize an asset in the amount of

A. $100,000

B. $115,500

C. $146,500

D. $158,500

Answer (B) is correct.

REQUIRED: The initial amount recognized for an intangible asset.

DISCUSSION: Cost includes the purchase price (including purchase taxes and import duties) and any directly attributable costs to prepare the asset for its intended use, such as legal fees. Thus, the intangible asset is initially recognized at $115,500 ($100,000 price + $5,000 value-added taxes + $10,500 of legal costs).

Answer (A) is incorrect. Purchase taxes and legal fees for registration also are capitalized. **Answer (C) is incorrect.** Training and research costs are expensed as incurred. **Answer (D) is incorrect.** Training and research costs and administrative salaries and other overhead costs are not directly attributable costs.

2. On June 30, Year 5, Finn, Inc., exchanged 2,000 shares of Edlow Corp. $30 par-value common stock for a patent owned by Bisk Co. The Edlow stock was acquired in Year 1 at a cost of $50,000. At the exchange date, Edlow common stock had a fair value of $40 per share, and the patent had a net carrying amount of $100,000 on Bisk's books. Finn should record the patent at

A. $50,000

B. $60,000

C. $80,000

D. $100,000

Answer (C) is correct.

REQUIRED: The amount at which a patent should be recorded.

DISCUSSION: When an intangible asset is acquired in an exchange transaction, initial recognition is at the fair value of the more clearly evident of the consideration given or the asset acquired. The fair value of the assets given in return for the patent was $80,000 (2,000 shares of stock × $40 per share fair value).

Answer (A) is incorrect. The acquisition cost of the stock is $50,000. **Answer (B) is incorrect.** The par value of the stock is $60,000. **Answer (D) is incorrect.** The net carrying amount of the patent is $100,000.

9.2 Intangible Assets Distinct from Goodwill -- Accounting Subsequent to Acquisition

3. Wall Company bought a trademark from Black Corporation on January 1 for $112,000. An independent consultant retained by Wall estimated that the remaining useful life is 50 years. Its unamortized cost on Black's accounting records was $56,000. Wall decided to write off the trademark over the maximum period allowed. However, the pattern of consumption of the economic benefits of the trademark is not reliably determinable. How much should be amortized for the year ended December 31?

A. $1,120

B. $1,400

C. $2,240

D. $2,800

Answer (C) is correct.

REQUIRED: The amount of amortization of a trademark for the first year.

DISCUSSION: If the consideration given is cash, an exchange transaction is measured by the amount of cash paid. If the consideration given is not cash, measurement is based on the more reliably measurable of the fair value of the consideration given or the fair value of the assets (or net assets) acquired. The foregoing guidance should be followed when initially measuring the "cost" of an intangible asset at its fair value. When the useful life of a recognized intangible asset to the reporting entity is finite, the asset is amortized over that useful life. The amortization method should reflect the pattern in which the economic benefits of the intangible asset are consumed. If the pattern is not reliably determinable, the straight-line method is used. Consequently, annual amortization is $2,240 ($112,000 ÷ 50 years).

Answer (A) is incorrect. The amount of $1,120 results from amortizing the unamortized cost on Black's books over 50 years. **Answer (B) is incorrect.** The amount of $1,400 results from amortizing the unamortized cost on Black's books over 40 years. **Answer (D) is incorrect.** The amount of $2,800 is based on a 40-year useful life.

4. After an impairment loss is recognized, the adjusted carrying amount of the intangible asset shall be its new accounting basis. Which of the following statements about subsequent reversal of a previously recognized impairment loss is correct?

A. It is prohibited.

B. It is required when the reversal is considered permanent.

C. It must be disclosed in the notes to the financial statements.

D. It is encouraged but not required.

Answer (A) is correct.

REQUIRED: The treatment of previously recognized impairment losses.

DISCUSSION: When an impairment of an intangible asset is recognized, the previous carrying amount of the asset is reduced by the impairment loss. The adjusted carrying amount is the new accounting basis. Thus, it cannot be increased subsequently for a change in fair value. This rule applies whether the intangible asset has a finite or an indefinite useful life.

Answer (B) is incorrect. Recognition of an impairment loss is required when it is considered permanent, that is, when the applicable impairment test is met. Any increase in the fair value of an intangible asset related to the previous impairment loss is not recognized. **Answer (C) is incorrect.** Reversal is prohibited, so disclosure is not necessary. **Answer (D) is incorrect.** It is not encouraged, required, or even permitted to make an adjustment to the accounting of an intangible asset for a reversal of a previously recognized impairment loss.

5. Tech Co. bought a trademark 2 years ago on January 2. Tech accounted for the trademark as instructed under the provisions of the Accounting Standards Codification during the current year. The intangible was being amortized over 40 years. The carrying amount at the beginning of the year was $38,000. It was determined that the cash flow will be generated indefinitely at the current level for the trademark. What amount should Tech report as amortization expense for the current year?

A. $0

B. $922

C. $1,000

D. $38,000

Answer (A) is correct.

REQUIRED: The amortization expense for a purchased trademark.

DISCUSSION: An intangible asset with an indefinite useful life to the reporting entity is not amortized.

6. During the year just ended, Jase Co. incurred research and development costs of $136,000 in its laboratories relating to a patent that was granted on July 1. Costs of registering the patent equaled $34,000. The patent's legal life is 20 years, and its estimated economic life is 10 years. In its December 31 balance sheet, what amount should Jase report for the patent, net of accumulated amortization?

A. $32,300

B. $33,150

C. $161,500

D. $165,000

Answer (A) is correct.

REQUIRED: The amount reported for the patent, net of accumulated amortization.

DISCUSSION: R&D costs are expensed as incurred. However, legal work in connection with patent applications or litigation and the sale or licensing of patents are specifically excluded from the definition of R&D. Hence, the legal costs of filing a patent should be capitalized. The patent should be amortized over its estimated economic life of 10 years. Amortization for the year equals $1,700 [($34,000 ÷ 10) × (6 ÷ 12)]. Thus, the reported amount of the patent at year end equals $32,300 ($34,000 – $1,700).

Answer (B) is incorrect. The amount of $33,150 results from using the 20-year legal life of the patent. **Answer (C) is incorrect.** The $136,000 of R&D costs should not be capitalized. **Answer (D) is incorrect.** The R&D costs should not be capitalized, and the useful life, not the legal life, should be used.

7. Gray Co. was granted a patent on January 2, Year 5, and appropriately capitalized $45,000 of related costs. Gray was amortizing the patent over its estimated useful life of 15 years. During Year 8, Gray paid $15,000 in legal costs in successfully defending an attempted infringement of the patent. After the legal action was completed, Gray sold the patent to the plaintiff for $75,000. Gray's policy is to take no amortization in the year of disposal. In its Year 8 income statement, what amount should Gray report as gain from sale of patent?

A. $15,000

B. $24,000

C. $27,000

D. $39,000

Answer (B) is correct.

REQUIRED: The amount reported as gain from the sale of a patent.

DISCUSSION: The patent was capitalized at $45,000 in Year 5. Annual amortization of $3,000 ($45,000 ÷ 15 years) for Year 5, Year 6, and Year 7 reduced the carrying amount to $36,000. The $15,000 in legal costs for successfully defending an attempted infringement may be capitalized, which increases the carrying amount of the patent to $51,000 ($36,000 + $15,000). Accordingly, the gain from the sale is $24,000 ($75,000 – $51,000).

Answer (A) is incorrect. The amount of legal costs for defending the patent is $15,000. **Answer (C) is incorrect.** The amount of $27,000 assumes amortization in the year of disposal. **Answer (D) is incorrect.** The amount of $39,000 results from not capitalizing the $15,000 in legal costs.

9.3 Goodwill

8. On January 2, Paye Co. acquired Shef Co. in a business combination that resulted in recognition of goodwill of $200,000 having an expected benefit period of 10 years. Shef is treated as a reporting unit, and the entire amount of the recognized goodwill is assigned to it. During the first quarter of the year, Shef spent an additional $80,000 on expenditures designed to maintain goodwill. Due to these expenditures, at December 31, Shef estimated that the benefit period of goodwill was 40 years. In its consolidated December 31 balance sheet, what amount should Paye report as goodwill?

A. $180,000

B. $200,000

C. $252,000

D. $280,000

Answer (B) is correct.

REQUIRED: The amount of goodwill in the balance sheet.

DISCUSSION: Goodwill is not recorded except in a business combination. Thus, only the $200,000 recognized at the acquisition date should be recorded as goodwill. It should not be amortized but should be tested for impairment at the reporting-unit level. The facts given suggest that the fair value of the reporting unit (Shef) is not less than its carrying amount. Hence, no impairment of goodwill has occurred, and goodwill is unchanged at $200,000. Moreover, the cost of internally developing, maintaining, or restoring intangible assets (including goodwill) that are not specifically identifiable, have indeterminate useful lives, or are inherent in a continuing business and related to an entity as a whole should be expensed as incurred.

Answer (A) is incorrect. The amount of $180,000 results when goodwill is amortized on the straight-line basis over 10 years. **Answer (C) is incorrect.** The amount of $252,000 results from amortizing an additional $80,000 of expenditures to maintain goodwill over 10 years. **Answer (D) is incorrect.** The amount of $280,000 results from adding $80,000 of expenditures for the maintenance of goodwill.

9. A company reported $6 million of goodwill in last year's statement of financial position. How should the company account for the reported goodwill in the current year?

A. Determine the current year's amortizable amount and report the current year's amortization expense.

B. Determine whether the fair value of the reporting unit is greater than the carrying amount and report a gain on goodwill in the income statement.

C. Determine whether the fair value of the reporting unit is less than the carrying amount and report an impairment loss on goodwill in the income statement.

D. Determine whether the fair value of the reporting unit is greater than the carrying amount and report the recovery of any previous impairment in the income statement.

Answer (C) is correct.

REQUIRED: The accounting for goodwill.

DISCUSSION: Goodwill must be tested for impairment at least annually. The impairment test compares the carrying amount of the reporting unit, including goodwill, with its fair value. A goodwill impairment loss is recognized for the amount by which the carrying amount of the reporting unit, including goodwill, exceeds its fair value. The loss is limited to the total amount of goodwill allocated to that reporting unit.

Answer (A) is incorrect. Goodwill is not amortized. **Answer (B) is incorrect.** Goodwill does not appreciate. **Answer (D) is incorrect.** An impairment of goodwill is not reversible.

9.4 Franchise Accounting

10. Helsing Co. bought a franchise from Anya Co. on January 1 for $204,000. An independent consultant retained by Helsing estimated that the remaining useful life of the franchise was a finite period of 50 years and that the pattern of consumption of benefits of the franchise is not reliably determinable. Its unamortized cost on Anya's books on January 1 was $68,000. What amount should be amortized for the year ended December 31, assuming no residual value?

A. $5,100

B. $4,080

C. $3,400

D. $1,700

Answer (B) is correct.

REQUIRED: The first-year amortization expense of the cost of a franchise.

DISCUSSION: A franchise is an intangible asset. The initial measurement of an intangible asset acquired other than in a business combination is at fair value. Thus, the "cost" to be amortized should be based on the more reliably measurable of the fair value of the consideration given or the fair value of the assets acquired. If the useful life is finite, the intangible asset is amortized over that period. Moreover, if the consumption pattern of benefits of the intangible asset is not reliably determinable, the straight-line method of amortization is used. Accordingly, given no residual value, the amortization expense is $4,080 ($204,000 consideration given ÷ 50-year finite useful life).

Answer (A) is incorrect. The amount of $5,100 is based on a 40-year period. **Answer (C) is incorrect.** The amount of $3,400 is the difference between the $204,000 franchise price and Anya's $68,000 unamortized cost, divided by 40 years. **Answer (D) is incorrect.** The amount of $1,700 equals the unamortized cost on Anya's books amortized over 40 years.

9.5 Research and Development

11. West, Inc., made the following expenditures relating to Product Y:

- Legal costs to file a patent on Product Y -- $10,000. Production of the finished product would not have been undertaken without the patent.
- Special equipment to be used solely for development of Product Y -- $60,000. The equipment has no other use and has an estimated useful life of 4 years.
- Labor and material costs incurred in producing a prototype model -- $200,000.
- Cost of testing the prototype -- $80,000.

What is the total amount of costs that will be expensed when incurred?

A. $280,000

B. $295,000

C. $340,000

D. $350,000

Answer (C) is correct.

REQUIRED: The total amount of costs that will be expensed when incurred.

DISCUSSION: R&D costs are expensed as incurred. However, legal work in connection with patent applications or litigation and the sale or licensing of patents are specifically excluded from the definition of R&D. The legal costs of filing a patent should be capitalized. West's R&D costs include those incurred for the design, construction, and testing of preproduction prototypes. Moreover, the cost of equipment used solely for a specific project is also expensed immediately. Thus, the total amount of costs that will be expensed when incurred is $340,000.

Answer (A) is incorrect. The amount of $280,000 omits the cost of the special equipment. **Answer (B) is incorrect.** The amount of $295,000 includes 1 year's straight-line depreciation on the special equipment instead of the full cost. **Answer (D) is incorrect.** The amount of $350,000 includes the legal costs of filing a patent.

12. In the year just ended, Ball Labs incurred the following costs:

Direct costs of doing contract R&D work for the government to be reimbursed by governmental unit	$400,000

R&D costs not included above were

Depreciation	$300,000
Salaries	700,000
Indirect costs appropriately allocated	200,000
Materials	180,000

What was Ball's total R&D expense for the year?

A. $1,080,000

B. $1,380,000

C. $1,580,000

D. $1,780,000

Answer (B) is correct.

REQUIRED: The total R&D expense.

DISCUSSION: Materials used in R&D, compensation costs of personnel, and indirect costs appropriately allocated are R&D costs that should be expensed immediately. The costs of equipment and facilities that are used for R&D activities and have alternative future uses, whether for other R&D projects or otherwise, are to be capitalized as tangible assets when acquired or constructed. Thus, the depreciation is also expensed immediately. However, this guidance does not apply to R&D activities conducted for others. Hence, the reimbursable costs are not expensed. Ball's total R&D expense is therefore $1,380,000 ($300,000 + $700,000 + $200,000 + $180,000).

Answer (A) is incorrect. The amount of $1,080,000 omits depreciation. **Answer (C) is incorrect.** The amount of $1,580,000 includes the reimbursable costs of R&D conducted for others but omits the indirect costs. **Answer (D) is incorrect.** The amount of $1,780,000 includes the reimbursable costs of R&D conducted for others.

9.6 Computer Software

13. Yellow Co. spent $12,000,000 during the current year developing its new software package. Of this amount, $4,000,000 was spent before it was at the application development stage and the package was only to be used internally. The package was completed during the year and is expected to have a 4-year useful life. Yellow has a policy of taking a full-year's amortization in the first year. After the development stage, $50,000 was spent on training employees to use the program. What amount should Yellow report as an expense for the current year?

A. $1,600,000

B. $2,000,000

C. $6,012,500

D. $6,050,000

Answer (D) is correct.

REQUIRED: The first year expense for new software developed to be used internally.

DISCUSSION: Costs incurred in the preliminary project stage for computer software to be used internally are expensed as incurred. During the application development stage, costs are capitalized. However, training costs are expensed. Accordingly, $8,000,000 ($12,000,000 total – $4,000,000 spent before application development) of the development cost was capitalized. Amortization is on a straight-line basis over the 4-year useful life of the software. Thus, given that a full-year's amortization is recognized in year one, the expense for the year is $6,050,000 [$4,000,000 preliminary project expense + ($8,000,000 ÷ 4) amortization + $50,000 training cost].

Answer (A) is incorrect. The amount of $1,600,000 results from using a 5-year useful life for the software. **Answer (B) is incorrect.** The amount of $2,000,000 results from failing to include the costs incurred before the application development stage and the costs of training. **Answer (C) is incorrect.** The amount of $6,012,500 results from improperly capitalizing training costs.

14. On December 31, Year 7, Byte Co. had capitalized software costs of $600,000 with an economic life of 4 years. Sales for Year 8 were 10% of expected total sales of the software. At December 31, Year 8, the software had a net realizable value of $480,000. In its December 31, Year 8, balance sheet, what amount should Byte report as net capitalized cost of computer software?

A. $432,000

B. $450,000

C. $480,000

D. $540,000

Answer (B) is correct.

REQUIRED: The net capitalized cost of computer software at year end.

DISCUSSION: The annual amortization is the greater of the amount determined using (1) the ratio of current gross revenues to the sum of current gross revenues and anticipated future gross revenues, or (2) the straight-line method over the remaining estimated economic life, including the current reporting period. At year end, the unamortized cost of each software product must be compared with the net realizable value (NRV) of that software product. Any excess of unamortized cost over NRV must be written off. The amount of amortization under the straight-line method is used because it is greater than the amount determined using the 10% ratio of current sales to expected total sales. Thus, Byte Co. had an unamortized cost of software of $450,000 [$600,000 capitalized cost – ($600,000 ÷ 4)] at December 31, Year 8. The $450,000 unamortized cost is lower than the $480,000 NRV, so $450,000 is the amount reported in the year-end balance sheet.

Answer (A) is incorrect. The amount of $432,000 equals the NRV at December 31, Year 8, minus amortization calculated as 10% of NRV. **Answer (C) is incorrect.** The NRV at December 31, Year 8, is $480,000. **Answer (D) is incorrect.** The amount of $540,000 assumes amortization at 10% with no adjustment for NRV.

Questions 15 and 16 are based on the following information. During the year just ended, Pitt Corp. incurred costs to develop and produce a routine, low-risk computer software product as follows:

Completion of detail program design	$13,000
Costs incurred for coding and testing to establish technological feasibility	10,000
Other coding costs after establishment of technological feasibility	24,000
Other testing costs after establishment of technological feasibility	20,000
Costs of producing product masters for training materials	15,000
Duplication of computer software and training materials from product masters (1,000 units)	25,000
Packaging product (500 units)	9,000

The guidance pertaining to accounting for the costs of computer software to be sold, leased, or otherwise marketed applies.

15. In Pitt's December 31 balance sheet, what amount should be capitalized as software cost subject to amortization?

A. $54,000

B. $57,000

C. $59,000

D. $69,000

Answer (C) is correct.

REQUIRED: The amount capitalized as software cost subject to amortization.

DISCUSSION: Costs incurred internally in creating a computer software product are expensed when incurred as research and development until technological feasibility has been established for the product. Afterward, all software production costs incurred until the product is available for general release to customers are capitalized and amortized separately for each product. Subsequently, the lower of unamortized cost or net realizable value at the end of the period is reported in the balance sheet. Hence, (1) the costs of completing the detail program design and establishing technological feasibility are expensed; (2) the costs of duplicating software, documentation, and training materials and packaging the product are inventoried; and (3) the costs of coding and other testing after establishing technological feasibility and the costs of producing product masters are capitalized and amortized. The amount capitalized as software cost subject to amortization is therefore $59,000 ($24,000 + $20,000 + $15,000).

Answer (A) is incorrect. Inventoriable costs plus the other testing costs equals $54,000. **Answer (B) is incorrect.** The sum of the costs expensed and the costs inventoried is $57,000. **Answer (D) is incorrect.** The amount of $69,000 assumes the costs of coding and testing to establish feasibility are capitalized and amortized.

16. In Pitt's December 31 balance sheet, what amount should be reported in inventory?

A. $25,000

B. $34,000

C. $40,000

D. $49,000

Answer (B) is correct.

REQUIRED: The amount reported in inventory.

DISCUSSION: Costs incurred internally in creating a computer software product are expensed when incurred as R&D until technological feasibility has been established. Afterward, all software production costs incurred until the product is available for general release to customers shall be capitalized and amortized. The costs of (1) duplicating the software, documentation, and training materials from the product masters and (2) physically packaging the product for distribution are capitalized as inventory. Hence, inventory should be reported at $34,000 ($25,000 duplication costs + $9,000 packaging costs).

Answer (A) is incorrect. The amount of $25,000 excludes packaging costs. **Answer (C) is incorrect.** The amount of $40,000 excludes packaging costs but includes costs of producing product masters. **Answer (D) is incorrect.** The amount of $49,000 includes costs of producing product masters.

9.7 Prepayments and Other Issues

17. An analysis of Thrift Corp.'s unadjusted prepaid expense account at December 31, Year 4, revealed the following:

- An opening balance at $1,500 for Thrift's comprehensive insurance policy. Thrift had paid an annual premium of $3,000 on July 1, Year 3.
- A $3,200 annual insurance premium payment made July 1, Year 4.
- A $2,000 advance rental payment for a warehouse Thrift leased for 1 year beginning January 1, Year 5.

In its December 31, Year 4, balance sheet, what amount should Thrift report as prepaid expenses?

A. $5,200

B. $3,600

C. $2,000

D. $1,600

Answer (B) is correct.

REQUIRED: The amount reported for prepaid expenses.

DISCUSSION: The $1,500 beginning balance of prepaid insurance expired on 6/30/Yr 4, leaving a $0 balance. The $3,200 annual insurance premium paid on 7/1/Yr 4 should be allocated equally to Year 4 and Year 5, leaving a $1,600 prepaid insurance balance. The $2,000 advance rental payment is an expense that is wholly deferred until Year 5. Consequently, the total of prepaid expenses at year end is $3,600 ($1,600 + $2,000).

Answer (A) is incorrect. Half of the $3,200 of prepaid insurance should be expensed in Year 4. **Answer (C) is incorrect.** Only half of the $3,200 of prepaid insurance should be expensed in Year 4. **Answer (D) is incorrect.** The prepaid rent is deferred until Year 5.

18. Roro, Inc., paid $7,200 to renew its only insurance policy for 3 years on March 1, Year 4, the effective date of the policy. At March 31, Year 4, Roro's unadjusted trial balance showed a balance of $300 for prepaid insurance and $7,200 for insurance expense. What amounts should be reported for prepaid insurance and insurance expense in Roro's financial statements for the 3 months ended March 31, Year 4?

	Prepaid Insurance	Insurance Expense
A.	$7,000	$300
B.	$7,000	$500
C.	$7,200	$300
D.	$7,300	$200

Answer (B) is correct.

REQUIRED: The amounts reported for prepaid insurance and insurance expense.

DISCUSSION: The entry to record the insurance renewal included a debit to insurance expense for $7,200, and the balance in prepaid insurance has expired. At year end, the expense and prepaid insurance accounts should be adjusted to reflect the expired amounts. The 3-year prepayment is amortized at $200 per month ($7,200 ÷ 36 months). Consequently, insurance expense for the period should be $500 ($300 prepaid insurance balance + $200 amortization of the renewal amount). The $7,000 unexpired amount should be debited to prepaid insurance.

Answer (A) is incorrect. The amount of $300 does not include the $200 expense for March. **Answer (C) is incorrect.** Neither the prepaid insurance nor the insurance expense amounts have been adjusted for the $200 expense for March. **Answer (D) is incorrect.** Prepaid insurance includes $300 that should be expensed.

STUDY UNIT TEN

PAYABLES AND TAXES

(25 pages of outline)

This study unit deals with different types of liabilities. The first five subunits apply basic accrual accounting procedures to the recognition and reporting of liabilities in the balance sheet. The next five subunits address the financial statement implications of the differences between accounting under GAAP and accounting under the federal tax code.

10.1 ACCOUNTS PAYABLE

1. **Definition**
   a. Accounts payable (trade payables) are **liabilities**. They are obligations to sellers incurred when an entity purchases inventory, supplies, or services on credit.
   b. Accounts payable are usually **noninterest-bearing** unless they are not settled when due or payable.
      1) They also are usually **not** secured by collateral.
2. **Current Liabilities**
   a. A current liability is an obligation that will be either paid using current assets or replaced by another current liability. Thus, a liability is classified as current if it is expected to be paid within the entity's operating cycle or 1 year, whichever is longer.
   b. Current liabilities (accounts payable) should be recorded at **net settlement value**. Thus, they are measured at the undiscounted amounts of cash expected to be paid to liquidate an obligation.
      1) Obligations that are callable by the creditor within 1 year because of a violation of a debt agreement also are classified as current liabilities.
   c. **Checks** written before the end of the period but not mailed to creditors should not be accounted for as cash payments for the period. The amounts remain current liabilities until control of the checks has been surrendered.

3. **Gross Method vs. Net Method**
   a. Cash discounts are offered to induce early payment. Purchases and related accounts payable may be recorded using the gross method or the net method.
   b. The **gross method** ignores cash discounts. It accounts for payables at their face amount.
      1) **Purchase discounts taken** are credited to a contra purchases account and closed to cost of goods sold.
   c. The **net method** records payables net of the cash (sales) discount for early payment.
      1) When the discount is taken (the payment is within the discount period), no additional adjustment is required.
      2) Purchase discounts lost is recognized (debited) when payment is not made within the discount period.
4. **Shipping Terms**
   a. The timing of recognition of accounts payable may depend on the shipping terms.
   b. When goods are shipped **FOB shipping point**, the buyer records inventory and a payable at the time of shipment.
   c. When goods are shipped **FOB destination**, the buyer records inventory and a payable when the goods are tendered at the destination.

EXAMPLE 10-1 Effect of Shipping Terms on Accounts Payable

Kew Co.'s accounts payable balance at December 31, Year 3, was $2.2 million before considering the following:

- Goods shipped to Kew **FOB shipping point** on December 22, Year 3, were lost in transit. The invoice cost of $40,000 was not recorded by Kew. On January 7, Year 4, Kew filed a $40,000 claim against the common carrier.
- On December 27, Year 3, a vendor authorized Kew to return, for full credit, goods shipped and billed at $70,000 on December 3, Year 3. The returned goods were shipped by Kew on December 28, Year 3. A $70,000 credit memo was received and recorded by Kew on January 5, Year 4.
- Goods shipped to Kew **FOB destination** on December 20, Year 3, were received on January 6, Year 4. The invoice cost was $50,000.

When goods are shipped FOB shipping point, inventory and a payable are recognized at the time of shipment. Hence, Kew should currently recognize a $40,000 payable for the goods lost in transit. The $70,000 purchase return should be recognized currently because the seller authorized the credit on December 27. However, the goods shipped FOB destination and not received until January should be excluded. Kew should not recognize inventory and a payable until the goods are tendered at the destination. Accordingly, the ending accounts payable balance is $2,170,000 ($2,200,000 + $40,000 – $70,000).

STOP & REVIEW

You have completed the outline for this subunit.
Study multiple-choice question 1 on page 311.

10.2 ACCRUED EXPENSES

1. **Accrual Entries**

   a. Ordinarily, accrued expenses meet **recognition criteria** in the current period but have **not been paid** as of year end. They are accounted for using basic accrual entries.

   b. Accruals may be used to facilitate accounting for expenses incurred but not paid at the end of an accounting period.

      1) For example, the year-end **accrual entry** for wages payable is

Wages expense	$XXX	
Wages payable		$XXX

2. **Reversing Entries**

   a. The reversing entry at the beginning of the next period is

Wages payable	$XXX	
Wages expense		$XXX

   b. No allocation between the liability and wages expense is needed when wages are paid in the subsequent period. The full amount of expenses paid in the next period can be debited to expense.

      1) The entry is simply

Wages expense	$XXX	
Cash		$XXX

3. **No Reversing Entries**

   a. If reversing entries are **not** made, payments during the year are recorded by **debiting expense** for the full amount.

      1) The entry is

Wages expense	$XXX	
Cash		$XXX

   b. At year end, the **liability** is adjusted to the balance owed at that date.

      1) For example, if the liability for accrued wages has decreased, the adjusting entry is

Wages payable	$XXX	
Wages expense		$XXX

EXAMPLE 10-2 Accrual with and without Reversing Entries

Mike Co.'s salaried employees are paid monthly. The payment is always on the fifth day of the next month. In Year 1, the total monthly salary was $100,000. In Year 2, the employees received a 5% raise to $105,000.

On December 31, Year 1, Mike must accrue a liability of $100,000 for December salaries expense that will be paid on January 5, Year 2.

Salaries expense	$100,000	
Salaries payable		$100,000

In Year 2, the journal entries recorded by Mike depend on its bookkeeping approach to expense accrual.

1) Reversing Journal Entries

January 1, Year 2 – Reversal of December 31, Year 1, entry

Salaries payable	$100,000	
Salaries expense		$100,000

January 5, Year 2 – Payment of December Year 1 salaries

Salaries expense	$100,000	
Cash		$100,000

February 5, Year 2, through December 5, Year 2: Monthly entry

Salaries expense	$105,000	
Cash		$105,000

December 31, Year 2 – Accrual of a liability for December Year 2 salaries

Salaries expense	$105,000	
Salaries payable		$105,000

NOTE: The annual salaries expense for Year 2 is $1,260,000 ($105,000 monthly salary × 12 months). The salaries payable balance on December 31, Year 2, is $105,000.

2) No Reversing Journal Entries

January 5, Year 2 – Payment of December Year 1 salaries

Salaries expense	$100,000	
Cash		$100,000

February 5, Year 2, through December 5, Year 2: Monthly entry

Salaries expense	$105,000	
Cash		$105,000

December 31, Year 2 – The liability is adjusted to the balance owed. The credit is $5,000 ($105,000 amount owed for December Year 2 – $100,000 unadjusted balance).

Salaries expense	$5,000	
Salaries payable		$5,000

NOTE: The annual salaries expense for Year 2 is $1,260,000 [$100,000 on 1/5/Year 2 + ($105,000 × 11 months) + $5,000 on 12/31/Year 2]. The salaries payable balance on December 31, Year 2, is $105,000 ($100,000 beginning balance + $5,000 adjustment on 12/31/Year 2).

4. **Effects of Nonaccrual**

   a. If an entity fails to accrue expenses at year end, **income** is overstated in that period and understated in the next period (when they are paid and presumably expensed).

      1) Moreover, expenses incurred but unpaid and not recorded result in understated **accrued liabilities** and possibly understated assets (for example, if the amounts should be inventoried).

         a) In addition, working capital (current assets – current liabilities) will be overstated, but cash flows will not be affected.

EXAMPLE 10-3 Year-End Accrued Liabilities

Windy Co. must determine the December 31, Year 2, year-end accruals for advertising and rent expenses. A $500 advertising bill was received January 7, Year 3. It related to costs of $375 for advertisements in December Year 2 and $125 for advertisements in January Year 3. A one-year lease, effective December 16, Year 2, calls for fixed rent of $1,200 per month, payable beginning 1 month from the effective date.

The $375 of advertising expense should be accrued in Year 2 because this amount can be directly related to events in that period. The $125 amount is related to events in Year 3 and should not be accrued in Year 2.

The fixed rental is due at mid-month. Thus, the fixed rental for the last half month of Year 2 ($1,200 ÷ 2 = $600) also should be accrued.

In its December 31, Year 2, balance sheet, Windy should report accrued liabilities of $975 ($375 + $600).

STOP & REVIEW

You have completed the outline for this subunit.
Study multiple-choice questions 2 and 3 on page 312.

10.3 CERTAIN TAXES PAYABLE

1. **Federal**
   a. **Federal unemployment tax** and the employer's share of **FICA taxes** are expenses incurred as employees earn wages. But they are only paid on a periodic basis to the federal government.
      1) Accordingly, liabilities should be accrued for both expenses, as well as for wages earned but not paid.

Payroll tax expense	$X,XXX	
Employer FICA taxes payable		$XXX
Federal unemployment taxes payable		XXX

   b. Income taxes withheld and the employees' share of FICA taxes are accrued as **withholding taxes** (payroll deductions), not as employer payroll taxes.
2. **State**
   a. Most states impose **sales taxes** on certain types of merchandise. Ordinarily, the tax is paid by the buyer but is collected and remitted by the seller.
   b. Most states require quarterly or monthly filing of sales tax returns and remittance of taxes collected.
3. **Local**
   a. **Property taxes** are usually expensed by monthly accrual over the fiscal period of the taxing authority.

STOP & REVIEW

You have completed the outline for this subunit.
Study multiple-choice questions 4 and 5 on page 313.

10.4 DEPOSITS AND OTHER ADVANCES

SUCCESS TIP

The AICPA has tested CPA candidates' knowledge of deposits and advances with questions that have often asked for the calculation of the liability amount. Use the noteboard to write out the appropriate T-accounts or journal entries showing the flow of the transactions. This may be helpful in answering these types of questions.

1. **Definition**
   a. A deposit or other advance is a **contract liability**. It does not qualify for revenue recognition.
   b. A contract liability is an obligation to transfer goods or services to a customer for which the consideration already has been received from the customer.
   c. Alternative descriptions of a contract liability, such as **deferred revenue**, may be used in the statement of financial position.
2. **Accounting Treatment**
   a. Cash advances (such as sales of gift certificates) are recorded as follows:

Cash	$XXX	
Contract liability (deferred revenue)		$XXX

   b. The entity should derecognize the contract liability and recognize revenue when the promised goods or services are transferred to the customer.

Contract liability	$XXX	
Revenue		$XXX

   c. Cash received from customers for **magazine subscriptions** creates a liability for unearned subscription revenue.

EXAMPLE 10-4 Advance Payments

Nepal Co. requires advance payments with special orders for machinery constructed to customer specifications. These advances are nonrefundable. Revenue is recognized when control of the machinery is transferred to the customer (e.g., when the order is shipped). Information for Year 2 is as follows:

Customer advances -- balance 12/31/Year 1	$236,000
Advances received with orders in Year 2	368,000
Advances applied to orders shipped in Year 2	328,000
Advances applicable to orders canceled in Year 2	100,000

In Nepal's December 31, Year 2, balance sheet, the amount reported as a current liability is $176,000 ($236,000 beginning balance + $368,000 advances received – $328,000 advances credited to revenue after shipment of orders – $100,000 for canceled orders) for customer advances. Deposits or other advance payments are contract liabilities because they were received before Nepal transferred machinery to customers. The nonrefundable advances applicable to canceled orders qualify for revenue recognition (debit the liability, credit revenue) because the entity's performance obligations have been satisfied.

d. If a customer option to acquire additional goods or services for free or at a discount provides a material right to the customer, the customer in effect pays the entity in advance for future goods or services. The following is the accounting for such an option:

1) The total transaction price is allocated to performance obligations based on their relative standalone selling prices (discussed in Study Unit 3, Subunit 4).

2) At contract inception, the consideration allocated to the option is recognized as a **contract liability** (e.g., deferred revenue).

3) Revenue is recognized when (a) those goods or services are transferred to the customer or (b) the option expires.

EXAMPLE 10-5 Customer's Material Right to Additional Goods

On October 1, Year 1, BGU Co. sold 50 computers for $940 each. The cost of each computer to BGU is $400. In the package of a computer, BGU includes a voucher for a $100 credit on future purchases of BGU products. The voucher expires on May 1, Year 2, and requires a minimum future purchase of $800. The transaction price is the same as the standalone selling price of the computer ($940). BGU determines that this voucher represents a material right. Based on its past experience, BGU estimates that 60% of customers will redeem vouchers. Thus, the estimated standalone selling price of the voucher is $60 ($100 × 60%). The total transaction price of $940 is allocated as follows:

Performance Obligation	Standalone Selling Price	Percent of Allocation	Allocated Transaction Price
Computer	$ 940	94% [$940 ÷ ($940 + $60)]	**$883.6** ($940 × 94%)
Voucher	60	6% [$ 60 ÷ ($940 + $60)]	**56.4** ($940 × 6%)
Total	$1,000	100%	**$940**

The following journal entries are recorded by BGU on October 1, Year 1:

Cash ($940 × 50)	$47,000	
Revenue ($883.6 × 50)		$44,180
Contract liability ($56.4 × 50)		2,820

Cost of goods sold ($400 × 50)	$20,000	
Computer inventory		$20,000

By the end of Year 1, 18 vouchers had been redeemed, and BGU still estimates that a total of 30 vouchers (50 × 60%) will be redeemed. By the end of Year 1, BGU recognizes revenue from redeemed vouchers of $1,692 [$2,820 × (18 ÷ 30)]. On the December 31, Year 1, balance sheet, the contract liability is reported at $1,128 ($2,820 – $1,692). The following journal entry records the redemption of 18 vouchers in Year 1.

Contract liability	$1,692	
Revenue		$1,692

STOP & REVIEW

You have completed the outline for this subunit.
Study multiple-choice questions 6 through 8 beginning on page 314.

10.5 WARRANTIES

1. **Overview**

   a. A warranty is a written guarantee of the integrity of a product or service. The seller may also agree to repair or replace a product or provide additional service.

      1) A warranty customarily is offered for a limited time, such as 2 years.
      2) It may or may not be sold separately from the product or service.

   b. A warranty that provides a customer assurance that a product will function as expected in accordance with agreed-upon specifications is an **assurance-type warranty**.

      1) A standard one-year computer warranty against manufacturing defects is an example of an assurance-type warranty.

   c. A warranty that provides a customer with a service in addition to the assurance that the product complies with agreed-upon specifications is a **service-type warranty**.

      1) A warranty against customer-inflicted damages, such as dropping the computer on the floor or into water, is an example of a service-type warranty.
      2) A service-type warranty is accounted for as a **separate** performance obligation in the contract.

2. **Classification of a Warranty as an Assurance- or Service-Type Warranty**

   a. A warranty that can be **purchased separately** by the customer is a **service-type warranty**.

      1) If a customer does **not** have the option to purchase a warranty separately, the warranty is an **assurance-type warranty**.

   b. A warranty required by law is an assurance-type warranty.

   c. The length of the warranty coverage period may indicate the type of warranty. A service-type warranty is more likely to have a longer coverage period. A longer warranty is more likely to provide service in addition to the assurance that the product complies with agreed-upon specifications.

   d. If an assurance-type warranty and a service-type warranty provided in the contract cannot be separated, the warranties are accounted for as a single performance obligation in a contract (that is, as a service-type warranty).

3. **Accounting for an Assurance-Type Warranty**

   a. An assurance-type warranty is **not** a separate performance obligation in a contract. Thus, no transaction price is allocated to the warranty.

   b. An assurance-type warranty creates a **loss contingency**. **Accrual accounting** should be used if

      1) Incurrence of warranty expense is probable,
      2) The amount can be reasonably estimated, and
      3) The amount is material.

c. A liability for warranty costs is recognized when the related revenue is recognized, i.e., on the day the product is sold.

1) Even if the warranty covers a period longer than the period in which the product is sold, the **entire liability** (expense) for the expected warranty costs must be recognized on the day the product is sold. The warranty liability (expense) must not be prorated over the annual periods covered by the warranty.

Beginning warranty liability	$XXX
Warranty expense recognized in the current period	XXX
Warranty payments in the current period	(XXX)
Ending warranty liability	$XXX

2) Actual payments for warranty costs reduce the amount of warranty liability recognized and do not affect warranty expense.

a) If the warranty payments for the period are greater than the amount of warranty liability recognized, the excess is recognized as warranty expense.

d. The following are **accrual-basis** entries for warranty expense estimated as a percentage of sales when the **warranty is not separable**:

1) To record a sale of product

Cash or accounts receivable	$XXX	
Sales revenue		$XXX

2) To record related warranty expense recognized on the day of sale

Warranty expense	$XXX	
Estimated warranty liability		$XXX

3) To record actual warranty expenditures paid in the current period

Estimated warranty liability	$XXX	
Cash		$XXX

EXAMPLE 10-6 Assurance-Type Warranty

In Year 1, a company began selling a product under a standard 2-year warranty. The estimated warranty costs are 3% of sales in the year of sale and 5% in the following year. Sales and actual warranty payments for Year 1 and Year 2 are as follows:

	Sales	Warranty Payments
Year 1	$300,000	$ 5,000
Year 2	500,000	37,000

In Year 1, warranty expense of $24,000 [$300,000 × (3% + 5%)] is recognized. The warranty liability of $19,000 ($24,000 – $5,000) is reported on the December 31, Year 1, balance sheet.

In Year 2, warranty expense of $40,000 [$500,000 × (3% + 5%)] is recognized. The warranty liability of $22,000 is reported on the December 31, Year 2, balance sheet.

Beginning warranty liability (1/1/Year 2)	$ 19,000
Warranty expense recognized in the current period	40,000
Warranty payments in the current period	(37,000)
Ending warranty liability (12/31/Year 2)	$ 22,000

4. **Accounting for a Service-Type Warranty**

   a. A service-type warranty is a **separate performance obligation in a contract**. Thus, a portion of the total transaction price is allocated to the service-type warranty.

      1) The total transaction price is allocated to the service-type warranty and the related product sold based on their estimated standalone selling prices.

   b. At contract inception, the consideration received for the service-type warranty is accounted for as an advance payment and a contract liability is recognized. The following entry is recorded on a sale of a product with a service-type warranty:

Cash	$XXX (total transaction price)	
Revenue		$XXX (transaction price allocated to the product)
Contract liability		XXX (transaction price allocated to the service-type warranty)

   c. Revenue from a service-type warranty is recognized over time (i.e., over the coverage period). The pattern of revenue recognized from a service-type warranty depends on the way the warranty performance obligation is satisfied.

      1) If warranty service is provided continuously over the warranty period, revenue is recognized on the **straight-line basis** over the coverage period.

      2) If warranty service costs are **not incurred on a straight-line basis**, revenue recognition over the contract's term should be proportionate to the estimated service costs.

      3) The following entry is recorded when revenue from a service-type warranty is recognized:

Contract liability	$XXX	
Revenue		$XXX

      4) The following entry is recorded when an entity pays for the costs related to the claims under the warranty:

Warranty expense	$XXX	
Cash		$XXX

STOP & REVIEW

You have completed the outline for this subunit.
Study multiple-choice questions 9 and 10 beginning on page 315.

10.6 INCOME TAX ACCOUNTING -- OVERVIEW

BACKGROUND 10-1 Divergence of Tax Code from GAAP

Until 1954, business income reported to the IRS and income reported on financial statements were essentially the same. In that year, accelerated depreciation for tax purposes was permitted for the first time. Since then, more and more provisions of the tax code have diverged from GAAP. The procedures necessary to calculate the amount owed for taxes and current-year tax expense are the subject of the next five subunits.

1. **Objectives**
   a. The objectives of accounting for income taxes are to recognize
      1) The amount of taxes currently payable or refundable
      2) Deferred tax liabilities and assets for the future tax consequences of events that have been recognized in the financial statements or tax returns
   b. To achieve these objectives, an entity uses the **asset-and-liability approach** to account for (1) income taxes currently payable or deductible and (2) deferred taxes.
2. **Interperiod Tax Allocation**
   a. Amounts in the entity's income tax return for a year include the tax consequences of most items recognized in the financial statements for the same year. But significant exceptions may exist.
   b. Revenues and expenses reported in financial statements prepared in accordance with GAAP are based on the **accrual method** of accounting. However, revenues and expenses reported in an income tax return are based on the **income tax basis** of accounting.
      1) The accrual basis of accounting reports the effects of transactions and other events and circumstances on the entity's resources and claims when they occur, not necessarily when the cash flows occur.
      2) Under the income tax basis of accounting, certain revenues and expenses are recognized when cash is received or paid, respectively. Recognition does **not** depend on when (a) goods are delivered or received or (b) services are rendered.
         a) Accordingly, **tax consequences** of some items may be recognized in **tax returns** for a year different from that in which their **financial-statement effects** are recognized (temporary differences).
         b) Moreover, some items may have tax consequences or financial-statement effects but never both (permanent differences).
   c. When tax consequences and financial-statement effects differ, income taxes currently payable or refundable also **may differ from** income tax expense or benefit.
      1) The accounting for these differences is **interperiod tax allocation**.
3. **Intraperiod Tax Allocation**
   a. Intraperiod tax allocation **is required**. Income tax expense (benefit) is allocated to
      1) Continuing operations,
      2) Discontinued operations,
      3) Other comprehensive income, and
      4) Items debited or credited directly to equity.

4. **Basic Definitions**
   a. **Income tax expense or benefit** is the sum of (1) current tax expense or benefit and (2) deferred tax expense or benefit.
   b. **Current tax expense or benefit** is the amount of **taxes paid or payable** (or refundable) for the year as determined by applying the enacted tax law to the taxable income or excess of deductions over revenues for that year.
   c. **Taxable income** is the income calculated under the tax code. Taxable income equals pretax accounting income adjusted for permanent and temporary differences.
   d. **Deferred tax expense or benefit** is the net change during the year in an entity's deferred tax amounts.
   e. A **deferred tax liability** records the deferred tax consequences of taxable temporary differences. It is measured using the enacted tax rate and enacted tax law.
   f. A **deferred tax asset** records the deferred tax consequences of deductible temporary differences and carryforwards. It is measured using the enacted tax rate and enacted tax law.
   g. A **valuation allowance** is the portion of a deferred tax asset for which it is more likely than not that a tax benefit will not be realized.
   h. A **temporary difference (TD)** results when the GAAP basis and the tax basis of an asset or liability differ.
      1) Differences in the two bases arise when items of income and expense are recognized in different periods under GAAP and under the tax code.
      2) The effect is that a taxable or deductible amount will occur in future years when the asset is recovered or the liability is settled.
         a) But some TDs may not be related to an asset or liability for financial reporting.
   i. A **permanent difference** is an event that is recognized either in pretax financial income or in taxable income **but never in both**. It does not result in a deferred tax amount.
5. **Basic Principles of Income Tax Accounting**
   a. A **current tax liability or asset** is recognized for the estimated taxes payable or refundable on current-year tax returns.
   b. A **deferred tax liability or asset** is recognized for the estimated future tax effects of temporary differences and carryforwards.
   c. **Measurement** of tax liabilities and assets is based on **enacted tax law**. The effects of future changes in that law are not anticipated.
   d. A deferred tax asset is reduced by a **valuation allowance**.

STOP & REVIEW

You have completed the outline for this subunit.
Study multiple-choice question 11 on page 316.

10.7 INCOME TAX ACCOUNTING -- TEMPORARY AND PERMANENT DIFFERENCES

SUCCESS TIP

The AICPA has frequently tested candidates' knowledge of the recognition and measurement of deferred income taxes. The AICPA has released CPA Exam questions that require calculations of deferred tax assets or deferred tax liabilities.

1. **Asset-and-Liability Approach**
   a. Income reported under **GAAP** (accrual basis) differs from income reported for **tax purposes** (income tax basis).
      1) The asset-and-liability approach accounts for the resulting temporary (but not permanent) differences.
   b. This approach recognizes the deferred tax consequences for balance sheet measurements and related income statement amounts.
      1) As a result of temporary differences, the tax bases of assets and liabilities differ from their carrying amounts reported on the financial statements. A deferred tax amount equals the tax rate times the difference between (a) the tax basis and (b) the carrying amount.

      (Tax basis – Carrying amount) × Tax rate = Deferred tax asset (liability)

      2) A positive difference results in recognition of a deferred tax asset, and a negative difference results in recognition of a deferred tax liability.
      3) In the equation above, tax bases and carrying amounts of assets will be included as positive amounts (illustrated in Example 10-7 on the next page). However, tax bases and carrying amounts of liabilities will be included as negative amounts (illustrated in Example 10-9 beginning on page 302).
   c. **Taxable temporary differences** result in future taxable amounts and deferred tax liabilities (DTL).

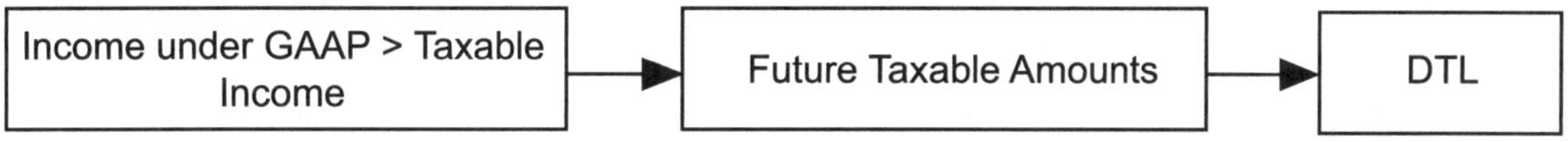

Figure 10-1

   d. **Deductible temporary differences** result in future deductible amounts and deferred tax assets (DTA).

Figure 10-2

2. **Deferred Tax Liabilities (DTLs) and Future Taxable Amounts**

   a. DTLs arise when **revenues or gains** are recognized under GAAP before they are included in taxable income. Examples include the following:

      1) Income recognized under the equity method for financial statement purposes and at the time of distribution in taxable income
      2) Sales revenue accrued for financial reporting and recognized on the installment basis for tax purposes
      3) Gains on involuntary conversion

DTL = Future taxable amount × Enacted tax rate

EXAMPLE 10-7 DTL Due to Temporary Differences in Revenue

In Year 1, Luxor Corp. recognizes $800,000 of sales on credit. The cash will be collected in Years 2 through 5 in the amounts of $300,000, $200,000, $200,000, and $100,000, respectively. For tax purposes, these sales are recognized only when the cash is actually collected. The amounts collected are those by which taxable income in Years 2 through 5 will exceed GAAP income. Accordingly, they are future taxable amounts. The enacted tax rate for Year 1 through Year 5 is 40%.

Year 1 excess of GAAP income over taxable income	$800,000
Future taxable amount in Year 2	$300,000
Future taxable amount in Year 3	200,000
Future taxable amount in Year 4	200,000
Future taxable amount in Year 5	100,000
Total future taxable amount	$800,000
Enacted tax rate	× 40%
Deferred tax liability -- 12/31/Year 1	**$320,000**

The total future taxable amount, i.e., the amount that will reverse, equals the current-period difference between GAAP income and taxable income.

Tax basis of accounts receivable on 12/31/Year 1	$ 0
Carrying amount (GAAP basis) on 12/31/Year 1	– 800,000
Difference	$(800,000)
Tax rate	× 40%
Deferred tax liability -- 12/31/Year 1 balance	**$ 320,000**

   b. DTLs also result when **expenses or losses** are deductible for tax purposes before they are recognized under GAAP. An example is accelerated tax depreciation of property.

EXAMPLE 10-8 DTL Due to Temporary Differences in Expenses

On January 1, Year 1, Mika Co. purchased a machine for $100,000. The machine will be depreciated over its 4-year useful life on a straight-line basis for financial reporting (25% a year under GAAP). The following accelerated depreciation percentages are used for tax purposes: Year 1 – 60%, Year 2 – 20%, Year 3 – 10%, and Year 4 – 10%. The tax rate for these years is 40%.

The Year 1 excess of GAAP (financial statement) income over taxable income of $35,000 [$100,000 × (60% – 25%)] will be reversed in Years 2-4. The result will be future taxable amounts.

Future taxable amount in Year 2: $100,000 × (20% tax rate – 25% GAAP)	$ 5,000
Future taxable amount in Year 3: $100,000 × (10% tax rate – 25% GAAP)	15,000
Future taxable amount in Year 4: $100,000 × (10% tax rate – 25% GAAP)	15,000
Total future taxable amount	$35,000
Enacted tax rate	× 40%
Deferred tax liability 12/31/Year 1	**$14,000**

-- Continued on next page --

EXAMPLE 10-8 -- Continued

Reported revenue was $90,000 in each of the Years 1-4. No expenses other than depreciation expense for the machine were incurred in Years 1-4.

Taxable Income	Income Tax Payable
Year 1: $30,000 ($90,000 – $60,000)	Year 1: $12,000 ($30,000 × 40%)
Year 2: $70,000 ($90,000 – $20,000)	Year 2: $28,000 ($70,000 × 40%)
Year 3: $80,000 ($90,000 – $10,000)	Year 3: $32,000 ($80,000 × 40%)
Year 4: $80,000 ($90,000 – $10,000)	Year 4: $32,000 ($80,000 × 40%)

Tax basis of the machine on 12/31/Yr 1	$ 40,000	($100,000 cost – $60,000 accum. dep.)
Carrying amount (GAAP basis) on 12/31/Yr 1	– 75,000	($100,000 cost – $25,000 accum. dep.)
Difference	$(35,000)	
Tax rate	× 40%	
Deferred tax liability -- 12/31/Yr 1 balance	**$ 14,000**	
Tax basis of the machine on 12/31/Yr 2	$ 20,000	($100,000 cost – $80,000 accum. dep.)
Carrying amount (GAAP basis) on 12/31/Yr 2	– 50,000	($100,000 cost – $50,000 accum. dep.)
Difference	$(30,000)	
Tax rate	× 40%	
Deferred tax liability -- 12/31/Yr 2 balance	**$ 12,000**	
Tax basis of the machine on 12/31/Yr 3	$ 10,000	($100,000 cost – $90,000 accum. dep.)
Carrying amount (GAAP basis) on 12/31/Yr 3	– 25,000	($100,000 cost – $75,000 accum. dep.)
Difference	$(15,000)	
Tax rate	× 40%	
Deferred tax liability -- 12/31/Yr 3 balance	**$ 6,000**	
Tax basis of the machine on 12/31/Yr 4	$ 0	($100,000 cost – $100,000 accum. dep.)
Carrying amount (GAAP basis) on 12/31/Yr 4	– 0	($100,000 cost – $100,000 accum. dep.)
Difference	$ 0	
Tax rate	× 40%	
Deferred tax liability -- 12/31/Yr 4 balance	**$ 0**	

<u>Journal entry -- 12/31/Yr 1</u>

Income tax expense -- current	$12,000	
Income tax expense -- deferred	14,000	
Income tax payable		$12,000
Deferred tax liability		14,000

<u>Journal entry -- 12/31/Yr 2</u>

Income tax expense -- current	$28,000	
Deferred tax liability ($14,000 – $12,000)	2,000	
Income tax payable		$28,000
Income tax expense -- deferred		2,000

<u>Journal entry -- 12/31/Yr 3</u>

Income tax expense -- current	$32,000	
Deferred tax liability ($12,000 – $6,000)	6,000	
Income tax payable		$32,000
Income tax expense -- deferred		6,000

<u>Journal entry -- 12/31/Yr 4</u>

Income tax expense -- current	$32,000	
Deferred tax liability ($6,000 – $0)	6,000	
Income tax payable		$32,000
Income tax expense -- deferred		6,000

NOTE: Given no permanent differences, the total income tax expense recognized each year in the financial statements is $26,000. It equals income before taxes of $65,000 ($90,000 – $25,000) times the tax rate of 40%.

3. **Deferred Tax Assets (DTAs) and Future Deductible Amounts**

   a. DTAs result when **revenues or gains** are included in taxable income before they are recognized under GAAP.

      1) Examples are unearned revenues such as rent and subscriptions received in advance.

DTA = Future deductible amount × Enacted tax rate

EXAMPLE 10-9 DTA Due to Temporary Differences in Revenue

On January 1, Year 1, Shunia Co. sold 4-year subscriptions to its industry journal for $40,000 in cash. In its financial statements, it will recognize annual revenue of $10,000 from these subscriptions on the straight-line basis. For tax purposes, revenue is recognized when the payment is received. Thus, $40,000 of taxable revenue was recognized in Year 1. The tax rate for these years is 40%.

The Year 1 excess of taxable income over GAAP (financial statement) income of $30,000 ($40,000 – $10,000) will be reversed in Years 2-4. The result will be future deductible amounts.

Future deductible amount in Year 2: $10,000 GAAP – $0 taxes	$10,000
Future deductible amount in Year 3: $10,000 GAAP – $0 taxes	10,000
Future deductible amount in Year 4: $10,000 GAAP – $0 taxes	10,000
Total future deductible amount	$30,000
Enacted tax rate	× 40%
Deferred tax asset 12/31/Year 1	**$12,000**

-- Continued on next page --

EXAMPLE 10-9 -- Continued

In addition to subscription revenue, reported annual revenue net of expenses from other activities was $100,000 for Years 1-4.

Taxable Income	Income Tax Payable
Year 1: $140,000 ($100,000 + $40,000)	Year 1: $56,000 ($140,000 × 40%)
Year 2: $100,000	Year 2: $40,000 ($100,000 × 40%)
Year 3: $100,000	Year 3: $40,000 ($100,000 × 40%)
Year 4: $100,000	Year 4: $40,000 ($100,000 × 40%)

Tax basis of unearned revenue (liability) on 12/31/Yr 1	$ 0	
Carrying amount of unearned revenue on 12/31/Yr 1	– (30,000)	($40,000 – $10,000)
Difference	$ 30,000	
Tax rate	× 40%	
Deferred tax asset -- 12/31/Yr 1 balance	**$ 12,000**	

Tax basis of unearned revenue (liability) on 12/31/Yr 2	$ 0	
Carrying amount of unearned revenue on 12/31/Yr 2	– (20,000)	($40,000 – $20,000)
Difference	$ 20,000	
Tax rate	× 40%	
Deferred tax asset -- 12/31/Yr 2 balance	**$ 8,000**	

Tax basis of unearned revenue (liability) on 12/31/Yr 3	$ 0	
Carrying amount of unearned revenue on 12/31/Yr 3	– (10,000)	($40,000 – $30,000)
Difference	$ 10,000	
Tax rate	× 40%	
Deferred tax asset -- 12/31/Yr 3 balance	**$ 4,000**	

Tax basis of unearned revenue (liability) on 12/31/Yr 4	$ 0	
Carrying amount of unearned revenue on 12/31/Yr 4	– 0	($40,000 – $40,000)
Difference	$ 0	
Tax rate	× 40%	
Deferred tax asset -- 12/31/Yr 4 balance	**$ 0**	

<u>Journal entry -- 12/31/Yr 1</u>

	Debit	Credit
Income tax expense -- current	$56,000	
Deferred tax asset	12,000	
Income tax payable		$56,000
Income tax expense -- deferred		12,000

<u>Journal entry -- 12/31/Yr 2</u>

	Debit	Credit
Income tax expense -- current	$40,000	
Income tax expense -- deferred	4,000	
Income tax payable		$40,000
Deferred tax asset ($12,000 – $8,000)		4,000

<u>Journal entry -- 12/31/Yr 3</u>

	Debit	Credit
Income tax expense -- current	$40,000	
Income tax expense -- deferred	4,000	
Income tax payable		$40,000
Deferred tax asset ($8,000 – $4,000)		4,000

<u>Journal entry -- 12/31/Yr 4</u>

	Debit	Credit
Income tax expense -- current	$40,000	
Income tax expense -- deferred	4,000	
Income tax payable		$40,000
Deferred tax asset ($4,000 – $0)		4,000

NOTE: Given no permanent differences, the total annual income tax expense recognized in the financial statements is $44,000. It equals income before taxes of $110,000 ($10,000 revenue from subscriptions + $100,000 other net revenue) times the tax rate of 40%.

b. DTAs also result when **expenses or losses** are recognized under GAAP before they are deductible for tax purposes. Examples include the following:

1) Credit loss expense recognized under the allowance method
2) Warranty costs
3) Startup and organizational costs

EXAMPLE 10-10 DTA Due to Temporary Differences in Expenses

In Year 1, Luxor accrued $70,000 of warranty costs for financial reporting purposes. From past experience, it expects these costs to be incurred in Years 2 through 5 as follows: $5,000, $15,000, $40,000, $10,000. For tax purposes, warranty costs are expensed as incurred.

Year 1 excess of taxable income over GAAP income	$ 70,000
Future deductible amount in Year 2	$ 5,000
Future deductible amount in Year 3	15,000
Future deductible amount in Year 4	40,000
Future deductible amount in Year 5	10,000
Total future deductible amount	$ 70,000
Enacted tax rate	× 40%
Deferred tax asset -- 12/31/Year 1	**$ 28,000**
Tax basis of warranty liability on 12/31/Year 1	$ 0
Carrying amount of warranty liability on 12/31/Year 1	– (70,000)
Difference	$ 70,000
Tax rate	× 40%
Deferred tax asset -- 12/31/Year 1 balance	**$ 28,000**

4. **Permanent Differences -- No Deferred Tax Consequences**

a. Permanent differences are never reversed. Therefore, they have no deferred tax consequences.

b. One category of permanent differences consists of income items included in **net income** but not taxable income. Examples include the following:

1) State and municipal bond interest
2) Proceeds from life insurance on key employees

c. Another category of permanent differences consists of items subtracted in calculating net income but **not taxable income**. Examples include the following:

1) Premiums paid for life insurance on key employees
2) Fines resulting from a violation of law

d. A third category of permanent differences consists of items subtracted in calculating taxable income but not net income. Examples include the following:

1) Percentage depletion of natural resources
2) The dividends-received deduction

5. **Valuation Allowance**

a. A valuation allowance reduces a **deferred tax asset**. It is recognized if it is **more likely than not** (probability > 50%) that some portion of the deferred tax asset will not be realized. The allowance should reduce the deferred tax asset to the amount that is more likely than not to be realized.

Income tax expense	$XXX	
Deferred tax asset -- valuation allowance		$XXX

1) A new judgment about realizability may require a change in the beginning balance. This revision ordinarily is an item of **income from continuing operations**.

IFRS DIFFERENCE

A deferred tax asset is recognized for most deductible TDs and for the carryforward of unused tax losses and credits, but only to the extent it is probable that taxable profit will be available. Thus, no valuation allowance is recognized.

STOP & REVIEW

You have completed the outline for this subunit.
Study multiple-choice questions 12 and 13 on page 317.

10.8 INCOME TAX ACCOUNTING -- APPLICABLE TAX RATE

1. **Applicable Tax Rates**

   a. A deferred tax amount is measured using the **enacted tax rate(s)** expected to apply when the liability or asset is expected to be settled or realized. In the U.S., the **applicable tax rate** is the **regular rate**.

EXAMPLE 10-11 Enacted Tax Rates

Using the data from Example 10-7 on page 300, assume that the enacted tax rates are 40% for Year 1, 35% for Year 2 through Year 4, and 30% for Year 5. Luxor Corp. calculates the December 31, Year 1, deferred tax liability (DTL) based on the enacted tax rates in effect when the temporary difference reverses.

	Future taxable amount		Enacted tax rate		
Year 2	$300,000	×	35%	=	$105,000
Year 3	200,000	×	35%	=	70,000
Year 4	200,000	×	35%	=	70,000
Year 5	100,000	×	30%	=	30,000
Year 1 DTL					$275,000

2. **Enacted Changes in Law or Rates**

   a. Such changes require an adjustment of a deferred tax amount in the period of the enactment. The effect is included in the amount of income tax expense or benefit allocated to continuing operations.

STOP & REVIEW

You have completed the outline for this subunit.
Study multiple-choice questions 14 and 15 on page 318.

10.9 INCOME TAX ACCOUNTING -- RECOGNITION OF TAX EXPENSE

1. **Calculating Taxable Income**

   a. Taxable income (or excess of deductions over revenue) equals pretax accounting income (or loss) adjusted for permanent and temporary differences.

Pretax accounting income		$XXX,XXX
Temporary differences:		
Subtract revenues recognized first under GAAP:		
Accrual sales (installment method for tax)	$(X,XXX)	
Equity method income	(X,XXX)	
Gain on involuntary conversion	(X,XXX)	(XX,XXX)
Subtract expenses recognized first on tax return:		
Excess tax depreciation	$(X,XXX)	(XX,XXX)
Add revenues recognized first on tax return:		
Unearned revenues (subscriptions, rent, etc.)	$ X,XXX	XX,XXX
Add expenses recognized first under GAAP:		
Excess financial statement depreciation	$ X,XXX	
Warranty costs	X,XXX	
Startup and organizational costs	X,XXX	
Credit loss expense using allowance method (direct write-off for tax)	X,XXX	XXX,XXX
Permanent differences:		
Subtract GAAP revenues that are not taxed:		
State and municipal bond interest	$(X,XXX)	
Proceeds from key officer life insurance	(X,XXX)	$(XX,XXX)
Subtract deductible expenses not recognized under GAAP:		
Percentage depletion of natural resources	$(X,XXX)	
Dividends-received deduction	(X,XXX)	(XX,XXX)
Add GAAP expenses that are not deductible:		
Premiums on key officer life insurance	$ X,XXX	
Fines resulting from violation of law	X,XXX	XX,XXX
Taxable income		$XXX,XXX

2. **Calculating Tax Expense or Benefit**

   a. Income tax expense or benefit reported on the income statement is the sum of the current component and the deferred component.

      1) **Current tax expense or benefit** is the amount of taxes paid or payable (or refundable) for the year based on the enacted tax law.

         Current tax expense or benefit:

         Taxable income (or excess of deductions over revenue) × Tax rate

      2) **Deferred tax expense or benefit** is the net change during the year in an entity's deferred tax amounts.

         Deferred tax expense or benefit:

         Changes in DTL balances ± Changes in DTA balances

3. **Basic Journal Entries**

   a. Current income tax expense is recorded as follows:

Income tax expense -- current	$XXX	
Income tax payable		$XXX

   b. Deferred income tax expense or benefit is recognized for the net change during the year in the deferred tax amounts (DTL and DTA) and recorded as follows:

<u>If the DTL balance increased during the year:</u>

Income tax expense -- deferred	$XXX	
Deferred tax liability		$XXX

<u>If the DTL balance decreased during the year:</u>

Deferred tax liability	$XXX	
Income tax expense -- deferred		$XXX

<u>If the DTA balance increased during the year:</u>

Deferred tax asset	$XXX	
Income tax expense -- deferred		$XXX

<u>If the DTA balance decreased during the year:</u>

Income tax expense -- deferred	$XXX	
Deferred tax asset		$XXX

   c. In the income statement, one line item is generally reported for the total amount of income tax expense or benefit (Current + Deferred) recognized for the period.

      1) The amounts of current income tax expense (or benefit) and deferred income tax expense (or benefit) are disclosed in the notes.

EXAMPLE 10-12 Effects of Changes in Deferred Tax Amounts

Lucas Company had the following deferred tax balances for the year just ended. The deferred tax asset is fully realizable. The company's taxable income was $1,000,000 for the year. The enacted tax rate is 40%.

	Beginning Balance	Ending Balance
Deferred tax asset	$ 9,000	$17,000
Deferred tax liability	13,000	23,000

Lucas calculates income tax expense for the year as follows:

- Current tax expense is $400,000 ($1,000,000 × 40%).
- Deferred tax expense is the net change in the deferred tax liability and asset balances for the year. The DTL balance increased by $10,000 ($23,000 – $13,000), and the DTA balance increased by $8,000 ($17,000 – $9,000). Thus, the net DTL increase is $2,000 ($10,000 – $8,000).

Lucas records the following entry:

Income tax expense -- current	$400,000	
Income tax expense -- deferred	2,000	
Deferred tax asset	8,000	
Income tax payable		$400,000
Deferred tax liability		10,000

STOP & REVIEW

You have completed the outline for this subunit.
Study multiple-choice questions 16 through 18 on page 319.

10.10 INCOME TAX ACCOUNTING -- OTHER ISSUES

1. **Net Operating Losses**

   a. Based on the CARES Act, depending on the year in which the net operating loss (NOL) arose, entities have several options for obtaining the tax benefit of the loss. For example,

      1) Carry forward the loss indefinitely or
      2) Carry the loss back 5 years and forward an unlimited number of years.

> **SUCCESS TIP**
>
> On the CPA Exam, the entity's option regarding NOLs will be indicated in the question.

   b. **Initial recognition of NOL carryforward**

      1) Carryforwards are deductions or credits that may be carried forward to reduce taxable income or taxes payable in a future year.

      2) A carryforward results in a **future deductible amount**, requiring recognition of a **deferred tax asset**.

      3) The journal entry is

Deferred tax asset	$XXX	
Income tax benefit from loss carryforward		$XXX

EXAMPLE 10-13 DTA Due to NOL Carryforward

Gaby Corp. incurred a $100,000 net operating loss in Year 1. The company determined that it is more likely than not that the full benefit of any loss carryforward will be realized. The tax rate is 21%, resulting in a tax benefit of $21,000 ($100,000 × 21%).

The company records the following journal entry:

Deferred tax asset	$21,000	
Income tax benefit from loss carryforward		$21,000

   c. **Realization of NOL carryforward**

      1) The amount of the NOL carryforward is **realized** in future periods by reducing the taxable income for these periods.

      2) Upon realization, the deferred tax asset reduces the amount of income tax payable in future periods and does not affect the total amount of income tax expense recognized.

EXAMPLE 10-14 Realization of NOL

Using the data from Example 10-13, assume that Gaby's taxable income in Year 2 was $240,000. The entire NOL carryforward from Year 1 of $100,000 is realized in Year 2. Thus, the Year 2 taxable income after realization of the NOL carryforward is $140,000 ($240,000 – $100,000). Year 2 current income tax expense is $29,400 ($140,000 × 21%). Year 2 deferred income tax expense is $21,000 (realization of deferred tax asset).

The company records the following journal entry:

Income tax expense -- current	$29,400	
Income tax expense -- deferred	21,000	
Income tax payable		$29,400
Deferred tax asset		21,000

NOTE: The total income tax expense in Year 2 is $50,400 ($29,400 + $21,000). This amount equals taxable income before realization of the NOL carryforward times the tax rate ($240,000 × 21% = $50,400).

d. **Carryback of NOLs**

1) If NOLs are carried back, the entity files an amended tax return that carries the loss back, offsetting some or all of that year's tax expense. The journal entry is

Income tax refund receivable (tax offset by carryback)	$XXX	
Income tax benefit from loss carryback		$XXX

2) Any current-year loss that remains after the 5-year carryback will be carried forward, resulting in recognition of a deferred tax asset.

EXAMPLE 10-15 Carryback of NOLs

Peace Company incurred a $500,000 net operating loss in Year 6. The tax rate for all years is 21%. The current-year tax benefit available for offsetting is $105,000 ($500,000 × 21%). The company has the following historical income tax information:

	Taxable Income		Tax Rate		Income Tax Paid
Year 1	$120,000	×	21%	=	$25,200
Year 2	50,000	×	21%	=	10,500
Year 3	100,000	×	21%	=	21,000
Year 4	40,000	×	21%	=	8,400
Year 5	60,000	×	21%	=	12,600
	$370,000				$77,700

Peace has elected to carry the loss back 5 years. The company determined that it is more likely than not that the full benefit of any loss carryforward will be realized. The company records the following journal entries:

Income tax receivable from carrying the NOL back 5 years:		
Income tax refund receivable	$77,700	
Income tax benefit from loss carryback		$77,700
Deferred tax asset for carrying the remaining loss forward:		
Deferred tax asset ($105,000 – $77,700)	$27,300	
Income tax benefit from loss carryforward		$27,300

2. **Financial Statement Presentation of Deferred Tax Amounts**
   a. In the statement of financial position, deferred tax liabilities and assets are classified as **noncurrent** amounts.
   b. Deferred tax liabilities and assets and any related valuation allowance are **netted** and presented as a single noncurrent amount.
      1) However, deferred tax amounts attributable to different tax jurisdictions must not be netted.
3. **Disclosures**
   a. The following are some of the required disclosures:
      1) Total deferred tax liabilities and total deferred tax assets
      2) Total DTA valuation allowance and the net annual change in it
      3) The significant components of income tax expense related to continuing operations
   b. No disclosures about permanent differences are required.
   c. The current income tax expense (or benefit) and deferred income tax expense (or benefit) recognized for the period must be disclosed in the financial statements or in the notes.
4. **Accounting for Uncertainty in Income Taxes**
   a. A **tax position** is one taken or to be taken in a **tax return**. It is reflected in financial statement measurements of tax assets and liabilities, whether current or deferred.
      1) For example, tax positions may include
         a) Decisions not to file,
         b) Income exclusions,
         c) Transaction exemptions,
         d) Income characterizations, or
         e) Shifts of income among jurisdictions.
   b. The evaluation of a tax position is a two-stage procedure:
      1) **Recognition threshold.** The financial statement effects are initially recognized if it is **more likely than not** (probability > 50%) that the position will be sustained upon examination based on its technical merits. It also may be recognized if **effective settlement** has occurred.
      2) **Measurement.** The entity recognizes the largest benefit that is **more than 50% likely** to be realized.
   c. Applying this guidance may result in recognition of a tax benefit different from the amount in the current tax return. Thus, **unrecognized tax benefits** are differences between a tax position in a tax return and the benefits recognized under GAAP.
      1) The result is a **contingent liability** (or reduction of a loss carryforward or refund). This result reflects the entity's possible future tax obligation because of a tax position not recognized in the financial statements.
      2) The entity ordinarily recognizes one or both of the following:
         a) An increased liability for taxes payable or a reduced refund receivable
         b) A decreased deferred tax asset or increased deferred tax liability
      3) A tax position recognized under this guidance may affect the **tax bases** of assets or liabilities and change (or create) **temporary differences**.

EXAMPLE 10-16 Uncertain Tax Position

In Year 1, Luxor Corp. took a deduction on its tax return for $15,000. The effective tax rate was 40%, resulting in a tax benefit of $6,000. Luxor believes that it is more likely than not that this deduction will be sustained upon examination. However, Luxor prefers not to litigate the matter and would accept a settlement offer. Luxor has considered the amounts and probabilities of the possible estimated outcomes as follows:

Possible Estimated Outcome	Individual Probability of Occurring (%)	Cumulative Probability of Occurring (%)
$6,000	5	5
5,000	25	30
4,000	25	55
3,000	20	75
2,000	10	85
1,000	10	95
0	5	100

Because $4,000 is the largest benefit that is more likely than not (probability > 50%) to be realized upon settlement, the entity recognizes a tax benefit of $4,000 in the financial statements.

STOP & REVIEW

You have completed the outline for this subunit.
Study multiple-choice questions 19 and 20 on page 320.

QUESTIONS

10.1 Accounts Payable

1. Lyle, Inc., is preparing its financial statements for the year ended December 31, Year 3. Accounts payable amounted to $360,000 before any necessary year-end adjustment related to the following:

- At December 31, Year 3, Lyle has a $50,000 debit balance in its accounts payable to Ross, a supplier, resulting from a $50,000 advance payment for goods to be manufactured to Lyle's specifications.
- Checks in the amount of $100,000 were written to vendors and recorded on December 29, Year 3. The checks were mailed on January 5, Year 4.

What amount should Lyle report as accounts payable in its December 31, Year 3, balance sheet?

A. $510,000

B. $410,000

C. $310,000

D. $210,000

Answer (A) is correct.

REQUIRED: The amount of accounts payable reported after year-end adjustments.

DISCUSSION: The ending accounts payable balance should include amounts owed as of December 31, Year 3, on trade payables. Although Lyle wrote checks for $100,000 to various vendors, that amount should still be included in the accounts payable balance because the company had not surrendered control of the checks at year end. The advance to the supplier was erroneously recorded as a reduction of (debit to) accounts payable. This amount should be recorded as a prepaid asset, and accounts payable should be credited (increased) by $50,000. Thus, accounts payable should be reported as $510,000 ($360,000 + $50,000 + $100,000).

Answer (B) is incorrect. The amount of $410,000 does not include the $100,000 in checks not yet mailed at year end. **Answer (C) is incorrect.** The amount of $310,000 does not include the $100,000 in checks, and it reflects the subtraction, not the addition, of the $50,000 advance. **Answer (D) is incorrect.** The amount of $210,000 results from subtracting the advance payment and the checks.

10.2 Accrued Expenses

2. Ross Co. pays all salaried employees on a Monday for the 5-day workweek ended the previous Friday. The last payroll recorded for the year ended December 31, Year 4, was for the week ended December 25, Year 4. The payroll for the week ended January 1, Year 5, included regular weekly salaries of $80,000 and vacation pay of $25,000 for vacation time earned in Year 4 not taken by December 31, Year 4. Ross had accrued a liability of $20,000 for vacation pay at December 31, Year 3. In its December 31, Year 4, balance sheet, what amount should Ross report as accrued salary and vacation pay?

A. $64,000

B. $68,000

C. $69,000

D. $89,000

Answer (D) is correct.

REQUIRED: The accrued salary and vacation pay.

DISCUSSION: The salary accrual at December 31, Year 4, was for a 4-day period (December 28-31). Thus, the accrued salary (amount earned in Year 4 but not paid until Year 5) should be $64,000 [$80,000 in salaries for a 5-day week × (4 days ÷ 5 days)]. Vacation pay ($25,000) for time earned but not taken in Year 4 was not paid until Year 5. Hence, $25,000, not $20,000, should have been accrued at year end. The total accrual is $89,000 ($64,000 + $25,000).

Answer (A) is incorrect. The amount of $64,000 does not include vacation pay. **Answer (B) is incorrect.** The amount of $68,000 equals the accrued Year 4 salary for a 3-day, rather than a 4-day, period, and the erroneous deduction of $20,000 for accrued Year 4 vacation time. **Answer (C) is incorrect.** The amount of $69,000 results from erroneously deducting $20,000.

3. In its Year 4 financial statements, Cris Co. reported interest expense of $85,000 in its income statement and cash paid for interest of $68,000 in its cash flow statement. There was no prepaid interest or interest capitalization at either the beginning or the end of Year 4. Accrued interest at December 31, Year 3, was $15,000. What amount should Cris report as accrued interest payable in its December 31, Year 4, balance sheet?

A. $2,000

B. $15,000

C. $17,000

D. $32,000

Answer (D) is correct.

REQUIRED: The accrued interest payable at year end.

DISCUSSION: The cash paid for interest was $68,000, including $15,000 of interest paid for Year 3. Consequently, $53,000 ($68,000 – $15,000) of the cash paid for interest related to Year 4. Interest payable is therefore $32,000 ($85,000 – $53,000).

Answer (A) is incorrect. The amount of $2,000 results from adding the $15,000 to $68,000 and subtracting that sum from the $85,000 interest expense. **Answer (B) is incorrect.** The interest paid for Year 3 is $15,000. **Answer (C) is incorrect.** The difference between the interest expense and cash paid out is $17,000.

10.3 Certain Taxes Payable

4. Bloy Corp.'s payroll for the pay period ended October 31, Year 4, is summarized as follows:

Department Payroll	Total Wages	Federal Income Tax Withheld	Amount of Wages Subject to Payroll Taxes: FICA	Amount of Wages Subject to Payroll Taxes: Unemployment
Factory	$ 60,000	$ 7,000	$56,000	$18,000
Sales	22,000	3,000	16,000	2,000
Office	18,000	2,000	8,000	--
	$100,000	$12,000	$80,000	$20,000

Assume the following payroll tax rates:

FICA for employer and employee	7% each
Unemployment	3%

What amount should Bloy accrue as its share of payroll taxes in its October 31, Year 4, balance sheet?

A. $18,200

B. $12,600

C. $11,800

D. $6,200

Answer (D) is correct.

REQUIRED: The amount to be accrued for payroll taxes.

DISCUSSION: The amount of wages subject to payroll taxes for FICA purposes is $80,000. At a 7% rate, the employer's share of FICA taxes equals $5,600 ($80,000 × 7%). Wages subject to unemployment payroll taxes are $20,000. At a 3% rate, unemployment payroll taxes equal $600 ($20,000 × 3%). Consequently, the total of payroll taxes is $6,200 ($5,600 + $600). A 7% employee rate also applies to the wages subject to FICA taxes. This amount ($80,000 × 7% = $5,600) should be withheld from the employee's wages and remitted directly to the federal government by the employer, along with the $6,200 in employer payroll taxes. The employee's share, however, should be accrued as a withholding tax (an employee payroll deduction) and not as an employer payroll tax.

Answer (A) is incorrect. The amount of $18,200 includes the federal income tax withheld. **Answer (B) is incorrect.** The amount of $12,600 is the sum of the federal income tax withheld and the unemployment tax. **Answer (C) is incorrect.** The amount of $11,800 includes the FICA employee taxes.

5. Under state law, Acme may pay 3% of eligible gross wages or it may reimburse the state directly for actual unemployment claims. Acme believes that actual unemployment claims will be 2% of eligible gross wages and has chosen to reimburse the state. Eligible gross wages are defined as the first $10,000 of gross wages paid to each employee. Acme had five employees, each of whom earned $20,000 during Year 4. In its December 31, Year 4, balance sheet, what amount should Acme report as accrued liability for unemployment claims?

A. $1,000

B. $1,500

C. $2,000

D. $3,000

Answer (A) is correct.

REQUIRED: The accrued liability for unemployment claims.

DISCUSSION: A contingent liability should be accrued when it is probable that a liability has been incurred and the amount can be reasonably estimated. Thus, Acme should accrue a liability for $1,000 [(5 employees × $10,000) eligible wages × 2%].

Answer (B) is incorrect. The amount of $1,500 is based on a 3% rate. **Answer (C) is incorrect.** The amount of $2,000 is based on the total wages paid to the employees. **Answer (D) is incorrect.** The amount of $3,000 is based on a 3% rate and the total wages paid to the employees.

10.4 Deposits and Other Advances

6. Barnel Corp. owns and manages 19 apartment complexes. On signing a lease, each tenant must pay the first and last months' rent and a $500 refundable security deposit. The security deposits are rarely refunded in total because cleaning costs of $150 per apartment are almost always deducted. About 30% of the time, the tenants are also charged for damages to the apartment, which typically cost $100 to repair. If a 1-year lease is signed on a $900 per month apartment, what amount would Barnel report as refundable security deposit?

A. $1,400

B. $500

C. $350

D. $320

Answer (B) is correct.

REQUIRED: The amount of the refundable security deposit.

DISCUSSION: The refundable security deposit is a liability. It involves a probable future sacrifice of economic benefits arising from a current obligation of a particular entity to transfer assets or provide services to another entity in the future as a result of a past transaction. The reported amount of the liability for the refundable security deposit ($500) is the probable future sacrifice of economic benefits. It may be in the form of (1) a $500 refund or (2) the sum of an estimated $320 refund, $150 of cleaning costs, and $30 of damages.

Answer (A) is incorrect. The amount of $1,400 equals the deposit plus the last month's rent, an amount that is not refundable. **Answer (C) is incorrect.** The amount of $350 does not reflect the expected value of cleaning costs. **Answer (D) is incorrect.** The amount of $320 does not reflect the expected value of cleaning costs or damages.

7. Marr Co. sells its products in reusable containers. The customer is charged a deposit for each container delivered and receives a refund for each container returned within 2 years after the year of delivery. Marr accounts for the containers not returned within the time limit as being retired by sale at the deposit amount. The information for Year 4 is as follows:

Container deposits at December 31, Year 3, from deliveries in

Year 2	$150,000	
Year 3	430,000	$580,000

Deposits for containers delivered in Year 4 $780,000

Deposits for containers returned in Year 4 from deliveries in

Year 2	$ 90,000	
Year 3	250,000	
Year 4	286,000	$626,000

In Marr's December 31, Year 4, balance sheet, the liability for deposits on returnable containers should be

A. $494,000

B. $584,000

C. $674,000

D. $734,000

Answer (C) is correct.

REQUIRED: The liability for deposits on returnable containers at year end.

DISCUSSION: At the beginning of Year 4, the contract liability for deposits on returnable containers is given as $580,000. This liability is increased by the $780,000 attributable to containers delivered in Year 4. The liability is decreased by the $626,000 attributable to containers returned in Year 4. Moreover, the 2-year refund period for Year 2 deliveries has expired. Accordingly, the liability should also be decreased for $60,000 ($150,000 – $90,000) worth of containers deemed to be retired. As indicated below, the liability for returnable containers at December 31, Year 4, is $674,000.

Deposits on Returnable Containers

Containers returned	$626,000	$580,000	12/31/Yr 3
Year 2 retired	60,000	780,000	Year 4 Containers delivered
		$674,000	12/31/Yr 4

Answer (A) is incorrect. The amount of $494,000 is the difference between total deposits for containers delivered in Year 4 and Year 4 deposits returned. **Answer (B) is incorrect.** The amount of $584,000 assumes that all Year 2 containers were retired. **Answer (D) is incorrect.** The amount of $734,000 omits the Year 2 containers retired by sale from the calculation.

8. Dunn Trading Stamp Company records stamp service revenue and provides for the cost of redemptions in the year stamps are sold to licensees. Dunn's past experience indicates that only 80% of the stamps sold to licensees will be redeemed. Dunn's liability for stamp redemptions was $6 million at December 31, Year 3. Additional information for Year 4 is as follows:

Stamp service revenue from stamps sold to licensees	$4,000,000
Cost of redemptions (stamps sold prior to 1/1/Yr 4)	2,750,000

If all the stamps sold in Year 4 were presented for redemption in Year 5, the redemption cost would be $2,250,000. What amount should Dunn report as a liability for stamp redemptions at December 31, Year 4?

A. $7,250,000

B. $5,500,000

C. $5,050,000

D. $3,250,000

Answer (C) is correct.

REQUIRED: The reported liability for stamp redemptions at year end.

DISCUSSION: The liability for stamp redemptions at the beginning of Year 4 is given as $6 million. This liability would be increased in Year 4 by $2,250,000 if all stamps sold in Year 4 were presented for redemption. However, because only 80% are expected to be redeemed, the liability should be increased by $1,800,000 ($2,250,000 × 80%). The liability was decreased by the $2,750,000 attributable to the costs of redemptions. Thus, the liability for stamp redemptions at December 31, Year 4, is $5,050,000 ($6,000,000 + $1,800,000 – $2,750,000).

Answer (A) is incorrect. The amount of $7,250,000 equals the beginning balance, plus stamp service revenue, minus redemptions of stamps sold before Year 4. **Answer (B) is incorrect.** The amount of $5,500,000 is based on an expected 100% redemption rate. **Answer (D) is incorrect.** The amount of $3,250,000 assumes that no stamps were sold in Year 4.

10.5 Warranties

9. Vadis Co. sells appliances that include a standard 3-year assurance-type warranty. Service calls under the warranty are performed by an independent mechanic under a contract with Vadis. Based on experience, warranty costs are estimated at $30 for each machine sold. When should Vadis recognize these warranty costs?

A. Evenly over the life of the warranty.

B. When the service calls are performed.

C. When payments are made to the mechanic.

D. When the machines are sold.

Answer (D) is correct.

REQUIRED: The recording of warranty costs.

DISCUSSION: An assurance-type warranty creates a loss contingency. Under the accrual method, a provision for warranty costs is made when the related revenue is recognized.

Answer (A) is incorrect. The accrual method matches the costs and the related revenues. **Answer (B) is incorrect.** When the warranty costs can be reasonably estimated, the accrual method should be used. Recognizing the costs when the service calls are performed is the cash basis. **Answer (C) is incorrect.** Recognizing costs when paid is the cash basis.

10. During Year 3, Rex Co. introduced a new product carrying a 2-year warranty against defects. The estimated warranty costs related to dollar sales are 2% within 12 months following sale and 4% in the second 12 months following sale. Sales and actual warranty expenditures for the years ended December 31, Year 3 and Year 4, are as follows:

	Sales	Actual Warranty Expenditures
Year 3	$ 600,000	$ 9,000
Year 4	1,000,000	30,000
	$1,600,000	$39,000

At December 31, Year 4, Rex should report an estimated warranty liability of

A. $0

B. $39,000

C. $57,000

D. $96,000

Answer (C) is correct.

REQUIRED: The estimated warranty liability at the end of the second year.

DISCUSSION: An assurance-type warranty creates a loss contingency. Because this product is new, the beginning balance in the estimated warranty liability account at the beginning of Year 3 is $0. For Year 3, the estimated warranty costs related to dollar sales are 6% (2% + 4%) of sales or $36,000 ($600,000 × 6%). For Year 4, the estimated warranty costs are $60,000 ($1,000,000 sales × 6%). These amounts are charged to warranty expense and credited to the estimated warranty liability account. This liability account is debited for expenditures of $9,000 and $30,000 in Year 3 and Year 4, respectively. Thus, the estimated warranty liability at 12/31/Yr 4 is $57,000.

Estimated Warranty Liability

		$ 0	1/1/Yr 3
Year 3 expenditures	$ 9,000	36,000	Year 3 expense
Year 4 expenditures	30,000	60,000	Year 4 expense
		$57,000	12/31/Yr 4

Answer (A) is incorrect. All warranties have not expired. **Answer (B) is incorrect.** The total warranty expenditures to date equals $39,000. **Answer (D) is incorrect.** The total warranty expense to date equals $96,000.

10.6 Income Tax Accounting -- Overview

11. Temporary differences arise when expenses are deductible for tax purposes

	After They Are Recognized in Financial Income	Before They Are Recognized in Financial Income
A.	No	No
B.	No	Yes
C.	Yes	Yes
D.	Yes	No

Answer (C) is correct.

REQUIRED: The situations in which temporary differences arise.

DISCUSSION: A temporary difference exists when (1) the reported amount of an asset or liability in the financial statements differs from the tax basis of that asset or liability, and (2) the difference will result in taxable or deductible amounts in future years when the asset is recovered or the liability is settled at its reported amount. A temporary difference may also exist although it cannot be identified with a specific asset or liability recognized for financial reporting purposes. Temporary differences most commonly arise when either expenses or revenues are recognized for tax purposes either earlier or later than in the determination of financial income.

10.7 Income Tax Accounting -- Temporary and Permanent Differences

12. Orlean Co., a cash-basis taxpayer, prepares accrual-basis financial statements. In its current-year balance sheet, Orlean's deferred income tax liabilities increased compared with those reported for the prior year. Assume that, for tax purposes, expenditures are deducted when actually paid. Which of the following changes would cause this increase in deferred income tax liabilities?

I. An increase in prepaid insurance
II. An increase in rent receivable
III. An increase in warranty obligations

A. I only.

B. I and II only.

C. II and III only.

D. III only.

Answer (B) is correct.

REQUIRED: The change(s) causing an increase in deferred income tax liabilities.

DISCUSSION: An increase in prepaid insurance signifies the recognition of a deduction on the tax return of a cash-basis taxpayer but not in the accrual-basis financial statements. The result is a temporary difference giving rise to taxable amounts in future years when the reported amount of the asset is recovered. An increase in rent receivable involves recognition of revenue in the accrual-basis financial statements but not in the tax return of a cash-basis taxpayer. This temporary difference also will result in future taxable amounts when the asset is recovered. A deferred tax liability records the tax consequences of taxable temporary differences. Hence, these transactions increase deferred tax liabilities. An increase in warranty obligations is a noncash expense recognized in accrual-basis financial statements but not on a modified-cash-basis tax return. The result is a deductible temporary difference and an increase in a deferred tax asset.

13. West Corp. leased a building and received the $36,000 annual rental payment on June 15, Year 4. The lease was classified as an operating lease. The beginning of the lease was July 1, Year 4. Rental income is taxable when received. West's tax rates are 30% for Year 4 and 40% thereafter. West had no other permanent or temporary differences. West determined that no valuation allowance was needed. What amount of deferred tax asset should West report in its December 31, Year 4, balance sheet?

A. $5,400

B. $7,200

C. $10,800

D. $14,400

Answer (B) is correct.

REQUIRED: The amount of deferred tax asset reported at year end.

DISCUSSION: The $36,000 rental payment is taxable in full when received in Year 4, but only $18,000 [$36,000 × (6 ÷ 12)] should be recognized in financial accounting income for the year. The result is a deductible temporary difference (deferred tax asset) arising from the difference between the tax basis ($0) of the liability for unearned rent and its reported amount in the year-end balance sheet ($36,000 – $18,000 = $18,000). The income tax payable for Year 4 based on the rental payment is $10,800 ($36,000 × 30% tax rate for Year 4), the deferred tax asset is $7,200 ($18,000 future deductible amount × 40% enacted tax rate applicable after Year 4 when the asset will be realized), and the income tax expense is $3,600 ($10,800 current tax expense – $7,200 deferred tax benefit). The deferred tax benefit equals the net change during the year in the entity's deferred tax liabilities and assets ($7,200 deferred tax asset recognized in Year 4 – $0).

Answer (A) is incorrect. The amount of $5,400 is based on a 30% tax rate. **Answer (C) is incorrect.** The income tax payable is $10,800. **Answer (D) is incorrect.** The amount of $14,400 would be the income tax payable if the 40% tax rate applied in Year 4.

10.8 Income Tax Accounting -- Applicable Tax Rate

14. Scott Corp. received cash of $20,000 that was included in revenues in its Year 1 financial statements, of which $12,000 will not be taxable until Year 2. Scott's enacted tax rate is 30% for Year 1, and 25% for Year 2. What amount should Scott report in its Year 1 balance sheet for deferred income tax liability?

A. $2,000

B. $2,400

C. $3,000

D. $3,600

Answer (C) is correct.

REQUIRED: The amount reported for deferred income tax liability.

DISCUSSION: This transaction gives rise to a taxable temporary difference. The resulting deferred tax liability should be measured using the enacted rate expected to apply to taxable income in the period in which the deferred tax liability is expected to be settled. Hence, the deferred tax liability is $3,000 ($12,000 taxable amounts × 25% rate applicable in Year 2).

Answer (A) is incorrect. The amount of $2,000 is 25% of $8,000, the amount taxable in Year 2. **Answer (B) is incorrect.** The amount of $2,400 is 30% of $8,000, the amount taxable in Year 1. **Answer (D) is incorrect.** The amount of $3,600 results from applying a 30% tax rate.

15. As a result of differences between depreciation for financial reporting purposes and tax purposes, the financial reporting basis of Noor Co.'s sole depreciable asset acquired in the current year exceeded its tax basis by $250,000 at December 31. This difference will reverse in future years. The enacted tax rate is 30% for the current year and 40% for future years. Noor has no other temporary differences. In its December 31 balance sheet, how should Noor report the deferred tax effect of this difference?

A. As an asset of $75,000.

B. As an asset of $100,000.

C. As a liability of $75,000.

D. As a liability of $100,000.

Answer (D) is correct.

REQUIRED: The deferred tax effect of the difference between the financial reporting basis and the tax basis.

DISCUSSION: The temporary difference arises because the excess of the reported amount of the depreciable asset over its tax basis will result in taxable amounts in future years when the reported amount is recovered. A taxable temporary difference results in a deferred tax liability. Because the enacted tax rate for future years is 40%, the deferred income tax liability is $100,000 ($250,000 × 40%).

Answer (A) is incorrect. The deferred income tax effect should be calculated using the 40% rate, and it is a liability. **Answer (B) is incorrect.** The deferred income tax effect is a liability. The temporary difference results in taxable, not deductible, amounts. **Answer (C) is incorrect.** The amount of $75,000 is based on the current-year tax rate.

10.9 Income Tax Accounting -- Recognition of Tax Expense

16. In Year 2, Ajax, Inc., reported taxable income of $400,000 and pretax financial statement income of $300,000. The difference resulted from $60,000 of nondeductible premiums on Ajax's officers' life insurance and $40,000 of rental income received in advance. Rental income is taxable when received. Ajax's effective tax rate is 30%. In its Year 2 income statement, what amount should Ajax report as income tax expense -- current portion?

A. $90,000

B. $102,000

C. $108,000

D. $120,000

Answer (D) is correct.

REQUIRED: The current income tax expense given nondeductible insurance premiums and taxable rent received in advance.

DISCUSSION: Current income tax expense or benefit is the amount of taxes paid or payable (or refundable) for the year based on enacted tax law applied to taxable income (or excess of deductions over revenues). Thus, current income tax expense is $120,000 ($400,000 × 30%).

Answer (A) is incorrect. The amount of $90,000 equals the effective tax rate times pretax financial statement income. **Answer (B) is incorrect.** The amount of $102,000 equals the effective tax rate times the excess of reported taxable income over the nondeductible insurance premiums. **Answer (C) is incorrect.** The amount of $108,000 equals the effective tax rate times the excess of reported taxable income over rent received in advance.

17. Quinn Co. reported a net deferred tax asset of $9,000 in its December 31, Year 1, balance sheet. For Year 2, Quinn reported pretax financial statement income of $300,000. Temporary differences of $100,000 resulted in taxable income of $200,000 for Year 2. At December 31, Year 2, Quinn had cumulative taxable temporary differences of $70,000. Quinn's effective income tax rate is 30%. In its December 31, Year 2, income statement, what should Quinn report as deferred income tax expense?

A. $12,000

B. $21,000

C. $30,000

D. $60,000

Answer (C) is correct.

REQUIRED: The deferred income tax expense.

DISCUSSION: Deferred tax expense or benefit is the net change during the year in the entity's deferred tax liabilities and assets. Quinn had a net deferred tax asset of $9,000 at the beginning of Year 2 and a net deferred tax liability of $21,000 ($70,000 × 30%) at the end of Year 2. The net change (a deferred tax expense in this case) is $30,000 ($9,000 reduction in the deferred tax asset + $21,000 increase in deferred tax liabilities).

Answer (A) is incorrect. The amount of $12,000 results from offsetting the deferred tax liability and the deferred tax asset. **Answer (B) is incorrect.** The deferred tax liability is $21,000. **Answer (D) is incorrect.** The amount of $60,000 is the current income tax expense for the year ($200,000 × 30%).

18. In its Year 4 income statement, Cere Co. reported income before income taxes of $300,000. Cere estimated that, because of permanent differences, taxable income for Year 4 would be $280,000. During Year 4, Cere made estimated tax payments of $50,000, which were debited to income tax expense. Cere is subject to a 30% tax rate. What amount should Cere report as income tax expense?

A. $34,000

B. $50,000

C. $84,000

D. $90,000

Answer (C) is correct.

REQUIRED: The amount to be reported for income tax expense.

DISCUSSION: A permanent difference does not result in a change in a deferred tax asset or liability, that is, in a deferred tax expense or benefit. Thus, total income tax expense equals current income tax expense, which is the amount of taxes paid or payable for the year. Income taxes payable for Year 4 equal $84,000 ($280,000 taxable income × 30%).

Answer (A) is incorrect. The amount of $34,000 equals the $84,000 of income taxes payable minus the $50,000 of income taxes paid. **Answer (B) is incorrect.** The amount of $50,000 equals income taxes paid, not the total current income tax expense. **Answer (D) is incorrect.** The amount of $90,000 is equal to the reported income of $300,000 times the tax rate.

10.10 Income Tax Accounting -- Other Issues

19. Brass Co. reported income before income tax expense of $60,000 for Year 2. Brass had no permanent or temporary differences for tax purposes. Brass has an effective tax rate of 30% and a $40,000 net operating loss carryforward from Year 1. What is the maximum income tax benefit that Brass can realize from the loss carryforward for Year 2?

A. $12,000

B. $18,000

C. $20,000

D. $40,000

Answer (A) is correct.

REQUIRED: The maximum tax benefit from a loss carryforward.

DISCUSSION: The $60,000 reported income from Year 2 can absorb the entire $40,000 loss carryforward from Year 1. Thus, the tax benefit is $12,000 ($40,000 × 30% tax rate).

Answer (B) is incorrect. The tax liability before the net operating loss carryforward is $18,000 ($60,000 × 30%). **Answer (C) is incorrect.** Taxable income is $20,000 ($60,000 – $40,000 NOL). **Answer (D) is incorrect.** The available net operating loss carryforward is $40,000.

20. At the end of Year 4, the tax effects of Thorn Co.'s temporary differences were as follows:

	Deferred Tax Assets (Liabilities)
Accelerated tax depreciation	$(75,000)
Additional costs in inventory for tax purposes	25,000
	$(50,000)

A valuation allowance was not considered necessary. Thorn anticipates that $10,000 of the deferred tax liability will reverse in Year 5. In Thorn's December 31, Year 4, balance sheet, what amount should Thorn report as noncurrent deferred tax liability?

A. $40,000

B. $50,000

C. $65,000

D. $75,000

Answer (B) is correct.

REQUIRED: The classification of deferred taxes on the balance sheet.

DISCUSSION: In the statement of financial position, deferred tax liabilities and assets are classified as noncurrent amounts. In addition, deferred tax liabilities and assets and any related valuation allowance are netted and presented as a single noncurrent amount. Thus, in Thorn's balance sheet, the deferred tax liability of $50,000 ($75,000 – $25,000) must be classified as noncurrent.

Answer (A) is incorrect. Deferred tax liabilities and assets and any related valuation allowance are netted and presented as a single noncurrent amount. **Answer (C) is incorrect.** Deferred tax liabilities and assets and any related valuation allowance are netted and presented as a single noncurrent amount. **Answer (D) is incorrect.** Deferred tax liabilities and assets and any related valuation allowance are netted and presented as a single noncurrent amount.

GLEIM

GO TO ONLINE COURSE

Access the **Gleim CPA Premium Review System** featuring our SmartAdapt technology from your Gleim Personal Classroom to continue your studies. You will experience a personalized study environment with exam-emulating multiple-choice questions.

STUDY UNIT ELEVEN

EMPLOYEE BENEFITS

(22 pages of outline)

The beginning of this study unit emphasizes accounting for defined benefit pensions. Postretirement benefits other than pensions are accounted for similarly. The remainder of the study unit covers other forms of employee compensation.

11.1 TYPES OF PENSION PLANS

BACKGROUND 11-1 Historical Events Affecting Employee Benefits

The major victory for the defined benefit pension plan was the so-called Treaty of Detroit, agreed to in 1950 between the United Auto Workers union and the three largest American automobile manufacturers. Management discovered that it was much easier to promise money in the future (i.e., increased pension benefits) than to pay higher salaries today. As life expectancies increased, however, Americans' retirement periods lasted longer and longer, and increased foreign competition ended the Detroit automakers' historic profits. These changes have put tremendous pressure on traditional defined benefit plans.

A historic change occurred on January 1, 1980, when the 401(k) account became available to all employees. Under this provision, workers could set aside pretax income and choose their own investments. However, many defined benefit plans that were entered into during years of prosperity are still in force. Current guidance is in FASB ASC 715.

1. **Overview**
   a. A **pension plan** is a **separate accounting entity** to which a sponsoring employer makes contributions. It invests the assets and makes payments to beneficiaries (but the assets and liabilities are the employer's).

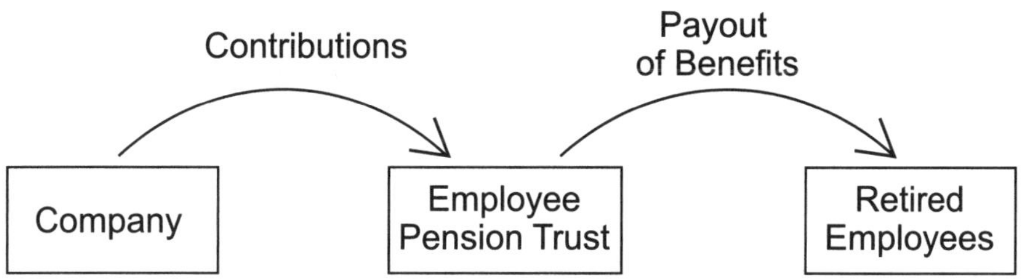

Figure 11-1

   b. The two basic types of pension plans are defined contribution plans and defined benefit plans.

2. **Defined Contribution Plan**

   a. A defined contribution plan provides an individual account for each participating employee. Benefits depend only on (1) the amount contributed to the plan by the employer and the employee and (2) the returns earned on investments of those contributions. Thus, the employer does not guarantee the amount of benefits that the employees will receive during retirement.

   b. The employer's only obligation is to make periodic deposits of the amounts defined by the plan's formula in return for services rendered by employees. Accordingly, employees bear the investment risk (the benefit of gain or risk of loss from assets contributed to the plan). The accounting is relatively easy.

   c. The employer's **annual pension expense** is the amount of the contribution determined by the plan's formula.

      1) The employer reports an **asset** only if the contribution is greater than the defined required contribution.

      2) The employer reports a **liability** only if the contribution is less than the required amount.

EXAMPLE 11-1 Entries for a Defined Contribution Plan

According to the pension agreement of a defined contribution plan, an employer must contribute $100,000 to the plan each year. The following are the employer's journal entries for different contributions:

1) The employer deposits $100,000 in the pension plan.

Pension expense	$100,000	
Cash		$100,000

2) The employer deposits $110,000 in the pension plan.

Pension expense	$100,000	
Prepaid expenses	10,000	
Cash		$110,000

3) The employer deposits $90,000 in the pension plan.

Pension expense	$100,000	
Cash		$90,000
Pension payable		10,000

3. **Defined Benefit Plan**

   a. A defined benefit plan defines an amount of pension benefit to be provided to each employee. The employer is responsible for providing the agreed benefits and therefore bears actuarial risk and investment risk.

   b. The benefits that the employer is required to pay depend on future events, such as (1) how long an employee or any survivor lives, (2) how many years of service the employee renders, and (3) the employee's compensation before retirement. Many of these events cannot be controlled by the employer.

   c. The accounting is **complex**. The exact amounts of future payouts are unknown and can only be estimated by using actuarial assumptions.

      1) Each year, entities with defined benefit plans must recognize pension expense, the funding provided, and the funded status of the plan.

   d. The assumption is that a pension plan is part of an **employee's compensation** earned when his or her services are rendered.

STOP & REVIEW

You have completed the outline for this subunit.
Study multiple-choice questions 1 and 2 on page 343.

11.2 DEFINED BENEFIT PLAN -- COMPONENTS OF PENSION EXPENSE

1. **Projected Benefit Obligation (PBO)**
   a. The PBO at a certain date is the actuarial present value of all benefits attributed by the **pension benefit formula** to employee services rendered prior to that date.
      1) The **measurement date** for benefit obligations and plan assets is generally the **balance sheet date**.
      2) The **actuarial present value** reflects the time value of money (through discounts for interest) and the probability of occurrence of future events. Events that may affect the amount of benefits to be paid include death, withdrawal, changes in future compensation, disability, and retirement.
   b. Assumptions about **discount (interest) rates** must be made to calculate the PBO.
      1) They reflect the rates at which benefit obligations can be settled, e.g., current prices of annuity contracts and rates on high-quality fixed investments.
2. **Fair Value of Plan Assets**
   a. These assets are invested by a trustee. They are segregated and restricted, generally in a trust, to provide for pension benefits.
   b. Plan assets change as a result of
      1) The return on investments (decrease or increase plan assets)
      2) Benefit payments (decrease plan assets)
      3) Contributions from the employer (increase plan assets)
3. **Income Statement -- Pension Expense (Cost)**
   a. The **required minimum** periodic pension expense (cost) consists of the following elements:

      + Service cost
      + Interest cost
      – Expected return on plan assets
      ± Amortization of net gain or loss
      ± Amortization of prior service cost or credit
      Net periodic pension expense

      1) The following is the entry to record annual service cost, interest cost, and expected return on plan assets (assuming service cost and interest cost are unfunded and their sum is greater than the expected return):

Pension expense	$XXX	
Pension liability		$XXX

b. The **service cost** component of pension expense is the actuarial present value of benefits attributed by the pension benefit formula to services rendered by employees **during the current period**. It is calculated by the plan's actuary.

1) Service cost increases the PBO.

2) Service cost increases pension expense and is unaffected by the funded status of the plan.

c. The **interest cost** component of pension expense is the increase in the PBO resulting from the passage of time. It equals the PBO at the beginning of the period times the **assumed discount rate**.

1) Interest cost increases pension expense.

Beginning PBO × Discount rate = Interest cost

EXAMPLE 11-2 Interest Cost Component of Pension Expense

The beginning PBO is $100,000, and the discount rate is 4%. The interest cost component of current-year pension expense is $4,000 ($100,000 × 4%). It increases the PBO and is recognized in the income statement as a component of pension expense.

d. The **expected return on plan assets** component of pension expense is the **fair value** of plan assets at the beginning of the period multiplied by the **expected long-term rate of return**.

Expected return = Fair value × Long-term rate

1) The expected return on plan assets decreases pension expense.

e. **Amortization of the Net Gain or Loss Component of Pension Expense**

1) Gains and losses result from (a) experience different from that assumed or (b) changes in actuarial assumptions. They are changes in the value of either (a) the PBO (what actuaries call **liability gains and losses**) or (b) the plan assets **(asset gains and losses)**.

2) A **liability gain or loss** can be determined from the PBO equation to the right.

a) A liability loss for the period results from an unexpected increase in the PBO.

b) A liability gain for the period results from an unexpected decrease in the PBO.

Beginning PBO
\+ Service cost
\+ Interest cost
\+ Prior service cost
– Prior service credit
– Benefits paid
± Liability gain or loss
Ending PBO

EXAMPLE 11-3 Liability Gain or Loss

The following data relate to Entity A's Year 1 PBO:

PBO -- January 1, Year 1	$250,000
PBO -- December 31, Year 1	$400,000
Benefits paid (on December 30, Year 1)	$20,000
Discount rate	5%
Service cost recognized in Year 1	$35,000
Prior service cost recognized in Year 1	$67,500

-- Continued on next page --

EXAMPLE 11-3 -- Continued

The liability loss for Year 1 can be derived from the following Year 1 PBO equation:

January 1, Year 1, PBO	$250,000
Service cost	35,000
Interest cost ($250,000 × 5%)	12,500
Prior service cost	67,500
Benefits paid in Year 1	(20,000)
Liability loss	**55,000**
December 31, Year 1, PBO	$400,000

3) The **actual return on plan assets** for the period is the difference between the beginning and ending fair values of plan assets, adjusted for contributions to plan assets and benefits paid.

a) The actual return on plan assets can be determined from the following plan assets equation:

Beginning fair value of plan assets
\+ Contributions
– Benefits paid
± **Actual return on plan assets**
Ending fair value of plan assets

b) An **asset gain or loss** for the period is the difference between the actual return on plan assets and the expected return on plan assets. An **asset loss** occurs when the expected return on plan assets is greater than the actual return on plan assets. An **asset gain** occurs when the actual return on plan assets is greater than the expected return on plan assets.

i) Actual return > Expected return → Asset gain
ii) Actual return < Expected return → Asset loss

EXAMPLE 11-4 Asset Gain or Loss

The following data relate to Entity A's Year 1 plan assets:

Beginning fair value of plan assets	$150,000
Ending fair value of plan assets	$170,000
Benefit payments made at year end	$20,000
Expected long-term rate of return on plan assets	8%
Contributions to plan assets made at year end	$15,000

Fair value of plan assets -- beginning of period	$150,000
Contributions during the period	15,000
Benefits paid	(20,000)
Actual return on plan assets	**25,000**
Ending fair value of plan assets	$170,000

The expected return on plan assets is $12,000 ($150,000 × 8%).

The actual return on plan assets is greater than the expected return on plan assets. Thus, the **asset gain** is $13,000 ($25,000 – $12,000).

c) Using the results from Example 11-3 and Example 11-4, Entity A's Year 1 net loss is $42,000 ($55,000 liability loss – $13,000 asset gain).

IFRS DIFFERENCE

1. **Interest income on plan assets** for the period is a component of the return on plan assets. It is recognized in profit or loss. It equals the fair value of plan assets at the beginning of the year (adjusted for contributions and benefits paid during the year) times the **same rate** used to discount the defined benefit obligation. Under U.S. GAAP, different interest rates may be used to calculate interest cost and the expected return on plan assets.
2. The remeasurement of plan assets for the period is the return on plan assets, excluding the interest income on plan assets.

   The remeasurement of plan assets can be determined from the plan assets equation. The following is an example:

Beginning fair value of plan assets	$100,000
Contributions	20,000
Benefits paid	(15,000)
Interest income plan assets	6,000
Remeasurement of plan assets	**9,000**
Ending fair value of plan assets	$120,000

   Remeasurements of plan assets are recognized in OCI. They are **never reclassified to profit or loss**. This accounting treatment also applies to remeasurements of defined benefit obligation.

4) The total of asset and liability gains or losses is the net gain or loss. An entity may choose among **three methods of accounting for the net gain or loss**.

   a) Net gains or losses can be recognized immediately in the statement of income in the period in which they arise as a component of pension expense. This method is permitted if it is applied consistently to all gains and losses on plan assets and obligations.

   b) Under the **corridor method**, gains or losses are recognized initially in **other comprehensive income (OCI)**. They are amortized in subsequent periods as a component of net pension expense. The corridor method determines the **minimum required amortization** of net gain or loss included in accumulated OCI that must be **reclassified**.

      i) The corridor is measured based on amounts at the beginning of the year. It equals 10% of the greater of (a) the PBO or (b) the fair value of plan assets (FVPA). The amount of the net gain or loss **outside of the corridor** is subject to required amortization.

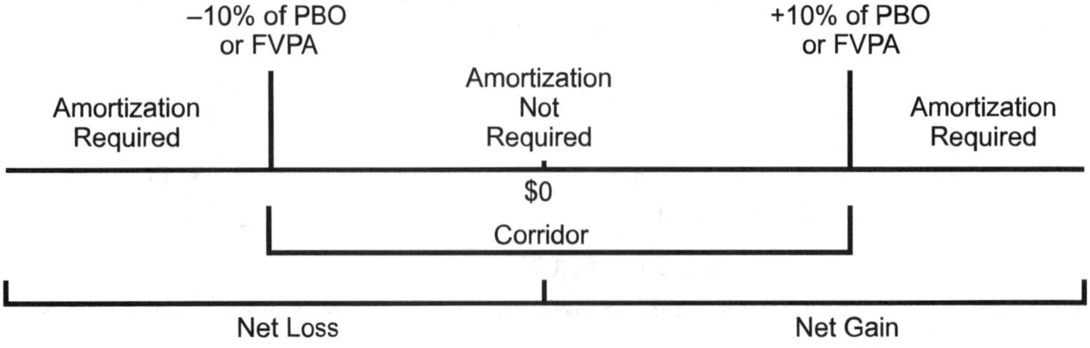

Figure 11-2

ii) The minimum required amortization equals the amount of the net gain or loss exceeding the corridor amount divided by the **average remaining service period** of active employees expected to receive benefits under the plan. E.g., the amortization of a net gain is calculated as follows:

$$\text{Amortization} = \frac{\text{Net gain} - [10\% \times (\text{Greater of PBO or FVPA})]}{\text{Average remaining service period}}$$

iii) The amortization of a **net gain** results in a decrease in pension expense. The following is the journal entry:

OCI	$XXX	
Pension expense		$XXX

iv) The amortization of a **net loss** results in an increase in pension expense. The following is the journal entry:

Pension expense	$XXX	
OCI		$XXX

EXAMPLE 11-5 Net Gain or Loss -- Corridor Method

The following data relate to Entity A's defined benefit pension plan:

	PBO	Fair Value of Plan Assets	Net Loss Included in Accumulated OCI
January 1, Year 1	$200,000	$180,000	$19,000
December 31, Year 1	260,000	240,000	
December 31, Year 2	250,000	245,000	

Entity A recognized a net loss of $21,000 in Year 1 and a net gain of $8,600 in Year 2. Entity A uses the corridor method of accounting for net gain or loss included in accumulated OCI. The average remaining service period for Years 1-3 is 10 years.

Year 1. No amortization of net loss included in accumulated OCI is required. The net loss at the beginning of the year ($19,000) is lower than the corridor amount of $20,000 ($200,000 × 10%).

Year 2. The beginning net loss included in accumulated OCI is $40,000 ($19,000 + $21,000). This exceeds the corridor amount of $26,000 ($260,000 × 10%). Required amortization of net loss in Year 2 is $1,400 [($40,000 – $26,000) ÷ 10]. This amount is reclassified from accumulated OCI to pension expense in Year 2.

Year 3. The beginning net loss included in accumulated OCI is $30,000 ($40,000 – $1,400 – $8,600). The corridor amount is $25,000 ($250,000 × 10%). Required amortization of net loss in Year 3 is $500 [($30,000 – $25,000) ÷ 10]. This amount is reclassified from accumulated OCI to pension expense.

c) Instead of the minimum amount calculated under the corridor method, any systematic method of amortizing net gains or losses included in accumulated OCI may be used if the following conditions are met:

i) The minimum amortization of net gain or loss is greater than the amount calculated under the corridor method.

ii) The method is applied consistently.

iii) The method is applied similarly to both gains and losses.

IFRS DIFFERENCE

Remeasurements of the net defined benefit liability (asset) are recognized in OCI. They are never reclassified to profit or loss in subsequent periods. Remeasurements include actuarial gains and losses. These are changes in the benefit obligation from

1) Adjustments for the differences between assumptions and actual results and
2) Changes in assumptions.

Remeasurements also include the remeasurement of plan assets. Accordingly, the corridor approach is not used.

f. **Amortization of the Prior Service Cost or Credit Component of Pension Expense**

1) **Prior service cost** is the cost of an amendment to (or initiation of) a pension plan that increases pension benefits granted to employees for services already rendered. It is a retroactive cost that increases the PBO.

   a) Prior service cost is recognized as a debit to OCI on the date of the plan amendment. OCI is a nominal account that is closed to accumulated OCI, a real account, at the end of the period.

   b) The journal entry on the amendment date is

Prior service cost -- OCI	$XXX	
Pension liability -- PBO		$XXX

2) The required **amortization of prior service cost** assigns an equal amount to each future period of service of each employee who is expected to receive benefits under the plan.

   a) The employer expects to realize economic benefits in future periods as a result of a plan amendment. Thus, prior service cost initially recognized in OCI must be allocated to future periods of service of employees active at the amendment date.

   b) The period for the amortization and reclassification of prior service cost from accumulated OCI to net pension expense begins on the date the prior service cost was initially recognized.

   c) The journal entry to amortize prior service cost is

Pension expense	$XXX	
Prior service cost -- OCI		$XXX

   d) To reduce the complexity and detail of the computations required, an employer may use an alternative approach that more rapidly amortizes prior service cost (e.g., straight-line amortization over the average remaining service period).

IFRS DIFFERENCE

Past service cost is recognized as **pension expense** at the earlier of when

1) The plan amendment or curtailment occurs or
2) An entity recognizes related restructuring costs or termination benefits.

Thus, past service cost is never included in OCI and never reclassified to profit or loss as it is amortized.

EXAMPLE 11-6 Prior Service Cost

On January 1, Year 1, Cannon Co. amended its defined benefit pension plan, resulting in an increase of $200,000 in the PBO. Cannon had 20 employees on the date of the amendment. Five employees are expected to leave at the end of each of the next 4 years (including the current year). Thus, the total service years expected to be rendered during the 4-year period equal 50 (20 + 15 + 10 + 5). The amortization fraction for the first year is therefore 20 ÷ 50. The minimum amortization equals the amount of the increase in the PBO multiplied by the amortization fraction. Accordingly, Cannon's minimum amortization of prior service cost for the first year is $80,000 [$200,000 × (20 ÷ 50)].

January 1, Year 1		
Prior service cost -- OCI	$200,000	
Pension liability -- PBO		$200,000
December 31, Year 1		
Pension expense	$80,000	
Prior service cost -- OCI		$80,000

3) **Prior service credit** is a plan amendment that **retroactively reduces benefits** and decreases the PBO. This decrease (prior service credit) is credited to OCI.
   a) First, it is used to reduce any prior service cost in accumulated OCI.
   b) Second, any remaining prior service credit is amortized as a component of pension expense on the same basis as prior service cost.
   c) Amortization of prior service credit decreases pension expense.

STOP & REVIEW

You have completed the outline for this subunit.
Study multiple-choice questions 3 and 4 on page 344.

11.3 DEFINED BENEFIT PLAN -- FUNDED STATUS OF PENSION PLANS

1. **Recognition of Funded Status**
   a. The statement of financial position must report the full under- or overfunded status of the pension plan as a liability or asset.
      1) OCI (presented in equity) must report unamortized gains or losses, prior service cost, and prior service credit.
   b. The funded status of a pension plan is the difference between the PBO and the fair value of plan assets at the reporting date.
      1) The **PBO** at the end of a period is calculated as follows:

+ Beginning PBO
+ Service cost
+ Interest cost
+ Prior service cost
– Prior service credit
– Benefits paid
± Changes in the PBO resulting from (a) experience different from that assumed (b) changes in assumptions
Ending PBO

      2) The **fair value of the plan assets** at the end of a period is calculated as follows:

+ Beginning fair value
+ Contributions
– Benefits paid
± Actual return on plan assets
Ending fair value

2. **Pension Liability or Asset**
   a. If the **pension is underfunded**, i.e., the PBO exceeds the fair value of the plan assets at the reporting date, the deficit must be recognized in the statement of financial position as a **liability**.

Pension liability = PBO – Fair value of plan assets

   b. If the **pension is overfunded**, i.e., the fair value of the plan assets at the reporting date exceeds the PBO, the excess must be recognized in the statement of financial position as an **asset**.

Pension asset = Fair value of plan assets – PBO

EXAMPLE 11-7 Funded Status of Pension Plan

On December 31, Year 1, Entity A determines the following information regarding its defined benefit plan:

PBO	$400,000
Fair value of plan assets	170,000

Entity A reports a $230,000 ($400,000 – $170,000) pension liability in its December 31, Year 1, financial statements.

Pension Accounting

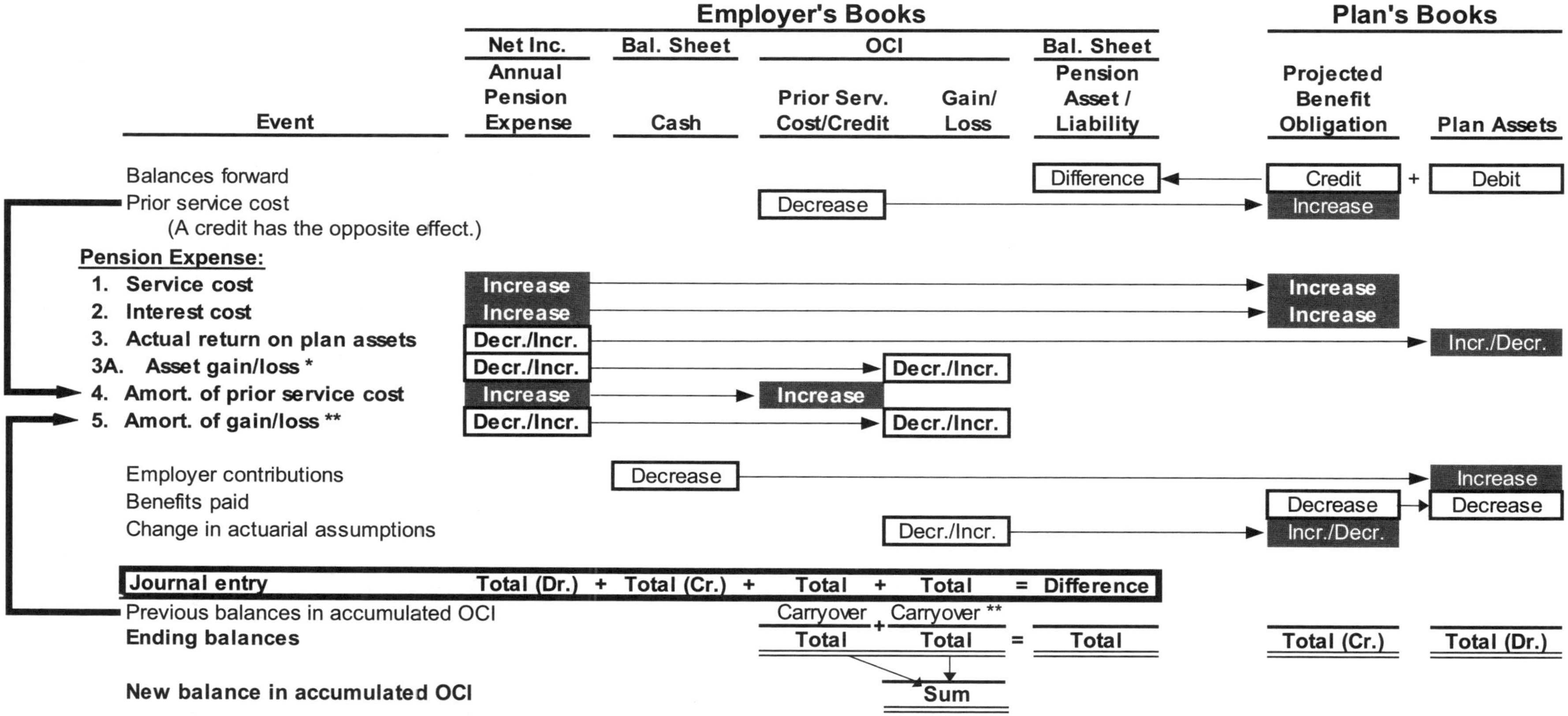

* The sum of items 3. and 3A. is the expected return on plan assets. Its use is allowed by the FASB for its smoothing effect.
Asset gain or loss = Actual return on plan assets – (Market-related value of plan assets × Expected rate of return)
= Actual return on plan assets – Expected return on plan assets

** Any carryover in accumulated OCI-G/L is tested for amortization. Assume 20-yr. avg. rem. serv. life and AOCI-G/L = $60,000

1. Begin. PBO	= $500,000	4. Corridor amount (10% of larger)	= $50,000
2. MRV of plan assets	= $400,000	5. Excess loss of AOCI-G/L balance over corridor amount	= $10,000 ($60,000 – $50,000)
3. Larger of above	= $500,000	6. Minimum amortization (excess G/L ÷ Avg. rem. serv. life)	= $500 ($10,000 ÷ 20 years)

Figure 11-3

c. An employer that sponsors multiple defined benefit plans must account for each plan separately and recognize (1) an asset for all overfunded plans and (2) a liability for all underfunded plans.

1) Generally, the asset and liability recognized must not be netted.

SUCCESS TIP

When testing candidates' knowledge of pensions, the AICPA has often presented questions requiring the determination of the pension's funded status amount through the calculations of both the projected benefit obligation and pension expense.

STOP & REVIEW

You have completed the outline for this subunit.
Study multiple-choice questions 5 through 8 beginning on page 345.

11.4 DISCLOSURES, PRESENTATION, AND OTHER ISSUES

1. **Required Disclosures**

a. An employer that sponsors one or more defined benefit plans must make certain disclosures. However, **nonpublic entities** are allowed to make reduced disclosures. Disclosure must be separate for pension plans and other postretirement plans, but amounts within each category are normally totaled. The following are among the required disclosures for **public entities**:

1) A **reconciliation of beginning and ending balances of the benefit obligation** (the PBO for defined benefit pension plans and the accumulated postretirement benefit obligation for other defined benefit postretirement plans)
2) A **reconciliation of beginning and ending balances of the fair value of plan assets**
3) The **funded status** of the plans and the amounts recognized in the balance sheet, with separate display of (a) assets and (b) current and noncurrent liabilities
4) Information about **plan assets**
5) The **accumulated benefit obligation** (the PBO with no assumption about future compensation) of a defined benefit pension plan
6) **Benefits** to be paid in each of the next 5 years and the total to be paid in years 6-10 based on the assumptions used to determine the benefit obligation at the current year end (future employee service is considered in the calculation)
7) **Net periodic benefit cost** recognized, showing separately each of its components and gain or loss recognized due to a settlement or curtailment
8) Separate amounts for
    a) Net gain (loss) and prior service cost (credit) recognized in **OCI for the period**,
    b) **Reclassification adjustments** of OCI recognized in net periodic benefit cost for the period, and
    c) Items still in **accumulated OCI** (net gain or loss, unamortized prior service cost or credit, and **the transition amount**)

9) Weighted-average **assumptions** about the discount rate, rate of compensation increase, and expected long-term rate of return, with specification of assumptions for calculating the benefit obligation and net benefit cost

2. **Income Statement Presentation**
   a. The **service cost** component of the periodic pension cost is reported in the same line item as other employee **compensation costs** and separately from other components of the periodic pension cost.
      1) It is reported **within** income from operations, if such a subtotal is presented in the income statement.
      2) Service cost is eligible for capitalization in assets when applicable (e.g., for production of inventory or an internally constructed fixed asset).
   b. The **other components** (besides service cost) of the periodic pension cost are reported **outside** a subtotal of income from operations, if one is presented. The other components are not eligible for capitalization in assets.
3. **Financial Statements of Employee Benefit Plans**
   a. The primary objective of a pension plan's financial statements is to provide financial information that is useful in assessing the plan's present and future ability to pay benefits when they are due.
   b. **A defined contribution plan** must present the following financial statements:
      1) A **statement of net assets available for benefits** of the plan as of the end of the plan year. This statement should present the total assets, total liabilities, and net assets available for benefits.
         a) The plan's net assets available to pay benefits equal the sum of participants' individual account balances.
      2) A **statement of changes in net assets available for benefits** of the plan for the year then ended. This statement should present the effects of significant changes in net assets during the year and must present, at a minimum, all of the following:
         a) Net appreciation or depreciation of the fair value of investments
         b) Contributions from employers, segregated between cash and noncash contributions
         c) Contributions from participants or other identified sources
         d) Benefits paid to participants
         e) Administrative expenses
         f) Payments to insurance entities to purchase contracts that are excluded from plan assets
   c. **A defined benefit plan** must present the following financial statements:
      1) A **statement of net assets available for benefits** of the plan as of the end of the plan year
      2) A **statement of changes in net assets available for benefits** of the plan for the year then ended

d. In addition, a defined benefit plan should provide information regarding the

   1) **Actuarial present value of accumulated plan benefits**, which may be presented in a separate statement or in a combined statement with the statement of net assets available for benefits

   2) **Changes in the actuarial present value of accumulated plan benefits** for the year then ended, which may be presented in a separate statement or in a combined statement with the statement of changes in net assets available for benefits

e. In a statement of net assets available for benefits,

   1) **Plan investments** (e.g., equity or debt securities and real estate) should be reported at their **fair value** at the reporting date.

   2) **Plan assets used in plan operations**, such as buildings, equipment, furniture, etc., are reported at historical cost minus accumulated depreciation.

f. The **statement of cash flows** is **not** required to be presented by the defined benefit plan entity or by the defined contribution plan entity.

STOP & REVIEW

You have completed the outline for this subunit.
Study multiple-choice questions 9 and 10 on page 347.

11.5 POSTRETIREMENT BENEFITS OTHER THAN PENSIONS

1. The accounting for **other postretirement employee benefits (OPEB)**, such as healthcare, is similar to pension accounting.

   a. Benefits depend on such factors as the

      1) Benefit formula,
      2) Life expectancy of the retiree and any beneficiaries and covered dependents, and
      3) Frequency and significance of events (e.g., illnesses) requiring payments.

   b. **Measurements** of plan assets and benefit obligations are generally made as of the balance sheet date.

   c. The costs are expensed during **the attribution period**, which begins on the **date of hire** unless the plan's benefit formula grants credit for service only from a later date.

      1) The end of the period is the **full eligibility date**.

EXAMPLE 11-8 Attribution Period of OPEB

An employer provides postretirement health insurance benefits to employees who have completed 20 years of service and have attained age 55 when they retire. The plan specifies that the attribution start date is the later of an employee's 35th birthday or his or her start date.

An employee is hired on August 5, Year 1, and turns 35 on January 9, Year 2. The employee's attribution period begins on January 9, Year 2.

2. **Benefit Obligations**

   a. The **expected postretirement benefit obligation (EPBO)** equals the **accumulated postretirement benefit obligation (APBO)** after the full eligibility date.

   b. The **EPBO** for an employee is the actuarial present value at a given date of the other postretirement employee benefits (OPEB) expected to be paid. Its measurement depends on the

      1) Anticipated amounts and timing of future benefits,
      2) Costs to be incurred to provide those benefits, and
      3) Extent the costs are shared by the employee and others (such as governmental programs).

   c. The **APBO** for an employee is the actuarial present value at a given date of the OPEB attributable to the employee's service as of that date.

      1) The APBO (as well as the EPBO and service cost) implicitly includes the consideration of **future salary progression**.
      2) An employer's obligation for OPEB must be **fully accrued** by the full eligibility date for all benefits even if the employee is expected to render additional service.

         a) The **full eligibility date** is reached when the employee has rendered all the services necessary to earn all of the expected benefits.
         b) Prior to that date, the EPBO exceeds the APBO.

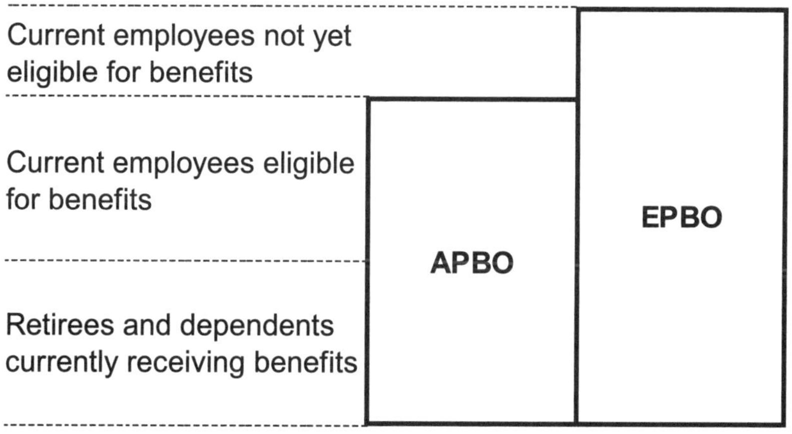

Figure 11-4

3. **Funded Status**

   a. The funded status of the plan must be recognized in the statement of financial position as the difference between the **fair value of plan assets and the APBO**.

      1) If the APBO exceeds the fair value of plan assets, a liability for the difference is reported.

4. **Net Periodic Postretirement Benefit Cost (NPPBC)**

   a. The possible components of the NPPBC of an employer sponsoring a defined benefit postretirement plan are similar to the elements of the required minimum periodic pension expense (covered in Subunit 11.2).

      1) Service cost
      2) Interest on the APBO
      3) Actual or expected return on plan assets
      4) Amortization of any prior service cost or credit included in accumulated OCI
      5) Gain or loss **component**

   b. **Service cost** increases NPPBC. It is the part of the **EPBO** attributed to services by employees during the period and is not affected by the level of funding.

      1) It is reported in the same line item as other compensation costs and separately from other components of NPPBC.

   c. **Interest cost** increases NPPBC. It is the change in the **APBO** during the period resulting solely from the passage of time.

      Interest cost = Beginning APBO × Discount rate

   d. **Prior service cost** is an increase in the APBO. It is incurred due to a **plan amendment** that provides improved benefits for prior service.

   e. A **prior service credit** retroactively reduces benefits and the APBO.

   f. The **gain or loss component** equals any gain or loss immediately recognized in NPPBC or the amortization of the net gain or loss from prior periods that was recognized in OCI.

   g. The accounting for the NPPBC is similar to the accounting for the elements of net periodic pension expense (covered in Subunit 11.2).

STOP & REVIEW

You have completed the outline for this subunit.
Study multiple-choice questions 11 and 12 on page 348.

11.6 COMPENSATED ABSENCES AND POSTEMPLOYMENT BENEFITS

1. **Compensated Absences**
   a. The accounting for compensated absences applies to employees' rights to receive compensation for future absences, such as vacations. It requires an accrual of a liability when four criteria are met:
      1) The payment of compensation is **probable**.
      2) The amount can be **reasonably estimated**.
      3) The benefits either **vest** or **accumulate**.
         a) Rights **vest** if they do not depend on employees' future service. The employer has an obligation to pay even if an employee provides no future service.
         b) Rights **accumulate** if earned but, if unused, may be carried forward to subsequent periods.
      4) The compensation relates to employees' **services** that have **already** been **rendered**.
   b. However, **sick pay benefits** that meet the criteria in item 1.a. are accrued only if the rights **vest**. If sick pay benefits accumulate but do not vest, an entity may (but need not) accrue a liability.
   c. The common way to **measure the liability** for compensated absences at the end of the reporting period is to multiply current employees' daily average wage rate by the number of vacation days earned and expected to be used in subsequent periods.
      1) In future periods, the wage rate may change. Thus, the amount paid for compensated absences may differ from the liability recognized. The difference is accounted for as a change in estimate and recognized in income.
      2) The liability should be classified as
         a) A **current liability** for the amount expected to be paid within 12 months after the end of the fiscal year and
         b) A **noncurrent liability** for the remaining amount.

EXAMPLE 11-9 Compensated Absences

Entity A provides each of its 500 employees 15 days of paid vacation a year. The unused annual leave may be rolled over for an unlimited time and is payable even upon termination. The employees' daily average wage rate is $150. During Year 1, each employee used an average of 12 vacation days. Entity A expects that 80% of unused accumulated vacation days will be used in Year 2 and the rest in Year 3.

On December 31, Year 1, Entity A must recognize a liability for paid vacation earned and not yet used by the employees. The amount of liability recognized is $225,000 [500 employees × (15 days accrued annually – 12 average days used annually) × $150 daily average wage]. The current portion is $180,000 ($225,000 × 80%), and the noncurrent portion is $45,000 ($225,000 – $180,000). The following is the journal entry:

Vacation pay expense	$225,000	
Compensated absences payable -- current liability		$180,000
Compensated absences payable -- noncurrent liability		45,000

IFRS DIFFERENCE

Short-term employee benefits are employee benefits (other than termination benefits), such as paid annual leave, sick leave, and wages, that are expected to be **settled wholly** before 12 months after the annual reporting period in which employees render the related services.

Using the data from Example 11-9, the entire liability for outstanding annual leave must be recognized at the end of Year 1 as a **long-term** liability because it is not expected to be settled wholly in Year 2. The long-term liability should be measured at the present value of the projected future cash flow.

2. **Postemployment Benefits**

   a. An employer should accrue a liability for postemployment benefits, such as severance pay, if all four criteria stated in the guidance on compensated absences are met.

EXAMPLE 11-10 Postemployment Benefits

Papina Co. developed reasonable estimates of its obligations for $450,000 in severance pay and $150,000 in job training benefits. Payment is probable, and the benefits relate to employees' services previously rendered. The job training benefits vest, and the severance pay benefits accumulate. Because all the criteria are met, Papina should accrue a liability of $600,000 for postretirement benefits.

STOP & REVIEW

You have completed the outline for this subunit.
Study multiple-choice questions 13 through 17 beginning on page 349.

11.7 SHARE-BASED PAYMENT

1. **Basic Accounting**

   a. This guidance applies to **share-based payment** transactions (with employees and nonemployees) involving receipt by the entity of **goods or services** in return for the following:

      1) Its **equity instruments**, e.g., shares or share options
      2) Incurrence of **liabilities** to suppliers that

         a) Are based on the **price** of the entity's equity instruments or
         b) May require **share settlement**

   b. Share-based payment awards are measured initially at the **grant-date fair value** of the equity instruments that an entity is obligated to issue.

      1) The **grant date** is the date at which a mutual understanding of the key terms and conditions of the award have been reached.

   c. Goods and services received from nonemployees for share-based payment awards are recognized in the same manner as if cash were paid for them.

2. **Stock Compensation -- Equity-Classified Awards**

   a. The estimated total compensation expense for equity awards is measured at the **grant-date fair value** of the equity instruments issued.

      1) This **compensation expense** is allocated over the **requisite service period**.

         a) The requisite service period is the period during which employees must perform services. It is most often the **vesting period**.

         b) The beginning of the requisite service period is usually the grant date.

         c) The **credit** is to a **paid-in capital** account. The following are typical journal entries:

<u>Recognition of expense during the requisite service period:</u>		
Compensation expense	$XXX	
Paid-in capital -- equity award		$XXX
<u>Issuance of shares:</u>		
Cash	$XXX	
Paid-in capital -- equity award	XXX	
Common stock		$XXX
Paid-in capital in excess of par		XXX
<u>Forfeitures or expiration of options:</u>		
Paid-in capital -- equity award	$XXX	
Paid-in capital -- forfeitures		$XXX

b. Total **compensation expense** at the end of the requisite service period is based on the number of equity instruments for which the requisite service was completed.

1) If during the entire requisite service period (vesting period) all the granted equity instruments expect to vest, the total compensation expense is equally allocated over the vesting period. Thus, an equal amount of compensation expense is recognized each period.

EXAMPLE 11-11 Share-Based Payment Award -- Equity Classification

On January 1, Year 1, Jeff Co. grants to each of its five executives 2,000 stock options. Each option permits the purchase of one share of Jeff's $1 par-value common stock at its current market price of $150. The executives must work for 2 more years for the options to vest. The options must be exercised within 10 years of the grant date. The fair value of each option on January 1, Year 1, is $62.

No journal entry is made on the grant date because no time has passed and no services associated with the options have been performed.

January 1, Year 1:
No entry

The total expected compensation expense equals the grant-date fair value of the options of $620,000 (5 executives × 2,000 options × $62 grant-date fair value per option). This total compensation expense is recognized evenly over the 2 years of the requisite service period (i.e., vesting period). Thus, $310,000 ($620,000 ÷ 2 years) of compensation expense is recognized each year. The following journal entries are recorded by Jeff at the end of Year 1 and Year 2:

December 31, Year 1, and December 31, Year 2:		
Compensation expense	$310,000	
Paid-in capital -- share options		$310,000

2) If the number of equity instruments expected to vest is changed during the requisite service period, the effect of a change is recognized through a cumulative catch-up adjustment that is included in compensation expense in the period of the change in estimate.

EXAMPLE 11-12 Share-Based Payment Award -- Equity Classification

Using the data from Example 11-11, assume that (1) one executive resigned on January 1, Year 2; (2) three executives exercised their options on July 1, Year 3; and (3), after 10 years, the remaining executive still has not exercised the options.

Because one executive left, the new estimated total compensation expense is $496,000 (4 executives × 2,000 options × $62 grant-date fair value per option). The Year 1 compensation expense would have been $248,000 ($496,000 ÷ 2). This change in estimate is accounted for prospectively, and no restatement of the Year 1 statements is appropriate. Accordingly, the Year 2 compensation expense is $186,000 ($496,000 new total compensation expense – $310,000 recognized in Year 1). The following journal entry is recorded by Jeff at the end of Year 2:

December 31, Year 2:		
Compensation expense	$186,000	
Paid-in capital -- share options		$186,000

When options are exercised, the total compensation expense is unaffected, and the market price of the stock is irrelevant. The following journal entry is recorded by Jeff when three executives out of four exercised their options:

July 1, Year 3:		
Cash (2,000 shares × 3 executives × $150 exercise price)	$900,000	
Paid-in capital -- share options [$496,000 × (3 ÷ 4)]	372,000	
Common stock (2,000 shares × $1 par value × 3 executives)		$ 6,000
Additional paid-in capital -- common stock		1,266,000

The following journal entry is recorded by Jeff when the remaining options are expired:

December 31, Year 10:		
Paid-in capital -- share options [$496,000 × (1 ÷ 4)]	$124,000	
Paid-in capital -- expired share options		$124,000

3) The number of equity instruments expected to vest may change due to the following **vesting conditions**:

   a) **Service conditions** pertain solely to rendering services for the designated period.

   b) **Performance conditions** relate to rendering services for a specified period and reaching objectives that relate solely to the employer's activities (e.g., achieving a stated growth rate).

   c) Market conditions (e.g., attaining a specified share price) do not affect vesting.

3. **Stock Compensation -- Liability-Classified Awards**

   a. An award may meet the criteria for classification as a **liability**. (Equity vs. liability classification is discussed in Study Unit 12, Subunit 6.)

   b. The **measurement date** for liabilities is the **settlement date**. Thus, after initial recognition at fair value, liabilities are **remeasured to fair value** at each reporting date through the date of settlement.

      1) **Periodic compensation expense** is based on the change (or part of the change, depending on the percentage of requisite service performed to date) in fair value of the liability.

      2) Under specific circumstances, certain liability awards may be measured based on **intrinsic value**.

Intrinsic value = Fair value of an underlying stock – Exercise price of an option

   c. **Share appreciation rights (SARs)** are examples of liability-classified awards. SARs allow employees to receive (e.g., in cash) the increase in the fair value of the shares directly from the employer.

      1) The employee receives compensation equal to the excess of the share's market price on the exercise date over the option price (generally the share's market price on the grant date).

EXAMPLE 11-13 Share-Based Payment Award -- Liability Classification

On January 1, Year 1, Sistina Co. grants its chief executive officer 5,000 share appreciation rights. The SARs entitle the CEO to cash for the difference between (1) the market price of its stock on December 31, Year 2, and (2) the stock market price on the grant date of $50. For simplicity, assume that Sistina measures the SARs based on their intrinsic value (Stock market price – Predetermined price of $50).

On December 31, Year 1, the market price of Sistina's stock was $65. Sistina must recognize a liability and compensation expense of $37,500 [5,000 shares × ($65 – $50) × (1 yr. ÷ 2 yrs.)].

December 31, Year 1:		
Compensation expense	$37,500	
Share-based compensation liability		$37,500

On December 31, Year 2, the stock price is $58. Sistina must recognize an additional liability and compensation expense of $2,500 {[5,000 shares × ($58 – $50) × (2 yrs. ÷ 2 yrs.)] – $37,500}.

December 31, Year 2:		
Compensation expense	$2,500	
Share-based compensation liability		$2,500

STOP & REVIEW

You have completed the outline for this subunit.
Study multiple-choice questions 18 through 20 beginning on page 351.

QUESTIONS

11.1 Types of Pension Plans

1. On December 31, Year 1, Entity A contributed $30,000 to a defined contribution pension plan. The contribution required by the plan's formula for Year 1 is $45,000. What is the effect of these events on Entity A's working capital?

A. Decrease of $45,000.

B. Decrease of $30,000.

C. Decrease of $15,000.

D. Increase of $15,000.

Answer (A) is correct.

REQUIRED: The effect of the events on working capital.

DISCUSSION: Entity A reports a liability (pension payable) for the difference between the contribution made and the contribution required by the pension formula (the expense recognized). The journal entry is

Pension expense	$45,000	
Cash		$30,000
Pension payable		15,000

The effect on working capital is a decrease of $45,000 that consists of (1) a decrease of $30,000 in current assets (cash) and (2) an increase of $15,000 in current liabilities (pension payable).

Answer (B) is incorrect. In addition to the $30,000 of cash contributed, Entity A also should recognize a current liability (pension payable) that decreases working capital. **Answer (C) is incorrect.** In addition to the $15,000 increase in current liabilities, the $30,000 of cash contributed also decreases working capital. **Answer (D) is incorrect.** The cash contribution and the recognition of a current liability decrease, not increase, working capital.

2. Which statement is true regarding a defined benefit pension plan?

A. A defined benefit plan defines the annual amount of cash that an employer must deposit to fulfill its pension obligation to employees.

B. No investment risk is borne by an employer.

C. At the end of the reporting period, an employer can measure exactly the total amount of pension benefits that it is responsible for providing to employees in the future.

D. The benefits to be paid to employees depend on events that are beyond the employer's control.

Answer (D) is correct.

REQUIRED: The true statement regarding a defined benefit pension plan.

DISCUSSION: A defined benefit plan defines an amount of pension benefits to be provided to each employee. This amount depends on future events, such as (1) how long the employee lives, (2) how many years of service the employee renders, and (3) the employee's compensation before retirement. Many of these events cannot be controlled by the employer.

Answer (A) is incorrect. A defined contribution plan, not a benefit plan, defines the annual amount that an employer has to deposit to fulfill its pension obligation to employees. **Answer (B) is incorrect.** The employer is responsible for providing the agreed future benefits to the employees. Accordingly, it bears the actuarial risk and investment risk. **Answer (C) is incorrect.** The total amount of benefits to be paid to employees is not precisely determinable but can only be estimated by using actuarial assumptions.

11.2 Defined Benefit Plan -- Components of Pension Expense

3. Which of the following components must be included in the calculation of pension expense recognized for a period by an employer sponsoring a defined benefit pension plan?

	Interest Cost	Expected Return on Plan Assets
A.	Yes	No
B.	Yes	Yes
C.	No	Yes
D.	No	No

Answer (B) is correct.

REQUIRED: The component(s), if any, to be included in pension expense.

DISCUSSION: The required minimum pension expense consists of the following elements:

+	Service cost
+	Interest cost
–	Expected return on plan assets
±	Amortization of net gain or loss
±	Amortization of prior service cost of credit
	Pension expense

Thus, both interest cost and expected return on plan assets are components of pension expense.

4. The following information pertains to Gali Co.'s defined benefit pension plan for Year 1:

Fair value of plan assets, beginning of year	$350,000
Fair value of plan assets, end of year	525,000
Employer contributions	110,000
Benefits paid	85,000

In computing pension expense, what amount should Gali use as actual return on plan assets?

A. $65,000

B. $150,000

C. $175,000

D. $260,000

Answer (B) is correct.

REQUIRED: The actual return on plan assets.

DISCUSSION: The actual return on plan assets is based on the fair value of plan assets at the beginning and end of the accounting period adjusted for contributions and payments during the period. The actual return for Gali is $150,000 ($525,000 – $350,000 – $110,000 + $85,000).

Answer (A) is incorrect. The amount of $65,000 results when benefits paid to employees are not included. **Answer (C) is incorrect.** The amount of $175,000 is the change in the fair value of plan assets without adjustment for contributions or benefits paid. **Answer (D) is incorrect.** The amount of $260,000 does not deduct employer contributions.

11.3 Defined Benefit Plan -- Funded Status of Pension Plans

5. The following is the only information pertaining to Kane Co.'s defined benefit pension plan:

Pension asset, January 1, Year 1	$ 2,000
Service cost	19,000
Interest cost	38,000
Actual and expected return on plan assets	22,000
Amortization of prior service cost arising in a prior period	52,000
Employer contributions	40,000

In its December 31, Year 1, balance sheet, what amount should Kane report as the unfunded or overfunded projected benefit obligation (PBO)?

A. $7,000 overfunded.

B. $15,000 underfunded.

C. $45,000 underfunded.

D. $52,000 underfunded.

Answer (A) is correct.

REQUIRED: The unfunded or overfunded PBO.

DISCUSSION: The employer must recognize the funded status of the plan as the difference between the fair value of plan assets and the PBO at year end. That amount is an asset or a liability. Current service cost and interest cost increase the PBO. The return on plan assets and contributions increase plan assets. Amortization of prior service cost arising in a prior period and recognized in accumulated OCI has no additional effect on the PBO or plan assets. However, it is a component of pension expense. The PBO was overfunded by $2,000 on January 1. It increased during the year by $57,000 ($19,000 + $38,000). Plan assets increased by $62,000 ($22,000 + $40,000). Accordingly, the plan is overfunded by $7,000 [$2,000 + ($62,000 – $57,000)] at year end. Kane should recognize a pension asset of $7,000 at year end.

Answer (B) is incorrect. The return on plan assets should be added to plan assets. **Answer (C) is incorrect.** The $45,000 underfunded includes prior service cost amortization. Prior service cost that arose in a prior period was reflected in the asset or liability recognized for the funded status of the plan at the beginning of the year. When prior service cost arises, the entry is to debit OCI, net of tax, and credit pension liability. **Answer (D) is incorrect.** The $52,000 underfunded is the prior service cost amortization.

6. An entity sponsors a defined benefit pension plan that is underfunded by $800,000. A $500,000 increase in the fair value of plan assets would have which of the following effects on the financial statements of the entity?

A. An increase in the assets of the entity.

B. An increase in accumulated other comprehensive income of the entity for the full amount of the increase in the value of the assets.

C. A decrease in accumulated other comprehensive income of the entity for the full amount of the increase in the value of the assets.

D. A decrease in the liabilities of the entity.

Answer (D) is correct.

REQUIRED: The effects of an increase in the fair value of plan assets that is less than the underfunded amount.

DISCUSSION: If a projected benefit obligation exceeds the fair value of plan assets, the amount of the underfunding must be recognized as a liability. If the pension plan is underfunded by $800,000, an increase in the fair value of plan assets of $500,000 reduces the underfunding to $300,000. Thus, the increase in the fair value of plan assets decreases but does not eliminate the pension liability.

Answer (A) is incorrect. Given that the projected benefit obligation is underfunded by $800,000, the fair value of plan assets would have to increase by more than $800,000 to increase the assets of the entity. For example, if the fair value of the plan assets, which are not assets of the sponsor, had increased by $900,000, the entity would recognize an asset of $100,000 for the overfunding. **Answer (B) is incorrect.** The full over- or underfunded status of the plan is reported as an asset or liability, respectively. Unamortized gains or losses, prior service cost, and prior service credit are reported in OCI. The total OCI for the period is transferred to accumulated OCI (a component of equity in the statement of financial position). Thus, the funded status of the plan does not affect accumulated OCI. **Answer (C) is incorrect.** The funded status of the plan does not affect accumulated OCI.

7. The following information pertains to Seda Co.'s pension plan:

Actuarial estimate of projected benefit obligation (PBO) at 1/1/Year 1	$72,000
Assumed discount rate	10%
Service cost for Year 1	$18,000
Pension benefits paid during Year 1	$15,000

If no change in actuarial estimates occurred during Year 1, Seda's PBO at December 31, Year 1, was

A. $67,800

B. $75,000

C. $79,200

D. $82,200

Answer (D) is correct.

REQUIRED: The projected benefit obligation at the end of the year.

DISCUSSION: Seda's ending PBO balance can be calculated as follows:

Beginning PBO balance	$ 72,000
Service cost	18,000
Interest cost ($72,000 × 10%)	7,200
Less: Benefits paid	(15,000)
Ending PBO balance	$ 82,200

Answer (A) is incorrect. The amount of $67,800 results from subtracting interest cost. **Answer (B) is incorrect.** The amount of $75,000 excludes interest cost. **Answer (C) is incorrect.** The amount of $79,200 ignores service costs and benefits paid.

8. Webb Co. implemented a defined benefit pension plan for its employees on January 1, Year 1. During Year 1 and Year 2, Webb's contributions fully funded the plan. The following data are provided for Year 4 and Year 3:

	Year 4 Estimated	Year 3 Actual
Projected benefit obligation, December 31	$750,000	$700,000
Accumulated benefit obligation, December 31	520,000	500,000
Plan assets at fair value, December 31	675,000	600,000
Projected benefit obligation in excess of plan assets	75,000	100,000
Pension expense	90,000	75,000
Employer's contribution	?	50,000

What amount should Webb contribute to report a pension liability of $15,000 in its December 31, Year 4, balance sheet?

A. $50,000

B. $60,000

C. $75,000

D. $100,000

Answer (B) is correct.

REQUIRED: The amount contributed to report an accrued pension liability.

DISCUSSION: A reported pension liability reflects an excess of the PBO over the fair value of the plan assets at the balance sheet date. If Webb projects this excess to be $75,000 ($750,000 – $675,000) at the end of Year 4 and wishes to report a liability of $15,000, a contribution of $60,000 ($75,000 – $15,000) will have to be made.

Answer (A) is incorrect. The Year 3 contribution is $50,000. **Answer (C) is incorrect.** The excess of the PBO over the plan assets is $75,000. **Answer (D) is incorrect.** The excess of the PBO for Year 3 is $100,000.

11.4 Disclosures, Presentation, and Other Issues

9. A public entity that sponsors a defined benefit pension plan must disclose in the notes to its financial statements a reconciliation of

A. The vested and nonvested benefit obligation of its pension plan with the accumulated benefit obligation.

B. The accrued or prepaid pension cost reported in its balance sheet with the pension expense reported in its income statement.

C. The accumulated benefit obligation of its pension plan with its projected benefit obligation.

D. The beginning and ending balances of the projected benefit obligation.

Answer (D) is correct.

REQUIRED: The employer disclosures required for a defined benefit pension plan.

DISCUSSION: One of the required disclosures by a public entity with a defined benefit pension plan is a reconciliation of the beginning and ending balances of the PBO. It should display separately the effects during the period of (1) service cost, (2) interest cost, (3) participants' contributions, (4) actuarial gains and losses, (5) foreign currency exchange rate changes, (6) benefits paid, (7) plan amendments, (8) business combinations, (9) divestitures, (10) curtailments, (11) settlements, and (12) special termination benefits.

Answer (A) is incorrect. Vested and nonvested amounts need not be disclosed. **Answer (B) is incorrect.** The employer must disclose the full funded status of the plan. Accrued/prepaid pension cost measures the extent of the funding of net period pension cost. **Answer (C) is incorrect.** The ABO must be disclosed but not with the PBO.

10. Note section disclosures in the financial statements of a public entity that sponsors a defined benefit pension plan for its employees are **not** required to include

A. The components of periodic pension cost.

B. The funded status of the plan.

C. Reclassification adjustments of other comprehensive income for the period.

D. A detailed description of the plan, including employee groups covered.

Answer (D) is correct.

REQUIRED: The note section disclosures by a public entity for a defined benefit pension plan that are not required.

DISCUSSION: The guidance on pension accounting originally required disclosure of a detailed description of the plan, including employee groups covered. However, the currently effective disclosure requirements do not require this disclosure.

Answer (A) is incorrect. Required disclosures by a public (not a nonpublic) entity include the net periodic benefit cost, showing separately each of its components and gain or loss recognized due to a settlement or curtailment. **Answer (B) is incorrect.** Required disclosures by a public (not a nonpublic) entity include the funded status of the plan and the amounts recognized in the balance sheet, with separate display of assets and current and noncurrent liabilities. **Answer (C) is incorrect.** Required disclosures by a public entity include reclassification adjustments of other comprehensive income as they are recognized in pension expense.

11.5 Postretirement Benefits Other than Pensions

11. Bounty Co. provides postretirement healthcare benefits to employees who have completed at least 10 years service and are aged 55 years or older when retiring. Employees retiring from Bounty have a median age of 62, and no one has worked beyond age 65. Fletcher is hired at 48 years old. The attribution period for accruing Bounty's expected postretirement healthcare benefit obligation to Fletcher is during the period when Fletcher is aged

A. 48 to 65.

B. 48 to 58.

C. 55 to 65.

D. 55 to 62.

Answer (B) is correct.

REQUIRED: The attribution period for accruing the expected postretirement healthcare benefit obligation to an employee.

DISCUSSION: The attribution period begins on the date of hire unless the plan's benefit formula grants credit for service only from a later date. The end of the period is the full eligibility date. If the exception does not apply, Fletcher's attribution period is from age 48, the date of hire, to age 58, the date of full eligibility.

12. An employer's obligation for postretirement health benefits that are expected to be fully provided to or for an employee must be fully accrued by the date the

A. Benefits are paid.

B. Benefits are utilized.

C. Employee retires.

D. Employee is fully eligible for benefits.

Answer (D) is correct.

REQUIRED: The full accrual date for postretirement health benefits that are expected to be fully paid.

DISCUSSION: Costs are expensed over the attribution period. It begins on the date of hire unless the plan's benefit formula states otherwise. It ends on the full eligibility date of the employee. This rule applies even if the employee is expected to render additional service. The full eligibility date is reached when the employee has rendered all the services necessary to earn all of the expected benefits.

11.6 Compensated Absences and Postemployment Benefits

13. North Corp. has an employee benefit plan for compensated absences that gives employees 10 paid vacation days and 10 paid sick days. Both vacation and sick days can be carried over indefinitely. Employees can elect to receive payment in lieu of vacation days; however, no payment is given for sick days not taken. At December 31 of the current year, North's unadjusted balance of liability for compensated absences was $21,000. North estimated that there were 150 vacation days and 75 sick days available at December 31. North's employees earn an average of $100 per day. In its December 31 balance sheet, what amount of liability for compensated absences is North required to report?

A. $36,000

B. $22,500

C. $21,000

D. $15,000

Answer (D) is correct.

REQUIRED: The amount of liability for compensated absences.

DISCUSSION: Vacation benefits earned but not yet taken must be accrued. However, a liability is not accrued for future sick pay unless the rights are vested. Thus, the estimated vacation days available at December 31 require a liability of $15,000 ($100 × 150 days).

Answer (A) is incorrect. The amount of $36,000 is the sum of the $15,000 liability for compensated absences and the unadjusted balance of liability for compensated absences. **Answer (B) is incorrect.** The sick days are not required to be included in the liability for compensated absences. **Answer (C) is incorrect.** The amount of $21,000 is the unadjusted balance of liability for compensated absences.

14. The following information relating to compensated absences was available from Graf Company's accounting records at December 31, Year 4:

- Employees' rights to vacation pay vest and are attributable to services already rendered. Payment is probable, and Graf's obligation was reasonably estimated at $110,000.
- Employees' rights to sick pay benefits do not vest but accumulate for possible future use. The rights are attributable to services already rendered, and the total accumulated sick pay was reasonably estimated at $50,000.

What amount is Graf required to report as the liability for compensated absences in its December 31, Year 4, balance sheet?

A. $160,000

B. $110,000

C. $50,000

D. $0

Answer (B) is correct.

REQUIRED: The amount to be reported as a liability for compensated absences at year end.

DISCUSSION: In general, GAAP require an accrual for compensated services when the compensation relates to services previously provided, the benefits either vest or accumulate, and payment is both probable and reasonably estimable. An exception is made for sick pay benefits, which must be accrued only if the rights vest. Because Graf's obligation for sick pay benefits relates to benefits that do not vest, no accrual for the $50,000 in accumulated sick pay should be recognized. Consequently, only the $110,000 obligation for employee rights to vacation pay should be recognized as part of the liability for compensated absences in the year-end balance sheet.

Answer (A) is incorrect. The amount of $160,000 includes the nonvesting sick pay benefits. **Answer (C) is incorrect.** The amount of $50,000 includes the nonvesting sick pay benefits but excludes the vacation pay. **Answer (D) is incorrect.** Zero excludes the vacation pay.

15. If the payment of employees' compensation for future absences is probable, the amount can be reasonably estimated, and the obligation relates to rights that vest, the compensation should be

A. Recognized when paid.

B. Accrued if attributable to employees' services whether or not already rendered.

C. Accrued if attributable to employees' services already rendered.

D. Accrued if attributable to employees' services not already rendered.

Answer (C) is correct.

REQUIRED: The additional criterion to be met to accrue an expense for compensated absences.

DISCUSSION: GAAP require an accrual when four criteria are met: (1) The payment of compensation is probable, (2) the amount can be reasonably estimated, (3) the benefits either vest or accumulate, and (4) the compensation relates to employees' services that have already been rendered.

16. At December 31, Year 2, Taos Co. estimates that its employees have earned vacation pay of $100,000. Employees will receive their vacation pay in Year 3. Should Taos accrue a liability at December 31, Year 2, if the rights to this compensation accumulated over time or if the rights are vested?

	Accumulated	Vested
A.	Yes	No
B.	No	No
C.	Yes	Yes
D.	No	Yes

Answer (C) is correct.

REQUIRED: The effect of accumulation and vesting on accrual of a liability for vacation pay.

DISCUSSION: GAAP require an accrual for compensated services when the compensation relates to services previously provided, the benefits either vest or accumulate, and payment is both probable and reasonably estimable. The single exception is for sick pay benefits, which must be accrued only if the rights vest.

Answer (A) is incorrect. Vesting meets one of the criteria for accrual of a liability. **Answer (B) is incorrect.** Either vesting or accumulation meets one of the criteria for accrual of a liability. **Answer (D) is incorrect.** Accumulation meets one of the criteria for accrual of a liability.

17. The following information pertains to Rik Co.'s two employees:

Name	Weekly Salary	Number of Weeks Worked in Year	Vacation Rights Vest or Accumulate
Ryan	$800	52	Yes
Todd	600	52	No

Neither Ryan nor Todd took the usual 2-week vacation during the year. In Rik's December 31 financial statements, what amount of vacation expense and liability should be reported?

A. $2,800

B. $1,600

C. $1,400

D. $0

Answer (B) is correct.

REQUIRED: The amount of vacation expense and liability.

DISCUSSION: An accrual is required when four criteria are met: (1) The payment of compensation is probable, (2) the amount can be reasonably estimated, (3) the benefits either vest or accumulate, and (4) the compensation relates to employees' services that have already been rendered. Hence, no accrual is made of Todd's vacation rights because they do not vest or accumulate. The liability reported should therefore be $1,600 ($800 weekly salary earned by Ryan × 2 weeks).

Answer (A) is incorrect. The amount of $2,800 includes Todd's vacation rights. **Answer (C) is incorrect.** The amount of $1,400 equals 1 week's salary for both Ryan and Todd. **Answer (D) is incorrect.** Zero excludes Ryan's vacation rights.

11.7 Share-Based Payment

Questions 18 and 19 are based on the following information. On December 21, Year 1, the board of directors of Oak Corporation approved a plan to award 600,000 share options to 20 key employees as additional compensation. Effective January 1, Year 2, each employee was granted the right to purchase 30,000 shares of the company's $2 par-value stock at an exercise price of $36 per share. The market price on that date was $32 per share. All share options vest at December 31, Year 4, the end of the 3-year requisite service period. They expire on December 31, Year 11. Based on an appropriate option-pricing formula, the fair value of the options on the grant date was estimated at $12 per option.

18. On January 1, Year 3, five key employees left Oak Corporation. During the period from January 1, Year 5, through December 31, Year 11, 400,000 of the share options that vested were exercised. The remaining options were not exercised. What amount of the previously recognized compensation expense should be adjusted upon expiration of the share options?

A. $2,400,000

B. $2,300,000

C. $100,000

D. $0

Answer (D) is correct.

REQUIRED: The adjustment to previously recognized compensation expense when share options are not exercised.

DISCUSSION: Total compensation expense for the requisite service period is not adjusted for expired options.

Answer (A) is incorrect. The amount of $2.4 million is the annual compensation expense recognized during each of the years of the requisite service period assuming no forfeitures. **Answer (B) is incorrect.** The amount of $2.3 million is the additional amount that would have been credited to additional paid-in capital if the 50,000 expired options had been exercised. **Answer (C) is incorrect.** The amount of $100,000 is the additional amount that would have been credited to common stock if the 50,000 expired options had been exercised.

19. What amount of compensation expense should Oak Corporation recognize in its annual income statement for the year ended December 31, Year 2?

A. $7,200,000

B. $6,400,000

C. $2,400,000

D. $1,200,700

Answer (C) is correct.

REQUIRED: The compensation expense recognized in Year 2.

DISCUSSION: Total compensation cost recognized during the requisite service period should equal the grant-date fair value of all share options for which the requisite service is rendered. GAAP require an entity to (1) estimate the number of share options for which the requisite service is expected to be rendered, (2) measure the cost of employee services received in exchange for those options at their fair value on the grant date, and (3) allocate that cost to the requisite service period. Given that all options vest at the same time (known as cliff vesting), the $7,200,000 (600,000 shares × $12 estimated fair value) total compensation cost should be allocated proportionately to the 3-year requisite service period. Thus, $2,400,000 ($7,200,000 ÷ 3) should be expensed in the annual income statement for the year ended December 31, Year 2.

Answer (A) is incorrect. The amount of $7,200,000 is the total estimated compensation cost for the entire requisite service period. **Answer (B) is incorrect.** The amount of $6,400,000 is total compensation expense based on the $32 market price. **Answer (D) is incorrect.** The amount of $1,200,000 is 600,000 shares times the $2 par value.

20. The measurement date for shares issued to employees in share option plans accounted for using the fair-value method is

A. The date on which options are granted to specified employees.

B. The earliest date on which both the number of shares to be issued and the option price are known.

C. The date on which the options are exercised by the employees.

D. The date the corporation forgoes alternative use of the shares to be sold under option.

Answer (A) is correct.

REQUIRED: The measurement date for shares issued after exercise of options if the accounting is in accordance with the fair-value method.

DISCUSSION: Under the fair-value method, compensation cost is measured at the grant date, which is when any needed approvals have been received, and the employer and employee "reach a mutual understanding of the key terms and conditions of a share-based payment award." This expense is based on the fair value of the award at that date and recognized over the requisite service period. This period is most often the period over which the vesting conditions are expected to be satisfied.

Answer (B) is incorrect. The earliest date on which the number of shares to be issued and the option price are known may coincide with, but does not define, the measurement date. **Answer (C) is incorrect.** The date on which the options are exercised by employees may coincide with, but does not define, the measurement date. **Answer (D) is incorrect.** The date the entity forgoes alternative use of the shares to be sold under option may coincide with, but does not define, the measurement date.

STUDY UNIT TWELVE

NONCURRENT LIABILITIES

(26 pages of outline)

This study unit covers traditional noncurrent liabilities (bonds and notes), including some securities that have characteristics of debt and equity. Unless the **fair value option** (outlined in Study Unit 5, Subunit 2) is elected, they are measured and accounted for in accordance with the guidance for interest on receivables and payables. The topics in this study unit are frequently tested.

12.1 TYPES OF BOND LIABILITIES

1. **Classification of Bonds**
   a. A bond is a formal contract to pay an amount of money (face amount) at the maturity date plus interest at the stated rate at specific intervals.
      1) All of the terms of the agreement are stated in an **indenture**.
   b. Bonds may be classified as follows:
      1) Nature of security
         a) **Mortgage bonds** are backed by specific assets, usually real estate.
         b) **Debentures** are backed only by the borrower's general credit.
         c) **Collateral trust bonds** are backed by specific securities.
         d) **Guaranty bonds** are guaranteed by a third party, e.g., the parent of the subsidiary that issued the bonds.
      2) Maturity pattern
         a) A **term bond** has a single maturity date at the end of its term.
         b) A **serial bond** matures in stated amounts at regular intervals.
      3) Ownership
         a) **Registered bonds** are issued in the name of the owner, who receives interest payments directly.
            i) When the owner sells the bonds, the certificates must be surrendered and new certificates must be issued.
         b) **Bearer bonds** (coupon bonds) are bearer instruments.
            i) Whoever presents the interest coupons is entitled to payment.
      4) Priority
         a) **Subordinated debentures** and **second mortgage bonds** are junior securities with claims inferior to those of senior bonds.
      5) Repayment provisions
         a) **Income bonds** pay interest contingent on the debtor's profitability.
         b) **Revenue bonds** are issued by governments and are payable from specific revenue sources.
         c) **Participating bonds** share in excess earnings of the debtor.

6) Valuation
   a) **Variable rate bonds** pay interest that is dependent on market conditions.
   b) **Zero-coupon** or **deep-discount bonds** are noninterest-bearing.
      i) Because they are sold at less than their face amount, an interest rate is imputed.
   c) **Commodity-backed bonds** are payable at prices related to a commodity, such as gold.

7) Redemption provisions
   a) **Callable bonds** may be repurchased by the issuer at a specified price before maturity.
      i) During a period of falling interest rates, the call provision allows the issuer to replace old high-interest debt with new low-interest debt.
      ii) Because only the issuer can benefit from the call provision, callable bonds generally have a higher yield than comparable noncallable bonds.
   b) **Convertible bonds** may be converted into equity securities of the issuer at the option of the holder (buyer) under specified conditions.

c. A bond indenture may require a **bond sinking fund** (a long-term investment).
   1) Payments into the fund plus the revenue earned on its investments provide the assets to settle bond liabilities.

STOP & REVIEW

You have completed the outline for this subunit.
Study multiple-choice questions 1 and 2 on page 379.

12.2 TIME VALUE OF MONEY

1. **Overview**

   a. Time value of money concepts are important in financial accounting. They affect the accounting for noncurrent receivables and payables (bonds and notes), leases, and certain employee benefits.

   b. A quantity of money to be received or paid in the future is worth less than the same amount now. The difference is measured in terms of interest calculated using the appropriate **discount rate**. Interest is the payment received by an owner of money from the current consumer to forgo current consumption.

   c. Standard tables have been developed to facilitate the calculation of present and future values. Each entry in one of these tables represents the factor by which any monetary amount can be modified to obtain its present or future value.

2. **Present Value (PV) of a Single Amount**

   a. The present value of a single amount is the value today of some future payment.

   b. It equals the future payment times the present value of 1 (a factor found in a standard table) for the given number of periods and interest rate.

EXAMPLE 12-1 Present Value of a Single Amount

	Present Value Factor of a Single Amount		
No. of Periods	6%	**8%**	10%
1	0.943	0.926	0.909
2	0.890	0.857	0.826
3	0.840	**0.794**	0.751
4	0.792	0.735	0.683
5	0.747	0.681	0.621

The present value of $1,000, to be received in 3 years and discounted at 8%, is $794 ($1,000 future value of a single amount × 0.794 present value factor).

This situation can be depicted as follows:

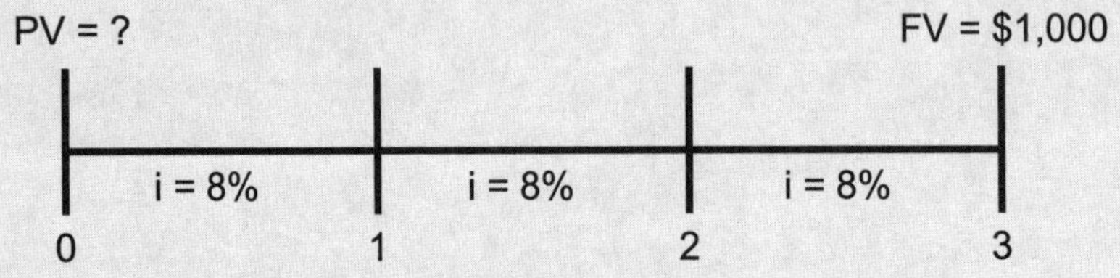

Figure 12-1

FV: Future value of a single amount (the amount to be paid or received in the future)

PV: Present value of a single amount

i: Interest rate

3. **Future Value (FV) of a Single Amount**

   a. The future value of a single amount is the amount available at a specified time in the future based on a single investment (deposit) today. The FV is the amount to be computed if one knows the present value and the appropriate discount rate.

   b. It equals the current payment times the future value of 1 (a factor found in a standard table) for the given number of periods and interest rate.

EXAMPLE 12-2 Future Value of a Single Amount

No. of Periods	Future Value Factor of a Single Amount 6%	8%	**10%**
1	1.060	1.080	1.100
2	1.124	1.166	1.210
3	1.191	1.260	1.331
4	1.262	1.360	**1.464**
5	1.338	1.469	1.610

The future value of $1,000 invested today for 4 years at 10% interest will be $1,464 ($1,000 present value of a single amount × 1.464 future value factor).

This situation can be depicted as follows:

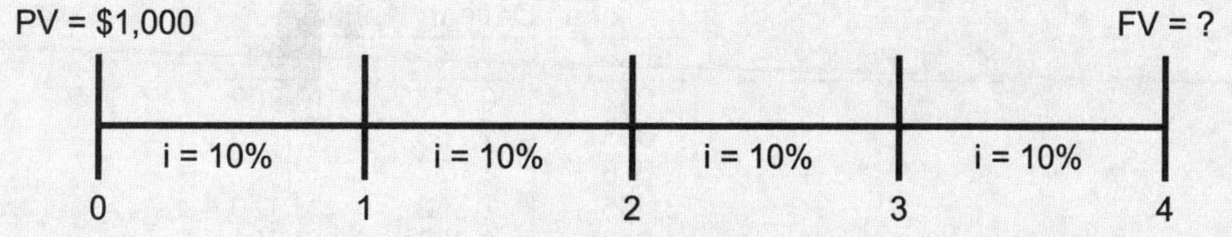

Figure 12-2

4. **Annuities**

a. An annuity is a series of equal payments at equal intervals of time, e.g., $1,000 at the end of every year for 10 years. The two types of annuities are ordinary annuities (annuity in arrears) and annuities due (annuity in advance).

1) An **ordinary annuity (annuity in arrears)** is a series of payments occurring at the **end** of each period. In an **annuity due (annuity in advance)**, the payments are made (received) at the **beginning** of each period.

b. The **present value of an annuity** is the value today of a series of future equal payments at equal intervals discounted at a given rate.

1) The first payment of an ordinary annuity is discounted, but the first payment of an annuity due is not discounted (since it was received today, it is worth its exact face amount, regardless of the discount rate).

2) A typical present value table is for an ordinary annuity, but the present value factor for an annuity due can be easily derived. The present value factor of an annuity due is equal to the present value factor of an ordinary annuity multiplied by (1 + i).

EXAMPLE 12-3 Present Value of an Annuity

	Present Value Factor of an Ordinary Annuity		
No. of Periods	6%	**8%**	10%
1	0.943	0.926	0.909
2	1.833	1.783	1.736
3	2.673	2.577	2.487
4	3.465	3.312	3.170
5	4.212	**3.993**	3.791

To calculate the present value of an **ordinary annuity** of five payments of $1,000 each discounted at 8%, multiply $1,000 by the appropriate factor ($1,000 payment per period × 3.993 present value factor of an ordinary annuity = **$3,993**).

This situation can be depicted as follows:

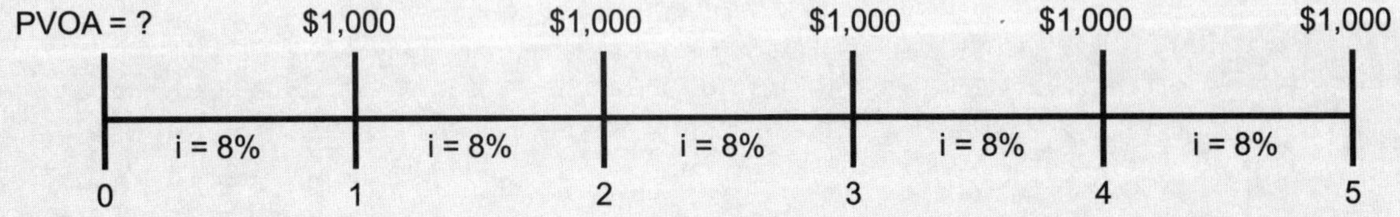

Figure 12-3

PVOA: Present value of an ordinary annuity

i: Interest rate

Using the same table, the present value of an **annuity due** of five payments of $1,000 each also may be calculated.

It equals **$4,312** [$1,000 payment per period × 3.993 present value factor of an ordinary annuity × (1 + 0.08)].

The present value of the annuity due ($4,312) is greater than the present value of the ordinary annuity ($3,993) because the payments occur 1 year sooner.

c. The **future value of an annuity** is the value that a series of equal payments will have at a certain moment in the future if the interest is earned at a given rate.

1) Interest is not earned for the first period of an ordinary annuity. Interest is earned on the first payment of an annuity due.

2) A typical future value table is for an ordinary annuity, but the future value factor for an annuity due can be easily derived. The future value factor of annuity due is equal to the future value factor of an ordinary annuity multiplied by (1 + i).

EXAMPLE 12-4 Future Value of an Annuity

	Future Value		
No. of Periods	**6%**	8%	10%
1	1.000	1.000	1.000
2	2.060	2.080	2.100
3	**3.184**	3.246	3.310
4	4.375	4.506	4.641
5	5.637	5.867	6.105

To calculate the FV of a 3-year **ordinary annuity** with payments of $1,000 each at 6% interest, multiply $1,000 by the appropriate factor ($1,000 × 3.184 = $3,184).

The FV of an **annuity due** also may be determined from the same table.

It equals $3,375 [$1,000 × 3.184 × (1 + 0.06)].

The future value of the annuity due ($3,375) is greater than the future value of an ordinary annuity ($3,184). The deposits are made earlier and therefore earn more interest.

STOP & REVIEW

You have completed the outline for this subunit.
Study multiple-choice questions 3 and 4 on page 380.

12.3 BONDS PAYABLE -- INITIAL MEASUREMENT

1. **Calculation of Proceeds**
   a. Of primary concern to an entity issuing bonds is the amount of cash that it will receive from investors on the day the bonds are sold.
      1) This amount is equal to the sum of the **present value of the cash flows** associated with the bonds discounted at the interest rate prevailing in the market at the time (called the market rate or effective rate).
         a) The cash flows associated with bonds are
            i) **Face amount** (present value of a single amount)
            ii) **Interest payments** (present value of an annuity)
      2) Using the effective rate as the discount rate ensures that the bonds' **yield to maturity** (that is, their ultimate rate of return to the investor) is equal to the rate of return prevailing in the market at the time of the sale.
   b. This present value calculation can result in cash proceeds equal to, less than, or greater than the face amount of the bonds, depending on the relationship of the bonds' stated rate of interest to the market rate.
      1) If the bonds' stated rate equals the market rate at the time of sale, the present value of the bonds will exactly equal their face amount, and the bonds are said to be sold **at par.**
2. **Issuance at a Premium**
   a. If the bonds' stated rate is greater than the current market rate, the cash proceeds are greater than the face amount, and the bonds are sold at a premium.

      Premium on bonds = Cash proceeds – Bonds' face amount

      1) Sometimes the issue price is an exact percentage of the face amount. In these cases, the bonds are said to be sold, for example, "at 101" or "at 102."
         a) Bonds issued "at 101" are issued at a price equal to 101% of the face amount.

EXAMPLE 12-5 Bonds Issued at a Premium

On January 1, Year 1, Pritzker, Inc., issues 200 8%, 5-year, $5,000 bonds when the prevailing interest rate in the market is 6%. The total face amount of bonds issued is therefore $1,000,000 ($5,000 face amount × 200 bonds). Annual cash interest payments of $80,000 ($1,000,000 face amount × 8% stated rate) will be made at the end of each year. The present value of the cash flows associated with this bond issue, discounted at the market rate of 6%, is calculated as follows:

Present value of face amount ($1,000,000 × 0.74726)	$ 747,260	
Present value of cash interest ($80,000 × 4.21236)	336,987	(rounded)
Cash proceeds from bond issue	$1,084,247	

Because the bonds are issued at a premium, the cash proceeds exceed the face amount. Pritzker records the following entry:

Cash (present value of cash flows)	$1,084,247	
Bonds payable (face amount)		$1,000,000
Premium on bonds payable (difference)		84,247

3. **Issuance at a Discount**

   a. If the bonds' stated rate is less than the current market rate, the cash proceeds are less than the face amount, and the bonds are sold at a discount.

      Discount on bonds = Bonds' face amount – Cash proceeds

      1) Sometimes the issue price is an exact percentage of the face amount. In these cases, the bonds are said to be sold, for example, "at 97" or "at 98."

         a) Bonds issued "at 99" are issued at a price equal to 99% of the face amount.

EXAMPLE 12-6 Bonds Issued at a Discount

On January 1, Year 1, Disler Co. issues 200 6%, 5-year, $5,000 bonds when the prevailing interest rate in the market is 8%. The total face amount of bonds issued is therefore $1,000,000 ($5,000 face amount × 200 bonds). Annual cash interest payments of $60,000 ($1,000,000 face amount × 6% stated rate) will be made at the end of each year. The present value of the cash flows associated with this bond issue, discounted at the market rate of 8%, is calculated as follows:

Present value of face amount ($1,000,000 × 0.68058)	$680,580	
Present value of cash interest ($60,000 × 3.99271)	239,566	(rounded)
Cash proceeds from bond issue	$920,146	

Because the bonds are issued at a discount, the cash proceeds are less than the face amount. Disler records the following entry:

Cash (present value of cash flows)	$920,146	
Discount on bonds payable (difference)	79,854	
Bonds payable (face amount)		$1,000,000

SUCCESS TIP

Stated Rate of Bonds	Cash Proceeds from Bonds	Bonds Issued at
Equals the market (effective) rate	Equals face amount	Par
Greater than the market (effective) rate	Greater than face amount	Premium
Lower than the market (effective) rate	Lower than face amount	Discount

4. **Bonds Sold between Interest Dates**

   a. When bonds are sold between interest payment dates, the buyer pays the issuer the amount of interest that has accrued since the last payment date.

EXAMPLE 12-7 Bonds Sold between Interest Dates

On November 1, Year 1, Bland Co. issues, at par, a 15-year bond with a face amount of $100,000. It has a stated rate of 9%, and interest is payable annually on July 1.

Annual interest on the bond is $9,000 ($100,000 face amount × 9% stated rate). On the next payment date (July 1, Year 2), Bland will pay the full annual interest of $9,000 to the buyer. The buyer therefore must pay Bland for the time during the most recent period that the buyer does not hold the bond (July 1-November 1, Year 1). The buyer includes accrued interest of $3,000 [$9,000 × (4 ÷ 12)] in the purchase price of the bond. The following entries will be recorded by Bland Co. and the buyer.

Bland Co.			Buyer		
November 1, Year 1:					
Cash	$103,000		Investment in bond	$100,000	
Bond payable		$100,000	Interest receivable	3,000	
Interest payable		3,000	Cash		$103,000
December 31, Year 1:					
Interest expense [$9,000 × (2 ÷ 12)]	$1,500		Interest receivable	$1,500	
Interest payable		$1,500	Interest income		$1,500
July 1, Year 2:					
Interest expense	$4,500		Cash	$9,000	
Interest payable	4,500		Interest receivable		$4,500
Cash		$9,000	Interest income		4,500

STOP & REVIEW

You have completed the outline for this subunit.
Study multiple-choice questions 5 and 6 on page 381.

12.4 BONDS PAYABLE -- SUBSEQUENT MEASUREMENT

1. **Balance Sheet Presentation**
   a. Bonds payable are reported in the balance sheet at their face amount (1) minus (plus) any unamortized discount (premium) and (2) minus any unamortized debt issuance costs.

Carrying amount of bonds payable = Face amount ± Unamortized premium (discount) – Unamortized debt issuance costs

2. **Effective Interest Method of Amortization**

SUCCESS TIP

CPA candidates should understand the effective interest method and expect to see a question asking for the calculation of interest expense. Remembering the associated journal entries will allow you to handle any question regarding the effective interest method with confidence.

   a. Bond discount or premium must be amortized using the effective interest method (unless the results of another method are not materially different).
      1) Under this method, interest expense changes every period, but the effective interest rate remains constant.

Annual interest expense = Carrying amount × Effective interest rate

      2) The cash paid for periodic interest also remains constant over the life of the bonds.

Cash interest paid = Face amount × Stated rate

   b. The difference between interest expense and cash interest paid is the discount or premium amortization.
      1) At the maturity date, the discount or premium is fully amortized, and the carrying amount of the bonds equals the face amount.

3. **Amortization Schedules**

   a. Premium amortized, total interest expense, and the carrying amount of the bonds **decrease** each period when amortizing a premium. The entry is

Interest expense	$XXX	
Premium on bonds payable	XXX	
Cash		$XXX

EXAMPLE 12-8 **Bonds Amortization Schedule -- Premium**

Pritzker, which issued bonds at a premium, uses the following amortization schedule:

Year	Beginning Carrying Amount	Times: Effective Rate	Equals: Interest Expense	Minus: Cash Paid	Equals: Premium Amortized	Ending Carrying Amount
1	$1,084,247	6%	$65,055	$80,000	$(14,945)	$1,069,302
2	1,069,302	6%	64,158	80,000	(15,842)	1,053,460
3	1,053,460	6%	63,208	80,000	(16,792)	1,036,668
4	1,036,668	6%	62,200	80,000	(17,800)	1,018,868
5	1,018,868	6%	61,132	80,000	(18,868)	1,000,000
					$(84,247)	

December 31, Year 1

Interest expense	$65,055	
Premium on bonds payable	14,945	
Cash		$80,000

December 31, Year 2

Interest expense	$64,158	
Premium on bonds payable	15,842	
Cash		$80,000

The bonds payable are reported on the December 31, Year 1, balance sheet at their carrying amount of $1,069,302.

   b. Discount amortized, total interest expense, and the carrying amount of the bonds **increase** each period when amortizing a discount. The entry is

Interest expense	$XXX	
Discount on bonds payable		$XXX
Cash		XXX

EXAMPLE 12-9 **Bonds Amortization Schedule -- Discount**

Disler, which issued bonds at a discount, uses the following amortization schedule:

Year	Beginning Carrying Amount	Times: Effective Rate	Equals: Interest Expense	Minus: Cash Paid	Equals: Discount Amortized	Ending Carrying Amount
1	$920,146	8%	$73,612	$60,000	$13,612	$ 933,758
2	933,758	8%	74,701	60,000	14,701	948,458
3	948,458	8%	75,877	60,000	15,877	964,335
4	964,335	8%	77,147	60,000	17,147	981,482
5	981,482	8%	78,519	60,000	18,519	1,000,000
					$79,854	

December 31, Year 1

Interest expense	$73,612	
Discount on bonds payable		$13,612
Cash		60,000

December 31, Year 2

Interest expense	$74,701	
Discount on bonds payable		$14,701
Cash		60,000

The bonds payable are reported on the December 31, Year 1, balance sheet at their carrying amount of $933,758.

4. **Interest on Bonds Paid More Often than Annually**

   a. Some bonds may pay interest more often than annually, e.g., semiannually. The accounting for these bonds is based on the number of periods in which interest is paid.

      1) The interest rates on bonds are provided on an annual basis. For the sake of simplicity, the stated rate and the market (effective) interest rate that apply to each period can be calculated as follows:

$$\frac{\text{Interest rate on an annual basis}}{\text{Number of times interest is paid per year}}$$

EXAMPLE 12-10 Interest on Bonds Paid Twice a Year

On January 1, Year 1, Eva Co. issued 5-year, 6%, $100,000 bonds. The bonds pay interest semiannually on July 1 and December 31. The bonds were issued to yield 10%. Thus, the market rate on the day of issuance was 10%. Because interest is paid twice a year, the interest is paid over 10 (5 years × 2) semiannual periods. The stated and effective interest rates on each period are 3% (6% ÷ 2) and 5% (10% ÷ 2), respectively.

The proceeds from the bonds equal the present value of the cash flows associated with the bond issue. These proceeds are calculated based on the following information: 10 periods, stated rate of 3%, cash interest payment each period of $3,000 ($100,000 × 3%), and market (effective) rate of 5%.

Bonds' face amount ($100,000) multiplied by the present value of $1 at 5% for 10 periods (0.614)	$61,400
Semiannual cash interest ($3,000) multiplied by the present value of an ordinary annuity of $1 at 5% for 10 periods (7.722)	23,166
Cash proceeds from bond issue	$84,566

January 1, Year 1		
Cash	$84,566	
Discount on bonds payable	15,434	
Bonds payable		$100,000

July 1, Year 1		
Interest expense ($84,566 × 5%)	$4,228	
Discount on bonds payable		$1,228
Cash		3,000

SUCCESS TIP

- When bonds are issued at a **premium**, interest expense for the period equals (1) cash interest paid during the period **minus** (2) premium amortized during the period.
- When bonds are issued at a **discount**, interest expense for the period equals (1) cash interest paid during the period **plus** (2) discount amortized during the period.

STOP & REVIEW

You have completed the outline for this subunit.
Study multiple-choice questions 7 through 9 beginning on page 382.

12.5 DEBT ISSUE COSTS

1. **Costs Included**
   a. Issue costs are incurred to bring debt to market. They include
      1) Printing and engraving costs,
      2) Legal fees,
      3) Accountants' fees,
      4) Underwriters' commissions,
      5) Registration fees, and
      6) Promotion costs.
2. **Accounting Treatment**
   a. Costs to issue debt securities must be reported in the balance sheet as a **direct deduction** from the **face amount of the debt**.

EXAMPLE 12-11 — Bond Issuance Costs

Ron Co. issued, at 98, 50 of its 10%, $1,000 bonds. Ron paid legal and registration fees of $2,000 to issue the bonds. On the issuance date, Ron records the following journal entries:

Cash (50 × $1,000 × 98%)	$49,000		Debt issue costs	$2,000	
Discount on bonds	1,000		Cash		$2,000
Bond payable (face amount)		$50,000			

On the face of the balance sheet, the bonds payable are reported at $47,000 ($50,000 face amount – $1,000 bond discount – $2,000 debt issue costs).

   b. Debt issue costs should be amortized over the term of the debt using the **effective interest method**. But the straight-line amortization method may be applied if the results are not materially different.

STOP & REVIEW

You have completed the outline for this subunit.
Study multiple-choice questions 10 and 11 on page 384.

12.6 SECURITIES WITH CHARACTERISTICS OF LIABILITIES AND EQUITY

1. **Classification**

   a. A liability results from a current obligation to transfer assets or provide services. Equity is the residual interest in the assets of an entity after subtraction of liabilities.

   b. Common stock or preferred stock that is not redeemable is treated as equity.

      1) Each confers a residual interest in entity assets, and no obligation exists to pay dividends or redeem the stock.

   c. Bonds are treated as liabilities.

      1) They represent an obligation to make interest and principal payments, with no residual interest in entity assets.

   d. The classification of a financial instrument as liability or equity is based on its specific characteristics, such as the way it is settled.

      1) A financial instrument that is settled by transferring **cash** is classified as a **liability**.

      2) A financial instrument that is settled by issuing a **fixed number** of shares is classified as equity. It is reported in the additional paid-in capital (APIC) account.

EXAMPLE 12-12 Classification of a Financial Instrument as Equity

On January 1, Year 1, Nerissa Co. received $5,000 for a promise to issue 100 of its own shares on July 1, Year 1. This financial instrument is classified as **equity** because it will be settled by issuing a fixed number of shares (100 shares).

      3) A financial instrument that is settled by issuing a **variable number of shares** is classified as a **liability** if

         a) The number of shares to be issued is based on a fixed monetary amount known at inception.

         b) The number of shares to be issued is inversely related to changes in the fair value of the issuer's shares. For example, the greater the issuer's market price per share, the lower the number of shares to be issued, and vice versa.

EXAMPLE 12-13 Classification of a Financial Instrument as Liability

On January 1, Year 1, Nerissa Co. received $5,000 for a promise to issue its own shares worth $6,000 on July 1, Year 1. This financial instrument is classified as a **liability**. The number of shares to be issued is variable and based on a fixed monetary amount known at inception ($6,000).

   e. However, the classification of the securities covered in the following outline is more complex because they have liability and equity components.

2. **Convertible Debt**

   a. Convertible debt may be exchanged for common stock of the issuer.

      1) Convertible debt may be more attractive to issuers than nonconvertible debt because it is usually issued at a lower interest rate.

   b. The debt and equity elements of convertible debt are treated as inseparable. The entire proceeds, typically cash, should be accounted for and reported as a liability until conversion.

3. **Detachable vs. Nondetachable Warrants**

   a. Like convertible debt, warrants allow a debtholder to obtain common shares.

      1) Unlike convertible debt, warrants require the debtholder to pay an additional amount to receive the shares.

   b. When warrants are **nondetachable**, their conversion feature is considered to be inseparable from the underlying debt, and the entire proceeds are attributed to debt.

   c. When debt is issued with **detachable** warrants, the proceeds must be allocated between the underlying debt and the warrants pro rata based on their relative fair values at the time of issuance.

      1) Allocate the proceeds pro rata to the debt.

$$\text{Cash proceeds received} \times \left(\frac{\text{FV of debt}}{\text{FV of debt + Warrants}}\right)$$

      2) Record the issuance of the debt.

Cash (see formula above)	$XXX	
Discount on bonds payable	XXX	
Bonds payable		$XXX

      3) Allocate the proceeds pro rata to the warrants.

$$\text{Cash proceeds received} \times \left(\frac{\text{FV of warrants}}{\text{FV of debt + Warrants}}\right)$$

      4) Record the issuance of the warrants.

Cash (see formula above)	$XXX	
Paid-in capital -- warrants		$XXX

      5) When the fair value of the warrants but not the debt is known, paid-in capital from warrants should be credited (increased) for the fair value of the warrants.

         a) The remainder is credited to the debt.

d. When the warrants are exercised, the journal entry is

Cash	$XXX	
Paid-in capital -- warrants	XXX	
Common stock		$XXX
Additional paid-in capital		XXX

EXAMPLE 12-14 Bonds with Detachable Warrants

On January 2, Matrix Co. issued $1,000,000 of 9% bonds for $1,040,000. Each $1,000 bond had 20 detachable warrants. Each warrant was redeemable for one share of Matrix $10 par-value stock at a price of $30. Directly after the issuance, the warrants were trading for $5 each.

The fair value of the 20,000 warrants [($1,000,000 ÷ $1,000) bonds × 20] was $100,000 (20,000 warrants × $5). Given that the fair value of the bonds is not known, the warrants are credited for $100,000. The remainder of the proceeds ($1,040,000 – $100,000 = $940,000) is assigned to the bonds.

To record the issuance of the bonds:

Cash	$940,000	
Discount on bonds payable	60,000	
Bonds payable		$1,000,000

To record the issuance of the warrants:

Cash	$100,000	
Paid-in capital -- warrants		$100,000

To record the exercise of the warrants:

Cash (20,000 × $30)	$600,000	
Paid-in capital -- warrants	100,000	
Common stock (20,000 × $10)		$200,000
Additional paid-in capital		500,000

STOP & REVIEW

You have completed the outline for this subunit.
Study multiple-choice question 12 on page 385.

12.7 EXTINGUISHMENT OF DEBT

1. **Early Extinguishment**
   a. Issuers sometimes retire debt before maturity, for example, to eliminate high-interest debt when rates are declining or to improve debt ratios.
   b. All extinguishments of debt before scheduled maturities are fundamentally alike and should be accounted for similarly.
   c. The carrying amount is the amount due at maturity, adjusted for unamortized premium or discount and unamortized issue costs.
   d. The reacquisition price is the amount paid on extinguishment, including any call premium and miscellaneous costs of reacquisition.
      1) An extinguishment may be done by exchanging new securities for the old (a refunding). The reacquisition price equals the total present value of the new securities.
2. **Gains or Losses**
   a. Gains or losses are recognized in earnings in the period of extinguishment.
      1) The gain or loss is measured by the difference between the reacquisition price and the carrying amount of the debt, which includes any unamortized debt issue cost.

EXAMPLE 12-15 Extinguishment of Debt

Debtor has a noncurrent note payable outstanding with a face amount of $1,000,000. When Debtor decides to extinguish the note at a cost of $1,050,000, the unamortized premium and debt issue costs are $20,000 and $12,500, respectively. Thus, the carrying amount of the note payable on that date is $1,007,500 ($1,000,000 face amount + $20,000 unamortized premium – $12,500 unamortized debt issue costs). Accordingly, the loss on extinguishment is $42,500 ($1,050,000 cost – $1,007,500).

Noncurrent note payable	$1,007,500	
Loss on extinguishment	42,500	
Cash		$1,050,000

3. **Derecognition**
   a. A debtor derecognizes a liability only if it has been extinguished. Extinguishment results only if the debtor
      1) Pays the creditor and is relieved of its obligation with respect to the liability or
      2) Is legally released from being the primary obligor, either judicially or by the creditor.

STOP & REVIEW

You have completed the outline for this subunit.
Study multiple-choice questions 13 and 14 beginning on page 385.

12.8 NONCURRENT NOTES PAYABLE

1. Notes payable are essentially accounted for the same as bonds. However,
   a. A note is payable to a single creditor, while bonds are payable to many creditors.
   b. Notes are usually of shorter duration than bonds.
   c. A loan agreement may require the debtor to pay principal and interest at specified intervals.
2. Any material premium or discount is amortized using the effective-interest method, as described in Subunit 12.4.
   a. Discount or premium, loan origination fees, etc., are amortized in accordance with the effective-interest method.
   b. Discount or premium is not an asset or liability separable from the related note.
      1) A discount or premium is therefore reported in the balance sheet as a direct subtraction from, or addition to, the face amount of the note.
3. Noncurrent notes that are payable in installments are classified as current to the extent of any principal payments due in the coming year.
   a. Payments not due in the current year are classified as noncurrent.
4. **Different Patterns of Repayments**
   a. Some notes require one principal payment at the end of the note's term plus periodic interest payments during the note's term (like a term bond).

EXAMPLE 12-16 Annual Interest Payments and Term-End Principal Payment

An entity agrees to give, in return for merchandise, a 3-year, $100,000 note bearing 8% interest paid annually. The effective interest rate is 6%. Because the note's stated rate exceeds the effective rate, the note will be issued at a premium.

The entity records the note at the present value of (1) a single payment of $100,000 in 3 years and (2) three interest payments of $8,000 each. These payments are discounted at the effective rate (five decimal places are used for increased accuracy).

Present value of principal ($100,000 × 0.83962)	$ 83,962
Present value of interest ($8,000 × 2.67301)	21,384
Present value of note	$105,346

The entry to record the note is

Inventory	$105,346	
Premium on note payable		$ 5,346
Note payable		100,000

b. Other notes require equal periodic principal payments plus interest. Each periodic payment includes an equal amount of return of principal and an amount of interest accrued on the beginning carrying amount.

EXAMPLE 12-17 Equal Periodic Payments Plus Interest

On January 1, Year 1, Shark Co. borrowed $120,000 on a 10% note payable to Bank. Three equal annual principal payments of $40,000 plus interest are paid beginning December 31, Year 1.

Year	Beginning Carrying Amount (a)	Interest Rate	Interest Payment/ Expense (b)	Principal Payment (c)	Total Payment (b) + (c)	Ending Carrying Amount (a) – (c)
1	$120,000	10%	$12,000	$40,000	$52,000	$80,000
2	80,000	10%	8,000	40,000	48,000	40,000
3	40,000	10%	4,000	40,000	44,000	0

c. A third type of note requires equal periodic cash payments. Each payment includes a principal component (i.e., return of principal) and an interest component.

EXAMPLE 12-18 Equal Periodic Cash Payments

On January 1, Year 1, Star Co. borrowed $120,000 on a 10% note payable to Bank. Three equal annual payments of $48,254 are paid beginning December 31, Year 1.

Year	Beginning Carrying Amount (a)	Interest Rate	Interest Payment/ Expense (b)	Total Payment (c)	Principal Payment (c) – (b) = (d)	Ending Carrying Amount (a) – (d)
1	$120,000	10%	$12,000	$48,254	$36,254	$83,746
2	83,746	10%	8,375	48,254	39,879	43,867
3	43,867	10%	4,387	48,254	43,867	0

NOTE: The proceeds from the note are equal to the present value of the cash payments associated with the note. The equal annual payment ($48,254) multiplied by the present value of an ordinary annuity of $1 at 10% for three periods (2.48685) equals the proceeds from the note of $120,000.

STOP & REVIEW

You have completed the outline for this subunit.
Study multiple-choice questions 15 and 16 beginning on page 386.

12.9 TROUBLED DEBT RESTRUCTURINGS

1. **Overview**

   a. A troubled debt restructuring (TDR) occurs when "the creditor for economic or legal reasons related to the debtor's financial difficulties grants a concession to the debtor that it would not otherwise consider" (ASC 310-40-20).

   b. A TDR can consist of either a settlement of the debt in full or a continuation of the debt with a modification in terms. TDRs almost always involve a loss to the creditor and a gain to the debtor.

2. **Settlement in Full with a Transfer of Assets**

   a. The **creditor recognizes a loss** equal to the difference between the fair value of the assets received and the net carrying amount of the receivable (Amortized cost basis – Allowance for credit losses).

      1) Thus, if the allowance method is used for recording debts expected to be uncollectible, the loss is net of the previously recognized credit loss expense related to the debt.

EXAMPLE 12-19 **TDR Settled with Assets -- Creditor**

Debtor gave a mortgage on its building to Creditor. The principal amount of Creditor's mortgage receivable is $5,000,000 (the amortized cost), and it has credited the related allowance for the uncollectible amount (i.e., allowance for credit losses) for $200,000. Thus, the carrying amount of the receivable is $4,800,000. Assume (for computational simplicity) that the carrying amount of Debtor's mortgage is $5,000,000. The building's fair value is $4,500,000, and its carrying amount on Debtor's balance sheet is $6,000,000. Debtor transfers the building to Creditor in full settlement of the debt.

<u>Creditor's entry:</u>		
Building (fair value)	$4,500,000	
Loss on receivable (difference)	300,000	
Allowance for credit losses (related amount)	200,000	
Mortgage receivable (principal)		$5,000,000

      2) If the creditor receives long-lived assets to be sold in full satisfaction, the assets are recorded at fair value minus cost to sell.

   b. The **debtor recognizes a gain on restructuring** when the carrying amount of the debt exceeds the fair value of the asset(s) given.

      1) The debtor also recognizes a **gain or loss on disposition** of the asset equal to the difference between the fair value of the assets given and their carrying amount.

EXAMPLE 12-20 **TDR Settled with Assets -- Debtor**

<u>Debtor's entry:</u>		
Mortgage payable (carrying amount)	$5,000,000	
Loss on disposition of building (Carrying amount – Fair value)	1,500,000	
Building (carrying amount)		$6,000,000
Gain on restructuring (Debt settled – Fair value of building)		500,000

NOTE: The total loss recognized by Debtor of $1,000,000 ($1,500,000 loss on disposition – $500,000 gain on restructuring) equals the excess of the carrying amount of the asset given ($6,000,000) over the carrying amount of the debt ($5,000,000).

   c. The creditor's total loss (Credit loss expense previously recognized + Current loss) equals the debtor's gain on restructuring.

3. **Settlement in Full with a Transfer of an Equity Interest**

   a. The creditor again recognizes a current loss equal to the difference between the fair value of the equity securities received and the net carrying amount of the receivable.

      1) The **debtor** recognizes a **gain** only on the restructuring (excess of the carrying amount of the debt over the fair value of the equity given).

EXAMPLE 12-21 TDR Settled with Equity Securities

Using the information from Examples 12-19 and 12-20, assume that Creditor receives Debtor common stock (100,000 shares at $10 par) with a fair value of $4,800,000. Because the fair value received ($4,800,000) equals the carrying amount ($5,000,000 – $200,000 allowance), Creditor recognizes no current loss.

Creditor's entry:		
Investment in common stock of debtor (fair value)	$4,800,000	
Allowance for credit losses (related amount)	200,000	
Mortgage receivable (principal)		$5,000,000
Debtor's entry:		
Mortgage payable (carrying amount)	$5,000,000	
Common stock (100,000 shares at $10 par)		$1,000,000
Additional paid-in capital (Fair value of stock – Total par value)		3,800,000
Gain on restructuring (Debt settled – Fair value of stock)		200,000

      2) As in the previous case, the creditor's total loss equals the debtor's gain on restructuring.

4. **Modification of Terms**

   a. Three changes in the terms of the loan are common:

      1) A reduction in the principal
      2) An extension of the maturity date
      3) A lowering of the interest rate

   b. The **debtor** accounts for the modification of terms based on the **undiscounted cash flows** (UCF) associated with the modified terms.

   c. The **creditor** accounts for the modification of terms based on the **discounted cash flows** associated with the modified terms.

      1) The discount rate used by the creditor is the **original (historical) contractual rate**.
      2) The credit losses recognized are recorded through an allowance for credit losses account.

5. **Modification of Terms when Future Cash Flows Exceed the Carrying Amount**

   a. **No gain** is recognized by the **debtor** when the **undiscounted cash flows** associated with the modified terms are **greater** than the carrying amount of the troubled debt.

EXAMPLE 12-22 **Modified Terms -- Debtor**

Instead of a full settlement as illustrated in Examples 12-19 and 12-20, Creditor agrees that (1) the mortgage principal will be reduced from $5,000,000 to $4,000,000, (2) the final maturity will be extended from 1 year to 5 years, and (3) the interest rate will be reduced from 8% to 6%. Interest continues to be paid at year end.

The new principal of $4,000,000 plus interest of $1,200,000 ($4,000,000 × 6% × 5 years) yields a UCF of $5,200,000. Because the UCF exceeds the carrying amount of the debt ($5,200,000 > $5,000,000), Debtor recognizes no gain. It continues making journal entries to record periodic interest payments and retirement of debt.

   b. The **creditor** must recognize the impairment of a loan when it is probable that the debtor will not be able to pay all the amounts (principal and interest) due in accordance with the original terms of the loan.

      1) The impairment loss is the difference between

         a) The **discounted expected cash flows** (DCF) reflecting an effective rate based on the **original contractual rate** and

         b) The net carrying amount of the receivable.

EXAMPLE 12-23 **Modified Terms -- Creditor Loss if Cash Flow > Carrying Amount**

The present value of the new principal, discounted at the original mortgage rate of 8% for 5 years, is $2,722,320 ($4,000,000 × .68058). The present value of the new annual interest payments, discounted at 8% for 5 years, is $958,250 ($4,000,000 × 6% × 3.99271).

Mortgage receivable (principal)	$5,000,000
Minus: Discounted principal	(2,722,320)
Minus: Discounted interest payments	(958,250)
Total impairment of receivable	$1,319,430

Given an existing credit in the allowance account of $200,000, Creditor records the current impairment loss as follows:

Credit loss expense ($1,319,430 – $200,000)	$1,119,430	
Allowance for credit losses		$1,119,430

      2) The creditor's loss does not equal the debtor's gain because no gain is recognized by the debtor when the future cash flows exceed the carrying amount of the debt.

6. **Modification of Terms when Future Cash Flows Are Less than the Carrying Amount**

   a. The **debtor** will recognize a **gain** if the total of the **undiscounted cash flows** (UCF) associated with the modified terms is **less** than the carrying amount of the troubled debt.

Gain = UCF – Carrying amount of the debt

EXAMPLE 12-24 Modified Terms -- Debtor Gain if Cash Flow < Carrying Amount

Instead of reducing the principal to $4,000,000, Creditor agrees to reduce the principal to $3,000,000. The principal of $3,000,000 plus interest of $900,000 ($3,000,000 × 6% × 5 years) yields UCF of $3,900,000.

Because the UCF are less than the carrying amount of the debt ($3,900,000 < $5,000,000), Debtor recognizes a gain equal to the difference.

Debtor's entry:		
Mortgage payable	$1,100,000	
Gain on restructuring		$1,100,000

   b. The **creditor's** current impairment loss is the difference between the DCF and the net carrying amount of the receivable.

EXAMPLE 12-25 Modified Terms -- Creditor Loss if Cash Flow < Carrying Amount

The present value of the principal, discounted at 8% for 5 years, is $2,041,740 ($3,000,000 × .68058). The present value of the new annual interest payments, discounted at 8% for 5 years, is $718,688 ($3,000,000 × 6% × 3.99271).

Mortgage receivable (carrying amount)	$5,000,000
Minus: Discounted principal	(2,041,740)
Minus: Discounted interest payments	(718,688)
Total impairment of receivable	$2,239,572

Given an existing credit in the allowance account of $200,000, Creditor records the current impairment loss as follows:

Creditor's entry:		
Credit loss expense ($2,239,572 – $200,000)	$2,039,572	
Allowance for credit losses		$2,039,572

   c. The creditor's impairment loss does not equal the debtor's gain (if any).

STOP & REVIEW

You have completed the outline for this subunit.
Study multiple-choice question 17 on page 387.

12.10 ASSET RETIREMENT OBLIGATIONS

1. **Overview**
   a. Certain long-lived tangible assets, such as mines or nuclear power plants, incur significant costs after the end of their productive lives.
   b. An asset retirement obligation (ARO) reflects a legal obligation arising from acquisition, construction, development, or normal operation of an asset.
      1) A legal obligation is one arising from an existing or enacted law, statute, ordinance, or contract.
2. **Initial Recognition and Measurement**
   a. An entity must recognize the fair value of a liability for an ARO. Upon initial recognition of such a liability, an entity must **capitalize** an **asset retirement cost (ARC)** by increasing the carrying amount of the related asset by the same amount as the liability recognized.
      1) The journal entry is

Asset	$XXX	
Liability for asset retirement obligation		$XXX

   b. If an item of property, plant, and equipment with an existing ARO is acquired, the entity credits a liability for that obligation and debits the carrying amount of the item for the same amount (the ARC) at the acquisition date. The effect is the same as if that obligation were incurred on that date.
   c. The fair value of the liability is **initially measured** by using an **expected present value technique**. The liability recognized equals the present value of the future cash flows expected to be paid to settle the obligation discounted at the **credit-adjusted risk-free rate**.

EXAMPLE 12-26 Initial Recognition and Measurement of ARO

On January 1, Year 1, Akula Co. acquired a plant for $200,000. The estimated useful life of the plant is 5 years with no salvage value. Akula is required by law to remove the plant and restore the land at the end of the plant's useful life. Akula estimates that the total cost to settle the liability for retirement of the plant is $50,000. Akula's credit-adjusted risk-free rate is 6%. The present value of $1 for a 5-year period at 6% is 0.7473. The present value of the future cash flows expected to be paid to settle the liability is $37,365 ($50,000 × 0.7473).

On January 1, Year 1, Akula recorded the following journal entry:

Plant ($200,000 + $37,365)	$237,365	
Cash		$200,000
Liability for plant retirement obligation		37,365

3. **Accounting Subsequent to Initial Recognition**
   a. After initial recognition, the ARC should be depreciated over the asset's useful life.
   b. In addition, the liability recognized must be adjusted periodically for (1) the passage of time (accretion expense) and (2) revisions in the original estimate.

EXAMPLE 12-27 Subsequent Accounting for ARO

By using the effective interest method, Akula Co. recognized the following accretion expenses in Years 1 through 5:

Year	Liability at Beginning of Year	Discount Rate	Accretion Expense	Liability at Year End
1	$37,365	6%	$2,242	$39,607
2	39,607	6%	2,375	41,982
3	41,982	6%	2,519	44,501
4	44,501	6%	2,670	47,171
5	47,171	6%	2,829	50,000

Akula recorded the following journal entries on December 31, Year 1:

	Debit	Credit
Depreciation expense ($237,365 ÷ 5)	$47,473	
Accumulated depreciation		$47,473
Accretion expense	$2,242	
Liability for plant retirement obligation		$2,242

The plant and related liability are reported on the December 31, Year 1, balance sheet as follows:

Noncurrent assets:		Noncurrent liabilities:	
Plant	$237,365	Liability for plant retirement obligation	$39,607
Accumulated depreciation	(47,473)		
Carrying amount	$189,892		

   c. At the end of the asset's useful life, the actual costs incurred to settle the liability may differ from the carrying amount of the liability on that date. The difference between the amount paid and the carrying amount of the liability for an ARO is recognized as a gain or loss on settlement of the ARO.

EXAMPLE 12-28 Settlement of ARO

At the end of the plant's service life, Akula Co. incurred costs of $55,000 for restoring the land. The journal entry is

	Debit	Credit
Asset retirement obligation	$50,000	
Loss on settlement of ARO	5,000	
Cash		$55,000

STOP & REVIEW

You have completed the outline for this subunit.
Study multiple-choice question 18 on page 388.

QUESTIONS

12.1 Types of Bond Liabilities

1. Blue Corp.'s December 31, Year 4, balance sheet contained the following items in the long-term liabilities section:

9.75% registered debentures, callable in Year 15, due in Year 20	$700,000
9.50% collateral trust bonds, convertible into common stock beginning in Year 13, due in Year 23	600,000
10% subordinated debentures ($30,000 maturing annually beginning in Year 10)	300,000

What is the total amount of Blue's term bonds?

A. $600,000

B. $700,000

C. $1,000,000

D. $1,300,000

Answer (D) is correct.

REQUIRED: The total amount of term bonds.

DISCUSSION: Term bonds mature on a single date. Thus, the registered bonds and the collateral trust bonds are term bonds, a total of $1,300,000 ($700,000 + $600,000).

Answer (A) is incorrect. The registered bonds are also term bonds. **Answer (B) is incorrect.** The collateral trust bonds are also term bonds. **Answer (C) is incorrect.** The collateral trust bonds, not the subordinated debentures, are term bonds.

2. Bonds payable issued with scheduled maturities at various dates are called

	Serial Bonds	Term Bonds
A.	No	Yes
B.	No	No
C.	Yes	No
D.	Yes	Yes

Answer (C) is correct.

REQUIRED: The name(s) for bonds issued with scheduled maturities at various dates.

DISCUSSION: Serial bonds are bond issues that mature in installments at various dates. Term bonds mature on a single date.

12.2 Time Value of Money

3. On December 30, Chang Co. sold a machine to Door Co. in exchange for a noninterest-bearing note requiring 10 annual payments of $10,000. Door made the first payment on December 30. The market interest rate for similar notes at date of issuance was 8%. Information on present value factors is as follows:

Number of Periods	Present Value of $1 at 8%	Present Value of Ordinary Annuity of $1 at 8%
9	0.50	6.25
10	0.46	6.71

In its December 31 balance sheet, what amount should Chang report as note receivable?

A. $45,000

B. $46,000

C. $62,500

D. $67,100

Answer (C) is correct.

REQUIRED: The carrying amount of a noninterest-bearing note receivable at the date of issuance.

DISCUSSION: The purchase agreement calls for a $10,000 initial payment and equal payments of $10,000 to be received at the end of each of the next 9 years. The amount reported for the receivable should consist of the present value of the nine future payments. The present value factor to be used is the present value of an ordinary annuity for nine periods at 8%, or 6.25. The note receivable should be recorded at $62,500 ($10,000 × 6.25).

Answer (A) is incorrect. The amount of $45,000 results from multiplying $90,000 ($10,000 payments × 9 years) by 0.50. **Answer (B) is incorrect.** The amount of $46,000 results from multiplying the $100,000 total by 0.46. **Answer (D) is incorrect.** The amount of $67,100 results from using the present value of an ordinary annuity of $1 at 8% for 10 years instead of 9 years.

4. For which of the following transactions would the use of the present value of an annuity due concept be appropriate in calculating the present value of the asset obtained or liability owed at the date of incurrence?

A. A finance lease is entered into with the initial lease payment due 1 month subsequent to the signing of the lease agreement.

B. A finance lease is entered into with the initial lease payment due upon the signing of the lease agreement.

C. A 10-year, 8% bond is issued on January 2 with interest payable semiannually on July 1 and January 1, yielding 7%.

D. A 10-year, 8% bond is issued on January 2 with interest payable semiannually on July 1 and January 1, yielding 9%.

Answer (B) is correct.

REQUIRED: The transaction for which the present value of an annuity due concept would be appropriate.

DISCUSSION: In an annuity due, the first payment is made at the beginning of the first period and is therefore not discounted. In an ordinary annuity, the first payment is made at the end of the first period and therefore is discounted. For annuities due, the first payment is included in the computation at its face value.

Answer (A) is incorrect. Given that the first payment is due 1 month from signing and not on the day of signing, an ordinary annuity, not an annuity due, is the relevant model. **Answer (C) is incorrect.** The bonds have just passed an interest payment (coupon) date. The next one is not for another 6 months. Given no immediate payment, the annuity is ordinary. Furthermore, the yield percentage is irrelevant to annuity. **Answer (D) is incorrect.** The initial payment is not due immediately.

12.3 Bonds Payable -- Initial Measurement

5. On November 1, Mason Corp. issued $800,000 of its 10-year, 8% term bonds dated October 1. The bonds were sold to yield 10%, with total proceeds of $700,000 plus accrued interest. Interest is paid every April 1 and October 1. What amount should Mason report for interest payable in its December 31 balance sheet?

A. $17,500

B. $16,000

C. $11,667

D. $10,667

Answer (B) is correct.

REQUIRED: The interest payable reported in the balance sheet.

DISCUSSION: Interest payable equals the face amount of the bonds, times the nominal (stated) interest rate, times the portion of the interest period included in the accounting period. The yield rate and sale between interest periods for an amount including accrued interest do not affect interest payable. Accordingly, interest payable equals $16,000 [($800,000 × 8%) × (3 ÷ 12 months)].

Answer (A) is incorrect. The amount of $17,500 equals 3 months of interest based on the yield rate and the sale proceeds (exclusive of accrued interest). **Answer (C) is incorrect.** The amount of $11,667 equals 2 months of interest based on the yield rate and the sale proceeds (exclusive of accrued interest). **Answer (D) is incorrect.** The amount of $10,667 equals the interest for 2 months.

6. The following information pertains to Camp Corp.'s issuance of bonds on July 1, Year 4:

Face amount	$800,000
Term	10 years
Stated interest rate	6%
Interest payment dates	Annually on July 1
Yield	9%

	At 6%	At 9%
Present value of 1 for 10 periods	0.558	0.422
Future value of 1 for 10 periods	1.791	2.367
Present value of ordinary annuity of 1 for 10 periods	7.360	6.418

What should the issue price be for each $1,000 bond?

A. $1,000

B. $943

C. $864

D. $807

Answer (D) is correct.

REQUIRED: The issue price for each bond.

DISCUSSION: The issue price of a bond equals the sum of the present values of the future cash flows (Principal + Interest). This amount is $807 [($1,000 face amount × .422 PV of 1 for 10 periods at 9%) principal + ($1,000 face amount × 6% stated rate × 6.418 PV of an ordinary annuity for 10 periods at 9%) interest].

Answer (A) is incorrect. The face amount is $1,000. **Answer (B) is incorrect.** The amount of $943 is the result of discounting the interest payments at 9% and the face amount at 6%. **Answer (C) is incorrect.** The amount of $864 is the result of discounting the interest payments at 6% and the face amount at 9%.

12.4 Bonds Payable -- Subsequent Measurement

7. How is the carrying amount of a bond payable affected by amortization of the following?

	Discount	Premium
A.	Increase	Increase
B.	Decrease	Decrease
C.	Increase	Decrease
D.	Decrease	Increase

Answer (C) is correct.
REQUIRED: The effect of discount and premium amortization on the carrying value of a bond payable.
DISCUSSION: The carrying amount of a bond payable is equal to its maturity (face) amount plus any unamortized premium or minus any unamortized discount. Amortization results in a reduction of the discount or premium. Consequently, the carrying amount of a bond is increased when discount is amortized and decreased when premium is amortized.

8. On January 1, Year 2, Oak Co. issued 400 of its 8%, $1,000 bonds at 97 plus accrued interest. The bonds are dated October 1, Year 1, and mature on October 1, Year 11. Interest is payable semiannually on April 1 and October 1. Accrued interest for the period October 1, Year 1, to January 1, Year 2, amounted to $8,000. On January 1, Year 2, what amount should Oak report as bonds payable, net of discount?

A. $380,300
B. $388,000
C. $388,300
D. $392,000

Answer (B) is correct.
REQUIRED: The bonds payable, net of discount.
DISCUSSION: A bond issued "at 97" is issued at a price equal to 97% of its face amount (400 bonds × $1,000 face amount × .97 = $388,000). At the issue date, no time has passed, so no amortization has occurred, and the accrued interest is credited to either interest payable or interest expense. The reported amount is therefore $388,000 ($400,000 – $12,000).
Answer (A) is incorrect. The amount of $380,300 deducts the accrued interest from the net bonds payable and adds 3 months of discount amortization. **Answer (C) is incorrect.** The amount of $388,300 includes 3 months of discount amortization. **Answer (D) is incorrect.** The amount of $392,000 equals face amount minus accrued interest.

9. On December 31, Year 1, Arnold, Inc., issued $200,000, 8% serial bonds, to be repaid in the amount of $40,000 each year. Interest is payable annually on December 31. The bonds were issued to yield 10% per year. The bond proceeds were $190,280 based on the present values at December 31, Year 1, of the five annual payments:

Due	Amounts Due		Present Value
Date	Principal	Interest	at 12/31/Yr 1
12/31/Yr 2	$40,000	$16,000	$ 50,900
12/31/Yr 3	40,000	12,800	43,610
12/31/Yr 4	40,000	9,600	37,250
12/31/Yr 5	40,000	6,400	31,690
12/31/Yr 6	40,000	3,200	26,830
			$190,280

Arnold amortizes the bond discount by the interest method. In its December 31, Year 2, balance sheet, at what amount should Arnold report the carrying amount of the bonds?

A. $139,380

B. $149,100

C. $150,280

D. $153,308

Answer (D) is correct.

REQUIRED: The carrying amount after year one of bonds issued at a discount.

DISCUSSION: The carrying amount of the bonds at the end of Year 1 equals the proceeds of $190,280. Interest expense for Year 2 at the 10% effective rate is thus $19,028. Actual interest paid is $16,000, discount amortization is $3,028 ($19,028 – $16,000), and the discount remaining at year end is $6,692 [($200,000 face amount – $190,280 issue proceeds) – $3,028 discount amortization]. Given that $40,000 in principal is paid at year end, the December 31, Year 2, carrying amount is $153,308 ($160,000 face amount – $6,692 unamortized discount).

Answer (A) is incorrect. The amount of $139,380 is the carrying amount of the bonds at December 31, Year 2, less the total amount due in Year 3. **Answer (B) is incorrect.** The amount of $149,100 is the difference between the face amount of the bonds and the total payment in Year 3. **Answer (C) is incorrect.** The amount of $150,280 results from reducing the carrying amount at December 31, Year 2, by the payment of principal during Year 3.

12.5 Debt Issue Costs

10. On March 1, Year 1, Cain Corp. issued, at 103 plus accrued interest, 200 of its 9%, $1,000 bonds. The bonds are dated January 1, Year 1, and mature on January 1, Year 11. Interest is payable semiannually on January 1 and July 1. Cain paid bond issue costs of $10,000. Cain should realize net cash receipts from the bond issuance of

A. $216,000

B. $209,000

C. $206,000

D. $199,000

Answer (D) is correct.

REQUIRED: The cash received from the issuance of a bond at a premium plus accrued interest.

DISCUSSION: The face amount of the bonds is $200,000 (200 bonds × $1,000 face amount). Excluding interest, the proceeds from the issuance of the bonds were $206,000 ($200,000 × 103%). Accrued interest for 2 months (January 1 through March 1) was $3,000 ($200,000 face amount × 9% coupon rate × 2/12). The net cash receipts from the issuance of the bonds were therefore equal to $199,000 ($206,000 bond proceeds + $3,000 accrued interest – $10,000 bond issue costs).

Answer (A) is incorrect. The amount of $216,000 equals the sum of the bond proceeds (excluding accrued interest) and the bond issue costs. **Answer (B) is incorrect.** The amount of $209,000 is the sum of the bond proceeds and the accrued interest. **Answer (C) is incorrect.** The amount of $206,000 is the sum of the bond proceeds (excluding accrued interest).

11. Lake Co. issued 3,000 of its 9%, $1,000 face amount bonds at 101 1/2. In connection with the sale of these bonds, Lake paid the following expenses:

Promotion costs	$ 20,000
Engraving and printing	25,000
Underwriters' commissions	200,000

What amount should Lake record as bond issue costs to be amortized over the term of the bonds?

A. $0

B. $220,000

C. $225,000

D. $245,000

Answer (D) is correct.

REQUIRED: The amount to be recorded as debt issue costs.

DISCUSSION: Debt issue costs include (1) printing costs, (2) underwriters' commissions, (3) attorney's fees, and (4) promotion costs (including preparation of a prospectus). The issue costs to be amortized equal $245,000 ($20,000 promotion costs + $25,000 printing costs + $200,000 underwriters' commissions). Debt issue costs are presented as a direct deduction from the related debt liability.

Answer (A) is incorrect. An amount of debt issue costs should be amortized. **Answer (B) is incorrect.** The $25,000 of printing costs also are debt issue costs that should be amortized. **Answer (C) is incorrect.** The $20,000 of promotion costs also are debt issue costs that should be amortized.

12.6 Securities with Characteristics of Liabilities and Equity

12. On December 30, Year 4, Fort, Inc., issued 1,000 of its 8%, 10-year, $1,000 face value bonds with detachable stock warrants at par. Each bond carried a detachable warrant for one share of Fort's common stock at a specified option price of $25.75 per share. Immediately after issuance, the market value of the bonds without the warrants was $1,080,000, and the market value of the warrants was $120,000. In its December 31, Year 4, balance sheet, what amount should Fort report as bonds payable?

A. $1,000,000

B. $975,000

C. $900,000

D. $880,000

Answer (C) is correct.

REQUIRED: The amount reported for bonds payable with detachable stock warrants.

DISCUSSION: The issue price of the bonds is allocated between the bonds and the detachable stock warrants based on their relative fair values. The market price of bonds without the warrants is $1,080,000, which is 90% [$1,080,000 ÷ ($1,080,000 + $120,000)] of the total fair value. Consequently, 90% of the issue price should be allocated to the bonds, and they should be reported at $900,000 ($1,000,000 × 90%) in the balance sheet.

Answer (A) is incorrect. The total proceeds equals $1,000,000. **Answer (B) is incorrect.** The amount of $975,000 is the result of deducting the option price of the stock from the issue price. **Answer (D) is incorrect.** The amount of $880,000 is the result of deducting the fair value of the warrants from the issue price.

12.7 Extinguishment of Debt

13. On June 30, Year 7, King Co. had outstanding 9%, $5,000,000 face value bonds maturing on June 30, Year 9. Interest was payable semiannually every June 30 and December 31. On June 30, Year 7, after amortization was recorded for the period, the unamortized bond premium and bond issue costs were $30,000 and $50,000, respectively. On that date, King acquired all its outstanding bonds on the open market at 98 and retired them. At June 30, Year 7, what amount should King recognize as gain before income taxes on redemption of bonds?

A. $20,000

B. $80,000

C. $120,000

D. $180,000

Answer (B) is correct.

REQUIRED: The amount of gain from the redemption of bonds.

DISCUSSION: The amount of gain or loss on the redemption of bonds is equal to the difference between the proceeds paid and the carrying amount of the debt. The carrying amount of the bonds is equal to the face amount, plus unamortized bond premium, minus unamortized bond issue costs. Thus, the carrying amount of the bonds is $4,980,000 ($5,000,000 + $30,000 – $50,000). The $80,000 gain is the difference between the carrying amount ($4,980,000) and the amount paid $4,900,000 ($5,000,000 × 98%).

Answer (A) is incorrect. The amount of $20,000 results from subtracting the unamortized bond premium and bond issue costs from the face amount of the bond. **Answer (C) is incorrect.** The amount of $120,000 results from adding the unamortized bond issue costs and subtracting the issue costs to find the carrying amount. **Answer (D) is incorrect.** The amount of $180,000 results from adding the unamortized bond issue costs and bond premium to find the carrying amount of the bond.

14. Ray Finance, Inc., issued a 10-year, $100,000, 9% note on January 1, Year 1. The note was issued to yield 10% for proceeds of $93,770. Interest is payable semiannually. The note is callable after 2 years at a price of $96,000. Due to a decline in the market rate to 8%, Ray retired the note on December 31, Year 3. On that date, the carrying amount of the note was $94,582, and the discounted amount of its cash flows based on the market rate was $105,280. What amount should Ray report as gain (loss) from retirement of the note for the year ended December 31, Year 3?

A. $9,280

B. $4,000

C. $(2,230)

D. $(1,418)

Answer (D) is correct.

REQUIRED: The amount of gain (loss) from the extinguishment of a note.

DISCUSSION: The amount of gain or loss resulting from the extinguishment of debt is the difference between the amount paid and the carrying amount of the note. Thus, a loss of $1,418 ($94,582 carrying amount – $96,000 amount paid) results from the extinguishment.

Answer (A) is incorrect. The difference between the discounted amount, based on the market rate, and the call price is $9,280. **Answer (B) is incorrect.** The difference between the face amount of the note and the call price is $4,000. **Answer (C) is incorrect.** The difference between the original amount received and the call price is $(2,230).

12.8 Noncurrent Notes Payable

Questions 15 and 16 are based on the following information. House Publishers offered a contest in which the winner would receive $1 million, payable over 20 years. On December 31, Year 4, House announced the winner of the contest and signed a note payable to the winner for $1 million, payable in $50,000 installments every January 2. Also on December 31, Year 4, House purchased an annuity for $418,250 to provide the $950,000 prize monies remaining after the first $50,000 installment, which was paid on January 2, Year 5.

15. In its Year 4 income statement, what should House report as contest prize expense?

A. $0

B. $418,250

C. $468,250

D. $1,000,000

Answer (C) is correct.

REQUIRED: The contest prize expense.

DISCUSSION: The contest prize expense equals $468,250 ($418,250 cost of the annuity + $50,000 first installment).

Answer (A) is incorrect. The sum of the cost of the annuity and the first installment must be recognized as an expense in Year 4. **Answer (B) is incorrect.** The amount of $418,250 does not include the $50,000 installment due in Year 5. **Answer (D) is incorrect.** The face amount of the note is $1,000,000.

16. In its December 31, Year 4, balance sheet, at what amount should House measure the note payable, net of current portion?

A. $368,250

B. $418,250

C. $900,000

D. $950,000

Answer (B) is correct.

REQUIRED: The amount at which the note payable should be measured.

DISCUSSION: Noninterest-bearing notes payable should be measured at their present value rather than their face amount. Thus, the measure of the note payable, net of the current portion, which has a nominal amount equal to its present value at December 31, Year 4, of $50,000, is its present value of $418,250 (debit annuity cost $418,250, debit discount $531,750, credit note payable $950,000). The present value of the noncurrent portion of the note is assumed to be the cash given for the annuity ($418,250) because no other right or privilege was exchanged.

Answer (A) is incorrect. The amount of $368,250 includes a reduction of $50,000 for the first installment. **Answer (C) is incorrect.** The amount of $900,000 equals the face amount of the note payable minus two installments. **Answer (D) is incorrect.** The amount of $950,000 equals the face amount of the note payable minus the first installment.

12.9 Troubled Debt Restructurings

17. For a troubled debt restructuring involving only a modification of terms, which of the following items specified by the new terms would be compared with the carrying amount of the debt to determine whether the debtor should report a gain on restructuring?

A. The total future cash payments.

B. The present value of the debt at the original interest rate.

C. The present value of the debt at the modified interest rate.

D. The amount of future cash payments designated as principal repayments.

Answer (A) is correct.

REQUIRED: The item used to determine the debtor's gain on a troubled debt restructuring.

DISCUSSION: When a troubled debt restructuring includes a modification of terms that results in future undiscounted cash flows less than the carrying amount of the debt, the debtor recognizes a gain equal to the difference. No gain is recognized if the future undiscounted cash flows are greater than the carrying amount of the debt.

12.10 Asset Retirement Obligations

18. On January 1, 10 years ago, Andrew Co. created a subsidiary for the purpose of buying an oil tanker depot at a cost of $1,500,000. Andrew expected to operate the depot for 10 years, at which time it is legally required to dismantle the depot and remove underground storage tanks. It was estimated that it would cost $150,000 to dismantle the depot and remove the tanks at the end of the depot's useful life. However, the actual cost to demolish and dismantle the depot and remove the tanks in the 10th year is $155,000. What amount of loss should Andrew recognize in its financial statements in Year 10?

A. None.

B. $5,000.

C. $150,000.

D. $155,000.

Answer (B) is correct.

REQUIRED: The settlement loss for an asset retirement obligation.

DISCUSSION: The asset retirement obligation (ARO) is recognized at fair value when incurred. An expected present value technique ordinarily is used to estimate the fair value. An amount equal to the ARO is the associated asset retirement cost (ARC). It is debited to the long-lived asset when the ARO is credited. The ARC is allocated to expense using the straight-line method over the life of the underlying asset (debit depreciation expense, credit accumulated depreciation). Furthermore, the entity recognizes accretion expense as an allocation of the difference between the maturity amount and the carrying amount of the ARO. Accretion expense for a period equals the beginning carrying amount of the ARO times the credit-adjusted risk-free interest rate. This amount is debited to accretion expense and credited to the ARO. At the end of the useful life of the underlying asset (the depot), the ARO should equal its maturity amount ($150,000). Moreover, the carrying amount of the ARC is zero. The total credits to accumulated depreciation equal the initial debit to record the ARC. Accordingly, given that the ARO liability after 10 years is $150,000, and the settlement cost is $155,000, the entry to record the settlement is to debit the ARO for $150,000, debit a loss for $5,000, and credit cash (or other accounts) for $155,000.

Answer (A) is incorrect. The actual settlement cost exceeded the ARO. **Answer (C) is incorrect.** The amount of $150,000 is the maturity amount of the ARO. **Answer (D) is incorrect.** The actual settlement cost equals $155,000.

STUDY UNIT THIRTEEN

LEASES AND CONTINGENCIES

(26 pages of outline)

A **lease** is a contractual agreement in which the **lessor** (owner) conveys to the **lessee** the right to control the use of specific **property, plant, or equipment** for a stated period in exchange for a stated payment. The lease standard does not apply to leases of intangible assets or inventory. The amount and timing of lease revenue recognized by the lessor and lease expenses recognized by the lessee depend on the initial classification of the lease.

13.1 LEASE CLASSIFICATION

1. **Basic Definitions**
   a. The **commencement date of the lease** is the date on which a lessor makes a leased asset available for use by a lessee.
   b. The **lease term** is the noncancelable period for which the lessee has the right to use the leased asset. Periods covered by an option to extend the lease are **included** in the lease term if (1) the lessee is reasonably certain to exercise that option or (2) the option is controlled by the lessor.
      1) The periods covered by the option to terminate the lease are included in the lease term only if the lessee is reasonably certain not to exercise that option.
   c. A **right-of-use asset** represents a **lessee's** right to use a leased asset for the lease term.
   d. **Lease payments** at the lease commencement date consist of the following:
      1) **Rental payments** are the periodic amounts owed by the lessee minus any incentives paid or payable to the lessee.
      2) A **purchase option** is the exercise price of an option to purchase the leased asset if the lessee is reasonably certain to exercise the option.
      3) **Penalties for terminating the lease** (nonrenewal penalties) are included if the lessee is expected to exercise the option to terminate the lease.
         a) For a lessee, the lease payments also include the amounts probable of being owed by the lessee under **residual value guarantees**.

e. The **guaranteed residual value** is a guarantee made to a lessor that the value of a leased asset returned to the lessor at the end of a lease term will be at least a specified amount. This residual value can be guaranteed by the lessee or any other third party unrelated to the lessor.

f. The **discount rate** for the lease is the **rate implicit in the lease**. If the lessee cannot determine the rate implicit in the lease, the lessee uses its **incremental borrowing rate**.

1) The **rate implicit in the lease** is the interest rate that on the lease commencement date causes (a) the fair value of the leased asset to equal (b) the present value of the lease payments plus the present value of the amount that the lessor expects to derive from the leased asset following the end of the lease term.

Fair value of the leased asset = **PV of the lease payments** + **PV of the amount that the lessor expects to derive from the leased asset following the end of the lease term**

a) The amount that a lessor expects to derive from the asset following the end of the lease term includes

i) The guaranteed residual value and
ii) The unguaranteed residual value of the leased asset.

2. **Lease Classification**

a. A lease is classified as a **finance lease by the lessee** and as a **sales-type lease by the lessor** if, at lease commencement, **at least one** of the **five criteria** below is met:

1) The lease **transfers ownership** of the leased asset to the lessee by the end of the lease term.

2) The lease includes an **option to purchase** the leased asset that the lessee is reasonably certain to exercise.

3) The lease term is for the major part of the remaining **economic life** of the leased asset.

a) A lease term of **75%** or more of the remaining economic life of the leased asset generally is considered to be a major part of its remaining economic life.

b) This criterion is inapplicable if the beginning of the lease term is at or near the end of the economic life of the leased asset. This period generally is considered to be the last 25% of the leased asset's total economic life.

4) The present value of the sum of (a) the **lease payments** and (b) any **residual value guaranteed by the lessee** equals or exceeds substantially all of the **fair value** of the leased asset.

a) A present value of **90%** or more of the fair value of the leased asset generally is considered to be substantially all of its fair value.

5) The leased asset is so specialized that it is expected to have **no alternative use** to the lessor at the end of the lease term.

b. When none of the five classification criteria described above are met, the lease is classified as

1) An **operating lease** by the **lessee**.
2) An **operating lease** or a **direct financing lease** by the **lessor**.

c. The lessor classifies a lease as a **direct financing lease** only when

1) The lease is not a sales-type lease,
2) The present value of the sum of (a) the lease payments and (b) any residual value guaranteed by the lessee **or any other third party** equals or exceeds substantially all of the fair value of the leased asset, and
3) It is probable that the lease payments and any residual value guarantee will be collected.

d. If the lease is **not** a direct financing lease, it is classified as an **operating lease** by the lessor.

1) Classification of a lease as a direct financing lease is rare. It happens only when the lease includes residual value guaranteed by a third party other than the lessee that results in meeting the "substantially all of the fair value" classification criterion (the 90% of the fair value of the leased asset criterion).

a) Thus, a lessor classifies a lease without residual value guaranteed by a third party (not the lessee) as either

i) A sales-type lease or
ii) An operating lease.

b) In most cases, when none of the five classification criteria are met (when the lease is not a sales-type lease), the **lessor classifies the lease as an operating lease**.

Decision Tree: Classification of the Lease by the Lessor

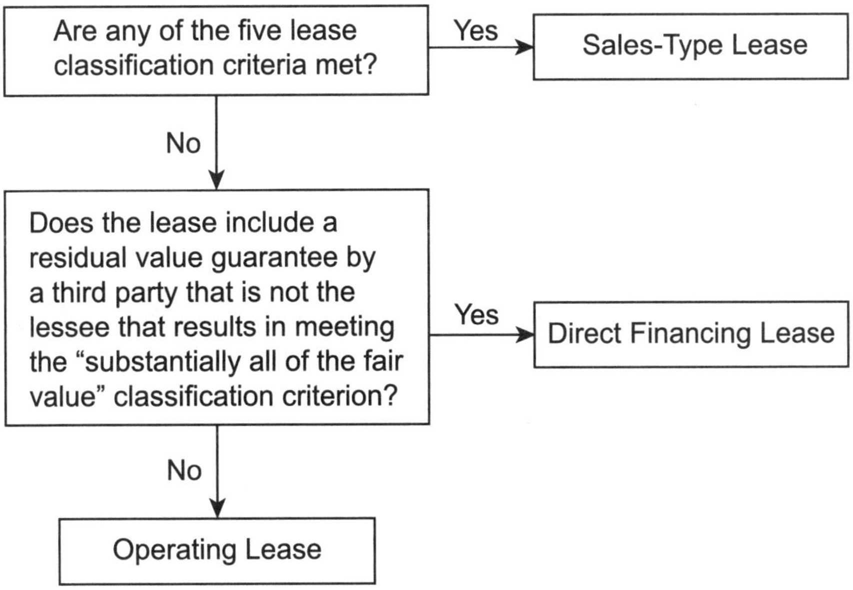

Figure 13-1

e. A **short-term lease** is a lease that, at the commencement date, has a lease term of **12 months or less** and does not include a purchase option that the lessee is reasonably certain to exercise.

1) As an accounting policy for **short-term leases**, a **lessee** may elect **not** to recognize the **right-of-use asset** and **lease liability**.

2) Under this short-term lease exception, the lessee recognizes lease payments as rent expense on the straight-line basis over the full lease term.

a) The lessee records the following journal entry:

Rent expense	$XXX	
Cash or rent payable		$XXX

EXAMPLE 13-1 Short-Term Lease -- Lessee

On October 1, Year 1, Gulf Co. entered into a 1-year lease contract for its warehouse. It elected not to recognize the right-of-use asset and lease liability for its short-term lease. The following are the lease terms:

- The first 2 months' rent are free.
- Monthly rent from December of Year 1 through September of Year 2 is $3,600.

The total rent expense over the lease term of $36,000 ($3,600 × 10 months) is recognized on a straight-line basis over the entire lease term of 12 months. Accordingly, from October of Year 1, monthly rent expense recognized is $3,000 ($36,000 total rent expense over the lease term ÷ 12-month lease term). Rent expense recognized is $9,000 ($3,000 × 3 months) in Year 1 and $27,000 ($3,000 × 9 months) in Year 2.

Decision Tree: Classification of the Lease by the Lessee

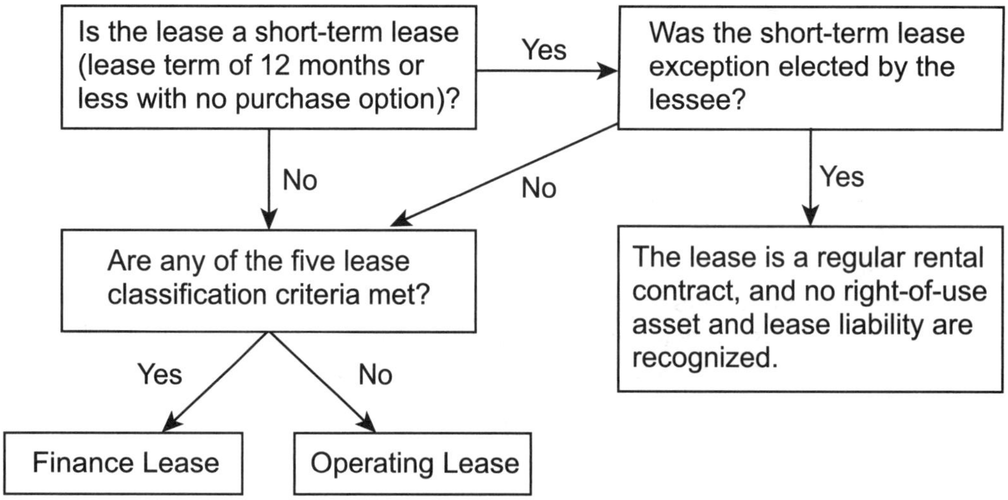

Figure 13-2

IFRS DIFFERENCE

1. An operating lease is not a classification option for the lessee. The lessee accounts for all leases, except for "short-term" leases and "low-value" leases, similarly to a finance lease under U.S. GAAP.
2. The lessee may elect to account for a lease of low-value assets (assets with value of $5,000 or less) the same way as for "short-term" leases. The lessee then recognizes lease payments as an expense on a straight-line basis over the lease term.

STOP & REVIEW

You have completed the outline for this subunit.
Study multiple-choice questions 1 and 2 on page 415.

13.2 LESSEE ACCOUNTING -- INITIAL MEASUREMENT

1. **General Rule**
   a. For **finance and operating leases**, a **lessee** must recognize a **lease liability** and a **right-of-use asset** at the lease commencement date.
   b. Finance and operating leases result in the **same accounting** for
      1) Initial recognition and measurement of the lease liability,
      2) Initial recognition and measurement of the right-of-use asset, and
      3) Subsequent measurement of the lease liability.
   c. The accounting for subsequent measurement of a right-of-use asset differs under finance and operating leases.
2. **Lease Liability**
   a. At the lease commencement date, a **lease liability** is measured at the **present value of the lease payments** to be made over the lease term.
   b. The lease payments are discounted using the discount rate for the lease.
      1) It is the rate implicit in the lease, if known to the lessee.
      2) If not, it is the lessee's incremental borrowing rate.

c. The lease payments used to calculate the lease liability depend on the specific terms of each lease contract.

1) If the lease includes a purchase option that the lessee is reasonably certain to exercise, the lease payments consist of the

a) Rental payments
b) Exercise price of the purchase option

2) If no purchase option exists, the lease payments may have the following three components:

a) Rental payments
b) Any penalties for terminating the lease (nonrenewal penalties)
c) Amounts probable of being owed by the lessee under residual value guarantees

NOTE: For the **"substantially all of the fair value"** lease classification criterion, the present value of the **full amount** of the residual value guaranteed by the lessee is included in the test. However, in measuring the lease liability, only the amounts **probable of being owed** by the lessee under residual value guarantees are included.

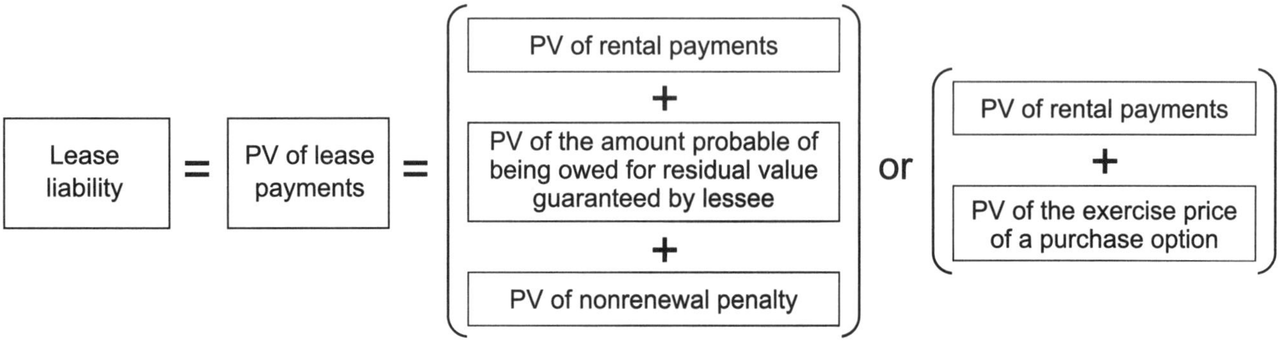

Figure 13-3

EXAMPLE 13-2 Residual Value Guaranteed by the Lessee

In a lease contract, a lessee guarantees that the residual value of the leased property at the end of the lease term is at least $50,000. At the lease commencement date, the lessee estimates that the value of the property at the end of the lease term will be only $40,000. Thus, it is probable that the lessee will owe $10,000 to the lessor under the residual value guarantee.

- To test the "substantially all of the fair value" lease classification criterion, the present value of the full amount of the $50,000 residual value guaranteed by the lessee is included.
- In the measurement of the lease liability, only the present value of the amount that is probable of being owed by the lessee under the residual value guarantee of $10,000 is included.

d. In a balance sheet, the total lease liability is allocated between current and noncurrent portions. The current portion at a balance sheet date is the reduction of the lease liability in the forthcoming year.

3. **Right-of-Use Asset**
   a. At the lease commencement date, a right-of-use asset is measured at the amount at which the lease liability was recognized plus initial direct costs incurred by the lessee.
   b. When no initial direct costs were incurred by the lessee, a **right-of-use asset equals the lease liability** recognized.
      1) The following journal entry is recorded by the lessee:

Right-of-use asset	$XXX	
Lease liability		$XXX

   c. Subsequent to initial recognition, the right-of-use asset is reported in the balance sheet at cost minus accumulated amortization and any impairment losses.

EXAMPLE 13-3 Finance Lease

On January 1, Year 1, Cottle, Inc., entered into a 3-year lease of a machine from Crimson, LLC. Cottle must pay Crimson three annual payments of $100,000 starting on December 31, Year 1. The machine's useful life from the lease commencement date is 5 years. The lease allows Cottle the option to purchase the machine at the end of the lease term for $15,000. Cottle is reasonably certain to exercise this purchase option. Cottle's incremental borrowing rate is 15%, but the rate implicit in the lease is 10%, which is known to Cottle.

- The present value factor for an ordinary annuity at 10% for 3 periods is 2.48685, and the present value of $1 at 10% for 3 periods is 0.7513.
- The present value factor for an ordinary annuity at 15% for 3 periods is 2.28323, and the present value of $1 at 15% for 3 periods is 0.65752.

The lease is a **finance lease** because it meets the lease classification criterion of including a purchase option that the lessee is reasonably certain to exercise. The rate implicit in the lease of 10% is used to calculate the present value of the lease payments because Cottle knows this rate.

PV of rental payments ($100,000 × 2.48685)	$248,685
PV of purchase option ($15,000 × 0.7513)	11,270
PV of lease payments	$259,955

Right-of-use asset	$259,955	
Lease liability		$259,955

EXAMPLE 13-4 Operating Lease -- Lessee

Using the scenario presented in Example 13-3, assume that (1) Cottle concludes that the contract is an **operating lease**, (2) the lease does not include a purchase option, (3) the rental payments are $100,000 at the end of Years 1 and 2 and $160,000 at the end of Year 3, and (4) the rate implicit in the lease is not known to Cottle.

Because Cottle does not know the rate implicit in the lease, it uses its **incremental borrowing rate** of 15% to calculate the present value of lease payments.

The PV of the rental payments is $267,774 [($100,000 × 2.28323) + ($60,000 × 0.65752)].

Right-of-use asset	$267,774	
Lease liability		$267,774

STOP & REVIEW

You have completed the outline for this subunit.
Study multiple-choice questions 3 and 4 on page 416.

13.3 LESSEE ACCOUNTING FOR FINANCE LEASES -- SUBSEQUENT MEASUREMENT

1. **Interest Expense and Amortization of a Lease Liability**

   a. Each periodic lease payment made by the lessee has two components: **interest expense** and the **reduction of the lease liability**.

      1) If the first periodic lease payment is made at the **commencement date** of the lease, its only component is the reduction of the lease liability. No interest expense is recognized for the first payment because no time has elapsed between the lease commencement date and the payment.

   b. **Interest expense** is calculated using the effective interest method (also known as the effective-rate method or the interest method).

      1) It is calculated as the carrying amount of the lease liability at the beginning of the period times the discount rate of the lease.

   Interest expense = Lease liability at the beginning of the period × Discount rate

   c. The **reduction of the lease liability** is the excess of the periodic lease payment over the interest expense recognized during the period.

   Reduction of lease liability = Periodic lease payment – Interest expense

EXAMPLE 13-5 Interest Expense and Amortization of Lease Liability

In Example13-3, the lease was classified as a **finance lease**. Cottle prepares the following amortization schedule and records the following journal entries:

Date	Period Beginning Lease Liability		Effective Interest Rate		Interest Expense		Cash Payment		Reduction of Lease Liability	Period Ending Lease Liability
1/1/Yr 1	$259,955	×	10%	=	$25,995	–	$100,000	=	$ 74,005	$185,950
1/1/Yr 2	185,950	×	10%	=	18,595	–	100,000	=	81,405	104,545
1/1/Yr 3	104,545	×	10%	=	10,455	–	115,000	=	104,545	0

The last payment on 12/31/Yr 3 is $115,000 ($100,000 annual rental payment + $15,000 exercise price of the option to purchase the machine).

12/31/Yr 1		
Interest expense	$25,995	
Lease liability	74,005	
Cash		$100,000

On December 31, Year 1, the carrying amount of the lease liability is **$185,950.** In its 12/31/Yr 1 balance sheet, Cottle reports a current lease liability of $81,405 and a noncurrent lease liability of $104,545.

12/31/Yr 2		
Interest expense	$18,595	
Lease liability	81,405	
Cash		$100,000

On December 31, Year 2, the carrying amount of the lease liability is **$104,545.** This entire amount is reported as a current liability in the 12/31/Yr 2 balance sheet because Cottle expects to pay the entire amount in Year 3.

12/31/Yr 3		
Interest expense	$ 10,455	
Lease liability	104,545	
Cash		$115,000 ($100,000 annual payment + $15,000 option price)

2. **Amortization of a Right-of-Use Asset**
   a. A lessee amortizes the right-of-use (ROU) asset on a **straight-line basis**.
   b. The right-of-use asset is amortized over the shorter of (1) its **useful life** or (2) the **lease term**.
      1) However, if, at the end of the lease term, (a) the ownership of the leased asset is transferred to the lessee or (b) the lessee is reasonably certain to exercise the purchase option, the amortization period is the **useful life of the leased asset**.

Lease Classification Criterion Satisfied	Amortization Period of the ROU Asset
Criterion 1 - Transfer of ownership	Useful life of the leased asset
Criterion 2 - Exercise of purchase option	Useful life of the leased asset
Criterion 3 - Major part of the remaining economic life	Shorter of ROU asset's useful life or lease term
Criterion 4 - Substantially all of the fair value	Shorter of ROU asset's useful life or lease term
Criterion 5 - No alternative use to the lessor	Shorter of ROU asset's useful life or lease term

EXAMPLE 13-6 Amortization of Right-of-Use Asset over Useful Life

In Example 13-5, Cottle is reasonably certain to exercise the option to purchase the machine. The right-of-use asset therefore is amortized over the useful life of the machine of 5 years. Annual amortization expense of $51,991 ($259,955 ÷ 5 years) is recognized by Cottle. The journal entry is

Amortization expense	$51,991	
Right-of-use asset		$51,991

In its 12/31/Yr 1 balance sheet, Cottle reports the right-of-use asset at **$207,964** ($259,955 initial cost – $51,991 accumulated amortization).

3. **Amortization of Leasehold Improvements**
   a. Leasehold improvements are amortized over the shorter of (1) their **useful life** or (2) the **remaining lease term**.
      1) If, at the end of the lease term, (a) the ownership of the leased asset is transferred to the lessee or (b) the lessee is reasonably certain to exercise a purchase option, the amortization period is the **useful life of the leasehold improvements**.
4. **Financial Statement Presentation**
   a. In the **income statement**, interest expense on a lease liability and amortization of a right-of-use asset must be **reported separately**.
   b. In the **statement of cash flows**, repayment of the principal portion of a finance lease liability is classified as a cash outflow from **financing activities**.
      1) Payment of **interest** on a lease liability is classified as a cash outflow **from operating activities**.
   c. In the footnotes to the financial statements, the lessee must disclose the **total finance lease cost** for the period. The total finance lease cost should be segregated between the amortization of the right-of-use assets and interest expense on the lease liabilities.

STOP & REVIEW

You have completed the outline for this subunit.
Study multiple-choice questions 5 through 7 beginning on page 417.

13.4 LESSEE ACCOUNTING FOR OPERATING LEASES -- SUBSEQUENT MEASUREMENT

1. **Finance Leases vs. Operating Leases**
   a. As noted in Subunit 13.2, accounting for finance leases and operating leases is **the same** for
      1) Initial recognition and measurement of the lease liability,
      2) Initial recognition and measurement of the right-of-use asset, and
      3) Subsequent measurement of the lease liability.
   b. The following are the **differences** in accounting for finance and operating leases:
      1) Subsequent accounting for (amortization of) the right-of-use asset
      2) Income statement presentation of interest expense and amortization of the right-of-use asset
      3) Statement of cash flow classification of cash lease payments
2. **Recognition of Lease Expense in Operating Leases**
   a. A **single (equal) lease expense** is recognized in each period. It is calculated so that the total undiscounted lease payments are allocated over the lease term on a **straight-line basis**.

Single periodic lease expense = Total undiscounted lease payments ($) ÷ Lease term (years)

      1) Initial direct costs incurred by the lessee are included in the total undiscounted lease payments. Thus, they are recognized in the single periodic lease expense on a straight-line basis over the lease term.
   b. The single periodic lease expense has two components, (1) interest expense on the lease liability and (2) amortization of the right-of-use asset.

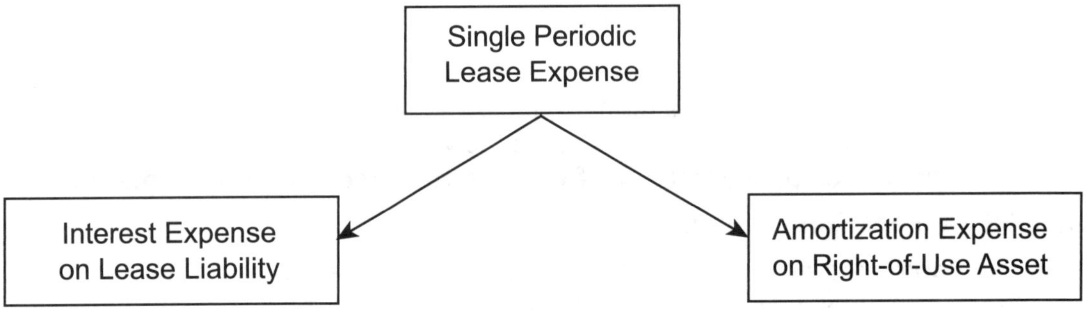

Figure 13-4

   c. In the **income statement**, a single amount for the total lease expense for the period is reported in income from continuing operations.
      1) Thus, interest expense for the lease liability and amortization expense for the right-of-use asset are **not reported separately**.
3. **Amortization of the Right-of-Use Asset**
   a. Amortization of the right-of-use asset is the difference between the (1) single periodic lease expense and (2) interest expense on the lease liability recognized for the period.

Amortization expense on right-of-use asset = Single periodic lease expense − Interest expense on lease liability

b. Interest expense equals the carrying amount of the lease liability at the beginning of the period times the discount rate of the lease.

EXAMPLE 13-7 Lessee's Operating Lease -- Amortization of the ROU Asset

On January 1, Year 1, Lor, Inc., entered into a 3-year lease for a building and determined that this contract is an **operating lease**. Based on the contract terms, Lor is required to pay three annual payments of $20,000 starting on December 31, Year 1. The building's remaining useful life is 30 years. The rate implicit in the lease is not known to Lor. Thus, Lor uses its incremental borrowing rate of 8% to measure the lease liability and right-of-use asset. The present value factor for an ordinary annuity at 8% for 3 periods is 2.5771.

- The lease liability and right-of-use (ROU) asset are recognized at the present value of the lease payments of **$51,542** ($20,000 × 2.5771).
- The single amount of annual lease expense is **$20,000** [($20,000 × 3) total undiscounted lease payments ÷ 3 years].

January 1, Year 1

ROU asset	$51,542	
Lease liability		$51,542

December 31, Year 1

The interest expense component of Year 1 lease expense is $4,124 ($51,542 × 8%). The amortization of the ROU asset component of Year 1 lease expense is $15,876 ($20,000 annual lease expense – $4,124 interest expense).

Lease liability	$15,876 ($20,000 lease payment – $4,124 interest expense)	
Lease expense	20,000	
Cash		$20,000
ROU asset		15,876

Lease expense of **$20,000** is recognized in the Year 1 income statement. The carrying amount of the lease liability and ROU asset on 12/31/Year 1 is **$35,666** ($51,542 – $15,876).

December 31, Year 2

The interest expense component of Year 2 lease expense is $2,853 ($35,666 × 8%). The amortization of the ROU asset component of Year 2 lease expense is $17,147 ($20,000 annual lease expense – $2,853 interest expense).

Lease liability	$17,147 ($20,000 lease payment – $2,853 interest expense)	
Lease expense	20,000	
Cash		$20,000
ROU asset		17,147

Lease expense of **$20,000** is recognized in the Year 2 income statement. The carrying amount of the lease liability and ROU asset on 12/31/Year 2 is **$18,519** ($35,666 – $17,147).

December 31, Year 3

The interest expense component of Year 3 lease expense is $1,481 ($18,519 × 8%). The amortization of the ROU asset component of Year 3 lease expense is $18,519 ($20,000 annual lease expense – $1,481 interest expense).

Lease liability	$18,519 ($20,000 lease payment – $1,481 interest expense)	
Lease expense	20,000	
Cash		$20,000
ROU asset		18,519

Lease expense of **$20,000** is recognized in the Year 3 income statement. The balance of the lease liability and ROU asset on 12/31/Year 3 is **$0** ($18,519 – $18,519).

NOTE: (1) When annual lease payments are paid in arrears and in equal amounts (annuity in arrears), the carrying amounts of the lease liability and right-of-use asset are the same throughout the entire lease term. (2) In the balance sheet, the lease liability should be allocated between current and noncurrent portions.

EXAMPLE 13-8 Lessee's Operating Lease -- Amortization of the ROU Asset

Using the data from Example 13-4, in which the lease was classified as an operating lease, the following is Cottle's accounting for the lease of a machine from Crimson:

- Total amount of undiscounted lease payments is **$360,000** ($100,000 + $100,000 + $160,000).
- The single amount of annual lease expense is **$120,000** ($360,000 ÷ 3 years).
- The amount of the lease liability and right-of-use (ROU) asset is initially recognized at the present value of lease payments of **$267,774** [($100,000 × 2.28323) + ($60,000 × 0.65752)].

<u>January 1, Year 1</u>

ROU asset	$267,774	
Lease liability		$267,774

<u>December 31, Year 1</u>

The interest expense component of Year 1 lease expense is $40,166 ($267,774 × 15%). The amortization of the ROU asset component of Year 1 lease expense is $79,834 ($120,000 annual lease expense – $40,166 interest expense).

Lease liability	$ 59,834 ($100,000 lease payment – $40,166 interest expense)	
Lease expense	120,000	
Cash		$100,000
ROU asset		79,834

Lease expense of **$120,000** is recognized in the Year 1 income statement. On December 31, Year 1, the carrying amount of the lease liability is **$207,940** ($267,774 – $59,834), and the carrying amount of the ROU asset is **$187,940** ($267,774 – $79,834).

<u>December 31, Year 2</u>

The interest expense component of Year 2 lease expense is $31,191 ($207,940 × 15%). The amortization of the ROU asset component of Year 2 lease expense is $88,809 ($120,000 annual lease expense – $31,191 interest expense).

Lease liability	$ 68,809 ($100,000 lease payment – $31,191 interest expense)	
Lease expense	120,000	
Cash		$100,000
ROU asset		88,809

Lease expense of **$120,000** is recognized in the Year 2 income statement. On December 31, Year 2, the carrying amount of the lease liability is **$139,131** ($207,940 – $68,809), and the carrying amount of the ROU asset is **$99,131** ($187,940 – $88,809).

<u>December 31, Year 3</u>

The interest expense component of Year 3 lease expense is $20,869 ($139,131 × 15%). The amortization of the ROU asset component of Year 3 lease expense is $99,131 ($120,000 annual lease expense – $20,869 interest expense).

Lease liability	$139,131 ($160,000 lease payment – $20,869 interest expense)	
Lease expense	120,000	
Cash		$160,000
ROU asset		99,131

Lease expense of $120,000 is recognized in the Year 3 income statement. On December 31, Year 3, the carrying amount of the lease liability is $0 ($139,131 – $139,131), and the carrying amount of the ROU asset is $0 ($99,131 – $99,131).

4. **Financial Statement Presentation**

   a. In the **balance sheet**, **finance lease liabilities** and **operating lease liabilities** must **not** be presented together in the same line item.

      1) They are presented in the balance sheet or disclosed in the notes, separately from each other and separately from other liabilities.

   b. In the **balance sheet**, **finance lease right-of-use assets** and **operating lease right-of-use assets** must **not** be presented together in the same line item.

      1) They are presented in the balance sheet or disclosed in the notes, separately from each other and separately from other assets.

   c. In the **statement of cash flows**, payments for operating leases (repayment of the lease liability and interest expense on the lease liability) are cash outflows from **operating activities**.

      1) Payments for leases classified as **short-term leases** are cash outflows from **operating activities**.

STOP & REVIEW

You have completed the outline for this subunit.
Study multiple-choice questions 8 and 9 on page 419.

13.5 LESSOR ACCOUNTING FOR SALES-TYPE LEASES

1. **Basic Definitions**

   a. The **lease receivable** is the (1) present value of the lease payments plus (2) the present value of the residual value guaranteed by the lessee or any other third party.

      Lease receivable = PV of lease payments + PV of guaranteed residual value

      1) The present value is calculated using the discount rate implicit in the lease.
      2) The lease receivable is the **revenue** recognized at the lease commencement date.

   b. The **unguaranteed residual value** is the amount that the lessor expects to derive from the leased asset at the end of the lease term that is not guaranteed by any party.

   c. The **net investment in the lease** is the present value of the total of cash and other assets that the lessor expects to receive over the lease term.

      1) It consists of (a) the lease receivable plus (b) the present value of unguaranteed residual value.

      2) Because the present value is calculated using the rate implicit in the lease, the net investment in the lease is the fair value of the leased asset.

Net investment in the lease = PV of lease payments + PV of guaranteed residual value + PV of unguaranteed residual value

Net investment in the lease = Lease receivable + PV of unguaranteed residual value = Fair value of the leased asset

d. **Selling profit or loss** on the lease is determined on the lease commencement date. Assuming no initial direct costs and prepayments, selling profit or loss (gross profit) is calculated as follows:

	Lease receivable	= Revenue
–	(Carrying amount of the leased asset – PV of unguaranteed residual value)	= Cost of goods sold
=	Selling profit or loss	

1) A lease can be classified as a sales-type lease even if it does not result in the recognition of any selling profit or loss.

2. **Initial Measurement**

a. On the lease commencement date, the lessor must **derecognize the leased asset** and **recognize** all of the following:

1) **Net investment in the lease**
2) **Selling profit or loss** calculated as

a) **Revenue** equal to the **lease receivable** minus

b) **Cost of goods sold**, which equals the carrying amount of the leased asset minus the present value of any unguaranteed residual value. Thus, when no residual value is unguaranteed, the cost of goods sold is the carrying amount of the leased asset.

b. The following journal entry is recorded at the lease commencement date:

Net investment in the lease	$XXX	
Cost of goods sold	XXX	
Revenue		$XXX
Leased asset		XXX

1) The leased asset (property held for lease) is derecognized (credit) at its carrying amount at the lease commencement date.

EXAMPLE 13-9 Sales-Type Lease

Alpha Co. sells and leases unspecialized machines. On January 1, Year 1, Alpha leased a machine to Beta Co. for 3 annual payments of $100,000 starting on December 31, Year 1. The machine's remaining useful life is 5 years. The expected residual value of the machine at the end of Year 3 is $30,000, and Beta guarantees this amount. At the inception of the lease, the fair value of the machine was $271,224 and the carrying amount was $250,000. The rate implicit in the lease is 10%. The present value factor for an ordinary annuity at 10% for 3 periods is 2.48685, and the present value of $1 at 10% for 3 periods is 0.7513.

PV of rental payments ($100,000 × 2.48685)	$248,685
PV of residual value guaranteed by the lessee ($30,000 × 0.7513)	22,539
Total	$271,224

Alpha classifies the lease as a **sales-type lease** because the "substantially all of the fair value of the leased asset" classification criterion was met. The sum of the present value of the lease payments and the present value of the residual value guaranteed by the lessee ($271,224) equals or exceeds substantially all of the fair value of the leased machine ($271,224). This classification criterion is the only one that was satisfied.

Alpha records the following journal entry on January 1, Year 1:

Net investment in the lease	$271,224		(fair value of the machine)
Cost of goods sold	250,000		(machine's carrying amount)
Revenue		$271,224	(lease receivable)
Machine		250,000	(machine's carrying amount)

EXAMPLE 13-10 Sales-Type Lease with Unguaranteed Residual Value

Soma Co. sells and leases unspecialized machines. On January 1, Year 1, Soma leased a machine to Viva Co. for 3 annual payments of $100,000 starting on December 31, Year 1. The machine's remaining useful life is 5 years. The expected residual value of the machine at the end of Year 3 is $40,000. The residual value guaranteed by Viva is $30,000. At the lease commencement date, the fair value of the machine was $278,737 and the carrying amount was $250,000. The rate implicit in the lease is 10%. The present value factor for an ordinary annuity at 10% for 3 periods is 2.48685, and the present value of $1 at 10% for 3 periods is 0.7513.

PV of rental payments ($100,000 × 2.48685)	$248,685
PV of residual value guaranteed by the lessee ($30,000 × 0.7513)	22,539
Total	$271,224

Soma classifies the lease as a **sales-type lease** because the "substantially all of the fair value of the leased asset" classification criterion was met. The sum of the present value of the lease payments and the present value of the residual value guaranteed by the lessee ($271,224) equals or exceeds substantially all of the fair value of the leased machine ($278,737).

$271,224 ÷ $278,737 = 97.3% > 90%

Soma records the following journal entry on January 1, Year 1:

Net investment in the lease	$278,737		(fair value of the machine)
Cost of goods sold	242,487		[$250,000 machine's carrying amount – ($10,000 × 0.7513) PV of unguaranteed residual value]
Revenue		$271,224	(lease receivable)
Machine		250,000	(machine's carrying amount)

NOTE: At the end of the lease term, the remaining balance of net investment in the lease account of $10,000 (assuming the residual value of the machine was $40,000) is reclassified to the appropriate asset account (machine).

c. When the collectibility of the lease payments and the residual value guaranteed by the lessee is not probable, the lessor does not derecognize the leased asset and does not recognize the net investment in the lease and selling profit or loss.

1) The lease payments received from the lessee are recognized as a deposit liability.

Cash	$XXX	
Deposit liability		$XXX

3. **Subsequent Measurement**

   a. Each periodic lease payment received has two components: **interest income** and the **reduction of net investment in the lease**.

   b. Interest income is calculated using the effective interest method.

      1) It equals the carrying amount of the net investment in the lease at the beginning of the period times the discount rate implicit in the lease.

Interest income = Net investment in the lease at the beginning of the period × Discount rate

   c. The reduction of the net investment in the lease is the difference between lease payments received from the lessee minus the interest income recognized.

Reduction of net investment in the lease = Periodic lease payment received – Interest income recognized

      1) If the first lease payment is received at the **commencement date** of the lease, its only component is the reduction of the net investment in the lease. No interest income is recognized for the first payment made at the lease commencement date.

   d. After the leased asset is derecognized, no depreciation expense for the leased asset is recognized by the lessor.

EXAMPLE 13-11 Sales-Type Lease -- Subsequent Measurement

Using the scenario from Example 13-9, assume that the residual value of the machine was $30,000 at the end of the lease term. Alpha records the following journal entries:

<u>December 31, Year 1</u>		
Cash	$100,000	
Interest income		$27,123 ($271,224 × 10%)
Net investment in the lease		72,877 ($100,000 – $27,123)

The carrying amount of the net investment in the lease on December 31, Year 1, is $198,347 ($271,224 – $72,877).

<u>December 31, Year 2</u>		
Cash	$100,000	
Interest income		$19,835 ($198,347 × 10%)
Net investment in the lease		80,165 ($100,000 – $19,835)

The carrying amount of the net investment in the lease on December 31, Year 2, is $118,182 ($198,347 – $80,165).

<u>December 31, Year 3</u>		
Cash	$100,000	
Machine	30,000	
Interest income		$ 11,818 ($118,182 × 10%)
Net investment in the lease		118,182 ($130,000 – $11,818)

The carrying amount of the net investment in the lease on December 31, Year 3, is $0 ($118,182 – $118,182).

4. **Financial Statement Presentation**

   a. In the **balance sheet**, the net investments in the lease assets resulting from sales-type and direct financing leases are aggregated and presented together.

      1) The net investment in the lease assets is presented separately from other assets in the balance sheet.

      2) The net investment in the lease account should be allocated between current and noncurrent portions. The current portion at a balance sheet date is the reduction of the net investment in the lease in the forthcoming year.

   b. In the **statement of cash flows**, cash receipts from all leases (sales-type, direct financing, and operating leases) are classified as cash inflows from **operating activities**.

STOP & REVIEW

You have completed the outline for this subunit.
Study multiple-choice questions 10 and 11 on page 420.

13.6 LESSOR ACCOUNTING FOR OPERATING AND DIRECT FINANCING LEASES

1. **Operating Lease**

   a. Lease payments are recognized as **lease (rental) income** by the lessor.

      1) If rental payments vary from a straight-line basis (e.g., if the first month is free), rental income should be recognized over the full lease term on the **straight-line basis**.

      2) Thus, an **equal amount of rental income** is recognized each period over the lease term as follows:

Rental income recognized each period = Total lease payments to be received ÷ Lease term

      3) The lessor records the following journal entry:

Cash or lease receivable	$XXX	
Rental (lease) income		$XXX

   b. The **leased asset** continues to be reported on the lessor's balance sheet. No net investment in the lease is recognized.

      1) The lessor depreciates the leased asset according to its normal depreciation policy for owned assets.

   c. Initial direct costs, such as realtor fees, are initially deferred by the lessor.

      1) Subsequently, they are expensed by the lessor over the lease term on a straight-line basis.

EXAMPLE 13-12 Lessor's Operating Lease

On January 1, Year 1, GO Co. leased its property for 3 years to RB Co. The lease is properly classified by GO as an operating lease. The following are the lease terms:

- First 4 months' rent is free.
- Monthly rent from May of Year 1 through December of Year 1 is $7,500.
- Monthly rent from January of Year 2 through December of Year 3 is $20,000.

The total lease payments to be received over the lease term of $540,000 [($7,500 × 8 months in Year 1) + ($20,000 × 24 months)] are recognized on a straight-line basis over the entire lease term of 36 months. Thus, from January of Year 1, monthly rental income recognized by GO is $15,000 ($540,000 ÷ 36-month lease term). Accordingly, annual rental (lease) income recognized by GO is $180,000 ($15,000 × 12 months).

2. **Direct Financing Lease**

   a. At the **lease commencement date**, the lessor derecognizes the carrying amount of the leased asset and recognizes the net investment in the lease.

      1) **No selling profit is recognized on the lease commencement date.** Any selling profit is deferred and reduces the initial amount of net investment in the lease.

      2) Assuming the lease does not result in a selling loss and no initial direct costs are incurred, the net investment in the lease equals the carrying amount of the leased asset, as shown in the journal entry below.

Net investment in the lease	$XXX	
Leased asset		$XXX

      3) Any **selling loss** is recognized in the income statement on the lease commencement date.

EXAMPLE 13-13 Direct Financing Lease

Dada Co. sells and leases unspecialized machines. On January 1, Year 1, Dada leased a machine to Nina Co. for 3 annual payments of $100,000 starting on December 31, Year 1. The machine's remaining useful life is 5 years. The expected residual value of the machine at the end of Year 3 is $70,000, and $45,000 of this amount was guaranteed by a third party other than Nina. At the lease commencement date, the fair value of the machine was $301,276, and the carrying amount was $250,000. The rate implicit in the lease is 10%. The present value factor for an ordinary annuity at 10% for 3 periods is 2.48685, and the present value of $1 at 10% for 3 periods is 0.7513. Dada believes that it is probable that the guaranteed residual value and the lease payments will be collected.

PV of rental payments ($100,000 × 2.48685)	$248,685
PV of residual value guaranteed by a third party other than Nina ($45,000 × 0.7513)	33,809
PV of unguaranteed residual value [($70,000 – $45,000) × 0.7513]	18,782
PV of cash and other assets that Dada expects to receive over the lease term	$301,276

-- Continued on next page --

EXAMPLE 13-13 -- Continued

The lease is classified by Dada as a **direct financing lease.** (1) No lease classification criterion for a sales-type lease is met, (2) it is probable that the lease payments and the guaranteed residual value will be collected, and (3) the present value of lease payments and the residual value guaranteed by a third party other than Nina of $282,494 ($248,685 + $33,809) exceeds substantially all of the fair value of the machine of $301,276.

$282,494 ÷ $301,276 = 94% > 90%

NOTE: If Nina (the lessee) guaranteed the residual value of $45,000, the lease would be classified by Dada as a sales-type lease.

- The lease receivable is $282,494 ($248,685 PV of lease payments + $33,809 PV of guaranteed residual value).
- Selling profit is $51,276 ($282,494 lease receivable + $18,782 PV of unguaranteed residual value – $250,000 carrying amount of the machine).
- Net investment in the lease is $250,000 ($301,276 fair value of the machine – $51,276 selling profit). Because no selling loss and initial direct costs were incurred, the net investment in the lease equals the carrying amount of the leased asset.

Dada records the following journal entry on January 1, Year 1:

Net investment in the lease	$250,000	
Leased asset		$250,000

b. **Subsequent** to the lease commencement date, each periodic cash payment received by the lessor includes both (1) interest income and (2) a reduction of the net investment in the lease.

1) Interest income equals the beginning balance of the net investment in the lease times a new discount rate that is used only for subsequent accounting.

a) The new discount rate is derived on the lease commencement date from the following equation:

Net investment in the lease recognized = **PV of cash and other assets the lessor expects to receive over the lease term**

IFRS DIFFERENCE

The lessor classifies all leases as either a finance lease (similar to a sales-type lease under U.S. GAAP) or an operating lease. IFRS does not distinguish between sales-type and direct financing leases. The selling profit that is deferred at lease commencement in a direct financing lease under U.S. GAAP will be recognized under IFRS when the lease is classified as a finance lease.

STOP & REVIEW

You have completed the outline for this subunit.
Study multiple-choice questions 12 and 13 on page 421.

13.7 INITIAL DIRECT COSTS AND SALE AND LEASEBACK TRANSACTIONS

SUCCESS TIP

Most of the CPA Exam questions about leases are **without** initial direct costs. However, knowing the effect of initial direct costs on accounting for leases may be useful if a question asks about it.

1. **Initial Direct Costs**
   a. **Initial direct costs** (IDCs) are incremental costs of a lease that would not have been incurred if the lease had not been obtained. An example is a commission.
   b. The following are the effects of initial direct costs on the accounting for leases:
      1) In the equation to calculate the **rate implicit in the lease** (defined in Subunit 13.1), **deferred IDCs** of the lessor are added to the fair value of the leased asset.
      2) In sales-type leases, **IDCs are expensed** when the fair value of the leased asset differs from its carrying amount.
         a) In this case, for the purpose of assessing the "substantially all of the fair value" lease classification criterion, the IDCs are excluded from the calculation of the rate implicit in the lease.
         b) If the fair value of the leased asset equals its carrying amount, IDCs are deferred and included in the calculation of the rate implicit in the lease. Thus, they are automatically included in the investment in the lease. They need not be added separately.
      3) In the initial calculation of the **right-of-use asset**, the IDCs of the lessee are added to the lease liability.
2. **Sale and Leaseback Transactions -- Basics**
   a. A sale-leaseback involves the sale of property by the owner (seller-lessee) and a lease of the property back from the buyer-lessor.

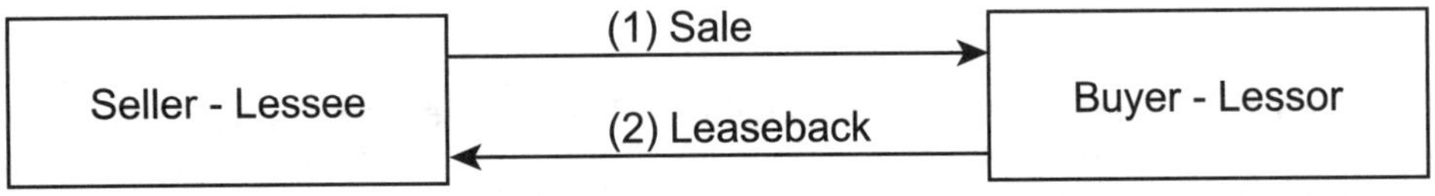

Figure 13-5

   b. The initial transfer of the asset to the buyer-lessor is **not a sale** of the asset if the leaseback is classified as a **finance lease** or a **sales-type lease**.
      1) Generally, the transfer of the asset is **not a sale** if, based on lease terms, the seller-lessee has the option to repurchase the asset.
   c. If the leaseback is classified as an **operating lease**, the initial transfer of the asset to the buyer-lessor can be accounted for as a **sale of an asset** if all the criteria for revenue recognition are met.
   d. If the initial transfer of the asset is a **sale**, the **seller-lessee** should
      1) Recognize the transaction price for the sale of the asset.
      2) Derecognize the carrying amount of the asset.
      3) Recognize any gain or loss on the sale of the asset, adjusted for off-market terms, if needed.
      4) Account for the leaseback of the asset.

3. **Sale and Leaseback Transactions -- The Transfer of an Asset Is a Sale**

   a. An entity needs to determine whether the sale-leaseback transaction is at fair value and based on market terms. The more readily determinable of the following should be considered:

      1) The difference between (a) the sale price of the asset and (b) its fair value.

      2) The difference between (a) the present value of the lease payments and (b) the present value of market rental payments.

   b. If the transaction is **at fair value**, the gain or loss on sale recognized by the seller-lessee is the difference between the selling price and the carrying amount of the asset.

Gain (loss) on sale = Selling price of the asset – Carrying amount of the asset

   c. When the sale-leaseback transaction is **not at fair value** and not based on market terms, off-market adjustments are needed to recognize the sale at fair value.

      1) The **off-market adjustment** equals the difference between the

         a) Fair value of an asset and its selling price or

         b) Present value of the lease payments and the present value of the market rental payments.

      2) The **gain or loss on sale** is adjusted for the off-market adjustment.

Gain (loss) on sale = Fair value of the asset – Carrying amount of the asset

      3) The buyer-lessor recognizes the purchased asset at its fair value.

   d. When the selling price of an asset (or leaseback payment) is **greater** than fair value (or market value), the difference is essentially **additional financing received from the buyer-lessor**.

      1) This additional financing should be accounted for **separately from the lease liability**.

      2) A financial liability (asset) is recognized by the seller-lessee (buyer-lessor) for the off-market adjustment (e.g., the excess of the selling price of an asset over its fair value).

EXAMPLE 13-14 Sale-and-Leaseback -- Initial Transfer Is a Sale

On January 1, Year 1, Zver Co. sold a machine with a remaining useful life of 10 years to Kasha Co. for $500,000. The carrying amount of the machine was $350,000, and its fair value was $410,000. At the same time, Zver (seller-lessee) entered into a contract with Kasha (buyer-lessor) for the right to use the machine (leaseback) for 2 years, with annual rental payments of $130,000 payable at the end of each year. A discount rate for the lease of 10% is used by both Zver and Kasha. The present value factor for an ordinary annuity at 10% for 2 periods is 1.73554.

Because no criterion to classify the leaseback as a sales-type lease or finance lease was met, the leaseback is classified as an operating lease. Thus, a gain on sale of the machine can be recognized by Zver. The transaction is not at fair value because the sale price of the machine is greater than its fair value. Zver essentially received additional financing from Kasha of $90,000 ($500,000 – $410,000). This financing should be accounted for separately from the lease liability by recognizing the following two components of each annual lease payment of $130,000:

- Annual payment for the additional financing of $51,857 ($90,000 ÷ 1.73554).
- Annual rental payment for the right to use the machine of $78,143 ($130,000 – $51,857). Because the lease is classified as an operating lease, $78,143 is the rental expense (revenue) recognized each period by Zver (Kasha).

Zver (seller-lessee) records the following journal entries:

<u>January 1, Year 1</u>		
Cash	$500,000	
Machine		$350,000
Gain on sale		60,000 ($410,000 fair value – $350,000 carrying amount)
Financial liability		90,000 ($500,000 sale price – $410,000 fair value)
Right-of-use (ROU) asset	$135,620	
Lease liability		$135,620 ($78,143 × 1.73554)
<u>December 31, Year 1</u>		
Interest expense	$ 9,000 ($90,000 × 10%)	
Financial liability	42,857 ($51,857 – $9,000)	
Cash		$51,857
Lease liability	$64,581 [$78,143 – ($135,620 × 10%)]	
Lease expense	78,143	
Cash		$78,143
ROU asset		64,581

In Zver's December 31, Year 1, balance sheet, the financial liability is reported at $47,143 ($90,000 – $42,857). The lease liability and ROU asset are reported at $71,039 ($135,620 – $64,581). In the Year 1 income statement, interest expense of $9,000 and lease expense of $78,143 are recognized.

<u>December 31, Year 2</u>		
Interest expense	$ 4,714 ($47,143 × 10%)	
Financial liability	47,143 ($51,857 – $4,714)	
Cash		$51,857
Lease liability	$71,039 [$78,143 – ($71,039 × 10%)]	
Lease expense	78,143	
Cash		$78,143
ROU asset		71,039

-- Continued on next page --

EXAMPLE 13-14 -- Continued

At the end of the lease term on December 31, Year 2, the carrying amount of the financial liability is $0 ($47,143 – $47,143). The carrying amounts of the lease liability and ROU asset also are $0 ($71,039 – $71,039). In the Year 2 income statement, interest expense of $4,714 and lease expense of $78,143 are recognized.

Kasha (buyer-lessor) records the following journal entries:

<u>January 1, Year 1</u>

Machine	$410,000 (at fair value)	
Financial asset	90,000 ($500,000 sale price – $410,000 fair value)	
Cash		$500,000

The lease is classified as an operating lease, and no journal entry for the lease is recorded by Kasha at the commencement date.

<u>December 31, Year 1</u>

Cash	$51,857		Cash	$78,143	
Interest income		$ 9,000 ($90,000 × 10%)	Rental income		$78,143
Financial asset		42,857 ($51,857 – $9,000)			

In the December 31, Year 1, balance sheet, a financial asset (loan receivable) is reported at $47,143 ($90,000 – $42,857). In the Year 1 income statement, interest income of $9,000 and rental income of $78,143 are recognized.

<u>December 31, Year 2</u>

Cash	$51,857		Cash	$78,143	
Interest income		$ 4,714 ($47,143 × 10%)	Rental income		$78,143
Financial asset		47,143 ($51,857 – $4,714)			

At the end of the lease term on December 31, Year 2, the carrying amount of the financial asset is $0 ($47,143 – $47,143). In the Year 2 income statement, interest income of $4,714 and rental income of $78,143 are recognized.

e. When the selling price of an asset (or leaseback payment) is **lower** than fair value (or market value), the difference is essentially a **rent prepaid by the seller-lessee**.

1) The off-market adjustment (the excess of the fair value of an asset over its selling price) is recognized by the seller-lessee as an **increase of the right-of-use asset**.

2) The buyer-lessor recognizes the prepaid rent as an asset. Subsequently, under an operating lease, the prepaid rent is recognized as rental income on a straight-line basis over the lease term.

IFRS DIFFERENCE

When the transfer of an asset is a sale, the gain recognized by the seller-lessee is limited to the amount of the gain that relates to the rights transferred to the buyer-lessor.

Using the data from Example 13-14, under IFRS, Zver would recognize on 1/1/Yr 1 a gain on sale of a machine of $40,153.

- Total gain on sale is $60,000 ($410,000 fair value – $350,000 carrying amount).
- The present value of rental payments of $135,620 ($78,143 × 1.73554) is for the right to use the machine retained by the seller-lessee (Zver).
- The right to use the machine transferred to the buyer-lessor (Kasha) is for $274,380 ($410,000 – $135,620).
- The gain recognized by the seller-lessee is $40,153 [$60,000 × ($274,380 ÷ $410,000)].

NOTE: On the CPA Exam, you probably will not be asked to calculate the gain on sale under IFRS. But you need to know conceptually the difference between IFRS and U.S. GAAP regarding gains on sale recognized.

4. **Sale and Leaseback Transactions -- The Transfer of an Asset Is Not a Sale**
   a. If the transfer of the asset is **not a sale**, the transaction is a financing transaction.
   b. The **seller-lessee** will continue to report the transferred asset and depreciate it. The initial proceeds received from the buyer-lessor are recognized as a financial liability (e.g., loan payable).
      1) Subsequently, each annual rental payment has the following two components:
         a) **Interest expense** equals the beginning of the period balance of the financial liability times the discount rate for the lease, and
         b) The **reduction of the financial liability** equals the difference between the periodic lease payment and interest expense recognized for the period.
   c. The **buyer-lessor** will not recognize the transferred asset. The amounts paid to the seller-lessee are recognized as a financial asset (e.g., loan receivable).
      1) Subsequently, each periodic rental payment received consists of interest income and a principal repayment of the financial asset.

STOP & REVIEW

You have completed the outline for this subunit.
Study multiple-choice questions 14 and 15 beginning on page 422.

13.8 CONTINGENCIES

1. **Definition**
   a. A contingency is "an existing condition, situation, or set of circumstances **involving uncertainty** as to possible gain (a gain contingency) or loss (a loss contingency) to an entity that will ultimately be resolved when one or more future events occur or fail to occur."
   b. A contingency may be
      1) **Probable.** Future events are likely to occur.
      2) **Reasonably possible.** The chance of occurrence is more than remote but less than probable.
      3) **Remote.** The chance of occurrence is slight.

2. **Probable Loss Contingencies**

   a. **Criteria for accrual.** A **contingent loss** must be accrued (debit loss and credit liability) when **two conditions are met**. Based on information available prior to the issuance of the financial statements, accrual is required if

      1) It is **probable** that, at a balance sheet date, an asset has been impaired or a liability has been incurred, and

      2) The amount of the loss can be **reasonably estimated**.

   b. **Measurement of the loss.** When the assessment of a **range of probable losses** is provided, the amount that appears to be a better estimate than any other within this range must be accrued.

      1) If no amount within that range appears to be a better estimate than any other, the **minimum** of the range should be accrued.

   c. **Disclosures.** Disclosure in the financial statements of the nature of the accrual and the amount or the range of loss is required.

3. **Reasonably Possible Loss Contingencies**

   a. **Disclosure** must be made if any condition to accrue a loss contingency is not met, but the probability of the loss is at least **reasonably possible**. The following should be disclosed:

      1) The nature of the contingency

      2) An estimate of the possible loss or range of loss or a statement that such an estimate cannot be made

EXAMPLE 13-15 Contingent Liability

(1) During Year 1, Crab Co. was sued by Apple Co. for patent infringement. At the end of Year 1, Crab's legal counsel believes that (a) an unfavorable outcome is probable, (b) an estimated amount of loss is in the range of $100,000 to $500,000, and (c) all amounts in the range are equally likely. In its December 31, Year 1, financial statements Crab Co. must

- Accrue a liability and recognize a loss of $100,000 (the minimum of the range).
- Disclose the nature of the contingency, the range of loss, and the exposure to an additional amount of loss of up to $400,000.

(2) Now assume that Crab's legal counsel believes that a loss of $200,000 is a better estimate than any other amount in the range of probable losses. In its December 31, Year 1, financial statements Crab Co. must

- Accrue a liability and recognize a loss of $200,000 (the better estimate within the range).
- Disclose the nature of the contingency, the range of loss, and the exposure to an additional amount of loss of up to $300,000.

(3) Now assume that Crab's legal counsel believes that an unfavorable verdict is only reasonably possible (but not probable). No liability is accrued and no loss is recognized. Disclosure of the nature of the contingency and the range of loss is required.

4. **Remote Loss Contingencies**
   a. These loss contingencies ordinarily are **not disclosed**.
   b. However, a **guarantee** (e.g., of the indebtedness of another or to repurchase receivables) must be disclosed even if the probability of loss is remote. The disclosure should include the nature and amount of the guarantee.
      1) A guarantee is a **noncontingent obligation** to perform after the occurrence of a triggering event or condition. It is coupled with a **contingent** obligation to make payments if such an event or condition occurs.
         a) Thus, **recognition of a liability** at the inception of a guarantee is required even when it is not probable that payments will be made.
      2) The **initial measurement** of a noncontingent obligation ordinarily is at **fair value**. If a contingent loss and liability also are required to be recognized, the liability recognized by the guarantor is the greater of the fair value measurement or the contingent liability amount.
   c. No accrual is permitted for general or unspecified business risks, for example, those related to national and international economic conditions. No disclosure is required.
5. **Unasserted Claims**
   a. With respect to unasserted claims, an entity must determine the degree of probability that a suit may be filed and the possibility of an unfavorable outcome.
   b. If it is probable that a suit will be filed against an entity and the two conditions to accrue a contingent liability are met (i.e., the loss is probable and can be reasonably estimated), a contingent loss must be accrued.
6. **Gain Contingencies**
   a. Gain contingencies are **recognized only when realized**.
      1) For example, an award of damages in a lawsuit is not realized if it is being appealed.
   b. A gain contingency must be adequately disclosed in the notes to the financial statements.

IFRS DIFFERENCE

Provisions are liabilities of uncertain timing or amount.

- **Recognition of provisions** is appropriate when (a) the entity has a legal or constructive present obligation resulting from a past event, (b) it is probable that an outflow of economic benefits will be necessary to settle the obligation, and (c) its amount can be reliably estimated.
- If the estimate of a provision is stated within a continuous range of possible outcomes, and each point in the range is as likely as any other, the **midpoint** is used.

A **contingent liability** is a possible obligation arising from past events. Its existence will be confirmed only by uncertain future events not wholly within the entity's control. A liability also is contingent if it is a present obligation that arises from past events but does not meet the recognition criteria (i.e., either a transfer of economic benefits is not probable or no reliable estimate can be made). A contingent liability must not be recognized. However, it should be disclosed unless the possibility of resource outflows is remote.

STOP & REVIEW

You have completed the outline for this subunit.
Study multiple-choice questions 16 through 20 beginning on page 424.

QUESTIONS

13.1 Lease Classification

1. Lease M does not contain a purchase option, but the present value of the lease payments is equal to 91% of the fair value of the leased asset. Lease P does not transfer ownership to the lessee by the end of the lease term, but the lease term is equal to 77% of the estimated economic life of the leased asset. How should the lessee classify these leases?

	Lease M	Lease P
A.	Finance lease	Operating lease
B.	Finance lease	Finance lease
C.	Operating lease	Finance lease
D.	Operating lease	Operating lease

Answer (B) is correct.

REQUIRED: The proper classification of leases.

DISCUSSION: A lease is classified as a finance lease by the lessee and as a sales-type lease by the lessor if, at lease commencement, at least one of the following five criteria is met: (1) The ownership of the leased asset is transferred to the lessee by the end of the lease term, (2) the lease includes an option to purchase the leased asset that the lessee is reasonably certain to exercise, (3) the lease term is for the major part (generally considered as 75%) of the remaining economic life of the leased asset, (4) the present value of the sum of the lease payments and any residual value guaranteed by the lessee equals or exceeds substantially all of the fair value (generally considered as 90%) of the leased asset, and (5) the leased asset is so specialized that it is expected to have no alternative use to the lessor at the end of the lease term. When no classification criterion is met, the lease is classified as an operating lease by the lessee. Thus, both lease M (91% of the fair value of the leased asset) and lease P (77% of the economic life of the leased asset) are classified as finance leases.

Answer (A) is incorrect. Lease P meets the 75% of the economic life of the leased asset classification criterion. **Answer (C) is incorrect.** Lease M meets the 90% of the fair value of the leased asset classification criterion. **Answer (D) is incorrect.** Lease P meets the 75% of the economic life of the leased asset classification criterion. Lease M meets the 90% of the fair value of the leased asset classification criterion.

2. Beal, Inc., intends to lease a machine from Paul Corp. Beal's incremental borrowing rate is 14%. The prime rate of interest is 8%. Paul's implicit rate in the lease is 10%, which is known to Beal. Beal computes the present value of the lease payments using

A. 8%

B. 10%

C. 12%

D. 14%

Answer (B) is correct.

REQUIRED: The discount rate used by the lessee to determine the present value of lease payments if the incremental borrowing rate and implicit rate are known.

DISCUSSION: The discount rate for the lease is the rate implicit in the lease. If the lessee cannot determine the rate implicit in the lease, the lessee uses its incremental borrowing rate. Because the implicit rate of 10% is known to Beal, it is used as the discount rate of the lease.

Answer (A) is incorrect. The prime rate (8%) is irrelevant. **Answer (C) is incorrect.** The rate of 12% is the average of the implicit rate and the incremental rate. **Answer (D) is incorrect.** The implicit rate is known to Beal. Thus, it must be used as the discount rate for the lease.

13.2 Lessee Accounting -- Initial Measurement

3. Robbin, Inc., leased a machine from Ready Leasing Co. The lease requires 10 annual payments of $10,000 beginning immediately. The lease contract specifies the rate implicit in the lease of 12% and a purchase option of $10,000 at the end of the tenth year, even though the machine's estimated value on that date is $20,000. Robbin is reasonably certain to exercise the purchase option. Robbin's incremental borrowing rate is 14%.

The present value of an annuity due of 1 at:
12% for 10 years is 6.328
14% for 10 years is 5.946

The present value of 1 at:
12% for 10 years is .322
14% for 10 years is .270

What amount should Robbin record as lease liability at the beginning of the lease term?

A. $62,160

B. $64,860

C. $66,500

D. $69,720

Answer (C) is correct.

REQUIRED: The amount that should be reported as a finance lease liability.

DISCUSSION: For a finance or an operating lease, a lessee initially must recognize a lease liability and a right-of-use asset. At the lease commencement date, a lease liability is measured at the present value of the lease payments to be made over the lease term. When the lease includes a purchase option that the lessee is reasonably certain to exercise, the lease is a finance lease. The lease payments therefore consist of rental payments and the exercise price of the purchase option. The discount rate for the lease is the rate implicit in the lease of 12% because it is known by Robbin. Thus, the lease liability is equal to $66,500 [($10,000 × 6.328) + ($10,000 × .322)].

Answer (A) is incorrect. The present value of the payment required by the purchase option and the annual lease payments should be discounted at 12% instead of 14%. **Answer (B) is incorrect.** The amount of the purchase option is $10,000, not the estimated value at that date. Also, the discount rate for both the option amount and the annual payments should be 12% instead of 14%. **Answer (D) is incorrect.** The payment required by the purchase option should be included in the present value of minimum lease payments, not the estimated value of the asset at the end of the lease.

4. Koby Co. entered into a lease with a vendor for equipment on January 2 for 7 years. The equipment has no guaranteed residual value. The lease required Koby to pay $500,000 annually on January 2, beginning with the current year. The present value of an annuity due for seven years was 5.35 at the inception of the lease. What amount should Koby recognize for the lease asset?

A. $500,000

B. $825,000

C. $2,675,000

D. $3,500,000

Answer (C) is correct.

REQUIRED: The amount recognized for the leased asset.

DISCUSSION: For finance and operating leases, a lessee must recognize a lease liability and a right-of-use asset at the lease commencement date. A right-of-use asset initially is measured at the amount at which the lease liability was recognized (i.e., present value of lease payments) plus initial direct costs incurred by the lessee. These payments include the initial payment at the inception of the lease. Thus, the annual payments constitute an annuity due. In the absence of a purchase option, guaranteed residual value, or nonrenewal penalty, the amount recognized as leased asset (right-of-use asset) is $2,675,000 ($500,000 annual payment × 5.35 present value of an annuity due for 7 years).

Answer (A) is incorrect. The annual payment is $500,000. **Answer (B) is incorrect.** The amount of $825,000 is the discount (nominal amount of the payments – their present value). **Answer (D) is incorrect.** The nominal amount (undiscounted sum) of the payments is $3,500,000.

13.3 Lessee Accounting for Finance Leases -- Subsequent Measurement

5. On January 1 of the current year, Tell Co. leased equipment from Swill Co. under a 9-year lease. The equipment had a cost of $400,000 and an estimated useful life of 15 years. Semiannual lease payments of $44,000 are due every January 1 and July 1. The present value of lease payments at the discount rate of the lease of 12% was $505,000, which equals the fair value of the equipment. What amount should Tell recognize as amortization expense on the right-of-use asset in the current year?

A. $26,667

B. $33,667

C. $44,444

D. $56,111

Answer (D) is correct.

REQUIRED: The amortization expense for a lease.

DISCUSSION: Tell Co. classifies the lease as a finance lease because the present value of the lease payments equals the fair value of the leased equipment. The right-of-use asset is initially measured at the present value of lease payments of $505,000. Under a finance lease when (1) the ownership of the leased asset is not transferred to the lessee, and (2) the lease does not include a purchase option that the lessee is reasonably certain to exercise, the right-of-use asset is amortized on a straight-line basis over the shorter of its useful life or lease term. Thus, annual amortization of the right-of-use asset is $56,111 ($505,000 ÷ 9 years).

Answer (A) is incorrect. The amount of $26,667 is based on the equipment's cost and estimated useful life. **Answer (B) is incorrect.** The amount of $33,667 is based on the estimated useful life, not the lease term. **Answer (C) is incorrect.** The amount of $44,444 is based on the equipment's cost.

6. On January 1, Year 4, Harrow Co., as lessee, signed a 5-year noncancelable equipment lease with annual payments of $100,000 beginning December 31, Year 4. Harrow treated this transaction as a finance lease. The five lease payments have a present value of $379,000 at January 1, Year 4, based on interest of 10%. What amount should Harrow report as interest expense for the year ended December 31, Year 4?

A. $37,900

B. $27,900

C. $24,200

D. $0

Answer (A) is correct.

REQUIRED: The interest to be recognized in the first year of a finance lease.

DISCUSSION: Under the effective-interest method, interest expense for the first year is $37,900 ($379,000 lease liability × 10% effective interest rate).

Answer (B) is incorrect. The amount of $27,900 assumes the initial payment was made immediately. **Answer (C) is incorrect.** The amount of $24,200 is one-fifth of the total interest ($500,000 – $379,000 PV). **Answer (D) is incorrect.** Interest must be accrued.

7. In the long-term liabilities section of its balance sheet at December 31, Year 3, Mene Co. reported a finance lease liability of $75,000, net of current portion of $1,364. Payments of $9,000 were made on both January 2, Year 4, and January 2, Year 5. Mene's incremental borrowing rate on the date of the lease was 11%, and the lessor's implicit rate, which was known to Mene, was 10%. In its December 31, Year 4, long-term liabilities section of the balance sheet, what amount should Mene report as a finance lease liability, net of current portion?

A. $66,000

B. $73,500

C. $73,636

D. $74,250

Answer (B) is correct.

REQUIRED: The finance lease liability, net of current portion.

DISCUSSION: The total lease liability on 12/31/Yr 3 was $76,364 ($75,000 noncurrent portion + $1,364 current portion). Each periodic lease payment made by the lessee has two components: interest expense and reduction of lease liability. After the Year 4 payment, which included the current portion, the lease liability was $75,000. Consequently, the Year 5 payment included interest of $7,500 ($75,000 carrying amount during Year 4 × 10% lessor's implicit rate, which is known to the lessee and a principal component of $1,500 ($9,000 cash – $7,500 interest). The latter is the current portion of the lease liability on 12/31/Year 4. The finance lease liability at December 31, Year 4, net of current portion, is therefore $73,500 ($75,000 – $1,500).

Answer (A) is incorrect. The amount of $66,000 results from treating the full $9,000 payment made in Year 5 as principal. **Answer (C) is incorrect.** The amount of $73,636 assumes the current portion is the same as the previous years'. **Answer (D) is incorrect.** The amount of $74,250 is based on an 11% rate.

13.4 Lessee Accounting for Operating Leases -- Subsequent Measurement

8. Oak Co. leased equipment for 9 years, agreeing to pay $50,000 at the start of the lease term on December 31, Year 4, and $50,000 annually on each December 31 for the next 8 years. The present value on December 31, Year 4, of the nine lease payments over the lease term, using the rate implicit in the lease, was $316,500. Oak knows that this rate is 10%. The December 31, Year 4, present value of the lease payments using Oak's incremental borrowing rate of 12% was $298,500. Oak made a timely second lease payment. The lease was classified as an operating lease by Oak. What amount should Oak report as a lease liability in its December 31, Year 5, balance sheet?

A. $350,000

B. $243,150

C. $228,320

D. $0

Answer (B) is correct.

REQUIRED: The amount to be reported as a lease liability for an operating lease.

DISCUSSION: For a finance or operating lease, a lessee initially must recognize a lease liability and a right-of-use asset. At the lease commencement date, a lease liability is measured at the present value of the lease payments to be made over the lease term. Subsequent to initial recognition, the lease liability is reduced for the excess of the periodic lease payment over the interest expense recognized during the period. Oak knows the implicit rate. Thus, the present value of the lease payments of this lease is $316,500, the amount based on the lessor's implicit rate. After the initial payment of $50,000, which contains no interest component, is deducted, the carrying amount during Year 5 is $266,500. Accordingly, the interest component of the next payment is $26,650 ($266,500 × 10% implicit rate), and the lease liability on December 31, Year 5, is $243,150 [$266,500 – ($50,000 – $26,650)].

Answer (A) is incorrect. The sum of the nine lease payments is $350,000. **Answer (C) is incorrect.** The amount of $228,320 is based on a 12% rate. **Answer (D) is incorrect.** Both finance and operating leases result in recognition of a lease liability at the lease commencement date.

9. On June 1, Oren Co. entered into a 5-year nonrenewable operating lease, commencing on that date, for office space and made the following payments to Rose Properties:

Bonus to obtain lease	$30,000
First month's rent	10,000
Last month's rent	10,000

The lease term requires monthly rent payments of $10,000. In its income statement for the year ended June 30, what amount should Oren report as lease expense?

A. $10,000

B. $10,500

C. $40,000

D. $50,000

Answer (B) is correct.

REQUIRED: The amount to be reported as lease expense for an operating lease.

DISCUSSION: In an operating lease, a single lease expense is recognized in each period. It is calculated so that the total undiscounted lease payments are allocated over the lease term on a straight-line basis. The rent expense in June is $10,000, the amount to be paid each month. The bonus to obtain the lease is an initial direct cost incurred by Oren. Initial direct costs incurred by the lessee are included in the total undiscounted lease payments. Thus, they are recognized in the single periodic lease expense on a straight-line basis over the lease term. Lease expense for June is $10,500 {$10,000 for the month's rent + [($30,000 ÷ 5) ÷ 12 amortization of the bonus]}.

Answer (A) is incorrect. The expense should include amortization of the bonus. **Answer (C) is incorrect.** The bonus should be amortized over the lease term benefited. **Answer (D) is incorrect.** The last month's rent payment should be deferred and expensed in the period it benefits. Also, the bonus should be amortized over the lease term.

13.5 Lessor Accounting for Sales-Type Leases

10. Farm Co. leased equipment to Union Co. on July 1, Year 4, and properly recorded the sales-type lease at $135,000, the present value of the lease payments discounted at 10%. The first of eight annual lease payments of $20,000 due at the beginning of each year of the lease term was received and recorded on July 3, Year 4. Farm had purchased the equipment for $110,000. What amount of interest revenue from the lease should Farm report in its Year 4 income statement?

A. $0

B. $5,500

C. $5,750

D. $6,750

Answer (C) is correct.

REQUIRED: The interest income recognized by the lessor in the first year of a sales-type lease.

DISCUSSION: Under the effective-interest method, interest revenue equals the carrying amount of the net investment in the lease at the beginning of the interest period multiplied by the interest rate used to calculate the present value of the lease payments. The present value of $135,000 is reduced by the $20,000 payment made at the inception of the lease, leaving a carrying amount of $115,000. Interest revenue for Year 4 is therefore $5,750 ($115,000 × 10% × 6/12).

Answer (A) is incorrect. Interest income for Year 2 is $5,750. **Answer (B) is incorrect.** The amount of $5,500 equals ($110,000 × 10% × 6/12). **Answer (D) is incorrect.** The amount of $6,750 equals ($135,000 × 10% × 6/12).

11. Winn Co. manufactures equipment that is sold or leased. On December 31, Year 4, Winn leased equipment to Bart for a 5-year period ending December 31, Year 9, at which date ownership of the leased asset will be transferred to Bart. Equal payments under the lease are $22,000 and are due on December 31 of each year. The first payment was made on December 31, Year 4. The normal sales price of the equipment is $77,000, and cost is $60,000. For the year ended December 31, Year 4, what amount of selling profit should Winn realize from the lease transaction?

A. $17,000

B. $22,000

C. $50,000

D. $33,000

Answer (A) is correct.

REQUIRED: The selling profit to be recognized by the lessor from a lease transaction.

DISCUSSION: Ownership of the leased equipment transfers to the lessee at the end of the lease term. Accordingly, one of the five criteria to classify the lease as a sales-type lease by the lessor is satisfied. Given no residual value or initial direct costs, selling profit for a sales-type lease is recognized for the excess of the fair value of the leased equipment over its carrying amount. Thus, a selling profit of $17,000 ($77,000 – $60,000) is recognized by Winn.

Answer (B) is incorrect. The amount of a periodic payment is $22,000. **Answer (C) is incorrect.** The amount of $50,000 equals the sum of the five periodic payments minus the equipment's cost. **Answer (D) is incorrect.** The amount of $33,000 equals the sum of the five periodic payments minus the normal sales price.

13.6 Lessor Accounting for Operating and Direct Financing Leases

12. On January 1, Year 1, Gee, Inc., leased a delivery truck from Marr Corp. under a 3-year operating lease. Total rent for the term of the lease will be $36,000, payable as follows:

$ 500 × 12 months = $ 6,000
$ 750 × 12 months = $ 9,000
$1,750 × 12 months = $21,000

All payments were made when due. In Marr's December 31, Year 2, balance sheet, the accrued rent receivable should be reported as

A. $0

B. $9,000

C. $12,000

D. $21,000

Answer (B) is correct.

REQUIRED: The amount to be included as rent receivable in the balance sheet.

DISCUSSION: For an operating lease, lease payments are recognized as rental income by the lessor. If rental payments vary from a straight-line basis, rental income should be recognized over the full lease term on a straight-line basis. An equal amount of rental income therefore is recognized each period over the lease term. This monthly rent revenue recognized is $1,000 [($6,000 + $9,000 + $21,000) ÷ 36 months]. At December 31, Year 2, cumulative revenue recognized is $24,000 ($1,000 × 24 months). Because cumulative cash received is $15,000 ($6,000 + $9,000), an accrued receivable for the $9,000 ($24,000 – $15,000) difference should be recognized.

Answer (A) is incorrect. The amount of $9,000 is equal to rent received during the year ended December 31, Year 2. **Answer (C) is incorrect.** The amount of $12,000 is rent revenue recognized each year. **Answer (D) is incorrect.** The amount of $21,000 is equal to the rent payments to be received in the following fiscal year.

13. On January 1, Year 4, Wren Co. leased a building to Brill under an operating lease for 10 years at $50,000 per year, payable the first day of each lease year. Wren paid $15,000 to a real estate broker as a finder's fee. The building is depreciated $12,000 per year. For Year 4, Wren incurred insurance and property tax expenses totaling $9,000. Wren's net rental income for Year 4 should be

A. $27,500

B. $29,000

C. $35,000

D. $36,500

Answer (A) is correct.

REQUIRED: The net rental income in the first year.

DISCUSSION: The net rental income equals the annual payment minus expenses. The finder's fee is an initial direct cost that should be deferred and subsequently expensed over the lease term on a straight-line basis. Accordingly, the net rental income for Year 4 is $27,500 [$50,000 annual rental – $12,000 depreciation – $9,000 insurance and taxes – ($15,000 ÷ 10 years) amortization of the finder's fee].

Answer (B) is incorrect. The amount of $29,000 omits amortization of the finder's fee. **Answer (C) is incorrect.** The amount of $35,000 equals rental income minus the full finder's fee. **Answer (D) is incorrect.** The amount of $36,500 excludes insurance and property taxes from the computation.

13.7 Initial Direct Costs and Sale and Leaseback Transactions

Questions 14 and 15 are based on the following information. On January 1, Year 1, White Co. sold a property with a remaining useful life of 20 years to Blue Co. for $900,000. At the same time, White entered into a contract with Blue for the right to use the property (leaseback) for a period of 6 years, with annual rental payments of $80,000 that approximate the market rental payments for similar properties. On January 1, Year 1, the carrying amount of the property was $680,000, and its fair value was $770,000. A discount rate for the lease of 10% is used by both White and Blue. The present value factor for an ordinary annuity at 10% for 6 periods is 4.3553. The lease does not transfer the property to White at the end of the lease term and does not include a purchase option.

14. What amount of lease expense for the right of use of the property is recognized by White in Year 1?

A. $80,000

B. $50,151

C. $13,000

D. $58,333

Answer (B) is correct.

REQUIRED: The lease expense for the right of use of property.

DISCUSSION: The leaseback is classified by White as an operating lease because none of the five criteria for classifying the lease as a finance lease were met. Because on January 1, Year 1, the selling price of the property was greater than its fair value, White received additional financing from Blue of $130,000 ($900,000 – $770,000) for the difference. Each annual lease payment includes both (1) the payment for the additional financing of $29,849 ($130,000 ÷ 4.3553) and (2) the payment for the right of use of the property of $50,151 ($80,000 – $29,849). If the leaseback is an operating lease, the payment for the right of use of the property is recognized as lease expense.

Answer (A) is incorrect. Because on January 1, Year 1, the selling price of the property was greater than its fair value, White received additional financing from Blue for the difference. Thus, each annual lease payment includes both the payment for the additional financing and the payment for the right of use of the property (which is the lease expense). **Answer (C) is incorrect.** The amount of $13,000 is the interest expense recognized in Year 1 on the additional financing received from Blue. **Answer (D) is incorrect.** The amount of $58,333 [$80,000 – ($130,000 ÷ 6 years)] assumes that the payment for the additional financing received from Blue is $21,667 ($130,000 ÷ 6 years) each year.

15. What amount of gain on sale of the property was recognized by White on January 1, Year 1?

A. $0

B. $130,000

C. $90,000

D. $220,000

Answer (C) is correct.

REQUIRED: The gain on sale recognized by the seller-lessee.

DISCUSSION: The leaseback is classified by White as an operating lease because none of the five criteria for classifying the lease as a finance lease were met. When the leaseback is classified as an operating lease, the initial transfer of the asset to the buyer-lessor can be accounted for as a sale of an asset, assuming all the criteria for revenue recognition were met. When the transaction is at fair value, a gain or loss on sale recognized by the seller-lessee is the difference between the selling price and the carrying amount of the property. But this transaction is not at fair value. The selling price of the property is greater than its fair value. The gain or loss on sale therefore is the difference between the fair value of the property and its carrying amount. Accordingly, a gain on sale of $90,000 ($770,000 fair value – $680,000 carrying amount) is recognized by White on January 1, Year 1.

Answer (A) is incorrect. The leaseback is classified by White as an operating lease because none of the five criteria to classify the lease as a finance lease were met. When the leaseback is classified as an operating lease, the initial transfer of the property to the buyer-lessor can be accounted for as a sale of the property, assuming all the criteria for revenue recognition were met. **Answer (B) is incorrect.** The amount of $130,000 is the excess of the selling price of the property over its fair value. It is the additional financing that White received from Blue. **Answer (D) is incorrect.** This transaction is not at fair value, because the sales price of the machine is greater than its fair value. Thus, the gain or loss on sale is calculated as the difference between the fair value of the property and its carrying amount.

13.8 Contingencies

16. Invern, Inc., has a self-insurance plan. Each year, retained earnings is appropriated for contingencies in an amount equal to insurance premiums saved less recognized losses from lawsuits and other claims. As a result of a Year 4 accident, Invern is a defendant in a lawsuit in which it will probably have to pay damages of $190,000. What are the effects of this lawsuit's probable outcome on Invern's Year 4 financial statements?

A. An increase in expenses and no effect on liabilities.

B. An increase in both expenses and liabilities.

C. No effect on expenses and an increase in liabilities.

D. No effect on either expenses or liabilities.

Answer (B) is correct.

REQUIRED: The effect on the financial statements of litigation with a probable unfavorable outcome.

DISCUSSION: A loss contingency is an existing condition, situation, or set of circumstances involving uncertainty as to the impairment of an asset's value or the incurrence of a liability as of the balance sheet date. Resolution of the uncertainty depends on the occurrence or nonoccurence of one or more future events. A loss should be debited and either an asset valuation allowance or a liability credited when the loss contingency is both probable and reasonably estimable. Thus, the company should accrue a loss and a liability.

17. Wyatt Co. has a probable loss that can only be reasonably estimated within a range of outcomes. No single amount within the range is a better estimate than any other amount. The loss accrual should be

A. Zero.

B. The maximum of the range.

C. The mean of the range.

D. The minimum of the range.

Answer (D) is correct.

REQUIRED: The contingent loss that should be accrued when a range of estimates is provided.

DISCUSSION: Because the loss is probable and can be reasonably estimated, it should be accrued if the amount is material. If the estimate is stated within a given range and no amount within that range appears to be a better estimate than any other, the minimum of the range should be accrued.

18. Bell Co. is a defendant in a lawsuit that could result in a large payment to the plaintiff. Bell's attorney believes that there is a 90% chance that Bell will lose the suit and estimates that the loss will be anywhere from $5,000,000 to $20,000,000 and possibly as much as $30,000,000. None of the estimates are better than the others. What amount of liability should Bell report on its balance sheet related to the lawsuit?

A. $0

B. $5,000,000

C. $20,000,000

D. $30,000,000

Answer (B) is correct.

REQUIRED: The liability of a defendant in a lawsuit.

DISCUSSION: A loss contingency is accrued by a debit to expense and a credit to a liability if it is probable that a loss will occur and the loss can be reasonably estimated. The $5,000,000 estimated loss is reported on the balance sheet, and the range of the contingent loss is disclosed in the notes. The loss is probable (likely to occur) given expert opinion that the chance of loss is 90%. When no amount within a reasonable estimated range is a better estimate than any other, the minimum is accrued.

19. In Year 4, hail damaged several of Toncan Co.'s vans. Hailstorms had frequently inflicted similar damage to Toncan's vans. Over the years, Toncan had saved money by not buying hail insurance and either paying for repairs or selling damaged vans and then replacing them. In Year 4, the damaged vans were sold for less than their carrying amount. How should the hail damage cost be reported in Toncan's Year 4 financial statements?

A. The actual Year 4 hail damage loss as a discontinued operation, net of income taxes.

B. The actual Year 4 hail damage loss in continuing operations, with no separate disclosure.

C. The expected average hail damage loss in continuing operations, with no separate disclosure.

D. The expected average hail damage loss in continuing operations, with separate disclosure.

Answer (B) is correct.

REQUIRED: The reporting of hail damage costs when a company is uninsured and sells the damaged item for a loss.

DISCUSSION: Because Toncan sold its damaged vans for less than their carrying amount, the company suffered a loss. The actual loss should be reported even though the company is uninsured against future hail damage and a contingency exists. With respect to future hailstorms, no asset has been impaired and no contingent loss should be recorded. Furthermore, this occurrence is not unusual or infrequent, and a separate disclosure is not needed.

Answer (A) is incorrect. Hail damage does not meet the definition of a discontinued operation. **Answer (C) is incorrect.** Toncan should report the actual loss incurred in Year 4. **Answer (D) is incorrect.** Toncan should report the actual loss, and a separate disclosure is not needed because this occurrence is not unusual or infrequent.

20. On February 5, Year 2, an employee filed a $2 million lawsuit against Steel Co. for damages suffered when one of Steel's plants exploded on December 29, Year 1. Steel's legal counsel expects the company will lose the lawsuit and estimates the loss to be between $500,000 and $1 million. The employee has offered to settle the lawsuit out of court for $900,000, but Steel will not agree to the settlement. In its December 31, Year 1, balance sheet, what amount should Steel report as liability from lawsuit?

A. $2,000,000

B. $1,000,000

C. $900,000

D. $500,000

Answer (D) is correct.

REQUIRED: The contingent loss that should be accrued when a range of estimates is provided.

DISCUSSION: Because the loss is probable and can be reasonably estimated, it should be accrued if the amount is material. If the estimate is stated within a given range, and no amount within that range appears to be a better estimate than any other, the minimum of the range should be accrued. Thus, Steel should report a $500,000 contingent liability.

Answer (A) is incorrect. The minimum of the range should be accrued. **Answer (B) is incorrect.** The minimum of the range should be accrued. **Answer (C) is incorrect.** The amount of $900,000 is the proposed settlement amount.

STUDY UNIT FOURTEEN

EQUITY

(18 pages of outline)

Corporate equity is more complex than partner or proprietor equity. Its major components are contributed capital, retained earnings, and accumulated other comprehensive income.

14.1 CLASSES OF EQUITY

1. **Reporting**

   a. Equity is reported on the face of the balance sheet.

EXAMPLE 14-1 Presentation of Equity

Capital stock:		
Preferred stock, $50 par value, 6% cumulative, 10,000 shares authorized, issued, and outstanding	$ 500,000	
Preferred stock, $40 par value, 7% cumulative, 5,000 shares authorized, issued, and outstanding, each convertible to 1 share of common stock	200,000	
Common stock, stated value $1 per share, 50,000 shares authorized, issued, and outstanding	50,000	
Common stock subscribed, 10,000 shares	10,000	
Common stock dividend distributable, 4,500 shares	4,500	
Stock warrants outstanding	1,500	
Total capital stock		$ 766,000
Additional paid-in capital:		
Excess over par -- preferred	$ 464,000	
Excess over par -- common	800,000	1,264,000
Total paid-in capital		$2,030,000
Retained earnings:		
Retained earnings -- unappropriated	$5,800,000	
Retained earnings -- appropriated for expansion	1,520,000	
Total retained earnings		7,320,000
Total paid-in capital and retained earnings		$9,350,000
Accumulated other comprehensive income		611,000
Minus: Receivable from stock subscription		(84,000)
Minus: Cost of treasury stock (5,000 common shares)		(100,000)
Total shareholders' equity		$9,777,000

2. **Stock Authorized, Issued, and Outstanding**

   a. Stock authorized is the maximum amount of stock that a corporation is legally allowed to issue.

      1) The charter (articles of incorporation) filed with the secretary of state of the state of incorporation indicates the classes of stock that may be issued and their authorized amounts in terms of shares or total dollar value.

   b. Stock issued is the amount of stock authorized that was actually issued by the corporation.

   c. Stock outstanding is the amount of stock issued that was purchased and is held by shareholders.

      1) Stock outstanding may be lower than stock issued as a result of the entity's repurchases of its own stock (treasury stock).

3. **Common Stock**

   a. The most widely used classes of stock are common and preferred. Common shareholders are entitled to receive **liquidating distributions** only after all other claims have been satisfied, including those of preferred shareholders.

   b. Common shareholders are not entitled to **dividends**.

      1) A corporation may choose not to declare dividends. Among the reasons are insufficient retained earnings to meet a legal requirement or the need to use cash for some other purpose.

   c. State statutes typically permit different classes of common stock with different rights or privileges, e.g., class A common with voting rights and class B common with no voting rights.

   d. If only one class of stock is issued, it is treated as common, and each shareholder must be treated equally.

   e. Common shareholders elect directors to the board.

4. **Preferred Stock**

   a. Preferred shareholders have the right to receive (1) dividends at a specified rate (before common shareholders may receive any) and (2) distributions before common shareholders (but after creditors) upon liquidation. But they tend not to have voting rights or to enjoy the same capital gains as the common shareholders.

BACKGROUND 14-1 Presentation of Preferred Stock

In the equity section, preferred stock is generally reported before common stock because it is a hybrid of debt and equity. This position reminds readers that, in liquidation, the claims of the preferred shareholders must be satisfied before the common shareholders can be paid.

   b. If a board issues preferred stock, it may establish different classes or series. Each may be assigned independent rights, dividend rates, and redemption prices.

   c. Holders of **convertible preferred stock** have the right to convert the stock into shares of another class (usually common stock) at a predetermined ratio set forth in the articles or bylaws.

   d. **Callable preferred stock** is issued with the condition that it may be called (redeemed or repurchased) by the issuer at a stated price and time. Issuers may establish a sinking fund for this purpose.

   e. **Mandatorily redeemable financial instruments (MRFIs)** are redeemable shares that embody an unconditional obligation to transfer assets at a fixed or determinable time or upon an event certain to occur.

      1) MRFIs must be accounted for as **liabilities** unless the redemption is required only upon the liquidation or termination of the entity.

5. **Equity Accounts**

   a. **Contributed capital** (paid-in capital) represents amounts invested by owners in exchange for stock (common or preferred).

      1) **Capital stock** (stated capital) is the **par value** (or stated value) of all shares issued and outstanding.

         a) Amounts for common and preferred stock are separately listed. Absent treasury stock, the number of shares may be determined by dividing these amounts by the related par value per share.

      2) **Additional paid-in capital** (paid-in capital in excess of par value) consists of amounts in excess of stated capital.

b. **Retained earnings** is increased by net income and decreased by (1) net losses, (2) cash or property dividends, (3) stock dividends, (4) split-ups effected in the form of a dividend, and (5) certain treasury stock transactions.

   1) Prior-period adjustments (error corrections) also are made to retained earnings.
   2) A change in accounting principle is applied retrospectively. The cumulative effect on all prior periods is reflected in the opening balances of assets, liabilities, and retained earnings (or other appropriate components of equity) for the first period presented.

c. Retained earnings amounts may be **appropriated** (restricted) at management's discretion to disclose that earnings are to be used for purposes other than dividends. An appropriation must be clearly displayed within equity.

   1) Purposes include (a) compliance with a bond indenture (bond contract), (b) retention of assets for internally financed expansion, (c) anticipation of losses, or (d) adherence to legal restrictions. For example, a state law may restrict retained earnings by an amount equal to the cost of treasury stock.
   2) The appropriation **does not set aside assets**. It limits the availability of dividends. A formal entry (debit retained earnings, credit retained earnings appropriated) or disclosure in a note may be made.
   3) Transfers to and from an appropriation do not affect net income.
      a) Costs and losses are not debited to an appropriation, and no amount is transferred to income.

d. **Treasury stock** is the entity's own stock that was repurchased by the entity subsequent to its initial issuance to shareholders.

   1) Treasury stock reduces the shares outstanding, not the shares authorized.
   2) It is commonly accounted for at cost (discussed later in this study unit).
   3) Treasury stock is not an asset, and dividends are never paid to these shares.

e. **Accumulated other comprehensive income** is a separate component of equity that includes items excluded from net income. Items in that component should be classified according to their nature. A list of items reported as other comprehensive income is in Study Unit 2, Subunit 3.

STOP & REVIEW

You have completed the outline for this subunit.
Study multiple-choice questions 1 and 2 on page 445.

14.2 ISSUANCE OF STOCK

1. **Par Value**

   a. The par value of stock is an arbitrary amount assigned by the issuer. Most states treat par value as **legal capital**, an amount unavailable for dividends.

      1) Common and preferred stock are reported in the financial statements at par value.

      2) When no-par stock is issued, most states require it to have a stated value equivalent to par value.

2. **Issuance of Stock**

   a. Cash is debited, the appropriate stock account is credited for the total par value, and additional paid-in capital (paid-in capital in excess of par) is credited for the difference.

EXAMPLE 14-2 Issuance of Stock

Parvenu Corp. issued 50,000 shares of its $1 par-value common stock. The market price of the stock was $17 per share on the day of issue.

Cash (50,000 shares × $17 market price)	$850,000	
Common stock (50,000 shares × $1 par value)		$ 50,000
Additional paid-in capital -- common (difference)		800,000

Parvenu also issued 10,000 shares of $50 par-value, 6% preferred stock. The market price at the time was $62 per share.

Cash (10,000 shares × $62 market price)	$620,000	
6% preferred stock (10,000 shares × $50 par value)		$500,000
Additional paid-in capital -- preferred (difference)		120,000

3. **Costs of Issuance**

   a. **Direct costs of issuing stock** (underwriting, legal, accounting, tax, registration, etc.) reduce the net proceeds received and additional paid-in capital. Equity interests and the issue costs inherent to them are permanent. Thus, they are not expensed.

EXAMPLE 14-3 Direct Costs of Issuing Stock

In the common stock issue illustrated above, Parvenu incurred direct issue costs of $10,000. The entry is the following:

Additional paid-in capital -- common	$10,000	
Cash		$10,000

      1) In contrast, **debt issue costs** reduce the carrying amount of the debt and are amortized. They benefit the entity only for the life of the debt, and the cost therefore must be systematically and rationally allocated over that life.

4. **Stock Subscriptions**

   a. A stock subscription is a contractual arrangement to sell a specified number of shares at a specified price at some future date.

      1) If payment is reasonably assured, the corporation recognizes an obligation to issue stock, and the subscriber undertakes to pay for the shares subscribed.

      2) A down payment is usually made. The shareholder cannot resell the stock or exercise voting rights until the subscription is paid in full.

EXAMPLE 14-4 Stock Subscriptions

Parvenu has issued 10,000 shares of its $1 par-value common stock on a subscription basis when the market price is $14 per share. The subscribers are required to make a 40% down payment, with the remainder due in 6 months.

Cash (10,000 shares × $14 market price × 40%)	$56,000	
Receivable from stock subscription (10,000 shares × $14 market price × 60%)	84,000	
Common stock subscribed (10,000 shares × $1 par value)		$ 10,000
Additional paid-in capital -- common (difference)		130,000

      3) The SEC requires that **stock subscriptions receivable** be reported as a **contra-equity account** unless collection has occurred before issuance of the financial statements. In that case, the account may be reported as an asset.

   b. When the subscription price is paid and the stock is issued, common stock subscribed is replaced with common stock.

EXAMPLE 14-5 Stock Subscriptions -- Full Payment

In the example above, the subscribers later make full payment. The entry is the following:

Cash	$84,000	
Common stock subscribed (balance)	10,000	
Receivable for stock subscription (balance)		$84,000
Common stock (10,000 shares × $1 par value)		10,000

      1) Thus, additional paid-in capital is increased when the stock is subscribed and is not affected when the stock is subsequently issued.

5. **Share-Based Payment for Goods or Services**

   a. Occasionally, stock is issued for goods received or services rendered.

      1) The transaction should be recorded at the **grant-date fair value** of the stock issued.

      2) The grant date is the date at which a mutual understanding of the key terms and conditions of the share-based payment award was reached.

EXAMPLE 14-6 Share-Based Payment for Services

Consultant agreed to perform an internal control study in return for 500 shares of Parvenu common stock. On the day the contract was signed, Parvenu common stock was trading at $12.50 per share. Consultant spent 39 hours on the study, and its normal billing rate is $160 per hour. At the time Consultant submitted the completed study to Parvenu's management, the stock was trading at $13.50 per share.

Parvenu records the transaction at the stock market price on the date the contract was signed.

Consulting expense (500 shares × $12.50 price at time of contract)	$6,250	
Common stock (500 shares × $1 par value)		$ 500
Additional paid-in capital -- common (difference)		5,750

6. **Donated Capital**

a. In general, contributions received must be recognized as revenues or gains in the period of receipt. They should be measured at fair value.

b. The receipt of a contribution of an **entity's own stock** is recorded at fair value as increases in both contributed capital and treasury stock.

1) Because these accounts offset, the transaction has no net effect on equity. Also, transactions in an entity's own stock cannot result in a gain or loss.

7. **Conversion of Convertible Preferred Stock**

a. When conversion occurs, all related amounts are removed from the books and replaced with amounts related to the new security.

1) Transactions in an entity's own stock may not result in a gain or loss. Thus, the conversion is reported using the **book value method**. The new shares are recorded at the carrying amount of the converted shares.

EXAMPLE 14-7 Conversion of Preferred Stock

Parvenu issued 5,000 shares of $40 par-value, 7% preferred stock, each share convertible into 5 shares of its $1 par-value common stock beginning 6 months after issue. The market price on the day of issue was $68 per share.

Cash (5,000 shares × $68 market price)	$340,000	
7% convertible preferred stock (5,000 shares × $40 par value)		$200,000
Additional paid-in capital -- preferred (difference)		140,000

Six months after the convertible preferred stock was issued, all the shareholders exercised their conversion privilege.

7% convertible preferred stock (balance)	$200,000	
Additional paid-in capital -- preferred (balance)	140,000	
Common stock (5,000 shares × 5 × $1 par value)		$ 25,000
Additional paid-in capital -- common (difference)		315,000

8. Combined Issuance

a. The proceeds of the combined issuance of different classes of securities are allocated based on the relative fair values of the securities.

EXAMPLE 14-8 Combined Issuance of Common Stock and Preferred Stock

Parvenu issued 2,000 shares of its $1 par-value common stock and 1,000 shares of its $50 par-value, 6% preferred stock for a lump sum of $99,000. At the time, the common stock was trading at $15 per share, and the preferred stock was trading at $60 per share.

Fair value of common stock (2,000 shares × $15 market price)	$30,000
Fair value of preferred stock (1,000 shares × $60 market price)	60,000
Total fair value issued	$90,000

Common stock is 33.3333% of the total ($30,000 ÷ $90,000), and preferred stock is 66.6667% ($60,000 ÷ $90,000). The proceeds are therefore assigned as $33,000 to common stock ($99,000 × 33.3333%) and $66,000 to preferred stock ($99,000 × 66.6667%). The sale is recorded as follows:

Cash (lump sum)	$99,000	
Common stock (2,000 shares × $1 par value)		$ 2,000
Additional paid-in capital -- common ($33,000 – $2,000)		31,000
6% preferred stock (1,000 shares × $50 par value)		50,000
Additional paid-in capital -- preferred ($66,000 – $50,000)		16,000

b. If the fair value of one class of securities is not known, the **incremental method** is used. The other securities are recorded at their fair values. The remaining proceeds are credited to the securities for which fair value is not determinable.

EXAMPLE 14-9 Combined Issuance -- Incremental Method

Simdyne, Inc., a closely held corporation, issued 5,000 shares of $2 par-value common stock and 8% bonds with a face amount of $100,000 for a lump sum of $120,000. Because no active market exists for Simdyne's stock, its fair value cannot be determined. If the bonds had been issued separately, they would have resulted in proceeds of $80,000.

Lump sum received	$120,000
Fair value of bonds	(80,000)
Remainder assigned to common stock	$ 40,000

The sale is recorded as follows:

Cash (lump sum)	$120,000	
Discount on bonds payable (difference)	20,000	
Bonds payable (face amount)		$100,000
Common stock (5,000 shares × $2 par value)		10,000
Additional paid-in capital -- common ($40,000 – $10,000)		30,000

STOP & REVIEW

You have completed the outline for this subunit.
Study multiple-choice questions 3 through 5 beginning on page 446.

14.3 STOCK WARRANTS AND STOCK RIGHTS

1. **Stock Warrants**
   a. A warrant is a certificate representing **a right to purchase shares** at a specified price within a specified period. Thus, it is an equity security. Warrants are usually attached to other securities.
2. **Preemptive Right**
   a. The preemptive right safeguards a shareholder's proportionate ownership. It is the **right to purchase a pro rata amount** of a new issuance of the same class of stock.
3. **Issuer's Accounting**
   a. In a rights offering, each shareholder is issued a warrant that is an option to buy a certain number of shares at a fixed price.
      1) When rights are issued for no consideration, the issuer makes only a memorandum entry.
         a) If rights previously issued without consideration are allowed to lapse, contributed capital is unaffected.
      2) Rights issued for consideration constitute share-based payment, discussed in detail in Study Unit 11, Subunit 7.
   b. If the **rights are exercised** and stock is issued, the issuer will reflect the proceeds received as a credit to (an increase in) common (preferred) stock at par value, with any remainder credited to additional paid-in capital.
   c. Transaction costs associated with the redemption of stock rights reduce equity.
4. **Recipient's Accounting**
   a. The recipient of stock rights must **allocate the carrying amount of the shares owned** between the shares and rights based on their relative fair values at the time the rights are received. The recipient then has three options:
      1) If the rights are exercised, the amount allocated to them becomes part of the carrying amount of the acquired shares.
      2) If the rights are sold, their carrying amount is credited, cash is debited, and a gain (loss) is credited (debited).
      3) If the rights expire, a loss is recorded.

STOP & REVIEW

You have completed the outline for this subunit.
Study multiple-choice questions 6 and 7 on page 447.

14.4 TREASURY STOCK -- ACQUISITION

SUCCESS TIP

The AICPA has released multiple CPA questions involving treasury stock calculations under both the cost and par-value methods. Successful candidates need to know the journal entries used by each method to be able to identify the correct debits and credits.

1. **Cost Method vs. Par-Value Method**
   a. Under the **cost method**, treasury shares are reported at their reacquisition price, and the journal entry is a debit to treasury stock and a credit to cash.
      1) On the balance sheet, treasury stock is reported separately as a reduction of total shareholders' equity.
      2) The cost method is much more common in practice.

   b. Under the **par-value method**, the acquisition is treated as a constructive retirement. All related amounts are removed from the books.
2. **Acquisition Price > Original Issue Price**
   a. Under the par-value method, if the acquisition price is greater than the original issue price, the difference is a reduction of retained earnings or a credit balance in paid-in capital (PiC) from treasury stock transactions.

EXAMPLE 14-10 Treasury Stock -- Cost Method vs. Par-Value Method

Parvenu reacquired 5,000 shares of its $1 par-value common stock for $20 per share. This stock had originally been issued at $17 per share. Parvenu had no prior treasury stock transactions.

Cost Method:		
Treasury stock (5,000 shares × $20 market price)	$100,000	
Cash (payment)		$100,000
Par-Value Method:		
Treasury stock (5,000 shares × $1 par value)	$ 5,000	
Additional paid-in capital -- common (5,000 shares × $16 original issue excess)	80,000	
Retained earnings (difference)	15,000	
Cash (payment)		$100,000

3. **Acquisition Price < Original Issue Price**

   a. Under the par-value method, if the acquisition price is less than the original issue price, additional paid-in capital is decreased (debited) for the difference between the acquisition price and the par value of the stock reacquired.

EXAMPLE 14-11 Treasury Stock -- Acquisition Price < Issue Price

Parvenu reacquired 5,000 shares of its $1 par-value common stock for $10 per share.

<u>Cost Method:</u>		
Treasury stock (5,000 shares × $10 market price)	$50,000	
Cash (payment)		$50,000
<u>Par-Value Method:</u>		
Treasury stock (5,000 shares × $1 par value)	$ 5,000	
Additional paid-in capital -- common (difference)	45,000	
Cash (payment)		$50,000

   b. However, if the acquisition price is less than the par value of stock reacquired, the difference is an increase in PiC from treasury stock transactions. (Gains and losses are not recognized on transactions in an entity's own stock.)

4. **Presentation**

   a. Treasury stock is not an asset. It is reported as a contra-equity account and decreases the total number of shares outstanding.

STOP & REVIEW

You have completed the outline for this subunit.
Study multiple-choice questions 8 and 9 on page 448.

14.5 TREASURY STOCK -- REISSUE

1. **Reissue Price > Cost**

    a. The excess is credited to paid-in capital from treasury stock transactions.

EXAMPLE 14-12 Treasury Stock -- Reissue Price > Cost

Parvenu reissued 1,000 shares of its treasury stock that had been acquired for $20 per share. At the time of reissue, the market price was $22 per share.

Cost Method:		
Cash (1,000 shares × $22 market price)	$22,000	
Treasury stock (1,000 shares × $20 cost)		$20,000
PiC from treasury stock transactions (difference)		2,000
Par-Value Method:		
Cash (1,000 shares × $22 market price)	$22,000	
Treasury stock (1,000 shares × $1 par value)		$ 1,000
PiC from treasury stock transactions (difference)		21,000

2. **Reissue Price < Cost**

    a. Under the cost method, the difference is debited to paid-in capital from treasury stock transactions to the extent of any credit balance. Otherwise, the debit is to retained earnings.

    b. Under the par-value method, the difference is credited to paid-in capital from treasury stock transactions.

EXAMPLE 14-13 Treasury Stock -- Reissue Price < Cost

Parvenu reissued 1,000 shares of its treasury stock that had been acquired for $20 per share. At the time of reissue, the market price was $18 per share. Parvenu had no prior reissuance of treasury stock. Thus, the accounting under the cost method includes a debit to retained earnings for the entire difference between the cost and the price of the reissued shares.

Cost Method:		
Cash (1,000 shares × $18 market price)	$18,000	
Retained earnings (difference)	2,000	
Treasury stock (1,000 shares × $20 cost)		$20,000
Par-Value Method:		
Cash (1,000 shares × $18 market price)	$18,000	
Treasury stock (1,000 shares × $1 par value)		$ 1,000
PiC from treasury stock transactions (difference)		17,000

SUCCESS TIP

The AICPA has also released a number of CPA questions addressing the reissue price and associated journal entries used when a corporation reissues previously purchased treasury stock.

STOP & REVIEW

You have completed the outline for this subunit.
Study multiple-choice questions 10 through 12 beginning on page 449.

14.6 RETIREMENT OF STOCK

1. Occasionally, a company decides to retire its own stock. The company may retire treasury stock it already owns or non-treasury stock it purchases. The journal entry to record this retirement includes the following:
   a. When treasury stock is retired, the treasury stock account is credited. When non-treasury stock is retired, cash or other consideration given is credited.
   b. The stock account is debited for the par or stated value.
   c. Additional paid-in capital is debited to the extent it exists from the original issuance.
   d. Any remainder is debited to retained earnings or credited to paid-in capital from stock retirement.

EXAMPLE 14-14 Acquisition and Retirement of Stock

Mainecat Co. reacquired 10,000 shares of its only class of common stock (par value $1 per share) for $50,000. The shares were issued at $10 per share. Mainecat uses the cost method to account for treasury stock transactions but has no current balances related to them. The following are the entries to record the acquisition and retirement of the shares:

Treasury stock	$50,000	
Cash		$50,000
Common stock	$10,000	
Additional paid-in capital -- common	90,000	
Treasury stock		$50,000
PiC from retirement of treasury stock		50,000

2. No gain or loss is reported on transactions involving an entity's own stock.
3. A retirement of treasury stock does not change the number of shares authorized.

STOP & REVIEW

You have completed the outline for this subunit.
Study multiple-choice question 13 on page 451.

14.7 CASH DIVIDENDS

1. Dividends may be distributed in the form of cash or property. (Stock dividends, discussed later in this study unit, are not a form of return on investment.)
   a. Dividends are paid on outstanding shares only, not on treasury stock.
2. **Relevant Dates**
   a. On the **date of declaration**, the board of directors formally approves a dividend.
      1) Unlike a stock dividend, a cash or property dividend cannot be withdrawn once declared. Thus, a cash or property dividend becomes a legal liability of the corporation on the date of declaration.
      2) The dividend is recorded by reclassifying a portion of retained earnings as a payable.
         a) In most states, a corporation may not declare a dividend in excess of its balance of retained earnings.
   b. All holders of the stock on the **date of record** are legally entitled to receive the dividend.
   c. The **date of payment** is the date on which the dividend is paid.

EXAMPLE 14-15 Dividend Declaration and Payment

On September 12, Parvenu's board of directors declared a $4 per-share dividend to be paid on October 15 to all holders of common stock as of October 1. On the date of declaration, Parvenu held 5,000 of its common shares in the treasury, and 45,000 shares were outstanding.

<u>September 12:</u>		
Retained earnings (45,000 shares outstanding × $4 per share)	$180,000	
Dividend payable		$180,000
<u>October 15:</u>		
Dividend payable	$180,000	
Cash		$180,000

3. **Dividends on Preferred Stock**
   a. Most preferred shares are issued with a **stated dividend rate**.
      1) The dividends on preferred stock equal the par value of the stock times its stated dividend rate.
   b. Unlike interest on debt, dividends on preferred stock are not a legal obligation of the corporation until the board chooses to declare them. Common shareholders may not receive a dividend unless the current-year preferred dividend has been paid.
   c. When a corporation has outstanding **cumulative preferred stock**, common shareholders may not receive a dividend until all preferred dividends in arrears have been paid.
      1) **Dividends in arrears** are preferred dividends that were not declared in prior years.
      2) Although they are not legal liabilities of the corporation, dividends in arrears must be disclosed either on the face of the balance sheet or in the notes, both in the aggregate and per share.

EXAMPLE 14-16 Dividends on Preferred Stock

On January 10 of the current year, Parvenu's board declared a $3 per-share dividend to all holders of common stock. Parvenu has not paid dividends on its 10,000 outstanding shares of $50 par-value, 6% cumulative preferred stock for the previous 2 years. Parvenu had 45,000 shares of common stock outstanding. On the date of declaration, Parvenu makes the following calculation:

Preferred dividends -- arrears (10,000 shares × $50 par value × 6% × 2 years)	$ 60,000
Preferred dividends -- current (10,000 shares × $50 par value × 6%)	30,000
Common dividends (45,000 shares × $3 per share)	135,000
Debit to retained earnings	$225,000

STOP & REVIEW

You have completed the outline for this subunit.
Study multiple-choice questions 14 and 15 on page 452.

14.8 PROPERTY DIVIDENDS AND LIQUIDATING DIVIDENDS

1. **Property Dividends**
   a. When a corporation declares a dividend consisting of tangible property, the property is first remeasured to fair value as of the date of declaration. The remeasurement to fair value is recognized in the income statement.

EXAMPLE 14-17 Property Dividend

Parvenu's board of directors resolved to distribute obsolete inventory from its warehouse to holders of common stock. The inventory had a carrying amount of $40,000 and a fair value of $10,000.

<u>Date of declaration:</u>		
Loss on inventory revaluation (Carrying amount – Fair value)	$30,000	
Inventory		$30,000
Retained earnings (fair value)	$10,000	
Property dividend payable		$10,000
<u>Date of distribution:</u>		
Property dividend payable	$10,000	
Inventory		$10,000

   b. The distribution of a property dividend affects retained earnings in two ways:
      1) Remeasurement of the property to fair value affects net income for the period.
      2) The decrease for the fair value of the property distributed.
         a) Thus, the total decrease in retained earnings as a result of a property dividend declaration equals the carrying amount of the property distributed.

2. **Liquidating Dividends**
   a. Dividends in excess of a corporation's retained earnings are liquidating dividends. They are not considered dividends but are treated as a return of capital.
      1) The effect of a liquidating dividend is to decrease contributed capital.
      2) Additional paid-in capital is debited first to the extent available before other contributed capital accounts are charged.

STOP & REVIEW

You have completed the outline for this subunit.
Study multiple-choice questions 16 and 17 beginning on page 452.

14.9 STOCK DIVIDENDS AND STOCK SPLITS

1. **Definitions**
   a. Stock dividends and stock splits are distributions of stock to current shareholders in return for no consideration.
      1) In a **stock dividend**, a portion of retained earnings is capitalized as part of paid-in capital.
         a) The **par value** of the shares is unchanged.
         b) An issuance of shares **less than 20% to 25%** of the previously outstanding common shares should be recognized as a **stock dividend**.
            i) The **SEC requires** an issuance of less than 25% by a public entity to be treated as a stock dividend.
         c) An issuance of **more than 20% to 25%** of the previously outstanding common shares (25% or more for public entities) more closely resembles a **stock split** than a dividend.
            i) An entity may be legally required to capitalize the par value of the additional shares issued. In this case, the term **stock split in the form of a dividend** should be used.
      2) In a **stock split**, no journal entry is made other than a memorandum entry.
         a) The **par value** of the shares is reduced.
   b. Stock dividends and stock splits do not affect the fair value of a shareholder's interest or the proportionate amount of that interest. Thus, the effect is simply a reclassification of equity.
      1) However, because more shares are outstanding, the fair value (and market price) per share is reduced.
2. **Stock Dividends**
   a. In accounting for a stock dividend, the fair value of the additional shares issued is reclassified from retained earnings to capital stock (at par value) and the difference to additional paid-in capital.

EXAMPLE 14-18 Stock Dividend

Parvenu's board of directors declared a 10% stock dividend on the 45,000 shares of common stock outstanding ($1 par value). The stock was trading for $15 per share at the declaration date.

Date of declaration:		
Retained earnings [(45,000 shares × 10%) × $15 market price]	$67,500	
Common stock dividend distributable [(45,000 shares × 10%) × $1 par value]		$ 4,500
Additional paid-in capital -- common (difference)		63,000
Date of distribution:		
Common stock dividend distributable	$4,500	
Common stock		$4,500

3. **Stock Split in the Form of a Dividend**

   a. The state of incorporation may require capitalization of retained earnings for a **stock split in the form of a dividend**, usually in an amount based on **par value**.

EXAMPLE 14-19 Stock Split in the Form of a Dividend

Use the information in Example 14-18, but assume that a 40% stock split in the form of a dividend was declared.

<u>Date of declaration:</u>		
Retained earnings [(45,000 shares × 40%) × $1 par value]	$18,000	
Common stock dividend distributable [(45,000 shares × 40%) × $1]		$18,000
<u>Date of distribution:</u>		
Common stock dividend distributable	$18,000	
Common stock		$18,000

4. **Stock Splits**

   a. The **primary purpose of** a stock split is to improve the stock's marketability by reducing its market price and proportionally increasing the number of shares outstanding.

   b. A stock split does not require an adjustment to retained earnings or paid-in capital and **does not affect total equity**.

EXAMPLE 14-20 Stock Split

Parvenu's board of directors declared a 2-for-1 common stock split. Prior to the stock split, Parvenu had 45,000 shares of $1 par-value common stock outstanding and 5,000 treasury shares. The laws of Parvenu's state of incorporation protect treasury stock from dilution. Thus, Parvenu reduces the par value of its common stock to $0.50 per share and issues 100,000 new shares: 90,000 to shareholders (45,000 × 2) and 10,000 to the treasury (5,000 × 2). Total equity is unchanged.

100,000 shares × $0.50 (new) = 50,000 shares × $1 (old)

   c. A **reverse stock split** reduces the number of shares outstanding, which serves to increase the fair value per share of those shares still outstanding.

5. **Other Issues**

   a. The **recipient** of a stock dividend or stock split should **not recognize income**. After receipt, the shareholder has the same proportionate interest in the corporation and the same total carrying amount as before the declaration.

   b. **Treasury stock** may be adjusted for stock dividends and splits to protect it from dilution. However, **some states prohibit** the payment of stock dividends on treasury stock.

STOP & REVIEW

You have completed the outline for this subunit.
Study multiple-choice questions 18 through 20 beginning on page 453.

QUESTIONS

14.1 Classes of Equity

1. Munn Corp.'s records included the following equity accounts:

Preferred stock, par value $15, authorized 20,000 shares	$255,000
Additional paid-in capital, preferred stock	15,000
Common stock, no par, $5 stated value, 100,000 shares authorized	300,000

In Munn's statement of equity, the number of issued and outstanding shares for each class of stock is

	Common Stock	Preferred Stock
A.	60,000	17,000
B.	60,000	18,000
C.	63,000	17,000
D.	63,000	18,000

Answer (A) is correct.

REQUIRED: The number of issued and outstanding shares of common and preferred stock.

DISCUSSION: If an entity does not hold any stock as treasury stock, the number of shares of each type of stock may be determined by dividing the amount allocated to each stock account by the related par value. The number of shares of preferred stock issued and outstanding is therefore 17,000 ($255,000 ÷ $15 par value), and the number of shares of common stock issued and outstanding is 60,000 ($300,000 ÷ $5 stated value).

Answer (B) is incorrect. The 18,000 shares of preferred would have a par value of $270,000. **Answer (C) is incorrect.** The 63,000 shares of common would have a stated value of $315,000. **Answer (D) is incorrect.** The 18,000 shares of preferred would have a par value of $270,000, and 63,000 shares of common would have a stated value of $315,000.

2. Which of the following financial instruments issued by a public company should be reported on the issuer's books as a liability on the date of issuance?

A. Cumulative preferred stock.
B. Preferred stock that is convertible to common stock 5 years from the issue date.
C. Common stock that contains an unconditional redemption feature.
D. Common stock that is issued at a 5% discount as part of an employee share purchase plan.

Answer (C) is correct.

REQUIRED: The financial instrument reported as a liability.

DISCUSSION: Mandatorily redeemable financial instruments (MRFIs) are redeemable shares that embody an unconditional obligation to transfer assets at a fixed or determinable time or upon an event certain to occur. MRFIs must be accounted for as liabilities.

Answer (A) is incorrect. Cumulative preferred stock is reported as equity, not a liability. Both common stock and preferred stock that is not unconditionally redeemable are treated as equity. **Answer (B) is incorrect.** Convertible preferred stock is reported as equity. **Answer (D) is incorrect.** Common stock that is issued at a 5% discount as part of an employee share purchase plan is still classified as equity. Both common stock and preferred stock that is not redeemable are treated as equity.

14.2 Issuance of Stock

3. On February 1, Hyde Corp., a newly formed company, had the following stock issued and outstanding:

- Common stock, no par, $1 stated value, 10,000 shares originally issued for $15 per share
- Preferred stock, $10 par value, 3,000 shares originally issued for $25 per share

Hyde's February 1 statement of equity should report

	Common Stock	Preferred Stock	Additional Paid-in Capital
A.	$150,000	$30,000	$45,000
B.	$150,000	$75,000	$0
C.	$10,000	$75,000	$140,000
D.	$10,000	$30,000	$185,000

Answer (D) is correct.

REQUIRED: The amounts of common stock, preferred stock, and additional paid-in capital to be reported in the statement of equity.

DISCUSSION: The common stock was issued for a total of $150,000 (10,000 shares × $15). Of this amount, $10,000 (10,000 shares × $1 stated value) should be allocated to the common stock, with the remaining $140,000 ($150,000 – $10,000) credited to additional paid-in capital. The preferred stock was issued for $75,000 (3,000 shares × $25), of which $30,000 (3,000 shares × $10 par value) should be allocated to the preferred stock and $45,000 ($75,000 – $30,000) should be allocated to additional paid-in capital. In the statement of equity, Hyde therefore should report $10,000 in the common stock account, $30,000 in the preferred stock account, and $185,000 ($140,000 + $45,000) as additional paid-in capital.

4. During the prior year, Brad Co. issued 5,000 shares of $100 par-value convertible preferred stock for $110 per share. One share of preferred stock can be converted into three shares of Brad's $25 par-value common stock at the option of the preferred shareholder. On December 31 of the current year, when the market value of the common stock was $40 per share, all of the preferred stock was converted. What amount should Brad credit to common stock and to additional paid-in capital -- common stock as a result of the conversion?

	Common Stock	Additional Paid-in Capital
A.	$375,000	$175,000
B.	$375,000	$225,000
C.	$500,000	$50,000
D.	$600,000	$0

Answer (A) is correct.

REQUIRED: The amounts credited to common stock and additional paid-in capital.

DISCUSSION: Brad recorded the issue of the convertible preferred stock with this entry:

	Debit	Credit
Cash (5,000 shares × $110 market value)	$550,000	
Preferred stock (5,000 shares × $100 par value)		$500,000
Additional paid-in capital -- preferred (difference)		50,000

Brad recorded the conversion as follows:

	Debit	Credit
Preferred stock (balance)	$500,000	
Additional paid-in capital -- preferred (balance)	50,000	
Common stock (5,000 shares × 3 × $25 par value)		$375,000
Additional paid-in capital -- common (difference)		175,000

Answer (B) is incorrect. The amount of $175,000 is credited to additional paid-in capital ($550,000 – $375,000). **Answer (C) is incorrect.** The amount of $500,000 is the par value of the preferred stock, not the common stock. **Answer (D) is incorrect.** The amount of $600,000 equals the fair value of the common stock at the date of conversion.

5. East Co. issued 1,000 shares of its $5 par-value common stock to Howe as compensation for 1,000 hours of legal services performed. Howe usually bills $160 per hour for legal services. On the date of issuance, the stock was trading on a public exchange at $140 per share. By what amount should the additional paid-in capital account increase as a result of this transaction?

A. $135,000

B. $140,000

C. $155,000

D. $160,000

Answer (A) is correct.

REQUIRED: The increase in additional paid-in capital.

DISCUSSION: When stock is issued in exchange for goods or services, the transaction is recorded at the grant-date fair value of the stock issued. The quoted price of the stock is used to measure the services received. The entry is to debit legal expense for $140,000 (1,000 shares × $140 market price), credit common stock for $5,000 (1,000 shares × $5 par value), and credit additional paid-in capital for the difference ($135,000).

Answer (B) is incorrect. The amount of $5,000 should be allocated to common stock. **Answer (C) is incorrect.** The fair value of the stock should be used to record the transaction. **Answer (D) is incorrect.** The amount of $5,000 should be allocated to common stock, and the fair value of the stock should be used to record the transaction.

14.3 Stock Warrants and Stock Rights

6. Blue Co. issued preferred stock with detachable common stock warrants at a price that exceeded both the par value and the fair value of the preferred stock. At the time the warrants are exercised, Blue's total equity is increased by the

	Cash Received upon Exercise of the Warrants	Carrying Amount of the Warrants
A.	Yes	No
B.	Yes	Yes
C.	No	No
D.	No	Yes

Answer (A) is correct.

REQUIRED: The effect of the exercise of warrants on total equity.

DISCUSSION: When shares of preferred stock with detachable common stock warrants are issued at a price that exceeds both the par value and the fair value of the preferred stock, the consideration received must be allocated between the preferred stock and the detachable warrants. The amount allocated to the stock warrants outstanding should be recorded in the equity section as contributed capital. At the time the warrants are exercised, contributed capital will reflect both the cash received upon the exercise of the warrants and the carrying amount of the warrants. Total equity, however, will be increased only by the amount of cash received because the carrying amount of the warrants is already included in total equity.

7. An entity issued rights to its existing shareholders without consideration. The rights allowed the recipients to purchase unissued common stock for an amount in excess of par value. When the rights are issued, which of the following accounts will be increased?

	Common Stock	Additional Paid-in Capital
A.	Yes	Yes
B.	Yes	No
C.	No	No
D.	No	Yes

Answer (C) is correct.

REQUIRED: The effect on common stock and additional paid-in capital when rights are issued without consideration.

DISCUSSION: When rights are issued without consideration, only a memorandum entry is made. Common stock and additional paid-in capital are affected only if the rights are exercised.

14.4 Treasury Stock -- Acquisition

8. Ten thousand shares of $10 par value common stock were issued initially at $15 per share. Subsequently, 1,000 of these shares were purchased as treasury stock at $13 per share. The cost method of accounting for treasury stock is used. What is the effect of the purchase of the treasury stock on the amount reported in the balance sheet on each of the following?

	Additional Paid-in Capital	Total Equity
A.	No effect	No effect
B.	No effect	Decrease
C.	Decrease	No effect
D.	Decrease	Decrease

Answer (B) is correct.
REQUIRED: The effect of the purchase of the treasury stock on additional paid-in capital and total shareholders' equity.
DISCUSSION: Under the cost method, the acquisition of treasury stock is recorded as a debit to treasury stock and a credit to cash equal to the amount of the purchase price. This transaction results in a decrease in both total assets and total equity. Additional paid-in capital is unaffected by the treasury stock purchase.

9. Lem Co., which accounts for treasury stock under the par-value method, acquired 100 shares of its $6 par value common stock for $10 per share. The shares had originally been issued by Lem for $7 per share. By what amount would Lem's additional paid-in capital from common stock decrease as a result of the acquisition?

A. $0

B. $100

C. $300

D. $400

Answer (B) is correct.
REQUIRED: The decrease in additional paid-in capital from an acquisition of treasury stock accounted for under the par-value method.
DISCUSSION: The entry for issuance of the stock was

Cash	$700	
Common stock ($6 per share)		$600
Additional paid-in capital		100

The par-value method treats a treasury stock purchase as a constructive retirement. Assuming no balance in paid-in capital from treasury stock transactions, the entry for the treasury stock purchase using the par-value method is

Treasury stock	$600	
Additional paid-in capital	100	
Retained earnings	300	
Cash		$1,000

Answer (A) is incorrect. Under the par-value method, the acquisition of treasury stock is accounted for by reducing additional paid-in capital by the amount recorded when the shares were originally issued. **Answer (C) is incorrect.** The amount of $300 is the debit to retained earnings. **Answer (D) is incorrect.** The amount of $400 is the sum of the debit to additional paid-in capital and the debit to retained earnings.

14.5 Treasury Stock -- Reissue

10. Selected information from the accounts of Row Co. at December 31, Year 4, follows:

Total income since incorporation	$420,000
Total cash dividends paid	130,000
Total value of property dividends distributed	30,000
Excess of proceeds over cost of treasury stock sold, accounted for using the cost method	110,000

In its December 31, Year 4, financial statements, what amount should Row report as retained earnings?

A. $260,000

B. $290,000

C. $370,000

D. $400,000

Answer (A) is correct.

REQUIRED: The amount to be reported as retained earnings.

DISCUSSION: Retained earnings is increased by net income and decreased by net losses, dividends, and certain treasury stock transactions. Thus, retained earnings is $260,000 ($420,000 – $130,000 – $30,000). Because Row uses the cost method to account for treasury stock, the $110,000 excess of proceeds over the cost of treasury stock sold does not affect retained earnings. Under the cost method, the excess should be credited to additional paid-in capital.

Answer (B) is incorrect. The amount of $290,000 fails to subtract the $30,000 in property dividends. **Answer (C) is incorrect.** The amount of $370,000 includes the $110,000 excess of proceeds over cost of treasury stock. **Answer (D) is incorrect.** The amount of $400,000 includes the $110,000 excess of proceeds over cost of treasury stock and does not subtract the $30,000 value of property dividends distributed.

11. Murphy Co. had 200,000 shares outstanding of $10 par common stock on March 30 of the current year. Murphy reacquired 30,000 of those shares at a cost of $15 per share and recorded the transaction using the cost method on April 15. Murphy reissued the 30,000 shares at $20 per share and recognized a $50,000 gain on its income statement on May 20. Which of the following statements is correct?

A. Murphy's comprehensive income for the current year is correctly stated.

B. Murphy's net income for the current year is overstated.

C. Murphy's net income for the current year is understated.

D. Murphy should have recognized a $50,000 loss on its income statement for the current year.

Answer (B) is correct.

REQUIRED: The true statement about the accounting for treasury stock transactions.

DISCUSSION: The cost method debits cash and credits treasury stock and paid-in capital from treasury stock transactions when a reissuance of shares is made for an amount in excess of cost. The credit to treasury stock is $450,000 (30,000 shares × $15), and the credit to paid-in capital from treasury stock transactions is $150,000 [$600,000 cash (debit) – $450,000 treasury stock (credit)]. The reason for the latter credit (an equity account) instead of a gain is that the effects of transactions in the entity's own stock are always excluded from net income or the results of operations. Thus, recognizing a gain on the reissuance of treasury stock overstates current net income.

Answer (A) is incorrect. Comprehensive income for the current year includes net income and items of other comprehensive income. Comprehensive income is therefore overstated if a gain is recognized in net income. **Answer (C) is incorrect.** Net income is overstated. **Answer (D) is incorrect.** No revenue, expense, gain, or loss is recognized on transactions in the entity's own stock.

Question 12 is based on the following information. Pugh Co. reported the following in its statement of equity on January 1:

Common stock, $5 par value, authorized 200,000 shares, issued 100,000 shares	$ 500,000
Additional paid-in capital	1,500,000
Retained earnings	516,000
	$2,516,000
Minus: Treasury stock, at cost, 5,000 shares	(40,000)
Total equity	$2,476,000

The following events occurred during the year:

May 1 -- 1,000 shares of treasury stock were sold for $10,000.
July 9 -- 10,000 shares of previously unissued common stock sold for $12 per share.
October 1 -- The distribution of a 2-for-1 stock split resulted in the common stock's per-share par value being halved.

Pugh accounts for treasury stock under the cost method. Laws in the state of Pugh's incorporation protect shares held in treasury from dilution when stock dividends or stock splits are declared.

12. In Pugh's December 31 statement of equity, the par value of the issued common stock should be

A. $550,000

B. $530,000

C. $275,000

D. $265,000

Answer (A) is correct.

REQUIRED: The par value of the issued common stock.

DISCUSSION: At the beginning of the year, 100,000 shares with a par value of $500,000 had been issued. These shares included the treasury stock (issued but not outstanding) accounted for at cost. Under the cost method, the par value recorded in the common stock account is unaffected by purchases and sales of treasury stock. On July 9, 10,000 shares of previously unissued common stock were sold. This transaction increased the aggregate par value to $550,000 (110,000 shares issued × $5). The 2-for-1 stock split reduced the par value per share by 50% but did not affect the aggregate par value of the issued stock. Thus, state law presumably did not require capitalization of retained earnings as a result of the stock split.

Answer (B) is incorrect. The par value of the issued and outstanding shares is $530,000. **Answer (C) is incorrect.** Half the par value of the issued stock is $275,000. **Answer (D) is incorrect.** Half the par value of the issued and outstanding stock is $265,000.

14.6 Retirement of Stock

13. Cross Corp. had 2,000 outstanding shares of 11% preferred stock, $50 par. These shares were not mandatorily redeemable. On August 8, Cross redeemed and retired 25% of these shares for $22,500. On that date, Cross's additional paid-in capital from preferred stock totaled $30,000. To record this transaction, Cross should debit (credit) its capital accounts as follows:

	Preferred Stock	Additional Paid-in Capital	Retained Earnings
A.	$25,000	$7,500	$(10,000)
B.	$25,000	--	$(2,500)
C.	$25,000	$(2,500)	--
D.	$22,500	--	--

Answer (C) is correct.

REQUIRED: The accounting for redemption and retirement of preferred stock.

DISCUSSION: Under the cost method, the entry to record a treasury stock purchase is to debit treasury stock at cost ($22,500) and credit cash. The entry to retire this stock is to debit preferred stock at par [(2,000 shares × 25%) × $50 = $25,000], debit additional paid-in capital from the original issuance ($30,000 × 25% = $7,500), credit treasury stock at cost ($22,500), and credit additional paid-in capital from stock retirement ($10,000). Thus, the net effect on additional paid-in capital is a $2,500 credit ($10,000 credit – $7,500 debit). No entry to retained earnings is necessary.

Answer (A) is incorrect. If the reacquisition price is less than the issuance price, a credit is made to additional paid-in capital, not retained earnings. **Answer (B) is incorrect.** Additional paid-in capital is debited to the extent it exists from the original issuance ($30,000 × 25% = $7,500), and a credit is made to additional paid-in capital for the stock retirement ($10,000). Retained earnings is not affected by this transaction. **Answer (D) is incorrect.** Preferred stock must be debited for the par value of the retired shares.

14.7 Cash Dividends

14. On January 15, Year 5, Rico Co. declared its annual cash dividend on common stock for the year ended January 31, Year 5. The dividend was paid on February 9, Year 5, to shareholders of record as of January 28, Year 5. On what date should Rico decrease retained earnings by the amount of the dividend?

A. January 15, Year 5.

B. January 31, Year 5.

C. January 28, Year 5.

D. February 9, Year 5.

Answer (A) is correct.

REQUIRED: The date to decrease retained earnings by the amount of the dividend.

DISCUSSION: On the date of declaration, a cash dividend becomes a legal liability of the corporation (unlike stock dividends, cash dividends cannot be rescinded). Thus, on January 15, a portion of retained earnings was reclassified as dividends payable.

15. At December 31, Year 3 and Year 4, Apex Co. had 3,000 shares of $100 par, 5% cumulative preferred stock outstanding. No dividends were in arrears as of December 31, Year 2. Apex did not declare a dividend during Year 3. During Year 4, Apex paid a cash dividend of $10,000 on its preferred stock. Apex should report dividends in arrears in its Year 4 financial statements as a(n)

A. Accrued liability of $15,000.

B. Disclosure of $15,000.

C. Accrued liability of $20,000.

D. Disclosure of $20,000.

Answer (D) is correct.

REQUIRED: The accounting for preferred dividends in arrears.

DISCUSSION: Dividends in arrears on preferred stock are not obligations of the company and are not recognized in the financial statements. However, the aggregate and per-share amounts of arrearages in cumulative preferred dividends should be disclosed on the face of the balance sheet or in the notes. The aggregate amount in arrears is $20,000 [(3,000 shares × $100 par × 5% × 2 years) – $10,000 paid in Year 4].

Answer (A) is incorrect. Dividends in arrears do not meet recognition criteria. **Answer (B) is incorrect.** The amount of $15,000 is the arrearage for 1 year. **Answer (C) is incorrect.** Dividends in arrears should be disclosed on the face of the balance sheet or in the notes, not accrued.

14.8 Property Dividends and Liquidating Dividends

16. On December 1, Year 4, Pott Co. declared and distributed a property dividend when the fair value exceeded the carrying amount. As a consequence of the dividend declaration and distribution, what are the accounting effects?

	Property Dividends Recorded at	Retained Earnings
A.	Fair value	Decreased
B.	Fair value	Increased
C.	Cost	Increased
D.	Cost	Decreased

Answer (A) is correct.

REQUIRED: The effects of a property dividend.

DISCUSSION: When a corporation declares a dividend consisting of tangible property, the property is first remeasured to fair value as of the date of declaration. The dividend should then be recognized as a decrease in (debit to) retained earnings and a corresponding increase in (credit to) a dividend payable. The distribution of the property dividend is recognized by a debit to property dividend payable and a credit to the property account.

Answer (B) is incorrect. Retained earnings is decreased. **Answer (C) is incorrect.** Retained earnings is decreased and the dividends are recorded at fair value. **Answer (D) is incorrect.** Property dividends are recorded at fair value.

17. A corporation declared a dividend, a portion of which was liquidating. How does this declaration affect each of the following?

	Additional Paid-in Capital	Retained Earnings
A.	Decrease	No effect
B.	Decrease	Decrease
C.	No effect	Decrease
D.	No effect	No effect

Answer (B) is correct.

REQUIRED: The effect of a dividend, a portion of which was liquidating, on additional paid-in capital and retained earnings.

DISCUSSION: The portion of a dividend that is liquidating results in a distribution in excess of the corporation's retained earnings. The effect of a liquidating dividend is to decrease contributed capital. Additional paid-in capital is debited first to the extent available before other contributed capital accounts are charged. Thus, declaration of a cash dividend, a portion of which is liquidating, decreases both additional paid-in capital and retained earnings.

Answer (A) is incorrect. Retained earnings is also decreased. **Answer (C) is incorrect.** Additional paid-in capital is also decreased. **Answer (D) is incorrect.** Both additional paid-in capital and retained earnings are decreased.

14.9 Stock Dividends and Stock Splits

18. Nest Co. issued 100,000 shares of common stock. Of these, 5,000 were held as treasury stock at December 31, Year 3. During Year 4, transactions involving Nest's common stock were as follows:

May 3 -- 1,000 shares of treasury stock were sold.
August 6 -- 10,000 shares of previously unissued stock were sold.
November 18 -- A 2-for-1 stock split took effect.

Laws in Nest's state of incorporation protect treasury stock from dilution. At December 31, Year 4, how many shares of Nest's common stock were issued and outstanding?

	Shares	
	Issued	Outstanding
A.	220,000	212,000
B.	220,000	216,000
C.	222,000	214,000
D.	222,000	218,000

Answer (A) is correct.

REQUIRED: The number of shares of common stock issued and outstanding.

DISCUSSION: In Nest's state, stock splits and dividends apply to treasury stock. Accordingly, the number of shares issued is 220,000 [(100,000 + 10,000) × 2]. The number of shares outstanding is 212,000 [(95,000 + 1,000 + 10,000) × 2].

Answer (B) is incorrect. The figure 216,000 does not properly account for the stock split on the treasury stock. **Answer (C) is incorrect.** The figure 222,000 includes 1,000 shares of treasury stock sold on May 3 twice [(100,000 + 1,000 + 10,000) × 2]. **Answer (D) is incorrect.** The figure 222,000 includes 1,000 shares of treasury stock sold on May 3 twice [(100,000 + 1,000 + 10,000) × 2]. Moreover, 218,000 shares outstanding includes 4,000 treasury stock shares that are not outstanding [(95,000 + 4,000 + 10,000) × 2].

19. Universe Co. issued 500,000 shares of common stock in the current year. Universe declared a 30% stock dividend. The market value was $50 per share, the par value was $10, and the average issue price was $30 per share. By what amount will Universe decrease shareholders' equity for the dividend?

A. $0

B. $1,500,000

C. $4,500,000

D. $7,500,000

Answer (A) is correct.

REQUIRED: The decrease in equity after declaration of a stock dividend.

DISCUSSION: When a stock dividend is declared, a portion of retained earnings is reclassified as contributed capital. The net effect on total equity is thus $0.

20. A company whose stock is trading at $10 per share has 1,000 shares of $1 par common stock outstanding when the board of directors declares a 30% common stock dividend. Which of the following adjustments should be made when recording the stock dividend?

A. Treasury stock is debited for $300.

B. Additional paid-in capital is credited for $2,700.

C. Retained earnings is debited for $300.

D. Common stock is debited for $3,000.

Answer (C) is correct.

REQUIRED: The recording of a stock dividend.

DISCUSSION: The board of directors declared a 30% common stock dividend. As this issuance is more than 25% of the previously outstanding common shares, it should be accounted for as a stock split in the form of a dividend. Generally (depending on the state of incorporation), the company will capitalize retained earnings in an amount based on the par value. Thus, the journal entry at the date of declaration will be:

Retained earnings (1,000 shares × 30%)	$300	
Common stock dividend distributable		$300

Answer (A) is incorrect. In a stock dividend, or stock split in the form of a dividend, a portion of retained earnings is capitalized as part of paid-in capital. In this case, the treasury stock account is unaffected. **Answer (B) is incorrect.** This issuance is not accounted for as a regular stock dividend. Because the issuance is more than 25% of the previously outstanding common shares, it should be accounted for as a stock split in the form of a dividend. **Answer (D) is incorrect.** In a stock dividend, or stock split in the form of a dividend, the common stock account is increased (credited), not decreased (debited).

GO TO ONLINE COURSE

Access the **Gleim CPA Premium Review System** featuring our SmartAdapt technology from your Gleim Personal Classroom to continue your studies. You will experience a personalized study environment with exam-emulating multiple-choice questions.

STUDY UNIT FIFTEEN

BUSINESS COMBINATIONS AND CONSOLIDATED FINANCIAL REPORTING

(20 pages of outline)

This study unit addresses the accounting for business combinations, the preparation of consolidated financial statements, and the accounting implications of other aspects of business combinations.

15.1 ACCOUNTING FOR BUSINESS COMBINATIONS -- OVERVIEW

1. **Definitions**
   a. A **business combination** (hereafter called a combination) is "a transaction or other event in which an acquirer obtains control of one or more businesses."
   b. **Control** is a controlling financial interest. It is the direct or indirect ability to determine the direction of management and policies of the investee. This usually means one entity's direct or indirect ownership of **more than 50%** of the outstanding voting interests of another entity.
   c. A **parent** is an entity that has a controlling financial interest in one or more **subsidiaries**.
   d. A **business** consists of an integrated set of activities and assets that can be conducted to provide a return of economic benefits directly to investors or others.
      1) The three elements of a business are inputs, processes, and outputs.
         a) Although businesses usually have outputs, outputs are **not** required for an integrated set to qualify as a business.
         b) To qualify as a business, the set must include an input and a substantive process that together significantly contribute to the ability to create output.
      2) When substantially all of the fair value of the gross assets acquired is concentrated in a single identifiable asset or group of similar identifiable assets, the set acquired does **not** constitute a business. This transaction is a regular asset acquisition.

3) The table below presents the differences between the accounting for (a) asset acquisitions and (b) business combinations.

Differences between Accounting for Asset Acquisitions and Business Combinations

	Business Combinations	Asset Acquisitions
Direct acquisition costs	Expensed as incurred	Capitalized to assets' cost
Goodwill	May be recognized	Never recognized
Initial recognition of assets acquired	Acquisition date fair value	Allocation of cost based on relative fair values

2. **Consolidated Reporting**

a. When one entity controls another, consolidated financial statements must be issued by a parent company regardless of the percentage of ownership.

1) **Consolidated statements** present amounts for the parent and subsidiary(ies) as if they were a single economic entity.

a) Separate parent and subsidiary statements may be used for internal purposes, but they are not in conformity with GAAP.

2) Consolidated reporting is required even when majority ownership is indirect, i.e., when a subsidiary holds a majority interest in another subsidiary.

EXAMPLE 15-1 Consolidated Entities

Each arrow below represents a percentage of a company's holding of another company's total outstanding voting interests.

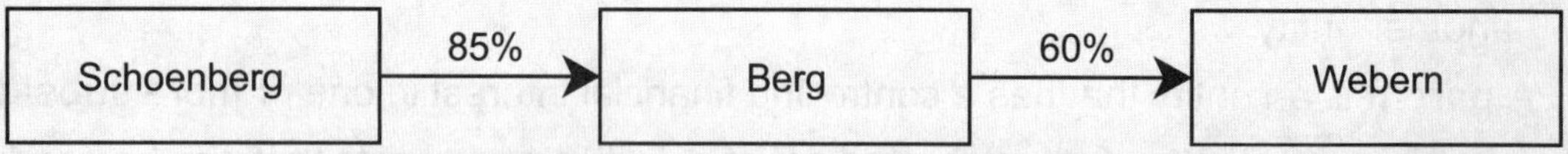

Figure 15-1

- The consolidated entity includes Schoenberg, Berg, and Webern. Schoenberg controls Berg, and Berg controls Webern.

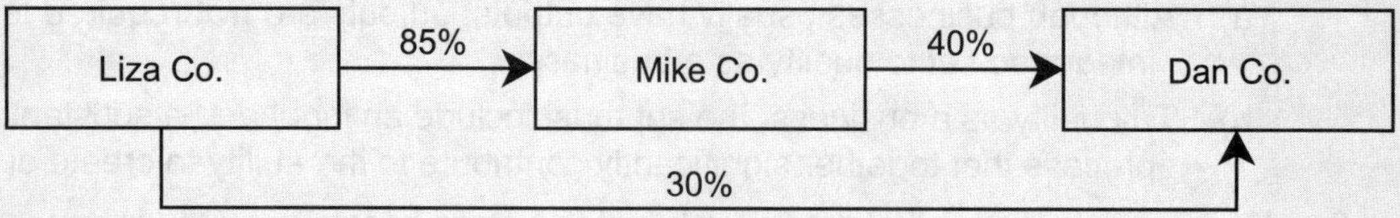

Figure 15-2

- Liza Co. controls Dan Co. because of its 30% direct and 40% indirect (through control of Mike Co.) ownership of Dan's outstanding voting interests. Thus, Liza consolidates Mike and Dan.

b. A parent and subsidiary may exist separately for an indefinite period, but consolidated financial statements must be issued that report them as a single entity.

c. Required consolidated reporting is an example of substance over form. Even if the two entities remain legally separate, the financial statements are more meaningful to users if they see the effects of control by one over the other.

3. **Recognition Principle**
   a. The acquirer must recognize the identifiable assets acquired, liabilities assumed, and noncontrolling interests in the acquiree.
   b. The assets and liabilities recognized must be **part of the exchange** and not the result of separate transactions.
      1) The acquirer must recognize only the consideration transferred for the acquiree.
      2) The acquirer also must identify amounts not part of the exchange and account for them according to their nature and relevant GAAP.
         a) A precombination transaction that primarily benefits the acquirer is most likely to be accounted for separately from the exchange.

EXAMPLE 15-2 Accounting for a Precombination Transaction

The acquiree undertakes to make severance payments to certain executives when an expected combination is completed. If the main purpose is to benefit the acquirer, the payments are not part of the exchange. If the main purpose is to benefit the acquiree or its former owners, the payments are included in accounting for the combination (i.e., in the fair value of the consideration transferred).

4. **Costs Associated with Business Combinations**
   a. **Acquisition-related costs**, such as finder's fees, professional and consulting fees, and general administrative costs, are expensed as incurred.
   b. Issue costs for securities are accounted for as follows:
      1) **Direct issue costs of equity** (underwriting, legal, accounting, tax, registration, etc.) reduce additional paid-in capital.
         a) Indirect costs of issue, records maintenance, and ownership transfers (e.g., a stock transfer agent's fees) are expensed.
      2) **Debt issue costs** are reported in the balance sheet as a direct deduction from the carrying amount of the debt.

EXAMPLE 15-3 Costs Associated with Business Combinations

On January 1, Year 1, Lipp Co. issued 100,000 shares of its $1 par-value common stock and transferred $300,000 in cash in exchange for all of Rahm Co.'s outstanding common stock. To finance the acquisition, Lipp issued bonds with a par value of $300,000. The following costs in relation to the acquisition were incurred by Lipp:

- Bond issue costs of $15,000
- Printer's fee of $10,000 for stock certificates
- Finder's and consulting fees of $40,000

Bond issue costs (debt issue costs) are reported in the balance sheet as a direct deduction from the carrying amount of the debt. The journal entry is

Debt issue costs	$15,000	
Cash		$15,000

A printer's fee for stock certificates is a direct issue cost of equity that reduces additional paid-in capital. The journal entry is

Additional paid-in capital	$10,000	
Cash		$10,000

Finder's and consulting fees are acquisition-related costs that must be expensed as incurred. The journal entry is

Business combination expense	$40,000	
Cash		$40,000

5. **Contingencies**

   a. Assets and liabilities arising from contingencies are recognized and measured at acquisition-date fair values.

EXAMPLE 15-4	**Contingent Liability**
Acquiree (AE) has been sued by former employees. Subsequent to the filing of the suit, Acquirer (AR) paid cash for all of AE's shares. At the acquisition date, AR will recognize a liability if, given all the relevant facts, it is probable that the suit will be lost.	

   b. The asset (liability) is derecognized when the contingency is resolved.

   c. The acquirer recognizes an **indemnification asset** when the seller contracts to pay for the result of a contingency or uncertainty related to an asset or liability.

EXAMPLE 15-5	**Indemnification Asset**
The seller in a business combination guarantees that the acquirer will not have to pay more than a certain amount to settle an assumed liability (the indemnified item). Because the liability is recognized at the acquisition date, it is measured at its acquisition-date fair value. Accordingly, the indemnification asset also is measured at fair value. No valuation allowance is necessary because fair value includes the effects of the uncertainty of collection.	

STOP & REVIEW

You have completed the outline for this subunit.
Study multiple-choice questions 1 and 2 on page 475.

15.2 ACCOUNTING FOR BUSINESS COMBINATIONS -- ACQUISITION METHOD

1. **Summary of the Accounting**

   a. A business combination must be accounted for using the **acquisition method**. It

      1) Determines the acquirer and the acquisition date.

      2) Recognizes and **measures at acquisition-date fair value** the

         a) Identifiable assets acquired,
         b) Liabilities assumed, and
         c) Any noncontrolling interest in the acquiree.

      3) Recognizes goodwill or a gain from a bargain purchase and measures it using the goodwill equation.

b. The consideration transferred in a business combination must be measured at **acquisition-date fair value**. It includes the
   1) Fair value of the assets transferred by the acquirer,
   2) Fair value of liabilities incurred by the acquirer to former owners of the acquiree (e.g., a liability for contingent consideration), and
   3) Fair value of equity interests (e.g., shares of common stock) issued by the acquirer.

EXAMPLE 15-6 Acquisition Cost

Platonic Corp. issues 10,000 shares of its common stock to acquire all of the outstanding common stock of Socratic Corp. (25,000 shares). Platonic's stock is currently trading at $12 per share, and Socratic's stock is trading at $3.80 per share.

Fair value of consideration given (10,000 shares × $12 market price)	$120,000

Platonic will record this acquisition at $120,000.

2. **Contingent Consideration**
   a. Contingent consideration is an obligation of the acquirer to transfer additional assets or equity securities to the former owners of an acquiree as part of the exchange for control of the acquiree if specified future events occur or conditions are met.
      1) For example, on the business combination date, the acquirer promises to pay the former shareholders of the acquiree an additional $100,000 next year if the current-year consolidated net income is greater than $500,000.
   b. On the business combination date, contingent consideration must be recognized at its **acquisition-date fair value**.
      1) The acquisition-date fair value of contingent consideration must be included in the total fair value of the consideration transferred and included in the calculation of goodwill.
      2) Future settlement of the contingent consideration has **no effect** on the amount of goodwill that was recognized on the business combination date.
   c. The classification of contingent consideration as a liability or as equity is based on the way it is settled (discussed in Study Unit 12, Subunit 6).
      1) Contingent consideration that is classified as a **liability** must be **remeasured to fair value** at each balance sheet date until it is settled.
         a) Changes in the fair value are recognized in the income statement.
      2) Contingent consideration that is classified as **equity** is **not** remeasured to fair value.

3. **Calculation of Goodwill or Gain from a Bargain Purchase**
   a. Goodwill is an intangible asset reflecting the future economic benefits arising from other assets acquired in a business combination that are not individually identified and separately recognized.
   b. At the acquisition date, the acquirer recognizes and measures goodwill or a gain from a bargain purchase using the **goodwill equation**.
      1) A **positive outcome** of the equation results in recognition of **goodwill** in the consolidated balance sheet.
      2) A **negative outcome** of the equation results in recognition of a **gain from a bargain purchase** in the consolidated income statement.
      3) All components of the goodwill equation are measured at **acquisition-date fair value**.
      4) The identifiable net assets acquired equal the identifiable assets acquired minus liabilities assumed.
      5) Below is the **goodwill equation**:

	Fair value of the consideration transferred
+	Fair value of any noncontrolling interest in the acquiree
+	Fair value of any previously held equity interest in the acquiree
–	Fair value of identifiable net assets acquired
	Positive outcome = Goodwill; Negative outcome = Gain from a bargain purchase

         a) A noncontrolling interest exists when less than 100% of the acquiree was acquired.
         b) A previously held equity interest exists when control of the acquiree was achieved in several transactions.

EXAMPLE 15-7 Goodwill

Platonic issued stock with a fair value of $120,000 to acquire all the outstanding stock of Socratic Corp. The carrying amount of Socratic's net assets is $100,000. This carrying amount equals the fair value of Socratic's net assets except that the fair values of inventory and property, plant, and equipment exceed their carrying amounts by $4,000 and $10,000, respectively. The acquisition-date fair value of the identifiable net assets acquired is $114,000 ($100,000 carrying amount of net assets acquired + $4,000 excess fair value of inventory + $10,000 excess fair value of PPE). Given no noncontrolling interest or prior equity interest, goodwill is calculated as follows:

Acquisition-date fair value of the consideration transferred	$120,000
Acquisition-date fair value of identifiable net assets acquired	(114,000)
Goodwill	**$ 6,000**

EXAMPLE 15-8 Gain from a Bargain Purchase

Using the information from Example 15-7, assume that the fair value of the PPE exceeded the carrying amount by $20,000. The acquisition-date fair value of the identifiable net assets acquired is $124,000 ($100,000 carrying amount of net assets acquired + $4,000 excess fair value of inventory + $20,000 excess fair value of PPE). Because the outcome of the goodwill equation below is negative, a gain from a bargain purchase of $4,000 is recognized.

Acquisition-date fair value of the consideration transferred	$ 120,000
Acquisition-date fair value of identifiable net assets acquired	(124,000)
Gain from bargain purchase	**$ (4,000)**

4. **Basic Aspects of the Acquisition Method**
   a. The acquirer is acquiring assets and assuming liabilities only. The acquiree's equity accounts are not relevant.
   b. Only the acquiree's identifiable assets acquired and liabilities assumed are recognized.
      1) Any goodwill on the books of the acquiree is not an identifiable asset recognized upon acquisition by the acquirer.
      2) However, the acquirer may recognize certain **intangible assets** that did not qualify for recognition by the acquiree.
         a) For example, on the business combination date, the acquirer may recognize intangible assets, such as a brand name or in-process research and development (IPR&D). These internally developed intangible assets have not been recognized in the financial statements of the acquiree because the costs to develop them (e.g., R&D costs) were expensed as incurred.
5. **Accounting for a Noncontrolling Interest (NCI)**
   a. A noncontrolling interest is a portion of equity (net assets) in a subsidiary not attributable to the parent. NCI is reported separately in the equity section of the parent's consolidated balance sheet.
   b. On the business combination date, the fair value of NCI can be calculated as total shares of common stock not acquired by the parent times the subsidiary's market price per share.

EXAMPLE 15-9 Goodwill Given an NCI

Use the information from Example 15-7, but assume that (1) Platonic transfers $108,000 for a 90% voting interest in Socratic; (2) the fair values exceed the carrying amounts of inventory and PPE by $4,000 and $10,000, respectively; and (3) the fair value of the noncontrolling interest (NCI) is $12,000. Platonic performs the following calculation:

Consideration transferred		$108,000
Noncontrolling interest		12,000
Acquisition-date fair value of net assets acquired:		
Carrying amount	$100,000	
Excess fair value -- inventory	4,000	
Excess fair value -- PPE	10,000	(114,000)
Goodwill		$ 6,000

IFRS DIFFERENCE

A noncontrolling interest (NCI) may be measured initially at (1) fair value or (2) a proportionate share of the fair value of the acquiree's identifiable net assets.

STOP & REVIEW

You have completed the outline for this subunit.
Study multiple-choice questions 3 and 4 beginning on page 476.

15.3 CONSOLIDATED FINANCIAL REPORTING -- ACQUISITION-DATE BALANCE SHEET

1. **Acquisition-Date Balance Sheet**

   a. A balance sheet should be prepared that reports the financial position of the consolidated entity at the acquisition date.

      1) Step 1 -- Determine the amount of goodwill or gain from bargain purchase recognized on the business combination.

EXAMPLE 15-10 Goodwill

On December 31, Year 0, Platonic and Socratic have the following condensed balance sheets:

	Platonic	Socratic		Platonic	Socratic
Current assets	$140,000	$ 40,000	Current liabilities	$ 60,000	$ 20,000
Noncurrent assets	180,000	80,000	Noncurrent liabilities	100,000	0
			Equity	160,000	100,000
Total assets	$320,000	$120,000	Total liabilities and equity	$320,000	$120,000

On January 1, Year 1, Platonic borrowed $120,000 on a 5-year balloon note and used the proceeds to purchase 80% of the outstanding common shares of Socratic. Platonic had no prior equity interest in Socratic. Assume that the carrying amounts of Socratic's assets and liabilities equal their fair values except that the fair value of land exceeds its carrying amount by $25,000. Also assume that the fair value of the noncontrolling interest (NCI) was $30,000.

Platonic performs the following calculation:

Consideration transferred		$120,000
Noncontrolling interest		30,000
Acquisition-date fair value of net assets acquired:		
Carrying amount	$(100,000)	
Excess fair value -- land	(25,000)	(125,000)
Goodwill		$ 25,000

      2) Step 2 -- Prepare the assets section of the consolidated balance sheet. Assets and liabilities are reported at 100% of their fair value even though an NCI exists.

EXAMPLE 15-11 Assets Section of the Balance Sheet

Consolidated assets are calculated as follows:

Current assets of parent	$140,000	Noncurrent assets of parent	$180,000
Current assets of subsidiary	40,000	Noncurrent assets of subsidiary	80,000
Consolidated current assets	$180,000	Excess fair value -- land	25,000
		Goodwill	25,000
		Consolidated noncurrent assets	$310,000

      3) Step 3 -- Prepare the liabilities section of the consolidated balance sheet.

EXAMPLE 15-12 Liabilities Section of the Balance Sheet

The new debt issued will be paid in one amount at the end of Year 5. Thus, it is classified as noncurrent debt.

Consolidated liabilities are calculated as follows:

Current liabilities of parent	$60,000	Noncurrent liabilities of parent	$100,000
Current liabilities of subsidiary	20,000	Noncurrent liabilities of subsidiary	0
Consolidated current liabilities	$80,000	New noncurrent debt	120,000
		Consolidated noncurrent liabilities	$220,000

4) Step 4 -- Determine the NCI. An NCI is not reported for every asset and liability. The entire NCI is reported as a single component of consolidated equity. (The fair value of the NCI was given in Example 15-10 as $30,000.)

5) Step 5 -- Because a combination is an acquisition of net assets, the subsidiary's equity accounts are eliminated. Thus, in the absence of a bargain purchase, the equity of the consolidated entity immediately after acquisition is the equity of the parent just prior to acquisition plus the fair value of the noncontrolling interest.

EXAMPLE 15-13 Consolidated Total Equity

Consolidated equity is calculated as follows:

Platonic's shareholders' equity	$160,000
Noncontrolling interest	30,000
Consolidated total equity	$190,000

6) Step 6 -- Prepare the acquisition-date balance sheet.

EXAMPLE 15-14 Acquisition-Date Balance Sheet

Platonic's condensed consolidated balance sheet at the acquisition date is as follows:

Consolidated current assets	$180,000	Consolidated current liabilities	$ 80,000
Consolidated noncurrent assets	310,000	Consolidated noncurrent liabilities	220,000
		Platonic's shareholders' equity	160,000
		Noncontrolling interest	30,000
Consolidated total assets	$490,000	Consolidated total liabilities and equity	$490,000

a) If the subsidiary holds shares of the common stock of the parent, this reciprocal investment must be eliminated. Subsidiary shareholdings in a parent are treated as treasury stock of the consolidated entity. Because no gain or loss on treasury stock transactions is recognized, reciprocal investments have no effect on the net income or retained earnings of the consolidated entity.

EXAMPLE 15-15 Reciprocal Investment

Assume that, on the date of acquisition, Socratic held 1,000 shares of Platonic common stock. In preparing the consolidated balance sheet, this holding is eliminated by a debit to treasury stock and a credit to investment in Platonic.

STOP & REVIEW

You have completed the outline for this subunit.
Study multiple-choice questions 5 through 9 beginning on page 478.

15.4 CONSOLIDATED FINANCIAL REPORTING -- NET INCOME AND CHANGES IN EQUITY

1. **Year-End Consolidated Financial Statements**
   a. After the close of the fiscal year in which the combination occurred, the consolidated entity prepares its first full set of consolidated financial statements.
   b. Year-end consolidated equity is affected by the net income earned, items of other comprehensive income, and the dividends paid by the consolidating entities.
   c. **Consolidation procedures.** The following steps must be performed when preparing consolidated financial statements:
      1) All line items of assets, liabilities, revenues, expenses, gains, losses, and OCI of a subsidiary are added item by item to those of the parent. These items are reported at the consolidated amounts.
      2) No investment in the subsidiary account is presented in the consolidated financial statements. Consolidated statements report the assets and liabilities of the subsidiary and the parent as if they are a single economic entity.
      3) All the equity of the subsidiary is eliminated (not presented in the consolidated financial statements).
      4) The periodic net income or loss and OCI of a consolidated subsidiary attributable to NCIs are presented separately from the periodic net income or loss and OCI attributable to the shareholders of the parent.
      5) Goodwill from the acquisition of a subsidiary is presented separately in noncurrent assets.
      6) Intraentity balances, transactions, income, and expenses must be eliminated in full (discussed in Subunit 15.5).
      7) NCI is reported separately in one line item in the equity section. The NCI must be adjusted for its proportionate share of
         a) The subsidiary's net income (an increase) or net loss (a decrease),
         b) Dividends declared by the subsidiary (a decrease), and
         c) Items of OCI recognized by the subsidiary.
      8) Adjustments should be made to report the subsidiary's assets and liabilities at amounts based on their acquisition-date fair values.

EXAMPLE 15-16 Reporting Based on Acquisition-Date Fair Value

On January 1, Year 1, Parent Co. acquired all of the outstanding shares of common stock of Son Co. On the acquisition date, the carrying amount of a building in Son's financial statements was $100,000, and its fair value was $120,000. Son depreciates this building using the straight-line depreciation method over 10 years with no salvage value.

In its December 31, Year 1, separate financial statements, Son reports the following amounts for the building:

December 31, Year 1, Son's separate financial statements	
Depreciation expense:	$10,000 = $100,000 ÷ 10 years
Building's carrying amount:	$90,000 = $100,000 – $10,000

-- Continued on next page --

EXAMPLE 15-16 -- Continued

However, the building and the related depreciation expense in the consolidated financial statements must be reported based on the $120,000 acquisition-date fair value of the building.

December 31, Year 1, consolidated financial statements	
Depreciation expense:	$12,000 = $120,000 ÷ 10 years
Building's carrying amount:	$108,000 = $120,000 – $12,000

When preparing the December 31, Year 1, consolidated financial statements, the first step of the consolidation procedures combines all assets, liabilities, and income statement items of the subsidiary with those of the parent. Thus, the following adjustments must be made by the parent to report the building and related depreciation expense in the December 31, Year 1, consolidated financial statements:

Increase depreciation expense by $2,000 ($12,000 – $10,000)
Increase the carrying amount of the building by $18,000 ($108,000 – $90,000)

2. **Consolidated Net Income**

a. The consolidated income statement must present separate amounts for the following:

1) Total consolidated net income
2) Net income attributable to the NCI
3) Net income attributable to the shareholders of the parent

EXAMPLE 15-17 Net Income Attributable to Shareholders of Parent and Subsidiary

The following are the separate statements of income of Platonic and Socratic, excluding Platonic's share of income from Socratic, for the year ended December 31, Year 1:

	Platonic	Socratic
Sales	$250,000	$120,000
Cost of goods sold	(120,000)	(70,000)
Selling and administrative expenses	(50,000)	(10,000)
Interest costs	(20,000)	0
Income tax expense	(21,000)	(14,000)
Net income	$ 39,000	$ 26,000

Assume that (1) the ownership percentages were the same as at the acquisition date (80%), (2) no items of other comprehensive income were recognized in Year 1, and (3) no intraentity transactions occurred during Year 1. Platonic's Year 1 consolidated statement of income is presented as follows:

Sales	$370,000
Cost of goods sold	(190,000)
Selling and administrative expenses	(60,000)
Interest costs	(20,000)
Income tax expense	(35,000)
Net income	$ 65,000
Net income attributable to NCI ($26,000 net income reported by Socratic × 20%)	(5,200)
Net income attributable to Platonic's shareholders [$39,000 + ($26,000 × 80%)]	$ 59,800

b. If an acquisition occurs after the first business day of the year, revenues, expenses, gains, losses, and OCI of the subsidiary are included in the financial statements of the consolidated entity only from the date of the acquisition.

3. **Dividends Paid**

   a. Consolidated dividends are those paid to parties outside the consolidated entity by the parent and the subsidiary.

      1) Dividends declared by the parent decreases the amount of consolidated retained earnings.

      2) The NCI's share of the subsidiary's dividends decreases the balance of the NCI.

      3) The parent's share of a subsidiary's dividends is not reported in the consolidated financial statements. No cash was paid outside of the consolidated entity.

EXAMPLE 15-18 Consolidated Dividends

Platonic and Socratic declared and paid $40,000 and $20,000 of dividends, respectively, during the year. Consolidated dividends paid are calculated as follows:

Dividends paid by parent	$40,000
Dividends paid by subsidiary	20,000
Parent's proportionate share of subsidiary's dividends ($20,000 × 80%)	(16,000)
Consolidated dividends paid	$44,000
NCI's share of subsidiary's dividends ($20,000 × 20%)	(4,000)
Decrease in consolidated retained earnings	$40,000

4. **Retained Earnings**

   a. Retained earnings of the consolidated entity at the acquisition date consist solely of the retained earnings of the parent. Equity amounts of the subsidiary are eliminated.

   b. Retained earnings of the consolidated entity at a subsequent reporting date consist of (1) acquisition-date retained earnings, plus (2) the net income (loss) for the subsequent period(s) attributable to the shareholders of the parent, minus (3) dividends paid by the parent to entities outside the consolidated entity.

EXAMPLE 15-19 Consolidated Retained Earnings

Platonic's equity balance of $160,000 just prior to acquisition consisted of common stock of $10,000, additional paid-in capital of $100,000, and retained earnings of $50,000. Consolidated retained earnings is calculated on December 31, Year 1, as follows:

Acquisition-date retained earnings of parent	$50,000
Consolidated net income attributable to parent's shareholders	59,800
Parent's dividends paid since acquisition date	(40,000)
Consolidated retained earnings at reporting date	$69,800

5. **Noncontrolling Interest**

   a. The NCI must be adjusted for its proportionate share of (1) the net income of the subsidiary included in consolidated net income, (2) items of consolidated other comprehensive income attributable to the subsidiary, and (3) dividends paid by the subsidiary.

EXAMPLE 15-20 NCI

Platonic owns 80% of Socratic. At the acquisition date, Platonic recognized $30,000 for the fair value of the NCI. During the current year, the subsidiary's net income and dividends paid were $26,000 and $20,000, respectively. The NCI at the reporting date is calculated as follows:

NCI at acquisition date	$30,000
Net income attributable to NCI ($26,000 × 20%)	5,200
NCI share in dividends paid by subsidiary ($20,000 × 20%)	(4,000)
Total NCI at reporting date	$31,200

6. **Consolidated Statement of Changes in Equity**

   a. This statement satisfies the requirement for a presentation of a reconciliation of the beginning and ending balances of (1) total equity, (2) equity attributable to the parent, and (3) equity attributable to the NCI.

EXAMPLE 15-21 Consolidated Statement of Changes in Equity

The following is Platonic's Year 1 consolidated statement of changes in equity:

		Platonic's Shareholders' Equity				
	Total	Retained Earnings	Accumulated OCI	Common Stock	APIC	NCI
Beginning balance	$190,000	$50,000	–	$10,000	$100,000	$30,000
Net income (loss)	65,000	59,800				5,200
Dividends paid	(44,000)	(40,000)	–	–	–	(4,000)
Ending balance	$211,000	$69,800	–	$10,000	$100,000	$31,200

STOP & REVIEW

You have completed the outline for this subunit.
Study multiple-choice questions 10 and 11 beginning on page 480.

15.5 CONSOLIDATED FINANCIAL REPORTING -- INTRAENTITY ELIMINATIONS

1. **Year-End Consolidated Financial Statements**
   a. Consolidating entities routinely conduct business with each other. The effects of these intraentity transactions must be eliminated in full during the preparation of the consolidated financial statements.
   b. Consolidated financial statements report the financial position, results of operations, and cash flows as if the consolidated entities were a single economic entity.
      1) Thus, all line items in the consolidated financial statements must be presented at the amounts that would have been reported **if the intraentity transactions had never occurred**.
   c. After adding together all the assets, liabilities, and income statement items of a parent and a subsidiary, **eliminating journal entries** for intraentity transactions must be recorded for proper presentation of the consolidated financial statements.
2. **Reciprocal Balances**
   a. In a consolidated balance sheet, reciprocal balances, such as receivables and payables, between a parent and a subsidiary are eliminated in their entirety, regardless of the portion of the subsidiary's stock held by the parent.

EXAMPLE 15-22 Intraentity Eliminations -- Reciprocal Balances

Platonic's separate balance sheet reports a $12,600 receivable from and an $8,500 payable to Socratic. Socratic's separate balance sheet reports an $8,500 receivable from and a $12,600 payable to Platonic. These balances are not reported on the consolidated balance sheet.

3. **Intraentity Inventory Transactions -- Gross Profit**
   a. Intraentity transactions that give rise to gross profit require more complex treatment.
      1) Profit from the sale of inventory between consolidating entities is a component of the net income of the entity that sold the inventory.
      2) However, the consolidated entity recognizes profit on this exchange only in proportion to the inventory that is sold to nonaffiliated parties. Accordingly, the gross profit included in the inventory remaining on the purchaser's books must be eliminated from consolidated net income.
      3) The year-end eliminating journal entry eliminates the gross profit recognized for the inventory remaining on the purchaser's books and reduces the inventory account to the balance it would have had if the intraentity transactions had never occurred.
         a) The **sales** account is debited (decreased) for the amount recognized by the seller on the intraentity sale.
         b) The **inventory** account is credited (decreased) for the amount equal to the unrealized intraentity gross profit (Seller's gross profit percentage × Inventory remaining on purchaser's books).
         c) The **cost of goods sold** account is credited (decreased) for the difference between a) and b). The total decrease in both the sales account and cost of goods sold account is exactly equal to the amount of gross profit eliminated.

Gross Profit Eliminated:

Inventory remaining on purchaser's books × Seller's gross profit percentage

EXAMPLE 15-23 Intraentity Eliminations -- Inventory Transaction

During the year, Platonic sold $100,000 of goods to Socratic on the same terms as sales made to third parties. Socratic sold 90% of this inventory to others. Socratic's cost of goods sold in connection with these outside sales was $90,000. Platonic had total sales of $800,000 and total cost of goods sold of $650,000 for the year.

Seller's gross profit percentage: [($800,000 – $650,000) ÷ $800,000] = 18.75%

Unsold inventory on purchaser's books	$ 10,000
Seller's gross profit percentage	× 18.75%
Unrealized intraentity gross profit	$ 1,875

The eliminating journal entry is as follows:

Sales	$100,000	
Inventory		$ 1,875
Cost of goods sold		98,125

d) If no inventory from an intraentity transaction remains on the purchaser's books at the end of the reporting period, no adjustment is necessary for unrealized gross profit in ending inventory. The only adjustment for the intraentity sale is to eliminate (1) the sale recognized by the seller and (2) the cost of goods sold recognized by the purchaser.

EXAMPLE 15-24 Intraentity Inventory Transaction -- None Retained

Using the data from Example 15-23, assume that Socratic (subsidiary) sold all of the inventory that was purchased from Platonic (parent) to third parties.

The year-end eliminating journal entry is as follows:

Sales	$100,000	
Cost of goods sold		$100,000

4. **Intraentity Noncurrent Assets Transactions**

   a. Transfers of noncurrent assets require elimination of any **gain or loss on sale** recognized on the intraentity transaction.

   b. All the accounts related to the asset transferred must be reported in the consolidated financial statements at the amounts that would have been reported if the intraentity transactions had never occurred.

      1) Thus, the **depreciation expense** recognized in the consolidated financial statements must be the depreciation expense as it would have been recognized in the seller's separate financial statements.

      2) If the original useful life and the depreciation method remain the same, the depreciation expense eliminated (added) is equal to the amount of gain (loss) on sale of equipment divided by the years of useful life remaining.

EXAMPLE 15-25 Intraentity Sale of Equipment

On the first day of its fiscal year, Platonic sold equipment to Socratic for $99,000. The equipment was originally purchased by Platonic 3 years ago for $120,000. Platonic depreciated the equipment using the straight-line method over 8 years with no salvage value. Socratic depreciates the equipment using the straight-line method over 5 years with no salvage value. The following steps must be performed to record the eliminating journal entry for proper presentation of the equipment in the year-end consolidated financial statements:

1. Eliminate the gain or loss on sale of the equipment that was recognized. Platonic recognized depreciation expense each year of $15,000 ($120,000 historical cost ÷ 8 years). Thus, the carrying amount of the equipment on the sale date in Platonic's separate financial statements was $75,000 ($120,000 historical cost – $45,000 accumulated depreciation). In its separate financial statements, Platonic recognized a gain on sale of **$24,000** ($99,000 transfer price – $75,000 seller's carrying amount). This gain must be eliminated (debited) in the eliminating journal entry.
2. The depreciation expense must be equal to the depreciation expense that would have been recognized by Platonic ($15,000) as if the intraentity transaction had never occurred. Because the equipment is on Socratic's books, the depreciation expense before the eliminating journal entry is $19,800 ($99,000 transfer price ÷ 5 years). Thus, the depreciation expense must be decreased (credited) in the eliminating journal entry by **$4,800** ($15,000 – $19,800). This amount is equal to the gain on sale recognized divided by the years of useful life remaining ($24,000 ÷ 5 = $4,800).
3. The cost of the equipment in the consolidated financial statements must be $120,000 (the amount that would have been reported if the intraentity transaction had never occurred). Thus, the equipment account must be increased (debited) in the eliminating journal entry by **$21,000** ($120,000 historical cost – $99,000 transfer price).
4. The accumulated depreciation balance in the consolidated financial statements must be $60,000 ($15,000 × 4). This amount would have been reported if the intraentity transaction had never occurred. Thus, the accumulated depreciation account must be increased (credited) in the eliminating journal entry by **$40,200** ($60,000 – $19,800).
5. The eliminating journal entry is as follows:

Equipment	$21,000	
Gain on sale of equipment	24,000	
Accumulated depreciation		$40,200
Depreciation expense		4,800

5. **Debt**

   a. When one entity holds the debt securities of another entity with which it is consolidated, the elimination is treated as an extinguishment of debt, with recognition of any resulting gain or loss.

      1) All accounts related to the debt, such as the maturity amount, interest receivable (payable), and interest income (expense), must be eliminated.

EXAMPLE 15-26 Intraentity Debt

Wagner, a holder of a $1 million Palmer, Inc., bond, collected the interest due on March 31 and then sold the bond to Seal, Inc., for $975,000. On that date, Palmer, a 75% owner of Seal, had a $1,075,000 carrying amount for this bond. The purchase was in substance a retirement of debt by the consolidated group for less than its carrying amount. The transaction resulted in a gain of $100,000 ($1,075,000 carrying amount – $975,000 price).

   b. The premium or discount on the debtor's and creditor's books, and any related amortization, is eliminated and recognized as a gain or loss on extinguishment in the period of purchase.

6. **Reciprocal Dividends**

   a. When consolidated entities hold reciprocal equity stakes, the portion of dividends paid to each other must be eliminated from the consolidated financial statements.

      1) The portion of the parent's dividends paid to outside parties reduces consolidated retained earnings.

      2) The portion of the subsidiary's dividends paid to outside parties reduces any noncontrolling interest.

Dividends	Consolidated Treatment
Parent's dividends to subsidiary	Eliminated
Subsidiary's dividends to parent	Eliminated
Parent's dividends to third parties	Reduces retained earnings
Subsidiary's dividends to third parties	Reduces NCI

SUCCESS TIP

The AICPA has released exam questions asking for the amount of a line item shown on the consolidated financial statements. When intraentity transactions are involved, determining the consolidated amount involves calculating the amount that must be eliminated for any intraentity transactions. Testable items include inventory; receivables; payables; property, plant, and equipment; accumulated depreciation; etc.

STOP & REVIEW

You have completed the outline for this subunit.
Study multiple-choice questions 12 through 16 beginning on page 482.

15.6 OTHER TOPICS RELATED TO BUSINESS COMBINATIONS

1. **Deconsolidation**
   a. A parent deconsolidates a subsidiary when it no longer has a controlling financial interest.
      1) Deconsolidation ordinarily occurs when the parent **no longer has more than 50%** of the outstanding voting interests of the other entity.
   b. Upon deconsolidation, the parent recognizes a gain or loss in the income statement. It equals the difference at the deconsolidation date between 1) and 2) below.
      1) The sum of the
         a) Fair value of the consideration received
         b) Fair value of any retained investment
         c) Carrying amount of any NCI
      2) The carrying amount of the subsidiary (including the carrying amount of goodwill).
   c. If b.1) is greater than b.2), a gain is recognized for the difference. If b.2) is greater than b.1), a loss is recognized.
   d. When control over the subsidiary is lost, the parent must cease to present consolidated financial statements and should perform all of the following at the deconsolidation date:
      1) Derecognize all the assets (including goodwill) and liabilities of the subsidiary at their carrying amounts.
      2) Derecognize the NCI in the former subsidiary at its carrying amount.
      3) Recognize the fair value of any consideration received from the transaction that results in deconsolidation.
      4) Recognize any gain or loss from the disposal transaction.
      5) Recognize any investment retained in the former subsidiary at its fair value.
2. **Variable Interest Entities (VIEs)**
   a. An investor must consolidate an investee in which it has a controlling financial interest.
      1) A **controlling financial interest** is the direct or indirect ability to determine the direction of management and policies through ownership, contract, or otherwise.
      2) The usual condition for a controlling financial interest is ownership of a majority voting interest. Thus, ownership by one reporting entity, directly or indirectly, **of more than 50%** of the outstanding voting shares of another entity generally is a condition for consolidation.
   b. Under certain circumstances, the voting interest test is not sufficient to determine which party has a controlling financial interest in the entity. For example,
      1) The entity's (investee's) equity is not sufficient to finance its activities without incurring additional debt (e.g., an entity's capital structure consists of 2% equity and 98% debt).
      2) The equity instruments (i.e., shares of common stock) do not have the normal equity characteristics that provide its holders with a potential controlling interest.

c. The variable interest model was developed to determine whether a controlling financial interest exists through arrangements that are not based solely on voting interests. Under this model, the party that has the power to direct the entity's most significant economic activities and the ability to participate in the entity's economic risks and rewards must consolidate the entity. This model includes the following steps:

   1) Identify the variable interest in the entity.
   2) Determine whether the entity is a variable interest entity (VIE).
   3) Identify the primary beneficiary of the VIE (the party that must consolidate the VIE).

d. **Variable interests** are investments or other interests that will (1) absorb portions of a variable interest entity's (VIE's) expected losses or (2) receive portions of the entity's expected residual returns. The following are common examples of variable interests:

   1) **Shares of common stock.** The equity investors provide capital to the entity and receive an ownership interest that exposes the investors to potential losses and potential returns of the entity. Thus, they are subject to the entity's economic risks and receive its rewards.
   2) **Guarantees of debt.** If the VIE cannot repay its debt, the party liable on the debt guarantee will incur a loss. Thus, this party is subject to the entity's economic risks.
   3) **Subordinated debt** issued by the VIE.

e. An entity is a VIE if it meets **any** of the following criteria:

   1) The total equity investment at risk is not sufficient to permit the entity to finance its activities without additional subordinated financial support.
   2) As a group, the holders of the equity investment at risk have one of the following three characteristics:
      a) Lack the power, through voting rights, to direct the activities that most significantly affect the entity's economic performance.
      b) Lack the obligation to absorb the entity's expected losses.
      c) Lack the right to receive the entity's expected residual returns.
   3) The entity is structured so that voting rights do not necessarily reflect the underlying economic reality. This situation occurs when
      a) The voting rights of some investors are not proportional to their share in expected losses or expected residual returns of entity and
      b) Substantially all of the entity's activities are on behalf of an investor that has disproportionately few voting rights.

f. The **primary beneficiary** is the reporting entity that is required to consolidate the VIE. **Only one** reporting entity (if any) is expected to be identified as the primary beneficiary of a VIE.

   1) The primary beneficiary has a controlling financial interest in a VIE if it has
      a) The power to direct activities that most significantly affect the economic performance of the VIE and
      b) The obligation to absorb losses or the right to receive benefits of the VIE that potentially could be significant to the VIE.

3. **Combined Financial Statements**

   a. Consolidated statements should be prepared only when the controlling financial interest is held by one of the consolidated entities. These financial statements report the financial information of the parent and all its subsidiaries as if they were a single economic entity.

   b. When consolidated statements are not prepared, combined financial statements may be more meaningful than the separate financial statements of commonly controlled entities.

      1) For example, combined statements are useful when one individual owns a controlling financial interest in several entities with related operations. They also may be used to present the statements of entities under common management.

   c. Combined statements are prepared in the same way as consolidated statements. However, the financial data of the parent is not reported in these statements.

      1) When they are prepared for related entities, e.g., commonly controlled entities, intraentity transactions and gains or losses are eliminated.

      2) Moreover, consolidation procedures are applied to such matters as (a) noncontrolling interests, (b) foreign operations, (c) different fiscal periods, and (d) income taxes.

EXAMPLE 15-27 Combined Financial Statements

Fructose Corp. owns 85% of the stock of Sucrose Co., 75% of Lactose Co., and 90% of Maltose Co. Fructose is considering selling its entire interest in all three subsidiaries to one buyer. The subsidiaries do not own each other's stock. Lactose has a $15,000 payable due from Sucrose, and Sucrose has $33,000 in profits and a $28,000 payable from its dealings with Maltose.

Fructose will issue one set of financial statements that reports consolidated information for all four entities. The $15,000 receivable (payable), the $33,000 in profits, and the $28,000 receivable (payable) are all eliminated from these statements.

Another set of statements also may be prepared that reports combined information only for Sucrose, Lactose, and Maltose. These statements also will eliminate the mutual receivable (payable) and profit amounts. These combined statements do not contain any of the financial data of Fructose.

STOP & REVIEW

You have completed the outline for this subunit.
Study multiple-choice questions 17 through 19 beginning on page 484.

QUESTIONS

15.1 Accounting for Business Combinations -- Overview

1. Primor, a manufacturer, owns 75% of the voting interests of Sublette, an investment firm. Sublette owns 60% of the voting interests of Minos, an insurer. In Primor's consolidated financial statements, should consolidation accounting or equity method accounting be used for Sublette and Minos?

A. Consolidation used for Sublette and equity method used for Minos.

B. Consolidation used for both Sublette and Minos.

C. Equity method used for Sublette and consolidation used for Minos.

D. Equity method used for both Sublette and Minos.

Answer (B) is correct.

REQUIRED: The method of accounting used by an entity that has a direct controlling interest in one entity and an indirect interest in another.

DISCUSSION: All entities in which a parent has a controlling financial interest through direct or indirect ownership of a majority voting interest ordinarily must be consolidated. However, a subsidiary is not consolidated when control does not rest with the majority owner. Primor has direct control of Sublette and indirect control of Minos and should consolidate both.

Answer (A) is incorrect. Primor has a controlling interest in Minos as well. **Answer (C) is incorrect.** Primor has a controlling interest in Sublette as well. **Answer (D) is incorrect.** Primor should consolidate both Sublette and Minos.

2. On August 31, Planar Corp. exchanged 100,000 shares of its $40 par value common stock for all of the net assets of Sistrock Co. The fair value of Planar's common stock on August 31 was $72 per share. Planar paid a fee of $320,000 to the consultant who arranged this acquisition. Direct costs of registering and issuing the equity securities amounted to $160,000. No goodwill or bargain purchase was involved in the acquisition. At what amount should Planar record the acquisition of Sistrock's net assets?

A. $7,200,000

B. $7,360,000

C. $7,520,000

D. $7,680,000

Answer (A) is correct.

REQUIRED: The fair value of the net assets acquired.

DISCUSSION: Acquisition-related costs, such as the $320,000 consultant's fee, are expensed as incurred. But exceptions are made for direct issue costs of securities accounted for under other GAAP. Thus, the direct issue costs of equity ($160,000) are debited to additional paid-in capital. The consideration transferred is measured at its fair value of $7,200,000 (100,000 shares of common stock issued × $72). Given that no goodwill or bargain purchase was involved, neither goodwill nor a gain is recognized. Consequently, the identifiable assets acquired and liabilities assumed are recorded at their net amount of $7,200,000. The journal entries are

Investment in Sistrock (100,000 × $72)	$7,200,000	
Common stock (100,000 × $40)		$4,000,000
Additional paid-in capital (difference)		3,200,000
Business combination expense	$320,000	
Additional paid-in capital	160,000	
Cash		$480,000

Answer (B) is incorrect. The fair value of the net assets acquired plus the registration and issuance costs equals $7,360,000. **Answer (C) is incorrect.** The fair value of the net assets acquired plus the consultant's fee equals $7,520,000. **Answer (D) is incorrect.** The fair value of the net assets acquired plus the registration and issuance costs and the consultant's fee equals $7,680,000.

15.2 Accounting for Business Combinations -- Acquisition Method

3. Alton Corporation purchased 100% of the shares of Jones Corporation for $600,000. Financial information for Jones Corporation is provided below.

	Jones Corporation ($000)	
	Carrying Amount	Fair Value
Cash	$ 50	$ 50
Accounts receivable	100	100
Inventory	150	100
Total current assets	$300	$250
Property, plant, and equipment (net)	500	600
Total assets	$800	$850
Current liabilities	$150	$150
Long-term debt	200	200
Total liabilities	$350	$350
Common stock	150	150
Paid-in capital	80	80
Retained earnings	220	
Total shareholders' equity	$450	
Total liabilities and shareholders' equity	$800	

The amount of goodwill resulting from this purchase, if any, would be

A. $200,000

B. $150,000

C. $100,000

D. $0

Answer (C) is correct.

REQUIRED: The amount of goodwill resulting from a purchase of an entity.

DISCUSSION: Goodwill is the excess of (1) the sum of the acquisition-date fair values of (a) the consideration transferred ($600,000), (b) any noncontrolling interest in the acquiree ($0), and (c) the acquirer's previously held equity interest in the acquiree ($0) over (2) the net of the acquisition-date fair values of the identifiable assets acquired ($850,000) and liabilities assumed ($350,000). The amount of goodwill is calculated as follows:

Consideration transferred	$600,000
Acquisition-date fair value of net assets acquired ($850,000 – $350,000)	(500,000)
Goodwill	$100,000

Answer (A) is incorrect. The amount of $200,000 is the goodwill that would have been recognized if the consideration transferred was $700,000. **Answer (B) is incorrect.** The amount of $150,000 is based on the carrying amount of the net assets acquired instead of their fair value. **Answer (D) is incorrect.** The consideration transferred is greater than the fair value of the net assets acquired.

4. Acquirer Corporation acquired for cash at $10 per share 100,000 shares of the outstanding common stock of Acquiree Company. The total fair value of the identifiable assets acquired minus liabilities assumed of Acquiree was $1.4 million on the acquisition date, including the fair value of its property, plant, and equipment (its only noncurrent asset) of $250,000. The consolidated financial statements of Acquirer Corporation and its wholly owned subsidiary must reflect

A. A deferred credit of $150,000.

B. Goodwill of $150,000.

C. A gain of $150,000.

D. A gain of $400,000.

Answer (D) is correct.

REQUIRED: The accounting for a bargain purchase.

DISCUSSION: When (1) the net of the acquisition-date fair values of the identifiable assets acquired and liabilities assumed exceeds (2) the sum of the acquisition-date fair values of (a) the consideration transferred, (b) any noncontrolling interest in the acquiree, and (c) the acquirer's previously held equity interest in the acquiree, the acquirer recognizes the excess as a gain from bargain purchase.

Acquisition-date fair value of consideration transferred (100,000 shares × $10)	$ 1,000,000
Acquisition-date fair value of identifiable net assets acquired	(1,400,000)
Gain from a bargain purchase	$ (400,000)

Answer (A) is incorrect. A deferred credit is never recognized for a bargain purchase. **Answer (B) is incorrect.** This acquisition results in a gain from bargain purchase, not goodwill. **Answer (C) is incorrect.** A gain of $150,000 results from reducing the fair value of the PPE to zero.

15.3 Consolidated Financial Reporting -- Acquisition-Date Balance Sheet

Questions 5 through 9 are based on the following information. On January 2, Parma borrowed $60,000 and used the proceeds to purchase 90% of the outstanding common shares of Seville. Parma had no prior equity interest in Seville. Ten equal principal and interest payments begin December 30. The excess of the implied fair value of Seville over the carrying amount of its identifiable net assets should be assigned 60% to inventory and 40% to goodwill. Moreover, the fair value of the noncontrolling interest (NCI) is 10% of the implied fair value of the acquiree. The following are the balance sheets of Parma and Seville on January 1:

	Parma	Seville
Current assets	$ 70,000	$20,000
Noncurrent assets	90,000	40,000
Total assets	$160,000	$60,000
Current liabilities	$ 30,000	$10,000
Noncurrent liabilities	50,000	--
Equity	80,000	50,000
Total liabilities and equity	$160,000	$60,000

5. On Parma's January 2 consolidated balance sheet, Parma's shareholders' equity should be

A. $80,000

B. $86,667

C. $90,000

D. $130,000

Answer (A) is correct.

REQUIRED: The equity in the consolidated balance sheet.

DISCUSSION: In the absence of a bargain purchase, the total equity of the consolidated entity immediately after acquisition is the equity of the parent just prior to acquisition plus the fair value of the NCI. An NCI is the equity in a subsidiary not attributable to the parent. Thus, the portion of the total consolidated equity that is attributable to the shareholders of the parent (Parma) equals the parent's (Parma's) equity just prior to the acquisition of $80,000.

Answer (B) is incorrect. Parma's equity at 1/1 plus the fair value of the noncontrolling interest equals $86,667. **Answer (C) is incorrect.** The total liabilities of the two entities at 1/1 equal $90,000. **Answer (D) is incorrect.** The sum of the equity amounts for Parma and Seville at 1/1 is $130,000.

6. On Parma's January 2 consolidated balance sheet, current liabilities equal

A. $50,000

B. $46,000

C. $40,000

D. $30,000

Answer (B) is correct.

REQUIRED: The consolidated current liabilities.

DISCUSSION: Consolidated current liabilities contain the current portion of the debt issued by Parma to finance the acquisition ($60,000 ÷ 10 equal principal payments = $6,000). Reported current liabilities equal $46,000.

Current liabilities of Parma	$30,000
Current liabilities of Seville	10,000
Current component of new debt	6,000
Consolidated current liabilities	$46,000

Answer (A) is incorrect. The pre-existing noncurrent debt is $50,000. **Answer (C) is incorrect.** The amount of $40,000 ignores the new borrowing. **Answer (D) is incorrect.** The amount of Parma's pre-existing current liabilities is $30,000.

7. On Parma's January 2 consolidated balance sheet, current assets equal

A. $100,000

B. $96,000

C. $90,000

D. $80,000

Answer (A) is correct.

REQUIRED: The consolidated current assets.

DISCUSSION: The implied fair value of the subsidiary is $66,667 ($60,000 cash paid by the parent ÷ 90%). The excess of this amount over the carrying amount of the subsidiary's identifiable net assets is $16,667 ($66,667 – $50,000). This amount is allocated $10,000 to inventory ($16,667 × 60%) and $6,667 to goodwill ($16,667 × 40%). Thus, the reported amount of the current assets is $100,000.

Current assets of Parma	$ 70,000
Current assets of Seville	20,000
Undervaluation of inventory	10,000
Consolidated current assets	$100,000

Answer (B) is incorrect. The amount of $96,000 assumes an assignment of $6,000 to inventory. **Answer (C) is incorrect.** The amount of $90,000 ignores the $10,000 excess of the fair value of inventory over its carrying amount. **Answer (D) is incorrect.** The amount of $80,000 excludes the carrying amount of Seville's current assets.

8. On Parma's January 2 consolidated balance sheet, noncurrent assets equal

A. $130,000

B. $134,000

C. $136,667

D. $140,000

Answer (C) is correct.

REQUIRED: The consolidated noncurrent assets.

DISCUSSION: The implied fair value of the subsidiary is $66,667 ($60,000 cash paid by the parent ÷ 90%). The excess of this amount over the carrying amount of the subsidiary's identifiable net assets is $16,667 ($66,667 – $50,000). This amount is allocated $10,000 to inventory ($16,667 × 60%) and $6,667 to goodwill ($16,667 × 40%). Thus, reported noncurrent assets equal $136,667.

Noncurrent assets of Parma	$ 90,000
Noncurrent assets of Seville	40,000
Goodwill	6,667
Consolidated noncurrent assets	$136,667

Answer (A) is incorrect. The amount of $130,000 ignores goodwill. **Answer (B) is incorrect.** The amount of $134,000 assumes that a 100% interest was acquired and that goodwill was therefore $4,000 [($60,000 – $50,000) × 40%]. **Answer (D) is incorrect.** The amount of $140,000 assumes that a 100% interest was acquired and that goodwill was $10,000.

9. Refer to the information on the preceding page(s). On Parma's January 2 consolidated balance sheet, the sum of the noncurrent liabilities and the NCI equal

A. $116,667

B. $110,667

C. $104,000

D. $50,000

Answer (B) is correct.

REQUIRED: The sum of the noncurrent liabilities and the NCI.

DISCUSSION: Consolidated noncurrent liabilities include the noncurrent portion of the debt issued by Parma to finance the acquisition ($60,000 – $6,000 = $54,000). Thus, reported noncurrent liabilities equal $104,000.

Noncurrent liabilities of Parma	$ 50,000
Noncurrent component of new debt	54,000
Consolidated noncurrent liabilities	$104,000

The implied fair value of the subsidiary is $66,667 ($60,000 cash paid by the parent ÷ 90%), and the NCI is $6,667 ($66,667 × 10%). The sum of the noncurrent liabilities and the NCI is therefore $110,667 ($104,000 + $6,667).

Answer (A) is incorrect. The amount of $116,667 is the sum of noncurrent liabilities (excluding the new borrowing) and the implied fair value of the subsidiary. **Answer (C) is incorrect.** The amount of $104,000 omits the NCI. **Answer (D) is incorrect.** The amount of $50,000 ignores the new borrowing and the NCI.

15.4 Consolidated Financial Reporting -- Net Income and Changes in Equity

10. On January 1, Year 4, Pane Corp. exchanged 150,000 shares of its $20 par value common stock for all of Sky Corp.'s common stock. At that date, the fair value of Pane's common stock issued was equal to the fair value of the identifiable assets acquired and liabilities assumed. Both corporations continued to operate as separate businesses, maintaining accounting records with years ending December 31. In its separate statements, Pane accounts for the investment using the equity method. Information from separate company operations follows:

	Pane	Sky
Retained earnings -- 12/31/Yr 3	$3,200,000	$925,000
Dividends paid -- 3/25/Yr 4	750,000	200,000

If consolidated net income was $800,000, what amount of retained earnings should Pane report in its December 31, Year 4, consolidated balance sheet?

A. $4,925,000

B. $4,125,000

C. $3,050,000

D. $3,250,000

Answer (D) is correct.

REQUIRED: The consolidated retained earnings.

DISCUSSION: Retained earnings of the consolidated entity at the acquisition date consist solely of the retained earnings of the parent. The consolidated entity does not report any equity amounts of the subsidiary. Retained earnings of the consolidated entity at the reporting date consist of acquisition-date retained earnings, plus consolidated net income (no NCI exists), minus consolidated dividends paid. Sky's dividends, if any, are paid solely to Pane. Thus, consolidated dividends (those paid outside the entity) consist entirely of those paid by Pane.

Acquisition-date retained earnings of Pane	$3,200,000
Consolidated net income since acquisition date	800,000
Consolidated dividends paid since acquisition date	(750,000)
Consolidated retained earnings at reporting date	$3,250,000

Answer (A) is incorrect. The amount of $4,925,000 includes Sky's retained earnings at 12/31/Yr 3 and does not reflect an adjustment for the dividends paid. **Answer (B) is incorrect.** The amount of $4,125,000 is the sum of the retained earnings of Pane and Sky at 12/31/Yr 3. **Answer (C) is incorrect.** The amount of $3,050,000 results from treating Sky's dividends as consolidated dividends.

11. On January 2 of the current year, Peace Co. paid $310,000 to purchase 75% of the voting shares of Surge Co. Surge held no shares in Peace. Peace reported retained earnings of $80,000, and Surge reported contributed capital of $300,000 and retained earnings of $100,000. The purchase differential was attributed to depreciable assets with a remaining useful life of 10 years. Peace used the equity method in accounting for its investment in Surge. Surge reported net income of $20,000 and paid dividends of $8,000 during the current year. Peace reported income, exclusive of its income from Surge, of $30,000 and paid dividends of $15,000 during the current year. What amount will Peace report as dividends declared and paid in its current year's consolidated statement of changes in equity?

A. $8,000

B. $15,000

C. $17,000

D. $23,000

Answer (C) is correct.

REQUIRED: The consolidated dividends declared and paid.

DISCUSSION: Peace acquired a greater than 50% share of the voting interests in Surge. Accordingly, Peace must consolidate Surge unless it does not have control. Moreover, the equity method is not appropriate except in parent-only statements. The consolidated statements should report only dividends paid to parties outside the consolidated entity. Because Peace acquired only 75% of the voting shares of Surge, a 25% noncontrolling interest exists. Thus, 25% of Surge's dividends were paid to parties outside the consolidated entity. Furthermore, all of Peace's dividends were paid to parties outside of the consolidated entity. Accordingly, consolidated dividends paid are calculated as follows:

Dividends paid by parent	$15,000
Dividends paid by subsidiary	8,000
Parent's proportionate share of sub's dividends ($8,000 × 75%)	(6,000)
Consolidated dividends paid	$17,000

Answer (A) is incorrect. The amount of $8,000 equals the dividends declared by Surge. **Answer (B) is incorrect.** The amount of $15,000 equals the dividends paid by Peace. **Answer (D) is incorrect.** The amount of $23,000 includes $6,000 of intraentity dividends.

15.5 Consolidated Financial Reporting -- Intraentity Eliminations

12. Wright Corp. has several subsidiaries that are included in its consolidated financial statements. In its December 31 trial balance, Wright had the following intraentity balances before eliminations:

	Debit	Credit
Current receivable due from Main Co.	$ 32,000	
Noncurrent receivable from Main Co.	114,000	
Cash advance to Corn Corp.	6,000	
Cash advance from King Co.		$ 15,000
Payable to King Co.		101,000

In its December 31 consolidated balance sheet, what amount should Wright report as intraentity receivables?

A. $152,000

B. $146,000

C. $36,000

D. $0

Answer (D) is correct.

REQUIRED: The amount reported as intraentity receivables.

DISCUSSION: In a consolidated balance sheet, reciprocal balances, such as receivables and payables, between a parent and a consolidated subsidiary are eliminated in their entirety, regardless of the portion of the subsidiary's stock held by the parent. Thus, Wright should report $0 as intraentity receivables.

Answer (A) is incorrect. The amount of $152,000 includes intraentity transactions in the consolidated financial statements. **Answer (B) is incorrect.** The effects of intraentity transactions should be completely eliminated in consolidated financial statements. **Answer (C) is incorrect.** Intraentity transactions should not be netted out in the consolidated financial statements.

13. Dunn Corp. owns 100% of Grey Corp.'s common stock. On January 2, Year 3, Dunn sold to Grey for $40,000 machinery with a carrying amount of $30,000. Grey is depreciating the acquired machinery over a 5-year life by the straight-line method. The net adjustments to compute Year 3 and Year 4 consolidated income before income tax are an increase (decrease) of

	Year 3	Year 4
A.	$(8,000)	$2,000
B.	$(8,000)	$0
C.	$(10,000)	$2,000
D.	$(10,000)	$0

Answer (A) is correct.

REQUIRED: The net adjustments to pretax comparative consolidated income resulting from an intraentity transaction.

DISCUSSION: In consolidated financial statements, intraentity transactions should be eliminated. Transfers of plant assets require elimination of any gain or loss on sale recognized. If the original useful life and depreciation method remain the same, the depreciation expense eliminated is equal to the amount of gain on sale of equipment divided by the years of useful life remaining. Thus, in Year 3 the $10,000 ($40,000 selling price – $30,000 carrying amount) gain and the $2,000 excess depreciation ($10,000 ÷ 5 years) should be eliminated. The $2,000 of excess depreciation should also be eliminated in Year 4. The net adjustment to Year 3 pretax consolidated income is an $8,000 decrease ($2,000 excess depreciation added back – $10,000 gain subtracted). In Year 4, the adjustment is a $2,000 increase resulting from adding back the excess depreciation.

Answer (B) is incorrect. The amount of $2,000 of excess depreciation should be added back in Year 4. **Answer (C) is incorrect.** The $8,000 net gain should be subtracted in Year 3. **Answer (D) is incorrect.** The $8,000 net gain should be subtracted in Year 3, and $2,000 of excess depreciation should be added back in Year 4.

14. Wagner, a holder of a $1 million Palmer, Inc., bond, collected the interest due on March 31, and then sold the bond to Seal, Inc., for $975,000. On that date, Palmer, a 75% owner of Seal, had a $1,075,000 carrying amount for this bond. What was the effect of Seal's purchase of Palmer's bond on the retained earnings and noncontrolling interest amounts reported in Palmer's March 31 consolidated balance sheet?

	Retained Earnings	Noncontrolling Interest
A.	$100,000 increase	$0
B.	$75,000 increase	$25,000 increase
C.	$0	$25,000 increase
D.	$0	$100,000 increase

Answer (A) is correct.

REQUIRED: The effect of the purchase by the subsidiary of the parent's debt.

DISCUSSION: The purchase was in substance a retirement of debt by the consolidated entity for less than its carrying amount. The transaction resulted in a constructive gain of $100,000 ($1,075,000 carrying amount – $975,000 price) and therefore a $100,000 increase in consolidated retained earnings. The noncontrolling interest was unaffected. The noncontrolling interest is based on the subsidiary's carrying amounts adjusted for subsidiary income and dividends. This transaction did not result in gain or loss for Seal.

Answer (B) is incorrect. The gain is not allocated. **Answer (C) is incorrect.** The noncontrolling interest is not affected. **Answer (D) is incorrect.** Retained earnings is increased by $100,000.

15. Zest Co. owns 100% of Cinn, Inc. On January 2, Zest sold equipment with an original cost of $80,000 and a carrying amount of $48,000 to Cinn for $72,000. Zest had been depreciating the equipment over a 5-year period using straight-line depreciation with no residual value. Cinn is using straight-line depreciation over 3 years with no residual value. In Zest's December 31 consolidating worksheet, by what amount should depreciation expense be decreased?

A. $0

B. $8,000

C. $16,000

D. $24,000

Answer (B) is correct.

REQUIRED: The decrease in depreciation expense on the consolidating worksheet.

DISCUSSION: Annual depreciation taken by the purchaser-subsidiary is $24,000 ($72,000 ÷ 3 years). Annual depreciation taken by the seller-parent was $16,000 ($80,000 ÷ 5 years). The $8,000 difference should be eliminated in the eliminating journal entry. Note that this amount is exactly equal to the gain on sale recognized of $24,000 ($72,000 – $48,000) divided by the years of useful life remaining (3 years).

Answer (A) is incorrect. The difference in depreciation arising from a sale within the consolidated entity must be eliminated. **Answer (C) is incorrect.** The annual depreciation recognized by the parent is $16,000. **Answer (D) is incorrect.** The annual depreciation recognized by the subsidiary is $24,000.

16. Jane Co. owns 90% of the common stock of Dun Corp. and 100% of the common stock of Beech Corp. On December 30, Dun and Beech each declared a cash dividend of $100,000 for the current year. What is the total amount of dividends that should be reported in the December 31 consolidated financial statements of Jane and its subsidiaries, Dun and Beech?

A. $10,000

B. $100,000

C. $190,000

D. $200,000

Answer (A) is correct.

REQUIRED: The total dividends reported in the consolidated financial statements.

DISCUSSION: The only dividends declared by the subsidiaries that are reported are those paid to noncontrolling interests. Beech has no NCIs because the parent (Jane) owns 100% of its shares. Accordingly, the dividends reported equal $10,000 ($100,000 declared by Dun × 10% noncontrolling ownership interest in Dun). The amount of dividends declared attributable to the noncontrolling interest is reported in the consolidated financial statements as a reduction in the NCI account.

Answer (B) is incorrect. The amount of $100,000 is the amount declared by Dun or Beech. **Answer (C) is incorrect.** The amount of $190,000 is the amount eliminated in the consolidation. **Answer (D) is incorrect.** The amount of $200,000 is the total declared by Dun and Beech.

15.6 Other Topics Related to Business Combinations

17. Acquiree Co. is a 90%-owned subsidiary of Acquirer Co. The carrying amounts of the noncontrolling interest and the subsidiary are $1,000,000 and $10,000,000, respectively. The subsidiary's fair value is $15,000,000. Acquirer transferred part of its interest to Third Co. on December 31 for $12,000,000 in cash but retained a noncontrolling interest equal to 20% of Acquiree's voting interests. The fair value of the retained interest, which gives Acquirer significant influence, is $3,000,000. The fair values and carrying amounts are as of December 31. Acquirer must account for this transaction by recognizing a

A. Gain of $5,000,000.

B. Gain of $6,000,000.

C. Gain of $1,000,000.

D. Loss of $3,000,000.

Answer (B) is correct.

REQUIRED: The gain or loss after a sale of the parent's controlling interest in a subsidiary with retention of significant influence.

DISCUSSION: The parent records a deconsolidation by recognizing a gain or loss in net income attributable to the parent. It equals the difference between (1) the sum of (a) the fair value of consideration received, (b) the fair value of any retained investment at the date of deconsolidation, and (c) the carrying amount of any noncontrolling interest (including accumulated other comprehensive income attributable to the noncontrolling interest at the date of deconsolidation and (2) the carrying amount of the subsidiary. Consequently, the gain is $6,000,000 [($12,000,000 + $3,000,000 + $1,000,000) – $10,000,000].

Answer (A) is incorrect. The carrying amount of NCIs must be included in the calculation of gain or loss on the deconsolidation. **Answer (C) is incorrect.** The amount of $1,000,000 assumes that the carrying amount of the subsidiary is $15,000,000. **Answer (D) is incorrect.** The amount of $3,000,000 is the difference between the consideration received and the fair value of the subsidiary.

18. Combined statements may be used to present the results of operations of

	Entities under Common Management	Commonly Controlled Entities
A.	No	Yes
B.	Yes	No
C.	No	No
D.	Yes	Yes

Answer (D) is correct.

REQUIRED: The use(s) of combined financial statements.

DISCUSSION: Combined (as distinguished from consolidated) statements of commonly controlled entities may be more meaningful than separate statements. For example, combined statements may be used (1) to combine the statements of several entities with related operations when one individual owns a controlling financial interest in them or (2) to combine the statements of entities under common management.

Answer (A) is incorrect. Common management justifies use of combined statements. **Answer (B) is incorrect.** Common control justifies use of combined statements. **Answer (C) is incorrect.** Either common management or common control justifies use of combined statements.

19. At December 31, S Corp. owned 80% of J Corp.'s common stock and 90% of C Corp.'s common stock. J's net income for the year was $200,000 and C's net income was $400,000. C and J had no interentity ownership or transactions during the year. Combined financial statements are being prepared for C and J in contemplation of their sale to an outside party. In the combined income statement, combined net income should be reported at

A. $420,000

B. $520,000

C. $560,000

D. $600,000

Answer (D) is correct.

REQUIRED: The combined net income.

DISCUSSION: Combined financial statements are appropriate when common management or common control exists for two or more entities not subject to consolidation. The calculation of combined net income is similar to the calculation for consolidated net income. Thus, combined net income should be recorded at the total of the net income reported by the combined entities, adjusted for any profits or losses from transactions between the combined entities. In the combined income statement issued for J Corp. and C Corp., net income should be reported at $600,000 ($200,000 + $400,000).

Answer (A) is incorrect. The amount of $420,000 is 70% of the combined net income. **Answer (B) is incorrect.** The amount of $520,000 equals 80% of the net income of J and 90% of the net income of C. **Answer (C) is incorrect.** The amount of $560,000 equals 80% of J's net income and 100% of C's net income.

GO TO ONLINE COURSE

Access the **Gleim CPA Premium Review System** featuring our SmartAdapt technology from your Gleim Personal Classroom to continue your studies. You will experience a personalized study environment with exam-emulating multiple-choice questions.

STUDY UNIT SIXTEEN

DERIVATIVES, HEDGING, AND OTHER TOPICS

(20 pages of outline)

Derivatives and hedge accounting, foreign currency transactions and translation, and financial statement analysis are topics listed in the AICPA's FAR blueprint.

16.1 DERIVATIVES AND HEDGING

BACKGROUND 16-1 Nature of a Derivative

A derivative is a bet on whether the value of something will go up or down. The purpose is either to speculate (incur risk) or to hedge (avoid risk). The value of a derivative changes as the value of the specified variable changes.

For example, a corn farmer can guarantee the price of his annual corn production using a derivative. In this case, the derivative is a hedge against the changes in the price of corn (to avoid risk).

1. **General Financial Market Terms**
   a. A **call option** is the right (but not an obligation) to purchase an asset at a fixed price (i.e., the exercise price or the strike price) on or before a future date (i.e., expiration date).
   b. A **put option** is the right (but not an obligation) to sell an asset at a fixed price (i.e., the exercise price or the strike price) on or before a future date (i.e., expiration date).
   c. The **exercise or strike price** is the agreed-upon price of exchange in an option contract.
   d. The **expiration date** is the date when the option may no longer be exercised.
   e. An **underlying** is the price, rate, or other variable (e.g., security price, commodity price, foreign exchange rate, etc.) specified in a derivative instrument.
   f. A **notional amount** is the number of units (e.g., number of securities, tons of commodity, etc.) specified in a derivative instrument.
   g. **Embedded** means that a derivative is contained within either (1) another derivative or (2) a financial instrument.
      1) For example, a mortgage has an embedded option. The mortgagor (the debtor) generally has the option to refinance the mortgage if interest rates decrease.
   h. The **spot price/rate** is the rate for immediate settlement of currencies, commodities, securities, etc.
   i. The **forward price/rate** is the rate for settlement of currencies, commodities, securities, etc., at some definite date in the future.

2. **Characteristics of a Derivative**

   a. A derivative is a financial instrument that has at least one **underlying** and at least one **notional amount** or payment provision, or both.

   b. No **initial net investment**, or one smaller than that necessary for contracts with similar responses to the market, is required.

   c. A derivative's terms require or permit net settlement or provide for the equivalent.

      1) **Net settlement** means that the derivative can be readily settled with only a net delivery of assets. Thus, neither party must deliver (a) an asset associated with its underlying or (b) an asset that has a principal, stated amount, etc., equal to the notional amount.

3. **Typical Derivatives**

   a. A **call option** allows the purchaser to benefit from an increase in the price of the underlying asset. The gain is the excess of the market price over the exercise price. The purchaser pays a premium for the opportunity to benefit from this appreciation.

   b. A **put option** allows the purchaser to benefit from a decrease in the price of the underlying asset. The gain is the excess of the exercise price over the market price. The purchaser pays a premium for the opportunity to benefit from the depreciation in the underlying.

      1) The price of an option (option fair value) consists of two components: the intrinsic value and the time value.

Option price = Intrinsic value + Time value

EXAMPLE 16-1 Call Option

On January 1, Year 1, Tom Co. acquired a call option that allows purchase of 100 shares of All Co.'s common stock on March 31, Year 1, at $20 per share. On March 31, Year 1, All's shares are trading at $25 per share.

The underlying:	The market price of All Co.'s shares of common stock
The underlying securities in the contract:	All Co.'s shares of common stock
The notional amount:	100 shares of All Co.'s common stock
The exercise/strike price:	$20 per share

On March 31, Year 1, the fair value of the call option is based on the difference between the market price per share and the exercise price of the option. Thus, the fair value of the option is $500 [100 × ($25 – $20)]. If net cash settlement is allowed, Tom will receive $500 in cash on March 31, Year 1.

NOTE: If the market price per share on March 31, Year 1, is lower than $20, there is no reason for Tom to exercise the option and purchase shares for $20 per share. Accordingly, the fair value of the option is $0.

c. A **forward contract** is an agreement for the purchase and sale of a stated amount of a commodity, foreign currency, or financial instrument at a stated price. Delivery or settlement is at a stated future date.

1) Forward contracts are usually specifically negotiated agreements and are not traded on regulated exchanges. Accordingly, the parties are subject to **default risk** (i.e., that the other party will not perform).

2) A forward contract to buy or sell foreign currency is called a forward exchange contract.

a) The fair value of this contract, both on the initial recognition date and the balance sheet date, is measured based on the **forward exchange rate** on those dates.

d. A **futures contract** is a forward-based agreement to make or receive delivery or make a cash settlement that involves a specified quantity of a commodity, foreign currency, or financial instrument during a specified time interval.

e. An **interest rate swap** is an exchange of one party's interest payments based on a **fixed rate** for another party's interest payments based on a **variable rate**. Moreover, most interest rate swaps permit **net settlement** because they do not require delivery of interest-bearing assets with a principal equal to the contracted amount.

1) An interest rate swap is appropriate when one counterparty prefers the payment pattern of the other. For example, a firm with **fixed-rate** debt may have revenues that vary with interest rates. It may prefer variable-rate debt so that its **debt service** will correlate directly with its **revenues**.

f. Certain **financial instruments**, e.g., accounts receivable, notes receivable, bonds, preferred stock, and common stock, are not derivatives. However, any of these instruments may be an underlying asset (security) in a derivative.

4. **Accounting for Derivatives**

a. Derivatives should be recognized as **assets or liabilities** depending on the terms of the contract.

b. **Fair value** is the only relevant measure for derivatives.

c. The accounting for changes in fair value of a derivative depends on

1) The **reasons for holding it**,
2) Whether the entity has elected to **designate** it as part of a hedging relationship, and
3) Whether it meets the **qualifying criteria** for the particular accounting.

d. Derivatives **not designated as a hedging instrument** are measured at **fair value through net income** (i.e., gains or losses on the remeasurement to fair value are recognized directly in earnings).

e. Derivatives designated as a hedging instrument are measured at fair value through net income or at fair value through OCI, depending on whether the hedge is

1) A fair value hedge,
2) A cash flow hedge, or
3) A foreign currency hedge.

5. **Hedge Accounting**

   a. The purchase or sale of a derivative or other instrument is a hedge if it is **expected to neutralize the risk** of (1) a recognized asset or liability, (2) an unrecognized firm commitment, or (3) a forecasted (anticipated) transaction.

      1) For example, a flour company buys and uses wheat in its product. It may wish to guard against increases in wheat costs when it has committed to sell at a price related to the current cost of wheat. If so, the company will purchase wheat futures contracts that will result in gains if the price of wheat increases (offsetting the actual increased costs).

   b. To qualify for **hedge accounting**, the hedging relationship must be **highly effective**. It should result in offsetting changes in the fair value (or cash flows) attributable to the hedged risk during the term of the hedge.

      1) When the hedge is determined to be highly effective, hedge accounting is applied to the **entire change in the fair value** of the hedging instrument.

   c. A fully **effective (perfect) hedge** results in no net gain or loss. It occurs when the gain or loss on the hedging instrument exactly offsets the loss or gain on the hedged item.

6. **Fair Value Hedges**

   a. A **fair value hedge** mitigates the exposure to changes in the **fair value** of a **recognized asset or liability** or of an **unrecognized firm commitment** that are attributable to a specified risk.

   b. Examples of hedged items are

      1) Fixed-rate investments and debt and
      2) Firm commitments to purchase or sell assets or incur liabilities.

   c. Gains and losses in relation to a fair value hedge must be accounted for as follows:

      1) Gains or losses from changes in the fair value of the **hedging instrument** (derivative) are recognized **immediately in earnings**.

      2) Gains or losses from changes in the fair value of the **hedged item** attributable to the hedged risk are recognized **immediately in earnings**.

         a) The gain or loss from the change in the fair value of the hedging instrument is reported in the same income statement line item as the earnings effect of the hedged item.

EXAMPLE 16-2 Fair Value Hedge of an Unrecognized Purchase Commitment

Kahli Co. is a crude oil dealer. On October 1, Year 1, Kahli signed a noncancelable contract to purchase on February 1, Year 2, 10,000 barrels of crude oil at $50 per barrel. On the same date, Kahli purchased for $20,000 a put option that allows it to sell 10,000 barrels of crude oil on February 1, Year 2, for $52 per barrel. Kahli purchased the put option to protect itself from the risk of recognizing losses on a firm purchase commitment if the market price of crude oil declined below the commitment price of $50 per barrel. (Study Unit 7, Subunit 7 contains information on accounting for firm purchase commitments.) Kahli sold this crude oil inventory on June 1, Year 2, for $51 per barrel.

-- Continued on next page --

EXAMPLE 16-2 -- Continued

The following are the spot prices of crude oil on the relevant dates:

October 1, Year 1	$50
December 31, Year 1	49
February 1, Year 2	46

For simplicity, ignore the time value and assume that the fair value of the option is based solely on its intrinsic value (Strike price of the option – Spot price of the crude oil). Thus, the fair value of the put option on October 1, Year 1, is $20,000 [($52 – $50) × 10,000].

This hedge is a highly effective fair value hedge. The put option is hedging against the decrease in the fair value of the purchase commitment.

October 1, Year 1

No journal entry is made for the purchase commitment

Put option (asset)	$20,000	
Cash		$20,000

December 31, Year 1

Loss on firm purchase commitment	$10,000 [($49 – $50) × 10,000]	
Liability for firm purchase commitment		$10,000

The fair value of the put option on December 31, Year 1, is its intrinsic value of $30,000 [($52 – $49) ×10,000]. Thus, the gain of $10,000 ($30,000 – $20,000) on the remeasurement of the put option to fair value is recognized. This gain exactly offsets the loss on the firm purchase commitment.

Put option	$10,000	
Loss on firm purchase commitment		$10,000

The gain from the change in the fair value of the hedging instrument is reported in the same income statement line item as the earnings effect of the hedged item.

February 1, Year 2

Loss on firm purchase commitment	$30,000 [($46 – $49) × 10,000]	
Liability for firm purchase commitment		$30,000
Liability for firm purchase commitment	$ 40,000 ($30,000 + $10,000)	
Crude oil inventory	460,000 ($46 × 10,000)	
Cash		$500,000 ($50 × 10,000)

The fair value of the put option on February 1, Year 2, is its intrinsic value of $60,000 [($52 – $46) × 10,000]. Thus, the gain on the remeasurement of the put option to fair value of $30,000 ($60,000 – $30,000) is recognized.

Put option	$30,000	
Loss on firm purchase commitment		$30,000

Because net settlement is allowed, Kahli received $60,000 on the option expiration date.

Cash	$60,000	
Put option		$60,000 ($20,000 + $10,000 + $30,000)

June 1, Year 2

Accounts receivable/cash	$510,000	
Sales		$510,000 ($51 × 10,000)

Cost-of-goods sold	$460,000	
Crude oil inventory		$460,000

7. **Cash Flow Hedges**

   a. A **cash flow hedge** mitigates the exposure to variability in the cash flows of a **recognized asset or liability** or of a **forecasted transaction** that is attributable to a specified risk.

      1) A forecasted transaction is probable, i.e., expected to occur, although no firm commitment exists. It does not (a) provide current rights or (b) impose a current obligation because no transaction or event has occurred.

      2) An example is an anticipated purchase or sale of inventory or item of property, plant, and equipment (a forecasted transaction).

   b. Gains or losses from changes in the fair value of the hedging instrument (derivative) are **recognized in OCI**.

   c. The amounts recognized in OCI (the gains or losses on the hedging instrument) are reclassified to earnings only when the hedged item affects earnings.

      1) After the reclassification of these gains or losses from accumulated OCI to earnings, they are reported in the income statement in the same line item as the earnings effect of the hedged item.

EXAMPLE 16-3 **Cash Flow Hedge of a Forecasted Transaction**

Kahli Co. is a crude oil dealer. On October 1, Year 1, Kahli anticipates that it will purchase 10,000 barrels of crude oil on December 31, Year 1. On the same date, Kahli purchased for $20,000 a call option that allows it to purchase 10,000 barrels of crude oil on December 31, Year 1, for $48 per barrel. Kahli acquired the crude oil inventory for its spot price on December 31, Year 1, and sold it on June 1, Year 2, for $56 per barrel.

The following are the spot prices of crude oil on the relevant dates:

October 1, Year 1	$50
December 31, Year 1	51

For simplicity, ignore the time value and assume that the fair value of the option is based solely on its intrinsic value (Spot price of crude oil – Strike price of the option). Thus, the fair value of the call option on October 1, Year 1, is $20,000 [($50 – $48) × 10,000].

By acquiring the call option, Kahli protects itself from the risk of changes in the cash flows that could result from an increase in crude oil prices. Thus, this hedge is classified as a cash flow hedge.

-- Continued on next page --

EXAMPLE 16-3 -- Continued

October 1, Year 1

Call option (asset)	$20,000		
Cash		$20,000	

December 31, Year 1

Remeasurement of the call option to fair value

The fair value of the call option on December 31, Year 1, is its intrinsic value of $30,000 [($51 – $48) × 10,000]. Thus, the gain of $10,000 ($30,000 – $20,000) on the remeasurement of the call option to fair value is recognized in OCI.

Call option	$10,000		
OCI		$10,000	

Inventory acquisition

Crude oil inventory	$510,000		($51 × 10,000)
Cash		$510,000	

Cash settlement of the call option

Cash	$30,000		[($51 – $48) × 10,000]
Call option		$30,000	($20,000 + $10,000)

June 1, Year 2

Inventory sale

Accounts receivable/cash	$560,000		
Sales		$560,000	($56 × 10,000)

Cost-of-goods sold	$510,000	
Crude oil inventory		$510,000

Reclassification of gains or losses on the hedging instrument from accumulated OCI to earnings when the hedged item affects earnings (when the crude oil inventory is sold)

OCI	$10,000	
Cost-of-goods sold		$10,000

The purchased crude oil was recorded in inventory. When the inventory was sold, its earnings effect was recognized in the cost-of-goods-sold account. Thus, the reclassification of the gain on the hedging instrument is from accumulated OCI to the cost-of-goods-sold account.

8. **Foreign Currency Hedges**
   a. Certain foreign currency exposures also may qualify for hedge accounting.
   b. A derivative may hedge the foreign currency exposure to variability in a foreign currency (exchange rate fluctuations) in different foreign currency transactions.
   c. A derivative may hedge the foreign currency exposure of **net investments in a foreign operation**. The accounting for gains and losses on the hedging instrument in a net investment hedge is accounted for similar to a cash flow hedge.
      1) Gains and losses on the change in the fair value of the hedging instrument is recognized in the currency translation adjustment section of OCI.
      2) Those amounts are reclassified from accumulated OCI to earnings only when the hedged item affects earnings.

9. **Embedded Derivatives**
    a. A common example is the conversion feature of convertible debt. It is a call option on the issuer's stock. Embedded derivatives must be **accounted for separately** from the host if
        1) The economic characteristics and risks of the embedded derivative are not clearly and closely related to the economic characteristics of the host;
        2) The hybrid instrument is **not remeasured at fair value** under otherwise applicable GAAP, with changes in fair value reported in earnings; and
        3) A freestanding instrument with the same terms as the embedded derivative is subject to the guidance on derivative instruments and hedging.
    b. If an embedded derivative is accounted for separately, the **host contract** is accounted for based on the accounting standards that apply to instruments of its type. The **separated derivative** should be accounted for under the guidance on derivative instruments and hedging.
        1) If the embedded derivative to be separated is **not reliably identifiable and measurable**, the entire contract must be measured at **fair value**, with gains and losses recognized in **earnings**.
        2) It may not be designated as a hedging instrument because nonderivatives usually do not qualify as hedging instruments.

10. **Derivatives and Hedging Disclosures**
    a. The guidance for disclosures about derivative instruments and hedging activities applies to all entities and all derivatives and hedged items.
    b. The following are some of the disclosures for every reporting period for which a statement of financial position is issued:
        1) **Objectives** of holding derivative instruments; their context, including each instrument's **primary risk exposure**; and the entity's related strategies.
            a) A distinction must be made between instruments (whether or not hedges) used for (1) risk management and (2) other purposes. The entity must disclose which hedging instruments are hedges of fair value, cash flows, or the net investment in a foreign operation. If derivatives are not hedges, their purpose must be described.
        2) Information about the **volume** of derivatives.
        3) **Location** and **gross fair values** of reported derivatives.
            a) These amounts are separately reported as assets and liabilities and classified as hedges and nonhedges. Within these classes, amounts are separately reported by type of derivative.
        4) **Location** and amounts of **gains and losses** on derivatives and hedged items.
            a) This information includes separate disclosures for (1) fair value hedges (hedging instruments and hedged items), (2) gains and losses on cash flow hedges and hedges of net investments that are currently recognized in OCI or reclassified from accumulated OCI, and (3) derivatives that are not used as hedges.
            b) The information is separately reported by type of derivative, with identification of line items.

STOP & REVIEW

You have completed the outline for this subunit.
Study multiple-choice questions 1 through 3 on page 507.

16.2 FOREIGN CURRENCY ISSUES

1. **Definitions**

   a. The **reporting currency** is the currency in which an entity prepares its financial statements.

   b. The **functional currency** is the currency of the primary economic environment in which the entity operates. Normally, that environment is the one in which it primarily generates and expends cash.

      1) For example, the functional currency of a foreign subsidiary might be the parent's currency if its cash flows directly and currently affect the parent's cash flows.

   c. **Foreign currency transactions** are fixed in a currency other than the functional currency. They result when an entity

      1) Buys or sells on credit;
      2) Borrows or lends; or
      3) For other reasons, acquires or disposes of assets, or incurs or settles liabilities, fixed in a foreign currency.

   d. A **foreign currency** is any currency other than the entity's functional currency.

   e. The **current exchange rate** is the rate used for currency conversion.

   f. The **transaction date** is the date when a transaction is recorded under GAAP.

   g. A **transaction gain (loss)** results from a change in exchange rates between the functional currency and the currency in which the transaction is denominated. It is the change in functional currency cash flows

      1) Actually realized on settlement and
      2) Expected on unsettled transactions.

   h. **Foreign currency translation** is the process of expressing in the reporting currency amounts that are (1) denominated in (fixed in units of) a different currency or (2) measured in a different currency.

      1) A consolidated entity may consist of separate entities operating in different economic and currency environments. Translation is necessary in these circumstances so that consolidated amounts are presented in one currency (the reporting currency of the parent company).

2. **Foreign Currency Transactions**

   a. The terms of a foreign currency transaction are stated in a currency different from the entity's functional currency.

      1) For example, if an entity whose functional currency is the U.S. dollar purchases inventory on credit from a German entity, payment is to be in euros.

   b. The **initial measurement** of the transaction must be in the reporting entity's functional currency.

      1) The exchange rate used is the rate in effect on the date the transaction was initially recognized.

EXAMPLE 16-4 Foreign Currency Transaction -- Initial Measurement

On November 15, Year 1, JRF Corporation, a U.S. entity, purchases and receives inventory from Paris Corporation, a French entity. The transaction is fixed in euros and calls for JRF to pay Paris €500,000 on January 15, Year 2. On November 15, Year 1, the euro-dollar exchange rate is $1.2 to €1.

November 15, Year 1:

Inventory	$600,000	
Accounts payable (€500,000 × 1.2 exchange rate)		$600,000

a) **A foreign currency transaction gain or loss** results from a change in the exchange rate between the date the transaction was recognized, the date of the financial statements, and the date the transaction is settled.

   i) This gain or loss is included in the income statement in the period the exchange rate changes. If the monetary aspect of the transaction has not yet occurred at the end of the reporting period, monetary items (accounts payable and accounts receivable) are measured at the period-end exchange rate.

EXAMPLE 16-5 Foreign Currency Transaction -- Gain or Loss

In continuation of Example 16-4, the euro-dollar exchange rate was $1.4 to €1 on December 31, Year 1, and $1.55 to €1 on January 15, Year 2.

December 31, Year 1 (financial statements day):

Loss on foreign currency transactions	$100,000	
Accounts payable [$600,000 – (€500,000 × 1.4 year-end exchange rate)]		$100,000

For the period between the initial recognition of the transaction (November 15, Year 1) and the date of the financial statements (December 31, Year 1), the dollar has depreciated against the euro. At that date, €500,000 euros cost $700,000 (€500,000 × 1.4). On December 31, Year 1, accounts payable is reported at $700,000, and the loss on foreign currency transactions is reported at $100,000.

January 15, Year 2 (transaction settlement day):

Accounts payable	$700,000	
Loss on foreign currency transactions [€500,000 × (1.55 – 1.4)]	75,000	
Cash (€500,000 × 1.55 settlement date exchange rate)		$775,000

The loss of $75,000 on foreign currency transactions is included in the Year 2 income statement.

NOTE: The total loss recognized on the exchange rate difference is $175,000 [€500,000 × (1.2 – 1.55)].

3. **Foreign Currency Translation**
   a. The method used to convert foreign currency amounts into units of the reporting currency is the **functional currency translation approach** (current-rate method).
   b. It is appropriate for use in accounting for and reporting the financial results and relationships of **foreign subsidiaries in consolidated statements**. This method
      1) Identifies the **functional currency** of the entity (the currency of the primary economic environment in which the foreign entity operates),
      2) Measures all elements of the statements in the functional currency, and
      3) Uses a **current exchange rate** for translation from the functional currency to the reporting currency.
   c. **Assets and liabilities** are translated at the exchange rate at fiscal year end.
   d. **Revenues, expenses, gains, and losses** are translated at the rates in effect when they were recognized. However, a **weighted-average rate** for the period may be used for these items.
4. **Translation Adjustments**
   a. Foreign currency translation adjustments for a foreign operation (translation gains and losses) are reported in **other comprehensive income** (OCI).
   b. When the investment in a foreign entity is sold, the amount of translation gains or losses attributable to this foreign operation is (1) removed from accumulated other comprehensive income and (2) recognized in measuring the gain or loss on the sale.
      1) When only part of the investment in a foreign entity is sold, a pro rata portion of the translation gains or losses is reported as part of a gain or loss on the sale.

5. **Remeasurement**

   a. If the books of a foreign entity are maintained in a currency not the functional currency, foreign currency amounts must be remeasured into the functional currency using the **temporal method**. They are then translated into the reporting currency using the **current-rate method**.

   b. **Nonmonetary** balance sheet items and related revenue, expense, gain, and loss amounts are remeasured at the **historical rate**.

      1) Examples are (a) equity securities carried at cost; (b) inventories carried at cost; (c) cost of goods sold; (d) prepaid expenses; (e) property, plant, and equipment; (f) depreciation; (g) intangible assets; (h) amortization of intangible assets; (i) deferred income; (j) common stock; (k) preferred stock carried at its issuance price; and (l) any noncontrolling interest.

   c. **Monetary** items are remeasured at the **current rate**.

      1) Examples of monetary items are

         a) Receivables,
         b) Payables,
         c) Inventories carried at market, and
         d) Marketable securities carried at fair value.

   d. Any **gain or loss** on remeasurement of monetary assets and liabilities is recognized in **current earnings** as part of continuing operations. This accounting treatment was adopted because gains or losses on remeasurement affect functional currency cash flows.

EXAMPLE 16-6 Foreign Currency Remeasurement and Translation

A U.S.-based conglomerate has a subsidiary in Norway that keeps its books using the krone (kr) (its local currency), but its primary operations involve Eurozone entities. Accordingly, to prepare its financial statements, the subsidiary must remeasure all unsettled transactions from kroner to euros. Then the parent must translate the subsidiary's financial statements denominated in euros into dollars ($).

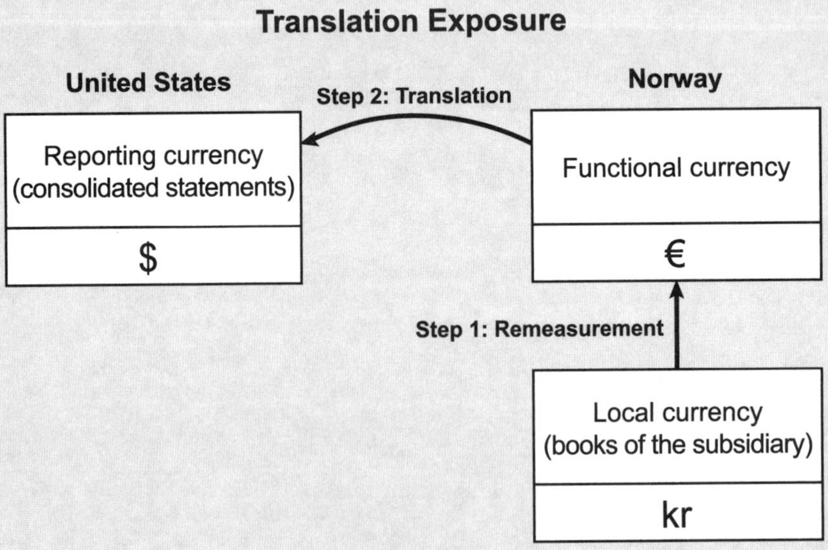

Figure 16-1

e. The financial statements of a foreign entity in a **highly inflationary economy** are remeasured into the reporting currency using the temporal method. Thus, the reporting currency is treated as if it were the functional currency.

f. **Transaction gains and losses** on the following are excluded from earnings and are reported in the same way as translation adjustments, that is, in **OCI**:

1) Transactions that are designated and effective as economic hedges of a **net investment in a foreign entity**

2) Transactions that are in effect **long-term investments** in foreign entities to be consolidated, combined, or accounted for by the equity method

6. **Tax Effects of Changes in Exchange Rates**

a. **Interperiod tax allocation** is necessary when transaction gains and losses result in temporary differences. Moreover, the tax consequences of translation adjustments are accounted for in the same way as temporary differences.

b. **Intraperiod tax allocation** is also required. For example, taxes related to transaction gains and losses and translation adjustments reported in OCI should be allocated to those items.

STOP & REVIEW

You have completed the outline for this subunit.
Study multiple-choice questions 4 through 9 beginning on page 508.

16.3 FINANCIAL STATEMENT ANALYSIS -- LIQUIDITY

The most common form of financial statement analysis is ratio analysis, in which two financial statement measures are compared.

1. **Liquidity**

a. Liquidity is a firm's ability to pay its current obligations as they come due and thus remain in business in the short run. Liquidity measures the ease with which assets can be converted to cash.

b. Liquidity ratios measure this ability by relating a firm's liquid assets to its current liabilities.

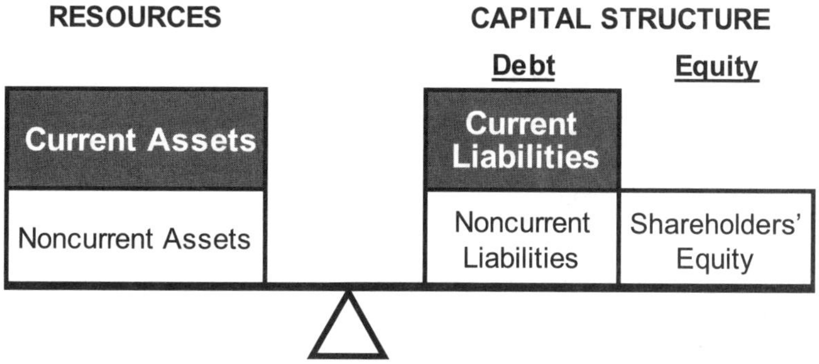

Figure 16-2

EXAMPLE 16-7 Balance Sheet

RESOURCES

	Current Year End	Prior Year End
CURRENT ASSETS:		
Cash and equivalents	$ 325,000	$ 275,000
Available-for-sale securities	165,000	145,000
Accounts receivable	120,000	115,000
Notes receivable	55,000	40,000
Inventories	85,000	55,000
Prepaid expenses	10,000	5,000
Total current assets	**$ 760,000**	**$ 635,000**
NONCURRENT ASSETS:		
Equity-method investments	$ 120,000	$ 115,000
Property, plant, and equip.	1,000,000	900,000
Minus: Accum. depreciation	(85,000)	(55,000)
Goodwill	5,000	5,000
Total noncurrent assets	**$1,040,000**	**$ 965,000**
Total assets	**$1,800,000**	**$1,600,000**

FINANCING

	Current Year End	Prior Year End
CURRENT LIABILITIES:		
Accounts payable	$ 150,000	$ 75,000
Notes payable	50,000	50,000
Accrued interest on note	5,000	5,000
Current maturities of L.T. debt	100,000	100,000
Accrued salaries and wages	15,000	10,000
Income taxes payable	70,000	35,000
Total current liabilities	**$ 390,000**	**$ 275,000**
NONCURRENT LIABILITIES:		
Bonds payable	$ 500,000	$ 600,000
Long-term notes payable	90,000	60,000
Employee-related obligations	15,000	10,000
Deferred income taxes	5,000	5,000
Total noncurrent liabilities	**$ 610,000**	**$ 675,000**
Total liabilities	**$1,000,000**	**$ 950,000**
SHAREHOLDERS' EQUITY:		
Preferred stock, $50 par	$ 120,000	$ 0
Common stock, $1 par	500,000	500,000
Additional paid-in capital	110,000	100,000
Retained earnings	70,000	50,000
Total shareholders' equity	**$ 800,000**	**$ 650,000**
Total liabilities and shareholders' equity	**$1,800,000**	**$1,600,000**

SUCCESS TIP

A candidate should know the formulas used to calculate the various financial ratios and be able to analyze the results. Certain ratios that may have more than one commonly agreed upon definition will be provided or defined by the AICPA, but you are expected to know simple ratios, such as the current ratio. Similarly, the numbers necessary to calculate a ratio often are not given directly. As a future CPA, you will be expected to determine these numbers using information given in the question and then calculate the ratio.

2. **Liquidity Ratios**

   a. The **current ratio** (also called the working capital ratio) is the most common measure of liquidity.

$$\frac{\text{Current assets}}{\text{Current liabilities}}$$

EXAMPLE 16-8 Current Ratio

Current year: $760,000 ÷ $390,000 = 1.95
Prior year: $635,000 ÷ $275,000 = 2.31

Although working capital increased in absolute terms ($10,000), current assets now provide less proportional coverage of current liabilities than in the prior year.

b. The **quick (acid-test) ratio** excludes inventories and prepaids from the numerator, recognizing that those assets are difficult to liquidate at their stated values. The quick ratio is thus a more conservative measure than the basic current ratio.

$$\frac{\text{Cash and equivalents} + \text{Marketable securities} + \text{Net receivables}}{\text{Current liabilities}}$$

EXAMPLE 16-9 Quick (Acid-Test) Ratio

Current year: ($325,000 + $165,000 + $120,000 + $55,000) ÷ $390,000 = 1.71
Prior year: ($275,000 + $145,000 + $115,000 + $40,000) ÷ $275,000 = 2.09

In spite of its increase in total working capital, the company's position in its most liquid assets deteriorated significantly.

3. **Effects of Transactions**

a. If a ratio is less than 1.0, the numerator is lower than the denominator.

1) A transaction that causes equal changes in the numerator and denominator will thus have a proportionally greater effect on the numerator, resulting in a change in the ratio in the same direction.

b. If a ratio is equal to 1.0, the numerator and denominator are the same.

1) A transaction that causes equal changes in the numerator and denominator results in no change in the ratio.

c. If a ratio is greater than 1.0, the numerator is higher than the denominator.

1) A transaction that causes equal changes in the numerator and denominator will thus have a proportionally greater effect on the denominator, resulting in a change in the ratio in the opposite direction.

Ratio range	Effect on ratio of equal increase to numerator and denominator	Effect on ratio of equal decrease to numerator and denominator
< 1.0	Increase	Decrease
= 1.0	No effect	No effect
> 1.0	Decrease	Increase

STOP & REVIEW

You have completed the outline for this subunit.
Study multiple-choice questions 10 through 12 beginning on page 511.

16.4 FINANCIAL STATEMENT ANALYSIS -- ACTIVITY

1. **Receivables Ratios**

EXAMPLE 16-10 Excerpt from an Income Statement

	Current Year	Prior Year
Net sales	**$1,800,000**	**$1,400,000**
Cost of goods sold	(1,650,000)	(1,330,000)
Gross profit	**$ 150,000**	**$ 70,000**

a. The **accounts receivable turnover ratio** is the number of times in a year the total balance of receivables is converted to cash.

$$\text{Accounts receivable turnover} = \frac{\text{Net credit sales}}{\text{Average balance in receivables}}$$

EXAMPLE 16-11 Accounts Receivable Turnover Ratio

All of the company's sales are on credit (see Example 16-7 on page 500). Net trade receivables at the balance sheet date of the second prior year were $105,000.

Current year: $1,800,000 ÷ [($120,000 + $115,000) ÷ 2] = 15.3 times
Prior year: $1,400,000 ÷ [($115,000 + $105,000) ÷ 2] = 12.7 times

The company turned over its trade receivables balance 2.6 more times during the current year, even as receivables were growing in absolute terms. Thus, the company's effectiveness at collecting accounts receivable has improved noticeably.

b. The **average collection period** (also called the **days' sales in receivables**) measures the average number of days that pass between the time of a sale and receipt of the invoice amount.

$$\text{Days' sales in receivables} = \frac{\text{Days in year}}{\text{Accounts receivable turnover ratio}}$$

EXAMPLE 16-12 Average Collection Period

Current year: 365 days ÷ 15.3 times = 23.9 days
Prior year: 365 days ÷ 12.7 times = 28.7 days

The denominator (calculated in Example 16-11 above) increased and the numerator is a constant. Consequently, days' sales must decrease. In addition to improving its collection practices, the company also may have become better at assessing the creditworthiness of its customers.

2. **Inventory Ratios**

   a. **Inventory turnover** measures the number of times in a year the total balance of inventory is converted to cash or receivables.

      1) Generally, the higher the inventory turnover rate, the more efficient the inventory management of the firm. A high rate may imply that the firm is not carrying excess levels of inventory or inventory that is obsolete.

$$\text{Inventory turnover} = \frac{\text{Cost of goods sold}}{\text{Average balance in inventory}}$$

EXAMPLE 16-13	**Inventory Turnover**

The balance in inventories at the balance sheet date of the second prior year was $45,000.

Current year: $1,650,000 ÷ [($85,000 + $55,000) ÷ 2] = 23.6 times
Prior year: $1,330,000 ÷ [($55,000 + $45,000) ÷ 2] = 26.6 times

The company did not turn over its inventories as many times during the current year. This is to be expected during a period of growing sales (and building inventory level) and so is not necessarily a sign of poor inventory management.

   b. **Days' sales in inventory** measures the average number of days that pass between the acquisition of inventory and its sale.

$$\text{Days' sales in inventory} = \frac{\text{Days in year}}{\text{Inventory turnover ratio}}$$

EXAMPLE 16-14	**Day's Sales in Inventory**

Current year: 365 days ÷ 23.6 times = 15.5 days
Prior year: 365 days ÷ 26.6 times = 13.7 days

The numerator is a constant, so the decreased inventory turnover means that days' sales in inventory increase. This common phenomenon occurs during a period of increasing sales.

3. **Operating Cycle**

   a. A firm's operating cycle is the amount of time that passes between the acquisition of inventory and the collection of cash on the sale of that inventory.

$$\text{Operating cycle} = \text{Days' sales in receivables} + \text{Days' sales in inventory}$$

EXAMPLE 16-15	**Operating Cycle**

Current year: 23.9 days + 15.5 days = 39.4 days
Prior year: 28.7 days + 13.7 days = 42.4 days

The company has managed to slightly reduce its operating cycle, even while increasing sales and inventories.

4. **Cash Conversion Cycle**

   a. A firm's cash conversion cycle is the amount of time that passes between the actual outlay of cash for inventory purchases and the collection of cash from the sale of that inventory.

   Average collection period
   \+ Days' sales in inventory
   – Average payables period
   = Cash conversion cycle

      1) The accounts payable turnover ratio is the number of times during a period that the firm pays its accounts payable.

$$\text{Accounts payable turnover} = \frac{\text{Cost of goods sold}}{\text{Average balance in accounts payable}}$$

      2) The average payables period (also called payables turnover in days, or payables deferral period) is the average time between the purchase of inventories and the payment of cash.

$$\text{Average payable period} = \frac{\text{Days in year}}{\text{Accounts payable turnover}}$$

   b. A difference between the operating cycle and the cash conversion cycle exists because the firm's purchases of inventory are made on credit. Thus, the cash conversion cycle is equal to the operating cycle minus the average payables period.

5. **Other Turnover Ratios**

   a. The total assets turnover and fixed assets turnover are broader-based ratios that measure the efficiency with which assets are used to generate revenue.

      1) Both cash and credit sales are included in the numerator.

$$\text{Total assets turnover} = \frac{\text{Net total sales}}{\text{Average total assets}}$$

$$\text{Fixed assets turnover} = \frac{\text{Net total sales}}{\text{Average net fixed assets}}$$

EXAMPLE 16-16 Other Turnover Ratios

Current year total assets turnover: $1,800,000 ÷ [($1,800,000 + $1,600,000) ÷ 2] = 1.06 times
Current year fixed assets turnover: $1,800,000 ÷ [($915,000 + $845,000) ÷ 2] = 2.04 times

NOTE: The current- and prior-year net carrying amounts of fixed assets are $915,000 ($1,000,000 – $85,000) and $845,000 ($900,000 – $55,000), respectively.

STOP & REVIEW

You have completed the outline for this subunit.
Study multiple-choice questions 13 through 17 beginning on page 512.

16.5 FINANCIAL STATEMENT ANALYSIS -- SOLVENCY, VALUATION, AND COMPARATIVE ANALYSIS

1. **Solvency and Leverage**
   a. Solvency is a firm's ability to pay its noncurrent obligations as they come due and thus remain in business in the long run (contrast with liquidity).
      1) Leverage in this context refers to the use of a high level of debt relative to equity in the firm's capital structure.
      2) An overleveraged firm risks insolvency.

$$\text{Debt-to-equity ratio} = \frac{\text{Total liabilities}}{\text{Total equity}}$$

   b. The ability to service debt out of current earnings is a key aspect of the successful use of leverage.

$$\text{Times-interest-earned ratio} = \frac{\text{Earnings before interest and taxes}}{\text{Interest expense}}$$

2. **Profitability Ratios**
   a. Profitability ratios measure how effectively the firm is using its resource base to generate a return.

$$\text{Profit margin on sales} = \frac{\text{Net income}}{\text{Sales}}$$

$$\text{Return on assets} = \frac{\text{Net income}}{\text{Average total assets}}$$

$$\text{Return on equity} = \frac{\text{Net income}}{\text{Average total equity}}$$

$$\text{Return on common equity} = \frac{\text{Net income} - \text{Preferred dividends}}{\text{Average common equity}}$$

3. **Corporate Valuation Measures**

   a. These ratios reflect and shape the stock market's assessment of a firm's current standing and future prospects.

$$\text{Basic earnings per share} = \frac{\text{Income available to common shareholders}}{\text{Weighted-average common shares outstanding}}$$

$$\text{Book value per common share} = \frac{\text{Net assets available to common shareholders}}{\text{Ending common shares outstanding}}$$

$$\text{Price-to-earnings ratio} = \frac{\text{Price per common share}}{\text{Basic EPS}}$$

SUCCESS TIP

The AICPA has traditionally tested financial ratios. Gleim materials contain CPA questions dating back to the mid 1980s that test candidates' knowledge of financial ratios, and the AICPA continues to release new questions on this topic. Successful CPA candidates have memorized the various ratios and are able to correctly answer the majority of financial ratio questions in the Gleim materials.

4. **Comparative Analysis**

   a. Comparative analysis involves both horizontal and vertical analysis. Horizontal (trend) analysis compares analytical data over a period of time. Vertical analysis makes comparisons among a single year's data.

   b. **Common-size financial statements** are used to compare entities of different sizes. Items on common-size financial statements are expressed as percentages of corresponding base amounts. A base amount is assigned the value of 100%.

      1) The **horizontal** form of common-size analysis is useful for evaluating trends. Each amount for subsequent years is stated as a percentage of a **base-year amount**.

      2) **Vertical** common-size analysis presents amounts for a single year expressed as percentages of a base amount on the **balance sheet** (e.g., total assets) and on the **income statement** (e.g., sales). Common-size analysis permits management to compare individual expenses or asset categories with those of other entities and with industry averages.

   c. Comparing an entity's performance with respect to its industry may identify strengths and weaknesses. Horizontal analysis of the industry may identify industry-wide trends and practices.

STOP & REVIEW

You have completed the outline for this subunit.
Study multiple-choice questions 18 and 19 on page 514.

QUESTIONS

16.1 Derivatives and Hedging

1. Which of the following is the characteristic of a perfect hedge?

A. No possibility of future gain or loss.

B. No possibility of future gain only.

C. No possibility of future loss only.

D. The possibility of future gain and no future loss.

Answer (A) is correct.

REQUIRED: The trait of a perfect hedge.

DISCUSSION: A hedge is used to avoid or reduce risks by creating a relationship by which losses on certain positions are expected to be counterbalanced in whole or in part by gains on separate positions in another market. A perfect hedge is completely effective. It has a complete negative correlation with the item being hedged and results in no net gain or loss.

Answer (B) is incorrect. A perfect hedge also has no possibility of future loss. **Answer (C) is incorrect.** A perfect hedge also has no possibility of future gain. **Answer (D) is incorrect.** A perfect hedge results in no net gain or loss.

2. Which of the following risks, if any, are inherent in an interest-rate swap agreement?

I. The risk of exchanging a lower interest rate for a higher interest rate

II. The risk of nonperformance by the counterparty to the agreement

A. I only.

B. II only.

C. Both I and II.

D. Neither I nor II.

Answer (C) is correct.

REQUIRED: The risks, if any, of an interest-rate swap.

DISCUSSION: An interest-rate swap is an exchange of fixed interest payments for payments based on a floating rate. The risks inherent in an interest-rate swap include both credit risk and market risk. Credit risk is the risk of accounting loss from a financial instrument because of the possibility that a loss may occur from the failure of another party to perform according to the terms of a contract. Market risk arises from the possibility that future changes in market prices may make a financial instrument less valuable or more onerous. Market risk therefore includes the risk that changes in interest rates will make the swap agreement less valuable or more onerous.

3. Which of the following financial instruments is **not** considered a derivative financial instrument?

A. Interest-rate swaps.

B. Currency futures.

C. Stock-index options.

D. Bank certificates of deposit.

Answer (D) is correct.

REQUIRED: The financial instrument not a derivative.

DISCUSSION: A derivative is a financial instrument or other contract that (1) has (a) one or more underlyings and (b) one or more notional amounts or payment provisions, or both; (2) requires either no initial net investment or an immaterial net investment; and (3) requires or permits net settlement. An underlying may be a specified interest rate, security price, commodity price, foreign exchange rate, index of prices or rates, or other variable. A notional amount is a number of currency units, shares, bushels, pounds, or other units specified. Settlement of a derivative is based on the interaction of the notional amount and the underlying. A certificate of deposit is a financial instrument of the issuing bank that is a type of promissory note. It has no underlying and requires a material net investment. Thus, it is not a derivative.

16.2 Foreign Currency Issues

4. Which of the following statements regarding foreign exchange gains and losses is true (where the exchange rate is the ratio of units of the functional currency to units of the foreign currency)?

A. An exchange gain occurs when the exchange rate increases between the date a payable is recorded and the date of cash payment.

B. An exchange gain occurs when the exchange rate increases between the date a receivable is recorded and the date of cash receipt.

C. An exchange loss occurs when the exchange rate decreases between the date a payable is recorded and the date of the cash payment.

D. An exchange loss occurs when the exchange rate increases between the date a receivable is recorded and the date of the cash receipt.

Answer (B) is correct.

REQUIRED: The true statement about foreign exchange gains and losses.

DISCUSSION: A foreign currency transaction gain or loss (commonly known as a foreign exchange gain or loss) is recorded in earnings. When the amount of the functional currency exchangeable for a unit of the currency in which the transaction is fixed increases, a transaction gain or loss is recognized on a receivable or payable, respectively. The opposite occurs when the exchange rate (functional currency to foreign currency) decreases.

Answer (A) is incorrect. The payable will become more expensive in the functional currency, resulting in a loss. **Answer (C) is incorrect.** The payable will become less expensive in the functional currency, resulting in a gain. **Answer (D) is incorrect.** An exchange gain occurs.

5. Fogg Co., a U.S. company, contracted to purchase foreign goods. Payment in foreign currency was due 1 month after the goods were received at Fogg's warehouse. Between the receipt of goods and the time of payment, the exchange rates changed in Fogg's favor. The resulting gain should be included in Fogg's financial statements as a(n)

A. Component of income from continuing operations.

B. Decrease in the carrying amount of the goods.

C. Deferred credit.

D. Item of other comprehensive income.

Answer (A) is correct.

REQUIRED: The accounting treatment of a foreign currency transaction gain.

DISCUSSION: This foreign currency transaction resulted in a payable stated in a foreign currency. The favorable change in the exchange rate between the functional currency and the currency in which the transaction was stated should be included in determining net income for the period in which the exchange rate changed. It should be classified as a component of income from continuing operations.

Answer (B) is incorrect. The historical cost of the goods is based on the exchange rate on the date the goods were purchased and received. The change in the payables between that date and the payment date is recognized in the income statement. **Answer (C) is incorrect.** The gain should not be deferred but should be recognized in the period in which the exchange rate changed. **Answer (D) is incorrect.** Translation adjustments, not transaction gains and losses, are included in OCI.

6. On September 22, Year 2, Yumi Corp. purchased merchandise from an unaffiliated foreign company for 10,000 units of the foreign company's local currency. On that date, the spot rate was \$.55. Yumi paid the bill in full on March 20, Year 3, when the spot rate was \$.65. The spot rate was \$.70 on December 31, Year 2. What amount should Yumi report as a foreign currency transaction loss in its income statement for the year ended December 31, Year 2?

A. \$0

B. \$500

C. \$1,000

D. \$1,500

Answer (D) is correct.

REQUIRED: The amount of foreign currency transaction loss to be reported in the income statement.

DISCUSSION: A receivable or payable stated in a foreign currency is adjusted to its current exchange rate at each balance sheet date. The resulting gain or loss should ordinarily be included in determining net income. It is the difference between the spot rate on the date the transaction originates and the spot rate at year end. Thus, the Year 2 transaction loss for Yumi Corp. is \$1,500 [10,000 units × (\$0.55 – \$0.70)].

Answer (A) is incorrect. A loss resulted when the spot rate increased. **Answer (B) is incorrect.** The amount of \$500 results from using the spot rates at December 31, Year 2, and March 20, Year 3. **Answer (C) is incorrect.** The amount of \$1,000 results from using the spot rates at September 22, Year 2, and March 20, Year 3.

7. Which of the following is debited to other comprehensive income (OCI)?

A. Discount on convertible bonds that are dilutive potential common stock.

B. Premium on convertible bonds that are dilutive potential common stock.

C. Cumulative foreign currency translation loss.

D. Organizational costs.

Answer (C) is correct.

REQUIRED: The item debited to OCI.

DISCUSSION: When the currency used to prepare a foreign entity's financial statements is its functional currency, the current rate method is used to translate the foreign entity's financial statements into the reporting currency. The translation gains and losses arising from applying this method are reported in OCI in the consolidated statements and are not reflected in income. Accumulated OCI is a component of equity displayed separately from retained earnings and additional paid-in capital in the statement of financial position. Because a cumulative foreign currency translation loss reduces the balance, it is a debit item.

Answer (A) is incorrect. A discount on bonds is a contra account to bonds payable in the liability section of the balance sheet. **Answer (B) is incorrect.** Premium on bonds is a contra account to bonds payable in the liability section. **Answer (D) is incorrect.** Organizational costs are expensed when incurred.

8. In preparing consolidated financial statements of a U.S. parent company with a foreign subsidiary, the foreign subsidiary's functional currency is the currency

A. In which the subsidiary maintains its accounting records.

B. Of the country in which the subsidiary is located.

C. Of the country in which the parent is located.

D. Of the environment in which the subsidiary primarily generates and expends cash.

Answer (D) is correct.

REQUIRED: The foreign subsidiary's functional currency.

DISCUSSION: The method used to convert foreign currency amounts into units of the reporting currency is the functional currency translation approach. It is appropriate for use in accounting for and reporting the financial results and relationships of foreign subsidiaries in consolidated statements. This method (1) identifies the functional currency of the entity (the currency of the primary economic environment in which the foreign entity operates), (2) measures all elements of the financial statements in the functional currency, and (3) uses a current exchange rate for translation from the functional currency to the reporting currency. The currency indicated by the relevant economic indicators, such as cash flows, sales prices, sales markets, expenses, financing, and intraentity transactions, may not be (1) the currency in which the subsidiary maintains its accounting records, (2) the currency of the country in which the subsidiary is located, or (3) the currency of the country in which the parent is located.

9. Toigo Co. purchased merchandise from a vendor in England on November 20 for 500,000 British pounds. Payment was due in British pounds on January 20. The spot rates to purchase 1 pound were as follows:

November 20	$1.25
December 31	1.20
January 20	1.17

How should the foreign currency transaction gain be reported on Toigo's financial statements at December 31?

A. A gain of $40,000 as a separate component of stockholders' equity.

B. A gain of $40,000 in the income statement.

C. A gain of $25,000 as a separate component of stockholders' equity.

D. A gain of $25,000 in the income statement.

Answer (D) is correct.

REQUIRED: The reporting of a foreign currency transaction gain.

DISCUSSION: Foreign currency transactions are recorded at the spot rate in effect at the transaction date. Transaction gains and losses are included in the income statement in the period the exchange rate changes. On November 20, the entity made the following entry:

Inventory (500,000 pounds × $1.25)	$625,000	
Accounts payable		$625,000

On December 31, the entity made the following entry:

Accounts payable [500,000 pounds × ($1.25 – $1.20)]	$25,000	
Foreign currency transaction gain		$25,000

Answer (A) is incorrect. The entity recognizes a gain in earnings of $15,000 [500,000 pounds × ($1.20 – $1.17)] on January 20. **Answer (B) is incorrect.** The only effect of the change in the spot rate during the period is recognized at the balance sheet date. **Answer (C) is incorrect.** The gain is recognized in earnings. Translation adjustments are recognized in OCI.

16.3 Financial Statement Analysis -- Liquidity

10. North Bank is analyzing Belle Corp.'s financial statements for a possible extension of credit. Belle's quick ratio is significantly better than the industry average. Which of the following factors should North consider as a possible limitation of using this ratio when evaluating Belle's creditworthiness?

A. Fluctuating market prices of short-term investments may adversely affect the ratio.

B. Increasing market prices for Belle's inventory may adversely affect the ratio.

C. Belle may need to sell its available-for-sale investments to meet its current obligations.

D. Belle may need to liquidate its inventory to meet its long-term obligations.

Answer (A) is correct.

REQUIRED: The possible limitation of using the quick ratio to evaluate creditworthiness.

DISCUSSION: The quick ratio equals cash plus short-term investment securities plus net receivables, divided by current liabilities. Because short-term investment securities are included in the numerator, fluctuating market prices of these investments may adversely affect the ratio if Belle holds a substantial amount of such current assets.

Answer (B) is incorrect. Inventory is excluded from the calculation of the quick ratio. **Answer (C) is incorrect.** If the available-for-sale securities are not current, they are not included in the calculation of the ratio. If they are classified as current, their sale to meet current obligations is consistent with normal current assets management practices. **Answer (D) is incorrect.** Inventory and noncurrent obligations are excluded from the calculation of the quick ratio.

11. A company's year-end balance sheet is shown below:

Assets	
Cash	$ 300,000
Accounts receivable	350,000
Inventory	600,000
Property, plant, and equipment (net)	2,000,000
	$3,250,000

Liabilities and Shareholder Equity	
Current liabilities	$ 700,000
Long-term liabilities	600,000
Common stock	800,000
Retained earnings	1,150,000
	$3,250,000

What is the current ratio as of December 31?

A. 1.79

B. 0.93

C. 0.67

D. 0.43

Answer (A) is correct.

REQUIRED: The current ratio.

DISCUSSION: The current ratio equals current assets divided by current liabilities [($300,000 + $350,000 + $600,000) ÷ $700,000 = 1.79].

Answer (B) is incorrect. Inventory is included in current assets. **Answer (C) is incorrect.** Retained earnings is not included in current liabilities. **Answer (D) is incorrect.** Accounts receivable and inventory are included in current assets.

12. Zenk Co. wrote off obsolete inventory of $100,000 during the year. What was the effect of this write-off on Zenk's ratio analysis?

A. Decrease in current ratio but not in quick ratio.

B. Decrease in quick ratio but not in current ratio.

C. Increase in current ratio but not in quick ratio.

D. Increase in quick ratio but not in current ratio.

Answer (A) is correct.

REQUIRED: The effect of writing off obsolete inventory.

DISCUSSION: Inventory is included in the numerator of the current ratio but not the quick ratio. Consequently, an inventory write-off decreases the current ratio but not the quick ratio.

16.4 Financial Statement Analysis -- Activity

13. Selected information for Clay Corp. for the year ended December 31 follows:

Average days' sales in inventories	124
Average days' sales in accounts receivable	48

The average number of days in the operating cycle for the year was

A. 172

B. 124

C. 86

D. 76

Answer (A) is correct.

REQUIRED: The number of days in the operating cycle.

DISCUSSION: The operating cycle is the time needed to turn cash into inventory, inventory into receivables, and receivables back into cash. It is equal to the sum of the number of days' sales in inventory and the number of days' sales in receivables. The number of days in Clay's operating cycle is thus 172 (124 + 48).

Answer (B) is incorrect. The average days' sales in inventories is 124. **Answer (C) is incorrect.** The amount of 86 days equals the sum of the average days' sales in inventories and the average days' sales in receivables, divided by 2. **Answer (D) is incorrect.** The amount of 76 days is the average days' sales in inventories minus the average days' sales in receivables.

14. The following financial ratios and calculations were based on information from Kale Co.'s financial statements for the current year:

Accounts receivable turnover
Ten times during the year

Total assets turnover
Two times during the year

Average receivables during the year
$200,000

What was Kale's average total assets for the year?

A. $2,000,000

B. $1,000,000

C. $400,000

D. $200,000

Answer (B) is correct.

REQUIRED: The average total assets.

DISCUSSION: The total assets turnover ratio (given as 2.0) equals net sales divided by average total assets. The accounts receivable turnover ratio (given as 10.0) equals net sales divided by average accounts receivable (it must be assumed that all sales are on credit). Given $200,000 of average accounts receivable, net sales must equal $2,000,000 ($200,000 × 10.0). Accordingly, average total assets equals $1,000,000 ($2,000,000 net revenue ÷ 2.0 total assets turnover).

Answer (A) is incorrect. The amount of $2,000,000 equals net revenue. **Answer (C) is incorrect.** The amount of $400,000 equals average accounts receivable times total assets turnover. **Answer (D) is incorrect.** The amount of $200,000 equals average receivables during the year.

Questions 15 through 17 are based on the following information. Selected data pertaining to Lore Co. for the Year 4 calendar year is as follows:

Net cash sales	$ 3,000
Cost of goods sold	18,000
Inventory at beginning of year	6,000
Purchases	24,000
Accounts receivable at beginning of year	20,000
Accounts receivable at end of year	22,000

15. The accounts receivable turnover for Year 4 was 5.0 times. What were Lore's Year 4 net credit sales?

A. $105,000

B. $107,000

C. $110,000

D. $210,000

Answer (A) is correct.

REQUIRED: The net credit sales.

DISCUSSION: Credit sales may be determined from the accounts receivable turnover formula (Credit sales ÷ Average accounts receivable). Credit sales are equal to 5.0 times average receivables [($20,000 + $22,000) ÷ 2], or $105,000.

Answer (B) is incorrect. The amount of $107,000 equals ending accounts receivable multiplied by the accounts receivable turnover ratio, minus cash sales. **Answer (C) is incorrect.** The amount of $110,000 equals ending accounts receivable multiplied by the accounts receivable turnover ratio. **Answer (D) is incorrect.** The amount of $210,000 equals beginning accounts receivable plus ending accounts receivable, multiplied by the accounts receivable turnover ratio.

16. What was Lore's inventory turnover for Year 4?

A. 1.2 times.

B. 1.5 times.

C. 2.0 times.

D. 3.0 times.

Answer (C) is correct.

REQUIRED: The inventory turnover ratio.

DISCUSSION: Inventory turnover is equal to cost of goods sold divided by average inventory. Ending inventory equals beginning inventory, plus purchases, minus cost of goods sold, or $12,000 ($6,000 + $24,000 – $18,000). Average inventory is $9,000 [($6,000 + $12,000) ÷ 2]. Inventory turnover is 2.0 times ($18,000 cost of goods sold ÷ $9,000 average inventory).

Answer (A) is incorrect. The amount of 1.2 times uses the average of beginning inventory and purchases. **Answer (B) is incorrect.** The amount of 1.5 times uses ending inventory instead of average inventory. **Answer (D) is incorrect.** The amount of 3.0 times uses beginning inventory instead of average inventory.

17. Lore would use which of the following to determine the average days' sales in inventory?

	Numerator	Denominator
A.	365	Average inventory
B.	365	Inventory turnover
C.	Average inventory	Sales divided by 365
D.	Sales divided by 365	Inventory turnover

Answer (B) is correct.

REQUIRED: The formula to calculate average day's sales in inventory.

DISCUSSION: The average days' sales in inventory is calculated by dividing the number of days in the year by the inventory turnover.

16.5 Financial Statement Analysis -- Solvency, Valuation, and Comparative Analysis

18. The following data pertain to Cowl, Inc., for the year ended December 31, Year 4:

Net sales	$ 600,000
Net income	150,000
Total assets, January 1, Year 4	2,000,000
Total assets, December 31, Year 4	3,000,000

What was Cowl's rate of return on assets for Year 4?

A. 5%

B. 6%

C. 20%

D. 24%

Answer (B) is correct.

REQUIRED: The rate of return on assets.

DISCUSSION: Return on assets equals net income ($150,000) divided by average total assets [($2,000,000 + $3,000,000) ÷ 2 = $2,500,000], or 6%.

Answer (A) is incorrect. A return of 5% results from using ending total assets instead of the average total assets. **Answer (C) is incorrect.** A return of 20% results from dividing net sales by ending total assets. **Answer (D) is incorrect.** A return of 24% results from using net sales rather than net income in the numerator.

19. The following is the equity section of Harbor Co.'s balance sheet at December 31:

Common stock $10 par, 100,000 shares authorized, 50,000 shares issued, of which 5,000 have been reacquired and are held in treasury	$ 450,000
Additional paid-in capital-common stock	1,100,000
Retained earnings	800,000
Subtotal	$2,350,000
Minus: Treasury stock (at cost)	(150,000)
Total stockholders' equity	$2,200,000

Harbor has insignificant amounts of convertible securities, stock warrants, and stock options. What is the book value per share of Harbor's common stock?

A. $31

B. $44

C. $46

D. $49

Answer (D) is correct.

REQUIRED: The book value per share of common stock.

DISCUSSION: The book value per share of common stock equals net assets available to common shareholders divided by ending common shares outstanding. Net assets available to common shareholders can also be stated as total equity minus liquidation value of preferred stock. Given no preferred shares, the numerator equals equity (assets minus liabilities). Thus, the book value per share of common stock is $49 [$2,200,000 equity ÷ (50,000 shares issued – 5,000 shares held in treasury)].

Answer (A) is incorrect. The amount of $31 results from not including retained earnings in the numerator. **Answer (B) is incorrect.** The amount of $44 results from including treasury shares in the denominator. **Answer (C) is incorrect.** The amount of $46 results from measuring the treasury shares at $10 per share and including those shares in the denominator.

STUDY UNIT SEVENTEEN

STATEMENT OF CASH FLOWS

(16 pages of outline)

This study unit covers the statement of cash flows. The first subunit explains the purposes of the statement and how cash flows are classified. The second subunit consists of questions that require the candidate to perform typical statement of cash flows calculations. The third subunit describes the direct and indirect methods of presenting operating cash flows. The fourth subunit provides extended examples of presenting operating cash flows under the direct and indirect methods.

17.1 STATEMENT OF CASH FLOWS -- CLASSIFICATIONS

BACKGROUND 17-1 Lack of Liquidity Not Revealed by Accrual Accounting

In 1969, in a desperate attempt to boost sales, the department store chain W.T. Grant drastically lowered its credit standards. As a result, sales boomed. However, during the economic downturn of 1970-71, customer accounts began to turn delinquent and cash inflows dried up. The company finally collapsed in 1974. Grant's creditors were caught completely unaware because the company's accrual-basis income statement had shown consistently positive results and Grant had never stopped paying a dividend. The Grant bankruptcy made the inadequacy of the traditional income statement for assessing liquidity glaringly obvious. This incident was one reason for the FASB's decision to require presentation of a statement of cash flows.

1. **Introduction**

   a. The **primary purpose** of a statement of cash flows is to provide information about the cash receipts and payments of an entity during a period. To achieve its primary purpose, the statement should provide information about cash inflows and outflows from **operating, investing, and financing activities** of an entity. This is the accepted order of presentation.

      1) The format reconciles the cash and cash equivalents balance at the beginning of the period with the balance at the end of the period.

EXAMPLE 17-1 Summary Statement of Cash Flows

The following is an example of the summarized format of the statement of cash flows (headings only). The amounts of cash and cash equivalents at the beginning and end of the year are taken from the balance sheet.

Entity A's Statement of Cash Flows for the Year Ended December 31, Year 1

Net cash provided by (used in) operating activities	$XXX
Net cash provided by (used in) investing activities	XXX
Net cash provided by (used in) financing activities	XXX
Net increase (decrease) in cash, cash equivalents, and restricted cash	$XXX
Cash, cash equivalents, and restricted cash at beginning of year (January 1, Year 1)	XXX
Cash, cash equivalents, and restricted cash at end of year (December 31, Year 1)	$XXX

b. A statement of cash flows is required as part of a full set of financial statements of most business and not-for-profit entities.

   1) If an entity reports financial position and results of operations, it must present a statement of cash flows for any period for which results of operations are presented.

   2) Cash flow per share is not reported.

c. The two ways of presenting the statement of cash flows are the **direct method** and the **indirect method**.

   1) The only difference between these two methods is their presentation of **net cash flows from operating activities**. The total cash flows from operating activities is the same regardless of which method is used.

2. **Treatment of Cash and Cash Equivalents**

   a. If an entity invests its cash in cash equivalents, it should use the descriptive term "cash and cash equivalents." Otherwise, the term "cash" is acceptable.

   b. **Cash equivalents** are readily convertible to known amounts of cash and are so near maturity that they present insignificant risk of changes in value because of changes in interest rates.

      1) Usually, investments with **original maturities of 3 months or less** qualify. Thus, a 3-year Treasury note meets the definition if purchased 3 months from maturity. However, if the note was purchased 3 years ago, it does not meet the definition when its remaining maturity is 3 months.

         a) Other examples of cash equivalents are Treasury bills, commercial paper, and money market funds.

         b) The statement of cash flows explains the change in cash, cash equivalents, and restricted cash during the period. However, exchanges of items within the category of cash, cash equivalents, and restricted cash need not be reported in the statement of cash flows.

   c. Not all qualifying investments must be classified as cash equivalents. An entity should **consistently apply a policy** for classifying cash equivalents.

      1) For example, an entity with operations that primarily involve investing in short-term, highly liquid investments may choose not to treat them as cash equivalents.

      2) Any change in policy is a change in accounting principle that requires retrospective application.

      3) The policy for determining which items are cash equivalents must be disclosed.

3. **Operating Activities**
   a. Operating activities are all transactions and other events that are **not financing or investing activities**. Cash flows from operating activities are primarily derived from the principal revenue-producing activities of the entity. They generally result from transactions and other events that enter into the determination of net income.
   b. The following are examples of **cash inflows** from operating activities:
      1) Cash receipts from the sale of goods and services (including collections of accounts receivable)
      2) Cash receipts from royalties, fees, commissions, and other revenue
      3) Cash received in the form of **interest** or **dividends**
      4) Cash receipts from certain loans and other debt and equity instruments of other entities that are **acquired specifically for resale in the short term**
   c. The following are examples of **cash outflows** from operating activities:
      1) Cash payments to suppliers for goods and services
      2) Cash payments to employees
      3) Cash payments to government for taxes, duties, fines, and other fees or penalties
      4) Payments of **interest on debt**
4. **Investing Activities**
   a. Cash flows from investing activities represent the extent to which expenditures have been made for resources intended to generate future income and cash flows.
   b. The following are examples of **cash outflows (and inflows)** from investing activities:
      1) Cash payments to acquire (cash receipts from sale of) property, plant and equipment; intangible assets; and other long lived assets
      2) Cash payments to acquire (cash receipts from sale and maturity of) equity and debt instruments of other entities for investing purposes
         a) Cash flows from purchases, sales, and maturities of available-for-sale debt securities and held-to-maturity debt securities are from investing activities.
      3) Cash advances and loans made to other parties (cash receipts from repayment of advances and loans made to other parties)
   c. Investing activities **exclude** transactions in cash equivalents and certain loans or other debt or equity instruments acquired specifically for resale in the short-term. These transactions are classified as operating activities.

5. **Financing Activities**

   a. Cash flows from financing activities generally involve the cash effects of transactions and other events that relate to the issuance, settlement, or reacquisition of the entity's debt and equity instruments.

   b. The following are examples of **cash inflows** from financing activities:

      1) Cash proceeds from issuing shares and other equity instruments (obtaining resources from owners)

      2) Cash proceeds from issuing loans, notes, bonds, and other short-term or long-term borrowings

   c. The following are examples of **cash outflows** from financing activities:

      1) Cash repayments of amounts borrowed

      2) Payments of **cash dividends**

      3) Cash payments to acquire or redeem the entity's own shares

      4) Cash payments by a lessee for a reduction of the outstanding liability relating to a finance lease

IFRS DIFFERENCE

Cash flows from **interest and dividends** should be separately disclosed and consistently classified. Total interest paid is disclosed whether it was expensed or capitalized. A **financial institution** customarily classifies interest paid or received and dividends received as operating items. For **entities other than financial institutions**, the following are the appropriate classifications:

	Operating	Financing	Investing
Interest paid	Yes	Yes	No
Interest received	Yes	No	Yes
Dividends paid	Yes	Yes	No
Dividends received	Yes	No	Yes

Reporting cash flow per share is not prohibited.

If bank overdrafts that are repayable on demand are part of an entity's cash management program, they are included in cash and cash equivalents, not in cash flows from financing activities.

6. **Noncash Investing and Financing Activities**

   a. Information about all **investing and financing activities** that affect recognized assets or liabilities **but not cash flows** must be disclosed. Given only a few transactions, disclosure may be on the same page as the statement of cash flows. Otherwise, they may be reported elsewhere in the statements with a clear reference to the statement of cash flows.

   b. The following are examples of noncash investing and financing activities:

      1) Conversion of debt to equity

      2) Acquisition of assets either by assuming directly related liabilities or by means of a finance lease

      3) Exchange of a noncash asset or liability for another

      4) Obtaining a building or investment asset by gift

STOP & REVIEW

You have completed the outline for this subunit.
Study multiple-choice questions 1 through 3 beginning on page 531.

17.2 STATEMENT OF CASH FLOWS -- CALCULATIONS

Many questions about the statement of cash flows ask for the calculation of the appropriate amount. This subunit consists entirely of such questions. Please review Subunit 17.1 before answering the questions.

STOP & REVIEW

You have completed the outline for this subunit.
Study multiple-choice questions 4 through 9 beginning on page 532.

17.3 DIRECT AND INDIRECT METHODS OF PRESENTING OPERATING CASH FLOWS

1. **The Direct Method**
   a. Under the direct method, the entity presents major classes of gross operating cash receipts and payments and their sum (net cash flow from operating activities). At a minimum, the following must be presented:
      1) Cash collected from customers
      2) Interest and dividends received
      3) Other operating cash receipts, if any
      4) Cash paid to employees and other suppliers of goods and services
      5) Interest paid
      6) Income taxes paid
      7) Other operating cash payments, if any
   b. If the direct method is used, the reconciliation of net income to net cash flow from operating activities (the operating section of the indirect method format) must be provided in a separate schedule.
   c. The direct method is preferable but not required. Although the FASB encourages use of the direct method, most entities apply the indirect method because the reconciliation must be prepared regardless of the method chosen.

SUCCESS TIP

The following equations will help you to convert the accrual-basis amounts in the income statement to the cash basis amount and the opposite:

Beginning accounts receivable	$XXX	Beginning accounts payable	$XXX
Sales (accrual basis)	XXX	Purchases (accrual basis)	XXX
Ending accounts receivable	(XXX)	Ending accounts payable	(XXX)
Cash collected from customers	$XXX	Cash paid to suppliers	$XXX
Beginning interest payable	$XXX	Ending prepaid expenses	$XXX
Interest expense (accrual basis)	XXX	Current-period expense (accrual basis)	XXX
Ending interest payable	(XXX)	Beginning prepaid expenses	(XXX)
Interest paid during the period	$XXX	Expenses paid during the period	$XXX

2. **The Indirect Method**

   a. Under the indirect method (also called the reconciliation method), the net cash flow from operating activities is determined by adjusting the net income of a business (or the change in the net assets of a not-for-profit entity) for the effect of the following:

      1) **Noncash revenue and expenses** that were **included in net income**, such as depreciation and amortization expenses, impairment losses, undistributed earnings of equity method investments, and amortization of discount and premium on bonds
      2) Items **included in net income** whose cash effects relate to **investing or financing cash flows**, such as gains or losses on sales of PPE items (related to investing activities) and gains or losses on extinguishment of debt (related to financing activities)
      3) All **deferrals** of past operating cash flows, such as changes during the period in inventory and deferred income
      4) All **accruals** of expected future operating cash flows, such as changes during the period in accounts receivable and accounts payable

   b. The reconciliation of net income to net cash flow from operating activities must disclose all **major classes** of reconciling items. For example, major classes of deferrals or accruals of operating cash flows must be separately disclosed. At a minimum, this disclosure reports changes in (1) accounts receivable and accounts payable related to operating activities and (2) inventories.

   NOTE: The net cash flow from operating activities is the same under both methods. The only difference is the presentation.

   c. Under the indirect method, an entity must provide a supplemental disclosure of the following amounts paid during the period:

      1) Interest paid (net of amounts capitalized)
      2) Income taxes paid

3. **Example of Direct and Indirect Methods**

EXAMPLE 17-2 Direct Method vs. Indirect Method

During Year 2, Bishop Corp. had the following transactions:

- Inventory (cost $9,000) was sold for $14,000, with $13,000 on credit and $1,000 in cash.
- Cash collected on credit sales to customers was $12,000.
- Inventory was purchased for $6,500.
- Bishop paid $8,500 to suppliers.

The following is Bishop's income statement for the year ended on December 31, Year 2:

Sales	$14,000
Cost of goods sold	(9,000)
Net income	**$ 5,000**

-- Continued on next page --

EXAMPLE 17-2 -- Continued

The following are Bishop's balance sheet accounts on December 31, Year 1, and December 31, Year 2:

	December 31			December 31	
Current assets	Year 1	Year 2	Current liabilities	Year 1	Year 2
Cash	$10,000	$14,500	Acc. payable	$ 5,000	$ 3,000
Net acc. receivable	6,000	7,000	Equity		
Inventory	14,000	11,500	Common stock	21,000	21,000
			Retained earnings	4,000	9,000
Total assets	$30,000	$33,000	Total liability and equity	$30,000	$33,000

a. The direct method presents the gross operating cash receipts and payments.

Bishop's Statement of Cash Flows for the Year Ended on December 31, Year 2
(Using the direct method)

Cash flows from operating activities:		
Cash received from customers ($12,000 + $1,000)	$13,000	
Cash paid to suppliers	(8,500)	
Net cash provided by operating activities		**$ 4,500**
Cash at beginning of year		10,000
Cash at end of year		**$14,500**

b. Under the indirect method, the net cash flow from operating activities is determined by adjusting net income for the period.

Bishop's Statement of Cash Flows for the Year Ended on December 31, Year 2
(Using the indirect method)

Cash flows from operating activities:			
Net income		$ 5,000	
Increase in accounts receivable ($6,000 – $7,000)	$(1,000)		(1)
Decrease in inventory ($11,500 – $14,000)	2,500		(2)
Decrease in accounts payable ($3,000 – $5,000)	(2,000)		(3)
Total adjustments		(500)	
Net cash provided by operating activities		**$ 4,500**	
Cash at beginning of year		10,000	
Cash at end of year		**$14,500**	

Explanation:

(1) The amount of accounts receivable increased during the year by $1,000, implying that cash collections were less than credit sales. The net income for the period is an accrual accounting amount. Thus, the increase in accounts receivable during the period must be subtracted from net income to determine the cash flow from operating activities.

(2) Inventory decreased by $2,500, implying that purchases were less than the amount of cost of goods sold. Thus, it must be added to net income to determine the cash flow from operating activities.

(3) Accounts payable decreased by $2,000, implying that cash paid to suppliers was greater than purchases. Thus, it must be subtracted from net income.

SUCCESS TIP

The following rules will help you to reconcile the net income to net cash flow from operating activities under the indirect method:

Increase in current operating liabilities	Added to net income
Decrease in current operating assets	Added to net income
Increase in current operating assets	Subtracted from net income
Decrease in current operating liabilities	Subtracted from net income

4. Example of Direct and Indirect Methods

EXAMPLE 17-3 **Direct Method vs. Indirect Method**

During Year 2, Knight Corp. had the following transactions:

- On December 31, Year 2, a machine was sold for $47,000 in cash. The machine was acquired by Knight on January 1, Year 1, for $50,000. Its useful life is 10 years with no salvage value, and it is depreciated using the straight-line method.
- On December 31, Year 2, the $31,500 due on a loan (Principal + Accumulated interest) was repaid. The term of the loan was 1 year from December 31, Year 1. The annual interest rate was 5%.
- During Year 2, Knight received $14,000 in cash for services provided to customers.

The following is Knight's income statement for the year ended on December 31, Year 2:

Revenue	$14,000
Depreciation expense ($50,000 ÷ 10)	(5,000)
Interest expense ($30,000 × 5%)	(1,500)
Gain on machine disposal [$47,000 – ($50,000 – $10,000)]	7,000
Net income	**$14,500**

The following are Knight's balance sheets on December 31, Year 1, and December 31, Year 2:

	December 31			December 31	
Current assets	Year 1	Year 2	Current liabilities	Year 1	Year 2
Cash	$10,000	$39,500	Loan	$30,000	$ 0
Fixed assets			Equity		
Machine at cost	50,000	0	Common stock	21,000	21,000
Accumulated depreciation	(5,000)	0	Retained earnings	4,000	18,500
Net fixed assets	$45,000	$ 0			
Total assets	$55,000	$39,500	Total liability and equity	$55,000	$39,500

a. The direct method presents the gross operating cash receipts and payments.

Knight's Statement of Cash Flows for the Year Ended on December 31, Year 2
(Using the direct method)

Cash flows from operating activities:		
Cash received from customers	$14,000	
Interest paid	(1,500)	
Net cash provided by operating activities		**$ 12,500**
Cash flows from investing activities:		
Proceeds from sale of machine	47,000	
Net cash provided by investing activities		**$ 47,000**
Cash flows from financing activities:		
Repayment of loan	(30,000)	
Net cash used in financing activities		**$(30,000)**
Net increase in cash during the year		**$ 29,500**
Cash at beginning of year		10,000
Cash at end of year		**$ 39,500**

-- Continued on next page --

EXAMPLE 17-3 -- Continued

b. Under the indirect method, the net cash flow from operating activities is determined by adjusting net income for the period.

Knight's Statement of Cash Flows for the Year Ended on December 31, Year 2
(Using the indirect method)

Cash flows from operating activities:			
Net income		$ 14,500	
Depreciation expense	$ 5,000		(1)
Gain on sale of machine	(7,000)		(2)
Total adjustments		(2,000)	
Net cash provided by operating activities		**$ 12,500**	
Cash flows from investing activities:			
Proceeds from sale of machine	47,000		
Net cash provided by investing activities		**$ 47,000**	
Cash flows from financing activities:			
Repayment of loan	(30,000)		
Net cash used in financing activities		**$(30,000)**	
Net increase in cash		**$ 29,500**	
Cash at beginning of year		10,000	
Cash at end of year		**$ 39,500**	

Explanation:

(1) **Depreciation expense** is a noncash expense included in net income. Thus, it must be added to net income to determine the net cash flow from operating activities.

(2) **Gain on sale of machine** is an item included in net income. Its cash effect is related to investing activities. Thus, it must be subtracted from net income to determine the net cash flow from operating activities.

SUCCESS TIP

The following rules will help you to reconcile net income to net cash flow from operating activities under the indirect method:

Noncash losses and expenses included in net income	Added to net income
Losses and expenses whose cash effects are related to investing or financing cash flows	Added to net income
Noncash gains and revenues included in net income	Subtracted from net income
Gains and revenues whose cash effects are related to investing or financing cash flows	Subtracted from net income

STOP & REVIEW

You have completed the outline for this subunit.
Study multiple-choice questions 10 through 13 beginning on page 535.

17.4 DIRECT AND INDIRECT METHODS -- EXTENDED EXAMPLES

EXAMPLE 17-4 Indirect Presentation

Dice Corp's consolidated balance sheet accounts as of December 31, Year 6 and Year 5, are presented below. Information relating to Year 6 activities is to the left.

Information Relating to Year 6 Activities

- Cash dividends of $240,000 were declared and paid by Dice in Year 6.
- The accounts receivable balances at the beginning and end of Year 6 were net of allowances for credit losses of $50,000 and $60,000, respectively. Dice wrote off $40,000 of accounts receivable during Year 6.
- Current investments consist of Treasury bills maturing on 6/30/Year 7. They were acquired for cash on December 31, Year 6.
- Equipment costing $400,000 and having a carrying amount of $140,000 was sold on January 1, Year 6, for $150,000 in cash. Additional plant assets were purchased in Year 6 for cash.
- Dice accounts for its interest in Thrice Corp. under the equity method. Its equity in Thrice's Year 6 earnings was $25,000. During Year 6, Dice received a $10,000 cash dividend from Thrice. At the end of Year 6, Dice sold part of its investment in Thrice for $135,000 in cash. Significant influence over Thrice was not lost as a result of the sale.
- The provision for Year 6 income taxes was $210,000.
- 10,000 shares of common stock were issued in Year 6 for $22 a share.

	December 31	
Assets	Year 6	Year 5
Cash	$ 195,000	$ 100,000
Current investments	300,000	0
Accounts receivable (net)	480,000	510,000
Inventory	680,000	600,000
Prepaid expenses	15,000	20,000
Equity method investment	215,000	300,000
Plant assets	1,730,000	1,000,000
Accumulated depreciation	(480,000)	(450,000)
Goodwill	90,000	100,000
Total assets	$3,225,000	$2,180,000
Liabilities and Equity		
Accounts payable	$ 825,000	$ 720,000
Interest payable	15,000	10,000
Income tax payable	20,000	30,000
Current debt	325,000	0
Deferred taxes	250,000	300,000
Common stock, $10 par	800,000	700,000
Additional paid-in capital	370,000	250,000
Retained earnings	620,000	170,000
Total liabilities and equity	$3,225,000	$2,180,000

The following computations are necessary to determine the net cash flows from operating, investing, and financing activities:

a. **Net income.** The starting point for presenting the net cash flow from operating activities is net income (loss) for the period. Net income can be calculated as follows:

Ending retained earnings	$620,000
Dividends declared	240,000
Beginning retained earnings	(170,000)
Year 6, net income	**$690,000**

1) The $240,000 of cash dividends paid in Year 6 are a cash outflow from financing activities.

-- Continued on next page --

EXAMPLE 17-4 -- Continued

b. **Accounts receivable.** The easiest way to determine the reconciling adjustment for accounts receivable is to calculate the change in their net amount (Accounts receivable – Allowance for credit losses). Net accounts receivable are current operating assets. A decrease in net accounts receivable of **$30,000** ($510,000 – $480,000) is **added** to net income to determine the net cash flow from operating activities.

c. **Plant assets.** The items that affect the presentation of cash flow from operating activities are depreciation expense, gain or loss on disposal, and impairment loss.

1) **Depreciation expense** for Year 6 can be calculated as follows:

Ending accumulated depreciation	$480,000
Accumulated depreciation on items sold	260,000
Beginning accumulated depreciation	(450,000)
Depreciation expense	**$290,000**

Depreciation expense is a noncash expense included in net income. Thus, **$290,000** is **added** to net income in determining the net cash flows from operating activities.

2) The **gain on disposal** of the equipment is **$10,000** ($150,000 cash received – $140,000 carrying amount). The cash effect is related to investing activities. Thus, it is **subtracted** from net income to determine the net cash flow from operating activities.

3) The $150,000 of cash proceeds from sale of equipment is a cash inflow from investing activities.

4) Plant assets purchased in Year 6 (cash outflow from investing activities) can be calculated as follows:

Ending plant assets at cost	$1,730,000
Plant assets sold at cost	400,000
Beginning plant assets at cost	(1,000,000)
Plant assets purchased	**$1,130,000**

NOTE: The following equation may be useful for deriving the required information if the data given in the question are for the carrying amount (Cost – Accumulated depreciation) of the PPE item.

Beginning carrying amount	$XXX
Purchases during the period	XXX
Depreciation expense	(XXX)
Disposals during the period	(XXX)
Ending carrying amount	**$XXX**

-- Continued on next page --

EXAMPLE 17-4 -- Continued

d. **Equity-method investment.** The carrying amount of the equity-method investment sold can be calculated as follows:

Beginning carrying amount	$300,000
Equity in Thrice's current year earnings	25,000
Dividends received from Thrice	(10,000)
Ending carrying amount	(215,000)
Carrying amount of investment sold	**$100,000**

1) **The gain on sale of the investment is $35,000** ($135,000 cash received – $100,000 carrying amount). The cash effect is related to investing activities. Thus, it is **subtracted** from net income in determining the net cash flows from operating activities.

2) **Undistributed earnings on equity-method investment.** Under the equity method, the investor's share of the investee's earnings is debited to the investment account and credited to income. A cash dividend from the investee is a return of an investment that results in a debit to cash and a credit to the investment. The undistributed earnings on the equity-method investments equal **$15,000** ($25,000 share in earnings – $10,000 dividends received). This amount is a noncash revenue included in net income. Thus, it is **subtracted** from net income in determining the net cash flow from operating activities.

3) The cash received on the sale of the investment of $135,000 is a cash inflow from investing activities.

e. **Goodwill.** Goodwill is not amortized. Thus, the **$10,000** decrease in the amount of goodwill ($100,000 beginning balance – $90,000 ending balance) must be a result of impairment. A loss on impairment of goodwill is a noncash loss included in net income. Thus, it is **added** to net income in determining the net cash flow from operating activities.

f. **Current investments.** The purchase of current investments for $300,000 is a cash outflow from investing activities.

g. **Common stock.** The proceeds from issuing common stock were $220,000 (10,000 × $22). This cash inflow from financing activities equals the sum of the increases in the common stock and additional paid-in capital accounts.

h. **Inventory** is a current operating asset. Inventory increased by **$80,000** ($680,000 – $600,000). This amount is **subtracted** from net income in determining the net cash flow from operating activities.

i. **Prepaid expenses** are current operating assets. Prepaid expenses decreased by **$5,000** ($15,000 – $20,000). This amount is **added** to net income in determining the net cash flow from operating activities.

j. **Accounts payable** is a current operating liability. Accounts payable increased by **$105,000** ($825,000 – $720,000). This amount is **added** to net income in determining the net cash flow from operating activities.

k. **Interest payable** is a current operating liability. Interest payable increased by **$5,000** ($15,000 – $10,000). This amount is **added** to net income in determining the net cash flow from operating activities.

l. **Income tax payable** is a current operating liability. Income tax payable decreased by **$10,000** ($20,000 – $30,000). This amount is **subtracted** from net income in determining the net cash flow from operating activities.

m. **Current debt.** The issuance of $325,000 of current debt ($325,000 – $0) is a cash inflow from financing activities.

n. The **deferred tax liability** decreased by **$50,000** ($250,000 – $300,000). The decrease in the deferred tax liability increases net income by decreasing income tax expense. This decrease is a noncash item included in net income. Thus, it is **subtracted** from net income in determining the net cash flow from operating activities.

-- Continued on next page --

EXAMPLE 17-4 -- Continued

Dice Corp.
Consolidated Statement of Cash Flows -- Indirect Method
for the Year Ended December 31, Year 6

Cash flows from operating activities:			
Net income for Year 6	$ 690,000	a.	
Decrease in accounts receivable	30,000	b.	
Depreciation expense	290,000	c1.	
Gain on disposal of equipment	(10,000)	c2.	
Gain on sale of investment	(35,000)	d1.	
Undistributed earnings of equity-method investment	(15,000)	d2.	
Loss on impairment of goodwill	10,000	e.	
Increase in inventories	(80,000)	h.	
Decrease in prepaid expenses	5,000	i.	
Increase in accounts payable	105,000	j.	
Increase in interest payable	5,000	k.	
Decrease in income tax payable	(10,000)	l.	
Decrease in deferred tax liability	(50,000)	n.	
Net cash provided by operating activities			**$ 935,000**
Cash flows from investing activities:			
Proceeds from sale of equipment	$ 150,000	c3.	
Purchases of plant assets	(1,130,000)	c4.	
Proceeds from sale of equity-method investment	135,000	d3.	
Purchases of current investments	(300,000)	f.	
Net cash used in investing activities			**$(1,145,000)**
Cash flows from financing activities:			
Dividends paid	$ (240,000)	a1.	
Proceeds from issuing common stock	220,000	g.	
Proceeds from current debt	325,000	m.	
Net cash provided by financing activities			**$ 305,000**
Net increase in cash			$ 95,000
Cash, beginning of year			100,000
Cash, end of year			**$ 195,000**

EXAMPLE 17-5 Direct Presentation

Additional information. Additional facts from Dice Corp.'s income statement for the year ended December 31, Year 6, are given below. These facts and the indirect presentation analysis from Example 17-4 are necessary to derive the amounts of the major classes of gross operating cash inflows and outflows required in a direct presentation.

Income Statement

Sales	$7,840,000
Cost of sales	(5,500,000)
Depreciation and impairment loss	(300,000)
Selling, general, administrative expenses	(1,100,000)
Interest expense	(140,000)
Equity in earnings of affiliate	25,000
Gain on disposal of equipment	10,000
Gain on sale of investments	35,000
Interest income	30,000
Income before income taxes	$ 900,000
Income tax expense	(210,000)
Net income	$ 690,000

a. **Cash collected from customers.** The beginning gross accounts receivable balance was $560,000 ($510,000 net beginning accounts receivable + $50,000 beginning allowance for credit losses). The ending gross accounts receivable balance was $540,000 ($480,000 net ending accounts receivable + $60,000 ending allowance for credit losses). Accounts receivable written off are recognized as a decrease of accounts receivable and the allowance for credit losses. Thus, in converting accrual basis sales to the amount of cash collected from customers (discussed further in the Gleim Success Tip on page 519), the amount of write-offs must be subtracted to eliminate noncash credits to accounts receivable.

Beginning gross accounts receivable	$ 560,000
Sales	7,840,000
Write-offs	(40,000)
Ending gross accounts receivable	(540,000)
Cash collected from customers	**$7,820,000**

b. **Cash paid to employees and suppliers** is derived as follows:

1) **Credit loss expense** is a noncash item included in selling, general, and administrative expenses and should be subtracted from them. Given that the allowance for credit losses increased by $10,000 ($60,000 – $50,000) despite $40,000 of write-offs, credit loss expense must have been $50,000.
2) An **increase in inventory** means that purchases exceeded cost of sales.
3) An **increase in accounts payable** indicates that purchases exceeded cash paid to suppliers. This amount is subtracted.
4) A **decrease in prepaid expenses** signifies recognition of a noncash expense related to a prior-period cash payment. Accordingly, this amount is subtracted.

-- Continued on next page --

EXAMPLE 17-5 -- Continued

Cost of sales		$5,500,000
Selling, general, administrative expenses	$1,100,000	
Noncash expense (credit loss)	(50,000)	
Net cash expenses		1,050,000
Inventory (12/31/Year 5)	$ (600,000)	
Inventory (12/31/Year 6)	680,000	
Net inventory increase from operations		80,000
Accounts payable (12/31/Year 5)	$ 720,000	
Accounts payable (12/31/Year 6)	(825,000)	
Net increase in accounts payable		(105,000)
Prepaid expenses (12/31/Year 5)	$ (20,000)	
Prepaid expenses (12/31/Year 6)	15,000	
Net decrease in prepaid expenses		(5,000)
Cash paid to employees and suppliers		**$6,520,000**

c. The cash dividend of $10,000 received, not the equity-based earnings recognized in net income, is included.

d. Interest income was $30,000. Given no interest receivable, cash interest collected also must have been $30,000.

e. The amount of interest paid can be calculated as follows (also discussed further in the Gleim Success Tip on page 519):

Beginning interest payable	$ 10,000
Interest expense	140,000
Ending interest payable	(15,000)
Interest paid	**$135,000**

f. Income taxes paid equaled tax expense ($210,000), plus the decrease in deferred taxes ($50,000), plus the decrease in taxes payable ($10,000), or $270,000.

NOTE: The amounts and the presentation of cash flows from investing and financing activities are the same regardless of whether the statement is presented according to direct or indirect method.

-- Continued on next page --

EXAMPLE 17-5 -- Continued

Dice Corp.
Consolidated Statement of Cash Flows -- Direct Method
for the Year Ended December 31, Year 6

Cash flows from operating activities:			
Cash collected from customers	$7,820,000	a.	
Cash paid to employees and suppliers	(6,520,000)	b.	
Cash dividend received	10,000	c.	
Interest received	30,000	d.	
Interest paid	(135,000)	e.	
Income taxes paid	(270,000)	f.	
Net cash provided by operating activities			**$ 935,000**
Cash flows from investing activities:			
Proceeds from sale of equipment	$ 150,000		
Proceeds from sale of equity-method investments	135,000		
Purchases of current investments	(300,000)		
Purchases of plant assets	(1,130,000)		
Net cash used in investing activities			**(1,145,000)**
Cash flows from financing activities:			
Proceeds from current debt	$ 325,000		
Proceeds from issuing common stock	220,000		
Dividends paid	(240,000)		
Net cash provided by financing activities			**305,000**
Net increase in cash			$ 95,000
Cash, beginning of year			100,000
Cash, end of year			**$ 195,000**

The difference between the direct and indirect method is the determination of operating cash flows. Compare the direct method format presented above with the indirect method format on page 527. The only difference is in how the $935,000 of cash provided by operations is calculated.

Dice Corp. has no noncash investing and financing transactions to report in supplemental disclosures.

STOP & REVIEW

You have completed the outline for this subunit.
Study multiple-choice questions 14 through 20 beginning on page 537.

QUESTIONS

17.1 Statement of Cash Flows -- Classifications

1. The primary purpose of a statement of cash flows is to provide relevant information about

A. Differences between net income and associated cash receipts and disbursements.

B. An entity's ability to generate future positive net cash flows.

C. The cash receipts and cash disbursements of an entity during a period.

D. An entity's ability to meet cash operating needs.

Answer (C) is correct.

REQUIRED: The primary purpose of a statement of cash flows.

DISCUSSION: The primary purpose is to provide information about the cash receipts and cash payments of a business entity during a period. This information helps investors, creditors, and other users to assess the entity's ability to generate net cash inflows, meet its obligations, pay dividends, and secure external financing. It also helps assess reasons for the differences between net income and net cash flow and the effects of cash and noncash financing and investing activities.

2. In a statement of cash flows, interest payments to lenders and other creditors should be classified as cash outflows for

A. Operating activities.

B. Borrowing activities.

C. Lending activities.

D. Financing activities.

Answer (A) is correct.

REQUIRED: The classification of interest payments to lenders and other creditors.

DISCUSSION: Cash receipts from sales of goods and services, interest on loans, and dividends on equity securities are from operating activities. Cash payments to (1) suppliers for inventory; (2) employees for services; (3) other suppliers for other goods and services; (4) governments for taxes, duties, fines, and fees; and (5) lenders for interest are also from operating activities.

Answer (B) is incorrect. Borrowing is not among the three categories of cash flows. **Answer (C) is incorrect.** Lending is not among the three categories of cash flows. **Answer (D) is incorrect.** Financing activities include (1) issuance of stock, (2) payment of distributions to owners, (3) treasury stock transactions, (4) issuance of debt, (5) repayment or other settlement of debt obligations, and (6) receipt of resources donor-restricted for long-term purposes.

3. In a statement of cash flows, payments to acquire debt instruments of other entities (other than cash equivalents and debt instruments acquired specifically for resale) should be classified as cash outflows for

A. Operating activities.

B. Investing activities.

C. Financing activities.

D. Lending activities.

Answer (B) is correct.

REQUIRED: The proper classification of payments.

DISCUSSION: Investing activities include the lending of money; the collection of those loans; and the acquisition, sale, or other disposal of (1) loans and other securities that are not cash equivalents and that have not been acquired specifically for resale and (2) property, plant, equipment, and other productive assets.

Answer (A) is incorrect. Operating activities are transactions and other events not classified as investing and financing activities. In general, the cash effects of operating activities (other than gains and losses) enter into the determination of income from continuing operations. **Answer (C) is incorrect.** Financing activities include the issuance of stock, the payment of dividends and other distributions to owners, treasury stock transactions, the issuance of debt, and the repayment or other settlement of debt obligations. It also includes receiving restricted resources that by donor stipulation must be used for long-term purposes. **Answer (D) is incorrect.** Cash flows result from investing, financing, or operating activities.

17.2 Statement of Cash Flows -- Calculations

4. Paper Co. had net income of $70,000 during the year. Dividend payment was $10,000. The following information is available:

Mortgage repayment	$20,000
Available-for-sale securities purchased	10,000 increase
Bonds payable-issued	50,000 increase
Inventory	40,000 increase
Accounts payable	30,000 decrease

What amount should Paper report as net cash provided by operating activities in its statement of cash flows for the year?

A. $0

B. $10,000

C. $20,000

D. $30,000

Answer (A) is correct.

REQUIRED: The net cash provided by operating activities.

DISCUSSION: The payment of dividends, the repayment of debt (the mortgage), and the issuance of debt (the bonds) are financing activities. The purchase of debt or equity instruments the (available-for-sale securities) is an investing activity. Operating cash flows exclude these financing and investing cash flows. Moreover, these items do not affect net income. Consequently, net cash provided by operating activities can be determined by adjusting net income for the changes in inventory and accounts payable. To account for the difference between cost of goods sold (a deduction from income) and cash paid to suppliers, a two-step adjustment is necessary. The difference between cost of goods sold and purchases is the change in inventory. The difference between purchases and the amount paid to suppliers is the change in accounts payable. Accordingly, the conversion of cost of goods sold to cash paid to suppliers requires subtracting the inventory increase and the accounts payable decrease. The net cash provided by operating activities is therefore $0 ($70,000 net income – $40,000 inventory increase – $30,000 accounts payable decrease).

Answer (B) is incorrect. The amount of $10,000 is the difference between the bond proceeds and the sum of the cash outflows for dividends paid, the mortgage repayment, and the securities purchase. **Answer (C) is incorrect.** The amount of $20,000 equals net income minus the bond proceeds. **Answer (D) is incorrect.** The amount of $30,000 equals net income minus the inventory increase.

5. New England Co. had net cash provided by operating activities of $351,000, net cash used by investing activities of $420,000, and cash provided by financing activities of $250,000. New England's cash balance was $27,000 on January 1. During the year, there was a sale of land that resulted in a gain of $25,000, and proceeds of $40,000 were received from the sale. What was New England's cash balance at the end of the year?

A. $27,000

B. $40,000

C. $208,000

D. $248,000

Answer (C) is correct.

REQUIRED: The cash balance at year end.

DISCUSSION: The cash balance at year end is $208,000 ($27,000 on January 1 + $351,000 provided by operations – $420,000 used by investing activities + $250,000 provided by financing activities). The proceeds from the land sale are included in the calculation of the cash used by investing activities.

Answer (A) is incorrect. The amount of $27,000 represents the cash balance on January 1. **Answer (B) is incorrect.** The amount of $40,000 equals the proceeds from the sale of land. **Answer (D) is incorrect.** The amount of $248,000 results from double-counting the land sale proceeds.

6. Green Co. had the following transactions at December 31:

Cash proceeds from sale of investment in bonds of Blue Co. classified as available-for-sale (carrying amount = $60,000)	$75,000
Dividends received on Grey Co. stock	10,500
Common stock purchased from Brown Co.	38,000

What amount should Green recognize as net cash from investing activities in its statement of cash flows at December 31?

A. $37,000

B. $47,500

C. $75,000

D. $85,500

Answer (A) is correct.

REQUIRED: The amount of net cash flows from investing activities.

DISCUSSION: The sale proceeds of available-for-sale debt securities ($75,000) are a cash inflow from an investing activity. Cash outflows from acquiring equity instruments ($38,000) also are from an investing activity. But cash inflows from operating activities include cash receipts in the form of dividends ($10,500). Thus, the net cash flow from investing activities is $37,000 ($75,000 – $38,000).

Answer (B) is incorrect. Cash inflows from operating activities include cash receipts in the form of dividends ($10,500). **Answer (C) is incorrect.** The purchase of common stock, a cash outflow of $38,000, is an investing activity. **Answer (D) is incorrect.** The purchase of common stock, a cash outflow of $38,000, is an investing activity. Cash inflows from operating activities include cash receipts in the form of dividends ($10,500).

Questions 7 and 8 are based on the following information. Kollar Corp.'s transactions for the year ended December 31, Year 6, included the following:

- Purchased real estate for $550,000 cash borrowed from a bank
- Sold available-for-sale debt securities for $500,000
- Paid dividends of $600,000
- Issued 500 shares of common stock for $250,000
- Purchased machinery and equipment for $125,000 cash
- Paid $450,000 toward a bank loan
- Reduced accounts receivable by $100,000
- Increased accounts payable by $200,000

7. Kollar's net cash used in investing activities for Year 6 was

A. $675,000

B. $375,000

C. $175,000

D. $50,000

Answer (C) is correct.

REQUIRED: The net cash used in investing activities.

DISCUSSION: The purchases of real estate and of machinery and equipment were uses of cash in investing activities. The sale of available-for-sale debt securities provided cash from an investing activity. Consequently, the net cash used in investing activities was $175,000 ($550,000 – $500,000 + $125,000). The reduction in accounts receivable and the increase in accounts payable were operating activities.

Answer (A) is incorrect. The amount of $675,000 omits the sale of securities. **Answer (B) is incorrect.** The amount of $375,000 results from either (1) improperly including the increase in accounts payable, a noncash transaction, as a use of cash in an investing activity ($550,000 cash borrowed – $500,000 sale of securities + $125,000 purchase of machinery + $200,000 increase in accounts payable) or (2) improperly calculating the net cash used in investing activities as the difference between the $500,000 sale of securities and the $125,000 purchase of machinery. **Answer (D) is incorrect.** The amount of $50,000 does not include the purchase of machinery and equipment.

8. Kollar's net cash used in financing activities for Year 6 was

A. $50,000

B. $250,000

C. $450,000

D. $500,000

Answer (B) is correct.

REQUIRED: The net cash used in financing activities.

DISCUSSION: The dividend payment and the payment of the bank loan were uses of cash in financing activities. The borrowing from the bank and the issuance of stock provided cash from financing activities. Thus, the net cash used in financing activities was $250,000 ($600,000 – $550,000 – $250,000 + $450,000).

Answer (A) is incorrect. The amount of $50,000 omits the issuance of stock and the repayment of the bank loan. **Answer (C) is incorrect.** The amount of $450,000 results from including the increase in accounts payable, a noncash transaction, as a use of cash in a financing activity. **Answer (D) is incorrect.** The amount of $500,000 excludes the issuance of stock.

9. Fara Co. reported bonds payable of $47,000 on December 31, Year 1, and $50,000 on December 31, Year 2. During Year 2, Fara issued $20,000 of bonds payable in exchange for equipment. There was no amortization of bond premium or discount during the year. What amount should Fara report in its Year 2 statement of cash flows for redemption of bonds payable?

A. $3,000

B. $17,000

C. $20,000

D. $23,000

Answer (B) is correct.

REQUIRED: The amount reported in the statement of cash flows for redemption of bonds payable.

DISCUSSION: Assuming no amortization of premium or discount, the net amount of bonds payable reported was affected solely by the issuance of bonds for equipment and the redemption of bonds. Given that $20,000 of bonds were issued and that the amount reported increased by only $3,000, $17,000 of bonds must have been redeemed. This amount should be reported in the statement of cash flows as a cash outflow from a financing activity.

Answer (A) is incorrect. The amount of $3,000 equals the increase in bonds payable. **Answer (C) is incorrect.** The amount of bonds issued is $20,000. **Answer (D) is incorrect.** The amount of $23,000 is the sum of the bonds issued and the increase in bonds payable.

17.3 Direct and Indirect Methods of Presenting Operating Cash Flows

10. Payne Co. prepares its statement of cash flows using the indirect method. Payne's unamortized bond discount account decreased by $25,000 during the year. How should Payne report the change in unamortized bond discount in its statement of cash flows?

A. As a financing cash inflow.

B. As a financing cash outflow.

C. As an addition to net income in the operating activities section.

D. As a subtraction from net income in the operating activities section.

Answer (C) is correct.

REQUIRED: The reporting of a change in unamortized bond discount in a statement of cash flows.

DISCUSSION: The amortization of bond discount (debit interest expense, credit discount) is a noncash item that reduces net income. In a statement of cash flows prepared using the indirect method, net operating cash flow is determined by adjusting net income. The indirect method begins with net income and then removes the effects of (1) deferrals of past operating cash receipts and payments, (2) accruals of estimated future operating cash receipts and payments, and (3) net income items not affecting operating cash flows. Thus, bond discount amortization should be added to net income in the reconciliation to net operating cash flow.

Answer (A) is incorrect. Amortization of bond discount is not a cash flow. **Answer (B) is incorrect.** Amortization of bond discount is not a cash flow. **Answer (D) is incorrect.** The amortization of bond discount is added to net income.

11. Dee's inventory and accounts payable balances at December 31, Year 2, increased over their December 31, Year 1, balances. Should these increases be added to or deducted from cash payments to suppliers to arrive at Year 2 cost of goods sold?

	Increase in Inventory	Increase in Accounts Payable
A.	Added to	Deducted from
B.	Added to	Added to
C.	Deducted from	Deducted from
D.	Deducted from	Added to

Answer (D) is correct.

REQUIRED: The effect of increases in inventory and accounts payable on the reconciliation of cash payments to suppliers to cost of goods sold.

DISCUSSION: A two-step adjustment is needed. The first step is to adjust for the difference between cash paid to suppliers and purchases. Because accounts payable increased, purchases must have been greater than cash paid to suppliers. Thus, the increase in accounts payable is an addition. The second step adjusts for the difference between purchases and cost of goods sold. Given that inventory increased, purchases must have exceeded cost of goods sold. Hence, the increase in inventories is a subtraction.

Question 12 is based on the following information. Royce Company had the following transactions during the fiscal year ended December 31, Year 2:

- Accounts receivable decreased from $115,000 on December 31, Year 1, to $100,000 on December 31, Year 2.
- Royce's board of directors declared dividends on December 31, Year 2, of $.05 per share on the 2.8 million shares outstanding, payable to shareholders of record on January 31, Year 3. The company did not declare or pay dividends for fiscal Year 1.
- Sold a truck with a net carrying amount of $7,000 for $5,000 cash, reporting a loss of $2,000.
- Paid interest to bondholders of $780,000.
- The cash balance was $106,000 on December 31, Year 1, and $284,000 on December 31, Year 2.

12. Royce Company uses the direct method to prepare its statement of cash flows at December 31, Year 2. The interest paid to bondholders is reported in the

A. Financing section, as a use or outflow of cash.

B. Operating section, as a use or outflow of cash.

C. Investing section, as a use or outflow of cash.

D. Debt section, as a use or outflow of cash.

Answer (B) is correct.

REQUIRED: The proper reporting of interest paid.

DISCUSSION: Payment of interest on debt is considered an operating activity, although repayment of debt principal is a financing activity.

Answer (A) is incorrect. Interest paid on bonds is an operating cash flow. **Answer (C) is incorrect.** Investing activities include the lending of money and the acquisition, sale, or other disposal of securities that are not cash equivalents and the acquisition, sale, or other disposal of long-lived productive assets. **Answer (D) is incorrect.** The statement does not have a debt section.

13. How should the amortization of bond discount on long-term debt be reported in a statement of cash flows prepared using the indirect method?

A. As a financing activities inflow.

B. As a financing activities outflow.

C. In operating activities as a deduction from income.

D. In operating activities as an addition to income.

Answer (D) is correct.

REQUIRED: The reporting of bond discount amortization in a statement of cash flows prepared using the indirect method.

DISCUSSION: Amortization of bond discount on long-term debt is presented in the operating activities section as an addition to net income. It is a noncash expense.

Answer (A) is incorrect. Amortization of bond discount is a noncash item presented in operating activities as an addition to income. **Answer (B) is incorrect.** Amortization of bond discount is a noncash item presented in operating activities as an addition to income. **Answer (C) is incorrect.** Amortization of bond discount is an addition to income. It is a noncash expense.

17.4 Direct and Indirect Methods -- Extended Examples

Questions 14 and 15 are based on the following information. Flax Corp. uses the direct method to prepare its statement of cash flows. Flax's trial balances at December 31, Year 6 and Year 5, are as follows:

Debits	December 31 Year 6	Year 5
Cash	$ 35,000	$ 32,000
Accounts receivable	33,000	30,000
Inventory	31,000	47,000
Property, plant, & equipment	100,000	95,000
Unamortized bond discount	4,500	5,000
Cost of goods sold	250,000	380,000
Selling expenses	141,500	172,000
General and administrative expenses	137,000	151,300
Interest expense	4,300	2,600
Income tax expense	20,400	61,200
	$756,700	$976,100

Credits	December 31 Year 6	Year 5
Allowance for credit losses	$ 1,300	$ 1,100
Accumulated depreciation	16,500	15,000
Trade accounts payable	25,000	17,500
Income taxes payable	21,000	27,100
Deferred income taxes	5,300	4,600
8% callable bonds payable	45,000	20,000
Common stock	50,000	40,000
Additional paid-in capital	9,100	7,500
Retained earnings	44,700	64,600
Sales	538,800	778,700
	$756,700	$976,100

- Flax purchased $5,000 in equipment during Year 6.
- Flax allocated one-third of its depreciation expense to selling expenses and the remainder to general and administrative expenses, which include the provision for credit losses.

14. What amount should Flax report in its statement of cash flows for the year ended December 31, Year 6, for cash collected from customers?

A. $541,800

B. $541,600

C. $536,000

D. $535,800

Answer (D) is correct.

REQUIRED: The cash collected from customers.

DISCUSSION: Collections from customers equal sales minus the increase in gross accounts receivable, or $535,800 ($538,800 – $33,000 + $30,000).

Answer (A) is incorrect. The amount of $541,800 results from adding the increase in receivables. **Answer (B) is incorrect.** The amount of $541,600 results from adding the increase in receivables and subtracting the increase in the allowance for credit losses, that is, from adding net accounts receivable. **Answer (C) is incorrect.** The amount of $536,000 results from subtracting net accounts receivable, a procedure that is appropriate when reconciling net income to net operating cash flow, not sales to cash collected from customers.

15. What amount should Flax report in its statement of cash flows for the year ended December 31, Year 6, for cash paid for income taxes?

A. $25,800

B. $20,400

C. $19,700

D. $15,000

Answer (A) is correct.

REQUIRED: The cash paid for income taxes.

DISCUSSION: To reconcile income tax expense to cash paid for income taxes, a two-step adjustment is needed. The first step is to add the decrease in income taxes payable. The second step is to subtract the increase in deferred income taxes. Hence, cash paid for income taxes equals $25,800 [$20,400 + ($27,100 – $21,000) – ($5,300 – $4,600)].

Answer (B) is incorrect. The amount of $20,400 is income tax expense. **Answer (C) is incorrect.** The amount of $19,700 equals income tax expense minus the increase in deferred income taxes. **Answer (D) is incorrect.** The amount of $15,000 results from subtracting the decrease in income taxes payable and adding the increase in deferred taxes payable.

Questions 16 and 17 are based on the following information. Royce Company had the following transactions during the fiscal year ended December 31, Year 2:

- Accounts receivable decreased from $115,000 on December 31, Year 1, to $100,000 on December 31, Year 2.
- Royce's board of directors declared dividends on December 31, Year 2, of $.05 per share on the 2.8 million shares outstanding, payable to shareholders of record on January 31, Year 3. The company did not declare or pay dividends for fiscal Year 1.
- Sold a truck with a net carrying amount of $7,000 for $5,000 cash, reporting a loss of $2,000.
- Paid interest to bondholders of $780,000.
- The cash balance was $106,000 on December 31, Year 1, and $284,000 on December 31, Year 2.

16. Royce Company uses the indirect method to prepare its Year 2 statement of cash flows. It reports a(n)

A. Source or inflow of funds of $5,000 from the sale of the truck in the financing section.

B. Use or outflow of funds of $140,000 in the financing section, representing dividends.

C. Deduction of $15,000 in the operating section, representing the decrease in year-end accounts receivable.

D. Addition of $2,000 in the operating section for the $2,000 loss on the sale of the truck.

Answer (D) is correct.

REQUIRED: The correct presentation of an item on a statement of cash flows prepared under the indirect method.

DISCUSSION: The indirect method determines net operating cash flow by adjusting net income for items that did not affect cash. Under the indirect method, the $5,000 cash inflow from the sale of the truck is shown in the investing section. A $2,000 loss was recognized and properly subtracted to determine net income. This loss, however, did not require the use of cash and should be added to net income in the operating section.

Answer (A) is incorrect. The $5,000 inflow is reported in the investing section. **Answer (B) is incorrect.** No outflow of cash dividends occurred in Year 2. **Answer (C) is incorrect.** The decrease in receivables should be added to net income.

17. The total of cash provided (used) by operating activities plus cash provided (used) by investing activities plus cash provided (used) by financing activities is

A. Cash provided of $284,000.

B. Cash provided of $178,000.

C. Cash used of $582,000.

D. Equal to net income reported for fiscal year ended December 31, Year 2.

Answer (B) is correct.

REQUIRED: The net total of cash provided and used.

DISCUSSION: The total of cash provided (used) by the three activities (operating, investing, and financing) should equal the increase or decrease in cash for the year. During Year 2, the cash balance increased from $106,000 to $284,000. Thus, the sources of cash must have exceeded the uses by $178,000.

Answer (A) is incorrect. The amount of $284,000 is the ending cash balance, not the change in the cash balance. It ignores the beginning balance. **Answer (C) is incorrect.** The cash balance increased during the year. **Answer (D) is incorrect.** Net income must be adjusted for noncash expenses and other accruals and deferrals.

18. Metro, Inc., reported net income of $150,000 for the current year. Changes occurred in several balance sheet accounts during the current year as follows:

Investment in Videogold, Inc., stock, all of which was acquired in the previous year, carried on the equity basis	$5,500 increase
Accumulated depreciation, caused by major repair to projection equipment	2,100 decrease
Premium on bonds payable	1,400 decrease
Deferred income tax liability (long-term)	1,800 increase

In Metro's current-year cash flow statement, the reported net cash provided by operating activities should be

A. $150,400

B. $148,300

C. $144,900

D. $142,800

Answer (C) is correct.

REQUIRED: The net cash provided by operating activities.

DISCUSSION: The increase in the equity-based investment reflects the investor's share of the investee's net income after adjustment for dividends received. Thus, it is a noncash revenue and should be subtracted in the reconciliation of net income to net operating cash inflow. A major repair provides benefits to more than one period and therefore should not be expensed. One method of accounting for a major repair is to charge accumulated depreciation if the useful life of the asset has been extended, with the offsetting credit to cash, a payable, etc. However, the cash outflow, if any, is from an investing activity. The item has no effect on net income and no adjustment is necessary. Amortization of bond premium is a noncash income statement item that reduces accrual-basis expenses and therefore must be subtracted from net income to arrive at net cash flow from operating activities. The increase in the deferred tax liability is a noncash item that reduces net income and should be added in the reconciliation. Accordingly, net cash provided by operations is $144,900 ($150,000 – $5,500 – $1,400 + $1,800).

Answer (A) is incorrect. The amount of $150,400 results from omitting the adjustment for the equity-based investment. **Answer (B) is incorrect.** The amount of $148,300 results from omitting the adjustment for the equity-based investment and improperly subtracting the decrease in accumulated depreciation. **Answer (D) is incorrect.** The amount of $142,800 results from improperly subtracting the decrease in accumulated depreciation.

19. Savor Co. had $100,000 in cash-basis pretax income for Year 2. At December 31, Year 2, accounts receivable had increased by $10,000 and accounts payable had decreased by $6,000 from their December 31, Year 1, balances. Compared to the accrual basis method of accounting, Savor's cash pretax income is

A. Higher by $4,000.

B. Lower by $4,000.

C. Higher by $16,000.

D. Lower by $16,000.

Answer (D) is correct.

REQUIRED: The relation of cash pretax income and accrual-basis pretax income.

DISCUSSION: The increase in accounts receivable indicates that cash-basis pretax income is $10,000 lower than accrual-basis pretax income. Revenues from the increase in receivables are reported as earned in an earlier period (Year 2) than the future related cash inflows. The decrease in accounts payable indicates that cash-basis pretax income is $6,000 lower than accrual-basis pretax income. The cash outflows related to the increase in payables occurred in Year 2, but the related expense was accrued in Year 1. Hence, cash pretax income is lower than accrual-basis income by $16,000.

Answer (A) is incorrect. The increase in receivables indicates that cash-basis pretax income is lower than accrual-basis pretax income. **Answer (B) is incorrect.** The decrease in accounts payable indicates that cash-basis pretax income is lower than accrual-basis pretax income. **Answer (C) is incorrect.** The increases in receivables and payables both indicate that cash-basis pretax income is lower than accrual-basis pretax income.

20. Tam Co. reported the following items in its year-end financial statements:

Capital expenditures	$1,000,000
Finance lease payments	125,000
Income taxes paid	325,000
Dividends paid	200,000
Net interest payments	220,000

What amount should Tam report as supplemental disclosures in its statement of cash flows prepared using the indirect method?

A. $545,000

B. $745,000

C. $1,125,000

D. $1,870,000

Answer (A) is correct.

REQUIRED: The amount of supplemental disclosures in a statement of cash flows prepared using the indirect method.

DISCUSSION: If an entity uses the indirect method to present its statement of cash flows, the interest paid (excluding amounts capitalized) and income taxes paid must be disclosed. The sum of these amounts is $545,000 ($220,000 + $325,000).

Answer (B) is incorrect. Dividends paid ($200,000) are not required to be included in the supplemental disclosures when the indirect method is used. **Answer (C) is incorrect.** The total of capital expenditures and finance lease payments is $1,125,000. **Answer (D) is incorrect.** The sum of all listed items is $1,870,000.

STUDY UNIT EIGHTEEN

GOVERNMENTAL ACCOUNTING -- MODIFIED ACCRUAL

(36 pages of outline)

Study Units 18 and 19 relate to state and local governments. Study Unit 18 is an overview of (1) the basic accounting system used by state and local governments, (2) the recognition rules and journal entries for financing activities, and (3) the content of the Comprehensive Annual Financial Report (CAFR).

18.1 REPORTING ENTITY, BASIS OF ACCOUNTING, AND FUNDS

BACKGROUND 18-1 GASB Hierarchy

The Governmental Accounting Standards Board (GASB) establishes GAAP for state and local governments in the U.S. The following is the hierarchy of authoritative GAAP:

1. GASB statements of Governmental Accounting Standards (GASBSs)
2. GASB technical bulletins, GASB implementation guides, and AICPA guidance cleared by the GASB

1. **Accountability Objective**
   a. Accountability is the primary objective of all governmental financial reporting. It is based on the public's right to know.
      1) **Fiscal accountability** is the responsibility of a government to justify that its actions comply with public decisions about obtaining and expending public resources in the short term.
      2) **Operational accountability** is the responsibility to report the extent to which accounting objectives have been met efficiently and effectively using available resources.
         a) It is also the responsibility to report whether those objectives can be met for the foreseeable future.
      3) **Interperiod equity** is a significant part of accountability. Financial resources received during a period should suffice to pay for the services provided during that period. Moreover, debt should be repaid during the period of usefulness of the assets acquired.
         a) Thus, governmental reporting should help users assess whether future taxpayers must pay for services already provided.
         b) Governmental reporting also should help users (e.g., citizens, lawmakers, and oversight bodies) to make economic, political, and social decisions.
            i) For example, revenue forecasts may help advocates for (or opponents of) spending for education or transportation.

2. **The Reporting Entity**

   a. **Financial accountability** is the primary criterion for defining the reporting entity.

   b. The reporting entity consists of the primary government and its component units.

      1) The **primary government** is financially accountable for the entities that make up its legal entity and certain other entities.

         a) Any state or general-purpose local government qualifies as a primary government.

         b) **Special-purpose governments (SPGs)** (such as school systems or fire departments) are legally separate entities that are primary governments or component units.

            i) Primary governments are required to be legally and fiscally independent and have a separately elected governing body.

         c) If an SPG is engaged in **one governmental program** (e.g., an assessment or drainage district), it may combine the government-wide and fund statements (listed in Subunit 18.3).

         d) If an SPG is engaged only in **business-type activities**, it reports the statements for **enterprise funds**. If it is engaged only in fiduciary activities, it reports the statements for **fiduciary funds**.

            i) **Public colleges and universities** must apply the guidance for special-purpose governments.

   c. A **component unit** is a legally separate organization for which the primary government is financially accountable.

      1) **Financial accountability** means that the primary government

         a) Appoints a voting majority of the governing body of the separate organization and

         b) Can impose its will on, or has a potential financial benefit or burden relationship with, the separate organization.

      2) Financial accountability also exists if the separate organization (a) is **financially dependent** on the primary government and (b) has a financial benefit or burden relationship with the primary government.

         a) For example, assume that a water district is financially dependent because a county must approve the issuance of its bonds. But if the district does not receive a subsidy from, or provide resources to, the county, it has no financial benefit or burden relationship with the primary government. Thus, in this example, the district is not a component unit of the county, even though its budget is fiscally dependent on the county.

d. A separate organization also must be treated as a component unit if its exclusion would cause the financial statements to be **misleading**.

e. **Reporting Component Units**

  1) The financial statements of the reporting entity should include information from all component units.

    a) This information should include the totals that would have been included in component unit statements.

  2) The statements of the reporting entity should **distinguish** between the primary government and most of its component units in a way that does not suggest that they are one legal entity.

    a) For this purpose, the government-wide financial statements should report information about **discretely** (individually) presented component units in separate rows and columns.

      i) The **equity interest** in a component unit must be reported as an **asset**.

    b) Information about fiduciary component units is reported only in the **fiduciary fund statements** of the primary government.

  3) But component units that are, in substance, the same as the primary government are reported using the **blending method**. Their balances and transactions are reported similarly to those of the primary government in the government-wide and fund statements.

    a) The primary government's **general fund** is the only general fund reported.

      i) The general fund of a blended component unit is reported as a **special revenue fund** of the primary government.

    b) Blending is appropriate only if

      i) The component unit's governing body is substantively the same as the primary government's, or

      ii) The component unit exclusively or almost exclusively benefits the primary government.

    c) Moreover, the primary government must have a financial benefit or burden relationship with the component unit or operational responsibility for it.

3. **Basis of Accounting -- Financial Statements of Governmental Funds**

   a. The basis of accounting is the timing of the recognition in the financial records of economic events or transactions. The basis of accounting of a fund depends on its measurement focus.

      1) This **measurement focus** is what is being measured or tracked by information in the financial statements.

   b. The **modified accrual** basis of accounting is used to report the governmental fund financial statements.

      1) The measurement focus is on **current financial resources**, that is, on determining financial position and changes in it.

      2) The reporting elements are sources, uses, and balances of current financial resources.

   c. In governmental funds, **revenues** increase fund financial resources. The primary examples of nonrevenue increases are **interfund transfers** (one-way asset flows with no repayment required) and **debt issue proceeds**. Under the modified accrual basis, revenue or another increase in financial resources (such as bond issue proceeds) is recognized when it is **susceptible to accrual**.

      1) **Revenue** (net of estimated uncollectible amounts) is accrued when it is measurable and available.

         a) **Available** means collectible within the current period or **soon enough thereafter** to be used to pay current liabilities.

            i) Ordinarily, material revenues are not recorded until received. However, they are accrued if receipt is delayed beyond the normal time.

         b) When a governmental fund records an asset, but the revenue is not available, a **deferred inflow of resources** is reported. It is a receipt of net assets that applies to a future period and is presented separately after liabilities in the government-wide statement of net position.

      2) **Expenditures** are decreases in fund financial resources.

         a) They usually are measurable and should be recognized when goods or services are acquired, i.e., when the related **liability is incurred**.

            i) But expenditures for principal and interest on **general long-term debt** usually are recognized only when those amounts are **due**.

         b) Expenditures do **not** result from (1) an interfund transfer or (2) expiration of a demand (redeemable) bond takeout arrangement.

            i) Transfers are covered in Subunit 18.2.

      3) Expenses are **not** recognized under the modified accrual basis of accounting.

4. **Basis of Accounting -- Other Financial Statements**

   a. The **accrual basis of accounting** is used to report the (1) government-wide, (2) proprietary fund, and (3) fiduciary fund statements.

      1) The measurement focus is on **economic resources**. The emphasis is on (a) a longer-term measure of operating results and (b) the cost of services.

      2) Thus, revenues and expenses are measured in the same way as in for-profit accounting.

   b. Under the accrual basis, most economic transactions and other events that can be measured are recognized without regard to cash flows.

      1) Moreover, an **expense** is recognized when goods or services are used or consumed instead of an expenditure when they are acquired.

         a) Acquired but unused goods and services are assets.

      2) Revenues, expenses, gains, losses, assets, deferred outflows of resources, liabilities, and deferred inflows of resources that result from **exchange** or exchange-like transactions are accrued when the exchange occurs.

      3) Except for revenues, recognition of the elements of **nonexchange** transactions is **not** affected by the basis of accounting. Nonexchange transactions are covered in Subunit 18.2.

   c. The cash basis is **not** used in governmental accounting except for miscellaneous cash items that are not measurable until cash is received or paid.

   d. **Transfers** are recognized in all affected funds when the interfund receivable and payable arise. Transfers are covered in Subunit 18.2.

5. **Funds**

   a. The diversity of governmental activities and the need for legal compliance require multiple accounting entities (funds).

   b. A **fund** is an independent, distinct fiscal and accounting entity with a self-balancing set of accounts. Items in a fund are segregated because they relate to activities or objectives that are subject to special regulations or limitations. A fund records

      1) Financial resources (including cash),
      2) Deferred outflows of resources,
      3) Liabilities,
      4) Deferred inflows of resources,
      5) Residual equities or balances, and
      6) Changes in them.

      An example of a governmental accounting balance sheet and a statement of revenues, expenditures, and changes in fund balances are located in Subunit 18.7.

   c. No more than the number of funds required by law and efficient financial administration should be created.

d. Funds are classified as governmental, proprietary, or fiduciary depending on their activities and objectives.

1) **Governmental funds** emphasize fiscal accountability. They account for the nonbusiness activities of a government and its current, expendable resources (most often taxes). Accordingly, they use the modified accrual accounting basis with a current financial resources measurement focus.

a) The **general fund** accounts for all financial resources except those required to be accounted for in another fund.

i) Only one general fund may be reported.

b) **Special revenue funds** account for restricted or committed inflows from specific revenue sources. Expenditure must be for a specified purpose (but not debt service or a capital project).

i) A government may have a special revenue fund for (a) road maintenance or (b) operation of its municipal auditorium.

ii) Donations for programs to be administered by the government also are accounted for in special revenue funds.

iii) A special revenue fund is **not** used for resources held as a fiduciary activity.

c) **Capital projects funds** account for financial resources restricted, committed, or assigned to be expended for capital purposes.

i) These resources include general obligation bond proceeds to be used for construction of major capital facilities, such as schools or bridges.

ii) The capital assets themselves are not accounted for in these funds.

iii) Other capital facilities may be financed through proprietary funds or certain trust funds.

d) **Debt service funds** account for resources restricted, committed, or assigned to paying principal and interest. But these funds do not account for the debt itself.

i) They also account for resources being accumulated for future principal and interest payments.

ii) A debt service fund is used if it is required by law.

e) **Permanent funds** account for resources that are restricted to the use of earnings (not principal) for the benefit of the government or its citizens.

i) An example is a perpetual-care fund for a public cemetery.

ii) Private-purpose trust funds are **not** permanent funds.

f) The reporting requirements for governmental funds are covered in Subunit 18.7.

2) **Proprietary funds** emphasize operational accountability. They account for the business-type activities of a government and its economic resources. Consequently, they use the accrual basis of accounting with an economic resources measurement focus. Proprietary funds serve defined customer groups and generally are financed through fees.

a) **Enterprise funds** account for activities that benefit outside parties (the reporting government is not the predominant participant) who are willing to pay for them, such as parking garages and utilities. They are the funds most like private businesses.

b) **Internal service funds** account for activities performed primarily for the benefit of other agencies, such as a centralized information technology department or motor pool.

i) Unless enterprise funds are the predominant participants in an internal service fund, the activities it accounts for generally are governmental, **not** business-type.

c) The reporting requirements for proprietary funds are described in Study Unit 19, Subunit 3.

3) **Fiduciary funds** provide operational information about the **fiduciary activities** of a government. They (a) have an economic resources measurement focus; (b) use accrual accounting; and (c) report capital assets, long-term liabilities, and deferred flows of resources.

a) **Pension (and other employee benefit)** trust funds report fiduciary activities for pensions, other postemployment benefit plans, and certain other employee benefit programs.

b) **Investment trust funds** report fiduciary activities involving (1) the external portion of investment pools and (2) individual investment accounts held in a trust meeting certain criteria.

c) **Private-purpose trust funds** report all fiduciary activities (1) not reported in the other fiduciary trust funds and (2) accounted for in a trust meeting certain criteria.

d) **Custodial funds** report fiduciary activities not required to be reported in the other fiduciary funds, such as tolls that will be paid to a private business.

e) The reporting requirements for fiduciary funds are covered in Study Unit 19, Subunit 4.

Fund Classification

Governmental Funds	Proprietary Funds	Fiduciary Funds
General Fund	Enterprise Funds	Pension (and other employee benefit) Trust Funds
Special Revenue Funds	Internal Service Funds	Investment Trust Funds
Capital Projects Funds		Private-Purpose Trust Funds
Debt Service Funds		Custodial Funds
Permanent Funds		

STOP & REVIEW

You have completed the outline for this subunit.
Study multiple-choice questions 1 through 4 beginning on page 577.

18.2 FUNDING SOURCES

1. **Overview of Nonexchange Transactions**
   a. **Revenue recognition** for a government is unlike that for a private entity.
      1) In a nonexchange transaction, a government gives or receives value (e.g., goods or services) without directly receiving or giving something of equal value in exchange.
      2) The timing of recognition of (a) assets, (b) deferred outflows of resources, (c) liabilities, (d) deferred inflows of resources, and (e) expenses or expenditures that result from nonexchange transactions is **not** affected by the basis of accounting (accrual or modified accrual).
      3) But **revenue** recognition on the **modified** accrual basis requires that (a) the criteria for nonexchange transactions be met and (b) the resources be **available**.
      4) The method of accounting for property taxes (recognition in the period for which they were levied) is **not** changed.
   b. All nonexchange transactions are classified into four categories.
      1) **Derived tax revenues** result from assessments imposed on exchange transactions (such as sales and income taxes).
         a) **Assets** are recognized at the earlier of (1) when the underlying exchange transaction occurs or (2) receipt of resources.
            i) Any resources received before the underlying exchange are reported as **liabilities**.
         b) **Revenues** (net of estimated refunds and uncollectibles) are recognized at the same time as the assets if the underlying exchange has occurred.

EXAMPLE 18-1 Governmental Fund Revenues

A state has the following information about revenues of its governmental funds:

- Revenues other than from sales taxes that became available in time to be used for payment of Year 3 liabilities:

From Year 1	$ 8,000,000
From Year 2	9,000,000
From Year 3	25,000,000

- Sales taxes collected by merchants in Year 3 but not remitted to the state until January Year 4: $12,000,000

-- Continued on next page --

EXAMPLE 18-1 -- Continued

Calculation of revenues not from sales taxes:

Governmental fund revenues are recognized when they are available to satisfy current liabilities. Given that the $8 million and $9 million of Year 1 and Year 2 revenues, respectively, did not become available until Year 3, they are included in the total amount of revenues recognized in Year 3 ($8,000,000 + $9,000,000 + $25,000,000 = $42,000,000).

Calculation of total revenues:

Recognition of derived tax revenues, such as sales taxes, occurs when the underlying exchanges occur. However, under the modified accrual basis of accounting, the sales tax collections also must be available (i.e., collectible within the current period or soon enough thereafter to be used to pay liabilities of the current period). Assuming that collectibility in the period following the fiscal year end meets this criterion (i.e., 60 days), the sales taxes should be recognized as revenues regardless of which basis of accounting (accrual or modified accrual) applies. Thus, the state should recognize total revenues of $54 million ($42 million + $12 million).

2) **Imposed nonexchange revenues** result from assessments imposed on nongovernmental entities (such as property taxes, fines, and forfeitures).
   a) **Assets** are recognized at the earlier of when (1) a legal claim to the resources exists or (2) resources are received.
   b) **Nonproperty tax revenues** are recognized when the assets are recognized unless time requirements apply.
      i) Given time requirements, revenues are recognized when (a) the resources are required to be used or (b) their use is first allowed.
      ii) Resources received or reported as received **before** the time requirements are met are **deferred inflows of resources**.
   c) Revenue is recognized in the governmental funds only if resources are **available**.
   d) **Property tax revenues** (net of estimated refunds and uncollectibles) are recognized in the period for which they were **levied**.
      i) The extension of time to meet the availability criterion ordinarily is not more than 60 days after year-end.
      ii) Resources received or reported as received **before** the period for which property taxes were levied are reported as **deferred inflows of resources**.

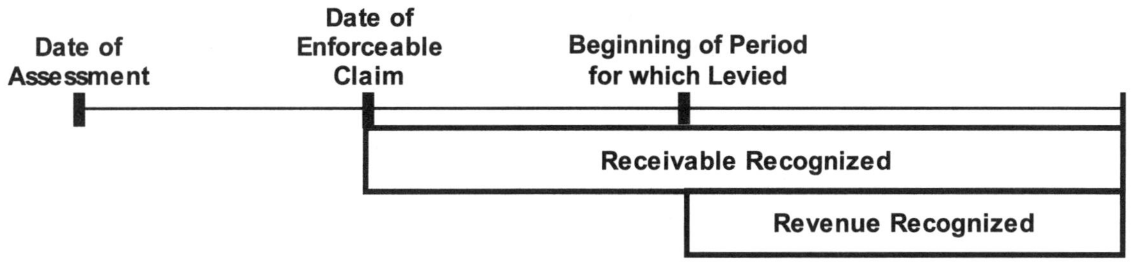

Figure 18-1

EXAMPLE 18-2 Property Tax Revenues

On November 1, a city assesses $110,000,000 of property taxes that are due December 1 and are levied for the subsequent calendar year.

<u>November 1:</u>
No entry

The city offers a discount to taxpayers who pay early. Any amounts received before they are legally due (December 1) must be recorded as a deferred inflow of resources.

<u>November 30:</u>		
Cash	$1,350,000	
Deferred inflow of resources -- property taxes		$1,350,000

On the day when the assessment is legally enforceable (the due date), the city recognizes a receivable (reduced by an allowance for uncollectibles). It also recognizes a deferred inflow of resources for the period in which the property taxes were levied.

<u>December 1:</u>		
Property taxes receivable	$108,000,000	
Deferred inflow of resources -- property taxes		$100,000,000
Allowance for uncollectible taxes		8,000,000

When the period for which the taxes were levied begins, the city debits deferred inflow of resources and recognizes the revenue.

<u>January 1:</u>		
Deferred inflow of resources -- property taxes	$101,350,000	
Revenues -- property taxes		$101,350,000

The following reconciles revenues to assessed property taxes:

Revenues	$101,350,000
Allowance for uncollectible taxes	8,000,000
Discount [($110,000,000 assessed – $108,000,000 receivable) – $1,350,000 deferred inflows of revenues]	650,000
Assessed property taxes	$110,000,000

SUCCESS TIP

The AICPA has released multiple CPA questions asking for the calculation of the amount of property tax revenue recognized by a governmental entity for a period of time.

3) **Voluntary nonexchange transactions** result from agreements entered into willingly by the parties. One party may be a nongovernmental entity.

   a) They are not imposed on any party.

   b) Fulfillment of eligibility requirements is essential.

   c) Examples include private donations to municipal museums and grants from charitable organizations to build inner-city recreational facilities.

4) **Government-mandated nonexchange transactions** occur when one government provides resources to a government at another level and requires that they be used for a specific purpose (such as federal grant money that state governments are required to spend on primary education).

   a) **Eligibility requirements** must be met before these transactions (other than advance payments) can occur and be accounted for. They are conditions set by the provider or by law and include the following:

      i) **Time requirements**

      ii) Incurrence of costs if resources are offered as reimbursements

      iii) Nature of recipient (e.g., a county or a school district)

      iv) Fulfillment of a contingency (e.g., raising a certain amount of other resources)

   b) If all eligibility (including time) requirements are met,

      i) Providers recognize expenses and liabilities (or decreases in assets) and

      ii) Recipients recognize revenues (net of uncollectible amounts) and receivables (or decreases in liabilities).

   c) If resources are transmitted before all eligibility requirements (excluding time) are met,

      i) Providers continue to report **assets** and
      ii) Recipients report **liabilities**.

   d) If resources are received **before** time requirements are met, but all other eligibility requirements are met,

      i) Providers report **deferred outflows of resources** and
      ii) Recipients report **deferred inflows of resources**.

EXAMPLE 18-3 Government-Mandated Nonexchange Transaction

State agrees to provide a grant to County for a sewage treatment plant. However, the recipient must incur $150,000 of allowable costs before qualifying for the grant. This reimbursement-type grant has two eligibility requirements: (1) the recipient is an authorized local government, and (2) the recipient incurs a specified amount of allowable costs. Accordingly, when County has made the qualifying expenditures, it has satisfied all eligibility requirements. It records the following entries in a special revenue fund:

Special revenue fund -- sewage		
Expenditures	$150,000	
Vouchers payable		$150,000
Due from State	$150,000	
Revenues		$150,000

2. **Exchange Transactions**

   a. Exchange revenues result from transactions in which each party receives benefits and incurs costs (each party receives and gives essentially equal values).

   b. Exchange revenues should be recognized according to conventional business principles (i.e., when goods or services are provided to the public or to another governmental entity). Exchange transactions include the following:

      1) A university receives funding for work described in an agreement.
      2) A sponsor shares research or receives benefits from the results of the research.
      3) A hospital provides medical services for a fee.

3. **Nonrevenue Sources of Funding**

   a. **Bonds**

      1) **Issuance of Debt**

         a) The proceeds of long-term debt are a nonrevenue source of funding.

         b) The accrual basis of accounting is used in the **government-wide financial statements**. Thus, they report all resources and obligations, both current and noncurrent.

            i) The receipt of cash and the related obligation are recognized. The inflow from a financing source is not.

EXAMPLE 18-4 Issuance of Construction Bonds

The state issues bonds to finance the construction of a new building.

Cash	$200,000,000	
Bonds payable		$200,000,000

            ii) Any premium received or discount paid upon issuance is recognized. Premiums and discounts are separate items related to and amortized over the life of the new debt.

         c) The modified accrual basis of accounting is used in the **governmental funds**. They have a current financial resources measurement focus, and bonds are not repaid with current financial resources.

            i) The fund that will expend the resources recognizes the receipt of cash and the related financing sources. The entry is in the following form:

Cash	$XXX	
Other financing uses (discount)	XXX	
Other financing sources (face amount)		$XXX
Other financing sources (premium)		XXX

EXAMPLE 18-5 Recognition in a Capital Projects Fund

Capital projects fund -- highway patrol headquarters building:

Cash	$202,000,000	
Other financing sources -- bond face amount		$200,000,000
Other financing sources -- bond issue premium		2,000,000

ii) The credit to other financing sources indicates that this inflow of resources is not a revenue.

iii) The premium is an inflow of additional resources. It is **not** amortized. But a bond indenture or law may require the premium to be applied to debt service.

d) Issue costs, debt insurance, etc., associated with the issuance of general long-term debt are recognized in governmental funds as expenditures (**not** as liabilities) when incurred. Thus, they are not capitalized and amortized.

i) Issue costs of proprietary fund debt (except amounts related to prepaid insurance costs) are expensed in the period incurred.

ii) In contrast, for-profit accounting amortizes debt issue costs over the debt term.

2) **Use of Bond Proceeds**

a) Payments for the project are made from the bond proceeds.

b) In the **government-wide financial statements**, the finished building (or construction-in-progress) is reported as a general capital asset.

c) In the **governmental funds**, payments to the contractor are recorded as expenditures.

i) The building is not capitalized in the governmental funds.

d) **Interest cost** incurred before the end of **construction** is recognized when incurred as interest expense (government-wide statements) or an expenditure (governmental funds).

EXAMPLE 18-6 Accounting for a Progress Payment

A progress payment is made for work done during the year.

Capital projects fund -- highway patrol headquarters building:

Expenditures -- capital outlay	$85,000,000	
Cash		$85,000,000

3) **Retirement of Debt**

a) The **government-wide financial statements** recognize (1) the reduction in assets and liabilities and (2) interest expense. But multiple entries are needed in the **governmental funds**.

EXAMPLE 18-7 **Government-Wide Financial Statements -- Retirement of Current Bond Principal**

The current portion of the bond principal is retired.

Bonds payable	$10,000,000	
Interest expense	700,000	
Cash		$10,700,000

EXAMPLE 18-8 **Governmental Funds -- Entries in the General Fund and Debt Service Fund**

General fund resources are committed to debt service.

General fund:		
Other financing uses -- interfund transfer to debt service fund	$10,700,000	
Due to debt service fund		$10,700,000
Debt service fund:		
Due from general fund	$10,700,000	
Other financing sources -- interfund transfer from general fund		$10,700,000

The resources are transferred.

General fund:		
Due to debt service fund	$10,700,000	
Cash		$10,700,000
Debt service fund:		
Cash	$10,700,000	
Due from general fund		$10,700,000

Expenditures are recorded when principal and interest are legally due.

Debt service fund:		
Expenditure -- bond principal	$10,000,000	
Expenditure -- bond interest	700,000	
Bonds payable		$10,000,000
Interest payable		700,000

The current portion of the debt is repaid.

Debt service fund:		
Bonds payable	$10,000,000	
Interest payable	700,000	
Cash		$10,700,000

b. **Special Assessments**

1) Governments may agree to construct physical improvements to benefit one or more property owners. The government issues debt, pays for the improvements with the proceeds, then repays the debt with reimbursements from the property owners.

EXAMPLE 18-9 Special Assessment Debt -- Government-Wide Statements

A city agrees to build roads, install street lights, and lay water and sewer lines for an employer who intends to build a factory. The city also is liable for the special assessment debt. Thus, it recognizes a general long-term liability and a capital asset.

The bonds are issued.

Cash	$10,000,000	
Bonds payable -- special assessment		$10,000,000

The improvements are finished.

Infrastructure assets	$10,000,000	
Cash		$10,000,000

When the bonds were issued, interest began accruing on them. This amount is added to what the factory owner owes for the improvements.

Special assessment receivable	$10,675,000	
Revenue -- special assessment		$10,675,000

The factory owner pays the assessment.

Cash	$10,675,000	
Special assessment receivable		$10,675,000

The bonds are retired and the portion of the interest that accrued while the project was underway is capitalized.

Bonds payable -- special assessment	$10,000,000	
Infrastructure assets	500,000	
Interest expense	175,000	
Cash		$10,675,000

2) In the **governmental funds**, resources are reported in the capital projects fund and the bonds are repaid from the debt service fund.

EXAMPLE 18-10 Special Assessment Debt -- Governmental Fund Statements

Certain entries are omitted below. These include entries reflecting the reduction of deferred inflows of resources that initially offset the assessment receivable. (Deferred inflows of resources is reduced as resources become available.)

The bonds are issued.

<u>Capital projects fund:</u>		
Cash	$10,000,000	
Other financing sources -- bonds payable		$10,000,000

The contractor is paid for building the improvements.

<u>Capital projects fund:</u>		
Expenditures -- special assessment	$10,000,000	
Cash		$10,000,000

The factory owner is assessed for the full amount including accrued interest.

<u>Debt service fund:</u>		
Special assessment receivable	$10,675,000	
Revenue -- special assessment		$10,675,000

The factory owner pays the assessment.

<u>Debt service fund:</u>		
Cash	$10,675,000	
Special assessment receivable		$10,675,000

The bonds are retired.

<u>Debt service fund:</u>		
Expenditure -- special assessment bond	$10,000,000	
Expenditure -- interest	675,000	
Cash		$10,675,000

c. **Interfund Activity**

1) Interfund activity involves internal events. **Transactions** are external events.

2) **Reciprocal interfund activities** are comparable to exchange and exchange-like transactions. They include interfund loans and interfund services.

a) **Interfund loans** result in interfund receivables and payables, not financing sources and uses.

i) Any amount not expected to be repaid reduces the interfund balances. It is reported as a **transfer**.

ii) Liabilities resulting from interfund activity are not general long-term liabilities and may be reported in governmental funds.

EXAMPLE 18-11 Interfund Loan

If the general fund lends $60,000 to an internal service fund for an equipment purchase, the following entries are made:

General fund:		
Interfund loan receivable -- current	$60,000	
Cash		$60,000
Internal service fund:		
Cash	$60,000	
Interfund loan payable -- current		$60,000

If the loan is noncurrent (not payable within 1 year), the receivable and the payable are designated as noncurrent. Furthermore, the receivable is an asset not spendable under the current appropriation. Thus, fund balance must be reclassified as follows:

General fund:		
Fund balance -- unassigned	$60,000	
Fund balance -- nonspendable		$60,000

Governmental fund balances are classified as (1) unassigned, (2) assigned, (3) committed, (4) restricted, and (5) nonspendable. These classifications are addressed in Study Unit 18.5.

b) **Interfund services provided and used** are sales and purchases at prices equivalent to external exchange values.

i) **Seller funds** recognize **revenues**, and **buyer funds** recognize **expenditures or expenses**.

ii) Unpaid amounts are **interfund receivables or payables**.

iii) However, when the general fund accounts for **risk-financing activity**, charges to other funds are treated as reimbursements.

- **Reimbursements** are repayments to payor funds by the funds responsible for specific resource outflows. They are not reported in the financial statements.

iv) In the **fund financial statements**, all transactions (those between activities and those within activities) are recognized.

- Transactions within activities are those involving only governmental funds or only business-type funds.
- Transactions between activities involve both governmental funds and business-type funds.

EXAMPLE 18-12 Interfund Services Provided and Used

A government pays for unemployment benefit coverage and computer processing time.

<u>General fund:</u>		
Expenditures -- unemployment compensation	$ 8,500,000	
Expenditures -- information services	15,500,000	
Cash		$24,000,000
<u>Enterprise fund -- unemployment compensation:</u>		
Cash	$ 8,500,000	
Revenues		$ 8,500,000
<u>Internal service fund -- information services:</u>		
Cash	$15,500,000	
Revenues		$15,500,000

v) In the **government-wide financial statements**, transactions within activities are **not** recognized.

- In Example 18-12, the transactions affecting the general fund and the enterprise fund are reported.
- The transactions affecting the internal service fund are entirely within the governmental activities section and are not reported.

EXAMPLE 18-13 Activity Types in Government-Wide Statements

<u>Governmental activities:</u>		
Expenses -- unemployment compensation	$8,500,000	
Cash		$8,500,000
<u>Business-type activities:</u>		
Cash	$8,500,000	
Revenues		$8,500,000

3) **Nonreciprocal Interfund Activity**

   a) **Interfund transfers** are one-way asset flows with no repayment required. They must be reported in the basic financial statements separately from revenues and expenditures or expenses.

      i) In a **governmental fund**, a transfer is an other financing use (source) in the transferor (transferee) fund. It is reported after excess (deficiency) of revenues over expenditures in the statement of revenues, expenditures, and changes in fund balances.

      ii) In a **proprietary fund**, the statement of revenues, expenses, and changes in fund net position reports interfund transfers separately after nonoperating revenues and expenses.

   b) The government-wide and the fund financial statements report transfers differently.

      i) Transfers **within the governmental activities section** are not reported in the government-wide statements. These transfers result in no overall change in governmental activities.

      ii) Transfers **between governmental activities and business-type activities** are reported in both the government-wide statements and the fund statements. These transfers result in overall changes in both classes of activities.

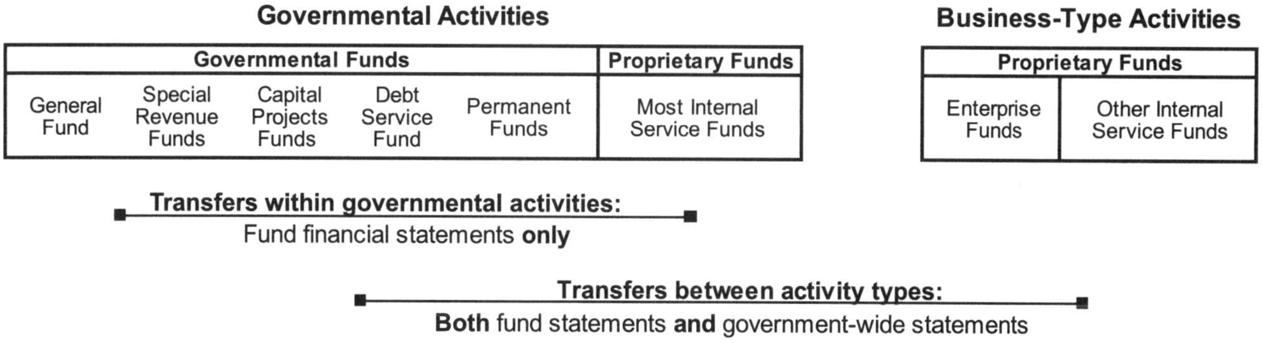

Figure 18-2

EXAMPLE 18-14 Transfers within Governmental Activities

A common interfund transfer is from the general fund to the debt service fund for the repayment of debts.

Fund financial statements. When the transfer is recognized, the transferor credits a payable, and the recipient debits a receivable.

General fund:		
Other financing uses -- transfer to debt service fund	$2,000,000	
Due to debt service fund		$2,000,000
Debt service fund:		
Due from general fund	$2,000,000	
Other financing sources -- transfer from general fund		$2,000,000

The following entries are recorded when the transfer is made:

General fund:		
Due to debt service fund	$2,000,000	
Cash		$2,000,000
Debt service fund:		
Cash	$2,000,000	
Due from general fund		$2,000,000

Government-wide financial statements. No entries.

EXAMPLE 18-15 Transfers between Activity Types

A government transfers resources from the general fund to an enterprise fund for a major expansion.

Fund financial statements. When the transfer is recognized, the accounting is similar to that used in Example 18-14.

General fund:		
Other financing uses -- transfer to municipal hospital fund	$130,000,000	
Due to municipal hospital fund		$130,000,000
Enterprise fund:		
Due from general fund	$130,000,000	
Interfund transfer from general fund		$130,000,000

The transfer of cash also is recorded in the same way.

General fund:		
Due to municipal hospital fund	$130,000,000	
Cash		$130,000,000
Enterprise fund:		
Cash	$130,000,000	
Due from general fund		$130,000,000

Government-wide statements. Additional entries are made. Resources have been transferred not only between funds but also between activities.

Governmental activities:		
Transfer to municipal hospital fund	$130,000,000	
Cash		$130,000,000
Business-type activities:		
Cash	$130,000,000	
Transfer from general fund		$130,000,000

STOP & REVIEW

You have completed the outline for this subunit.
Study multiple-choice questions 5 through 9 beginning on page 578.

18.3 ANNUAL FINANCIAL REPORTS

1. **A comprehensive annual financial report (CAFR)** should be prepared. It covers all funds and activities of the primary government and provides an overview of the discretely presented component units of the reporting entity. The CAFR includes introductory, financial, and statistical sections.
2. The **introductory section** contains the following:
    a. Letter of transmittal from the appropriate government officials
    b. Organization chart
    c. Names of principal officers
3. The **financial section** contains the following:
    a. Independent auditor's report
    b. Management's discussion and analysis (MD&A)
        1) MD&A is **required supplementary information**. It is analysis of financial activities based on **currently known** facts, decisions, or conditions expected to significantly affect financial position or results of operations.
            a) MD&A compares the current and prior years, with an emphasis on the current year, based on government-wide information. The focus is on the **primary government**.
            b) MD&A requirements are stated in general terms to encourage reporting of only the most relevant information.
        2) MD&A discusses the basic financial statements, including (a) their relationships to each other, (b) differences in the information provided, and (c) analyses of relationships between information in the fund statements and the government-wide statements.

c. Basic financial statements

1) **Government-wide financial statements**

a) Statement of net position
b) Statement of activities

2) **Fund financial statements**

a) **Governmental funds financial statements**

i) Balance sheet (with reconciliation to government-wide statement of net position)

ii) Statement of revenues, expenditures, and changes in fund balances (with reconciliation to government-wide statement of activities)

b) **Proprietary funds financial statements**

i) Statement of net position
ii) Statement of revenues, expenses, and changes in fund net position
iii) Statement of cash flows

NOTE: Only proprietary funds have a statement of cash flows.

c) **Fiduciary funds financial statements** (including fiduciary component units)

i) Statement of fiduciary net position
ii) Statement of changes in fiduciary net position

3) **Notes to the financial statements**

a) Notes are an integral part of the basic financial statements. They disclose information essential to fair presentation not reported in the statements. The focus is on the primary government's

i) Governmental activities,
ii) Business-type activities,
iii) Major funds, and
iv) Nonmajor funds in the aggregate.

b) The notes include a **summary of significant accounting policies**.

c) Disclosure of significant accounting policies is required when (1) a selection has been made from existing acceptable alternatives; (2) a policy is unique to the industry in which the government operates, even if the policy is predominantly followed in that industry; and (3) GAAP have been applied in an unusual or innovative way.

EXAMPLE 18-16 Summary of Significant Accounting Policies

A depreciation method is a selection from existing acceptable alternatives and should be included in a summary of significant accounting policies. But financial statement disclosure of accounting policies should not duplicate details presented elsewhere in the financial statements, such as the composition of inventories and capital assets.

d. **Required supplementary information (RSI)** other than MD&A

1) RSI other than MD&A is presented in a separate section of the CAFR after the notes to the basic financial statements.

2) RSI includes (a) schedules, (b) statistical data, (c) **budgetary comparison schedules**, and (d) other information that is an essential part of financial reporting. It should be presented with, but not as a part of, the basic financial statements of a governmental entity.

a) Budgetary comparisons generally should be presented for the **general fund** and each major special revenue fund that has a legally adopted annual budget. The schedules include the following stated on the government's budgetary basis:

i) Original appropriated budget
ii) Final appropriated budget as adjusted by authorized changes
iii) Actual inflows, outflows, and balances

NOTE: A separate column to report the variance between the final budget and actual amounts is encouraged but not required.

b) Essential disclosures also include information about **infrastructure** assets reported using the modified approach.

e. Combining statements and individual fund statements and schedules

1) **Combining statements** are included in the CAFR by fund type when the primary government has more than one (a) nonmajor governmental or enterprise fund or (b) internal service or fiduciary fund.

a) For example, a government with two or more internal service funds presents (for those funds only) the following combining statements: (1) net position; (2) revenues, expenses, and changes in fund net position; and (3) cash flows.

2) Combining statements also are included when the reporting entity has more than one nonmajor discretely presented component unit.

3) **Individual fund statements** are reported when (a) the primary government has just one nonmajor fund of a given type or (b) prior-year or budgetary comparisons are not included in RSI.

4. The **statistical section** focuses on the primary government.

a. It reports information in five categories:

1) Financial trends indicate changes in financial position over time.

2) Revenue capacity is an entity's ability to produce own-source revenues (e.g., taxes but not shared revenues).

3) Debt capacity relates to the entity's debt burden and the ability to issue new debt.

4) Demographic and economic information pertains to the socioeconomic environment.

5) Operating information provides context.

b. Narrative explanations should provide analysis of the quantitative data.

c. Ten years of selected financial, economic, and other data are required to be presented in the statistical section.

5. Minimum Requirements for General-Purpose External Financial Reporting

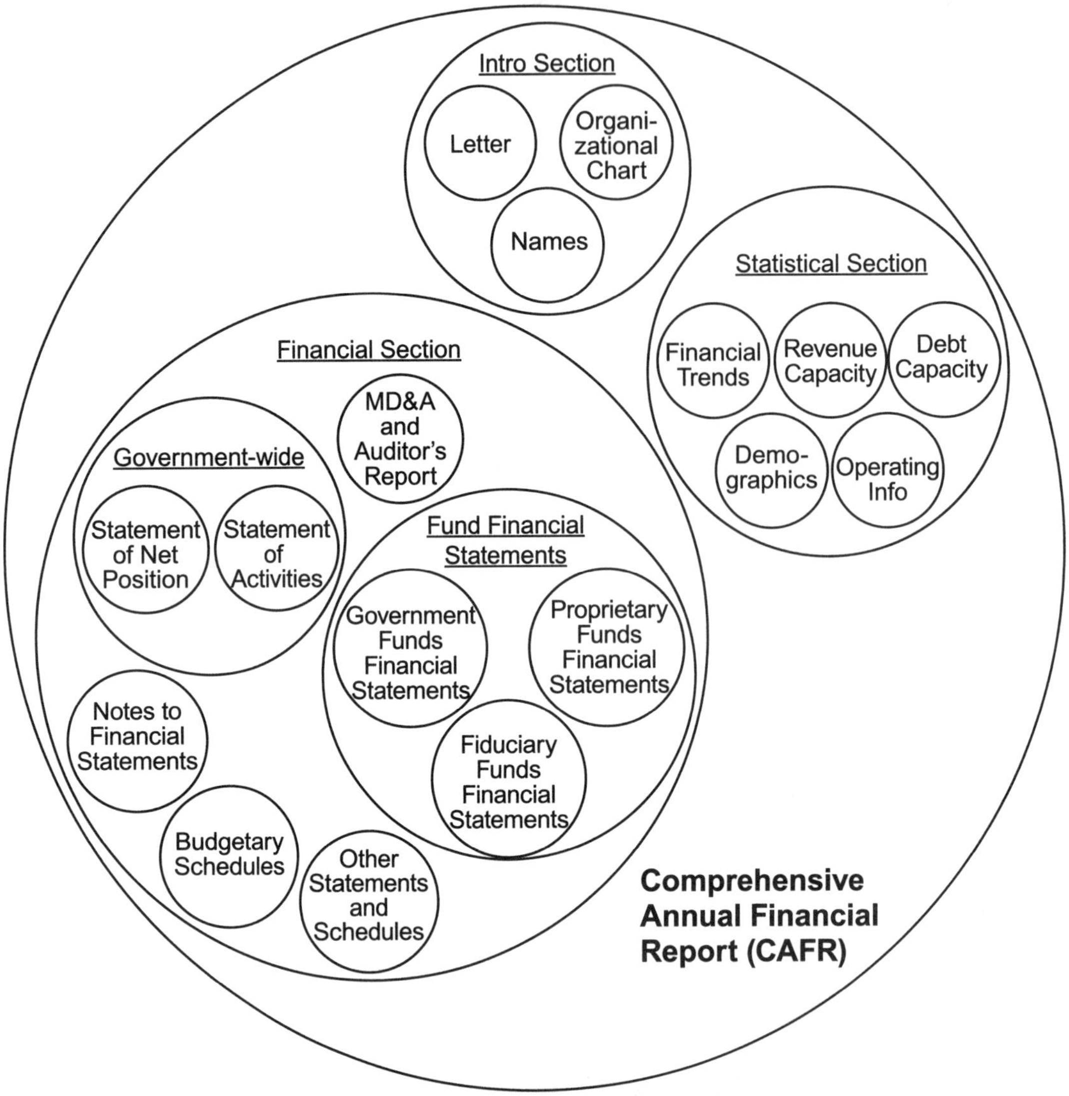

Figure 18-3

Memory Aids

Intro Section	
Lots	**L**etter
Of	**O**rganizational Chart
Nutrients	**N**ames

CAFR	
Indiana	**I**ntro Section
Farms	**F**inancial Section
Soybeans	**S**tatistical Section

Financial Section	
Many	**M**D&A and Auditor's Report
Green	**G**overnment-Wide
Fields	**F**und Financial Statements
Should	Other **S**tatements and **S**chedules
Never	**N**otes
Brown	**B**udgetary Schedules

Statistical Section	
Farmers'	**F**inancial Trends
Revenues	**R**evenue Capacity
Decrease	**D**ebt Capacity
During	**D**emographics
October	**O**perating Information

STOP & REVIEW

You have completed the outline for this subunit.
Study multiple-choice questions 10 through 12 on page 581.

18.4 BUDGETARY ACCOUNTS

1. **Budgetary Accounting**

   a. The budget is a statement of financial intent indicating how the government plans to raise revenue and expend its resources. For most governments, the emphasis of budgeting and appropriations is on planning and control of **governmental funds**.

   b. The budget ordinarily is **legally enforceable** against the financial managers.

      1) The budget also is a basis for evaluating performance. Actual expenditures or expenses are compared with amounts budgeted.

   c. Budgets should be prepared for varying periods of time and from multiple perspectives. Examples of budgets include the following:

      1) An **annual budget** controls financial operations, preferably through the accounting system.

      2) A **long-term budget** is a planning document that contains estimates of revenues and expenditures or expenses (ordinarily over a 4-to-6-year period). It emphasizes major program or capital outlays, with the latter referred to as **capital budgets**.

      3) The **appropriated budget** incorporates the legislatively granted expenditure authority and the related estimates of revenue.

      4) The **flexible budget** distinguishes between fixed and variable amounts.

         a) A series of flexible budgets is prepared for **proprietary funds**. Each contains alternative budget estimates based on varying levels of output.

      5) The **fixed budget** is appropriate for governmental funds in which expenditures and level of activity are set by legislative authorization.

2. **Budget Integration**

   a. Most governments integrate their budgets into the accounting system.

      1) Budget integration should be done for the following governmental funds:

         a) The general fund
         b) Special revenue funds
         c) Other funds with numerous transactions

   b. Common terminology and classifications must be used consistently throughout the budget, the accounts, and the financial reports of each fund.

      1) The budget should include every fund of the government.

      2) The basis of accounting for the budget preferably should correspond to the basis of accounting used by the fund for which the budget is being prepared.

      3) However, if the law requires another basis, governments often keep supplemental records that permit reporting in accordance with GAAP.

3. **Budgetary Accounts**

   a. Despite being formally integrated into the accounting system, the budgetary amounts are reversed at year-end and are **not reported** in the financial statements. The following are the principal accounts used in the entry to record the **annual budget**:

      1) **Estimated revenues** is an anticipatory asset (a debit).

         a) It records the amount expected to be collected from a government's main sources of revenue, such as taxes, fees, and fines.

      2) **Estimated other financing sources** is an anticipatory asset (a debit) that includes the sources of financing other than revenues.

         a) Examples are

            i) The face amount of long-term debt,

            ii) Debt issuance premium,

            iii) Receipt of interfund transfers, and

            iv) Sales of capital assets not qualifying as special items. **Special items** are (a) within management's control and (b) either unusual or infrequent but not both.

      3) **Estimated other financing uses** is an anticipatory liability (a credit) used to record an expected flow of resources to another fund.

         a) Examples are (1) debt issuance discount and (2) interfund transfers out.

      4) **Appropriations** is an anticipatory liability (a credit). It records the amount authorized to be spent by the government for the fiscal period.

         a) Unless a balanced budget or deficit is planned, estimated revenues exceed appropriations. The excess allows for some flexibility if revenues are lower, or expenditures higher, than expected.

      5) **Budgetary fund balance** is the difference (fund equity) between the anticipatory assets and anticipatory liabilities of a governmental fund. It records the budgeted change in fund equity for the year.

EXAMPLE 18-17 Budgetary Accounts

A state adopts its budget for the year. The following entries record the budget for the general fund and one of the special revenue funds:

General fund:		
Estimated revenues -- sales taxes	$2,400,000,000	
Estimated other financing sources -- face amount of bonds	400,000,000	
Appropriations		$2,100,000,000
Estimated other financing uses -- transfer to debt service fund		600,000,000
Budgetary fund balance		100,000,000
Special revenue fund -- highway maintenance:		
Estimated revenues -- vehicle license fees	$ 130,000,000	
Appropriations -- salaries		$ 40,000,000
Appropriations -- wages		20,000,000
Appropriations -- road equipment		40,000,000
Appropriations -- construction materials		20,000,000
Budgetary fund balance		10,000,000

b. As conditions change during the year, a portion of the fund balance may be moved to appropriations to acknowledge new circumstances in the budget.

EXAMPLE 18-18 Additional Appropriation

The state discovers that it has underestimated the amount of materials needed to maintain its roads. The authorization to spend more on materials must be recognized in the budget.

Special revenue fund -- highway maintenance:		
Budgetary fund balance	$5,000,000	
Appropriations -- construction materials		$5,000,000

4. **Year-End Closing**

a. The budgetary entries are reversed.

EXAMPLE 18-19 Reversing of Budgetary Entries

General fund:		
Appropriations	$2,100,000,000	
Estimated other financing uses -- transfer to debt service fund	600,000,000	
Budgetary fund balance	100,000,000	
Estimated revenues -- sales taxes		$2,400,000,000
Estimated other financing sources -- bond proceeds		400,000,000

The mid-year amendment to the budget for construction materials is reflected in the reversal entry for the special revenue fund.

Special revenue fund -- highway maintenance:		
Appropriations -- salaries	$40,000,000	
Appropriations -- wages	20,000,000	
Appropriations -- road equipment	40,000,000	
Appropriations -- construction materials	25,000,000	
Budgetary fund balance	5,000,000	
Estimated revenues -- vehicle license fees		$130,000,000

STOP & REVIEW

You have completed the outline for this subunit.
Study multiple-choice questions 13 through 15 on page 582.

18.5 CLASSIFICATION OF FUND BALANCE

1. Fund balance is reported only for a **governmental fund**. It is classified according to the limits on the specific purposes for which resources may be spent. A negative residual amount should not be reported for nonspendable, restricted, committed, or assigned fund balances in any fund. The following is the hierarchy of classifications:
   a. **Nonspendable.** This classification includes amounts that either (1) are in a form (e.g., inventory, prepayments, or long-term loans) that is not spendable or (2) must be kept intact (e.g., the principal of a permanent fund).
      1) But, if the proceeds of such an item are restricted, committed, or assigned, they are presented in one of those classifications.
   b. **Restricted.** This classification includes amounts that may be spent only for specific purposes established by
      1) A constitutional mandate,
      2) Enabling legislation, or
      3) An external provider.
   c. **Committed.** These amounts may be spent only for specific purposes established by a formal act of the entity's highest decision maker (e.g., a county commission).
      1) This decision maker may redirect the resources by following the necessary due process procedures.
   d. **Assigned.** This classification includes amounts **not** nonspendable, restricted, or committed.
      1) Amounts are only reported as assigned in the general fund if they are intended to be used for a specific purpose.
      2) Expenditure is limited only by the entity's intent to use such amounts for specific purposes.
      3) An example of an assignment is an appropriation of fund balance to offset a budget deficit expected in the next year.
         a) The amount should equal no more than the excess of expected expenditures over expected revenues.
      4) An assignment should not create a deficit in unassigned fund balance.

e. **Unassigned.** The general fund is the **only** fund that reports a positive balance (the sum of the amounts not classified elsewhere). The reason is that amounts reported in other governmental funds have been restricted, committed, or assigned, e.g., for debt payment or construction projects.

1) In other governmental funds, this classification is used only for a deficit balance, e.g., when expenditures exceed amounts restricted, committed, or assigned to the fund.

EXAMPLE 18-20 Fund Balance Classifications

City of Lemonville
General Fund
Balance Sheet
December 31, 20X4

Assets	$1,520,000	
Deferred outflows of resources	254,000	
Total assets and deferred outflows of resources		$1,774,000
Liabilities	$1,172,000	
Deferred inflows of resources	528,000	
Total liabilities and deferred inflows of resources		$1,700,000
Fund balance		
Nonspendable:		
Inventory	$ 22,000	
Prepayments	13,000	
Principal of permanent fund	10,000	
Restricted:		
Federal social services mandate	5,200	
Committed	13,000	
Assigned	4,500	
Unassigned	6,300	
Total fund balance		$ 74,000
Total liabilities, deferred inflows of resources, and fund balance		$1,774,000

STOP & REVIEW

You have completed the outline for this subunit.
Study multiple-choice question 16 on page 583.

18.6 ENCUMBRANCES

1. **Encumbrances**

   a. A government commits to expend resources when a contract is signed or a purchase order is approved. The amount (an estimate of actual cost) then may be formally recorded in a **budgetary** account called an **encumbrance**.

      1) By contrast, a for-profit entity does not accrue a payable until the goods are delivered or the service is performed.

   b. Encumbrance accounting may be used only for internal purposes in **governmental** funds, especially general and special revenue funds.

   c. **Reporting.** If amounts previously have been encumbered and classified as restricted, committed, or assigned, no separate display is needed in those classifications.

      1) If an encumbered amount has **not** been restricted, etc., it is not classified as unassigned. Instead, it is included in committed or assigned fund balance.

      2) An encumbrance is **not** reported in the body of the statements. Encumbering an amount does not further limit the specific purposes for which it may be used.

         a) For example, an encumbered amount is reported not as committed for encumbrances but with other such amounts having the same purpose.

      3) Significant encumbrances are disclosed in the **notes**.

   d. The encumbrance entry is to debit encumbrances and credit encumbrances outstanding.

EXAMPLE 18-21 Recognition of an Encumbrance

The state has contracted to purchase road maintenance equipment.

Special revenue fund -- highway maintenance:		
Encumbrances	$750,000	
Encumbrances outstanding		$750,000

   e. When the goods are delivered or the services are performed, two entries are made.

      1) The encumbrance entry is reversed.

EXAMPLE 18-22 Reversal of an Encumbrance

The state takes delivery of the equipment.

Special revenue fund -- highway maintenance:		
Encumbrances outstanding	$750,000	
Encumbrances		$750,000

      2) The legal obligation to pay is recognized.

         a) Governmental funds debit **expenditures** rather than expenses and credit **vouchers payable** rather than accounts payable for the actual cost of the goods or services.

EXAMPLE 18-23 Recognition of a Liability

The equipment costs less than anticipated.

Special revenue fund -- highway maintenance:		
Expenditures -- road equipment	$745,000	
Vouchers payable		$745,000

SUCCESS TIP

When the AICPA has tested encumbrance accounting, it has asked questions about the journal entries for the different transactions in the encumbrance process. Calculations of the amounts used in these journal entries also have been required.

2. **Year-End Closing**

   a. A government may intend, or be required, to honor outstanding encumbrances. But encumbrances are **not** reported in the financial statements.

EXAMPLE 18-24 Year-End Closure of Outstanding Encumbrances

At year end, the state has $12,750,000 of outstanding encumbrances.

Special revenue fund -- highway maintenance:		
Encumbrances outstanding	$12,750,000	
Encumbrances		$12,750,000

1) A government may reclassify fund balance to acknowledge in its financial statements the claim on next period's resources of commitments made during the reporting period.

EXAMPLE 18-25 Reclassification of Fund Balance

The state reclassifies a portion of fund balance equal to outstanding encumbrances.

Special revenue fund -- highway maintenance:		
Fund balance -- assigned	$12,750,000	
Fund balance -- committed		$12,750,000

In the general fund, the residual fund balance account is unassigned fund balance. Thus, the reclassification could be to assigned fund balance or committed fund balance.

   b. Common anticipated liabilities, such as wages payable and payroll taxes payable, need not be encumbered because of the controls in place for such expenditures.

3. **Summary**

	Governmental Funds	Proprietary Funds	Fiduciary Funds
Budgetary Accounting	General and special revenue funds; other funds with many transactions; rarely in debt service funds	Rarely	If similar to special revenue funds
Outlays Encumbered	General and special revenue funds; possibly other funds	No	No

STOP & REVIEW

You have completed the outline for this subunit.
Study multiple-choice questions 17 and 18 on page 584.

18.7 GOVERNMENTAL FUNDS REPORTING

1. **Measurement Focus and Basis of Accounting**
    a. Governmental funds emphasize sources, uses, and balances of current financial resources.
        1) In these funds, (a) **expendable** assets are assigned to funds based on their intended use, (b) **current** liabilities are assigned to funds from which they will be paid, and (c) the difference is the **fund balance**.
        2) Thus, the governmental funds are reported using the **current financial resources** measurement focus and the **modified accrual** basis of accounting.
2. **Major vs. Nonmajor Fund Reporting**
    a. Governmental and proprietary fund financial statements emphasize **major funds**. But major fund reporting does **not** apply to **internal service funds**.
        1) Each major fund is presented in a separate column.
            a) The main operating fund (the general fund) is always a major fund.
        2) Nonmajor funds are aggregated in one column.
        3) Combining statements are not required for nonmajor funds.
        4) Any individual governmental or enterprise fund **must** be reported as major if
            a) Total assets, liabilities, revenues, or expenditures or expenses (excluding extraordinary items) of the fund are **at least 10%** of the corresponding element total (assets, etc.) for all funds of its category (i.e., all governmental or all enterprise funds), **and**
            b) An element that met the 10% standard above is **at least 5%** of the corresponding element total for all governmental and enterprise funds.
        5) To determine whether major fund criteria are met,
            a) Deferred outflows of resources are combined with assets and
            b) Deferred inflows of resources are combined with liabilities.
    b. Any governmental or enterprise fund believed to be particularly important to users also may be reported in the same way as a major fund.
3. **General Fund**
    a. The general fund accounts for all resources not required to be reported elsewhere.
    b. The reporting entity has **only one** general fund.

4. **Special Revenue Funds**

   a. Special revenue funds account for **restricted or committed** proceeds of specific sources of revenue. Expenditure must be for a specified purpose (but not debt service or a capital project).

      1) Thus, the basis of the fund is a **substantial inflow** from restricted or committed revenue sources.
      2) Examples of resources accounted for are federal grants, shared revenue, and gasoline taxes.
      3) The following are examples of the uses of special revenue funds:

         a) Operation of a municipal auditorium
         b) Upkeep of a zoo
         c) Road maintenance

   b. Donations provided for programs to be administered by the government also are accounted for in special revenue funds.
   c. A special revenue fund is **not** used for the resources of a trust held as a fiduciary activity.
   d. The general fund of a **blended** component unit is reported as a special revenue fund.
   e. Special revenue funds are **not** required unless legally mandated.

5. **Capital Projects Funds**

   a. Capital projects funds account for financial resources **restricted, committed, or assigned** to be expended for capital purposes.

      1) These resources include general obligation bond proceeds to be used to acquire or construct major capital facilities for general government use (e.g., schools, bridges, or tunnels).

   b. Capital projects financed by proprietary funds or in trust funds are accounted for in those funds.
   c. The assets themselves are **not** accounted for in these funds.

6. **Debt Service Funds**

   a. Debt service funds account for resources **restricted, committed, or assigned** to payment of the principal and interest.
   b. They are required if

      1) They are legally mandated, or
      2) The resources are for payment of principal and interest due in future years.

   c. If the government has no obligation on **special assessment debt**, the debt service transactions are accounted for in a **custodial fund**.

7. **Permanent Funds**

   a. Permanent funds account for resources that are **restricted** to the use of **earnings** for the benefit of the government or its citizens.

      1) An example is a perpetual-care fund for a public cemetery.

   b. Permanent funds are **not** private-purpose trust funds.

      1) Private-purpose trust funds are reported with the other **fiduciary funds**.

8. **Balance Sheet**

   a. A balance sheet is required for governmental funds. It should be in balance sheet format with a **total column.**

Balance Sheet Format

Assets + Deferred outflows of resources	=	Liabilities + Deferred inflows of resources + Fund balances

   b. **Fund balances** should be classified as nonspendable, restricted, committed, assigned, or unassigned.

EXAMPLE 18-26 Balance Sheet

	General Fund	Special Revenue Fund	Capital Projects Fund	Debt Service Fund	All Nonmajor Funds	Total Governmental Funds
ASSETS AND DEFERRED OUTFLOWS OF RESOURCES						
Assets:						
Cash	$ 852,000	$580,000	$671,000	$410,000	$103,000	$2,616,000
Investments	108,000	134,000	145,000	124,000	100,000	611,000
Deferred outflows of resources	$ 101,000	$ 80,000	$ 50,000	$ 73,000	$ 38,000	$ 342,000
Total assets and deferred outflows of resources	**$1,061,000**	**$794,000**	**$866,000**	**$607,000**	**$241,000**	**$3,569,000**
LIABILITIES, DEFERRED INFLOWS OF RESOURCES, AND FUND BALANCES						
Liabilities:						
Accounts payable	$ 672,000	$508,000	$108,000	$310,000	$ 50,000	$1,648,000
Due to other funds	150,000	105,000	315,000	109,000	60,000	739,000
Deferred inflows of resources	$ 139,000	$150,000	$108,000	$150,000	$100,000	$ 647,000
Total liabilities and deferred inflows of resources	$ 961,000	$763,000	$531,000	$569,000	$210,000	$3,034,000
Fund balance:						
Nonspendable						
Inventories	$ 70,000	$ 0	$ 0	$ 0	$ 0	$ 70,000
Committed						
Encumbrances	20,000	13,000	125,000	8,000	5,000	171,000
Debt service	0	0	0	0	13,000	13,000
Assigned						
Special revenue funds	0	18,000	210,000	0	12,000	240,000
Capital projects funds	0	0	0	30,000	1,000	31,000
Unassigned						
General fund	10,000	0	0	0	0	10,000
Total fund balances	$ 100,000	$ 31,000	$335,000	$ 38,000	$ 31,000	$ 535,000
Total liabilities, deferred inflows of resources, and fund balances	**$1,061,000**	**$794,000**	**$866,000**	**$607,000**	**$241,000**	**$3,569,000**

9. **Statement of Revenues, Expenditures, and Changes in Fund Balances**

   a. This statement is required. It reports inflows, outflows, and balances of current financial resources. The focus is on major fund reporting.

EXAMPLE 18-27 Statement of Revenues, Expenditures, and Changes in Fund Balances

	General Fund	Special Revenue Fund	Capital Projects Fund	Debt Service Fund	All Nonmajor Funds	Total Governmental Funds
REVENUES						
Property taxes	$1,300,000	$ 0	$ 0	$ 0	$ 218,000	$ 1,518,000
Public service taxes	450,000	0	0	0	0	450,000
Fees and fines	208,000	0	0	0	0	208,000
Intergovernmental	530,000	240,000	0	0	158,000	928,000
Investment earnings	124,000	180,000	459,000	397,000	150,000	1,310,000
Etc.	729,000	321,000	0	597,000	491,000	2,138,000
Total revenues	**$3,341,000**	**$741,000**	**$ 459,000**	**$ 994,000**	**$1,017,000**	**$ 6,552,000**
EXPENDITURES						
Current:						
General governmental	$ 109,000	$ 0	$ 130,000	$ 329,000	$ 100,000	$ 668,000
Public safety	130,000	0	0	0	210,000	340,000
Public works	210,000	0	0	0	130,000	340,000
Etc.	220,000	150,000	0	0	125,000	495,000
Debt service:						
Principal	0	0	0	0	104,000	104,000
Interest and other charges	0	0	0	0	122,000	122,000
Capital outlay	0	0	327,000	231,000	201,000	759,000
Total expenditures	**$ 669,000**	**$150,000**	**$ 457,000**	**$ 560,000**	**$ 992,000**	**$ 2,828,000**
Excess (deficiency) of revenues over expenditures	**$2,672,000**	**$591,000**	**$ 2,000**	**$ 434,000**	**$ 25,000**	**$ 3,724,000**
OTHER FINANCING SOURCES (USES)						
Proceeds of refunding bonds	$ 0	$ 0	$ 0	$ 0	$1,200,000	$ 1,200,000
Proceeds of long-term capital-related debt	0	0	2,300,000	0	409,000	2,709,000
Payment to bond refunding escrow agent	0	0	0	0	529,000	529,000
Transfers in	170,000	0	0	0	1,790,000	1,960,000
Transfers out	(120,000)	(50,000)	(75,000)	0	(520,000)	(765,000)
Total other financing sources and uses	**$ 50,000**	**$ (50,000)**	**$2,225,000**	**$ 0**	**$3,408,000**	**$ 5,633,000**
SPECIAL ITEM						
Gain on disposal of operations	$ 150,000	$ 0	$ 0	$ 0	$ 0	$ 150,000
Net changes in fund balances	**$2,872,000**	**$541,000**	**$2,227,000**	**$ 434,000**	**$3,433,000**	**$ 9,507,000**
Fund balances – beginning	2,400,000	120,000	1,750,000	2,190,000	2,900,000	9,360,000
Fund balances – ending	**$5,272,000**	**$661,000**	**$3,977,000**	**$2,624,000**	**$6,333,000**	**$18,867,000**

b. **Revenues** are classified in this statement by major source and **expenditures** by, at a minimum, function.

   1) **Debt issue costs** (e.g., underwriter's fees) paid from the proceeds are expenditures.

      a) Issue costs (e.g., rating agency fees) paid from existing resources also are expenditures (but not until the liability is incurred).

c. **Other financing sources and uses** include

   1) The face amount of long-term debt,
   2) Issuance premium or discount,
   3) Some payments to escrow agents for bond refundings,
   4) Interfund transfers,
   5) Sales of capital assets (unless the sale is a special item), and
   6) Debt refundings.

d. **Special and extraordinary items** are reported separately after other financing sources and uses.

   1) Special items are transactions or other events that are (a) within the control of management and (b) either unusual in nature or infrequent in occurrence but not both.

      a) Significant transactions or other events that are either unusual or infrequent but **not** within the control of management should be (1) separately identified in the appropriate revenue or expenditure category or (2) disclosed in the notes.

   2) Extraordinary items are transactions or other events that are unusual in nature and infrequent in occurrence.

   3) If both special items and extraordinary items occur in the same fiscal year, special items are reported before extraordinary items.

STOP & REVIEW

You have completed the outline for this subunit.
Study multiple-choice questions 19 and 20 on page 585.

QUESTIONS

18.1 Reporting Entity, Basis of Accounting, and Funds

1. Lake County received the following proceeds that are legally restricted to expenditure for specified purposes:

Levies on affected property owners to install sewers	$500,000
Gasoline taxes to finance road repairs	900,000

What amount most likely will be accounted for in Lake's special revenue funds?

A. $1,400,000

B. $900,000

C. $500,000

D. $0

Answer (B) is correct.
REQUIRED: The amount to be recorded in special revenue funds.
DISCUSSION: Special assessments for construction activity may be accounted for in a capital projects fund or other appropriate fund. The gasoline taxes are special revenues received from the state government to be expended for a specific purpose and are properly recorded in the special revenue funds. However, special revenue funds need not be used unless they are legally required.
Answer (A) is incorrect. The amount of $1,400,000 includes the special assessment for a capital project. **Answer (C) is incorrect.** The amount of $500,000 is the special assessment for a capital project. **Answer (D) is incorrect.** The amount of $0 is based on the assumption that neither revenue source is accounted for in special revenue funds.

2. Kew City received a $15,000,000 federal grant to finance the construction of a center for rehabilitation of drug addicts. The proceeds of this grant should be accounted for in the

A. Special revenue funds.

B. General fund.

C. Capital projects funds.

D. Trust funds.

Answer (C) is correct.
REQUIRED: The fund used to account for a federal grant to finance the construction of a center for rehabilitation of drug addicts.
DISCUSSION: A capital projects fund is used to account for the receipt and disbursement of resources restricted to the acquisition of major capital facilities (other than those financed by proprietary and trust funds) through purchase or construction.
Answer (A) is incorrect. Special revenue funds do not record resources to be used for major capital facilities. **Answer (B) is incorrect.** The general fund does not record resources to be used for major capital facilities. **Answer (D) is incorrect.** A grant for a drug rehabilitation center is not accounted for in a trust fund. A trust fund accounts for assets held as a fiduciary activity.

3. A local governmental unit could use which of the following types of funds?

	Fiduciary	Proprietary
A.	Yes	No
B.	Yes	Yes
C.	No	Yes
D.	No	No

Answer (B) is correct.
REQUIRED: The types of funds that could be used by a local government.
DISCUSSION: The three categories of fund types that can be used by a state or local government are (1) governmental (general, special revenue, debt service, capital projects, and permanent funds), (2) proprietary (internal service and enterprise funds), and (3) fiduciary (pension and other employee benefit trust, investment trust, private-purpose trust, and custodial funds).

4. In the fund financial statements of which of the following fund types of a city government are revenues and expenditures recognized on the same basis of accounting as the general fund?

A. Private-purpose trust.

B. Internal service.

C. Enterprise.

D. Debt service.

Answer (D) is correct.

REQUIRED: The fund that recognizes revenues and expenditures in the same manner as the general fund.

DISCUSSION: A debt service fund is the only type of fund listed that is classified as a governmental fund. The other funds are proprietary or fiduciary. The modified accrual basis is used to prepare the financial statements for governmental funds. Proprietary and fiduciary funds are reported on the accrual basis.

Answer (A) is incorrect. A private-purpose trust fund is a fiduciary fund. Its financial statements are prepared on the same basis as those of proprietary funds. **Answer (B) is incorrect.** An internal service fund is a proprietary fund. Its financial statements are prepared using the accrual basis of accounting. **Answer (C) is incorrect.** An enterprise fund is a proprietary fund. Its financial statements are prepared using the accrual basis of accounting.

18.2 Funding Sources

5. During the current year, Knoxx County levied property taxes of $2,000,000, of which 1% is expected to be uncollectible. The following amounts were collected during the current year:

Prior year taxes collected within the first 60 days of the current year	$ 50,000
Prior year taxes collected between 60 and 90 days into the current year	120,000
Current year taxes collected in the current year	1,800,000
Current year taxes collected within the first 60 days of the subsequent year	80,000

What amount of property tax revenue should Knoxx County report in its government-wide statement of activities?

A. $1,800,000

B. $1,970,000

C. $1,980,000

D. $2,000,000

Answer (C) is correct.

REQUIRED: The property tax revenue reported in the government-wide statement of activities.

DISCUSSION: Regardless of whether the accrual or modified accrual basis of accounting is used, revenue from a property tax assessment is recognized in the period for which it was levied. However, the accrual basis is used to prepare the government-wide statement of activities. Recognition is net of estimated refunds and uncollectible amounts. Consequently, current-year property tax revenue recognized on the accrual basis is $1,980,000 [$2,000,000 levied × (100% – 1% estimated to be uncollectible)]. The amounts (1) collected currently but levied for a prior year and (2) levied for the current year and collected in the subsequent year are accrual basis revenue of the prior year and the current year, respectively.

Answer (A) is incorrect. The amount of $1,800,000 is the current-year levy collected in the current year. **Answer (B) is incorrect.** The amount of $1,970,000 is the amount collected in the current year. **Answer (D) is incorrect.** The amount of $2,000,000 is the total levied. But 1% of the total levy is expected to be uncollectible.

6. The following information pertains to Cobb City.

Year 6 governmental fund revenues that became measurable and available in time to be used for payment of Year 6 liabilities (including $2,000,000 from Year 4 and Year 5)	$16,000,000
Sales taxes collected by merchants in Year 6 but not remitted to Cobb City until January Year 7	3,000,000

For the year ended December 31, Year 6, Cobb City should recognize revenues in its governmental fund financial statements of

A. $14,000,000

B. $16,000,000

C. $17,000,000

D. $19,000,000

Answer (D) is correct.

REQUIRED: The amount of revenues to be recorded.

DISCUSSION: Governmental fund revenues are recognized when the resources are measurable and available to satisfy current liabilities. The $16 million of Year 6 revenues is measurable and available to pay current liabilities, and the amounts included from Year 4 and Year 5 transactions did not meet the recognition criteria until Year 6. Thus, $16,000,000 should be recognized for the year ended December 31, Year 6. Sales taxes are derived tax revenues. Recognition of such revenues occurs when (1) the underlying exchanges occurred and (2) the resources are available. When the modified accrual basis is used, the resources (the sales tax collections) also must be available (collectible within the current period or soon enough thereafter to be used to pay liabilities of the current period). Collection in the month following the December 31 fiscal year end meets the availability criterion (i.e., 60 days). Thus, $3 million of sales taxes should be recognized as revenues regardless of which basis of accounting (accrual or modified accrual) applies. Total revenues recognized are $19 million ($16 million + $3 million).

Answer (A) is incorrect. The amount of $14,000,000 excludes the revenues from Year 4 and Year 5 transactions and the sales taxes. **Answer (B) is incorrect.** The amount of $16,000,000 assumes that the sales taxes are not available. **Answer (C) is incorrect.** The amount of $17,000,000 assumes that previous years' revenues available in Year 6 should be subtracted.

7. On March 2, Year 4, the city of Finch issued 10-year general obligation bonds at face amount, with interest payable March 1 and September 1. The proceeds were to be used to finance the construction of a civic center over the period April 1, Year 4, to March 31, Year 5. During the fiscal year ended June 30, Year 4, no resources had been provided to the debt service fund for the payment of principal and interest. On June 30, Year 4, Finch should report the construction in progress for the civic center in the

	Capital Projects Fund	Government-Wide Statement of Net Position
A.	Yes	Yes
B.	Yes	No
C.	No	No
D.	No	Yes

Answer (D) is correct.

REQUIRED: The reporting of construction in progress.

DISCUSSION: Expenditures for the construction project but not the resulting general capital assets should be reported in the capital projects fund. The construction in progress is a general capital asset if it results from expenditure of governmental fund financial resources and is not related to activities reported in nongovernmental funds. Ultimately, the completed project should be reported in the government-wide statement of net position at historical cost, including ancillary charges. The expenditures should not be reported in the governmental funds balance sheet.

Answer (A) is incorrect. Expenditures but not in-progress assets are reported in the capital projects fund. General capital assets are not reported in governmental funds. **Answer (B) is incorrect.** The completed and in-progress assets are reported in the government-wide statement of net position, not in the capital projects fund. **Answer (C) is incorrect.** The completed and in-progress assets are reported in the government-wide statement of net position.

8. In Year 8, Menton City received $5,000,000 of bond proceeds to be used for capital projects. Of this amount, $1,000,000 was expended in Year 8 with the balance expected to be expended in Year 9. When should the bond proceeds be recorded in a capital projects fund?

A. $5,000,000 in Year 8.

B. $5,000,000 in Year 9.

C. $1,000,000 in Year 8 and $4,000,000 in Year 9.

D. $1,000,000 in Year 8 and in the general fund for $4,000,000 in Year 8.

Answer (A) is correct.

REQUIRED: The date(s) bond proceeds should be recorded in a capital projects fund.

DISCUSSION: The capital projects fund is a governmental fund. In this fund, the face amount of (1) long-term debt, (2) issuance premium or discount, and (3) certain other items are reported as other financing sources and uses. Thus, the entry in the capital projects fund to record receipt of the bond proceeds in Year 8 is a debit to cash and a credit to other financing sources -- bond issue proceeds for $5,000,000.

9. The renovation of Fir City's municipal park was accounted for in a capital projects fund. Financing for the renovation, which was begun and completed during the current year, came from the following sources:

Grant from state government	$400,000
Proceeds from general obligation bond issue	500,000
Transfer from Fir's general fund	100,000

In its governmental fund statement of revenues, expenditures, and changes in fund balances for the current year, Fir should report these amounts as

	Revenues	Other Financing Sources
A.	$1,000,000	$0
B.	$900,000	$100,000
C.	$400,000	$600,000
D.	$0	$1,000,000

Answer (C) is correct.

REQUIRED: The amounts to be reported in the governmental fund statement of revenues, expenditures, and changes in fund balances.

DISCUSSION: In governmental funds, revenues increase fund financial resources. The primary examples of nonrevenue increases are (1) interfund transfers and (2) debt issue proceeds. Thus, revenues of a capital projects fund include grants. The grant (a voluntary nonexchange transaction) is recognized when all eligibility requirements, including time requirements, have been met. When modified accrual accounting is used, as in a capital projects fund, the grant also must be available. Other financing sources include proceeds from bonds and incoming interfund transfers. Thus, revenues of $400,000 and other financing sources of $600,000 ($500,000 + $100,000) are reported in the governmental fund statement of revenues, expenditures, and changes in fund balances.

Answer (A) is incorrect. The proceeds from the bond issue and the transfer from the general fund should be reported under other financing sources. **Answer (B) is incorrect.** The proceeds from bond issue should be reported under other financing sources. **Answer (D) is incorrect.** The grant should be reported under revenues.

18.3 Annual Financial Reports

10. Which of the following is one of the three standard sections of a governmental comprehensive annual financial report?

A. Investment.

B. Actuarial.

C. Statistical.

D. Single audit.

Answer (C) is correct.

REQUIRED: The standard section of a CAFR.

DISCUSSION: The three standard sections of a state or local government's CAFR are the introductory section, the financial section, and the statistical section. The statistical section reports (1) financial trends, (2) revenue capacity, (3) debt capacity, (4) demographic and economic information, and (5) operating information.

Answer (A) is incorrect. An investment section is not a standard section of a CAFR. **Answer (B) is incorrect.** An actuarial section is not a standard section of a CAFR. **Answer (D) is incorrect.** A single audit section is not a standard section of a CAFR. But the financial section does include the independent auditor's report.

11. Which of the following should be included in the introductory section of a local government's comprehensive annual financial report?

A. Auditor's report.

B. Management letter.

C. Engagement letter.

D. Letter of transmittal.

Answer (D) is correct.

REQUIRED: The item included in the introductory section of a local government's CAFR.

DISCUSSION: A state or local government must prepare a CAFR. It (1) covers all funds and activities of the primary government and (2) provides an overview of the discretely presented component units of the reporting entity. The CAFR includes introductory, financial, and statistical sections. The introductory section contains (1) a letter of transmittal from the appropriate government officials, (2) an organization chart, and (3) names of principal officers.

Answer (A) is incorrect. The financial section contains the auditor's report. **Answer (B) is incorrect.** The financial section contains management's discussion and analysis (MD&A). **Answer (C) is incorrect.** The engagement letter is not included in the CAFR.

12. Financial reporting by general-purpose governments includes presentation of management's discussion and analysis as

A. Required supplementary information after the notes to the financial statements.

B. Part of the basic financial statements.

C. A description of currently known facts, decisions, or conditions expected to have significant effects on financial activities.

D. Information that may be limited to highlighting the amounts and percentages of change from the prior to the current year.

Answer (C) is correct.

REQUIRED: The nature of MD&A.

DISCUSSION: MD&A is required supplementary information (RSI) that precedes the basic financial statements and provides an overview of financial activities. It is based on currently known facts, decisions, or conditions and includes comparisons of the current and prior years, with an emphasis on the current year, based on government-wide information. Currently known facts are those of which management is aware at the audit report date.

Answer (A) is incorrect. MD&A precedes the basic financial statements. **Answer (B) is incorrect.** MD&A is not part of the basic financial statements. **Answer (D) is incorrect.** MD&A should state the reasons for change from the prior year, not merely the amounts or percentages of change.

18.4 Budgetary Accounts

13. When Rolan County adopted its budget for the year ending June 30, Year 1, $20 million was recorded for estimated revenues control. Actual revenues for the year ended June 30, Year 1, amounted to $17 million. In closing the budgetary accounts at June 30, Year 1,

A. Revenues control should be debited for $3 million.

B. Estimated revenues control should be debited for $3 million.

C. Revenues control should be credited for $20 million.

D. Estimated revenues control should be credited for $20 million.

Answer (D) is correct.

REQUIRED: The journal entry to close estimated revenues control and revenues control.

DISCUSSION: Estimated revenues control is an anticipatory asset recognized by a debit upon the adoption of the budget. Revenues control is a nominal account in which revenues are credited when they meet the recognition criteria. At year end, both accounts are closed. Because no other entries are made to estimated revenues control, the closing entry credits the account for the initial amount.

Answer (A) is incorrect. The amount of $3 million is the effect on the fund balance of the difference between actual and estimated revenues. **Answer (B) is incorrect.** Estimated revenues control is credited for the initial amount. **Answer (C) is incorrect.** The year-end entry to close the budgetary accounts should include a debit to revenues control for the amount of actual revenues recognized.

14. For the budgetary year ending December 31, Maple City's general fund expects the following inflows of resources:

Property taxes, licenses, and fines
Proceeds of debt issue
Interfund transfers for debt service

In the budgetary entry, what amount should Maple record for estimated revenues?

A. $9,000,000

B. $10,000,000

C. $14,000,000

D. $15,000,000

Answer (A) is correct.

REQUIRED: The amount of estimated revenues.

DISCUSSION: Estimated revenues is an anticipatory asset and is debited for the amount expected to be collected from a governmental body's main sources of revenue. In the general fund, the main sources of revenue are taxes, fees, penalties, etc. ($9,000,000). Expected proceeds from the issuance of debt is an other financing source. An expected transfer from a different fund is an other financing source.

Answer (B) is incorrect. The amount of $10,000,000 incorrectly includes the interfund transfers to the debt source fund (an other financing use). **Answer (C) is incorrect.** The amount of $14,000,000 incorrectly includes the debt issue proceeds (an other financing source). **Answer (D) is incorrect.** The amount of $15,000,000 incorrectly includes the debt issue proceeds (an other financing source) and interfund transfers to the debt service fund (an other financing use).

15. A city taxes merchants for various central district improvements. Which of the following accounting methods, if any, assist in assuring that these revenues are expended legally?

	Fund Accounting	Budgetary Accounting
A.	Yes	No
B.	No	Yes
C.	No	No
D.	Yes	Yes

Answer (D) is correct.

REQUIRED: The accounting methods, if any, assuring that tax revenues are legally expended.

DISCUSSION: To ensure budgetary control and accountability, budgetary accounts are integrated into the accounting system of a governmental entity. Such integration is necessary in (1) general, (2) special revenue, and (3) other annually budgeted governmental funds with many revenues, expenditures, and transfers. Accordingly, funds and budgetary accounts are useful for assuring fiscal accountability.

18.5 Classification of Fund Balance

16. The following information pertains to Park Township's general fund at December 31:

Total assets, including $200,000 of cash	$1,000,000
Total liabilities	600,000
Encumbrances	100,000

Appropriations do not lapse at year end. At December 31, what amount should Park report as unassigned fund balance in its general fund balance sheet?

A. $200,000

B. $300,000

C. $400,000

D. $500,000

Answer (B) is correct.

REQUIRED: The amount to be reported as unassigned fund balance in the general fund.

DISCUSSION: Appropriations encumbered at year end are reported in the balance sheet as committed or assigned fund balance (as appropriate). Accordingly, the amount of the unassigned fund balance in the general fund is equal to the amount of assets available to finance expenditures of the current or succeeding year. Funds that are (1) nonspendable, (2) restricted, (3) committed, or (4) assigned must be removed from the unassigned fund balance. Because $600,000 is needed to cover liabilities and $100,000 is reported in assigned or committed fund balance, the unassigned fund balance is $300,000 ($1,000,000 total assets – $600,000 liabilities – $100,000 assigned or committed).

Answer (A) is incorrect. The amount of $200,000 is the cash available. **Answer (C) is incorrect.** The amount of $400,000 does not reflect the amount encumbered. **Answer (D) is incorrect.** The amount of $500,000 is net position (Assets – Liabilities), plus the amount encumbered.

18.6 Encumbrances

17. A budgetary fund balance of a government's general fund is classified for encumbrances in excess of a balance of encumbrances. This accounting indicates

A. An excess of vouchers payable over encumbrances.

B. An excess of purchase orders over invoices received.

C. An excess of appropriations over encumbrances.

D. A recording error.

Answer (D) is correct.

REQUIRED: The reason a budgetary fund balance exceeds the encumbrance balance.

DISCUSSION: The budgetary fund balance account is a general ledger budgetary account sometimes used to record the anticipated change in fund balance at the beginning of the period. Encumbrances is debited and encumbrances outstanding is credited to record commitments related to unperformed executory contracts and unfulfilled purchase orders. When the expenditure is recorded, the encumbrance entry is reversed. At year end, any remaining encumbrances may be eliminated if the legal authority of appropriations expires. If (1) encumbrances will be honored by the entity, and (2) encumbered amounts have not been restricted, committed, or assigned, they are reclassified from unassigned fund balance to committed or assigned fund balance, as appropriate. They are not reported as encumbrances in the financial statements. (But significant encumbrances should be disclosed.) However, none of these entries involves budgetary fund balance, a nominal account that is (1) debited (credited) at the beginning of the year and (2) credited (debited) at year end for the budgeted change in fund balance. Thus, a recording error must exist if a budgetary fund balance is classified for any purpose.

Answer (A) is incorrect. An excess of vouchers payable over encumbrances indicates that expenditures exceeded encumbrances. **Answer (B) is incorrect.** An excess of purchase orders over invoices received indicates an excess of encumbrances over expenditures. **Answer (C) is incorrect.** An excess of appropriations over encumbrances equals the amount of permissible expenditures.

18. During its fiscal year ended June 30, Cliff City issued purchase orders totaling $5 million, which were properly charged to encumbrances at that time. Cliff received goods and related invoices at the encumbered amounts totaling $4.5 million before year end. The remaining goods of $500,000 were not received until after year end. Cliff paid $4.2 million of the invoices received during the year. The amount of Cliff's encumbrances outstanding in the general fund at June 30 was

A. $0

B. $300,000

C. $500,000

D. $800,000

Answer (C) is correct.

REQUIRED: The amount of encumbrances outstanding.

DISCUSSION: When a commitment is made to expend general fund resources, encumbrances is debited and encumbrances outstanding is credited. When the goods or services are received and the liability is recognized, this entry is reversed, and an expenditure is recorded. Because goods totaling $500,000 were not received at year end, encumbrances outstanding total $500,000 ($5,000,000 – $4,500,000).

Answer (A) is incorrect. Not all of the goods related to the encumbrance amounts were received during the year. **Answer (B) is incorrect.** The amount of $300,000 is the excess of goods received over the amount actually paid on the invoices during the year. **Answer (D) is incorrect.** The amount of $800,000 is the excess of total encumbrances over the amount paid on the invoices.

18.7 Governmental Funds Reporting

19. The focus of certain fund financial statements of a local government is on major funds. Accordingly,

A. Major internal service funds must be presented separately in the statement of net position for proprietary funds.

B. The main operating fund is always reported as a major fund.

C. Combining statements for nonmajor funds are required.

D. Enterprise funds not meeting the quantitative criteria are not eligible for presentation as major funds.

Answer (B) is correct.

REQUIRED: The true statement about major fund reporting.

DISCUSSION: The focus of reporting of governmental and proprietary funds (but not internal service funds) is on major funds. The main operating fund (e.g., the general fund) is always reported as a major fund, and any governmental or enterprise funds believed to be particularly important to users also may be reported in this way. These funds must be reported as major if they meet the quantitative thresholds.

Answer (A) is incorrect. Major fund reporting requirements apply to governmental and enterprise funds but not to internal service funds. **Answer (C) is incorrect.** Combining statements for nonmajor funds are not required but may be reported as supplementary information. **Answer (D) is incorrect.** A government may report any governmental or enterprise individual fund as major if it is particularly important.

20. A capital projects fund of a local government must be reported as major if

A. Total assets of that fund are 5% of the total assets of all governmental funds and 2% of the total assets of all governmental and enterprise funds combined.

B. Total expenditures of that fund are 10% of the total expenditures of all governmental funds and 2% of the total expenditures of all governmental and enterprise funds combined.

C. Total liabilities of that fund are 10% of the total liabilities of all governmental funds and 5% of the total liabilities of all governmental and enterprise funds combined.

D. Total revenues of that fund are 6% of the total revenues of all governmental funds and 3% of the total revenues of all governmental and enterprise funds combined.

Answer (C) is correct.

REQUIRED: The criteria for requiring major fund reporting of a capital projects fund.

DISCUSSION: Any fund must be reported as major if total revenues, expenditures or expenses, assets, or liabilities (excluding extraordinary items) of the fund (1) are at least 10% of the corresponding element total (assets, etc.) for all funds of the same category or type, that is, for all governmental or all enterprise funds, and (2) the same element that met the 10% standard is at least 5% of the corresponding element total for all governmental and enterprise funds in the aggregate.

STUDY UNIT NINETEEN

GOVERNMENTAL ACCOUNTING -- FULL ACCRUAL

(29 pages of outline)

This study unit is the second related to the state and local governments content area. It describes reporting requirements for government-wide, proprietary, and fiduciary financial statements and accounts and journal entries for various transactions specific to governmental entities.

The presentation assumes knowledge of the information in Study Unit 18.

19.1 CHARACTERISTIC TRANSACTIONS OF GOVERNMENTAL ENTITIES

1. **Outlays for Operations vs. Outlays for Capital Assets**
   a. In the **governmental funds**, whether an expenditure is for services used immediately or for a general capital asset is irrelevant.
      1) The focus of governmental-fund reporting is on the disposition of current-period resources. Thus, such outlays are expenditures rather than expenses.

EXAMPLE 19-1 Operations or Capital Assets Outlays -- Governmental Funds

An entry for the purchase of road maintenance equipment is similar to an entry to pay for extra office space.

General fund		
Expenditures -- rent	$20,000	
Vouchers payable		$20,000
Special revenue fund -- highway maintenance		
Expenditures -- road equipment	$745,000	
Vouchers payable		$745,000

   b. In the **government-wide financial statements**, all economic resources are reported.
      1) The services used in the current period are debited to an expense, and the noncurrent asset is capitalized.

EXAMPLE 19-2 Operations or Capital Assets Outlays -- Government-Wide Statements

The entries for road maintenance equipment and rental expense are as follows:

Rental expense	$20,000	
Vouchers payable		$20,000
Road equipment	$745,000	
Vouchers payable		$745,000

2. **Supplies and Prepaid Items**

   a. In the **governmental fund financial statements**, inventories of supplies and prepaid items present an accounting challenge.

      1) They are not expendable available financial resources, but they represent economic benefits retained by the entity.

         a) The two methods in common use for accounting for supplies and prepayments are described below.

      2) The **purchases method** is a modified accrual accounting treatment. It is used with a periodic system.

EXAMPLE 19-3 Purchases Method

Supplies and prepayments are recognized as expenditures at the time of purchase.

General Fund		
Expenditures -- supplies	$200,000	
Expenditures -- insurance	400,000	
Vouchers payable		$600,000

Assuming no beginning balances, i.e., increases in inventory and prepaid insurance, the year-end entries are

General Fund		
Inventory of supplies	$ 95,000	
Prepaid insurance	190,000	
Other financing sources -- inventory increase		$ 95,000
Other financing sources -- prepayment increase		190,000
Unassigned fund balance	$285,000	
Fund balance -- nonspendable for increase in supplies inventory		$ 95,000
Fund balance -- nonspendable for increase in prepaid insurance		190,000

Prepaid insurance is debited. The GASB has not specifically identified prepayments as items classified as deferred outflows of resources.

      3) The **consumption method** is essentially an accrual accounting treatment. It is used with a periodic or perpetual system.

EXAMPLE 19-4 Consumption Method

Using the perpetual system, supplies and prepayments are recognized as assets at the time of purchase and payment, respectively.

General Fund		
Inventory of supplies	$200,000	
Prepaid insurance	400,000	
Vouchers payable		$600,000

During the period, issuances of inventory are recognized by debits to expenditures and credits to inventory. At year end, the following entries recognize (1) an inventory shortage of $5,000 based on a physical count and (2) the expired portion of prepaid insurance ($210,000):

General Fund		
Expenditures	$215,000	
Inventory of supplies		$ 5,000
Prepaid insurance		210,000

b. In the **government-wide financial statements**, the accrual method is used to account for supplies and prepaid items.

1) An asset is recognized at the time of purchase, and an expense (not an expenditure) is recognized for the usage of the asset or the passage of time.

EXAMPLE 19-5 Government-Wide Funds -- Supplies and Prepaid Items

Based on the same numbers and facts from the previous examples, an asset is recognized at the time of purchase.

Enterprise Fund		
Inventory of supplies	$200,000	
Prepaid insurance	400,000	
Vouchers payable		$600,000

During the period, issuances of inventory are recognized by debits to cost of goods sold (an expense, not expenditure) and credits to inventory.

Enterprise Fund		
Accounts receivable	$150,000	
Cost of goods sold	100,000	
Inventory of supplies		$100,000
Sales		150,000

The ending balance of inventory of supplies (before adjusting for the shortage) is $100,000.

At year end, the following entries recognize (1) an inventory shortage of $5,000 based on a physical count and (2) the expired portion of prepaid insurance ($210,000):

Enterprise Fund		
Cost of goods sold	$ 5,000	
Insurance expenses	210,000	
Inventory of supplies		$ 5,000
Prepaid insurance		210,000

The ending balances of inventory of supplies and prepaid insurance are $95,000 and $190,000, respectively.

3. **Capital Leases**

a. The GASB adopted the FASB's guidelines for classifying leases as capital or operating. Thus, when any of the four capitalization criteria is met, a governmental unit, whether as a lessee or lessor, must recognize a capital lease.

SUCCESS TIP

The GASB adopted the FASB's previous guidance on lease accounting. The FASB's new lease pronouncement is testable in 2021 and is covered extensively in Study Unit 13. However, the GASB's new lease pronouncement (Statement 87) is not testable until Q3 2021.

b. **Lessee Accounting**

1) In **government-wide, proprietary fund, and trust fund** financial statements, a capital lease is recognized in the same way as in a purchase.

a) The leased asset is capitalized at the present value of the minimum lease payments, and a long-term liability is recognized for any remainder after a cash payment at the lease's inception.

EXAMPLE 19-6 Lessee -- Capital Lease: Accrual Entries

A government enters into a long-term capital lease for equipment. The present value of the minimum lease payments is $120,000.

Equipment -- capital lease	$120,000	
Cash		$ 10,000
Capital lease obligation		110,000

At the end of the first year, a portion of the lease is amortized.

Interest expense	$9,000	
Capital lease obligation	1,000	
Cash		$10,000

2) The financial statements of **governmental funds**, with their focus on current financial resources, do not recognize the long-term nature of a leased asset and its related obligation.

EXAMPLE 19-7 Lessee -- Capital Lease: Modified Accrual

The initiation of the lease is recorded as follows:

Expenditures -- leased assets	$120,000	
Cash		$ 10,000
Other financing sources -- capital lease		110,000

The payment at the end of the first year is recorded as follows:

Expenditures -- interest	$9,000	
Expenditures -- principal	1,000	
Cash		$10,000

c. **Lessor Accounting**

1) In **government-wide, proprietary fund, and trust fund** financial statements, the lessor's accounting also follows the guidance above.

2) In the financial statements of **governmental funds**, a lease receivable is recognized to the extent it represents another financing source that is measurable and available. The rest is deferred.

a) Furthermore, the noncurrent receivable is not a general capital asset. Thus, it is reported in the fund accounting for the lease.

4. **Compensated Absences**

   a. When governments grant their employees paid time off, the salary rate used to calculate the liability should be the rate in effect at the end of the fiscal period.

      1) In **governmental funds financial statements**, only the portion of compensated absences that employees will use in the next fiscal period is recognized. This portion must be paid with current financial resources.

      2) In government-wide financial statements, the entire liability must be recognized.

EXAMPLE 19-8 Compensated Absences

General fund		
Expenditures -- compensated absences	$91,000	
Liability -- compensated absences		$91,000
Government-wide financial statements		
Expenses -- compensated absences	$750,000	
Liability -- compensated absences		$750,000

5. **Works of Art and Historical Treasures**

   a. The accounting measurement of a work of art or historical treasure obtained by a government depends on whether the item is purchased or donated.

      1) If the item is **purchased**, it is recorded at historical cost.

EXAMPLE 19-9 Work of Art -- Government-Wide Statements

A government pays $12,000,000 for a work of art for its museum. A similar item with equivalent service potential recently sold at auction for $14,000,000.

Government-wide financial statements		
Work of Art	$12,000,000	
Cash		$12,000,000

         a) If the museum in which the item is displayed is operated as an **enterprise fund**, i.e., an admission fee is charged, the asset generates revenue.

         b) If the museum is accounted for in the **general fund**, the modified accrual basis of accounting requires the transaction to be recorded as an expenditure.

EXAMPLE 19-10 Work of Art -- General Fund

The government operates its museum as a governmental activity.

General fund		
Expenditures -- work of art	$12,000,000	
Cash		$12,000,000

      2) If a work of art or historical treasure is **donated**, it is recorded at **acquisition value**. This measurement attribute is defined in item 6.d. on the next page.

EXAMPLE 19-11 Donated Work of Art

If the government accounts for the museum in an enterprise fund, the following entry is recorded in the government-wide financial statements and the proprietary fund financial statements:

Work of art	$14,000,000	
Revenue -- donation		$14,000,000

If the government accounts for the museum in the general fund, the item is not capitalized.

b. Although the recognition of works of art and historical treasures as **assets** is encouraged, capitalization is optional in some circumstances.

1) A government may record the acquisition (whether by purchase or donation) of a work of art or historical treasure as an **expense** if the collection to which the object is being added meets these three criteria:

a) The collection is held for public exhibition, education, or research in furtherance of public service rather than financial gain;

b) The collection is protected, kept unencumbered, cared for, and preserved; and

c) The collection is subject to an organizational policy that requires the proceeds from sales of collection items to be used to acquire other items for collections.

2) Only collections or items that are exhaustible are **depreciated**.

6. **Capital Assets and Long-Term Liabilities**

a. **Governmental funds** have a current financial resources measurement focus.

1) Such noncurrent items as capital assets and long-term liabilities are **not** reported in governmental funds.

b. **Proprietary funds** have an economic resources measurement focus. The capital assets and long-term liabilities specifically related to proprietary fund activities are accounted for on the accrual basis.

1) They are reported in those funds and in the government-wide statements.

c. **Fiduciary funds** hold resources as a fiduciary activity in certain trust funds and custodial funds.

1) The capital assets and long-term liabilities specifically related to fiduciary funds are reported in the fund financial statements but **not** in the government-wide statements.

d. **Capital assets** are tangible and intangible assets used in operations that have initial useful lives beyond one reporting period.

1) **Depreciation** of capital assets is required except for (a) land, (b) works of art and historical treasures that are inexhaustible, and (c) infrastructure assets accounted for using the modified approach.

a) Depreciation is recognized in the government-wide, proprietary fund, and fiduciary fund statements.

2) Purchased capital assets are reported at historical cost, including other charges (e.g., freight-in or site preparation).

3) Donated capital assets are measured at acquisition value (an entry price).

a) **Acquisition value** is (1) the price that would be paid to acquire an **asset** with equivalent service potential in an orderly market transaction at the acquisition date or (2) the amount at which a **liability** could be liquidated with the counterparty at the acquisition date.

4) **Infrastructure assets** are stationary capital assets that can be preserved for a longer time than most capital assets.

a) Examples include roads, bridges, tunnels, sidewalks, water and sewer systems, drainage systems, and lighting systems. But buildings are not infrastructure assets unless they are ancillary parts of a network or subsystem of a network.

b) The treatment of public infrastructure assets is similar to that for other capital assets.

   i) In the **government-wide** financial statements, they are reported as assets.

   ii) In the **governmental funds** financial statements, they are reported as expenditures. They are not current financial resources.

c) Like works of art and historical treasures, some infrastructure assets may have lives so long that they are in effect inexhaustible and therefore **nondepreciable**.

d) The **modified approach** is an alternative to depreciation for very long-lived infrastructure assets.

   i) Infrastructure assets that are part of a network or subsystem of a network (eligible infrastructure assets) need **not** be depreciated. However, the government must (a) use an asset management system with certain characteristics and (b) document that the assets are being preserved approximately at an established condition level disclosed by the government.

   ii) The modified approach allows a government to **record maintenance costs** instead of recording depreciation expense.

   iii) Additions to and improvements of infrastructure assets still are capitalized.

EXAMPLE 19-12 Modified Approach

A private corporation built a solar power system for $12,000,000 and donated the system to a local government in Year 2. A similar system with equivalent service potential recently sold at auction for $14,000,000. The system is expected to last for so long that it is in effect inexhaustible and therefore nondepreciable. The local government elected the modified approach to account for the system. The government spent $100,000 in routine maintenance of the system in both Year 2 and Year 3. In Year 3, the government spent $250,000 to add new sensors to the system. The following entries are recorded in the government-wide financial statements:

For the donation in Year 2:

Proprietary Fund		
Solar power system	$14,000,000	
Revenue -- donation		$14,000,000

The donated asset is recorded at the acquisition value of $14,000,000.

For the maintenance in Year 2:

Proprietary Fund		
Maintenance expense	$100,000	
Cash		$100,000

No depreciation expense is recorded under the modified approach.

For the addition in Year 3:

Proprietary Fund		
Solar power system	$250,000	
Cash		$250,000

The addition of the sensors is capitalized.

For the maintenance in Year 3:

Proprietary Fund		
Maintenance expense	$100,000	
Cash		$100,000

No depreciation is recorded for the solar power system and the capitalized addition of the sensors.

e. **General capital assets** are all capital assets not reported in the proprietary funds or the fiduciary funds. Thus, they usually result from expenditure of governmental fund financial resources.
   1) General capital assets are reported **only** in the governmental activities column of the government-wide statement of net position.
f. **General long-term liabilities** are secured by the government's general credit and revenue-raising powers. They include all unmatured long-term liabilities not directly related to, and not expected to be paid from, proprietary funds and fiduciary funds.
   1) The following are examples of general long-term liabilities:
      a) Unmatured principal amounts of general obligation debt (such as bonds, warrants, and notes)
      b) Noncurrent portions of liabilities for capital leases, compensated absences, claims and judgments, and pensions
      c) Special assessment debt for which the government is obligated in some manner, except for any portion to be paid from an enterprise fund
      d) Other commitments not recorded as current liabilities in governmental funds
   2) General long-term liabilities are reported **only** in the governmental activities column of the government-wide statement of net position.

7. **Deferred Outflows and Inflows of Resources**
   a. Some items accounted for as assets and liabilities by nongovernmental entities must be reported by a governmental entity as deferred outflows and inflows of resources.
      1) For example, in nongovernmental accounting, revenues received but not earned are liabilities, and prepayments of expenses are assets.
   b. A **deferred outflow of resources** is a consumption of net assets that applies to a future reporting period.
   c. A **deferred inflow of resources** is an acquisition of net assets that applies to a future reporting period.
   d. Deferred outflows of resources are presented separately following **assets**, and deferred inflows of resources are presented separately following **liabilities**, in a statement of net position or a governmental fund balance sheet.
      1) A **statement of net position** is presented in the (a) government-wide statements, (b) proprietary fund statements, and (c) fiduciary fund statements.

e. Classification as a deferred outflow or inflow of resources is limited to items **specifically** identified in GASB pronouncements. The following are examples of transactions that generally qualify for this treatment:

1) Certain nonexchange transactions. (This subject is covered in Study Unit 18, Subunit 2.)

a) Imposed nonexchange revenue transactions (e.g., property taxes collected prior to the period for which they are levied)

b) Government-mandated nonexchange transactions and voluntary nonexchange transactions (e.g., government grants received for which all eligibility requirements have not yet been met)

2) Certain leases

a) Any gain or loss recognized in a sale-leaseback transaction must be accounted for as a deferred inflow or outflow of resources and recognized in a systematic and rational manner over the lease term.

3) Assets associated with **unavailable** revenues in governmental funds

a) Governmental fund resources should be recognized when they are measurable and available. Thus, if an asset is recognized in a governmental fund but the revenue is not available, a deferred inflow of resources (a credit) is reported.

4) Assets and liabilities associated with pensions (e.g., long-term obligations for pension benefits)

8. **Investments**

a. Investments ordinarily are measured at **fair value**.

1) An investment is a security or other asset that

a) Is held primarily for income and profit and

b) Has a service capacity based only on the ability to generate cash or be sold for cash.

b. The GASB has adopted the FASB's definition of fair value and approach to fair value measurement as described in Study Unit 4, Subunit 7. The following are examples of items measured at fair value:

1) Equity securities

2) Debt securities

3) Land and other real estate held by endowments, including permanent and term endowments, and permanent funds

c. Examples of items **not** required to be measured at fair value are the following:

1) Money-market investments
2) Held-to-maturity debt securities
3) Equity-method investments in common stock

STOP & REVIEW

You have completed the outline for this subunit.
Study multiple-choice questions 1 through 6 beginning on page 615.

19.2 GOVERNMENT-WIDE FINANCIAL STATEMENTS

1. **Overview**

   a. Government-wide financial statements report information about the government **as a whole**. Thus, they do not display funds or fund types.

      1) Government-wide statements also do **not** report information about **fiduciary activities**, including fiduciary component units.

         a) The assets of a fiduciary fund are held as a fiduciary activity.

   b. The primary government is distinguished from its discretely presented component units.

   c. The governmental activities and business-type activities of the primary government are separately presented.

      1) **Governmental activities** normally are financed by nonexchange revenues (taxes, etc.). They are reported in governmental and internal service funds.

      2) **Business-type activities** are financed at least in part by fees charged to external parties for goods and services. They are reported in enterprise funds.

2. **Measurement Focus and Basis of Accounting**

   a. The **economic resources** measurement focus and the **accrual** basis of accounting are used to measure and report all of the following:

      1) Assets (capital and financial)
      2) Deferred outflows of resources
      3) Liabilities
      4) Deferred inflows of resources
      5) Revenues
      6) Expenses
      7) Gains
      8) Losses

3. **Eliminations and Reclassifications**
   a. Preparation of the government-wide statements requires that certain interfund activity and fund balances be eliminated or reclassified.
   b. Certain **interfund amounts**, e.g., receivables and payables, are eliminated from the governmental and business-type activities columns of the statement of net position.
      1) The exceptions are **net residual amounts** due between the two types of activities.
         a) However, the total primary government column excludes internal balances.
            i) The statement of net position on page 598 is an example of the elimination of internal balances. The statement of activities on page 600 is an example of the elimination of transfers.
   c. **Internal service funds** report activities that provide goods or services on a cost-reimbursement basis to (1) other funds or functions of the primary government or (2) other governments.
      1) Their activities ordinarily are more governmental (e.g., financing goods or services for other funds) than business-type. Thus, although internal service funds are **proprietary** funds, they are reported in the **governmental activities** column in the government-wide statements to the extent they are not eliminated.
         a) When the activities of governmental funds and internal service funds are both governmental, the effects of transactions between them must be eliminated.
   d. Eliminations are not made in the statement of activities for the effects of **interfund services provided and used** between functions.
      1) An example is the sale of power by a utility (an enterprise fund) to the general government.
   e. Flows of resources between the **primary government** and its **blended** component units are reclassified as internal activity based on the requirements for interfund activity.
      1) Flows between the primary government and its **discretely presented** component units (unless they affect the statement of net position only) are treated as **external transactions** (as revenues and expenses).
   f. Receivables from or payables to **fiduciary funds** are reclassified as receivables from or payables to **external parties**.
      1) The reason is that fiduciary funds report only balances held as fiduciary activities.
4. **Statement of Net Position**
   a. The statement reports **all financial and capital resources**. The GASB prefers the following format:

$$\begin{array}{rl} & \text{(Assets + Deferred outflows of resources)} \\ - & \underline{\text{(Liabilities + Deferred inflows of resources)}} \\ = & \underline{\underline{\text{Net position}}} \end{array}$$

      1) **Net position**, not equity or fund balance, is reported.

EXAMPLE 19-13 Sample Statement of Net Position -- December 31, 20X1

	Primary Government			
ASSETS	**Governmental Activities**	**Business-Type Activities**	**Total**	**Component Units**
Cash and cash equivalents	$20,400,000	$13,876,000	$34,276,000	$ 107,000
Investments	4,520,000	0	4,520,000	101,000
Derivative instrument -- rate swap	1,140,000	968,000	2,108,000	401,000
Receivables (net)	5,502,000	3,987,000	9,489,000	507,000
Internal balances	530,000	0	530,000	0
Inventories	307,000	299,000	606,000	420,000
Equity interest in joint venture	142,000	121,000	263,000	10,000
Capital assets, net	4,201,000	2,975,000	7,176,000	521,000
Total assets	**$36,742,000**	**$22,226,000**	**$58,968,000**	**$2,067,000**
DEFERRED OUTFLOWS OF RESOURCES				
Accumulated decrease in fair value of hedging derivatives	$ 2,012,000	$ 1,015,000	$ 3,027,000	$1,104,000
LIABILITIES				
Accounts payable and accrued expenses	$ 1,342,000	$ 405,000	$ 1,747,000	$ 801,000
Internal balances	0	530,000	530,000	0
Advances from grantors	1,470,000	0	1,470,000	98,000
Forward contract	1,502,000	0	1,502,000	91,000
Long-term liabilities:				
Due within 1 year	2,508,000	1,501,000	4,009,000	106,000
Due in more than 1 year	5,142,000	3,104,000	8,246,000	670,000
Total liabilities	**$11,964,000**	**$ 5,540,000**	**$17,504,000**	**$1,766,000**
DEFERRED INFLOWS OF RESOURCES				
Accumulated increase in fair value of hedging derivatives	$ 2,430,000	$ 514,000	$ 2,944,000	$ 108,000
Deferred service concession arrangement receipts	530,000	146,000	676,000	281,000
Total deferred inflows of resources	**$ 2,960,000**	**$ 660,000**	**$ 3,620,000**	**$ 389,000**
NET POSITION				
Net investment in capital assets	$ 4,201,000	$ 2,975,000	$ 7,176,000	$ 521,000
Restricted for:				
Transportation and public works	3,987,000	0	3,987,000	802,000
Debt service	643,000	3,975,000	4,618,000	0
Housing and community redevelopment	4,754,000	0	4,754,000	0
Other purposes	2,430,000	0	2,430,000	0
Unrestricted (deficit)	7,815,000	10,091,000	17,906,000	(307,000)
Total net position	**$23,830,000**	**$17,041,000**	**$40,871,000**	**$1,016,000**

b. Presentation of assets and liabilities in order of relative liquidity is encouraged.

1) Separate display of current and noncurrent assets and liabilities (a classified statement) also is acceptable.

c. Net position should be displayed as three components:

1) **Net investment in capital assets** includes capital assets, net of accumulated depreciation, reduced by outstanding debt related to acquiring, constructing, or improving the assets. Related deferred inflows and outflows of resources also are included.

a) However, significant (1) **unspent debt proceeds** or (2) deferred inflows of resources may exist at the end of the period. The part of the debt or deferred inflows related to the unspent amount then is excluded from the net investment in capital assets.

i) Accordingly, that part of the debt or deferred inflows should be classified in the same net position component as the unspent amount (restricted or unrestricted).

2) **Restricted net position** equals restricted assets minus related liabilities and deferred inflows of resources. The restrictions are imposed by external entities (creditors, grantors, or other governments) or by law (constitutional provisions or **enabling legislation**).

a) If permanent endowments or permanent fund principal amounts are included, restricted net position should be displayed as expendable and nonexpendable.

i) **Nonexpendable** means that the restriction is retained in perpetuity.

3) **Unrestricted net position** is the net of (a) assets, (b) deferred outflows of resources, (c) liabilities, and (d) deferred inflows of revenue not included in the other components of net position. Thus, it is a residual category.

a) Unrestricted net position includes items that may be internally committed or assigned. These commitments and assignments are not reported on the face of the statements.

5. **Statement of Activities**

a. The statement of activities displays **net (expense) revenue** for each function.

1) It reports the relative financial burden on the taxpayers for each function.

2) The net (expense) revenue for each governmental or business-type function equals expenses (at a minimum, the **direct expenses** of the function) minus program revenues.

b. The minimum levels of detail for activities accounted for in governmental funds and in enterprise funds are by **function** and by **different identifiable activities**, respectively.

1) An identifiable activity has a specific revenue stream and related expenses, gains, and losses separately accounted for. Whether it is different ordinarily depends on the goods, services, or programs that the activity provides.

c. **Direct expenses** must be reported by function.

1) **Indirect expenses** may or may not be allocated.

2) **Depreciation** specifically identifiable with a function is a direct expense. Depreciation of capital assets **shared by functions** is allocated as a direct expense.

a) Depreciation of capital assets that **serve all functions** is not required to be included in direct expenses of the functions. It may be displayed on a separate line in the statement of activities or as part of the general government function. It may or may not be allocated.

b) Depreciation of infrastructure assets is not allocated to other functions.

3) **Interest on general long-term liabilities** is usually an indirect expense.

EXAMPLE 19-14 **Statement of Activities**

		Program Revenues			Net (Expense) Revenue and Changes in Net Position			
					Primary Government			
Functions/Programs	Expenses	Charges for Services	Operating Grants and Contributions	Capital Grants and Contributions	Governmental Activities	Business-type Activities	Total	Component Units
Primary government:								
Governmental activities:								
General government	$ 500,000	$ 368,000	$ 59,000	$ 0	$ (73,000)	$ 0	$ (73,000)	$ 0
Public safety	1,200,000	480,000	530,000	32,000	(158,000)	0	(158,000)	0
Public works	1,320,000	43,000	0	260,000	(1,017,000)	0	(1,017,000)	0
Engineering services	485,000	63,000	0	0	(422,000)	0	(422,000)	0
Etc.	2,300,000	530,000	270,000	520,000	(980,000)	0	(980,000)	0
Total governmental activities	$ 5,805,000	$ 1,484,000	$ 859,000	$ 812,000	$ (2,650,000)	$ 0	$ (2,650,000)	$ 0
Business-type activities:								
Water	$ 980,000	$ 440,000	$ 0	$ 720,000	$ 0	$ 180,000	$ 180,000	$ 0
Sewer	320,000	930,000	0	83,000	0	693,000	693,000	0
Parking facilities	380,000	275,000	0	0	0	(105,000)	(105,000)	0
Total business-type activities	$ 1,680,000	$ 1,645,000	$ 0	$ 803,000	$ 0	$ 768,000	$ 768,000	$ 0
Total primary government	**$ 7,485,000**	**$ 3,129,000**	**$ 859,000**	**$ 1,615,000**	**$ (2,650,000)**	**$ 768,000**	**$ (1,882,000)**	**$ 0**
Component units:								
Landfill	$ 540,000	$ 820,000	$ 0	$ 50,000	$ 0	$ 0	$ 0	$ 330,000
Public school system	1,300,000	73,000	430,000	0	0	0	0	(797,000)
Total component units	**$ 1,840,000**	**$ 893,000**	**$ 430,000**	**$ 50,000**	**$ 0**	**$ 0**	**$ 0**	**$ (467,000)**
General revenues:								
Taxes:								
Property taxes levied for general purposes					$ 2,100,000	$ 0	$ 2,650,000	$ 0
Property taxes levied for debt service					500,000	0	428,000	0
Franchise fees					310,000	0	630,000	0
Public service taxes					820,000	0	421,000	0
Payment from City					0	0	0	280,000
Grants and contributions not restricted to specific programs					275,000	0	438,000	328,000
Investment earnings					325,000	56,000	370,000	53,000
Miscellaneous					35,000	72,000	48,000	3,000
Special item – gain on sale of land					420,000	0	439,000	0
Transfers					43,000	(43,000)	0	0
Total general revenues, special items, and transfers					**$ 4,828,000**	**$ 85,000**	**$ 5,424,000**	**$ 664,000**
Change in net position					$ 2,178,000	$ 853,000	$ 3,542,000	$ 197,000
Net position – beginning					4,020,000	2,380,000	3,420,000	343,000
Net position – ending					**$ 6,198,000**	**$ 3,233,000**	**$ 6,962,000**	**$ 540,000**

d. **Program revenues** include (1) charges for services, (2) program-specific operating grants and contributions, and (3) program-specific capital grants and contributions.

1) They also may include investment earnings specifically restricted to a given program.

2) **Charges for services** are program revenues resulting from charges to customers, applicants, or others who (a) directly benefit from what is provided (goods, services, or privileges) or (b) are otherwise directly affected.

a) Thus, **fines and forfeitures** are charges for services because they are paid by persons directly affected by a program or service.

b) Charges for services are assigned to a given function if the function generates those revenues.

3) **Grants and contributions** are assigned to a given function if the revenues are restricted to it.

e. **General revenues** are not required to be reported as program revenues. They are reported separately after total net (expense) revenue for all functions.

1) All taxes, including those levied for a special purpose, are general revenues.

2) General revenues are reported at the bottom of the statement of activities to determine the change in net position for the period.

f. The following are reported separately at the bottom of the statement of activities: (1) contributions to endowments, (2) contributions to permanent fund principal, (3) transfers between governmental and business-type activities, and (4) special and extraordinary items.

1) **Extraordinary items** are unusual in nature and infrequent in occurrence.

2) **Special items** are reported separately before extraordinary items. They are significant transactions or other events that are

a) Unusual or infrequent but not both and
b) **Within the control of management**.

3) Significant transactions or other events that are unusual or infrequent but not within the control of management should be disclosed in the notes.

6. **Reconciliation: Total Governmental Fund Balances to Net Position of Governmental Activities**

a. A summary reconciliation of (1) the **total governmental fund balances** to (2) the **net position of governmental activities** in the government-wide statement of net position must be prepared.

1) This summary should be presented at the bottom of the statement or in a schedule.

b. **General capital assets and general long-term liabilities** not currently due are reconciling items because they are not reported on the balance sheet. Thus, (1) the **current financial** resources measurement focus of the governmental funds balance sheet is reconciled with (2) the **economic** resources measurement focus of the government-wide statement of net position.

EXAMPLE 19-15 Total Governmental Fund Balances to Net Position of Governmental Activities

Total governmental fund balances	$18,867,000
Amounts reported for *governmental activities* in the statement of net position in the government-wide statements differ from governmental fund amounts because	
Capital assets are not financial resources. They are not reported in the governmental funds.	4,170,000
Other long-term assets are not available to pay for current-period expenditures and are reported as deferred inflows of resources, which reduce fund balances. (The balance sheet formula in Study Unit 18, Subunit 7, illustrates this relationship.) Thus, other long-term assets are added to total governmental fund balances in the reconciliation to net position of governmental activities.	745,000
Internal service funds are proprietary funds used by management to charge the costs of certain activities, such as insurance and telecommunications, to individual funds. The assets and liabilities of the internal service funds are not included in the governmental funds, but they are included in governmental activities in the statement of net position.	710,000
Long-term liabilities, including bonds payable, not due and payable in the current period are not reported in the governmental funds.	(12,255,000)
Net position of governmental activities	**$ 12,237,000**

Study Unit 18, Subunit 7, covers governmental fund financial statements.

EXAMPLE 19-16 Net Increase in Fund Balance to Change in Net Position

Tree City reported a $1,500 net increase in fund balance for governmental funds for the current year. During the year, Tree purchased general capital assets of $9,000 and recorded depreciation expense of $3,000. What amount should Tree report as the change in net position for governmental activities?

The $1,500 net increase in the fund balance for governmental funds reflects a $9,000 expenditure (modified accrual basis of accounting) for general capital assets. These assets are not reported in the fund statements. The effect of the expenditure is a decrease in current financial resources of $9,000.

However, the government-wide statements report an expense of $3,000 (accrual basis of accounting) for depreciation and a depreciated asset with a carrying amount of $6,000 ($9,000 cost – $3,000 depreciation). The effect is a decrease in economic resources of $3,000.

Reconciling the net increase in fund balance to the change in net position therefore requires adding $6,000 ($9,000 modified accrual basis expenditure – $3,000 accrual basis expense). The change in net position is $7,500 ($1,500 + $6,000 reconciling item).

Net increase in governmental fund balance	$1,500
Expenditure	9,000
Expense	(3,000)
Change in net position for governmental activities	$7,500

7. **Reconciliation: Net Change in Governmental Fund Balances to Change in Net Position of Governmental Activities**

   a. A summary reconciliation of (1) the **net change in governmental fund balances** to (2) the **change in net position of governmental activities** in the government-wide statement of activities must be prepared.

      1) This summary should be presented at the bottom of the statement or in a schedule.

EXAMPLE 19-17 Net Change in Governmental Fund Balances to Change in Net Position of Governmental Activities

Net change in fund balances -- total governmental funds	$9,507,000
Amounts reported for *governmental activities* in the statement of activities in the government-wide statements differ from amounts included in the net change in fund balances. The following are examples:	
Governmental funds report **capital outlays** as expenditures. However, in the statement of activities, the cost of those assets is allocated over their estimated useful lives as depreciation expense. The reconciling amount equals the excess of capital outlays over depreciation in the current period.	759,000
In the statement of activities, only the **gain on a sale of an asset** (Sale proceeds – Asset cost) is reported. But in the governmental funds, the proceeds from the sale increase financial resources. Thus, the cost of the asset is subtracted from the net change in fund balances in the reconciliation to the change in net position of governmental activities.	(240,000)
Revenues in the statement of activities that do not provide current financial resources are not reported as revenues in the funds.	470,000
Bond proceeds increase current financial resources in the governmental funds. But issuing debt increases long-term liabilities in the statement of net position with no effect on the statement of activities. Repayment of bond principal is an expenditure in the governmental funds that reduces fund balance. But the repayment reduces long-term liabilities in the statement of net position without recognition of an expense in the statement of activities. Thus, the excess of the proceeds over the repayments is subtracted from the net change in fund balances in the reconciliation to the change in net position of governmental activities.	(1,480,000)
Some expenses reported in the statement of activities do not require the use of current financial resources and therefore are not reported as expenditures in governmental funds.	(1,020,000)
Internal service funds are used by management to charge the costs of certain activities, such as insurance and telecommunications, to individual funds. Although internal service funds are proprietary, their activities ordinarily are governmental. Accordingly, the net revenue (expense) of the internal service funds is reported in the governmental activities column. For example, net expense is subtracted from the net change in governmental fund balances in the reconciliation to the change in net position of governmental activities.	(480,000)
Change in net position of governmental activities	**$7,516,000**

Study Unit 18, Subunit 7, covers governmental fund financial statements.

STOP & REVIEW

You have completed the outline for this subunit.
Study multiple-choice questions 7 through 10 beginning on page 617.

19.3 PROPRIETARY FUNDS REPORTING

1. **Measurement Focus and Basis of Accounting**
   a. The emphasis of proprietary funds is on (1) operating income, (2) changes in net position (or cost recovery), (3) financial position, and (4) cash flows.
      1) Moreover, these funds customarily do **not** record a budget and encumbrances.
   b. The **economic resources** measurement focus and the **accrual** basis of accounting are required in the proprietary fund financial statements.
2. **Enterprise Funds**
   a. Enterprise funds may be used for (1) any activities for which fees are charged to external users or (2) certain fiduciary activities.
      1) Business activities (including enterprise funds) may report assets and a liability otherwise reportable in a **custodial fund** (a fiduciary fund) in the statement of net position. But the assets ordinarily should be expected to be held for no more than three months.
         a) If this reporting is adopted, significant additions and deductions should be separately reported as operating cash inflows and outflows, respectively, in the statement of cash flows.
   b. The **criteria** to determine whether an activity must be reported as an enterprise fund (1) are applied in the context of the activity's principal revenue sources and (2) emphasize **fees charged to external users**. An activity is reported in an enterprise fund if any of the following criteria is met:
      1) The activity is financed with debt, and the only security is a pledge of the activity's net revenues from fees and charges.
      2) Capital and other costs of providing services are legally required to be recovered from fees and charges, not taxes or similar revenues.
      3) Pricing policies set fees and charges to recover capital and other costs.
   c. The following are examples of enterprise fund activities:
      1) Public transportation systems
      2) State-run lotteries
      3) Public utilities (water, sewage, or electricity)
      4) Unemployment compensation funds
      5) Emergency services
      6) Government-owned healthcare facilities
   d. Journal entries are virtually the same as in any business. **Major fund** reporting is required for enterprise funds.

3. **Internal Service Funds**

   a. They may be used for activities that provide goods and services to other subunits of the primary government and its component units or to other governments on a **cost-reimbursement basis**.

      1) However, if the reporting government is **not** the predominant participant, the activity should be reported as an **enterprise fund**.

   b. The following are examples of internal service fund activities:

      1) Information technology support
      2) Central purchasing and warehousing
      3) Motor pool maintenance
      4) Photocopying and printing
      5) Self-insurance for payment of claims and judgments

   c. **Billings for goods and services** are recorded as operating revenues. These activities are considered to be interfund services provided and used.

   d. Journal entries are virtually the same as for any business.

      1) The initial allocation of resources may come from (a) an interfund transfer (i.e., an amount not to be repaid) or (b) an interfund loan.

         a) To record an interfund transfer from the general fund and an interfund loan from an enterprise fund, the entry might be

Cash	$800,000	
Interfund transfer from the general fund		$200,000
Due to enterprise fund		600,000

   e. **Major fund** reporting is **not** required for internal service funds.

      1) The combined totals for all internal service funds are reported in a separate column (usually labeled as governmental activities) to the right of the total enterprise funds column in each proprietary fund financial statement.

4. **Statement of Net Position**

   a. Governments are encouraged to use the following net position format:

Assets	$ 58,438,000	
Deferred outflows of resources	3,027,000	
Total		$61,465,000
Liabilities	$(16,974,000)	
Deferred inflows of resources	(3,620,000)	
Total		(20,594,000)
Net position		$40,871,000

   b. Assets and liabilities must be **classified** as current or long-term.

   c. Net position should be reported in three components:

      1) Net investment in capital assets
      2) Restricted (with display of major categories)
      3) Unrestricted

   d. **Capital contributions** (such as grants or contributions by developers) should **not** be displayed as a separate component.

   e. **Designations** should **not** be shown on the face of the statements.

   f. **Capital assets** of proprietary funds and **long-term liabilities** directly related to, and expected to be paid from, proprietary funds are reported in

      1) The government-wide statement of net position and
      2) The proprietary fund statement of net position.

5. **Statement of Revenues, Expenses, and Changes in Fund Net Position**

   a. **Revenues** are reported by major source either

      1) **Net** with disclosure of discounts and allowances or
      2) **Gross** with discounts and allowances reported beneath the revenue amounts.

   b. **Operating** items are included in the following separate subtotals:

      1) Revenues
      2) Expenses
      3) Income (loss)

   c. **Nonoperating revenues and expenses** are reported after operating income (loss).

      1) An example of a nonoperating revenue is the receipt of an unrestricted grant from another government (a nonreciprocal transfer).
      2) Another example is receipt of a state appropriation in a government-mandated nonexchange transaction.

   d. The following are reported separately **after** nonoperating revenues and expenses:

      1) Revenues from capital contributions
      2) Revenues from additions to the principal of term and permanent endowments

         a) A term endowment is temporarily restricted.
         b) A permanent endowment is principal that cannot be expended.

      3) Special and extraordinary items (Study Unit 18, Subunit 7, and Subunit 19.2, contain relevant outlines.)
      4) Transfers (Study Unit 18, Subunit 2, contains an outline of nonreciprocal interfund activity.)

e. The sequence of items described on the previous page should be followed in each column of the statement.

EXAMPLE 19-18 Statement of Revenues, Expenses, and Changes in Fund Net Position

Sample: December 31, 20X1

	Business-Type Activities -- Enterprise Funds			
	Regional Transit System	**Regional Utilities**	**Totals**	**Governmental Activities -- Internal Service Funds**
Operating revenues:				
Charges for services	$3,480,000	$ 1,082,000	$4,562,000	$ 988,000
Miscellaneous	0	980,000	980,000	639,000
Total operating revenues	$3,480,000	$ 2,062,000	$5,542,000	$ 1,627,000
Operating expenses:				
Personal services	$ 500,000	$ 309,000	$ 809,000	$ 670,000
Contractual services	278,000	132,000	410,000	480,000
Utilities	123,000	562,000	685,000	320,000
Repairs and maintenance	520,000	798,000	1,318,000	238,000
Other supplies and expenses	418,000	276,000	694,000	349,000
Insurance claims and expenses	0	0	0	135,000
Depreciation	760,000	370,000	1,130,000	785,000
Total operating expenses	$2,599,000	$ 2,447,000	$5,046,000	$ 2,977,000
Operating income (loss)	$ 881,000	$ (385,000)	$ 496,000	$(1,350,000)
Nonoperating revenues (expenses):				
Interest and investment revenue	$1,300,000	$ 1,453,000	$2,753,000	$ 1,364,000
Miscellaneous revenue	0	1,290,000	1,290,000	980,000
Interest expense	(850,000)	(1,465,000)	(2,315,000)	(1,398,000)
Miscellaneous expense	0	(1,298,000)	(1,298,000)	(965,000)
Total nonoperating revenue (expenses)	$ 450,000	$ (20,000)	$ 430,000	$ (19,000)
Income (loss) before contributions and transfers	$1,331,000	$ (405,000)	$ 926,000	$(1,369,000)
Capital contributions	1,650,000	0	1,650,000	1,340,000
Transfers out	(1,870,000)	(978,000)	(2,848,000)	(1,280,000)
Change in net position	$1,111,000	$(1,383,000)	$ (272,000)	$(1,309,000)
Total net position -- beginning	980,000	1,209,000	2,189,000	1,890,000
Total net position -- ending	$2,091,000	$ (174,000)	$1,917,000	$ 581,000

f. A government should consistently follow appropriate **definitions of operating items**. The presentation in a cash flows statement should be considered in defining these items.

1) For example, an item **not** classified as an operating cash flow most likely should be treated as a nonoperating revenue or expense.

g. **Reconciliation**

1) Net position and changes in net position are reported in the proprietary fund statements for total enterprise funds. They ordinarily are the same as the corresponding amounts for business-type activities in the government-wide statements. However, any differences should be reconciled.

a) For example, although **internal service funds** are proprietary funds, the activities they account for generally are governmental.

i) Thus, they should be included in the governmental activities column in the government-wide statement of activities.

ii) But, if enterprise funds are the **predominant participants** in the internal service funds, this presentation is not appropriate.

iii) Accordingly, internal service fund transactions must be reclassified from governmental to business-type activities. The purpose is to reconcile the amounts for total enterprise funds to amounts in the government-wide statements.

6. **Statement of Cash Flows**

a. The guidance for preparing the cash flows statement is similar to that for nongovernmental entities (covered in Study Unit 17).

1) This section is intended only as a concise statement of the differences.

b. A statement of cash flows is required for

1) Proprietary funds and

2) Entities engaged in **business-type activities**, e.g., governmental utilities, governmental healthcare providers, and public colleges and universities.

c. Cash flows should be classified as operating, financing, and investing, but financing cash flows are reported in separate categories.

1) **Noncapital financing activities** include borrowings (and repayments of debt, including interest) for purposes other than acquiring, constructing, or improving capital assets. Cash flows may include

a) Grants and subsidies received or paid,

b) Property tax receipts,

c) Debt proceeds, and

d) Cash received from or paid to other funds (excluding flows from interfund services provided or used).

2) **Capital and related financing activities** include (a) receipts of grants, contributions, and proceeds of sale of capital assets and (b) borrowings (and repayments of debt, including interest) for

a) Acquiring, constructing, or improving capital assets;

b) Acquiring and disposing of capital assets used to provide goods or services; and

c) Paying for capital assets obtained on credit.

3) **Operating activities** are activities **not** classified as financing or investing. In general, operating activities affect operating income. They include
   a) Loan activities not intended as investments but as **program loans** made to fulfill a governmental responsibility (e.g., student loans),
   b) Interfund services provided and used, and
   c) Selling goods or services.
4) **Investing activities** include (a) making and collecting loans (other than program loans) and (b) acquiring and disposing of debt and equity instruments.
   a) **Cash interest** and dividends received as returns on nonprogram loans, equity securities, etc., are inflows from investing activities.

d. Investing, capital, and financing activities may affect recognized assets or liabilities but not result in cash flows in the current period.
   1) These activities should be presented in a separate schedule. Space permitting, this schedule may be presented on the same page as the statement of cash flows. Examples of **noncash transactions** are
      a) Acquiring assets by assuming directly related liabilities (e.g., mortgages) or entering into a capital lease and
      b) Exchanging noncash assets or liabilities for other noncash assets or liabilities.

e. The **direct method** (including a **reconciliation** of operating income to operating cash flows) should be used to report operating cash flows. The indirect method is **not** permitted.
   1) The major classes of gross operating cash receipts and payments and their sum (net cash flow from operating activities) are reported. The following are the **minimum classes** to be reported:
      a) Cash receipts from customers
      b) Cash receipts from interfund services provided
      c) Other operating cash receipts
      d) Cash payments to employees for services
      e) Cash payments to other suppliers of goods or services
      f) Cash payments for interfund services used
      g) Other operating cash payments

SUCCESS TIP

A statement of cash flows is required for proprietary funds and entities engaged in business-type activities. The other fund types do not have to present this statement because they are operated as governmental entities, not as commercial businesses.

STOP & REVIEW

You have completed the outline for this subunit.
Study multiple-choice questions 11 through 15 beginning on page 620.

19.4 FIDUCIARY FUNDS REPORTING

SUCCESS TIP

The AICPA has released CPA questions that test candidates' knowledge of the various fiduciary funds and their required financial statements. These questions have been mainly conceptual, but a few have required calculations.

1. **Measurement Focus and Basis of Accounting**
   a. The **economic resources** measurement focus and the **accrual** basis of accounting are required in the fiduciary fund financial statements.
2. **Nature of Fiduciary Funds**
   a. Fiduciary funds emphasize net position and changes in net position. They are used to report **fiduciary activities**.
      1) The complex criteria for identifying fiduciary activities often address
         a) The government's control of assets,
         b) The source of the assets (e.g., not from revenues generated by the government itself), and
         c) The beneficiaries (e.g., not the government itself).
      2) All fiduciary funds, including fiduciary component units, are reported only in the statements of fiduciary net position and changes in fiduciary net position. Thus, information about fiduciary activities is excluded from the government-wide statements.
   b. The fiduciary funds are the
      1) Pension (and other employee benefit) trust funds,
      2) Investment trust funds,
      3) Private-purpose trust funds, and
      4) Custodial funds.
         a) A **trust fund** differs from a **custodial fund** because of a trust agreement (or equivalent) with certain terms.

3. **Pension (and Other Employee Benefit) Trust Funds**
   a. These funds report fiduciary activities of (1) pension plans (defined benefit or contribution), (2) other postemployment benefit plans, or (3) other employee benefit plans.
   b. A governmental entity that provides a **defined benefit pension plan** administered through a trust applies principles similar to those for nongovernmental entities.
      1) The liability to employees is measured as follows:

	Total pension liability (actuarial present value of projected payments based on past service)
–	Plan's fiduciary net position
=	**Net pension liability**

         a) Actuarial **valuations** of the total liability must be done at least every 2 years.
         b) Projected benefits must be discounted using a **long-term expected rate of return** on plan investments. But a tax exempt, high quality municipal bond rate must be used if the fiduciary net position is not projected to suffice to pay benefits.
         c) This outline applies to accounting by single and agent employers who do not have a special funding situation.
            i) A **single** employer uses a plan that provides benefits to employees only of that employer.
            ii) An **agent** employer participates in a multi-employer plan that (a) pools plan assets but (b) maintains separate employer accounts.
            iii) A **cost-sharing** employer also participates in a multi-employer plan. But the plan assets can be used to pay benefits to employees of any employer that provides pensions through the plan.
         d) This outline does **not** address **special funding** situations. These are legal responsibilities of nonemployers to provide pensions to employees of one or more other entities. Moreover, (1) the amount of the required contribution is not dependent on an event unrelated to pensions, **or** (2) the employer is the only entity required to contribute directly to the pension plan.
            i) The employer must make accounting adjustments for nonemployer contributions.
         e) Also beyond the scope of this outline are the requirements for reporting by (1) governmental pension plans and (2) governmental plans and employers for other post employment benefits.
      2) **Pension expenses** and deferred inflows and outflows of resources primarily result from changes in the net pension liability.
         a) Most such changes are expensed in the period of change.
         b) The effects of certain changes are expensed over the current and future periods:
            i) Changes in assumptions and
            ii) Differences between expected and actual experience.
         c) Changes in the net pension liability **not** included in pension expense are reported as deferred inflows or outflows.

c. A governmental employer that provides a **defined contribution pension plan** should report (1) a plan description, (2) a summary of significant accounting policies, and (3) information about investment concentrations.

   1) The plan description should identify the plan as a defined contribution plan and disclose in the notes to the financial statements the number of participating employers and other contributing entities.

   2) The description also should include

      a) The classes of employees covered and the total current membership,

      b) A brief description of plan provisions and the authority under which they are established (or may be amended), and

      c) Contribution requirements.

   3) An employer recognizes **pension expense** equal to contributions to employees' accounts required by the benefit terms (net of forfeited amounts).

      a) A change in the pension liability is recognized for the difference between (1) pension expense and (2) amounts paid.

4. **Investment Trust Funds**

   a. An investment trust fund is used to report fiduciary activities involving the external portion of an **investment pool** (the portion belonging to legally separate entities not part of the government's reporting entity). Moreover, the government should report each external pool as a separate fund.

      1) An investment trust fund also should be used for individual investment accounts provided to legally separate entities not part of the same reporting entity. This arrangement makes specific investments for individual entities.

         a) In contrast, an investment pool commingles the moneys of the legally separate entities.

   b. Most investments are reported at **fair value**. It is an exit price defined as "the price that would be received to sell an asset or paid to transfer a liability in an orderly transaction between market participants at the measurement date."

      1) The GASB has adopted the FASB's approach to fair value measurement described in Study Unit 4, Subunit 7.

5. **Private-Purpose Trust Funds**

   a. These funds are used for all other trust arrangements meeting the criteria for fiduciary activities.

      1) An example is a fund for escheat property. Property escheats when it reverts to a governmental entity in the absence of legal claimants.

6. **Custodial Funds**

   a. These funds report fiduciary activities not required to be reported in a trust fund.

      1) They account for grants and other financial assistance to be transferred to, or spent on behalf of, a secondary recipient if the recipient government acts purely as a conduit, that is, if it receives the monies and transmits them without having any administrative or direct involvement in the program.
      2) When capital improvements are financed by special assessment debt, the debt service transactions for which the government is not obligated should be reported in a custodial fund in the statement of fiduciary net position, not a debt service fund.
      3) Other examples are (a) the external portion of an investment pool not held in a trust and (b) sales taxes collected for other governments.

7. **Fiduciary Fund Financial Statements**

   a. These statements include information about all fiduciary funds and similar component units. The statements report information in a separate column for each type of fiduciary fund but **not** by major fund.

      1) The **notes** present financial statements for individual defined benefit pension and other postemployment benefit plans unless separate GAAP reports have been issued.

   b. A **statement of fiduciary net position** is required for fiduciary funds. For each type of fiduciary fund, it presents net position as follows:

	Assets
+	Deferred outflows of resources
–	Liabilities
–	Deferred inflows of resources
=	Net position

      1) The statement does not present the three components of net position reported in the government-wide statement of net position or in the proprietary fund statement of net position.
      2) **Capital assets** of fiduciary funds and **long-term liabilities** directly related to, and expected to be paid from, fiduciary funds are reported in the statement of fiduciary net position, **not** in the government-wide statement of net position.

   c. A **statement of changes in fiduciary net position** is required for fiduciary funds. The following is presented for each type of fiduciary fund:

	Additions
–	Deductions
=	Net increase (decrease) in fiduciary net position

      1) **Additions** should be disaggregated by source (if applicable), such as
         a) Investment earnings,
         b) Investment costs, and
         c) Net investment earnings.
      2) **Deductions** should be disaggregated by type with separate display of administrative costs.
      3) Single aggregated totals for additions and deductions (e.g., property taxes collected for, or distributed to, other governments) of custodial funds may be reported if the resources are expected to be held for no more than 3 months.

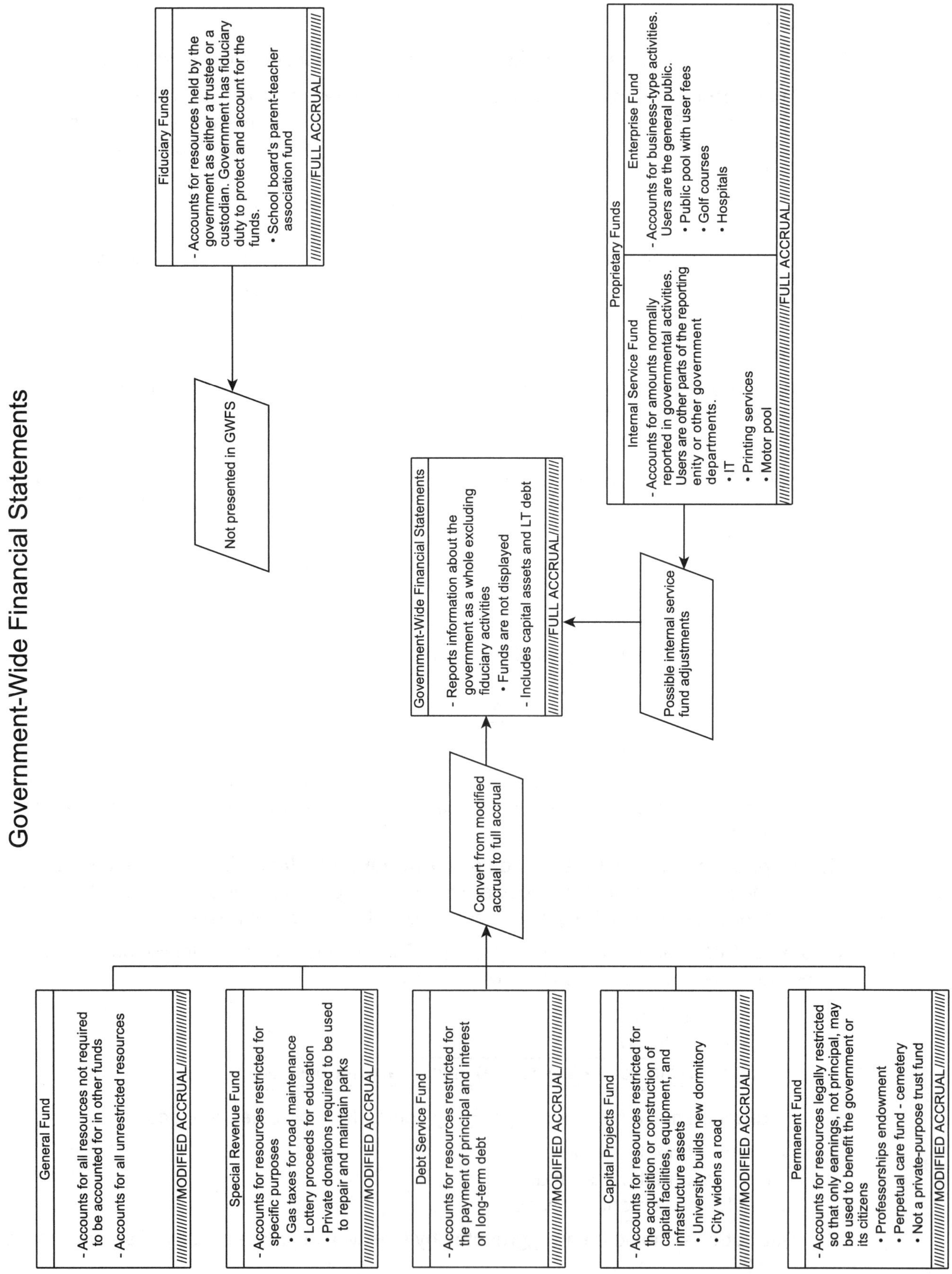
Government-Wide Financial Statements
General Fund
- Accounts for all resources not required to be accounted for in other funds
- Accounts for all unrestricted resources
MODIFIED ACCRUAL
Special Revenue Fund
- Accounts for resources restricted for specific purposes
• Gas taxes for road maintenance
• Lottery proceeds for education
• Private donations required to be used to repair and maintain parks
MODIFIED ACCRUAL
Debt Service Fund
- Accounts for resources restricted for the payment of principal and interest on long-term debt
MODIFIED ACCRUAL
Capital Projects Fund
- Accounts for resources restricted for the acquisition or construction of capital facilities, equipment, and infrastructure assets
• University builds new dormitory
• City widens a road
MODIFIED ACCRUAL
Permanent Fund
- Accounts for resources legally restricted so that only earnings, not principal, may be used to benefit the government or its citizens
• Professorships endowment
• Perpetual care fund - cemetery
• Not a private-purpose trust fund
MODIFIED ACCRUAL
Convert from modified accrual to full accrual
Government-Wide Financial Statements
- Reports information about the government as a whole excluding fiduciary activities
• Funds are not displayed
- Includes capital assets and LT debt
FULL ACCRUAL
Possible internal service fund adjustments
Proprietary Funds
Internal Service Fund
- Accounts for amounts normally reported in governmental activities. Users are other parts of the reporting enity or other government departments.
• IT
• Printing services
• Motor pool
Enterprise Fund
- Accounts for business-type activities. Users are the general public.
• Public pool with user fees
• Golf courses
• Hospitals
FULL ACCRUAL
Fiduciary Funds
- Accounts for resources held by the government as either a trustee or a custodian. Government has fiduciary duty to protect and account for the funds.
• School board's parent-teacher association fund
FULL ACCRUAL
Not presented in GWFS

Figure 19-1

STOP & REVIEW

You have completed the outline for this subunit.
Study multiple-choice questions 16 through 20 beginning on page 622.

QUESTIONS

19.1 Characteristic Transactions of Governmental Entities

1. If a capital asset is donated to a governmental unit, the asset is accounted for in an enterprise fund, and eligibility requirements are met, it should be recorded

A. At the donor's carrying amount as revenue.

B. At acquisition value as revenue.

C. At the lower of the donor's carrying amount or estimated fair value as deferred inflows of resources.

D. As a memorandum entry only.

Answer (B) is correct.

REQUIRED: The recording of capital assets accounted for in an enterprise fund that are donated to a governmental unit.

DISCUSSION: If a capital asset is donated to a governmental unit, it should be recorded at its acquisition value (an entry price). It is the price that would be paid to acquire an asset with equivalent service potential in an orderly market transaction at the acquisition date. In any voluntary nonexchange transaction, assets and revenues are recognized when all eligibility requirements (including time requirements) are met. Because an enterprise fund uses the accrual basis, the resources need not be available.

Answer (A) is incorrect. The donor's carrying amount may not reflect the asset's acquisition value at the time of the governmental unit's receipt of the asset. **Answer (C) is incorrect.** The asset should be recorded at acquisition value as revenue. **Answer (D) is incorrect.** The acquisition value of the donated asset should be recognized.

2. Dayne County's general fund had the following disbursements during the year:

Payment of principal on long-term debt	$100,000
Payments to vendors	500,000
Purchase of a computer	300,000

What amount should Dayne County report as expenditures in its governmental funds statement of revenues, expenditures, and changes in fund balances?

A. $300,000

B. $500,000

C. $800,000

D. $900,000

Answer (D) is correct.

REQUIRED: The amount classified as expenditures.

DISCUSSION: Expenditures are recognized in the fund financial statements of a governmental fund under the modified accrual basis. They are decreases in (uses of) expendable available financial resources of a governmental fund. Expenditures are usually measurable and should be recognized when the related liability is incurred. However, expenditures for principal and interest on general long-term debt are usually recognized when those amounts are due. The liabilities for payments to vendors and the computer purchase were most likely incurred in the current year. The liability for payment of the principal on long-term debt was most likely due in the current year. Thus, general fund expenditures equal $900,000 ($100,000 + $500,000 + $300,000).

Answer (A) is incorrect. The purchase of a computer is not the only expenditure. **Answer (B) is incorrect.** The payments to vendors are not the only expenditures. **Answer (C) is incorrect.** The payment on long-term debt also should be considered an expenditure.

3. Kingwood Town, at the beginning of the year, paid $22,000 cash for a flatbed trailer to be used in the general operations of the town. The expected useful life of the trailer is 6 years with an estimated $7,000 salvage value. Which of the following amounts should be reported?

A. $15,000 increase in equipment in the general fund.

B. $15,000 increase in general capital assets.

C. $22,000 increase in general capital assets.

D. $22,000 increase in equipment in the general fund.

Answer (C) is correct.

REQUIRED: The recording of the purchase of equipment for general operations.

DISCUSSION: Capital assets related to proprietary funds are accounted for in the government-wide financial statements and in the fund financial statements. Capital assets related to fiduciary funds are reported only in the statement of fiduciary net position. All other capital assets are general capital assets reported only in the governmental activities column in the government-wide statement of net position. Capital assets are recorded at historical cost or at estimated fair value if donated. Thus, general capital assets should be debited for $22,000, the historical cost of the equipment.

Answer (A) is incorrect. Capital assets are not reported in the general fund, and the assets are recorded at historical cost. **Answer (B) is incorrect.** Capital assets are reported at historical cost, not historical cost minus salvage value. **Answer (D) is incorrect.** Capital assets are not reported in the general fund.

4. The City of Bell entered into a capital lease agreement on December 31, Year 4, to acquire a capital asset. Under this agreement, Bell is to make three annual payments of $75,000 each on principal, plus interest of $22,000, $15,000, and $8,000 at the end of Year 5, Year 6, and Year 7, respectively. At the beginning of the lease, what amount should be debited to expenditures control in Bell's general fund?

A. $270,000

B. $225,000

C. $75,000

D. $97,000

Answer (B) is correct.

REQUIRED: The amount that should be debited to expenditures control in the general fund.

DISCUSSION: General capital assets that are acquired by capital lease are recorded in the same manner as those acquired by outright purchase. The asset is reported only in the governmental activities column of the government-wide statement of net position. It is measured in accordance with nongovernmental GAAP. In the general fund, when a capital lease represents the acquisition of a general capital asset, the transaction is reported by debiting an expenditure and crediting an other financing sources -- capital lease at the present value of the minimum lease payments ($75,000 annual principal repayment × 3 years = $225,000).

Answer (A) is incorrect. The amount of $270,000 includes the interest payments. **Answer (C) is incorrect.** The amount of $75,000 is the amount of one annual payment. **Answer (D) is incorrect.** The amount of $97,000 is the first annual payment plus the first interest payment.

5. Lys City reports a general long-term compensated absences liability in its financial statements. The salary rate used to calculate the liability should normally be the rate in effect

A. When the unpaid compensated absences were earned.

B. When the compensated absences are to be paid.

C. At the balance sheet date.

D. When the compensated absences were earned or are to be paid, or at the balance sheet date, whichever results in the lowest amount.

Answer (C) is correct.

REQUIRED: The salary rate used to calculate the liability for compensated absences.

DISCUSSION: The compensated absences liability should be calculated based on the pay or salary rates in effect at the balance sheet date. However, the employer might pay employees for their compensated absences at other than their pay or salary rates. For example, payment might be at a lower amount established by contract, regulation, or policy. That other rate determined at the balance sheet date should be used to calculate the liability.

6. The portion of capital improvement special assessment debt maturing in 5 years, to be repaid from general resources of the government, should be reported in the

A. General fund.

B. Government-wide statement of net position.

C. Custodial fund.

D. Capital projects fund.

Answer (B) is correct.

REQUIRED: The reporting of long-term special assessment debt.

DISCUSSION: If the government is obligated for capital improvement special assessment debt, it should be reported as a general long-term liability only in the governmental activities column of the government-wide statement of net position (except for any portion related to, and expected to be paid from, an enterprise fund). The public benefit portion (the amount repayable from general resources of the government) is treated in the same manner as other general long-term liabilities.

Answer (A) is incorrect. Governmental funds have a current resources focus. **Answer (C) is incorrect.** The debt service transactions of special assessment debt for which the government is not obligated are reported in a custodial fund in the statement of fiduciary net position. **Answer (D) is incorrect.** General long-term liabilities are not reported in governmental funds.

19.2 Government-Wide Financial Statements

7. Which of the following activities should be excluded when governmental fund financial statements are converted to government-wide financial statements?

A. Proprietary activities.

B. Fiduciary activities.

C. Government activities.

D. Enterprise activities.

Answer (B) is correct.

REQUIRED: The activities excluded from government-wide financial statements.

DISCUSSION: Fiduciary funds provide operational information about fiduciary activities. Information about fiduciary funds, including fiduciary component units, is excluded from the government-wide financial statements. Consequently, they are reported only in the fund statements (statements of fiduciary net position and changes in fiduciary net position).

Answer (A) is incorrect. Proprietary activities presumably include activities of proprietary funds (enterprise funds and internal service funds). Proprietary fund activities of internal service funds are usually reported in the governmental activities column. Activities of enterprise funds are reported in the business-type activities column. **Answer (C) is incorrect.** The government-wide statement of activities displays columns for governmental activities and business-type activities. **Answer (D) is incorrect.** Business-type activities are reported in enterprise funds and in the government-wide statements.

8. In the government-wide statement of net position, restricted capital assets should be included in the

A. Expendable component of restricted net position.

B. Nonexpendable component of restricted net position.

C. Net investment in capital assets, net of related debt, component of net position.

D. Designated component of net position.

Answer (C) is correct.

REQUIRED: The classification of restricted capital assets in the statement of net position.

DISCUSSION: Net position has three components: (1) net investment in capital assets, net of related debt, accumulated depreciation, and deferred inflows and outflows of resources; (2) restricted net position; and (3) unrestricted net position. Net investment in capital assets includes unrestricted and restricted capital assets. However, debt related to significant unspent proceeds is classified in the same net position component as those proceeds.

Answer (A) is incorrect. Restricted net position is subject to constraints imposed by external entities (creditors, grantors, or other governments) or by law (constitutional provisions or enabling legislation). If permanent endowments or permanent fund principal amounts are included, restricted net position should be displayed as expendable and nonexpendable. Nonexpendable means that the restriction is retained in perpetuity. However, capital assets must be included in net investment in capital assets even if they are restricted and expendable. **Answer (B) is incorrect.** Capital assets must be included in the net investment in capital assets even if they are restricted and nonexpendable. **Answer (D) is incorrect.** Designations of net position are not reported on the face of the statement.

9. Government-wide financial statements are prepared using the

	Economic Resources Measurement Focus	Current Financial Resources Measurement Focus	Accrual Basis	Modified Accrual Basis
A.	Yes	No	Yes	No
B.	No	Yes	No	Yes
C.	Yes	No	No	Yes
D.	No	Yes	Yes	No

Answer (A) is correct.

REQUIRED: The measurement focus and basis of accounting used in government-wide financial statements.

DISCUSSION: Government-wide financial statements are prepared using the economic resources measurement focus and the accrual basis of accounting and should report all of the government's assets, liabilities, revenues, expenses, gains, and losses. The economic resources focus measures revenues and expenses in the same way as in for-profit accounting. It also emphasizes a longer-range measure of revenues earned or levied (and accrued immediately if measurable) and cost of services. The accrual basis recognizes most transactions when they occur, regardless of when cash is received or paid.

10. In preparing Chase City's reconciliation of the statement of revenues, expenditures, and changes in fund balances to the government-wide statement of activities, which of the following items should be subtracted from changes in fund balances?

A. Capital assets purchases.

B. Payment of long-term debt principal.

C. Internal service fund increase in net assets.

D. Book value of capital assets sold during the year.

Answer (D) is correct.

REQUIRED: The subtraction from changes in fund balances in the reconciliation to the government-wide statement of activities.

DISCUSSION: In the statement of activities, only the gain or loss on the sale of a capital asset is reported. (The acquisition was recorded in the governmental funds as an expenditure for its full amount.) But in the governmental funds, the proceeds are recorded as an increase in resources. Consequently, the change in net position (statement of activities) differs from the change in fund balances by the carrying amount of the capital assets sold. This item requires a reconciling subtraction from the change in fund balance.

Answer (A) is incorrect. Governmental funds report capital outlays as expenditures (decreases in the fund balance). The reconciling item is the amount by which these expenditures exceeded the depreciation recognized in the statement of activities for the current period. This item is added to the net change in fund balances. **Answer (B) is incorrect.** The payment of long-term debt principal is an expenditure in the governmental funds (debt service fund). This transaction does not affect the change in net position reported in the statement of activities. Thus, this item is added to the net change in fund balances. **Answer (C) is incorrect.** Internal service funds are proprietary funds that account for activities performed primarily for the benefit of agencies accounted for in other funds. Examples are a motor pool and an information technology department. In the preparation of the statement of activities, the effects of internal service activities must be eliminated to avoid double counting. The purpose is to prevent recognition of both the activities of the internal service fund and the charges made to the participating funds or functions. Thus, the preparation of the statement of activities essentially involves reducing (through an intraentity elimination) the balance of the internal service fund to zero. The effect on the reconciliation is an addition to the net change in fund balances because of the elimination of charges to governmental funds by a proprietary fund.

19.3 Proprietary Funds Reporting

11. The statement of revenues, expenses, and changes in fund net position for proprietary funds

A. Combines special and extraordinary items in a subtotal presented before nonoperating revenues and expenses.

B. Must report revenues at gross amounts, with discounts and allowances disclosed parenthetically.

C. Distinguishes between operating and nonoperating revenues and expenses.

D. Must define operating items in the same way as in the statement of cash flows.

Answer (C) is correct.

REQUIRED: The true statement about the statement of revenues, expenses, and changes in fund net position.

DISCUSSION: A statement of revenues, expenses, and changes in fund net position is the required operating statement for proprietary funds. Operating and nonoperating revenues and expenses should be distinguished, and separate subtotals should be presented for operating revenues, operating expenses, and operating income.

Answer (A) is incorrect. Nonoperating revenues and expenses are presented immediately after operating income (loss). Moreover, special and extraordinary items are reported separately. **Answer (B) is incorrect.** Revenues are reported by major source either net with disclosure of discounts and allowances or gross with discounts and allowances reported beneath the revenue amounts. **Answer (D) is incorrect.** A government should consistently follow appropriate definitions of operating items. Considerations in defining these items are (1) the principal purpose of the fund and (2) their presentation in a cash flows statement. However, the classification in the statement of cash flows is not controlling.

12. The following transactions were among those reported by Corfe City's electric utility enterprise fund for the year just ended:

Capital contributed by subdividers	$ 900,000
Cash received from customer households	2,700,000
Proceeds from sale of revenue bonds	4,500,000

In the proprietary funds statement of cash flows for the year ended December 31, what amount should be reported as cash flows from the electric utility enterprise fund's capital and related financing activities?

A. $4,500,000

B. $5,400,000

C. $7,200,000

D. $8,100,000

Answer (B) is correct.

REQUIRED: The amount reported as cash flows from capital and related financing activities.

DISCUSSION: Cash flows should be classified as operating, noncapital financing, capital and related financing, or investing. Operating activities include producing and delivering goods and providing services. Thus, cash from customer households is a revenue item reported under cash flows from operating activities. Capital and related financing activities include acquiring and disposing of capital assets, borrowing and repaying money related to capital asset transactions, etc. Assuming the sale of revenue bonds and the capital contributions by subdividers are for the acquisition or improvement of capital assets, the amount to report under capital and related financing activities is $5,400,000 ($900,000 + $4,500,000).

Answer (A) is incorrect. The amount of $4,500,000 omits the capital contributed by subdividers. **Answer (C) is incorrect.** The amount of $7,200,000 includes customer fees revenue and omits capital contributed by subdividers. **Answer (D) is incorrect.** The amount of $8,100,000 includes customer fees.

13. The GASB has established criteria for the required reporting of activities as enterprise funds. Based on these criteria, and assuming the amounts involved are derived from principal revenue sources, enterprise fund reporting is most likely to be optional if

A. Fees are charged to external users for goods or services.

B. The activity is financed with debt, and the only security is a pledge of the activity's net revenues from fees and charges.

C. The activity's costs are legally required to be recovered from fees and charges.

D. The activity's pricing policies set fees and charges to recover costs.

Answer (A) is correct.

REQUIRED: The circumstances in which enterprise fund reporting is most likely to be optional.

DISCUSSION: Enterprise funds must be used if one of three criteria (applied in the context of the activity's principal revenue sources) is satisfied. The criteria primarily emphasize fees charged to external users. (1) The activity should be reported as an enterprise fund if it is financed with debt, and the only security is a pledge of the activity's net revenues from fees and charges. If the debt also is secured by the full faith and credit of a related governmental entity, the debt is not payable solely from the activity's net revenues. (2) The activity also should be reported as an enterprise fund if its costs (including capital costs) of providing services are legally required to be recovered from fees and charges, not taxes or similar revenues. (3) Furthermore, the activity should be reported as an enterprise fund if its pricing policies set fees and charges to recover its costs (including capital costs).

Answer (B) is incorrect. Securing the financing of an activity by fees and charges satisfies a criterion for required enterprise fund reporting. **Answer (C) is incorrect.** A legal requirement to recover costs from fees and charges satisfies a criterion for required enterprise fund reporting. **Answer (D) is incorrect.** A policy that sets fees and charges to recover costs satisfies a criterion for required enterprise fund reporting.

14. Dogwood City's water enterprise fund received interest of $10,000 on long-term investments. How should this amount be reported on the statement of cash flows?

A. Operating activities.

B. Noncapital financing activities.

C. Capital and related financing activities.

D. Investing activities.

Answer (D) is correct.

REQUIRED: The classification of interest received on long-term investments in the statement of cash flows.

DISCUSSION: Reporting of cash flows of proprietary funds and entities engaged in business-type activities, e.g., governmental utilities, is required. Cash inflows should be classified as operating, noncapital financing, capital and related financing, and investing. Investing activities include making and collecting loans (other than program loans) and acquiring and disposing of debt and equity instruments. Cash inflows from investing activities include interest and dividends received as returns on loans (not program loans), debt of other entities, equity securities, and cash management or investment pools.

Answer (A) is incorrect. Operating activities are all transactions and other events that are not classified as either financing or investing activities. In general, operating activities involve transactions and other events the effects of which are included in the determination of operating income. **Answer (B) is incorrect.** Noncapital financing activities include borrowings for purposes other than acquiring, constructing, or improving capital assets and debt. **Answer (C) is incorrect.** Capital and related financing activities include borrowings and repayments of debt related to (1) acquiring, constructing, or improving capital assets; (2) acquiring and disposing of capital assets used to provide goods or services; and (3) paying for capital assets obtained on credit.

15. Lily City uses a pay-as-you-go approach for funding postemployment benefits other than pensions. The city reports no other postemployment benefits (OPEB) liability at the beginning of the year. At the end of the year, Lily City reported the following information related to OPEB for the water enterprise fund:

Benefits paid	$100,000
Annual required contribution	500,000
Unfunded actuarial accrued liability	800,000

What amount of expense for OPEB should Lily City's water enterprise fund report in its fund level statements?

A. $100,000

B. $500,000

C. $600,000

D. $1,400,000

Answer (B) is correct.

REQUIRED: The OPEB expense reported in the fund level statements.

DISCUSSION: Lily City's water enterprise fund should report the amount of the annual required contribution (ARC) of $500,000 as an expense in its fund level statements. The ARC is the employer's periodic required contribution to a defined benefit OPEB plan. The ARC is the sum of the normal cost and an amortization payment for the unfunded actuarial accrued liability.

Answer (A) is incorrect. The postretirement benefit obligation is accrued during the period of employment. The amount of the benefits paid does not equal the current expense. **Answer (C) is incorrect.** The amount of benefits paid is not the total current expense. A postretirement benefit obligation is accrued during the period of employment. **Answer (D) is incorrect.** The full amount of the unfunded actuarial accrued liability is not expensed in the current period. An unfunded actuarial accrued liability is amortized, and the current amortization payment is included in the annual required contribution. The benefits paid of $100,000 do not constitute a current expense. Under GASB, entities are not required actually to pay the annual required contribution each year.

19.4 Fiduciary Funds Reporting

16. Fish Road property owners in Sea County are responsible for special assessment debt that arose from a storm sewer project. If the property owners default, Sea has no obligation regarding debt service, although it does bill property owners for assessments and uses the monies it collects to pay debt holders. What fund type should Sea use to account for these collection and servicing activities?

A. Custodial.

B. Debt service.

C. Special revenue funds.

D. Capital projects.

Answer (A) is correct.

REQUIRED: The reporting of debt service transactions of a special assessment issue.

DISCUSSION: When capital improvements are financed by special assessment debt, the debt service transactions of a special assessment issue for which the government is not obligated should be reported in a custodial fund in the statement of fiduciary net position, not a debt service fund. This reporting reflects the government's limited responsibility to act as an agent for the assessed property owners and the bondholders.

17. Glen County uses governmental fund accounting and is the administrator of a multiple-jurisdiction deferred compensation plan covering both its own employees and those of other governments participating in the plan. This plan is an eligible deferred compensation plan under the U.S. Internal Revenue Code and Income Tax Regulations and meets the criteria for a pension (and other employee benefit) trust fund. Glen has legal access to the plan's $40 million in assets, of which $2 million pertain to Glen and $38 million pertain to the other participating governments. In Glen's balance sheet, what amount should be reported in a custodial fund for plan assets and as a corresponding liability?

A. $0

B. $2,000,000

C. $38,000,000

D. $40,000,000

Answer (A) is correct.

REQUIRED: The deferred compensation plan assets and liability to record in a custodial fund.

DISCUSSION: The plan should be reported in a pension (and other employee benefit) trust fund in the statements of fiduciary net position and changes in fiduciary net position if it meets the criteria for that fund type. Pension (and other employee benefit) trust funds report fiduciary activities for pensions, other postemployment benefit plans, and certain other employee benefit programs. This treatment is in accordance with a tax law amendment that required all assets and income of the plan to be held in trust for the exclusive benefit of participants and their beneficiaries. Consequently, no amounts should be reported in a custodial fund.

18. River City has a defined contribution pension plan. How should River report the pension plan in its financial statements?

A. Amortize any transition asset over the estimated number of years of current employees' service.

B. Disclose in the notes to the financial statements the amount of the pension benefit obligation and the net position available for benefits.

C. Disclose in the notes to the financial statements the classes of employees covered and the employer's and employees' obligations to contribute to the fund.

D. Accrue a liability for benefits earned but not paid to fund participants.

Answer (C) is correct.

REQUIRED: The method for reporting a defined contribution pension plan.

DISCUSSION: A defined contribution pension plan must report (1) a plan description, (2) a summary of significant accounting policies, and (3) information about investment concentrations. The plan description should identify the plan as a defined contribution plan and disclose the number of participating employers and other contributing entities. The description also should include (1) the classes of employees covered, (2) the total current membership, (3) a brief description of plan provisions, (4) the authority under which they are established (or may be amended), and (5) contribution requirements.

Answer (A) is incorrect. No transition asset arises under a defined contribution plan. **Answer (B) is incorrect.** A pension benefit obligation arises under a defined benefit pension plan. **Answer (D) is incorrect.** Under a defined contribution plan, the governmental employer's obligation is for contributions, not benefits.

19. Taxes collected and held by Franklin County for a separate school district are accounted for in which fund?

A. Special revenue.

B. Internal service.

C. Trust.

D. Custodial.

Answer (D) is correct.

REQUIRED: The fund that collects and holds taxes for a separate school district.

DISCUSSION: Fiduciary fund reporting emphasizes net position and changes in net position. Fiduciary funds report fiduciary activities. The criteria for identifying these activities ordinarily emphasize (1) whether the government controls the assets of the activity and (2) the beneficiaries in the fiduciary relationship. Custodial funds report fiduciary activities not reported in (1) pension (and other employee benefit) trust funds, (2) investment trust funds, or (3) private-purpose trust funds. Accordingly, custodial funds generally report fiduciary activities not involving a trust or the equivalent. For example, tax custodial funds are used when a governmental entity is the collection agent of taxes for disbursement to other governmental units, e.g., school districts or special taxing districts.

Answer (A) is incorrect. Special revenue funds are governmental funds that account for proceeds of specific revenue sources legally restricted to expenditure for specified purposes. **Answer (B) is incorrect.** Internal service funds are proprietary funds that may be used to provide goods and services to other subunits of the primary government or to other governments on a cost-reimbursement basis. **Answer (C) is incorrect.** A trust fund differs from a custodial fund because of the presence of a trust agreement (or equivalent) with certain characteristics.

20. Which of the following is a required financial statement for an investment trust fund?

A. Statement of revenues, expenditures, and changes in fiduciary net position.

B. Statement of activities.

C. Statement of revenues, expenses, and changes in fiduciary net position.

D. Statement of changes in fiduciary net position.

Answer (D) is correct.

REQUIRED: The required financial statement for an investment trust fund.

DISCUSSION: Investment trust funds report fiduciary activities involving (1) the external portion of investment pools and (2) individual investment accounts held in a trust meeting certain criteria. Separate statements of fiduciary net position and changes in fiduciary net position should be presented for each such fund. The external portion belongs to legally separate entities not included in the reporting entity.

Answer (A) is incorrect. Fiduciary funds emphasize net position and changes in net position, not revenues and expenditures. **Answer (B) is incorrect.** A statement of activities is presented in the government-wide financial statements. **Answer (C) is incorrect.** Fiduciary funds emphasize net position and changes in net position, not revenues and expenses.

STUDY UNIT TWENTY

NOT-FOR-PROFIT ACCOUNTING AND REPORTING

(20 pages of outline)

This study unit addresses accounting and reporting by **nongovernmental not-for-profit entities (NFPs)** in accordance with GAAP established by the FASB. An NFP has the following characteristics:

- Contributors of significant resources to the NFP do not expect a proportionate return.
- The NFP has operating purposes other than providing goods or services for profit.
- The NFP has no ownership interests similar to those of a business entity.

Among the many kinds of NFPs are (1) educational institutions, (2) healthcare entities, (3) cultural organizations, (4) voluntary health and welfare entities, (5) federated fundraising organizations, (6) unions, (7) political parties, and (8) public broadcasting stations.

20.1 FINANCIAL STATEMENTS

1. **Financial Reporting Model**
   a. The primary purpose of financial statements of an NFP is to provide relevant information serving the common interest of donors, creditors, and other external resource providers.
      1) This information should help to asses the NFP's (a) services, (b) ability to continue providing those services, and (c) stewardship and other aspects of performance.
      2) This information should be provided about
         a) Assets, liabilities, and net assets;
         b) Changes in net assets;
         c) Flows of economic resources;
         d) Cash flows, borrowing and repayment of borrowing, and other factors affecting liquidity; and
         e) Service efforts.
   b. Reporting is based on a **net assets model**.
      1) Net assets equals the excess or deficiency of assets over liabilities. Net assets is classified as
         a) With donor restrictions or
         b) Without donor restrictions.
   c. The following are an NFP's general-purpose financial statements:
      1) A **statement of financial position** is equivalent to a for-profit entity's balance sheet.
         a) The **elements** are assets, liabilities, and net assets. The statement presents information about the elements and their relationships at a moment in time.
         b) The elements investments by owners and distributions to owners are **not** included.
      2) A **statement of activities** is an operating statement equivalent to a for-profit entity's income statement. Its **elements** are revenues, expenses, gains, and losses. Comprehensive income is **not** an element of an NFP's statement of activities. The statement provides information about
         a) The effects of transactions and other events and circumstances that change the amount and nature of net assets.
         b) The relationships among those transactions, etc.
         c) How resources are used to provide programs and services.
      3) A **statement of cash flows** is similar to the statement reported by for-profit entities.
   d. Fund terminology is not used because the emphasis is on net assets and changes in net assets taken as a whole.
      1) Reporting by **fund groups** therefore is **not** required for external reporting. But disaggregating information by fund groups is allowed.
   e. Presentation of **comparative** statements is encouraged but **not** required.
   f. An outline of the **objectives** of financial reporting for NFPs is in Study Unit 1, Subunit 3.

2. **Statement of Financial Position**

   a. The items bolded in the example below must be presented.

EXAMPLE 20-1 Consolidated Statement of Financial Position

The American National Red Cross
Consolidated Statement of Financial Position
June 30, 20X2 (with comparative information as of June 30, 20X1)
(in thousands)

Assets	20X2	20X1
Current assets:		
Cash and cash equivalents	$ 52,905	$ 372,662
Investments	626,872	695,856
Trade receivables, including grants, net of allowance for credit losses of $5,657 in 20X2 and $3,818 in 20X1	216,517	222,430
Contributions receivable	70,011	66,977
Inventories, net of allowance for obsolescence of $4,105 in 20X2 and $1,382 in 20X1	113,876	126,382
Collateral under securities loaned agreements	--	110,943
Other current assets	24,922	28,901
Total current assets	$1,105,103	$1,624,151
Investments	1,356,851	1,309,580
Contributions receivable	16,030	14,134
Land, buildings, and other property, net	1,050,793	1,077,945
Other assets	249,184	227,771
Total assets	**$3,777,961**	**$4,253,581**
Liabilities and net assets		
Current liabilities:		
Accounts payable and accrued expenses	$ 281,012	$ 333,223
Current portion of debt	14,400	14,418
Postretirement benefits	3,991	4,147
Payables under securities loaned agreements	--	110,943
Other current liabilities	164,121	185,134
Total current liabilities	$ 463,524	$ 647,865
Debt	538,958	558,963
Pension and postretirement benefits	1,001,636	667,987
Other liabilities	178,620	186,843
Total liabilities	**$2,182,738**	**$2,061,658**
Net assets:		
Net assets without donor restrictions	$ 133,687	$ 655,029
Net assets with donor restrictions	1,461,536	1,536,894
Total net assets	**$1,595,223**	**$2,191,923**
Commitments and contingencies		
Total liabilities and net assets	$3,777,961	$4,253,581

b. The minimum required classes of net assets are (1) those with donor restrictions and (2) those without donor restrictions.

1) Although these classes may be disaggregated, the NFP must report amounts for (a) each of the two classes and (b) total net assets.

2) A **donor-imposed restriction** is a stipulation that is more specific than the limits resulting from (a) the nature of the entity, (b) its environment, or (c) its organizational objectives (e.g., those stated in bylaws).

a) Some restrictions are **temporary**. For example, a stipulation may require resources to be used (1) in a later period or after a specific date (**time** restriction), (2) for a specific purpose (**purpose** restriction), or (3) both.

i) Other restrictions are **perpetual**. For example, the stipulation may require resources to be maintained in perpetuity.

ii) A law may extend donor-imposed restrictions, for example, to investment returns.

3) A governing board of an NFP may limit use of part of its net assets **without donor restrictions** by

a) Establishing an endowment **(a board-designated endowment fund)** or

b) Self-imposing specific earmarks **(board-designated net assets)**, e.g., for investment, contingencies, or construction of fixed assets.

4) Information about the nature and amounts of **restrictions** must be provided on the face of the statement or in the notes. Also, to report different types of restrictions, separate line items may be included in (a) net assets with donor restrictions or (b) the notes. The following are examples:

a) Support of particular operating activities

b) Investment for a specified term (term endowments)

c) Use in a specified future period

d) Acquisition of long-lived assets

e) Assets, e.g., land or works of art, to be used for a specified purpose, preserved, and not sold

f) Assets to be invested to provide permanent income (e.g., **donor-restricted perpetual endowments**)

EXAMPLE 20-2 Temporary Restriction

A disease-fighting charity may receive a grant specifying that the amount must be used for vaccinations in Africa for 5 years. Any balance remaining at the end of that time may be used for any purpose the board deems appropriate.

EXAMPLE 20-3 Perpetual Restriction

In Example 20-2, the entity may receive a grant that must be invested in AAA-grade bonds in perpetuity, with the income being spent on vaccinations in Africa (a donor-restricted perpetual endowment).

c. **Assets** must be combined into reasonably homogeneous groups.

   1) Assets (including cash) that are donor-restricted to long-term use must **not** be classified with assets without donor restrictions that are currently available.
   2) The nature and amount of limitations on the use of **cash and cash equivalents** should be disclosed in the notes or on the statement of financial position.
   3) The guidance for reporting current and noncurrent assets and liabilities applies to for-profit entities and NFPs.

d. Receivables from exchange transactions must be measured at net realizable value if amounts are due within 1 year.

e. **Property, plant, and equipment (PPE)** consist of long-lived tangible assets.

   1) The amount initially recognized for contributed PPE includes all costs incurred to place the assets in use, e.g., freight and installation costs.
   2) NFPs recognize depreciation on most items of PPE.
      a) **Depreciation** expense decreases net assets without donor restrictions. A donor's time restriction on a depreciable asset expires as the economic benefits are used.
   3) Land used as a building site and certain individual works of art and historical treasures with very long useful lives are **not** depreciated.
      a) A **work of art** or **historical treasure** is nondepreciable only if verifiable evidence supports the conclusions that
         i) It has cultural, aesthetic, or historical value worth preserving perpetually.
         ii) The holder has the means of, and is, preserving its full service potential.
      b) However, the capitalized costs of major preservation or restoration efforts should be depreciated.

f. Contributions of **works of art, historical treasures, and similar items** are recognized as assets and as revenues or gains if they are **not** collection items.

   1) If the amount capitalized is not presented separately on the statement of financial position, it must be disclosed.
   2) **Collections** are works of art, historical treasures, and similar items that are
      a) Held for public exhibition, education, or research to further public service rather than for financial gain;
      b) Protected, kept unencumbered, cared for, and preserved; and
      c) Subject to a policy that requires the proceeds of items sold to be used for acquisitions of new collection items, the direct care of existing items, or both.
   3) The NFP must disclose its policy for proceeds when items are removed from a collection.

4) An NFP may choose to (a) capitalize its collections, (b) capitalize prospectively items acquired after a certain date, or (c) not capitalize collections.

a) Capitalization of part of the collections is **not** permitted.

5) If an NFP does **not capitalize collections**,

a) No assets or contribution revenues or gains are recognized.

b) The costs (proceeds) of the collection items purchased (sold) are recognized separately as a decrease (an increase) in the appropriate class of net assets. The entry for purchase with net assets without donor restrictions is

Net assets without donor restrictions	$XXX	
Cash		$XXX

c) The proceeds from insurance recoveries for collection items are recognized as an increase in the appropriate class of net assets.

d) Cash flows from purchases, sales, and insurance recoveries of uncapitalized collection items are reported in the investing activities section of the statement of cash flows.

6) If collections are capitalized **prospectively**, proceeds from sales and insurance recoveries of items not previously capitalized are reported separately.

g. **Liabilities** also must be combined into reasonably homogeneous groups.

1) An NFP must recognize a liability for (a) its **unconditional promise to give** or (b) an amount received in an **agency transaction**.

3. **Statement of Activities**

a. The statement of activities reports the **changes** in (1) net assets and (2) the categories of net assets for the reporting period.

1) Revenues, expenses, gains, and losses must be combined into reasonably homogeneous groups.

a) They also must be reported as increases or decreases in (1) net assets with donor restrictions or (2) net assets without donor restrictions.

2) Other events, e.g., expirations of donor-imposed time or purpose restrictions, result in **reclassification of net assets**.

a) They are reported separately as **net assets released from restrictions**.

i) A reclassification of net assets is displayed as an increase in one net assets class and a decrease in the other. The reclassification entry does not include cash flows.

EXAMPLE 20-4 Net Assets Released from Restrictions

A patron gave an art museum $100,000 to award fellowships to graduate art students. When the NFP received the contribution, it should have been classified as net assets with donor restrictions because it was to be used for a specified purpose. When the purpose is fulfilled by awarding fellowships, the restriction expires. The amount then should be reclassified as a decrease in net assets with donor restrictions and an increase in net assets without donor restrictions. The reduction of net assets (the expense incurred by awarding fellowships) is reflected by decreasing net assets without donor restrictions.

EXAMPLE 20-5 **Consolidated Statement of Activities**

The American National Red Cross
Consolidated Statement of Activities
Year Ended June 30, 20X2
(with summarized information for the year ended June 30, 20X1)
(in thousands)

	Without Donor Restrictions	With Donor Restrictions	Totals 20X2	Totals 20X1
Operating revenues and gains				
Contributions:				
Corporate, foundation, and individual giving	$ 224,373	$ 213,395	$ 437,768	$ 685,947
United Way and other federated	31,024	69,203	100,227	111,273
Legacies and bequests	51,359	43,270	94,629	81,548
Services and materials	18,537	18,887	37,424	35,272
Products and services:				
Biomedical	2,153,870	--	2,153,870	2,189,663
Program materials	136,876	--	136,876	139,222
Contracts, including federal government	82,552	--	82,552	112,804
Investment income	27,098	31,002	58,100	49,584
Other revenues	63,628	5,443	69,071	65,222
Net assets released from restrictions	438,468	(438,468)	--	--
Total operating revenues and gains	**$3,227,785**	**$ (57,268)**	**$3,170,517**	**$3,470,535**
Operating expenses				
Program services:				
(1) Services to the Armed Forces	$ 53,045	$ --	$ 53,045	$ 57,403
(2) Biomedical services	2,239,784	--	2,239,784	2,195,108
(3) Community services	77,538	--	77,538	90,558
(4) Domestic disaster services	279,190	--	279,190	282,974
(5) Health and safety services	195,596	--	195,596	203,735
(6) International relief and development services	186,726	--	186,726	340,106
Total program services	**$3,031,879**	**$ --**	**$3,031,879**	**$3,169,884**
Supporting activities:				
(7) Fundraising	172,407	--	172,407	127,019
(8) Management and general	140,847	--	140,847	142,682
Total supporting services	**$ 313,254**	**$ --**	**$ 313,254**	**$ 269,701**
Total operating expenses	**$3,345,133**	**$ --**	**$3,345,133**	**$3,439,585**
Change in net assets from operations	(117,348)	(57,268)	(174,616)	30,950
Nonoperating gains (losses)	(18,424)	(18,090)	(36,514)	193,157
Pension-related changes other than net periodic benefit cost	(385,570)	--	(385,570)	8,929
Change in net assets	**$ (521,342)**	**$ (75,358)**	**$ (596,700)**	**$ 233,036**
Net assets, beginning of year	655,029	1,536,894	2,191,923	1,958,887
Net assets, end of year	$ 133,687	$1,461,536	$1,595,223	$2,191,923

NOTE: Items (1)-(8) are functional expenses.

b. **Revenues** are reported as increases in net assets without donor restrictions unless the use of the assets received is restricted by the donor.

EXAMPLE 20-6	Classification of Revenues
Fees for services and investment income ordinarily are without donor restrictions.	
Income from a perpetual or term endowment ordinarily increases net assets with donor restrictions.	

1) The **gross** amounts of revenues and expenses from the entity's **ongoing major or central operations** are reported.
   a) But **investment returns** not related to program services must be reported net of external, and direct internal, expenses.
2) The accounting for **contributions** is described in Subunit 20.2.

c. **Exchange transactions** must be accounted for in accordance with the guidance for **revenue from contracts with customers** discussed in Study Unit 3, Subunit 4.
1) Resources received in exchange transactions must be classified as revenues in net assets without donor restrictions even if the provider (e.g., a government) limits their use.

d. **Gains and losses** on assets or liabilities are changes in net assets without donor restrictions unless their use is restricted explicitly by the donor or by law.
1) Gains and losses may be reported as **net** amounts if they result from
   a) Peripheral or incidental transactions or
   b) Other events and circumstances largely beyond the NFP's control.

e. Most **expenses** are reported as decreases in net assets without donor restrictions.
1) An exception is **investment expense**. It must be netted against investment return (not related to program services) and reported in the same net asset category.
2) A statement of activities or the notes must provide information about expenses by **functional** classification (program services and supporting activities).
   a) All NFPs must report information about **all** expenses in one place: (1) the statement of activities, (2) a schedule in the notes, or (3) a separate statement.
   b) An analysis must be presented that disaggregates functional expense classifications by **natural** expense classifications (e.g., salaries, rent, interest, electricity, awards and grants to others, supplies, professional fees, and depreciation).
3) Some **expense recognition** issues are unique to NFPs.
   a) **Fundraising** costs, including the costs of special events, are expensed as incurred even if they result in contributions in future periods.
   b) How costs related to sales are displayed depends on whether the sales are a major activity or an incidental activity.
      i) For example, a **major** fundraising activity should report and display separately the revenues from sales and the related cost of sales.
      ii) If sales relate to a **program** service or a **supporting** activity, the cost of sales is a program expense or a supporting expense, respectively.

f. Certain other categories of changes in net assets may be useful.

1) Examples are

a) Operating and nonoperating,
b) Recurring and nonrecurring,
c) Recognized and unrecognized, and
d) Expendable or nonexpendable.

2) If an intermediate operating measure (e.g., operating profit or operating income) is used, it must be in a financial statement that at a minimum reports the change in net assets without donor restrictions.

4. **Functional Classification of Expenses**

a. **Program services** distribute goods and services to beneficiaries, customers, or members to fulfill the purposes of the entity.

1) Those services are the major purpose and output of the entity and often relate to several major programs.

b. **Supporting activities** of an NFP are **not** program services. They usually include the following:

1) Management and General

a) Oversight and business management
b) Budgeting, financing, and related activities
c) Recordkeeping
d) Most management and administrative activities

2) Fundraising

a) Publicity and conducting campaigns
b) Maintenance of donor lists
c) Special events
d) Preparing and distributing related materials
e) Other solicitation activities

3) Membership Development

a) Soliciting for members and dues
b) Member relations

c. Some expenses relate to more than one major program or supporting activity.

1) **Direct** identification (assignment) of specific expenses (direct expenses) with programs, services, or support activities is preferable when feasible. Otherwise, **allocation** (indirect expenses) must be rational and systematic, and the result must be reasonable.

a) For example, the cost of a direct-mail solicitation may need to be allocated between fundraising (a supporting activity) and the NFP's educational mission (a program service).

5. **Statement of Cash Flows**

   a. The guidance in Study Unit 17 for reporting a statement of cash flows applies to **all NFPs** and business entities. For example, the term **"income statement"** includes a statement of activities, and the term **"net income"** includes the change in net assets. The outline in this section includes the guidance specific to NFPs.

EXAMPLE 20-7 **Consolidated Statement of Cash Flows**

The American National Red Cross
Consolidated Statement of Cash Flows
Year Ended June 30, 20X2 (with comparative information for the year ended June 30, 20X1)
(in thousands)

	20X2	20X1
Cash flows from operating activities:		
Change in net assets	$(596,700)	$ 233,036
Adjustments to reconcile change in net assets to net cash used in operating activities:		
Depreciation and amortization	78,925	83,331
Provision for credit losses on accounts receivable	2,954	1,252
Provision for obsolete inventory	2,930	(495)
Net gain on sales of property	(938)	(2,699)
Net investment and derivative gain (loss)	24,784	(192,075)
Pension-related changes other than net periodic benefit cost	385,570	(8,929)
Perpetually restricted contributions	(34,748)	(22,032)
Changes in operating assets and liabilities:		
Receivables	(1,971)	(123,257)
Inventories	9,576	3,869
Other assets	(17,434)	(78,999)
Accounts payable and accrued expenses	(52,211)	(37,821)
Other liabilities	(35,949)	192,930
Pension and postretirement benefits	(52,077)	(81,229)
Net cash used in operating activities	**$(287,289)**	**$ (33,118)**
Cash flows from investing activities:		
Purchases of property	$ (55,299)	$ (74,452)
Proceeds from sales of property	4,464	6,407
Purchases of investments	(277,416)	(158,583)
Proceeds from sales of investments	281,058	222,948
Net cash used in investing activities	**$ (47,193)**	**$ (3,680)**
Cash flows from financing activities:		
Contributions with donor restrictions	$ 34,748	$ 20,932
Proceeds from borrowings	--	20,109
Repayments of debt	(20,023)	(38,785)
Net cash provided by financing activities	**$ 14,725**	**$ 2,256**
Net decrease in cash and cash equivalents	$(319,757)	$ (34,542)
Cash and cash equivalents, beginning of year	372,662	407,204
Cash and cash equivalents, end of year	**$ 52,905**	**$ 372,662**
Supplemental disclosures of cash flow information:		
Cash paid during the year for interest	$ 18,590	$ 21,342
Noncash investing and financing transactions:		
Donated stock and beneficial interest in perpetual trust	4,267	1,499

b. **Cash inflows from operating activities** include receipts of contributions without donor restrictions.

   1) NFPs and for-profit entities also treat **interest** and **dividends** on investments without donor restrictions as operating cash flows.

   2) Either the direct or indirect method of presenting cash flows from operating activities may be used.

      a) If the direct method is used, a reconciliation to the indirect method is permitted but **not** required.

   3) Operating activities may include **agency transactions**.

      a) In an agency transaction, the NFP receives assets in a voluntary transfer but has little discretion in their use.

c. **Cash inflows from financing activities** include receipts of resources that are donor-restricted for long-term purposes.

   1) Accordingly, cash donor-restricted to (a) acquiring, constructing, or improving long-lived assets (e.g., a building or equipment) or (b) establishing or increasing a donor-restricted endowment fund is a cash inflow from a financing activity. Moreover, it is also reported as a cash **outflow** from an **investing** activity.

      a) Receipts of investment income (cash interest and dividends) that are donor-restricted for such purposes also are financing cash inflows.

d. **Investing activities** include cash flows from purchases, sales, and insurance recoveries of unrecognized, noncapitalized **collection items**.

e. **Noncash** investing and financing activities, e.g., receipt of a contribution of a building, securities, or recognized collection items, are separately disclosed.

f. Restrictions may prevent items otherwise qualifying as **cash equivalents** from being classified as such.

   1) An example is a short-term, highly liquid investment purchased with resources donor-restricted to long-term investment.

STOP & REVIEW

You have completed the outline for this subunit.
Study multiple-choice questions 1 through 11 beginning on page 645.

20.2 CONTRIBUTIONS

NOTE: The accounting for contributions applies to NFPs and businesses (but not transfers from governments to businesses).

1. A **contribution** is an unconditional, voluntary, and nonreciprocal transfer of assets (or a reduction, cancellation, or settlement of liabilities). It also may be an unconditional promise to give.
    a. A contribution is **not**
        1) An investment by, or a distribution to, an owner.
        2) An involuntary nonreciprocal transfer (e.g., taxes).
        3) An **exchange transaction**, a reciprocal transfer in which each party receives and sacrifices **approximately commensurate value**.
            a) A resource provider (contributor) often receives indirect value in the form of positive sentiment from the donation or a public benefit. But that sentiment or benefit is **not** commensurate value.
            b) In an exchange transaction, the potential public benefit is secondary to the direct benefit to the resource provider.
            c) EXAMPLE: An exchange transaction likely exists if the resource provider and recipient agree on the amount of assets transferred for commensurate value.
            d) EXAMPLE: A contribution likely is made if the recipient solicits assets without intending to give commensurate value or the resource provider has full discretion regarding the amount of assets.
    b. A **promise to give** is an oral or written agreement to contribute assets to another entity. It is **unconditional** if it depends only upon the passage of time or a demand by the promisee for performance.
        1) Sufficient verifiable **documentation** must exist.
        2) An ambiguous promise is unconditional if it is unconditional and legally enforceable.

c. A **donor-imposed condition** is a **barrier** that must be overcome before the recipient is entitled to the assets. If it is not overcome, the contributor must have a **right of return** of the assets or the promisor a **right of release** from its obligation.

1) A conditional promise to give is **not** recognized until the condition is substantially met (i.e., the barrier is overcome).

a) A transfer of assets before the condition is met is a **conditional contribution**. It is accounted for as a refundable advance until the condition is (1) substantially met or (2) explicitly waived by the donor.

Assets	$XXX	
Liability-refundable advances		$XXX

2) Whether a contribution is conditional must be determinable from an **agreement**. It should be sufficiently clear that the recipient has an entitlement **only** if it has overcome the barrier.

a) Without an apparent indication of a barrier, the agreement does **not** contain a right of return or release. It is therefore an unconditional contribution.

b) However, a donor stipulation that is ambiguous and not clearly unconditional is presumed to be conditional.

3) The following **indicators** may be useful in determining whether a barrier exists:

a) A **measurable performance-related** barrier may consist of a specified service level, output, or outcome.

b) An **other measurable** barrier may be an identified event, e.g., a matching requirement.

c) The recipient's **limited discretion** over the conduct of an activity may extend to (1) guidelines about qualifying expenses or (2) a protocol that must be followed.

d) A stipulation related to the **purpose of the agreement** may be a barrier, e.g., a homeless shelter's serving a specified number of meals. But administrative and trivial stipulations (e.g., routine reporting) are not barriers.

2. A contribution is usually recognized by the donor and the donee (a) at the same time (when made or received, respectively) or, (b) if conditional, when the barrier is overcome.

3. **Contributions received** ordinarily are accounted for when received at **fair value**.

a. Debits are to

1) **Assets** (e.g., cash or other assets),

2) **Liabilities** (e.g., for payment of an NFP's debt), or

3) **Expenses** (e.g., services when the contribution is received and used at the same time).

b. Credits are to income, specifically to

1) **Revenues** if the transactions are part of the NFP's ongoing major or central operations, e.g., soliciting contributions.

2) **Gains** if the transactions are peripheral or incidental.

c. The difference between the amount ultimately received and the fair value is recognized as an adjustment of the original contributions.

4. **Present value** may be used to measure the fair value of an unconditional promise to give cash.
   a. Interest accruals are recognized using the interest method as
      1) Contribution revenue by donees and
      2) Contribution expense by donors.

Contributions (pledges) receivable	$20,000,000	
Contribution revenue -- net assets with donor restrictions		$16,454,000
Discount		3,546,000

   b. However, unconditional promises to give expected to be collected in less than 1 year may be recognized at **net realizable value** (that is, minus an estimated uncollectible amount).
   c. The recipient of an unconditional promise to give must disclose the allowance for **uncollectible promises receivable**. But the allowance excludes amounts determined to be uncollectible when the receivable was measured initially.

EXAMPLE 20-8 Uncollectible Promises Receivable

On December 31, Year 1, the end of NFP's fiscal year, it received unconditional promises to give in the amount of $100,000. NFP determines that (1) the estimated future cash inflows are $80,000 and (2) their present value is $60,000. The entry is

Contributions receivable	$80,000	
Contribution revenue -- net assets with donor restrictions		$60,000
Discount		20,000

5. **Contributions of services** are recognized if they either
   a. Create or enhance **nonfinancial assets** (e.g., buildings) or
   b. Require special skills, are provided by those having such skills, and usually would be purchased if not donated.

EXAMPLE 20-9 Contributions of Services

An animal shelter is an NFP that receives contributed services from the following individuals measured at their normal billing rates:

Veterinarian provides volunteer animal care	$8,000
A board member who is a CPA volunteers to prepare books for audit	4,500
Registered nurse volunteers as receptionist	3,000
Teacher provides volunteer dog walking	2,000

What amount should the shelter record as contribution revenue?

The services provided by the veterinarian and the CPA are recognized as contribution revenue. The services provided by the registered nurse and the teacher are not. Veterinary services and bookkeeping (1) require special skills, (2) are provided by persons with such skills, and (3) otherwise would be paid for by an animal shelter. Thus, the animal shelter should record $12,500 ($8,000 + $4,500) as contribution revenue.

Expenses	$12,500	
Contribution revenue -- net assets without donor restrictions		$12,500

6. A contribution of **utilities**, such as electricity, is a contribution of other assets, not services. A simultaneous receipt and use of utilities should be recognized in the period of receipt and use.

Expense	$XXX	
Revenue -- net assets without donor restrictions		$XXX

7. If an NFP **capitalizes collections**, contributions of collection items received are recognized as assets and as revenues or gains in the appropriate net asset class. They are measured at fair value.

Assets -- collections	$XXX	
Contribution revenue -- net assets with donor restrictions		$XXX

8. **Contributions made** are recognized at fair value when made as (a) expenses and (b) decreases of assets or increases in liabilities.

9. **Reporting Contributions**

   a. An NFP distinguishes between (1) contributions received with donor-imposed restrictions and (2) those without such restrictions.

      1) **Donor-restricted support** consists of contribution revenues or gains that increase net assets with donor restrictions.

      2) Contribution revenues or gains without donor restrictions increase net assets without donor restrictions.

      3) An NFP must recognize the **expiration** of a donor-imposed restriction on a contribution in the period when it expires. **Expiration** occurs when

         a) The time stipulated has lapsed,
         b) The purpose stipulated has been fulfilled, or
         c) Both.

      4) Under the **simultaneous release** accounting policy, an NFP may elect to report donor-restricted contributions whose **restrictions** are met in the same period as support within net assets without donor restrictions. The NFP must

         a) Have a similar policy for investment gains and income,
         b) Report consistently, and
         c) Disclose the policy.

            i) The election of the simultaneous release policy also may be made for contributions that were **initially conditional** (assuming the condition was met). However, the NFP is **not** required to elect that policy for (a) other donor-restricted contributions or (b) investment gains and income (if the reporting is consistent and the policy is disclosed).

   b. **Unconditional promises to give**, with payments due in **future** periods, are reported as donor-restricted support unless the donor clearly intended support for current activities.

      1) Unconditional promises to give cash in future years usually increase net assets with donor restrictions.

   c. Contributions restricted to acquisition of long-term assets are reported initially as donor-restricted support.

      1) Unless a donor has stipulated a time restriction on the use of such assets, donor restrictions expire when the assets are placed in service.

      2) An NFP must **not** imply a time restriction that expires over the term of a long-lived asset.

EXAMPLE 20-10 Contribution of Long-Term Assets to Support Donee's Mission

On June 30, Year 4, Donee, an NFP, received a building and the land on which it was constructed as a gift from Donor. The building is intended to support the entity's education and training mission or any other purpose consistent with the entity's mission. Immediately prior to the contribution, the fair values of the building and land were appraised at $350,000 and $150,000, respectively. Donor's carrying amounts on June 30, Year 4, were $290,000 and $75,000, respectively.

The terms of this gift allow the long-lived assets to be used for any purpose consistent with the NFP's mission. A policy implying time restrictions on gifts of long-lived assets is not permitted. Thus, the contribution increased net assets without donor restrictions.

10. **Agency transactions** are types of exchange transactions in which the NFP acts as an agent, trustee, or intermediary for a third party who may be a donor or donee. An **agent** acts for or on behalf of another. An **intermediary** merely facilitates the transfer of assets from the donor to the donee beneficiary and is **not** an agent, trustee, donor, or donee.

    a. Financial assets received in an agency transaction should be reported as increases in assets and liabilities. Distributions should be reported as decreases.

Asset	$XXX	
Liability		$XXX

    1) If the assets are nonfinancial, the recipient has the option not to recognize the assets and liabilities.

EXAMPLE 20-11 Agency Transaction

A nongovernmental not-for-profit entity received financial assets during its annual campaign that were specifically pledged by the donor to another nongovernmental not-for-profit entity. Thus, the transfer is an agency transaction. The NFP is an intermediary, a facilitator of the transfer of financial assets from the donor to the donee beneficiary. Consequently, amounts received in the agency transaction should be reported as increases in assets and liabilities.

11. An **exchange transaction** is a reciprocal transfer in which one entity receives assets, services, or satisfaction of a liability(ies) by transferring other assets, performing services, or incurring another obligation(s).

    a. The cost of **premiums** given to potential donors in a mass fundraising appeal is a fundraising expense if the premiums are not given in exchange for contributions.

Fundraising expenses -- premium expense	$ 20	
Cash	1,399,980	
Premium inventory		$ 20
Revenue -- sales		1,399,980

    1) The cost of premiums given to acknowledge contributions also is a fundraising expense if the cost is immaterial in relation to the contributions. But the cost of premiums that is not immaterial is a cost of sales, and the transaction is part exchange and part contribution.

    2) Total contribution revenue is the excess of total contributions received over the costs of fundraising premiums.

b. **Dues** from members may have elements of a contribution and an exchange if members receive tangible or intangible benefits from membership. Dues and **nonrefundable fees** received in exchange transactions are recognized as revenues in accordance with the guidance for revenue from contracts with customers.

EXAMPLE 20-12 Nonrefundable Fees

In Year 3, a not-for-profit trade association enrolled five new member companies, each of which was obligated to pay nonrefundable initiation fees of $1,000. These fees were receivable by the association in Year 4. Three of the new members paid the initiation fees in Year 3, and the other two new members paid their initiation fees in Year 4. Annual dues (excluding initiation fees) received by the association from all of its members always have covered the organization's costs of services provided to members. The reasonable expectation is that future dues will cover all costs of the organization's future services to members. Average membership duration is 10 years because of mergers, attrition, and economic factors. What amount of initiation fees from these five new members should the association recognize as revenue in Year 4?

Membership dues received or receivable in exchange transactions that relate to several accounting periods should be allocated and recognized as revenue in those periods as the performance obligation is satisfied. The entity applies the input method based on time elapsed. The nonrefundable initiation and life membership fees are recognized as revenue when they are receivable because the entity has no performance obligations to satisfy. Thus, the $5,000 in nonrefundable initiation fees should be recognized as revenue when assessed and reported as such in the Year 4 statement of activities.

Deferred revenue -- fees paid in advance	$3,000	
Cash	2,000	
Fee revenue		$5,000

c. **Grants, awards, or sponsorships** are contributions if (1) the resource providers receive no value or (2) the value is incidental to the public benefit.

1) The transfers are exchange transactions if the public benefit is secondary.

d. Resources received in **exchange transactions** are classified as revenues in net assets without donor restrictions even when resource providers limit the use of the resources (limitations are not donor-imposed restrictions and contributions).

12. A **donation on behalf of a beneficiary** is a contribution of cash or other financial assets to an NFP that agrees to use it on behalf of a third party.

a. If the donor explicitly grants **variance power**, the NFP records the asset and contribution revenue at fair value. Variance power is the **unilateral** power to redirect the use of the assets to another beneficiary.

b. If the donor does **not** grant variance power, the NFP recognizes an asset and a **liability** to the beneficiary, which also recognizes an asset.

Common stock -- X Corp.	$XXX	
Liability -- beneficiary Y		$XXX

1) If the assets are **nonfinancial**, such as materials or supplies, the recipient is **not** required to recognize the assets and the liability. The NFP must disclose this accounting policy and apply it consistently.

c. If the recipient and the beneficiary are **financially interrelated**, the nontrustee recipient recognizes the fair value of the assets as a contribution.

1) NFP organizations are financially interrelated if (a) one has the ability to influence the operating and financial decisions of the other and (b) one has an ongoing economic interest in the other.

2) Below is a summary of journal entries for the recipient:

		Grants variance power			
		Yes		No	
Financially interrelated	Yes	Asset	Contribution	Asset	Contribution
	No	Asset	Contribution	Asset	Liability

EXAMPLE 20-13 Donation without Variance Power for Beneficiary

A family lost its home in a fire. In December Year 3, a donor sent money to NFP to purchase furniture for the family. The donor did not explicitly grant NFP the unilateral power to redirect the use of the assets. During January Year 4, NFP purchased this furniture. How should NFP report the receipt of the money in its Year 3 financial statements?

The recipient and beneficiary presumably are **not** financially interrelated. Furthermore, the donor explicitly does **not** grant the recipient variance power. Accordingly, the donation is an agency transaction, and the NFP is a pass-through entity. Because NFP was not explicitly granted variance power, it is an agent or trustee acting on behalf of the third-party donee and has little or no discretion in use of the cash. Thus, NFP should account for the transfer as a liability, not a contribution.

13. Under **split-interest agreements (SIAs)**, such as trusts or other arrangements, NFPs may share benefits with the donor or third-party beneficiaries.

a. SIAs may be revocable or irrevocable.

b. **Distributions** are made to beneficiaries during the term of the agreement.

c. At the end of the agreement, the remaining assets are distributed to or retained by either the NFP or another beneficiary.

d. If the NFP has a **lead interest**, it receives distributions during the agreement's term, for example, the life of a designated person, a specified number of years, or in perpetuity.

1) If it has a **remainder interest**, the donor (or others designated by the donor) receives those distributions, and the NFP receives all or part of the assets remaining at the end of the agreement.

EXAMPLE 20-14 SIA

Donor contributes debt and equity securities to a trust administered by a third party. The NFP receives quarterly cash payments (the lead interest) over the 10-year duration of the trust. Payments equal a specified percentage of the fair value of the donated assets (the trust corpus). At the end of the 10-year term, the remaining assets revert to the donor (the remainder interest).

STOP & REVIEW

You have completed the outline for this subunit.
Study multiple-choice questions 12 through 15 beginning on page 650.

20.3 INVESTMENTS

SUCCESS TIP

Laws address the use of the investment return on donor-restricted endowment funds. The majority of jurisdictions follow a statutory version of the relevant uniform act (Uniform Prudent Management of Institutional Funds Act of 2006, or UPMIFA). Others follow trust law. One issue is whether the investment return is available to be spent.

The outline and questions in this subunit assume that UPMIFA applies. However, if the endowment is subject to trust law, the original gift and net appreciation generally are unavailable to be spent. But ordinary income (interest, dividends, etc.) generally may be spent assuming no purpose or other donor restriction.

1. **Purchased** debt and equity securities initially are measured at acquisition **cost** (excluding transaction costs).
   a. Debt and equity securities received as contributions or through agency transactions initially are measured at **fair value**.
      1) If a debt or equity security is acquired by contribution, it is recognized as an asset and as a revenue or gain when received.
      2) An NFP may hold an investment as an agent with little or no discretion in how income and realized and unrealized gains and losses are used. The NFP therefore must report those activities as agency transactions (changes in assets and liabilities), **not** as changes in net assets.
2. Gains and losses, dividends, interest, and other investment income are reported in the statement of activities as changes in net assets without donor restrictions. But, if they are **donor-restricted** (or if they are subject to a **law** that extends donor restrictions), they are reported as changes in net assets with donor restrictions.
   a. Under the **simultaneous release** accounting policy, donor-restricted gains and investment income may be reported as increases in net assets without donor restrictions if the **restrictions expire** in the period the gains and income are recognized. The NFP must
      1) Have a similar policy for contributions received,
      2) Report consistently, and
      3) Disclose the policy.
   b. Investment return not related to program services must be reported net of related external, and direct internal, investment expenses.
3. Study Unit 5, Subunit 3, outlines the guidance for subsequent measurement of **equity securities**.
4. Subsequent measurement of **debt securities** is at fair value in the statement of financial position.

5. A **donor-restricted endowment fund** is created by a donor stipulation requiring a gift to be invested for a specified period or in perpetuity.
   a. This definition excludes **board-designated** endowment funds.
   b. Classifying a donor-restricted endowment fund within net assets with donor restrictions or net assets without donor restrictions depends on (1) the donor's specific stipulation and (2) the applicable law.
      1) Without a donor or legal restriction, **investment return** generally is free of donor restrictions. But most donor-restricted endowment funds are subject to the UPMIFA. This statute **extends** a donor restriction to use of the assets, including the return, until **appropriation for expenditure** by the governing board.
         a) Thus, without contrary language in the gift instrument, the assets in the fund (including the return) are net assets with donor restrictions until appropriation.
         b) An appropriation reduces net assets with donor restrictions if all time and purpose restrictions have been met. The result is a reclassification to net assets without donor restrictions.
            i) Appropriation occurs upon **approval** for expenditure unless a legal interpretation states otherwise.
      2) An **underwater endowment fund** has a reporting-date fair value less than the amount (a) of the gift or (b) required by the donor or a law that extends donor restrictions.
         a) The accumulated **losses** are included with that fund in net assets with donor restrictions.

EXAMPLE 20-15 Perpetual Endowment Fund Subject to Majority Legal Rules

A nongovernmental not-for-profit entity received a $2 million gift from a donor who specified that it be used to create an endowment fund to be invested in perpetuity. The income from the fund is to be used to support a specific program in the second year and beyond. Income from investments purchased with the gift was $40,000 during the first year. At the end of the first year, the fair value of the investments was $2,010,000. What is the net effect on net assets with donor restrictions at year end?

The applicable state law follows the majority rule, and the donor gave no instruction on use of the appreciation of the fund investments. In these circumstances, the income increases net assets with donor restrictions because the time and purpose restrictions have not been met. Also, (1) the jurisdiction follows the majority legal rule that extends donor restrictions to use of the investment return, and (2) no amount was appropriated for expenditure by the governing board. Accordingly, the $10,000 gain on the perpetual endowment and the $40,000 of income increase net assets with donor restrictions by $50,000.

STOP & REVIEW

You have completed the outline for this subunit.
Study multiple-choice questions 16 through 19 beginning on page 652.

QUESTIONS

20.1 Financial Statements

1. Forkin Manor, a nongovernmental not-for-profit entity (NFP), wants to reformat its financial statements using terminology that is more readily associated with for-profit entities. The director believes that the term "operating profit" and the practice of segregating recurring and nonrecurring items more accurately depict the NFP's activities. Under what condition will Forkin be allowed to use "operating profit" and to segregate its recurring items from its nonrecurring items in its statement of activities?

A. The NFP reports the change in net assets without donor restrictions for the period.

B. A parenthetical disclosure in the notes implies that the NFP is seeking for-profit entity status.

C. Forkin receives special authorization from the Internal Revenue Service that this wording is appropriate.

D. At a minimum, the NFP reports the change in net assets with donor restrictions for the period.

Answer (A) is correct.

REQUIRED: The condition allowing an NFP to use the term "operating profit" and to segregate recurring and nonrecurring items in its statement of activities.

DISCUSSION: In its statement of activities, an NFP may use such classifications as (1) operating and nonoperating, (2) expendable and nonexpendable, (3) recognized and unrecognized, and (4) recurring and nonrecurring. Furthermore, if an intermediate operating measure (e.g., operating income or operating profit) is used, it must be in a financial statement that at a minimum reports the change in net assets without donor restrictions.

Answer (B) is incorrect. The NFP need not seek for-profit status to report in the described manner. **Answer (C) is incorrect.** The NFP need not obtain IRS authorization to report in the described manner. **Answer (D) is incorrect.** The NFP must report the changes in the two classes of net assets regardless of whether additional classifications are included in the statement of activities.

2. A complete set of general-purpose external financial statements issued by a nongovernmental not-for-profit entity must include

A. Statements of financial position as of the beginning and end of the reporting period, a statement of cash flows, and a statement of activities.

B. A statement of financial position as of the end of the reporting period and a statement of revenues, expenditures, and changes in fund balances.

C. A statement of financial position as of the end of the reporting period, a statement of cash flows, and a statement of activities.

D. Statements of financial position as of the beginning and end of the reporting period, comparative statements of cash flows, and comparative statements of activities.

Answer (C) is correct.

REQUIRED: The statements included in a complete set of financial statements of NFPs.

DISCUSSION: A complete set of financial statements of an NFP must include (1) a statement of financial position as of the end of the reporting period, (2) a statement of activities and a statement of cash flows for the reporting period, and (3) accompanying notes.

Answer (A) is incorrect. The statement of financial position must be as of the end of the reporting period. **Answer (B) is incorrect.** A statement of revenues, expenditures, and changes in fund balances is reported for the governmental funds of a state or local governmental entity. **Answer (D) is incorrect.** The statement of financial position must be as of the end of the reporting period, and comparative statements are not required.

3. Net assets is an element of the financial statements of nongovernmental not-for-profit entities (NFPs). It

A. Is the residual interest in the assets of an NFP after subtracting its liabilities.

B. Is the change in equity during a period from transactions and other events and circumstances not involving resource providers.

C. Differs from equity in businesses because it is not a residual interest.

D. Consists of the probable future economic benefits obtained or controlled by a particular entity as a result of past transactions or events.

Answer (A) is correct.

REQUIRED: The definition of the net assets element of the financial statements of NFPs.

DISCUSSION: Net assets equals the residual interest in the assets of an entity that remains after subtracting its liabilities. In an NFP, which has no ownership interest, net assets is classified at a minimum as net assets without donor restrictions and net assets with donor restrictions.

Answer (B) is incorrect. Comprehensive income is the change in equity of a business during a period from transactions and other events and circumstances from nonowner sources. **Answer (C) is incorrect.** Equity and net assets are residuals. **Answer (D) is incorrect.** Assets, not net assets, are probable future economic benefits obtained or controlled by a particular entity as a result of past transactions or events.

4. At the beginning of the year, the Baker Fund, a nongovernmental not-for-profit corporation, received a $125,000 contribution restricted to youth activity programs. During the year, youth activities generated revenues of $89,000 and had program expenses of $95,000. What amount should Baker report as net assets released from restrictions for the current year?

A. $0

B. $6,000

C. $95,000

D. $125,000

Answer (C) is correct.

REQUIRED: The net assets released from restrictions for the current year.

DISCUSSION: At the time the contribution was made, net assets with donor restrictions increased by $125,000. The restriction stated that the funds were to be used for youth activity programs. The amount of actual program expenses for the year ($95,000) is reported under net assets released from restrictions.

Answer (A) is incorrect. The incurrence of program expenses reduced net assets with donor restrictions by fulfilling the purpose of the restriction to the extent the resources were used. **Answer (B) is incorrect.** The amount of $6,000 is the excess of program expenses over revenues generated by youth activities. **Answer (D) is incorrect.** The purpose of the restriction was fulfilled only to the extent the contribution was used for the stated purpose.

5. The following information was reported by a nongovernmental not-for-profit entity at the end of its current fiscal year:

Gross accounts receivable	
January 1	$ 37,500
December 31	49,300
Sales on account and cash sales	359,000
Uncollectible accounts	2,000

No accounts receivable were written off or recovered during the year. If the direct method is used in the statement of cash flows, cash collected from customers is

A. $372,800

B. $370,800

C. $347,200

D. $345,200

Answer (C) is correct.

REQUIRED: The cash collected from customers.

DISCUSSION: Collections from customers equal sales revenue adjusted for the change in gross accounts receivable and write-offs and recoveries. Because no accounts receivable were written off or recovered during the year, no adjustment for these transactions is needed. Accounts receivable increased by $11,800 ($49,300 – $37,500). This amount is an excess of revenue recognized over cash received. Cash collected from customers is $347,200 ($359,000 – $11,800).

Answer (A) is incorrect. The amount of $372,800 results from adding the increase in accounts receivable and the uncollectible accounts balance. **Answer (B) is incorrect.** The amount of $370,800 results from adding the increase in accounts receivable. **Answer (D) is incorrect.** The amount of $345,200 results from subtracting the uncollectible accounts balance.

6. A nongovernmental not-for-profit entity has the following current information to be reflected in its statement of cash flows:

	January 1	December 31
Accounts receivable	$9,500	$16,000
Allowance for credit losses	300	700
Prepaid rent expense	7,200	4,400
Accounts payable	8,700	10,700

The current-year change in net assets is $55,000. Net cash provided by operating activities in the statement of cash flows should be

A. $49,600

B. $56,200

C. $53,000

D. $53,700

Answer (D) is correct.

REQUIRED: The net cash provided by operating activities.

DISCUSSION: The change in net assets should be adjusted for the effects of items properly included in its determination but having either a different effect or no effect on net operating cash flow. The increase in gross accounts receivable should be subtracted. The increase indicates that revenues exceeded cash received. The increase in the allowance for credit losses should be added. This amount is a noncash expense. The decrease in prepaid rent expense should be added. The cash was paid in a prior period, but the expense is recognized currently as a noncash item. The increase in accounts payable should be added. It indicates that liabilities and related expenses were recognized without cash outflows. The net cash provided by operating activities is therefore $53,700.

$55,000	Change in net assets
(6,500)	Increase in gross AR
400	Increase in allowance for credit losses
2,800	Decrease in prepaid rent
2,000	Increase in accounts payable
$53,700	Net cash provided by operating activities

Answer (A) is incorrect. The amount of $49,600 results from subtracting the increase in accounts payable. **Answer (B) is incorrect.** The amount of $56,200 results from adding the change in accounts receivable and subtracting the changes in the other balances. **Answer (C) is incorrect.** The amount of $53,000 results from subtracting the change in the allowance for credit losses.

7. Functional expenses recorded in the general ledger of ABC, a nongovernmental not-for-profit entity, are as follows:

Soliciting prospective members	$45,000
Printing membership benefits brochures	30,000
Soliciting membership dues	25,000
Maintaining donor list	10,000

What amount should ABC report as fundraising expenses?

A. $10,000

B. $35,000

C. $70,000

D. $110,000

Answer (A) is correct.

REQUIRED: The fundraising expenses.

DISCUSSION: The major functional classes of expenses for an NFP are program services and supporting activities. An analysis also must be presented that disaggregates functional expense classifications by natural expense classifications (e.g., salaries, interest, rent, and depreciation). Supporting activities include (1) management and general, (2) fundraising, and (3) membership-development activities. Fundraising expenses include maintaining donor lists ($10,000). Soliciting members and dues and printing membership benefits brochures are membership-development activities.

Answer (B) is incorrect. The amount of $35,000 includes the cost of soliciting dues, a membership-development activity. **Answer (C) is incorrect.** The amount of $70,000 is the cost of soliciting members and dues. **Answer (D) is incorrect.** Only the cost of the donor list is an expense of fundraising.

Question 8 is based on the following information. NFP, a nongovernmental not-for-profit entity, reported a change in net assets of $300,000 for the current year. Changes occurred in several balance sheet accounts as follows:

Equipment	$25,000 increase
Accumulated depreciation	40,000 increase
Note payable	30,000 increase

Additional Information:

- During the current year, NFP sold equipment costing $25,000, with accumulated depreciation of $12,000, for a gain of $5,000.
- In December of the current year, NFP purchased equipment costing $50,000 with $20,000 cash and a 12% note payable of $30,000.
- Depreciation expense for the year was $52,000.

8. In NFP's current-year statement of cash flows, net cash provided by operating activities should be

A. $340,000

B. $347,000

C. $352,000

D. $357,000

Answer (B) is correct.

REQUIRED: The net cash provided by operating activities in the statement of cash flows.

DISCUSSION: The FASB's guidance for presenting a statement of cash flows applies to a nongovernmental not-for-profit entity. For example, "net income" includes the change in net assets. An NFP should adjust the change in net assets for the effects of items that have no effect on net cash provided by operating activities. Depreciation is included in the determination of the change in net assets but has no cash effect. Thus, depreciation should be added. The sale of equipment resulted in a gain included in the determination of the change in net assets, but the cash effect is classified as an inflow from an investing activity. Thus, the gain should be subtracted. The cash outflow for the purchase of equipment is from an investing activity and has no effect on the change in net assets. It requires no adjustment. The net cash provided by operating activities is $347,000 ($300,000 change in net assets + $52,000 depreciation – $5,000 gain).

Answer (A) is incorrect. The amount of $340,000 reflects addition of the accumulated depreciation. **Answer (C) is incorrect.** The amount of $352,000 results from not subtracting the gain. **Answer (D) is incorrect.** The amount of $357,000 results from adding the gain.

9. A nongovernmental not-for-profit entity borrowed $5,000, which it used to purchase a truck. In which section of the entity's statement of cash flows should the transaction be reported?

A. In cash inflow and cash outflow from investing activities.

B. In cash inflow and cash outflow from financing activities.

C. In cash inflow from financing activities and cash outflow from investing activities.

D. In cash inflow from operating activities and cash outflow from investing activities.

Answer (C) is correct.

REQUIRED: The section of the statement of cash flows in which the purchase of a truck is reported by an NFP.

DISCUSSION: The borrowing is a cash inflow from a financing activity because it results from issuing debt. The purchase of the truck is a cash outflow from an investing activity because it involves the acquisition of property, plant, or equipment or other productive assets.

10. In its fiscal year ended June 30, Year 4, Barr College, a large nongovernmental not-for-profit entity, received $100,000 designated by the donor for scholarships for superior students. On July 26, Year 4, Barr selected the students and awarded the scholarships. How should the July 26 transaction be reported in Barr's statement of activities for the year ended June 30, Year 5?

A. As both an increase and a decrease of $100,000 in net assets without donor restrictions.

B. As a decrease only in net assets without donor restrictions.

C. By footnote disclosure only.

D. Not reported.

Answer (A) is correct.

REQUIRED: The treatment by a private not-for-profit entity of funds received and used for a designated purpose.

DISCUSSION: When the NFP received the contribution, it should have been classified as net assets with donor restrictions because it was to be used for a specified purpose. When the purpose is fulfilled, the restriction expires. The amount then should be reclassified as a decrease in net assets with donor restrictions and an increase in net assets without donor restrictions. When the scholarships are awarded, net assets without donor restrictions is decreased.

Answer (B) is incorrect. Net assets without donor restrictions also must be increased. **Answer (C) is incorrect.** A donation must be reported on the face of the statement of activities. **Answer (D) is incorrect.** This donation must be reported as (1) an increase and a decrease in net assets without donor restrictions and (2) a decrease in net assets with donor restrictions when its purpose is fulfilled and the scholarships are awarded.

11. On January 1, Year 4, a nongovernmental not-for-profit botanical society received a gift of an exhaustible fixed asset with an estimated useful life of 10 years and no salvage value. The donor's cost of this asset was $20,000, and its fair value at the date of the gift was $30,000. What amount of depreciation of this asset should the society recognize in its Year 4 financial statements?

A. $3,000

B. $2,500

C. $2,000

D. $0

Answer (A) is correct.

REQUIRED: The amount of depreciation to be recognized in the financial statements.

DISCUSSION: NFPs must recognize depreciation. Moreover, contributions are recorded at their fair value when received. Assuming the straight-line method is used, the amount of depreciation that the NFP should recognize is $3,000 [($30,000 fair value – $0 salvage value) ÷ 10 years].

Answer (B) is incorrect. Annual straight-line depreciation for this asset is $3,000. **Answer (C) is incorrect.** The amount of $2,000 results from using cost as the depreciable basis of the asset. **Answer (D) is incorrect.** NFPs recognize depreciation on most property and equipment.

20.2 Contributions

12. During the current year, Mill Foundation, a nongovernmental not-for-profit entity, received $100,000 in unrestricted contributions from the general public. Mill's board of directors stipulated that $75,000 of these contributions would be used to create an endowment. At the end of the current year, how should Mill report the $75,000 in the net assets section of the statement of financial position?

A. Permanently restricted.

B. Net assets without donor restrictions.

C. Temporarily restricted.

D. Donor restricted.

Answer (B) is correct.

REQUIRED: The reporting of unrestricted contributions designated as an endowment.

DISCUSSION: An internal decision to designate a portion of net assets without donor restrictions as an endowment is not a restriction. If the contributions had been restricted by the donor, the classification of the assets would have been net assets with donor restrictions.

Answer (A) is incorrect. The contributions were not restricted by the donors. **Answer (C) is incorrect.** The contributions were unrestricted because the endowment was designated by the board. **Answer (D) is incorrect.** The board of directors, not the donors, designated a portion of the contributions as an endowment.

13. NFP has received a $2,000,000 research grant from a government. NFP may retain the rights to the research and is permitted to publish the findings. However, NFP must (1) follow a certain protocol (regulations established by the government), (2) incur specified qualifying expenses, (3) forfeit unspent money, and (4) report the research findings to the government. This transfer of assets to NFP from a government is

A. An unconditional contribution.

B. An exchange transaction.

C. A conditional contribution.

D. A conditional exchange transaction.

Answer (C) is correct.

REQUIRED: The nature of a governmental grant.

DISCUSSION: An exchange transaction is a reciprocal transfer in which each party receives and sacrifices approximately commensurate value. But the government (resource provider) does not receive commensurate value. NFP retains the rights to the research, and the government receives only an indirect benefit. NFP and the public receive the direct (primary) benefit. The transaction is a conditional contribution to the extent the assets are received before the condition is met. The agreement (donor stipulation) states a barrier that must be overcome before the recipient is entitled to the assets. This condition is deemed to exist because of certain indicators (e.g., a protocol to be followed and incurrence of qualifying expenses). They established that a barrier exists in the form of limits on the recipient's discretion over the conduct of the research activity. Before the condition is substantially met (or explicitly waived), NFP recognizes a refundable advance (liability). After the condition is substantially met, NFP recognizes contribution revenue. The transfer of assets is then unconditional as well as voluntary and nonreciprocal.

Answer (A) is incorrect. The agreement contains indicators of the existence of a barrier (a condition) that must be overcome before the recipient is entitled to the assets. **Answer (B) is incorrect.** The government did not receive commensurate value. **Answer (D) is incorrect.** The guidance regarding conditions applies to contributions, not exchange transactions.

14. During the current year, a voluntary health and welfare entity received $300,000 in pledges without donor-imposed restrictions. Of this amount, $100,000 has been designated by donors for use next year to support operations. If 15% of the pledges without donor-imposed restrictions are expected to be uncollectible, what amount of support that increases net assets without donor restrictions should the entity recognize in its current-year financial statements?

A. $300,000

B. $270,000

C. $200,000

D. $170,000

Answer (D) is correct.

REQUIRED: The current-year support that increases net assets without donor restrictions to be recognized.

DISCUSSION: Only $200,000 of the pledged total constitutes support that increases net assets without donor restrictions. These pledges may be recognized at net realizable value (NRV) if their collection is expected in less than 1 year. The NRV of these pledges is $170,000 [$200,000 × (1.0 – .15 estimated uncollectible)].

Answer (A) is incorrect. The amount of $300,000 is the total amount of pledges. **Answer (B) is incorrect.** The amount of $100,000 of the pledges is restricted until the next year. **Answer (C) is incorrect.** The amount of $200,000 does not reflect the estimated uncollectible pledges.

15. In July Year 3, Katie irrevocably donated $200,000 cash to be invested and held in trust by a church. Katie stipulated that the revenue generated from this gift be paid to Katie during Katie's lifetime. After Katie dies, the principal is to be used by the church for any purpose chosen by its governing body. The church received interest of $16,000 on the $200,000 for the year ended June 30, Year 4, and the interest was remitted to Katie. In the church's June 30, Year 4, annual financial statements,

A. $200,000 should be reported as revenue.

B. $184,000 should be reported as revenue.

C. $16,000 should be reported as revenue.

D. The gift and its terms should be disclosed only in notes to the financial statements.

Answer (A) is correct.

REQUIRED: The accounting for a donation of cash to be invested to pay income to the donor for life and then to pay the principal to the donee.

DISCUSSION: An NFP should report an irrevocable split-interest agreement. Assets under the control of the NFP are recorded at fair value at the time of initial recognition, and the contribution is recognized as revenue. Because the NFP has a remainder interest, it should not recognize revenue from receipt of the income of the trust. Thus, the NFP should recognize revenue of $200,000 (the presumed fair value of the contributed cash).

Answer (B) is incorrect. The contribution is not reduced by the income paid to the donor. **Answer (C) is incorrect.** The income paid to the donor is not revenue of the NFP. **Answer (D) is incorrect.** The contribution should be recognized at fair value.

20.3 Investments

16. On December 31 of the current year, Communities Organized for Social Improvement (COSI), a not-for-profit entity, holds an investment in common stock of one publicly traded entity and an investment in debt securities of another. The not-for-profit entity holds the common stock as a long-term investment and has the intent and the ability to hold the debt securities until maturity.

	Investment in Common Stock	Investment in Debt Securities
Original cost	$50,000	$35,000
Amortized cost		28,000
Fair value	63,000	40,000

In the December 31 statement of financial position for the current year, COSI should value these investments as

	Investment in Common Stock	Investment in Debt Securities
A.	$50,000	$28,000
B.	$50,000	$40,000
C.	$63,000	$28,000
D.	$63,000	$40,000

Answer (D) is correct.

REQUIRED: The amount to be recorded by an NFP for investments in equity and debt securities.

DISCUSSION: GAAP applying to accounting for certain investments held by NFPs require them to measure investments in equity securities with readily determinable fair values and all investments in debt securities at fair value in the statement of financial position.

Answer (A) is incorrect. The investment in common stock should not be measured at original cost. The investment in debt securities should not be measured at amortized cost. **Answer (B) is incorrect.** The investment in common stock should not be measured at original cost. **Answer (C) is incorrect.** The investment in debt securities should not be measured at amortized cost.

17. Lane Foundation, a voluntary health and welfare entity, received a perpetual endowment of $500,000 in Year 3 from Gant Enterprises. The endowment assets were invested in publicly traded securities, and Gant did not specify how gains and losses from dispositions of endowment assets were to be treated. No donor-imposed restrictions were placed on the use of dividends received and interest earned on fund resources. In Year 4, Lane realized gains of $50,000 on sales of fund investments and received total interest and dividends of $40,000 on fund securities. Lane's governing board has not appropriated any part of the investment return. If the Uniform Prudent Management of Institutional Funds Act (UPMIFA) applies, what amount of these capital gains, interest, and dividends increases net assets without donor restrictions?

A. $0

B. $40,000

C. $50,000

D. $90,000

Answer (A) is correct.

REQUIRED: The amount of capital gains, interest, and dividends that increases net assets without donor restrictions.

DISCUSSION: The donor did not specify how income (interest and dividends), gains, and losses were to be treated. Nevertheless, the NFP is subject to UPMIFA. This statute extends a donor restriction (i.e., on the endowment held in perpetuity) to use of the assets, including the return, until appropriation for expenditure by the governing board. Thus, without other language in the gift instrument, the assets in the fund (including the return) are net assets with donor restrictions until appropriation. An appropriation reduces net assets with donor restrictions if all time and purpose restrictions have been met. The result is a reclassification to net assets without donor restrictions. Without a contrary legal interpretation, appropriation occurs upon approval for expenditure. In the absence of an appropriation by the governing board, the NFP's capital gain, interest, and dividends therefore increase net assets with donor restrictions, not net assets without donor restrictions.

Answer (B) is incorrect. The amount of $40,000 (interest and dividends) increases net assets with donor restrictions. **Answer (C) is incorrect.** The amount of $50,000 (capital gains) increases net assets with donor restrictions. **Answer (D) is incorrect.** The amount of $90,000 (capital gains, interest, and dividends) increases net assets with donor restrictions.

18. A voluntary health and welfare entity received a $500,000 perpetual endowment at the beginning of the year. The donor stipulated that the income be used for a mental health program. Also, no reporting date fair value was stipulated by the donor or required by law. The endowment fund reported a $60,000 net decrease in fair value and $30,000 of investment income. The entity spent $45,000 on the mental health program during the year. What amount of change in net assets with donor restrictions should the entity report?

A. $75,000 decrease.

B. $15,000 decrease.

C. $440,000 increase.

D. $470,000 increase.

Answer (C) is correct.

REQUIRED: The change in net assets with donor restrictions from receipt of a perpetual endowment with a purpose restriction on income.

DISCUSSION: The $500,000 contribution to a perpetual endowment is an increase in net assets with donor restrictions. The income is subject to a donor-imposed purpose restriction. However, if the restriction is met in the period the income is recognized, it may be reported as an increase in net assets without donor restrictions if the entity (1) has a similar policy for reporting contributions received, (2) reports consistently, and (3) discloses the policy. Assuming these criteria were satisfied, the restriction on the $30,000 of investment income expired when it was spent (with an additional $15,000, presumably from other sources). The endowment fund is underwater because its reporting date fair value ($500,000 gift – $60,000 = $440,000) is less than the amount of the gift. (No reporting date fair value was stipulated by the donor or required by law.) The loss is included with the fund in net assets with donor restrictions. The effect on net assets with donor restrictions of (1) creation of the endowment (an increase of $500,000 in net assets with donor restrictions), (2) the receipt and expenditure in the same period of income (an increase of $30,000 in net assets without donor restrictions), and (3) the loss on the principal of the endowment (a decrease of $60,000 in net assets with donor restrictions) is $440,000.

Answer (A) is incorrect. The amount of $75,000 is the sum of the fair value decrease and the excess of spending over income. **Answer (B) is incorrect.** The amount of $15,000 is the excess of the amount spent over the income. **Answer (D) is incorrect.** The amount of $470,000 equals the contribution (perpetual endowment) minus the excess of the fair value decrease over the income.

19. A voluntary health and welfare entity received a $700,000 perpetual endowment during the year. The donor stipulated that the income and investment appreciation be used to maintain its senior center. The endowment fund reported a net investment appreciation of $80,000 and investment income of $50,000. The entity spent $60,000 to maintain its senior center during the year. What amount of change in net assets with donor restrictions should the entity report?

A. $50,000

B. $770,000

C. $130,000

D. $70,000

Answer (B) is correct.

REQUIRED: The change in net assets with donor restrictions reported by a VHWE that received a perpetual endowment with a purpose restriction on appreciation and income.

DISCUSSION: The $700,000 contribution to a perpetual endowment is an increase in net assets with donor restrictions. Income or appreciation from donor-restricted perpetual endowments is an increase in donor-restricted support if the donor restricts its use. However, if the restriction expires in the period the income and appreciation are recognized, it may be reported as net assets without donor restrictions if the entity (1) has a similar policy for reporting contributions received, (2) reports consistently, and (3) discloses its accounting policy. Assuming these criteria were satisfied, the donor-imposed restriction on the income and gains is deemed to have expired but only to the extent it was expended during the year. Accordingly, the change in net assets with donor restrictions was $70,000 ($80,000 gain + $50,000 income – $60,000 spent). The total change in net assets with donor restrictions is $770,000 ($700,000 contribution to a permanent endowment + $70,000 unexpended gain and income).

Answer (A) is incorrect. The amount of $50,000 is the VHWE's investment income. **Answer (C) is incorrect.** The amount of $130,000 is the sum of the appreciation and income. **Answer (D) is incorrect.** The amount of $70,000 equals the sum of the unexpended gain and income.

APPENDIX A
IFRS DIFFERENCES

The following appendix summarizes the most testable differences between IFRS and U.S. GAAP.

Topic	IFRS	U.S. GAAP	Page
Interim financial reporting	Each interim period is a discrete reporting period.	Each interim period is treated primarily as an integral part of an annual period.	110
Investment in equity securities			
• Accounting for investment in equity securities that does not result in significant influence or control over the investee	The investment is measured at fair value through profit or loss (as under U.S. GAAP). The investor may irrevocably elect at initial recognition to measure the investment that is not held for trading at fair value through OCI. The holding gains and losses accumulated in OCI are never reclassified to profit or loss.	The investment is measured at fair value through net income. When the fair value is not readily determinable, the investment may be measured at cost minus impairment (if any), plus or minus changes resulting from observable price changes for the identical or a similar investment of the same issuer.	141
Equity method of accounting			
• Accounting method for significant influence investments (20%-50% ownership but not control)	The equity method is applied for such investments.	The investor may choose either the (1) fair value option (FVO) or (2) equity method to account for such investments.	142
Inventories			
• Cost flow methods	LIFO is not permitted.	LIFO is an acceptable method.	200
• Measurement	Inventory is measured at the lower of cost or net realizable value (NRV). NRV is the estimated selling price minus estimated costs of completion and disposal.	Measurement of inventory depends on the cost method used. (1) Inventory accounted for using LIFO or the retail inventory method is measured at the lower of cost or market. (2) Inventory accounted for using any other cost method (e.g., FIFO or average cost) is measured at the lower of cost or net realizable value.	205
• Reversals of an inventory write-down	An inventory write-down may be reversed in subsequent periods but not above original cost.	Reversals of write-downs of inventory are prohibited in subsequent periods.	205

Topic	IFRS	U.S. GAAP	Page
• Measurement at interim periods	An inventory loss from a decline below cost must be recognized in the interim period in which it occurred even if no loss is reasonably expected for the year.	An inventory loss from a decline below cost may be deferred in the interim period if no loss is reasonably anticipated for the year. Nontemporary inventory losses from a decline below cost must be recognized at the interim date. If the loss is recovered in another quarter, it is recognized as a gain and treated as a change in estimate. The amount recovered is limited to the losses previously recognized.	207
<u>Property, plant, and equipment (PPE)</u>			
• Accounting policies	PPE items may be accounted for under either the (1) cost model or (2) revaluation model. The same accounting policy must apply to an entire class of PPE.	PPE items are accounted for using the cost model. They are reported at historical cost minus accumulated depreciation and impairment losses.	226
• The revaluation model	An item of PPE whose fair value can be reliably measured may be carried at a revalued amount equal to fair value at the revaluation date (minus subsequent accumulated depreciation and impairment losses). Revaluation is needed whenever fair value and the asset's carrying amount differ materially. A revaluation increase must be recognized in other comprehensive income and accumulated in equity as revaluation surplus. But the increase must be recognized in profit or loss to the extent it reverses a decrease of the carrying amount of the same asset that was recognized in profit or loss. A revaluation decrease must be recognized in profit or loss. But the decrease must be recognized in other comprehensive income to the extent of any credit in revaluation surplus for the same asset.	The revaluation model is not permitted.	226

Topic	IFRS	U.S. GAAP	Page
• Investment property	Investment property is property (land, building, part of a building, or both) held by the owner or by the lessee under a finance lease to earn rental income or for capital appreciation or both. Investment property may be accounted for according to (1) the cost model or (2) the fair value model. If the fair value model is chosen as the accounting policy, all of the entity's investment property must be measured at fair value at the end of the reporting period. A gain or loss resulting from a change in the fair value of investment property must be recognized in profit or loss for the period in which it occurred. Investment property that is accounted for according to the fair value model is not depreciated.	Investment property is not separately defined. Thus, it is accounted for using the cost model applied to other items of PPE.	227
• Component depreciation	Each part of an item with a cost significant to the total cost must be depreciated separately.	Component depreciation is permitted but not required under U.S. GAAP.	236
<u>Impairment of assets</u>			
• Test for impairment	One-step impairment test. The carrying amount of an asset is compared with its recoverable amount. An impairment loss is recognized equal to the excess of the carrying amount over the recoverable amount. The recoverable amount is the greater of an asset's (1) fair value minus cost to sell or (2) value in use. Value in use of the asset is the present value of its expected cash flows.	Two-step impairment test. Step (1). The carrying amount of an asset is not recoverable if it exceeds the sum of the undiscounted future cash flows expected from the use and disposition of the asset. Step (2). If the carrying amount is not recoverable, an impairment loss may be recognized. It equals the excess of the carrying amount of the asset over its fair value.	245
• Reversals of impairment loss	An impairment loss may be reversed in a subsequent period if a change in the estimates used to measure the recoverable amount has occurred. The reversal of an impairment loss is recognized immediately in profit or loss as income from continued operations.	A previously recognized impairment loss must not be reversed.	245

Topic	IFRS	U.S. GAAP	Page
Intangible assets			
• Accounting policies	Intangible assets may be accounted for under either the (1) cost model or (2) revaluation model. The revaluation model can be applied only if the intangible asset is traded in an active market.	Intangible assets are accounted for using the cost model. They are reported at historical cost minus accumulated amortization and impairment losses.	261
• Test for impairment – Intangible asset with finite useful life	One-step impairment test. The same test as for items of PPE. The carrying amount of an asset is compared with its recoverable amount. An impairment loss may be reversed in a subsequent period if a change in the estimates used to measure the recoverable amount has occurred.	Two-step impairment test. The same test as for items of PPE. A previously recognized impairment loss must not be reversed.	262
• Test for impairment – Intangible asset with indefinite useful life other than goodwill	A qualitative assessment is not an option. One-step impairment test. The same test as for items of PPE. The carrying amount of an asset is compared with its recoverable amount.	An entity may first perform a qualitative assessment to determine whether it is necessary to perform the quantitative impairment test. The quantitative test compares the carrying amount with the fair value of an asset. An impairment loss is recognized equal to the excess of the carrying amount over the fair value.	263
• Test for impairment – Goodwill	A qualitative assessment is not an option. The test for impairment of a cash-generating unit (CGU) to which goodwill has been allocated is whether the carrying amount of the CGU (including allocated goodwill) exceeds its recoverable amount. Thus, the test has one step. An impairment loss for a CGU is allocated first to reduce allocated goodwill to zero and then pro rata to other assets of the CGU.	An entity may first perform a qualitative assessment to determine whether it is necessary to perform the quantitative impairment test. The fair value of a reporting unit is compared with its carrying amount, including goodwill. A goodwill impairment loss is recognized for the amount that the carrying amount of a reporting unit, including goodwill, exceeds its fair value. The loss is limited to the total amount of goodwill allocated to that reporting unit.	268

Topic	IFRS	U.S. GAAP	Page
• Research and development costs (other than computer software)	Research costs must be expensed as incurred. Development costs may result in recognition of an intangible asset if the entity can demonstrate the (1) technical feasibility of completion of the asset, (2) intent to complete, (3) ability to use or sell the asset, (4) way in which it will generate probable future economic benefits, (5) availability of resources to complete and use or sell the asset, and (6) ability to measure reliably expenditures attributable to the asset.	Research and development (R&D) costs must be expensed as incurred.	270
<u>Income tax accounting</u>			
• Valuation allowance	No valuation allowance is recognized.	A valuation allowance reduces a deferred tax asset. It is recognized if it is more likely than not (probability > 50%) that some portion of the asset will not be realized.	305
<u>Defined benefit pension plan</u>			
• Return on plan assets	No expected return on plan assets is recognized. Instead, interest income on plan assets for the period is recognized in profit or loss. This interest income is calculated by using the same rate used to discount the defined benefit obligation.	The expected return on plan assets component of pension expense is the fair value of plan assets at the beginning of the period multiplied by the expected long-term rate of return.	326
• Actuarial gains and losses	Remeasurements of the net defined benefit liability (asset) are recognized in OCI. They are never reclassified to profit or loss in subsequent periods. Remeasurements include actuarial gains and losses.	An entity may choose among three methods of accounting for the net actuarial gain or loss. (1) The corridor method. (2) Net gains or losses can be recognized immediately in the statement of income in the period in which they arise as a component of pension expense. (3) Any systematic method of amortizing net gains or losses included in accumulated OCI may be used.	327

Topic	IFRS	U.S. GAAP	Page
• Prior service cost or credit	Past service cost or credit is recognized as a component of pension expense in the period in which it arises.	Prior service cost or credit is initially recognized in accumulated other comprehensive income. Subsequently, the amount recognized is amortized and reclassified from accumulated OCI to net pension expense. The required amortization of prior service cost or credit assigns an equal amount to each future period of service of each employee who is expected to receive benefits under the plan.	329
<u>Leases</u>			
• Accounting by lessee	The lessee accounts for all leases, except for "short-term" leases and "low-value" leases, similar to a finance lease under U.S. GAAP. The lessee may elect to account for a lease of low-value assets (assets with a value of $5,000 or less) the same way as "short-term" leases.	The lease is classified by the lessee as an operating lease or a finance lease. As an accounting policy for "short-term" leases, a lessee may elect not to recognize the right-of-use asset and lease liability. A "low-value" lease is not a classification option for the lessee.	393
• Accounting by lessor	The lessor classifies a lease as a finance lease (similar to sales-type lease under U.S. GAAP) or an operating lease. A direct financing lease is not a classification option for the lessor.	The lessor classifies a lease as a sales-type lease, an operating lease, or a direct financing lease.	407
<u>Contingent liability or provision</u>			
• Estimate stated within a range	If the estimate of a provision is stated within a continuous range of possible outcomes and each point in the range is as likely as any other, the midpoint is used.	If the estimate is stated within a range and no amount within that range appears to be a better estimate than any other, the minimum should be accrued.	414
<u>Noncontrolling interest (NCI)</u>			
• Measurement of NCI on the business combination date	A NCI may be measured at (1) fair value or (2) a proportionate share of the fair value of the acquiree's identifiable net assets.	A NCI is measured at its acquisition-date fair value.	461

Topic	IFRS	U.S. GAAP	Page
Statement of cash flows			
• Classification of dividends paid	Dividends paid are classified as cash outflows either from (1) operating activities or (2) financing activities.	Dividends paid are cash outflows from financing activities.	518
• Classification of interest paid	Interest paid is classified as a cash outflow either from (1) operating activities or (2) financing activities.	Interest paid is a cash outflow from operating activities.	518
• Classification of interest and dividends received	Interest and dividends received are classified as cash inflows either from (1) operating activities or (2) investing activities.	Interest and dividends received are cash inflows from operating activities.	518

NOTE:

1) To succeed on the exam, you should be familiar with all differences between IFRS and U.S. GAAP described in the book.
2) Questions that apply to IFRS include phrases such as "under IFRS" or "according to IFRS."

For example, this AICPA-released question from 2016 tests a concept that is treated differently under IFRS:

EXAMPLE
From CPA Exam

At the end of Year 1, a company reduced its inventory cost from $100 to its net realizable value of $80. As of the end of Year 2, the inventory was still on hand and its net realizable value increased to $150. Under IFRS, what journal entry should the company record for Year 2 to properly report the inventory value?

A. Debit inventory for $20 and credit expense for $20.
B. Debit inventory for $70 and credit expense for $70.
C. Debit inventory for $70, credit retained earnings for $50, and credit expense for $20.
D. Debit inventory for $20, debit expense for $30, and credit retained earnings for $50.

Answer (A) is correct. Under IFRS, inventories are measured at the lower of cost or net realizable value (NRV). NRV is the estimated selling price less the estimated costs of completion and disposal. At the end of Year 1, a loss on write-down of $20 ($100 cost – $80 NRV) was recognized. NRV is assessed each period. Accordingly, a write-down may be reversed but not above original cost. The write-down and reversal are recognized in profit or loss. Therefore, only the original $20 write-down can be reversed by debiting inventory for $20 and crediting the expense account for $20.

Answer (B) is incorrect. Under IFRS, a write-down may be reversed but not above original cost.

Answer (C) is incorrect. Under IFRS, reversing a write-down is a current-period event, so retained earnings is not directly affected.

Answer (D) is incorrect. Reversing written-down inventory does not incur any expense.

APPENDIX B
AICPA UNIFORM CPA EXAMINATION BLUEPRINTS WITH GLEIM CROSS-REFERENCES

The AICPA has indicated that the Blueprints have several purposes, including to

- *Document the minimum level of knowledge and skills necessary for initial licensure.*
- *Assist candidates in preparing for the Exam by outlining the knowledge and skills that may be tested.*
- *Apprise educators about the knowledge and skills candidates will need to function as newly licensed CPAs.*
- *Guide the development of Exam questions.*

For your convenience, we have reproduced the AICPA's Financial Blueprint. We also have provided cross-references to the study units in this book that correspond to the Blueprint's coverage.

FINANCIAL ACCOUNTING AND REPORTING (FAR)

Area I – Conceptual Framework, Standard-Setting and Financial Reporting (25-35%)

A. CONCEPTUAL FRAMEWORK AND STANDARD-SETTING FOR BUSINESS AND NONBUSINESS ENTITIES

1. Conceptual framework - SU 1
2. Standard-setting process - SU 1

B. GENERAL-PURPOSE FINANCIAL STATEMENTS: FOR-PROFIT BUSINESS ENTITIES

1. Balance sheet/statement of financial position - SU 2
2. Income statement/statement of profit or loss - SU 2
3. Statement of comprehensive income - SU 2
4. Statement of changes in equity - SU 2
5. Statement of cash flows - SU 17
6. Notes to financial statements - SU 4
7. Consolidated financial statements (including wholly owned subsidiaries and noncontrolling interests) - SU 15
8. Discontinued operations - SU 3
9. Going concern - SU 4

C. GENERAL-PURPOSE FINANCIAL STATEMENTS: NONGOVERNMENTAL, NOT-FOR-PROFIT ENTITIES

1. Statement of financial position - SU 20
2. Statement of activities - SU 20
3. Statement of cash flows - SU 20
4. Notes to financial statements - SU 20

D. **PUBLIC COMPANY REPORTING TOPICS (U.S. SEC REPORTING REQUIREMENTS, EARNINGS PER SHARE AND SEGMENT REPORTING)** - SU 1, SUs 3-4

E. **FINANCIAL STATEMENTS OF EMPLOYEE BENEFIT PLANS** - SU 11

F. **SPECIAL PURPOSE FRAMEWORKS** - SU 2

Area II – Select Financial Statement Accounts (30-40%)

A. **CASH AND CASH EQUIVALENTS** - SU 5

B. **TRADE RECEIVABLES** - SU 6

C. **INVENTORY** - SU 7

D. **PROPERTY, PLANT AND EQUIPMENT** - SU 8

E. **INVESTMENTS**

1. Financial assets at fair value - SU 5
2. Financial assets at amortized cost - SUs 5-6
3. Equity method investments - SU 5

F. **INTANGIBLE ASSETS – GOODWILL AND OTHER** - SU 9

G. **PAYABLES AND ACCRUED LIABILITIES** - SU 10, SU 12

H. **LONG-TERM DEBT (FINANCIAL LIABILITIES)**

1. Notes and bonds payable - SU 12
2. Debt covenant compliance - SU 2

I. **EQUITY** - SU 14

J. **REVENUE RECOGNITION** - SU 1, SU 3

K. **COMPENSATION AND BENEFITS**

1. Compensated absences - SU 11
2. Retirement benefits - SU 11
3. Stock compensation (share-based payments) - SU 11

L. **INCOME TAXES** - SU 10

Area III – Select Transactions (20-30%)

A. **ACCOUNTING CHANGES AND ERROR CORRECTIONS** - SU 3
B. **BUSINESS COMBINATIONS** - SU 15
C. **CONTINGENCIES AND COMMITMENTS** - SU 13
D. **DERIVATIVES AND HEDGE ACCOUNTING (E.G. SWAPS, OPTIONS, FORWARDS)** - SU 16
E. **FOREIGN CURRENCY TRANSACTIONS AND TRANSLATION)** - SU 16
F. **LEASES** - SU 13
G. **NONRECIPROCAL TRANSFERS** - SU 20
H. **RESEARCH AND DEVELOPMENT COSTS** - SU 9
I. **SOFTWARE COSTS** - SU 9
J. **SUBSEQUENT EVENTS** - SU 4
K. **FAIR VALUE MEASUREMENTS** - SU 4
L. **DIFFERENCES BETWEEN IFRS AND U.S. GAAP** - App A

Area IV – State and Local Governments (5-15%)

A. STATE AND LOCAL GOVERNMENT CONCEPTS

1. Conceptual framework - SU 1, SU 18
2. Measurement focus and basis of accounting - SUs 18-19
3. Purpose of funds - SUs 18-19

B. FORMAT AND CONTENT OF THE FINANCIAL SECTION OF THE COMPREHENSIVE ANNUAL FINANCIAL REPORT (CAFR)

1. Government-wide financial statements - SU 19
2. Governmental funds financial statements - SU 18
3. Proprietary funds financial statements - SU 19
4. Fiduciary funds financial statements - SUs 18-19
5. Notes to financial statements - SU 18
6. Management's discussion and analysis - SU 18
7. Budgetary comparison reporting - SU 18
8. Required supplementary information (RSI) other than management's discussion and analysis - SU 18
9. Financial reporting entity, including blended and discrete component units - SU 18

C. DERIVING GOVERNMENT-WIDE FINANCIAL STATEMENTS AND RECONCILIATION REQUIREMENTS - SUs 18-19

D. TYPICAL ITEMS AND SPECIFIC TYPES OF TRANSACTIONS AND EVENTS: MEASUREMENT, VALUATION, CALCULATION AND PRESENTATION IN GOVERNMENTAL ENTITY FINANCIAL STATEMENTS

1. Net position and components thereof - SU 19
2. Fund balances and components thereof - SU 18
3. Capital assets and infrastructure assets - SU 19
4. General and proprietary long-term liabilities - SUs 18-19
5. Interfund activity, including transfers - SU 18
6. Nonexchange revenue transactions - SU 18
7. Expenditures and expenses - SU 18
8. Special items - SU 19
9. Budgetary accounting and encumbrances - SU 18
10. Other financing sources and uses - SU 18

APPENDIX C
OPTIMIZING YOUR SCORE ON THE TASK-BASED SIMULATIONS (TBSs)

Each section of the CPA Exam contains multiple testlets of Task-Based Simulations. The number of TBS testlets and the number of TBSs in each testlet are the same for each exam section except BEC.

TBSs per Exam Section

	Testlet 3	Testlet 4	Testlet 5	Total
AUD	2	3	3	8
BEC	2	2	N/A*	4
FAR	2	3	3	8
REG	2	3	3	8

*Testlet 5 of BEC is Written Communications.

Task-Based Simulations are constructive response questions with information presented either with the question or in separate exhibits. Question responses may be in the form of entering amounts into a spreadsheet, choosing the correct answer from a list in a pop-up box, completing accounting or tax forms, or reviewing and completing or correcting a draft of a document. In the AUD, FAR, and REG exam sections, you will also have to complete a Research task, which requires you to research the relevant authoritative literature and cite the appropriate guidance as indicated. You will not have to complete a Research task in BEC.

It is not productive to practice TBSs on paper. Instead, you should use your online Gleim CPA Review Course to complete truly interactive TBSs that emulate exactly how TBSs are tested on the CPA Exam. As a CPA candidate, you must become an expert on how to approach TBSs, how to budget your time in the TBS testlets, and the different types of TBSs. This appendix covers all of these topics for you and includes examples of typical TBSs. Use this appendix only as an introduction to TBSs, and then practice hundreds of exam-emulating TBSs in your Gleim CPA Review Course.

Task-Based Simulations -- Toolbar Icons and Operations

The following information and toolbar icons are located at the top of the testlet screen of each TBS. All screenshots are taken from the AICPA Sample Test (www.aicpa.org). The examples that follow are taken from our online course. The CPA Exam, the Sample Test, and all screenshots are Copyright 2020 by the AICPA with All Rights Reserved. The AICPA requires all candidates to review the Sample Tests and Tutorials before sitting for the CPA Exam.

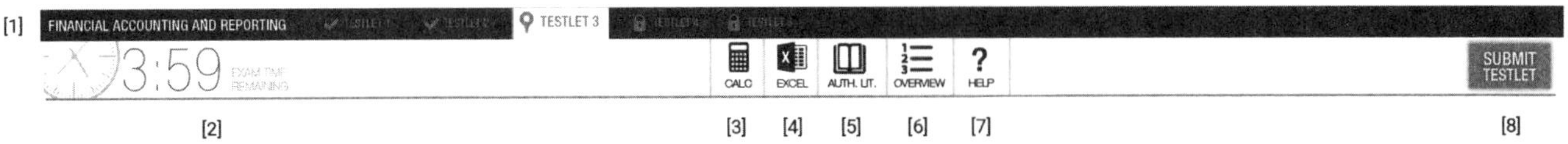

1. **Exam Section and Testlet Number:** The testlet number will always be 3, 4, or 5 for the simulations.
2. **Time Remaining:** This information box displays how much time you have remaining in the entire exam. Consistently check the amount of time remaining to stay on schedule.
3. **Calculator:** The calculator icon launches a basic tool for simple computations. It is similar to calculators used in common software programs. The calculator tape is saved and accessible throughout the entire testlet; it does not clear until a new testlet is entered or the "Clear Tape" function is employed. Numbers (but not text) can be copied and pasted between the calculator, any exhibits, the question content and answer fields, and Excel.

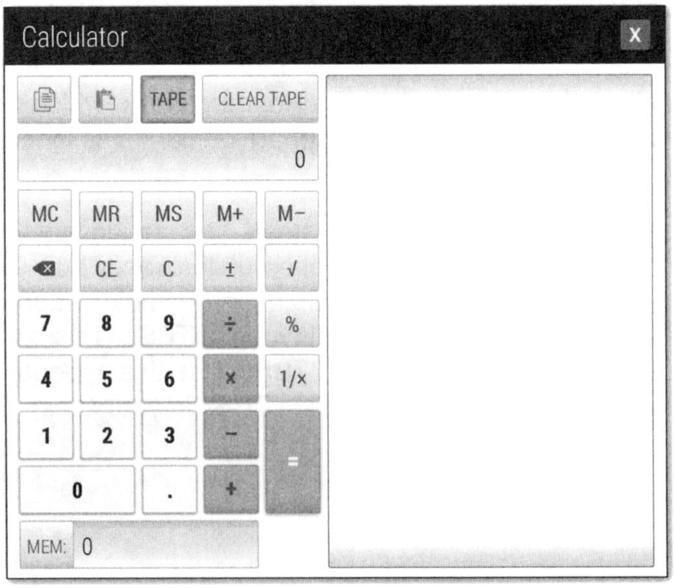

4. **Excel:** Instead of the proprietary spreadsheet used previously, candidates will now have access to the desktop version of Excel, which launches by clicking the spreadsheet icon found in the top toolbar.
   - The exam spreadsheet will perform the same essential functions as a regular desktop Excel spreadsheet.
   - Candidates can easily transfer data out of and into Excel, for example, by copying from Excel and pasting to the answer fields of a simulation or into the calculator, and vice versa. Excel will retain all of the information entered while in a testlet, even if Excel is closed and/or when navigating between simulations. Excel will only clear when beginning a new testlet. There is also an option to manually save any work.
   - Work done and calculations performed within Excel will not be graded. Many of Excel's less relevant features and some functions of Excel that may threaten user security will not work.

5. **Authoritative Literature:** The Authoritative Literature for AUD, FAR, and REG is available in every TBS testlet. You can use either the table of contents or the search function to locate the correct guidance. The table of contents will not populate until a source has been selected.
   - An extremely useful feature is that candidates can bookmark a document by clicking the bookmark icon next to the document title. All bookmarked documents will be listed in a section that appears above the table of contents, and hovering over the bookmarked items reveals the full title in a pop-up box.
   - The Advanced Search options have been altered to include the following:
     - "All of these words:" multiple words at a time, in no particular order
     - "This exact phrase:" exact words in an exact order
     - "Any of these words:" one or more of the entered words in no particular order
     - "None of these words:" none of the words entered
   - Clicking the "Search within:" box next to the search bar allows candidates to limit their search to a specific folder or sub-folder. Within the Advanced Search field, candidates must once again click the "Search within:" box in order to limit their search to a designated sub-folder, even if the "Search within:" box is activated for the basic search.
   - The search function of the Authoritative Literature tool can be used at a basic level to find words or numbers. A search can be enhanced with an asterisk, which searches for anything starting with the word, or with a question mark in place of a character, which indicates that any character can appear in that specific position in the search term. Up to three question marks can be used.

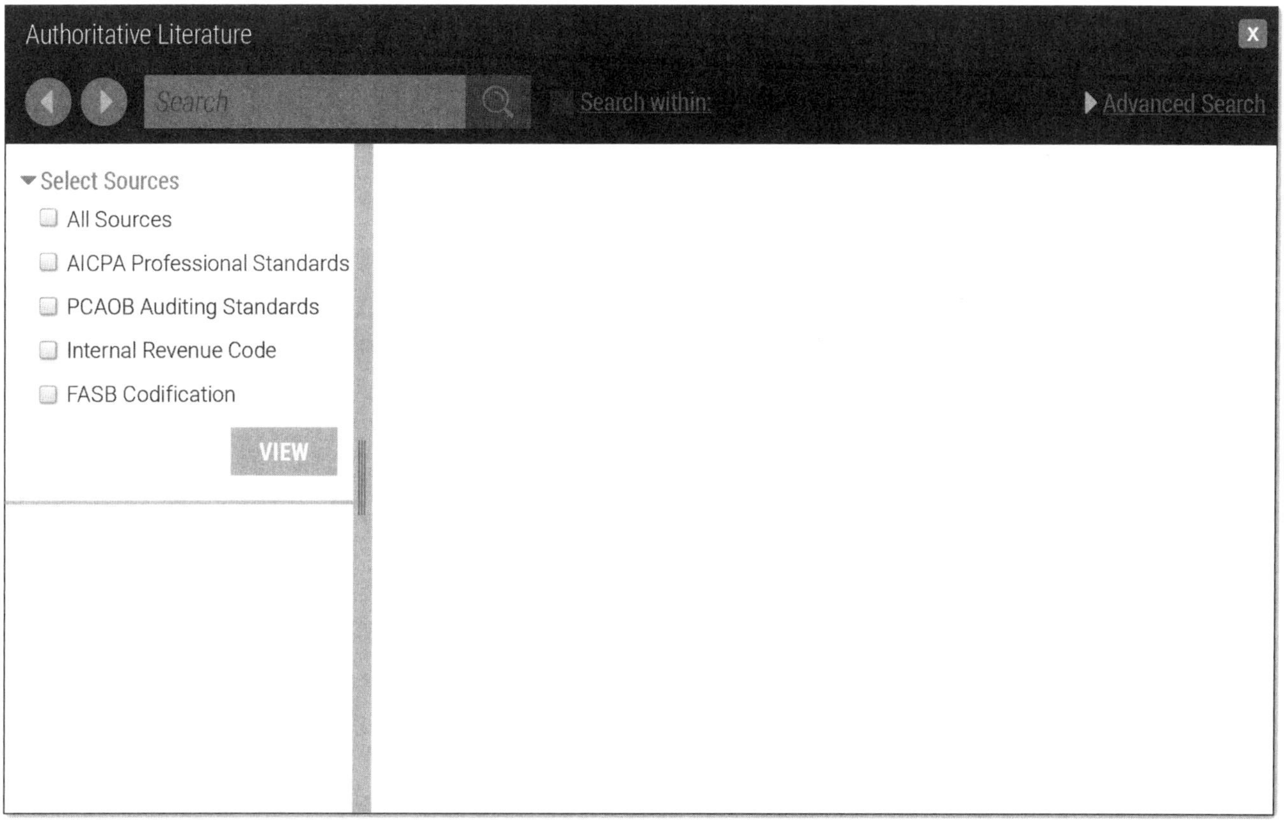

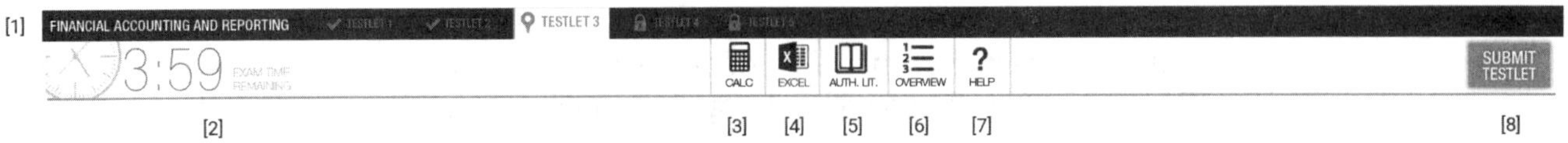

6. **Overview:** The overview lets you review and navigate the questions within a testlet. You can also use it to view, add, and remove bookmarks.

7. **Help:** The help icon provides important information about certain functions and tool buttons specific to the type of task you are working in. It also provides directions and general information but does not include information related specifically to the test content. It can be navigated via either the table of contents or the search bar.

8. **Submit Testlet:** There are two options when you choose this icon from the toolbar.
   - In any of the first four testlets, you will be asked to select either Return to Testlet or Submit Testlet. Return to Testlet allows you to review and change your answers in the current testlet. Submit Testlet takes you to the next testlet. After submitting your testlet, you will receive a prompt that allows for an optional break.
   - In the final testlet, you will be asked to select either Return to Testlet or Quit Exam. Choose Quit Exam if you wish to complete the exam. You will not be able to return to any testlet, and you will not receive credit for any unanswered questions. To prevent accidentally ending your exam, you will be asked to verify your selection, or you can choose Go Back. Upon verifying you wish to End Exam, you will be required to leave the test center with no re-admittance.

Navigation between simulations within a testlet is done using the number and arrow buttons directly beneath the toolbar or the arrow buttons at the bottom of the simulation. You can navigate between simulations within a testlet at any time before you submit the testlet.

Clicking on a number will take you to the corresponding simulation. Clicking on the bookmark icon beside the number on the left will flag the simulation to remind you to return to it before submitting the testlet.

Workspace: Task-Based Simulations have a designated workspace where all of the exam tools and exhibits open.

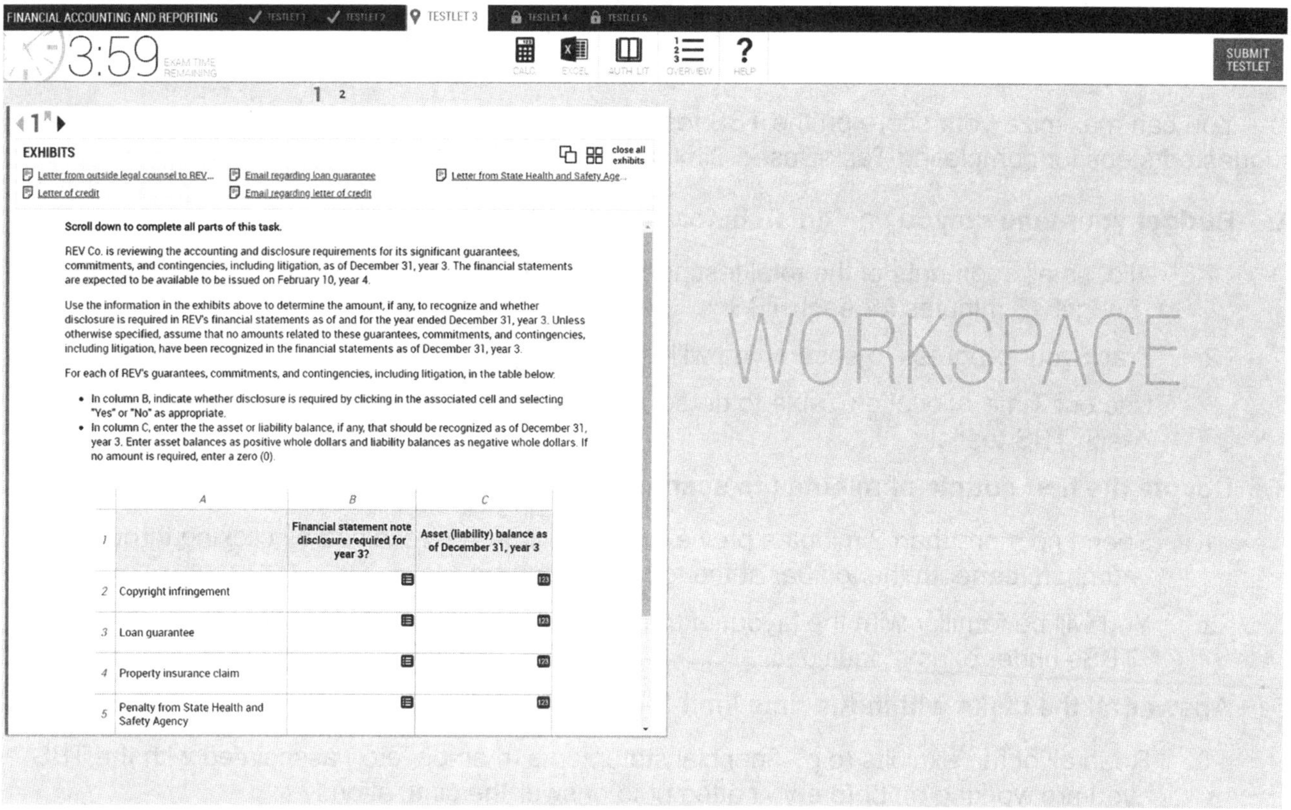

You can have multiple exam tools and exhibits open simultaneously, and you are able to freely resize and move each window.

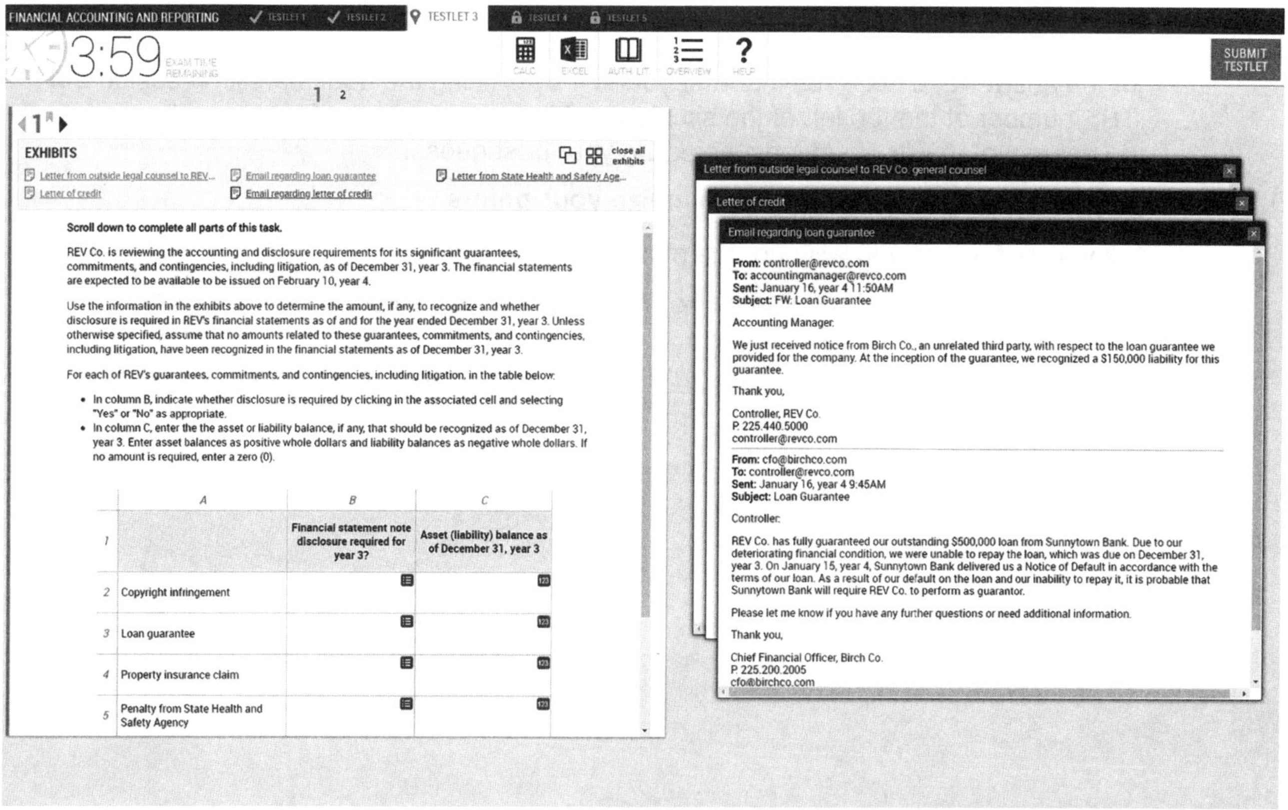

Answering Task-Based Simulations

Do not be intimidated by TBSs. Just learn the material and practice answering the different question types. Knowing **how** to work through the simulations is nearly as important as knowing what they test.

You can maximize your score on the TBS testlets of each exam section by following these suggested steps for completing Task-Based Simulations.

A. **Budget your time so you can finish before time expires.**

   1. Allot small segments of the total testing time to each specific task. We recommend you budget 18 minutes for each TBS.
   2. Track your progress to ensure you will have enough time to complete all the tasks.
   3. Use our Time Allocation Table to determine the time at which you need to start and finish each TBS testlet.

B. **Devote the first couple of minutes to scanning each TBS.**

   1. Spend no more than 2 minutes previewing the TBSs you received by clicking through the numbers beneath the toolbar at the top of the screen.
   2. You will be familiar with the layout of the TBSs if you have been practicing with Gleim TBSs under exam conditions.

C. **Answer all the tasks within the time limit for each testlet.**

   1. Read all of the exhibits (e.g., financial statements, memos, etc.) associated with the TBS you are working on before you attempt to answer the simulation.
      a. We have included detailed directions on using exhibits as source documents in the next section on Document Review Simulations. Much of those instructions can also be used when answering regular TBSs that contain exhibits.
   2. Do not skip any of the questions within a TBS. Make an educated guess if you are unsure of the answer and set a reminder for yourself by clicking the bookmark icon beside the TBS number at the top left of the simulation. There is no penalty for incorrect answers, so do not move on without at least selecting your best guess.

D. **Spend any remaining time wisely to maximize your points.**

   1. Ask yourself where you will earn the most points.
   2. Move from task to task systematically, reviewing and completing each one. Focus specifically on any TBS you flagged.
   3. Move on to the next TBS within the testlet or to the next testlet at the end of 18 minutes.

DOCUMENT REVIEW SIMULATIONS

Within the Task-Based Simulation testlets included in each CPA Exam section, you may find a Document Review Simulation (DRS). You are required to review various exhibits to determine the best phrasing of a particular document. The document will contain underlined words, phrases, sentences, or paragraphs that may or may not be correct. You then must select answer choices that indicate which (if any) changes you believe should be made in the underlined words, phrases, sentences, or paragraphs.

The DRSs always include the actual document you must review and correct and one or more exhibits. Exhibits vary from one DRS to the next because they contain the information to be used as sources for your conclusions. For example, these exhibits may be financial statements, emails, letters, invoices, memoranda, or minutes from meetings. You must read each DRS exhibit so that you are always aware of the resources available.

Answering Document Review Simulations

A. **Familiarize yourself with every part of the DRS.**

Review each exhibit so you know what information is available. If your subject-matter preparation has been thorough, you should be able to identify quickly the most relevant information in each part of the DRS.

B. **Address every underlined portion of text in the DRS.**

You must make an answer selection for every modifiable section of a DRS because each counts as a separate question. You will know an answer has been selected when you see that the white outline in the blue icon has changed to a white checkmark.

C. **Read the underlined section and answer choices carefully and completely.**

Each underlined portion of text may have four to seven answer choices that may include the options to revise the text, retain the original text, or delete the text. Verify that each word or amount is correct in your choice before making your final selection.

D. **Clearly understand the information in the exhibits.**

Quickly survey the various items; then analyze the most relevant facts specifically and refer to them to reduce the possible answer choices. Keep in mind that the relevant information may be presented or worded differently than the document you are revising.

E. **Double-check that you have officially responded to each underlined portion of text.**

If you have time, go through the entire DRS once more to confirm that every underlined section has a white checkmark next to it.

MANAGING TIME ON THE TBSs

Managing your time well during the CPA Exam is critical to success, so you must develop and practice your time management plan before your test date. The only help you will receive during your actual CPA Exam is a countdown of the hours and minutes remaining. When there are less than 2 minutes left in an exam section, the exam clock will begin to include the seconds and turn red, but you should be doing your final review by that point.

Each of the testlets on the exam is independent, and there are no time limits on individual testlets. Therefore, you must budget your time effectively to complete all five testlets in the allotted 4 hours.

The key to success is to become proficient in answering all types of questions in an average amount of time. When you follow our system, you'll have 2-17 minutes of total extra time (depending on the section) that you will be able to allocate as needed.

Each exam will begin with three introductory screens that you must complete in 10 minutes. Time spent in the introductory screens does not count against the 240 minutes you get for the exam itself. Then you will have two MCQ testlets. Each testlet contains half the total number of MCQs for that section (36/testlet for AUD, 31/testlet for BEC, 33/testlet for FAR, and 38/testlet for REG). Based on the total time of the exam and the amount of time needed for the other testlets, you should average 1.25 minutes per MCQ.

The final three testlets in AUD, FAR, and REG will have eight TBSs each: two in Testlet #3, three in Testlet #4, and three in Testlet #5. BEC will have four TBSs in two testlets, then a final testlet of three Written Communications (WCs). We suggest you allocate approximately 18 minutes to answering each TBS. On BEC, budget 25 minutes for each of the three WCs (20 minutes to answer, 5 minutes to review and perfect your response).**

To make the most of your testing time during the CPA Exam, you will need to develop a time management system and commit to spending a designated amount of time on each question. To assist you, please refer to the Gleim Time Management System.

The table below shows how many minutes you should expect to spend on each testlet for each section. Remember, you cannot begin a new testlet until you have submitted a current testlet, and once you have submitted a testlet, you can no longer go back to it.

Time Allocation per Testlet (in minutes)

Testlet	Format	AUD	BEC**	FAR	REG
1	MCQ	45	38*	41*	47*
2	MCQ	45	38*	41*	47*
3	TBS	36	36	36	36
15-Minute Break					
4	TBS	54	36	54	54
5	TBS/WC	54	75	54	54
Total		234	223	226	238
Extra Time		6	17	14	2
Total Time Allowed		240	240	240	240

*Rounded down

**BEC candidates may prefer to allocate more time to the TBSs and reduce the 17 minutes of extra review time after the WCs. In this case, we suggest 20 minutes per TBS, for a total time of 40 minutes in Testlet 3 and 40 minutes in Testlet 4, leaving 9 minutes of final review after the WCs.

The exam screen will show hours:minutes remaining. Focus on how much time you have, NOT the time on your watch. Using the times on the previous page, you would start each testlet with the following hours:minutes displayed on-screen:

Completion Times and Time Remaining

	AUD	BEC**	FAR	REG
Start	4 hours 0 minutes	4 hours 0 minutes	4 hours 0 minutes	4 hours 0 minutes
After Testlet 1	3 hours 15 minutes	3 hours 22 minutes	3 hours 19 minutes	3 hours 13 minutes
After Testlet 2	2 hours 30 minutes	2 hours 44 minutes	2 hours 38 minutes	2 hours 26 minutes
After Testlet 3	1 hour 54 minutes	2 hours 8 minutes	2 hours 2 minutes	1 hour 50 minutes
15-Minute Break				
After Testlet 4	1 hour 0 minutes	1 hour 32 minutes	1 hour 8 minutes	0 hours 56 minutes
After Testlet 5	0 hours 6 minutes	0 hours 17 minutes	0 hours 14 minutes	0 hours 2 minutes

Next, develop a shorthand for hours:minutes. This makes it easier to write down the times on the noteboard you will receive at the exam center.

	AUD	BEC**	FAR	REG
Start	4:00	4:00	4:00	4:00
After Testlet 1	3:15	3:22	3:19	3:13
After Testlet 2	2:30	2:44	2:38	2:26
After Testlet 3	1:54	2:08	2:02	1:50
15-Minute Break				
After Testlet 4	1:00	1:32	1:08	0:56
After Testlet 5	0:06	0:17	0:14	0:02

The following pages of this appendix contain eight example TBSs. We have included a variety of TBS types, including Research, Numeric Entry, Option List, Global Response Grid, and DRS, along with suggestions on how to approach each type. The answer key and our unique answer explanations for each TBS appear at the end of this appendix.

Again, do not substitute answering TBSs in your Gleim CPA Review Course with answering the TBSs presented here. Refer to these TBSs only for guidance on how to answer this difficult element of the exam. It is vital that you practice answering TBSs in the digital environment of our online course so that you are comfortable with such an environment during your CPA Exam.

**BEC candidates may prefer to allocate more time to the TBSs and reduce the 17 minutes of extra review time after the WCs. In this case, we suggest 20 minutes per TBS, for a total time of 40 minutes in Testlet 3 and 40 minutes in Testlet 4, leaving 9 minutes of final review after the WCs.

RESEARCH

This type of TBS requires that you research within the Authoritative Literature, which is accessible at the top of the TBS toolbar (shown below), to find the best supporting guidance for the presented scenario. Although there is only one question to answer in the Research TBS, it counts as much as a TBS with multiple questions, so you must treat it with the same gravity as any other TBS. Our suggested steps on how to answer this task type follow:

1. Read through the given scenario to identify the question being asked and, within that, the key terms to search for in the literature. In this example, the question is asking for the proper accounting treatment of application development stage costs, so the key terms are internal use, software, and development.
2. Select the source(s) relevant to the question being asked; then click "View." For this question, we want to look within the FASB codification.
3. Type the key term(s) into the search box and click the magnifying glass.
4. Review the first 10 results. Use your knowledge of the topic to decide whether the search results fit the question you are researching. Often, the first search will not yield the correct answer, and it is necessary to narrow your scope.
5. Restrict your search to only the most relevant section of the literature by using the "Search within" function. To do so, choose the section of the literature from the table of contents that is most likely to contain the related literature. Click on that section, type your term into the search box, select the "Search within" checkbox, and click the magnifying glass. This will populate the results with only matches from that specific section. For example, this Research question refers to the creation of a software application for internal use, which would be recorded as an asset to the company. Therefore, Assets is the section to search within.
6. From these streamlined results, select the exact paragraph that corresponds to the given scenario and enter your response using the on-screen formatting prompts.

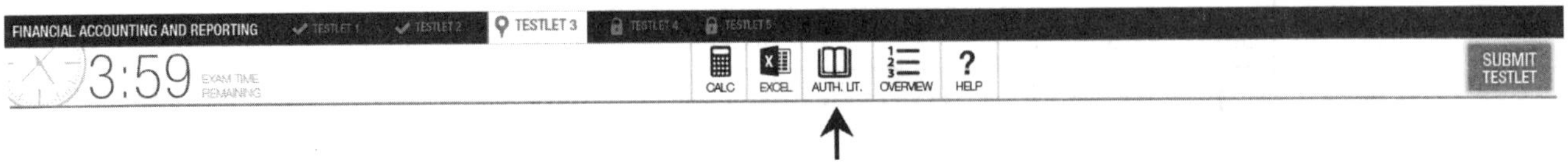

Crank Co. is a software developer that has accumulated costs related to developing a software application for internal use. The development is past the preliminary project stage and into the application development stage.

Which section of the Accounting Standard Codification best helps Crank's controller determine the proper accounting treatment of the application development stage costs?

FASB ASC [ ] - [ ] - [ ] - [ ]

BANK RECONCILIATION: NUMERIC ENTRY 1

The following three TBSs are all Numeric Entries. This type of TBS requires that you calculate and then respond with some kind of number, e.g., an amount of currency, a ratio, etc. After clicking a cell, a field will appear that will automatically format your response. Be sure to review the formatted response before finalizing your answer. There are also options to cancel an entry or reset the cell to blank. Some Numeric Entry TBSs may also require Option List-type responses, which are in essence multiple-choice questions.

The following information pertains to Company A's December 31, Year 1, bank reconciliation:

- Check #217 for $4,000 was drawn on the company's account, payable to a vendor, dated and recorded in the company's books on December 31, Year 1, but not mailed until January 9, Year 2.
- Deposits in transit are $5,200.
- Outstanding checks are $8,980.
- On December 31, Year 1, the bank charged the company $500 for service fees. The company received a notice about this charge during Year 2.
- The balance per bank statement received shows that a customer check for $4,600 had been returned due to insufficient funds.
- Check #221 for $800, written by the company, was erroneously cleared by the bank on December 31, Year 1, for $80.
- On November 1, Year 1, one of the company's customers deposited $700 directly to the company's bank account. The bookkeeper recorded this transaction as follows:

Accounts receivable	$700	
Bank account		$700

Using the information above, prepare Company A's December 31, Year 1, bank reconciliation. Enter the correct amounts in the shaded cells below. Indicate negative amounts by using a leading minus (-) sign. If no entry is necessary, enter a zero (0) or leave the cell blank.

	Bank	Books
Balance per Bank Statement / Books (December 31, Year 1)	$32,400	$27,600
1. Check #217		
2. Deposits in transit		
3. Outstanding checks		
4. Service fees charged by the bank		
5. Nonsufficient funds checks		
6. Check #221		
7. Deposit on November 1, Year 1		
8. **Correct cash balance**		

INTANGIBLE ASSETS -- IMPAIRMENT TEST: NUMERIC ENTRY 2

For each of the following independent situations described below, calculate the amount of impairment loss that should be recognized in Company A's December 31, Year 4, financial statements. Enter in the shaded cells the applicable dollar value. If no impairment loss is recognized, enter a zero (0). Enter all amounts as positive values.

Situation	Impairment loss
1. On December 31, Year 4, Company A estimates that the carrying amount of its patent may not be recoverable. The patent was purchased on January 1, Year 1, for $50,000, and its useful life is 10 years. On January 1, Year 3, Company A paid $24,000 in legal fees for a successful defense of the patent. The sum of the undiscounted expected future cash flows from the patent and the patent's fair value on December 31, Year 4, are $40,000 and $35,000, respectively.	
2. Company A bought a trademark 4 years ago on January 1 for $80,000. The useful life of the trademark is indefinite, and no impairment loss was previously recognized. On December 31, Year 4, the company determined that it is necessary to perform the quantitative impairment test for the trademark. The fair value of the trademark on that date was $75,000.	
3. On January 1, Year 2, Company A purchased a franchise with a finite useful life of 5 years for $60,000. On December 31, Year 4, the company estimates that the carrying amount of the franchise may not be recoverable. The sum of the undiscounted expected future cash flows from the franchise and the franchise's fair value on December 31, Year 4, are $25,000 and $22,000, respectively.	

OPERATING CASH FLOW: NUMERIC ENTRY 3

Presented below are the balance sheet accounts of Kern, Inc., as of December 31, Year 2 and Year 1, and their net changes.

	Year 2	Year 1	Net Change
Assets			
Cash	$ 471,000	$ 307,000	$ 164,000
Trading debt securities, at cost	150,000	250,000	(100,000)
Securities fair value adjustment (trading)	(10,000)	(25,000)	15,000
Accounts receivable, net	550,000	515,000	35,000
Inventories	810,000	890,000	(80,000)
Investments in Word Corp., at equity	420,000	390,000	30,000
Property, plant, and equipment	1,145,000	1,070,000	75,000
Accumulated depreciation	(345,000)	(280,000)	(65,000)
Patent, net	109,000	118,000	(9,000)
Total assets	$3,300,000	$3,235,000	$ 65,000
Liabilities and Shareholders' Equity			
Accounts payable and accrued liabilities	$ 845,000	$ 960,000	$ (115,000)
Note payable, noncurrent	600,000	900,000	(300,000)
Deferred income taxes	190,000	190,000	---
Common stock, $10 par value	850,000	650,000	200,000
Additional paid-in capital	230,000	170,000	60,000
Retained earnings	585,000	365,000	220,000
Total liabilities and shareholders' equity	$3,300,000	$3,235,000	$ 65,000

Additional Information:

1. On January 2, Year 2, Kern sold equipment costing $45,000, with a carrying amount of $28,000, for $18,000 cash.
2. On March 31, Year 2, Kern sold one of its trading security holdings for $119,000 cash. Cash flows from purchases, sales, and maturities of Kern's trading securities are from investing activities. No other transactions involved trading securities.
3. On April 15, Year 2, Kern issued 20,000 shares of its common stock for cash at $13 per share.
4. On July 1, Year 2, Kern purchased equipment for $120,000 cash.
5. Kern's net income for Year 2 is $305,000. Kern paid a cash dividend of $85,000 on October 26, Year 2.
6. Kern acquired a 20% interest in Word Corp.'s common stock during Year 1. There was no goodwill attributable to the investment, which is appropriately accounted for by the equity method. Word reported net income of $150,000 for the year ended December 31, Year 2. No dividend was paid on Word's common stock during Year 2.

For the following operating cash flow items, enter in the shaded cells the amounts that will be reported in Kern's statement of cash flows. Indicate negative numbers by using a leading minus (-) sign.

Cash flows from operating activities:	**Amount**
Net income	$305,000
Adjustments to reconcile net income to net cash provided by operating activities:	
1. Depreciation	
2. Amortization of patent	
3. Loss on sale of equipment	
4. Equity in income of Word Corp.	
5. Gain on sale of trading securities	
6. Decrease in securities fair value adjustment	
7. Increase in accounts receivable	
8. Decrease in inventories	
9. Decrease in accounts payable and accrued liabilities	
10. Net cash provided by operating activities	

EPS: OPTION LIST 1

The following two TBSs are Option Lists, which are in essence multiple-choice questions. This type of task requires that you select a response from a list of choices. Some Option List TBSs may also require Numeric Entry type responses.

At the beginning of Year 1, Mike Co. had 100,000 shares of $1 par-value common stock outstanding. Mike's Year 1 net income before the effects of the independent transactions described below was $350,000.

For each transaction, select from the option list provided the appropriate effect, if any, on Mike's Year 1 basic earnings per share (BEPS). For the diluted earnings per share (DEPS), indicate whether it is lower, greater, or equal to the BEPS amount in Year 1. Each choice may be used once, more than once, or not at all. Do not leave any box empty; all the boxes must be filled.

Assume that Mike is required to report both BEPS and DEPS.

Transaction	BEPS	DEPS
A. On March 1, Year 1, Mike issued 20,000 new shares of common stock.		
B. On January 1, Year 1, Mike issued to its employees call options to purchase 10,000 shares of Mike's common stock at $14 per share. No options were exercised during Year 1. The Year 1 average market price per share of Mike's common stock was $12.		
C. On January 1, Year 1, Mike issued 10,000 shares of $100 par, 5% cumulative convertible preferred stock. The conversion ratio is 1 share of preferred stock to 1 share of common stock. Mike did not declare preferred dividends in Year 1. No conversion of preferred stock occurred in Year 1.		
D. On September 1, Year 1, Mike repurchased 20,000 shares of its common stock for $500,000. Mike accounts for treasury stock using the cost method.		

BEPS Option List
Increase
Decrease
No effect

DEPS Option List
Greater
Lower
Equal

CLASSIFICATION OF CASH FLOWS: OPTION LIST 2

Select from the option list provided the best classification for each activity below. Each choice may be used once, more than once, or not at all.

Cash flow	Classification
1. Purchase of available-for-sale debt securities	
2. Purchase of land	
3. Dividends distributed to shareholders	
4. Equipment acquired through finance lease	
5. Sale of trading securities	
6. Collection of trade receivables	
7. Equipment acquired through purchase	
8. Dividends received	
9. Interest paid	
10. Interest received	
11. Retirements of bond principal	
12. Issuance of preferred shares	

Option List
Operating activity
Investing activity
Financing activity
Noncash investing and financing activities
Not reported on statement of cash flows
Depends on nature and purpose

NONCURRENT NOTES PAYABLE: GLOBAL RESPONSE GRID

In Global Response Grid simulations, each distinct question has its own response table. This Journal Entry TBS is a type of Global Response Grid that uses both Numeric Entry and Option List questions. In journal entries, such as this one, each entry will additionally have a "No Entry Required" checkbox in the upper left corner. If no entry is required for a given question, click the box and all the cells will be grayed out.

Drake, Inc., has two loans recorded on its books. Loan 1 was obtained on January 1, Year 1, and Loan 2 was entered into on January 1, Year 2. Drake's year end is December 31.

For the situations related to the loans below, prepare the appropriate journal entries. Each loan should be accounted for independent of the other loan.

To prepare each required journal entry:

- Click on a cell in the Account Name column and select from the option list the appropriate account. Each account may be used once or not at all.
- Enter the corresponding debit or credit amount in the associated column.
- Enter all amounts as positive values. Round all amounts to the nearest whole number.
- Not all rows in the table might be needed to complete each journal entry.
- If no journal entry is needed, check the "No entry required" box at the top of the table as your response.

Loan 1

Loan 1 is a 4%, 5-year balloon loan for $3,000,000 with interest due and paid annually on December 31. Drake records interest annually on December 31. Drake incorrectly recorded the journal entry for the Year 1 interest expense and payment as a debit to accrued interest payable and a credit to cash. Prepare the net journal entry to correct Year 1 and properly record the interest attributable to the loan as of and for the year ended December 31, Year 2.

□ No Entry Required

Account Name	Debit	Credit

Option List
Accounts receivable
Accrued interest payable
Cash
Comprehensive expense
Comprehensive income
Interest expense
Paid-in capital
Prepaid interest
Retained earnings

-- Continued on next page --

-- Continued from previous page --

Loan 2

Loan 2 is an 8%, $1,000,000 loan with interest due annually on December 31. Drake did not record or pay the required Year 2 interest payment until January 1, Year 3. Prepare the journal entry Drake should record at December 31, Year 2.

□ No Entry Required

Account Name	Debit	Credit

Option List
Accounts receivable
Accrued interest payable
Cash
Comprehensive expense
Comprehensive income
Interest expense
Paid-in capital
Prepaid interest
Retained earnings

DOCUMENT REVIEW SIMULATION (DRS)

This type of TBS requires that you analyze certain words or phrases in a document to decide whether to (1) keep the current text, (2) replace the current text with different text, or (3) delete the text. You must review various exhibits (e.g., financial statements, emails, invoices, etc.) presented with the original document in order to find the information necessary for each response.

close all exhbits

EXHIBITS

- Attorney Invoice
- Acquisition Announcement
- Valuation Letter
- Balance Sheet
- Share Prices

Millennium Capital Management, Inc., (MCM) acquired a 90% interest in NextGen, Inc. MCM's Financial Manager, Matthew Steven, has prepared a draft memo to the CFO, Hannah Jordan, advising her on how the company should account for certain aspects of the acquisition. Mr. Steven would like you to review the draft memo and make any necessary revisions to comply with generally accepted accounting principles. Using the information from the exhibits on the following pages, select the option from the list provided that corrects each underlined portion of the memo. If the underlined text is already correct in the context of the document, select *[Original Text]* from the list.

To: Hannah Jordan, CFO
From: Matthew Steven, Financial Manager
Re: Accounting for Acquisition of NextGen

The fair value of the consideration that MCM transferred to acquire its interest in NextGen is $9,000,000.

- [A] *[Original Text]* $9,000,000.
- [B] $8,000,000.
- [C] $10,000,000.
- [D] $9,500,000.
- [E] $8,500,000.

We must expense the $190,000 payment to Jacob, Sullivan, & Duke.

- [A] *[Original Text]* expense the $190,000 payment
- [B] capitalize the $190,000 payment
- [C] expense $150,000 of the payment
- [D] expense $135,000 of the payment
- [E] expense $40,000 of the payment

On its acquisition-date consolidated balance sheet, MCM will report a noncontrolling interest of $900,000 in NextGen.

- [A] *[Original Text]* report a noncontrolling interest of $900,000 in NextGen.
- [B] not report a noncontrolling interest in NextGen.
- [C] report a noncontrolling interest of $433,000 in NextGen.
- [D] report a noncontrolling interest of $1,000,000 in NextGen.
- [E] report a noncontrolling interest of $962,500 in NextGen.

-- Continued on next page --

-- Continued from previous page --

On the date of MCM's acquisition of a 90% interest in NextGen, MCM will recognize goodwill of $500,000 on the acquisition.

- [A] *[Original Text]* recognize goodwill of $500,000 on the acquisition.
- [B] recognize goodwill of $5,670,000 on the acquisition.
- [C] recognize goodwill of $1,000,000 on the acquisition.
- [D] recognize goodwill of $5,170,000 on the acquisition.
- [E] not recognize any goodwill on the acquisition.

DRS: EXHIBITS

MILLENNIUM CAPITAL MANAGEMENT, INC.

Always ahead of the curve

January 15, 20XX

To our shareholders:

Acquisition Announcement

Millennium Capital Management, Inc., ("MCM") is pleased to announce that on January 14, 20XX, we acquired from NextGen, Inc., ("NextGen") shareholders a 90% interest in NextGen, which is a public company.

Board Approval

MCM's board of directors unanimously approved this acquisition on January 13, 20XX.

Consideration

In consideration for a 90% interest in NextGen, MCM issued 100,000 shares of its common stock to NextGen shareholders in exchange for 450,000 shares of NextGen common stock. This transaction occurred on January 14, 20XX.

Regulatory Approval

This acquisition passed federal regulatory review on January 12, 20XX, and is in full compliance with all applicable laws, statutes, and regulations.

Sincerely,

Joseph Prince, CEO

GSG Financial Advisory Services

SUMMARY VALUATION REPORT: NextGen, Inc.

January 14, 20XX

Millennium Capital Management, Inc.
Attn: Joseph Prince, CEO

Mr. Prince:

In accordance with our engagement letter, we performed a valuation of NextGen, Inc., ("NextGen") to ascertain the fair values of its identifiable assets and liabilities. The fair values are based on the most appropriate markets relative to NextGen's identifiable assets and liabilities.

Accordingly, we assess the fair value of NextGen's identifiable assets and liabilities at $35,000,000 and $25,000,000, respectively. The fair value of every asset equaled its book value except for Land and Buildings. The fair value for Land exceeded its book value by $1,500,000, and the fair value for Buildings (net of accumulated depreciation) exceeded its book value by $4,170,000. The fair value of every liability equaled its book value.

Also in accordance with our engagement letter, this valuation report is a summary of the full report, which is available upon your request.

In closing, we would like to take this opportunity to thank you for trusting us to undertake this valuation. Should there be any areas that need clarification, please do not hesitate to contact us.

Sincerely,

Michael Carter, CPA/ABV
Managing Partner
GSG Financial Advisory Services

NextGen, Inc.
Balance Sheet
January 14, 20XX

Assets		
Current assets		
Cash	$530,000	
Accounts receivable, net of allowance for doubtful accounts	$1,500,000	
Inventories	$3,800,000	
Supplies on hand	$750,000	
Prepaid expenses	$300,000	
Total current assets		$6,880,000
Noncurrent assets		
Investment in bonds	$2,500,000	
Equipment, net of accumulated depreciation	$5,000,000	
Land	$3,000,000	
Buildings, net of accumulated depreciation	$11,950,000	
Total noncurrent assets		$22,450,000
Total assets		$29,330,000
Liabilities and Stockholders' Equity		
Current liabilities		
Accounts payable	$1,000,000	
Income taxes payable	$2,000,000	
Accrued salaries, wages, and other liabilities	$2,000,000	
Deposits received from customers	$500,000	
Total current liabilities		$5,500,000
Noncurrent liabilities		
Note payable	$19,500,000	
Total noncurrent liabilities		$19,500,000
Total liabilities		$25,000,000
Stockholders' equity		
Common—		
Authorized, issued, and outstanding, 500,000 shares of $1.00 par value	$500,000	
Additional paid-in capital	$3,500,000	
Retained earnings	$330,000	
Total stockholders' equity		$4,330,000
Total liabilities and stockholders' equity		$29,330,000

MILLENNIUM CAPITAL MANAGEMENT, INC.

Always ahead of the curve

January 14, 20XX

To: Joseph Prince, CEO; Samuel Lamon, General Counsel
From: Hannah Jordan, CFO
Re: Share Prices

The listed share prices* of MCM and NextGen on the requested dates are shown below:

	MCM	**NextGen**
Preliminary discussions date (01/01/20XX)	$75.00	$18.00
Regulatory approval date (01/12/20XX)	$80.00	$18.50
Board approval date (01/13/20XX)	$85.00	$19.25
Acquisition date (01/14/20XX)	$95.00	$20.00

*Reflect stock market closing prices on respective dates

Sincerely,

Hannah Jordan, CFO
Millennium Capital Management

Jacob, Sullivan, & Duke LLP
Attorneys at Law

Your mergers and acquisitions experts since 1934

INVOICE

Date: 01/13/20XX
Invoice No.: 12442
Matter: Acquisition
File No.: M-27

PAID
Date: 01/14/20XX
Accounts payable supervisor: *REB*
Controller: SEG

Bill to: Millennium Capital Management, Inc.

Due date: Due upon receipt

Professional Services

Details		**Amount***
Acquisition-related fees (consultation, agreement review, meeting attendance)		$150,000.00
Direct issue costs of stock		40,000.00
	Total	**$190,000.00**

*Itemized fees report available on request.

ANSWERS 1 OF 6

1. Research (1 Gradable Item)

Answer: FASB ASC 350-40-25-2

Application Development Stage

25-2 Internal and external costs incurred to develop internal-use computer software during the application development stage shall be capitalized.

2. Bank Reconciliation (8 Gradable Items)

1. Books: $4,000. The $4,000 check that was not mailed until January 9, Year 2, should be added back to the balance. This predated check is still within the control of the company and should not decrease the cash account.
2. Bank: $5,200. Deposits in transit are items known to the company but not known to the bank. A time lag may occur between deposit of receipts and the bank's recording of the transaction. The amount of deposits in transit is $5,200 ($2,000 + $1,755 + $1,445). In the bank reconciliation procedure, these receipts are added to the bank balance to arrive at the true balance.
3. Bank: $(8,980). Outstanding checks are checks written by the company that have not yet cleared the bank. The amount of outstanding checks is $8,980 ($2,900 + $2,240 + $2,040 + $1,800). These amounts are subtracted from the bank balance to arrive at the true balance.
4. Books: $(500). Items known to the bank but not known to the company generally include service charges. Service charges cannot be recorded in the books until the bank statement is received. These amounts are subtracted from the book balance to arrive at the true balance.
5. Books: $(4,600). Customer checks returned for insufficient funds are items known to the bank but not always known to the company until the bank statement is received. These amounts are subtracted from the book balance to arrive at the true balance.
6. Bank: $(720). The bank has wrongly charged the company for $720 ($800 – $80) less than it should have. This amount is subtracted from the bank balance to arrive at the true balance.
7. Books: $1,400. The bookkeeper erroneously credited, instead of debited, the bank account for $700. Thus, to arrive at the true balance, $1,400 must be added (debited) to the book balance.
8. Correct cash balance: $27,900. The correct cash balance is the outcome of the bank reconciliation ($27,900 = $32,400 + $5,200 – $8,980 – $720 = $27,600 + $4,000 – $500 – $4,600 + $1,400).

3. Intangible Assets -- Impairment Test (3 Gradable Items)

1. $13,000. Legal fees incurred in the successful defense of a patent should be capitalized as part of the cost of the patent and then amortized over its remaining useful life. Thus, the carrying amount of the patent on December 31, Year 4, is $48,000 [($50,000 ÷ 10) × 6 + ($24,000 ÷ 8) × 6]. An amortized intangible asset is reviewed for impairment when events or changes in circumstances indicate that its carrying amount may not be recoverable. An impairment loss is recognized only if the carrying amount is not recoverable and is greater than the patent's fair value. Thus, the impairment test has two steps. First, the carrying amount of the patent ($48,000) exceeds the undiscounted cash flows expected from the patent ($40,000). Second, the impairment loss equals the difference between the carrying amount of the patent and its fair value [($48,000 – $35,000) = $13,000].
2. $5,000. An intangible asset with an indefinite useful life must not be amortized. The impairment test for an intangible asset that is not subject to amortization consists of a comparison of its fair value with its carrying amount. Thus, the impairment loss recognized is $5,000 ($80,000 – $75,000).
3. $0. The carrying amount of the franchise on December 31, Year 4, is $24,000 {$60,000 – [($60,000 ÷ 5) × 3]}. The carrying amount of the franchise ($24,000) is lower than the undiscounted expected future cash flows from the franchise ($25,000). Thus, the carrying amount is recoverable, and no impairment loss is recognized.

ANSWERS 2 OF 6

4. Operating Cash Flow (10 Gradable Items)

Cash flows from operating activities:	
Net income	$305,000
Adjustments to reconcile net income to net cash provided by operating activities:	
1. Depreciation	82,000
2. Amortization of patent	9,000
3. Loss on sale of equipment	10,000
4. Equity in income of Word Corp.	(30,000)
5. Gain on sale of trading securities	(19,000)
6. Decrease in securities fair value adjustment	(15,000)
7. Increase in accounts receivable	(35,000)
8. Decrease in inventories	80,000
9. Decrease in accounts payable and accrued liabilities	(115,000)
10. Net cash provided by operating activities	272,000

1. $82,000. Accumulated depreciation at the end of Year 1 was $280,000. Of this amount, $17,000 ($45,000 – $28,000) was eliminated when equipment was sold at the beginning of Year 2. Thus, the change during the year was $82,000 [$345,000 – ($280,000 – $17,000)]. This amount is the depreciation recognized for Year 2. It is added to net income because it is a noncash expense.
2. $9,000. The net change in the patent's carrying amount is a decrease of $9,000. It is added to net income because it is a noncash expense.
3. $10,000. The loss on the sale of equipment ($28,000 CA – $18,000 = $10,000) is a noncash item.
4. $(30,000). The equity in the income of the investee [($150,000 × 20%) = $30,000] is a noncash revenue item that decreases net income in the reconciliation.
5. $(19,000). The $19,000 gain ($119,000 – $100,000 CA) is from an investing activity, so it is subtracted from net income.
6. $(15,000). The unrealized holding gain ($25,000 – $10,000 year-end FV adjustment) is a noncash item subtracted from net income.
7. $(35,000). The $35,000 increase in net accounts receivable implies that cash collections were less than the related revenues. Thus, it is subtracted from net income.
8. $80,000. The $80,000 decrease in inventories indicates that purchases were less than cost of goods sold. It is added to net income.
9. $(115,000). The $115,000 decrease in accounts payable and accrued liabilities indicates that the cash paid to suppliers exceeded purchases. It is subtracted from net income. Thus, the net effect of the changes in inventories and accounts payable and accrued liabilities is that cash paid to suppliers was $35,000 more than cost of goods sold.
10. $272,000. The net provided is $272,000.

ANSWERS 3 OF 6

5. EPS (8 Gradable Items)

1. (A) BEPS – Decrease. As a result of the issuance of new shares, the weighted-average number of common shares outstanding increases. BEPS and DEPS decrease by the same amount.
2. (A) DEPS – Equal. As a result of the issuance of new shares, the weighted-average number of common shares outstanding increases. BEPS and DEPS decrease by the same amount.
3. (B) BEPS – No effect. The call options were not exercised during the year. No new shares of common stock were issued, and BEPS is unaffected.
4. (B) DEPS – Equal. The DEPS calculation includes the effects of dilutive potential common shares (PCS). Call options are dilutive only if the average market price for the period of the common shares is greater than the exercise price of the options. But the average market price of the common shares ($12) is lower than the exercise price of the options ($14). These call options are antidilutive and have no effect on the calculation of DEPS.
5. (C) BEPS – Decrease. BEPS is calculated as income available to common shareholders divided by the weighted-average number of common shares outstanding. Income available to common shareholders is reduced by the dividends accumulated for the current period on cumulative preferred stock. Without the issuance of cumulative preferred stock, BEPS in Year 1 equals $3.5 ($350,000 ÷ 100,000). As a result of the issuance, income available to common shareholders is $300,000 [$350,000 – (10,000 shares × $100 × 5%)], and BEPS is $3 ($300,000 ÷ $100,000).
6. (C) DEPS – Equal. DEPS includes the effects of dilutive potential common shares (PCS). Dilution is a reduction of BEPS resulting from the assumption that convertible securities (e.g., preferred stock or debt) were converted. BEPS before the conversion is $3 ($300,000 income available to common shareholders ÷ 100,000 weighted-average number of common shares outstanding). The conversion of cumulative preferred stock results in adjustment of the BEPS numerator to add back any convertible preferred dividends that were declared or accumulated. Thus, the BEPS numerator increases by $50,000 to $350,000. The conversion also results in adjustment of the BEPS denominator. It is increased to include the weighted-average number of additional shares of common stock that would have been outstanding if the convertible preferred stock had been converted. Thus, BEPS denominator is increased by 10,000 to 110,000 (100,000 + 10,000). The assumed conversion of cumulative convertible preferred stock results in BEPS of $3.18 ($350,000 ÷ 110,000). Because cumulative convertible preferred stock is antidilutive (the conversion results in an increase in BEPS), they have no effect on DEPS and should not be included in the calculation of DEPS.
7. (D) BEPS – Increase. Treasury stock reduces the weighted-average number of common shares outstanding. Consequently, BEPS and DEPS increase as a result of the repurchase of Mike's own common stock.
8. (D) DEPS – Equal. Treasury stock reduces the weighted-average number of common shares outstanding. BEPS and DEPS increase as a result of the repurchase of Mike's own common stock.

ANSWERS 4 OF 6

6. Classification of Cash Flows (12 Gradable Items)

1. Investing activity. Cash flows from purchases, sales, and maturities of available-for-sale and held-to-maturity debt securities are from investing activities. They are reported gross for each classification of security in the cash flows statement.
2. Investing activity. Investing activities include (a) making and collecting loans; (b) acquiring and disposing of debt or equity instruments; and (c) acquiring and disposing of property, plant, and equipment and other productive assets (but not materials in inventory) held for or used in the production of goods or services.
3. Financing activity. Financing activities include (a) issuance of stock, (b) payment of dividends, (c) treasury stock transactions, (d) incurrence of debt, (e) repayment or other settlement of debt obligations, and (f) the exercise of share options resulting in excess tax benefits.
4. Noncash investing and financing activities. Some transactions affect recognized assets or liabilities but not cash flows. They are reported in related disclosures. The acquisition of equipment subject to a finance lease is such an activity.
5. Depends on nature and purpose. Cash flows from purchases, sales, and maturities of trading securities (securities bought and held primarily for sale in the near term) are classified based on the nature and purpose for which the securities were acquired.
6. Operating activity. Operating activities are all transactions and other events that are not financing or investing activities. In general, they involve producing and delivering goods and providing services. Their effects normally are reported in earnings.
7. Investing activity. Investing activities include (a) making and collecting loans; (b) acquiring and disposing of debt or equity instruments; and (c) acquiring and disposing of property, plant, and equipment and other productive assets (but not materials in inventory) held for or used in the production of goods or services.
8. Operating activity. Operating activities are all transactions and other events that are not financing or investing activities. In general, they involve producing and delivering goods and providing services. Their effects normally are reported in earnings.
9. Operating activity. Operating activities are all transactions and other events that are not financing or investing activities. In general, they involve producing and delivering goods and providing services. Their effects normally are reported in earnings.
10. Operating activity. Operating activities are all transactions and other events that are not financing or investing activities. In general, they involve producing and delivering goods and providing services. Their effects normally are reported in earnings.
11. Financing activity. Financing activities include (a) issuance of stock, (b) payment of dividends, (c) treasury stock transactions, (d) incurrence of debt, (e) repayment or other settlement of debt obligations, and (f) the exercise of share options resulting in excess tax benefits.
12. Financing activity. Financing activities include (a) issuance of stock, (b) payment of dividends, (c) treasury stock transactions, (d) incurrence of debt, (e) repayment or other settlement of debt obligations, and (f) the exercise of share options resulting in excess tax benefits.

ANSWERS 5 OF 6

7. Noncurrent Notes Payable (2 Gradable Items)

1. Loan 1 – Any error related to a prior period discovered after the statements are, or are available to be, used must be reported as an error correction by restating the prior-period statements. Restatement requires retrospective application. The carrying amounts of (1) assets, (2) liabilities, and (3) retained earnings at the beginning of the first period reported are adjusted for the cumulative effect of the error on the prior periods. In Year 1, interest expense of $120,000 ($3,000,000 × 4%) should have been recognized on Loan 1. Instead, Drake debited accrued interest payable for $120,000. Thus, the journal entry recorded in Year 2 to adjust the beginning balances for the cumulative effect of the error is the following:

   Retained earnings debit $120,000. The cumulative effect of the error on Year 1 income is $120,000. Because the correct net income in Year 1 should have been $120,000 lower, the beginning balance of Year 2 retained earnings must be debited (decreased) by this amount.

   Accrued interest payable credit $120,000. Year 1 interest was paid, so no accrued interest payable should have been debited. To remove this balance, Drake must credit accrued interest payable for $120,000.

   Drake paid $120,000 in cash for Year 2 interest expense on Loan 1. The following is the journal entry:

   Interest expense debit $120,000.

   Cash credit $120,000.

2. Loan 2 – Year 2 interest expense on Loan 2 is $80,000 ($1,000,000 × 8%). Because Drake did not pay this amount by the end of Year 2, it should be accrued as interest payable. The following is the journal entry:

   Interest expense debit $80,000.

   Accrued interest payable credit $80,000.

8. Document Review (4 Gradable Items)

1. A. *[Original Text]* $9,000,000. The fair value of the 450,000 shares of NextGen common stock acquired by MCM is $9,000,000.

   B. $8,000,000. The fair value of the consideration would be $8,000,000, using MCM's share price on the regulatory approval date ($80 on 1/12/20XX). However, MCM's share price on the acquisition date ($95 on 1/14/20XX) is the correct fair value measure.

   C. $10,000,000. The fair value of NextGen's net assets is $10,000,000.

   D. **Correct:** $9,500,000. The consideration transferred in a business combination is measured as the sum of the acquisition-date fair values of (1) the assets transferred by the acquirer, (2) the liabilities incurred by the acquirer to former owners of the acquiree, and (3) the equity interests issued by the acquirer. MCM neither transferred assets to NextGen nor incurred liabilities to NextGen's former owners. However, MCM did transfer 100,000 shares of its common stock for its interest in NextGen. On the acquisition date (1/14/20XX), MCM's common stock was trading at $95 per share. Therefore, the fair value of the consideration that MCM transferred to acquire its interest in NextGen is $9,500,000 (100,000 shares × $95).

   E. $8,500,000. The fair value of the consideration would be $8,500,000, using MCM's share price on the board approval date ($85 on 1/13/20XX). However, MCM's share price on the acquisition date ($95 on 1/14/20XX) is the correct fair value measure.

ANSWERS 6 OF 6

2. A. *[Original Text]* expense the $190,000 payment. MCM only must expense the portion of the payment attributed to acquisition-related costs ($150,000), not the entire $190,000 payment.

   B. capitalize the $190,000 payment. Neither the $190,000 payment nor any portion thereof represents a capitalizable expense.

   C. **Correct:** expense $150,000 of the payment. Acquisition-related costs are expensed as incurred. In contrast, direct issue costs of equity are not expensed as incurred but reduce additional paid-in capital. The $190,000 payment consists of $150,000 of acquisition-related fees and $40,000 of direct issue costs of stock. Therefore, MCM must expense $150,000 of the $190,000 payment to Jacob, Sullivan, & Duke.

   D. expense $135,000 of the payment. Although MCM must expense its acquisition-related costs of $150,000, the amount expensed is not limited to MCM's percentage interest in NextGen (90% × $150,000 = $135,000).

   E. expense $40,000 of the payment. The portion of the payment attributed to direct issue costs of stock (i.e., direct issue costs of equity) is $40,000. Direct issue costs of equity are not expensed as incurred but reduce additional paid-in capital.

3. A. *[Original Text]* report a noncontrolling interest of $900,000 in NextGen. The amount of $900,000 is 90% of the noncontrolling interest of $1,000,000.

   B. not report a noncontrolling interest in NextGen. MCM will report a noncontrolling interest because it only acquired a 90% interest in NextGen.

   C. report a noncontrolling interest of $433,000 in NextGen. The amount of $433,000 is 10% of the book value of NextGen's net identifiable assets.

   D. **Correct:** report a noncontrolling interest of $1,000,000 in NextGen. On its acquisition-date consolidated balance sheet, an acquirer with a controlling interest in an acquiree must report the acquisition-date fair value (FV) of any noncontrolling interest (NCI) in the acquiree. A controlling interest is established, among other means, when an entity acquires more than 50% of the outstanding voting interest of another entity. The acquisition-date FV of the NCI is measured as the FV of the acquiree's outstanding common stock not held by the acquirer on the acquisition date. Accordingly, the FV of the NCI on 1/14/20XX is $1,000,000 [10% × (500,000 shares of NextGen outstanding common stock × $20 market price per share)].

   E. report a noncontrolling interest of $962,500 in NextGen. The amount of $962,500 is the FV of the noncontrolling interest on the board approval date of 1/13/20XX [10% × (500,000 shares of NextGen outstanding common stock × $19.25 market price per share)].

4. A. **Correct:** *[Original Text]* recognize goodwill of $500,000 on the acquisition. Goodwill equals the excess of the sum of the acquisition-date fair values of (1) the acquirer's consideration transferred, (2) any noncontrolling interest (NCI), and (3) any previously held equity interest in the acquiree over the acquisition-date fair value of the acquiree's net identifiable assets. The acquisition-date fair values of MCM's consideration transferred and the NCI were $9,500,000 and $1,000,000, respectively, and MCM did not previously hold equity in NextGen. The acquisition-date fair value of NextGen's net identifiable assets was $10,000,000. Therefore, on the acquisition date, MCM will recognize goodwill of $500,000 [($9,500,000 + $1,000,000) – $10,000,000].

   B. recognize goodwill of $5,670,000 on the acquisition. MCM will not recognize goodwill equal to the excess of the acquisition-date fair value of NextGen's net identifiable assets ($10,000,000) over the book value of NextGen's net identifiable assets ($4,330,000).

   C. recognize goodwill of $1,000,000 on the acquisition. MCM will not recognize goodwill equal to the excess of the acquisition-date fair value of NextGen's net identifiable assets ($10,000,000) over the acquisition-date fair value of NextGen stock received ($9,000,000).

   D. recognize goodwill of $5,170,000 on the acquisition. MCM will not recognize goodwill equal to the excess of its consideration transferred ($9,500,000) over the acquisition-date book value of NextGen's net identifiable assets ($4,330,000).

   E. not recognize any goodwill on the acquisition. MCM will recognize goodwill on its acquisition of a 90% interest in NextGen because the sum of the acquisition-date fair values of (1) its consideration transferred and (2) the noncontrolling interest in NextGen exceeds the acquisition-date fair value of NextGen's net identifiable assets.

INDEX